The New York

Intellectuals

The Rise and Decline

of the Anti-Stalinist

Left from the 1930s

to the 1980s

. . . .

BY ALAN M. WALD

The University of North Carolina Press

Chapel Hill & London

The New York Intellectuals

Library of Congress Cataloging-in-Publication Data

Wald, Alan M., 1946–

  The New York intellectuals.

  Bibliography: p.

  Includes index.

  1. Socialists—New York (N.Y.)—History—
20th century.   2. Intellectuals—New York (N.Y.)—
History—20th century.   I. Title.

HX92.N5W35 1987   320.5'32'097471   86-24922

ISBN 0-8078-1716-3

ISBN 0-8078-4169-2 (pbk.)

Some portions of this book have appeared in somewhat different
form in *Jewish Social Studies* 38 (1976); *Antioch Review* 35
(1977); *Prospects* 3 (1977); *Literature at the Barricades*
(University of Alabama Press, 1982), pp. 187–203; and
Centennial Review 29 (1985).

Jmb
3-7-89

TO CELIA

Contents

. . . .

A section of photographs follows page 164.

Acknowledgments

. . . .

I am grateful to the following libraries for assistance and in some cases for permission to quote from letters and manuscripts: American Academy and Institute of Arts and Letters; Archives of Labor History and Urban Affairs, Wayne State University; Boston Public Library; Butler Library, Columbia University; Charles Patterson Van Pelt Library, University of Pennsylvania; Frank Melville, Jr. Memorial Library, State University of New York at Stony Brook; Guy W. Bailey Library, University of Vermont; Harvard University Records Office; Haverford College Library; Hoover Institute, Stanford University; Houghton Library, Harvard University; Humanities Research Center, University of Texas; Labadie Collection, University of Michigan; Leon Trotsky Institute, Grenoble, France; Library of Congress; Library of Social History, New York City; Middlebury College Library; Mills College Library; Museum of Social Science, Paris; Northwestern University Library; Tamiment Library, New York University; Tufts University Library; University of California, Los Angeles, Research Library; University of Delaware Library; University of Illinois Library; University of Massachusetts, Amherst, Library; University of Oregon Library; University of Tennessee Library; University of Washington Library; Wisconsin State Historical Society; Yale University Library. The following individuals generously gave me access to their private collections: Daniel Aaron, Cambridge, Massachusetts; George Breitman, New York City; Robert Gorham Davis, Cambridge, Massachusetts; James T. Farrell, New York City; Albert Glotzer, New York City; Walter Lippmann, Los Angeles; and George Novack, New York City. I appreciate the assistance of Cassandra Johnson in obtaining and allowing me to use photographs from the Sylvia Salmi Collection.

The following people participated in personal interviews, many of them tape-recorded: Lionel Abel; Sherry Abel; Nathan Adler; John Archer; Erwin Bauer; Estar Bauer; David Bazelon; Irving Beinin; Michael Blankfort; Dorothy Breitman; George Breitman; Alexander Buchman; Nicholas Calas; Joel Carmichael; Noam Chomsky; Phil Clark; Bert Cochran; Malcolm Cowley; Charles Curtiss; Lillian Curtiss; Hope Hale Davis; Robert Gorham Davis; Farrell

Dobbs; Ross Dowson; Hal Draper; F. W. Dupee; John Dwyer; Dorothy Eisner; James T. Farrell; Cleo Ferguson; Leslie Fiedler; Pauline Firth; Max Geldman; Emanuel Geltman; Milton Genecin; Tybie Genecin; Martin Glaberman; Frank Glass; Nathan Glazer; Albert Glotzer; Maggie Glotzer; Walter Goldwater; Sam Gordon; James Gotesky; Barbara Gray; Clement Greenberg; Horace Gregory; Al Hansen; Joseph Hansen; Reba Hansen; Elinor Rice Hays; David Herreshoff; Davis Herron; Elsa-Ruth Herron; Helen Hirschberg; Rod Holt; Irving Howe; Louis Jacobs; Sarah Jacobs; Julius Jacobson; Phyllis Jacobson; DeMila Jenner; Matthew Josephson; Alfred Kazin; Almeda Kirsch; Stanley Kunitz; Suzanne La Follette; Joe Lee; Morris Lewit; Sylvia Lewit; Robert Littman; Ethel Lobman; Frank Lovell; Mary McCarthy; Dwight Macdonald; John McDonald; Ernest Mandel; Felix Morrow; George Novack; George Perle; William Phillips; Hugo Rasmussen; Harry Ring; Harry Roskolenko; Muriel Rukeyser; Edward Sagaran; Sylvia Salmi; Irving Sanes; Meyer Schapiro; Morris U. Schappes; Ralph Schoenman; Philip Selznick; Paul N. Siegel; Donald Slaiman; Ray Sparrow; Bette Swados; Virgil Thomson; Jean Tussey; Doris VanZleer; Adelaide Walker; Beatrice Warren; Jac Wasserman; Stan Weir; Myra Tanner Weiss; George Weissman; B. J. Widick; Bernard Wolfe.

The following people shared information with me through correspondence and phone conversations: Herbert Aptheker; David Aronson; Mary Anne Ashley; Carleton Beals; Julian Behrstock; Jeanna Belkin; Daniel Bell; Saul Bellow; Louis Berg; Shirley Biagi; Earle Birney; Peter Bloch; Edgar Branch; Cleanth Brooks; Pierre Broué; Spencer Brown; Stanley Brown; James Burnham; Grace Carlson; Eleanor Clark; Sylvia Cohen; Jack Conroy; Lewis Coser; Alex P. Daspit; Peter Davis; Hugo DeWar; Caroline Durrieux; Ernest Erber; Clifton Fadiman; Lewis Feuer; Leona Finestone; Jack Fischel; Maxwell Geismar; Jules Geller; Richard Gillam; Tom Glazer; Boyer Gonzales; Rubin Gotesky; Peter Graham; C. Hartley Grattan; Louis Graver; Louis Hacker; Albert Halper; Robert Heilman; Granville Hicks; Fred Hochberg; John Hollander; Eric Homberger; Sidney Hook; Quincy Howe; Carlos Hudson; David Hurwood; Charles Hyneman; Harold Isaacs; Paul Jacobs; Marlene Kadar; Alice Kahler; Garson Kanin; Harold Kaplan; Peter Boris Kauffman; Harvey Klehr; Hilton Kramer; William Krehm; Elinor Langer; Richard La Pan; Melvin J. Lasky; Donald Lazere; William Lewis III; Michael Löwy; Eugene Lyons; Nancy Macdonald; Seymour Martin Lipset; Staughton Lynd; Lois Mahier; Jerre Mangione; Ed Medard; Seymour Melman; Howard Mitchum; Arthur Mizener; Jeanne Morgan; Belle Myer; Helen Neville; Russell Nye; William O'Neill; Shirley Pasholk; Cleo Paturis; Victor Perlo; Nunzio Pernicone; Stanley Plastrik; T. R. Poole; Earl Raab; Philip Rahv; Paul Rasmussen; Jack A. Robbins; Selden Rodman; Richard Rorty; Winifred Rorty; Harold Rosenberg; Richard Rovere; Roscoe J. Saville; Carl Schier; Arthur Schlesinger, Jr.; Janet Sharistanian; Mark Sharron; Jesse Simons; Anne Solow; Davidson Sommers; George Spiro; Eliot Stanley; Arne Swabeck; Edith Tarcov; Harvey Teres; Diana Trilling; Lionel Trilling; Martin Upham; Eric Voegelin; Harold Vorhees; Nathan Walker; Robert Penn Warren; Douglas Webb; Allen Weinstein; Morton G. White; Ralph Wickiser; Leonard Wilcox; Calder Willingham; Eleanor Wolff; Virginia Xanthos; Milton Zaslow; Arthur Zipser.

The following people provided various kinds of technical assistance and offered suggestions about the content of the book: Bazel Allen; Jeff Beneke; Anne-Marie Bouché; Edgar Branch; Robert Buckeye; David Cooper; Bill Costley; Harold Cruse; Stuart Dick; John Dobson; Ellen Dunlap; Les Evans; Dianne Feeley; Milton Fisk; Alan Freeman; Marilyn Gagron; Joel Geier; James Gindin; David Hollinger; Jane Holzka; Nancy Johnson; Robert Johnson-Lally; Mark Krupnick; Robert Langston; Paul Le Blanc; Ralph Levitt; Walter Lippmann; Brian Lloyd; S. A. Longstaff; Cleo Paturis; Warner Pflug; Daniel Pope; Eric Poulos; Rodolphe Prager; Paula Rabinowitz; Peter Railton; Gérard Roche; Barbara Shapiro; Mark Shechner; Tony Smith; Frank Thompson; Edward Weber; Neda Westlake; Stephen Whitfield; Brooke Whiting. Joanna Misnik aided with translations. The Rackham Graduate School at the University of Michigan provided me with two research assistants, Geoff Cummins and William Ferral, who prepared transcriptions of tape-recorded interviews and located library materials. On several occasions I presented the gist of my argument in public symposia, and I received useful criticism from the following respondents: Robert Brenner, John Diggins, Robert Fitrakis, Martin Glaberman, Nathan Huggins, Chris Huxley, Mel Rothenberg, Wally Seccombe, and Michael Wreszin.

The funding enabling this research was provided by a 1982–83 fellowship from the American Council of Learned Societies, several contributions from the Robert H. Langston Foundation, and a Research Grant from the Rackham Graduate School at the University of Michigan.

Portions of the manuscript were criticized at various times by Jeff Beneke, Paul Breines, George Breitman, Howard Brick, Paul Buhle, Neil Chacker, Robert Gorham Davis, James T. Farrell, David Finkel, Michael Folsom, James Gilbert, Albert Glotzer, Laurence Goldstein, Elinor Rice Hays, Sidney Hook, Irving Howe, Julius

Jacobson, Phyllis Jacobson, Berta Langston, Ralph Levitt, Michael Löwy, Ernest Mandel, John McDonald, Leonard Michaels, Felix Morrow, George Novack, David Reid, Irving Sanes, Meyer Schapiro, Morris U. Schappes, Mark Shechner, Louis Sinclair, Henry Nash Smith, Diana Trilling, Lionel Trilling, Celia Wald, Haskell Wald, Douglas Webb, B. J. Widick, and Bernard Wolfe. My debt for such generous assistance is enormous, but I wish to emphasize that none of these individuals is responsible for the opinions expressed in this book. In addition, I wish to give particular mention to Patrick Quinn, who selflessly devoted many hours to carefully scrutinizing every aspect of my work; Berta Langston, whose unflagging moral support has been indispensable; George Breitman, who generously gave me the benefit of his unparalleled knowledge of the history of American Trotskyism; James T. Farrell, who sent me informative and encouraging letters on this subject nearly once a week from 1974 until his death; and Ernest Mandel, whose writings on socialist theory and practice have helped to guide me through the maze of contemporary politics since the late 1960s. At the University of North Carolina Press, I again had the privilege of benefiting from the efficiency and reliability of Iris Tillman Hill, and I am grateful to Sandra Eisdorfer for her work on the manuscript.

This book challenges the conventional wisdom established through a plethora of memoirs and earlier studies about a crucial episode in contemporary intellectual history; its publication is bound to produce controversy, and its author is likely to be scrutinized with some ruthlessness in at least two areas. First, his accuracy will be questioned by those of his subjects still alive, as well as by their friends and associates. Such questioning, however, is welcome; while I have gone to unusual lengths to check and recheck facts with numerous participants in the events discussed, as well as with a variety of scholars, I will happily acknowledge any legitimate corrections of the historical record. I apologize in advance for any errors that remain.

Second, those who disagree with the central argument of the book may attempt to disparage or dismiss the author's perspective by stamping it with a simplistic political label that elides the subtlety of the argument. While I have tried to be unambiguous about my purpose and point of view in preparing this study, I especially regret that there is inadequate space to develop concretely the political perspective I espouse as an alternative to that of the social democratic figures in the closing chapters, Irving Howe and Harvey Swados, for whom I obviously have more sympathy than I have for the neoconservatives to their right. Readers who recognize the in-sufficiency of labels will find further elaborations of my general perspective in two essays appearing just as this book goes to press: Robert Brenner's "The Paradox of Social Democracy: The American Case," in *The Year Left* (1985), pp. 32–86, and Ralph Miliband and Marcel Liebman's "Beyond Social Democracy," in *Socialist Register 1985/86: Social Democracy and After* (1986), pp. 476–89. Noam Chomsky's *Turning the Tide* (1985) and Mike Davis's *Prisoners of the American Dream* (1986) are additional sources. Moreover, for assistance in formulating my general approach to the subject of politics and intellectuals, as well as for providing models in the application of contemporary Marxist theory, I wish to acknowledge the considerable influence of Perry Anderson's *Considerations on Western Marxism* (1976) and *Arguments within English Marxism* (1980), and Michael Löwy's chapter "Towards a Sociology of the Anticapitalist Intelligentsia," in *Georg Lukács: From Romanticism to Bolshevism* (1979).

A Note on the Text and the Illustrations

. . . .

An important obstacle to the study of political culture in the United States of the 1930s and after is the mystification of the terms "Communism" and "communism." The capitalization or noncapitalization of the letter "c" makes a qualitative difference in the meaning of the term, to which the reader must be ever alert.

In 1967, thirty years after the break of *Partisan Review* magazine from the Communist Party, Philip Rahv, the journal's central editor, felt the need to clarify in a public symposium in *Commentary* that "it was not communism, in its doctrinal formulations by Marx, or even Lenin, that we broke away from, but the Soviet embodiment of it known as Stalinism." In other words, Rahv and his circle broke from Communism (by which they meant the official Soviet-dominated movement, which they characterized as Stalinist), but for some years remained communists (by which they meant general adherents of the revolutionary ideas of Marx and Lenin).

Following Rahv, this study uses the terms "Communism" and "Communists" (uppercase "C") to refer to official doctrines and adherents of parties of the Soviet-dominated Third International, which after the late 1920s can be characterized as "Stalinist." In contrast, "communism" and "communists" (lowercase "c") refer to doctrines and adherents of the broader movement growing out of the Russian Revolution of October 1917, which includes not only the Stalinist current but also Trotskyists (the most important for this book), Bukharinists, and council communists.

Since one aim of this book is to vivify an important politico-cultural experience as expressed through the lives and work of a talented group of intellectuals, a portfolio of photographs has been inserted in the text. Most of these photographs come from the private collection of the late Sylvia Salmi, although a few are from libraries and individuals who responded to requests. Unfortunately, the vast majority of the photographs were undated and in most cases it was impossible to offer a sound guess of the year in which they were taken or to identify the exact setting.

Even though the photographs exhibit the men and women at various stages of their lives, from youth to old age, it was decided to present the photographs roughly in order of the appearance of the individuals in the narrative. In some cases, there are two photographs that show the man or woman at different ages. The appearance or nonappearance of photographs of individuals, or the number of pictures printed, is not necessarily an indication of the centrality of the person to the narrative; the decision to include photographs was also based on the availability of the photographs and their quality.

The New York Intellectuals

You think you are
doing the pushing,
But it is you who are
being pushed.

—Mephistopheles in
Goethe's *Faust*

INTRODUCTION

Political Amnesia

Today's younger generation of intellectuals consists of the late arrivals to the generation that made its appearance as American "Marxists" and which has lived its entire life with Marxism (including, of course, anti-Marxism) as its central theme and interest. Without Marxism this generation is not only dull—it is nothing. It does not exist.

—Harold Rosenberg,
"Death in the
Wilderness," 1965[1]

. . . .

In late 1933, Sidney Hook, a thirty-one-year-old assistant professor of philosophy at New York University, wrote the political program for a new revolutionary communist party. The organization that would be launched in just a few months was called the American Workers Party. Hook, widely believed to be the only Marxist professor in the United States at the time and one of the few Jews to hold a university appointment in the humanities, thought that the need for such a new party was exigent. "Despite its best revolutionary intentions," his program declared, "the Communist Party has neither advanced the cause of revolutionizing the situation of the masses, nor has it done anything to advance the immediate interests of the producing classes." In short, the Communist Party "has brought disgrace to the term Communism."[2] Hook presented additional motivation for the new party in an article published shortly thereafter in the Marxist journal *Modern Monthly*, edited by V. F. Calverton: "It seems to me that only communism can save the world from its social evils; it seems to me to be just as evident that

3

the official Communist Party or any of its subsidiary organizations cannot be regarded as a Marxist, critical, or revolutionary party today. The conclusion is, therefore, clear: the time has come to build a new communist party and a new communist international."[3]

Ten months after publishing this statement, Hook became the victim of an intense antiradical campaign promoted by the conservative newspaper publisher William Randolph Hearst. Hearst's *New York American* ran a series publicizing Hook's role (and also that of his New York University colleague James Burnham) as a guiding spirit of the American Workers Party, and demanding that he be ousted from his teaching position. In response, Hook turned to a Trotskyist-led organization called Non-Partisan Labor Defense, which organized a protest rally of 2,500 to denounce Hearst's red-baiting activities.[4]

Yet twenty years later, in 1953, this same Sidney Hook, now fifty-one years old, a full professor, and the former chairman of the New York University Philosophy Department, published a book called *Heresy, Yes—Conspiracy, No.* Its thesis was that "communism . . . is the greatest menace to human freedom in the world today." Hook unabashedly called upon faculty and administrators to enforce "a policy of exclusion of members of the Communist Party and similar groups" from teaching in schools and universities.[5] Even as he wrote this book, Hook still considered himself a liberal socialist. Two decades later, he campaigned for Richard Nixon, and in 1980 he proudly endorsed Ronald Reagan, who in turn sent warm greetings to Hook's eightieth birthday party in the fall of 1982.[6]

This political odyssey, a strange blend of the paradigmatic and the idiosyncratic, requires comment. First, Hook's move from left to right is familiar to those who have studied the deradicalization of twentieth-century American intellectuals, a middle-class stratum increasingly tied to the professions. But the same pattern appears among a cross-section of an entire generation born in the first two decades of this century, including white-collar workers, radicalized owners of small businesses, and industrial workers. What distinguishes intellectuals from the others is not the overall direction of their movement but the suddenness of their shifts, the extremes to which they went, and the fact that, as intellectuals, they articulate their new views at every stage, sometimes blithely contradicting what they had earlier professed. Thus, an understanding of the causes and consequences of Hook's evolution from revolution to reconciliation has broad implications for the understanding of our political culture.

Hook's evolution is distinctive among the left intelligentsia of the 1930s for its failure to exemplify the "God that failed" motif. In contrast to most ex-Communists and fellow-travelers, Hook's disillusionment with the Soviet Union as the fatherland of socialism somewhat predated his public emergence as a revolutionary Marxist. His political activity in the early and mid-1930s, especially before the eruption of the Moscow purge trials, was devoted to developing a revolutionary communist left in opposition to official Communism, or "Stalinism," as Soviet communism was already being called by such Marxist and Trotskyist-influenced opponents as Hook. Yet what appears in this instance to be Hook's personal idiosyncrasy vis-à-vis the mainstream radical intellectuals of the 1930s turns out to be paradigmatic for the formative years of the group known today as the "New York Intellectuals." It is precisely the attempt by the founders of the tradition of the New York intellectuals to develop an anti-Stalinist revolutionary communism that distinguishes them from the pure and simple anti-Communists of the 1930s and after, despite the efforts of some in later years to obliterate, to trivialize, or to misrepresent this crucial episode of their lives. Moreover, it was the abandonment of an opposition to Stalinism on anticapitalist premises that sapped the movement of its most positive qualities in the years following World War II. Hook and many others became fanatical adherents of a more sophisticated version of the anticommunist ideology that was promoted by the United States government, business, and conservative elements to smooth the transition in the changing world role of the United States from a semi-isolationist stance to the major imperialist power; subsequently, this "liberal anticommunism" took on a life of its own.[7]

A good example of an inaccurate representation of this history is contained in a 1984 letter to the *New York Times Book Review* by Sidney Hook and Arnold Beichman. They argue for the centrality of the *New Leader* in the tradition of the anti-Stalinist left, in response to a piece by Nathan Glazer, which recognized *Partisan Review*'s right to that role.[8] From the perspective of the political frame of reference used by the New York intellectuals themselves during their formative years, a frame of reference that is resurrected and embraced in this book, the *New Leader* was generally regarded as a halfway house for right-wing social-democratic anticommunists from which virtually no one returned. If the *New Leader* had actually been central to the anti-Stalinist left from its inception, then Clement Greenberg's oft-quoted remark that "anti-Stalinism . . . started out more or less as Trotskyism" would be false.[9] There would, in fact, be little difference between the anti-Stalinism of

Hook and his associates in the 1930s and their views in the 1980s, a myth that some might like to foster for the sake of appearing politically consistent, rather than acknowledging the subsequent sequence of turnabouts and gyrations in their orientation. Obscured would be the profound difference between anti-Communism (originally, opposition by revolutionary Marxists to Soviet Communism, after the rise of Stalin, as a deformation or perversion of socialism) and anticommunism (in the United States, an ideological mask for discrediting movements for radical social change and supporting the status quo by amalgamating these movements with Soviet crimes, expansionism, and subversion).[10]

Simply put, without Trotskyism there would have never appeared an anti-Stalinist left among intellectuals in the mid-1930s; there would only have been the anticommunist movement already existing, one associated with the essentially Menshevik politics of various social democratic organizations, with David Dubinsky and Sidney Hillman in the needle trades unions, and with publications such as the *New Leader* and the *Jewish Daily Forward*. But it is inconceivable that Menshevism had the power to inspire such young writers as Sidney Hook and Philip Rahv, who were drawn to the Russian Revolution, because Menshevism denied the validity of that revolution while Trotskyism, despite its opposition to Stalin's policies, celebrated its significance and achievements. Trotskyism made it possible for these rebellious intellectuals to declare themselves on the side of the revolution (as opposed to the side of the social democrats who had just then succumbed to the Nazis without resistance), and yet also to denounce Stalin from the left as the arch betrayer of Lenin's heritage.[11] In a certain sense their position anticipated the one promoted three decades later by the Soviet dissident Roy Medvedev: that one can be a Leninist and for democracy at the same time.

Regrettably, scholars, biographers, and literary critics have missed entirely the centrality of this political phase in their continuing efforts to analyze and assess the New York intellectuals. Instead, most of the studies to date are brief and vague about the revolutionary politics of the group, according disproportionate attention to important but secondary issues such as Jewish immigrant origins and literary tastes. Of course, the approach of Hook and Beichman, asserting anticommunist social democracy as the consistent and determining factor in the history of the group, is highly unusual. The more typical misreading of the evolution of the New York intellectuals determines membership in the circle by the extent of their involvement in *Partisan Review*. My own contention is that the New York intellectuals must be understood as an outgrowth of the tradition of the anti-Stalinist left as it passed through an excruciatingly difficult political period.

Since the late 1960s, there has been a steady stream, now swelling to a torrent, of books and articles about this group. Sometimes the New York intellectuals are called the "New York family." In popular usage, the term usually refers to a loose circle of intellectuals whose preeminent forums have been *Partisan Review, Commentary*, and *Dissent*. Contributors to these journals who were old enough to be politically active in the 1930s tended to become, like Hook, not only anti-Stalinists but also revolutionary Marxists of one persuasion or another. In the cultural arena, most defended the modernist avant-garde, even if they felt strong allegiances to other traditions. In the 1980s, many—including not only Hook but other former Trotskyists and Trotskyist sympathizers such as Lionel Abel, Saul Bellow, Irving Kristol, Melvin J. Lasky, and Seymour Martin Lipset—are associated with the neoconservative "Committee for the Free World" led by Midge Decter and her husband, *Commentary* editor Norman Podhoretz. This is a predominantly pro-Reagan organization that achieved considerable notoriety when in April 1981 it ran an advertisement in the *New York Times* to "applaud American policy in El Salvador." Other surviving New York intellectuals are not quite so right wing, but very few consider themselves to be politically to the left of the Democratic Party, a position that was assumed at the outset of their careers.

Appraisals of the New York intellectuals have been made by at least a dozen scholars, and there have been book-length studies of such individuals as Hannah Arendt (who entered the tradition at a later date), Saul Bellow, Max Eastman, James T. Farrell, Clement Greenberg, Mary McCarthy, Dwight Macdonald, Delmore Schwartz, Lionel Trilling, and Edmund Wilson.[12] Even more striking has been the production of autobiographical and semiautobiographical works by the New York intellectuals themselves. Such memoirs include not only the acclaimed trilogy by Alfred Kazin, the sensational revelations of Norman Podhoretz (another latecomer), and the ironical "confessions" published by Mary McCarthy and Dwight Macdonald in the 1950s, but also numerous books and sketches by Lionel Abel, William Barrett, Daniel Bell, Leslie Fiedler, Albert Halper, Michael Harrington, Sidney Hook, Irving Howe, Irving Kristol, George Novack, William Phillips, Harry Roskolenko, Diana Trilling, Lionel Trilling, and Bernard Wolfe.[13]

The widespread and continuing interest in the New York intellectuals by students and scholars of radical political and cultural history—not to mention those of the reading public fascinated by intimate revelations about the lives of the literary mandarins of our time—is obviously because of the mark these writers have made on American culture. The *New York Times Book Review* described *Partisan Review* as "the best literary magazine in America" when one of its founders, Philip Rahv, died in 1973.[14] Further evidence of the importance of the New York intellectuals on the national scene during recent decades has been provided by such political and sociological studies as Charles Kadushin's *The American Intellectual Elite* (1974), Peter Steinfels's *The Neo-Conservatives* (1979), Philip Green's *The Pursuit of Inequality* (1981), William L. O'Neill's *A Better World—The Great Schism: Stalinism and the American Intellectuals* (1982), and Richard Pells's *The Liberal Mind in a Conservative Age* (1985).

One purpose of this book is to help understand how and why the New York intellectuals, a group of one-time rebels and outsiders, became so well integrated into American culture. It documents the process by which the views of former revolutionaries came into harmony with the dominant ideology of the liberal intelligentsia during the Cold War, an ideology typified by Arthur Schlesinger, Jr.'s *The Vital Center* (1949). Once this happened, the skills and experience they had acquired as polemicists and ideologists during their radical years, and especially as authorities on communism with an insider's knowledge, enabled them to move rapidly into seats of cultural power during the 1950s. In more recent decades, some even came to have access to national power. Irving Kristol, for example, became an intellectual consultant to the Nixon administration, Nathan Glazer's work was much admired by the Reagan administration, and neoconservative articles in *Commentary* influenced White House policy in the 1980s.

The study that informs this book, however, would have been necessary even if its subjects had not received so much notoriety in recent years. This work approaches the history of the New York intellectuals with a view to reconstructing an important and vastly misunderstood chapter in the history of literary radicalism and the Marxist intellectual tradition in the United States. It proposes, from a contemporary Marxist point of view, to help cure a certain political amnesia that has hitherto prevented a full understanding of the achievements and mistakes of an earlier generation.

In light of the neoconservative self-portrait being created by many of the New York intellectuals, one is tempted to conclude that they have a stake in perpetuating an amnesia that avoids a forthright disclosure of their previous political history as revolutionary but anti-Stalinist Marxists. Thus it is not surprising that many young radical intellectuals in search of a Marxist tradition among the American intelligentsia have turned elsewhere. They imagine that anti-Stalinism automatically leads to reconciliation with capitalism, an erroneous judgment that fails to account for the fact that the *entire* spectrum of the radical left—including Communists, Trotskyists, anarchists, and radical social democrats—moved rightward for largely social, not ideological, reasons. This misconception accounts for the recent infatuation, following the decline of the New Left in the 1970s, with the history of American Communism, particularly during the Popular Front era, an infatuation that is reflected in the many favorable references in radical journals to the scholarship of Paul Buhle, Vivian Gornick, Maurice Isserman, Mark Naison, and others.[15]

The New York intellectuals are often scornfully dismissed by contemporary radicals. Even when they are treated with some sympathy and understanding, their legacy is so confused that what is most relevant, worthwhile, and enduring in their tradition is sometimes missed.[16] William O'Neill's *A Better World*, for example, presents his heroes, the "anti-Stalinists" in the 1940s, without ever discussing the revolutionary Marxist and Trotskyist past of the central figures.[17] In *The Liberal Mind in a Conservative Age*, Richard Pells considers the "anti-Stalinist" intellectuals only in terms of their "retreat from socialism."[18] James Atlas, in a 1985 *New York Times Magazine* essay, "The Changing World of the New York Intellectuals," favorably quotes Norman Birnbaum's statement that "a New York intellectual was one who wrote for, edited, or read *Partisan Review*." [19]

The most recent study, Alexander Bloom's *Prodigal Sons: The New York Intellectuals and Their World* (1986), explains the phenomenon of the New York intellectuals primarily in terms of upwardly mobile Jews. Like all exaggerations, this approach has a strong element of truth in that some of the central figures in the group really were from poor immigrant backgrounds, and the incorporation of this sector of American society into the mainstream of intellectual life after World War II is an element that must be theorized along with other components of the New York intellectuals' tradition. But upwardly mobile Jews comprised a disproportionate number of intellectuals involved in *all* radical movements in New York in the 1930s. The veterans of the *New Masses* and *New Leader* were not qualitatively different in their Jewish composition from those of the *Partisan Review*. The case for a unique association between Jewish intellectuals (including their background and literary style) and the New York intellectuals' tradition will have to be made, if it can be made, on more specific grounds than on the percentage of Jewish editors and contributors to the key publications.[20]

It is, of course, the post–World War II political evolution of the New York intellectuals that confuses these scholars and also makes it so difficult to convince young radicals that the New York intellectuals' contribution to politics and culture in the 1930s should be critically assimilated as one of the more useful components of a rich Marxist heritage. Hook is an authentic although less desirable representative of that tradition. There are certain obvious continuities between his present neoconservative posture and some of the positions taken by the New York intellectuals in their previous incarnations. But if one understands the changes in political orientation on their part just prior to, during, and especially after World War II, it becomes clear that their ultimate evolution was not the only one possible.

In fact, only by understanding the peculiar nature of their transformation can one come to grips with the most contradictory and confusing aspect of the New York intellectuals: that a group of individuals who mainly began their careers as revolutionary communists in the 1930s could become an institutionalized and even hegemonic component of American culture during the conservative 1950s while maintaining a high degree of collective continuity. This pendular evolution by so many New York intellectuals suggests, from a radical point of view, that their politics were deceptive from the beginning. Politically oriented members of the generation of the 1960s and 1970s find it hard to believe that such neoconservative and right-wing social democratic figures among the New York intellectuals as Kristol and Hook once considered themselves genuine Marxist revolutionaries and at the same time expressed an uncompromising opposition to Stalinism. The contemporary generation of the left fails to understand that it was not anti-Stalinism per se that was responsible for changing these intellectuals into Cold War liberals in the 1950s and neoconservatives in the 1970s, but a host of historical and social factors that terminated their revolutionary socialist perspectives. Thus it is crucial to demonstrate that the political and cultural content of the group's anti-Stalinism meant different things at different times.

It was by successive stages that the New York intellectuals moved from a distinct variety of communism in the 1930s to a distinct variety of liberalism by the 1950s; from advocating socialist revolution to endorsing American capitalism. At the beginning, most of the intellectuals were anti-Stalinist communists; by the mid-1950s, most had become anticommunist liberals. Nonetheless, individuals who were not members of the original core joined the group at various points, but the newcomers were assimilated into a group drifting in a conservative direction.

This shift—in which certain doctrinal elements appear to remain the same in form while being utterly transformed in content—represents the most significant bond between such disparate members of the group as Lionel Trilling, a devout academic of immigrant Jewish parentage, who was markedly evasive in his political pronouncements, and James T. Farrell, an Irish-American, generally hostile to academe, who was at times abrasive in his political declarations. In fact, the appellation "New York intellectuals" began as a somewhat mystifying euphemism for a group originally called the "Trotskyist intellectuals."[21] After all, many in the group came from cities other than New York (James T. Farrell, Saul Bellow, and Isaac Rosenfeld were all from Chicago), while others, such as Benjamin Stolberg and James Rorty, would be classified by most cultural historians as journalists rather than intellectuals. Historically, the phrase "New York intellectuals" was episodically used to refer to nonparty Trotskyist sympathizers and allies during the 1930s and early 1940s. By the 1950s, when it had wider currency, the point of reference was those former revolutionaries who had achieved some reputation in New York intellectual journals, combined with newer friends and associates who identified in various ways with that former experience. Thus Max Eastman, a crucial figure in the formation of the anti-Stalinist left, is never considered a "New York intellectual," while Alfred Kazin, who was only peripherally involved in the 1930s and never sympathetic to Trotskyism, is sometimes mistaken as a representative figure.

One reason for the ascendancy of the term "New York intellectuals" has to do with their changing status. During the 1930s, when they coalesced as a distinct grouping, most had not gained the prominence that they acquired in later years. Sidney Hook, James T. Farrell, Louis Hacker, Lewis Corey, and Edmund Wilson enjoyed national reputations at the time, but Lionel Trilling did not publish his first book, *Matthew Arnold*, until 1939, and Meyer Schapiro, Philip Rahv, Mary McCarthy, Harold Rosenberg, Lionel Abel, among others, had yet to publish a book. Fame and influence came only after they had excised their anti-Stalinism from the context of revolutionary Marxism and quasi-Trotskyist politics in which it had been fashioned. It was precisely this political transformation that constituted the binding moment in their evolution and signaled their entrance as a significant force in American intellectual history. From that time on, claims of being an "anti-Stalinist" left were inauthentic, a rhetorical ploy to gain a hearing in liberal and left-wing circles. With only a few exceptions, these intellectuals had become anticommunist liberals who were embarked on an increasingly right-wing trajectory.

Among other purposes, this book tries to explain the social context in which this transformation occurred. The Moscow trials and the relentless growth of fascism caused some in the group to become demoralized in the late 1930s. Then came World War II, whose complex nature disoriented many of the intellectuals and caused some to repudiate long-held positions. Finally, the postwar environment—filled with disappointments and fear as well as opportunities for new careers in publishing and academe—precipitated the final stage in their collective change of political allegiance. Remarkably, even though most individuals made this shift in a staggered sequence—each denouncing the others for their apostasies before themselves following suit—they remained a coherent, distinguishable group. Despite broad variations in political orientation, ranging from the affiliation of Max Eastman and James Burnham with *National Review* to the social democratic views of Irving Howe, Meyer Schapiro, and others grouped around *Dissent*, the New York intellectuals' tradition had become such a clearly demarcated ideological force that Norman Podhoretz and others of a younger generation could assimilate it secondhand and perpetuate some of its features in the decades that followed World War II.

A book that undertakes such a vast subject as the political and cultural implications of the rise and decline of anti-Stalinist Marxism among intellectuals in New York between the early 1930s and the 1980s must be clear about its focus, priorities, and limitations. Among the questions explored in this book are the following: What was the nature of theories of Stalinism and anti-Stalinism formulated by various New York intellectuals? Did these theories change? What connections existed between evolving political attitudes and the creative practice of the intellectuals? What were the precise political engagements of the intellectuals, especially in regard to Marxist political organizations? Was the project of creating an anti-Stalinist left doomed from the start, viable only at a certain historical moment and for certain limited purposes? Has it properly attained its logical culmination in the existing worldviews that exist today around *Partisan Review*, *Dissent*, and *Commentary*?

Many individuals, famous and forgotten, wend their way across the pages of this book, and numerous subsidiary issues receive consideration. Therefore, it is impossible to provide complete biographical and critical studies of all the intellectuals included; I have focused instead on those aspects of their careers that are most relevant or that have received inaccurate or inadequate attention from other scholars. Thus, even though the chapters of the book proceed chronologically, I sometimes return to earlier episodes or jump forward to later ones in order to present the overall shape of an intellectual career. The book's primary objective is to explain the political trajectory of creative, independent-minded literary intellectuals who attempted to develop and sustain an anti-Stalinist Marxism. Consequently, I have not emphasized the impact of anti-Stalinist Marxism in areas such as the trade union movement, nor have I dealt extensively with those components of the anti-Stalinist left that were a step removed from the Trotskyist-influenced core that evolved into the New York intellectuals (such as the Bukharinist theoreticians Will Herberg and Bertram D. Wolfe, and council communists such as Paul Mattick).

To many members of the current generation, the questions addressed above are still burning ones. I hope that this book will enable readers to see the dilemma whole, in terms of both the strengths and weaknesses of its subjects. Perhaps it can help resolve the tension that many contemporary radicals feel between their anticapitalist and anti-Stalinist predilections. It may also assist efforts to avoid the sorts of dogmatically pure doctrinairism and the insufferable self-righteousness characteristic of all too many politically minded people both on the left and on the right. Perhaps this book will also help allay the process of deradicalization that eventually overtakes almost all whose lives are based in institutions of teaching, scholarship, and publishing during conservative periods.

At the same time, this book undertakes other tasks as well. It examines many intriguing people, ranging from the lesser-known Herbert Solow to the more famous Hook and Howe; it considers some psychological dimensions of deradicalization; it discusses a variety of literary and cultural issues; and it analyzes the antinomies of revolutionary internationalism and Jewish identity. In order to integrate all these themes into a coherent narrative, it was necessary to overcome a major obstacle to reconstructing the lives, activities, and values of the creators and perpetuators of the New York intellectual tradition: the politics of memory.

Some may consider the expression "the politics of memory" a euphemism for lying about one's past actions and motivations, but the phenomenon is more complex. Individuals sometimes perceive or remember facets of their lives inaccurately for psychological or emotional reasons beyond their conscious control. The frequent sublimation of the personal into the political is one of the themes of Daniel Aaron's essay, "The Treachery of Recollection," written after the completion of his well-known study, *Writers on the Left: Episodes in American Literary Communism* (1961). Aaron came away from his research with the profound conviction that "some writers joined or broke from the [Communist] Movement because of their wives, or for careerist reasons, or because they read their own inner disturbances into the realities of social dislocation. To put it another way, the subject matter of politics . . . was often the vehicle for non-political emotions and compulsions."[22] Yet when interviewed or in writing their memoirs, intellectuals were rarely candid enough to offer such "low" motives as explanations for their lofty political commitments and breaks.

Another variant of the politics of memory was described by Dwight Macdonald and Philip Rahv in the early 1940s when they noticed that a growing number of profoundly disillusioned ex-Marxist intellectuals, such as James Burnham, were writing articles and books in which they fundamentally misrepresented doctrines for which they had been articulate exponents only a few years before. The two *Partisan Review* editors diagnosed this phenomenon as "'cultural amnesia' . . . in which the victim, as the result of some great shock, simply *cannot recall* the most elementary truths from his past experience."[23]

A third example of what might more accurately be called "political amnesia" occurs when an individual, sometimes without the slightest calculation, attempts for pragmatic reasons to assign a spurious consistency to his or her political career by focusing on secondary aspects of their earlier thought and omitting, minimizing, or reinterpreting what was primary. In the early 1950s Floyd Dell recalled his feelings about the deceptive manner in which his old *Masses* comrade Max Eastman had reneged on his opposition to World War I, just as the *Masses* was suppressed by the U.S. government and the *Liberator* was proposed as a replacement: "You quoted . . . some earlier editorial writings to show that your recent views [in support of World War I] had been expressed earlier. . . . your sincerity was not doubted, but it was felt that there *was* a change, fortunate for all of us, since it permitted the continuation of the magazine under a new name."[24]

In the course of research for this book, I found that the most common manifestations of the politics of memory involved a modification of the past to validate some present political conviction. For example, a number of ex-revolutionary Marxists of Jewish background had become pro-Israel after 1948 and had substituted either Zionism or some other form of Jewish ethnic identity for the revolutionary internationalism to which they had once adhered. They tended to recall the Marxist movement of the 1930s, including not just the Communists but also the Trotskyists, as being almost "anti-Semitic." They now believed that the semiofficial policy of those movements denied Jews a cultural identity, even though they championed such identities for Irish-Americans and Afro-Americans. Moreover, they recalled that the Trotskyist movement paid little attention to Hitler's war against the Jews. The fact that many radical Jews assumed non-Jewish names for party or professional reasons is cited as further evidence of a bias against Jewish ethnicity in the movement, and perhaps even a manifestation of Jewish self-hatred: Irving Horenstein became Irving Howe; Joseph Friedman became Joe Carter; Albert Glotzer became Albert Gates; Emanuel Geltman became Emanuel Garrett; Felix Mayorwitz became Felix Morrow; and so on.

On the other hand, veteran radicals who still adhered to some form of internationalism or universalism, or who at least had not adopted any form of Judeocentrism, remembered very differently. For example, they pointed out that Trotsky was among the first to predict that World War II would lead to the extermination of millions of Jews and that it was the Trotskyists alone who mobilized thousands in the streets of New York against German-American Bund activities. Trotskyists, they remembered, had published article after article in their papers and magazines excoriating anti-Semitism and analyzing what was then called "the Jewish question."[25]

The point is not that one version of the past is wholly true and the other wholly false; it is that sometimes the past is remembered selectively, in accord with the needs of the ideological outlook one has at a given moment or had at some significant moment in the past. The contemporary cultural historian must try to recreate a whole through the use of all available evidence—documents, publications, and correspondence—as well as a wide range of personal interviews, and not be misled by an affinity or dislike for one or another political person.

For example, understanding the mixed motives of memoirists, not entirely ideological but not free of ideology either, is important in assessing several heated exchanges that have occurred over various aspects of Lionel Trilling's career. Since her husband's death, Diana Trilling has been especially active in "correcting" the record to conform with her own recollections. Her exchange with Sidney

Hook in the June 1976 issue of *Encounter* is characteristic. In a memoir of Whittaker Chambers, Hook referred to a lunchtime discussion of the Communist theory of "social fascism" between Lionel Trilling and Chambers. Mrs. Trilling wrote a protest letter denying the possibility of such an encounter, insisting that "Lionel was not at all the kind of person who undertook, as other of our friends did, to argue the theories of political radicalism." Then followed a bizarre battle of memories between Hook and Diana Trilling, involving a vegetarian restaurant, a 1934 New York City telephone directory, and an item from the *New York Times* obituary file.[26]

However, the issue in dispute here may be significant. Mrs. Trilling is attempting, as she has elsewhere, to minimize the degree of anti-Stalinist revolutionary political commitment on the part of herself and her husband, taking advantage of the fact that, because of the passage of time and Lionel's own cautious temperament, records are scarce, participants in the events are deceased, and some intimates of the Trilling circle are inclined to perpetuate the same questionable image. Hook, who left a much longer public record of his Communist and post-Communist revolutionary activities and has therefore fewer inhibitions in demonstrating that he was not alone in such "youthful indiscretions," tends to be more forthright about his own involvement. Yet even Hook is susceptible to significant lapses. Although he has carefully documented his break with the Communist Party in early 1933, his memory of the subsequent five or six years of revolutionary communist activity is blurred. For example, he has no recollection at all of signing a 1936 manifesto, "Socialism in Our Time." This pamphlet, printed by the Trotskyist publishing house, endorses Norman Thomas's presidential campaign on grounds that are unambiguously revolutionary:

> Undoubtedly the struggle for socialism will be a hard-fought battle, for the capitalists will not willingly relinquish their power and privileges to the people. But only by wresting State power from the capitalists can we begin the task of building a new social order. Only by recognizing that the State power is one of the weapons with which the struggle between the two major classes is fought out, can we successfully undertake the transformation of our society.[27]

A tendency on the part of some of the New York intellectuals to downplay the depth of their radical involvement in order to minimize the extent to which they have reneged on their youthful ideals is elevated to a larger scale in William Phillips's *A Partisan View:*

Five Decades of the Literary Life (1983). Phillips's autobiography gives the impression that he and his friends were always more or less liberal socialists who were deceived and manipulated by dishonest Leninists. For example, in describing the extent of his association with the Communist Party, Phillips says that he had first heard about the John Reed Clubs as a left-wing organization in 1934 (the clubs had been established in 1929). He reports that, after joining, he was surprised to learn that the clubs were closely associated with the Communist Party.

Yet the January 1933 issue of the *Communist*, the theoretical organ of the party, contains a 3,000-word essay by Phillips denouncing the Spanish philosopher Ortega y Gasset as a social fascist backed by Wall Street and a slanderer of the Soviet Union.[28] This article would have had to have been written and accepted in 1932, and it is difficult to believe that the *Communist*'s editorial board would have agreed to publish a piece by a person entirely unknown to the movement. It also seems unlikely that Phillips would have made such a submission without some awareness of important party activities among writers, such as those of the New York John Reed Club. Furthermore, the essay indicates that Phillips had been carefully studying the ultraleft "Third Period" political line and trying to apply it to cultural issues. In his memoir he also forgets to mention that his closest collaborator at the time, Philip Rahv, and his wife, Edna, were party members until the mid-1930s.[29] It seems likely, in brief, that Phillips had an earlier and more intimate association with the party than he remembers.

Here the politics of memory operates to suggest that Phillips was sufficiently close to the Communists to gain expert inside information yet not close enough so that one is struck by the extreme zigzags in his political career, which in fact there were. A similar process is apparent in his discussion of Trotskyism. He claims that James Burnham, a frequent contributor to and advisory board member of *Partisan Review* until the 1950s, was only "briefly" a Trotskyist after *Partisan Review* broke with the Communists in 1936–37.[30] In fact, from December 1934 until the spring of 1940, Burnham was one of the top leaders of the Trotskyists, functioning in their three successive organizations: the Workers Party of the United States, the *Appeal* Group of the Socialist Party, and the Socialist Workers Party. He also coedited the Trotskyist theoretical organ *New International* during this time and wrote a number of important Trotskyist pamphlets.

As for Phillips's own Trotskyist associations, it is true that he never joined a Trotskyist organization, but the substantial correspondence with Trotsky from Rahv and Macdonald on behalf of all the members of the *Partisan Review* editorial board reflects the board's close political agreement with Trotsky's International Left Opposition. For example, on 23 August 1937 Macdonald wrote: "[A]ll of us are opponents of Stalinism and committed to a Leninist program of action. We believe in the need for a new party to take the place of the corrupted Comintern."[31] Phillips taught a class sponsored by the Socialist Workers Party as late as 1939.[32] That same year, Phillips joined with intellectuals in the Socialist Workers Party to form the League for Cultural Freedom and Socialism, an organization of revolutionary writers and artists inspired by a manifesto issued by Trotsky, André Breton, and Diego Rivera. None of these facts appears in Phillips's memoir.

Even when he includes excerpts from *Partisan Review*'s first editorial—after its post-Stalinist reorganization in 1937—to demonstrate the magazine's "combination of social concerns and literary standards," Phillips omits all reference to the magazine's anticapitalist political thrust.[33] He might have included the following statement of the journal's early editorial policy: "Our program is the program of Marxism, which in general terms means being for the revolutionary overthrow of capitalist society, for a workers' government, and for international socialism. In contemporary terms it implies the struggle against capitalism in all its modern guises and disguises, including bourgeois democracy, fascism, and reformism (social democracy, Stalinism)."[34]

When confronted with such omissions, the memoirist may insist that he or she was not covering up but simply that such omitted facts or episodes "weren't very important" in the larger scheme of things. In some instances this may be so, but when there is a pattern of omissions that results in a certain impression that seems to serve an ideological necessity of the present moment, then the historian has good reason to suspect that the politics of memory has played a part in reassembling past experience.

The politics of memory also plays certain tricks on memoirists who are driven to recast the past, in part, according to current political exigencies. For example, some present-day neoconservatives choose to present themselves as having a special "expertise" about the politics of the radical movement, a spurious claim that can backfire when original experiences have been overlayed by decades of anti-Marxist thinking. Such is the case with William Barrett, a *Partisan Review* editor in the late 1940s and author of *The Truants: Adventures Among the Intellectuals* (1982), who was more distant from the radical movement than the other *Partisan Review* editors but who nonetheless wishes to present himself as an authoritative interpreter of their tradition. For example, at one point Barrett explains why he had "mixed feelings" about Trotsky's Theory of Permanent Revolution even when he was a self-proclaimed Marxist: "If the revolution is permanent and unceasing, then next week you reverse what you have revolutionized last week."[35] To anyone who has the slightest familiarity with Trotsky's most famous theoretical contribution, this statement will be astonishing. Trotsky, like all Marxists, believed that social relations and institutions would continue to evolve after the working class took power, but the essence of the Theory of Permanent Revolution, derived in part from Marx, involved an analysis of the dynamic of social change in economically underdeveloped countries. Trotsky theorized that in such countries during the age of imperialism the proletariat was the only class capable of carrying out political and social tasks (such as land reform and national unification) earlier associated with the radical bourgeoisie.[36] What Barrett is describing in this passage is something more akin to Mao's "Cultural Revolution" in the 1960s, or, worse, to Stalin's slanders against Trotsky's internationalist policies in the 1920s.

It is also doubtful that Barrett understands, or ever understood, the basic Trotskyist critique of Stalinism, since Barrett writes that socialism is no longer an option for him because, having repudiated Trotskyism, he now realizes that "the dictatorial course of socialist revolution can no longer be dismissed as an aberration due to the personality of Stalin."[37] Trotsky, of course, took into account Stalin's role as an individual but never claimed that Stalin's personality was what transformed the political character of the Russian Revolution. In *The Revolution Betrayed* (1937), he clearly describes the encircling conditions and economic class forces that precipitated the crystallization of a bureaucratic caste in the Soviet Union, for which Stalin served as chief spokesman.

These blunders occur despite Barrett's repeated references to himself as having been a Marxist since the early 1930s—indeed, as one who was "passionately arguing Marxist theory" even in the 1940s.[38] In a 1982 *New York Times* interview, Barrett even refers to himself as having been in his *Partisan Review* days "a Marxist with a Trotskyist orientation."[39] Apparently this fanfare about his Marxist expertise is necessary to give credibility to the familiar premise stated early in the book that only former Marxists can understand the truly pernicious nature of Marxism and the Soviet Union. But it is difficult to find much that Barrett gets right in his book in regard to either Marxist political or cultural matters. For example, 1937 is cited as the year of "the last of Stalin's purges," when in fact the sensational Bukharin trial did not begin until 1938.[40] Barrett states that when *Partisan Review* was relaunched in 1937, the Communist Party advocated "a cultural doctrine of social realism and proletarian culture," although this line had actually been discarded two years earlier in favor of the People's Front, with its Hollywood and Broadway stars, which was one of the reasons why Phillips and Rahv became disenchanted with the party.[41] Barrett describes the Communists' and fellow-travelers' view of the Soviet Union in the late 1940s as a "Worker's State," even though their official doctrine was that such a stage had been superseded by "socialism" a decade earlier.[42]

Like Phillips, Barrett's description of the deradicalization of James Burnham is also somewhat skewed. He tells us that in the late 1930s Burnham reached the conclusion that socialism should not be theorized as "inevitable" but only as a "moral idea." According to Barrett, Burnham published these views in the "Trotskyist organ" and Trotsky "thundered furiously" from Mexico that people who worried about "moral ideas" had succumbed to "petty-bourgeois revisionism." At this point "Burnham was promptly read out of the party" and responded with an essay called "Lenin's Heir" that "appeared in *Partisan Review* in 1939."[43]

Barrett has the facts so jumbled here that it would take several pages to set all of them straight. Burnham acknowledged that he had never agreed with dialectical and historical materialism but had considered the matter unimportant until a dispute broke out in the Trotskyist movement over what policy socialists should take toward the Soviet Union in the early days of World War II. Burnham was never "read out" of any party but joined a faction in the Trotskyist movement that split in 1940 to form the Workers Party, from which he speedily resigned of his own volition. "Lenin's Heir" was published in 1945, so it hardly could have been part of a factional polemic with Trotsky who was assassinated in 1940.[44]

Many of the above sorts of errors can be corrected simply by checking the records; inaccurate dates, misleading summaries of theoretical positions, the claim that someone was expelled from an organization when he or she resigned, and so on, can be caught by a careful researcher. But other judgments about the past and about different stances are more directly bound up in an individual's political orientation both at the time of the event and at the time the recollection is offered. Moreover, there is the problem of gauging an individual's frame of reference; Midge Decter's 1982 *Commentary* magazine attack on Irving Howe's autobiography as the work of an irresponsible utopian reminds us that one person's moderate is another person's extremist.[45]

Some comments on the method of research and analysis used in this book may help to explain how it comes to grips with the politics of memory. This study began with an interest in writers and politics on the left. It soon became apparent that accomplished writers and artists, as well as full-time scholars, had little time for political activism. They tended to be linked to political movements and activities through more activist but lesser-known political friends. Possibly these friends remained lesser-known because so much of their energy went into political organizing, although in some cases problems in their own intellectual work compelled them to find fulfillment in political activity. Behind the friends were committees, and behind the committees were various left-wing parties. Behind these parties came the press of social forces and historical events.

Thus I came to recognize that no simple claims could be made about the degree and nature of my subjects' political commitments based on their public political statements and memoirs alone; a fairly detailed reconstruction of personal relationships and the background of political activity would be required for the disclosure of at least some of the subtleties. In the case of the left-wing anti-Stalinist intellectuals of the 1930s, the influence of Trotsky was central and this influence was mediated through various political groups. Despite their small size, such groups were often the aquifer of currents of political thought among the intellectuals; like the small magazines of that time and after, they were sometimes the source of ideas and analyses that trickled upward to nourish the political thinking of unaffiliated radicals. This is one of the reasons why I have devoted serious attention to Trotskyist political figures such as James P. Cannon and Max Shachtman, normally slighted or caricatured in previous studies, as well as to a number of party intellectuals who have never been, and who would never want to be, associated with the New York intellectuals.

In this book I have emphasized networks and associations as one aspect of the way in which intellectuals become drawn to certain political ideas, but I also believe that ideas and theories matter and that some ideas and theories matter more than others because they more adequately interpret complex reality. This does not, however, by any means eliminate all the mediating factors that come into play in shaping one's perspective, such as family background, personal loyalties, sexual attraction, psychology (especially the desire for attention and for security), and accident. The Marxism that informs this study aspires to probe a multiplicity of such causes without indulging in the fallacy of psychoanalysis at long distance.

Such an approach is crucial if the story of the deradicalization of the New York intellectuals is to be presented in its full complexity and not as a tale of good and bad cowboys, with black-hatted opportunists battling white-hatted saints. From the point of view of developing a socialist movement in the United States, their story is a tragedy (with some comic relief), not a morality play. Even the most notorious apologists for the status quo among the New York intellectuals today are at least partially under the delusion that in some way the defense of the inegalitarian social order from which they have so benefited is consistent with the best interests of humankind. To characterize their transformation from left to right as an "economic sell-out" would be a vulgar caricature, though not without some element of truth. More central to the lives of intellectuals, however, is the need for a vision to sustain their work. Thus the failures of this group are more aptly characterized as stemming from a blindness to the social functions served by the post-1940s ideologies they promoted—ideologies most often touted as some sort of nonideological breakthrough. On the other hand, I do not intend to make a brief for the absolute purity of all Marxist commitment; intransigent loyalists of left-wing parties and factions, especially leaders and full-time functionaries, can receive their own kinds of benefits—in terms of a modest power, a sense of moral righteousness, and satisfying work—from defending their political organization and its ideology.

Still, it should be unambiguous that my political sympathies are with Marxist commitment. While this book does not claim to have overcome the partisanship that other scholars pretend to transcend, I have made every effort to examine the central controversies evenhandedly and to interrogate all sources with equal care. At various times I have tried to imagine myself in the same position as the figures in this study, and within the areas of my intellectual competence I have tried to indicate what I think the preferable course of action might have been. To a certain extent, writing a book such as this is an imaginative act, involving skills such as one might use when writing a historical novel.

In this book the term "intellectual" is used rather specifically. An intellectual is defined not by personal attributes but by social function; an intellectual is one who is occupationally involved in the production and dissemination of ideas. As Karl Mannheim, Joseph Schumpeter, and others have emphasized, intellectuals are not a class; they are bonded together by their education and have some group attributes but tend to ally with more powerful social forces.[46] While there are many intellectual workers (in distinction to manual workers) in our society, authentic intellectuals are the creative sector among those intellectual workers who produce intellectual products.[47] Most often an intellectual will be an interdisciplinary generalist as opposed to a narrow specialist or technician. In this study I will almost always be referring to people in the professions of teaching, journalism, and editing intellectual magazines, or, in a few instances, "political intellectuals," that is, full-time party members whose task is to disseminate ideas. Everyone, of course, uses his or her brain to indulge ideas, so everyone is intellectual to one degree or another. However, it is not true that everyone who *is* intellectual performs the *social function* of an intellectual. Antonio Gramsci, one of the leading theoriticians of intellectuals, provided a useful analogy in the section of his *Prison Notebooks* on intellectuals: all of us cook or sew to one degree or another in our daily lives, but few of us have the social function of being cooks or tailors.[48]

Finally, this book rejects a position fashionable on the left at the moment, popularized by James Weinstein and others, that American radicals must abandon their traditional preoccupation with the significance and legacy of the Russian Revolution. James Gilbert, in reviewing Irving Howe's intellectual autobiography, *A Margin of Hope* (1982), in the socialist paper *In These Times*, complained of the Old Left that "many American intellectuals . . . were more concerned with the Soviet Union than with their own country."[49] This is an exaggeration, but it is true that slavish imitation of "foreign models" and ignorance about peculiar features of the United States have vitiated our indigenous American socialist movements. On the other hand, so have various forms, sometimes unconscious, of national chauvinism and the abandonment of an internationalist perspective. The point is that it is futile to evade the knotty problems of theory and practice that have ensnared our political ancestors rather than learn from them and try to do a bit better. We can ignore the "Russian Question," but it will not ignore us. A failure to understand the nature of the Soviet Union (is it imperialist? belligerent? wholly reactionary? an acceptable ally for victims of U.S. aggression?) has led to catastrophes on the radical left—disorientation and deradicalization. Meanwhile, the same basic type of revolution, with a majority of peasants in an economically underdeveloped country and a leadership professing Leninism, keeps recurring to this day.

My own study of the left in the United States from the 1930s to the present convinces me more than ever that an understanding of these worker-peasant revolutions, especially the 1917 one, is crucial for the survival of a healthy socialist movement in the United States. Did not a misunderstanding of Stalinism—first excessively "pro" and then excessively "anti"—destroy a generation of socialists? Later, in a repeat performance of the late 1930s, those New Leftists who uncritically cheered the accomplishments of China and Vietnam crumbled into apathy and worse because they did not anticipate the ways in which these worker-peasant revolutions might evolve. In Chapters 5, 6, and 9, I give further consideration to this problem.

In summary, the purpose of this book is to combat the political amnesia of a predecessor generation in the hope of reasserting the possibility and the potential of a tradition of radical political and cultural activity that is both Marxist and anti-Stalinist. The approach is to reconstruct and interpret more than fifty years of political and cultural activity by the founders and continuators of an intellectual tradition that initiated and subsequently abandoned this project. Such an effort starts with the delineation of the core groups and the process of evolution that led to the formation of the culturally significant intellectual circle that established the tradition of anti-Stalinist Marxism. Thus we begin by examining the activities of a coterie of young intellectuals who coalesced in the 1920s around a cultural enterprise devoted to the exploration of Jewish identity in the modern age.

PART I

Origins
of the
Anti-Stalinist
Left

CHAPTER I
Jewish Internationalists

> Like Marx, Rosa Luxemburg and Trotsky strove, together with their non-Jewish comrades, for the universal, as against the particularist, and for the internationalist, as against the nationalist, solutions to the problems of their time.
>
> —Isaac Deutscher, "The Non-Jewish Jew"[1]

. . . .

THE NON-JEWISH JEWS

A substantial number of studies have been devoted to probing the social and historical roots of modern Jewish radicalism. Despite the variety of conclusions such studies have yielded, most analyses usually begin by noting the dilemma of young Jewish intellectuals who have attempted to escape the confines of the religio-cultural ghetto, only to confront an alien society toward which they feel ambivalent if not hostile.[2] Political radicalism with its internationalist élan has often served as a magnetic pole of attraction to such intellectuals, especially in a period of social upheaval. One of the most important yet least documented developments in the evolution of modern American culture concerns just such a group of Jewish intellectuals. Seeking to forge a liberal Jewish cultural movement under the aegis of "cultural pluralism" in the 1920s, they found themselves propelled first toward Communism and then toward Trotskyism during the 1930s. Their experience produced several of the earliest pioneers of the anti-Stalinist left who later achieved national prominence as New York intellectuals.

In their origins and outlook, as recorded in the pages of the *Menorah Journal* between 1923 and 1931, these intellectuals shared many characteristics with the archetype that Isaac Deutscher depicts in his 1958 essay "The Non-Jewish Jew." Deutscher used this term to describe rationalist Jews—such as Spinoza, Marx, and Freud —who lived "on the borderlines of various civilizations, religions, and national cultures," and who were shaped by the cross-fertilization of such diverse influences.[3] More specifically, as these particular Jewish-American intellectuals gained confidence in their ideas and deepened their political commitments, they progressively shed ambivalent feelings about their ethnic backgrounds while embracing a universalist internationalism. As they increasingly came to terms with their Jewish origins in a positive way (some, in fact, felt a special empathy with Jewish history because of its record of struggle against oppression), they refused to credit any specifically Jewish trait or achievement as inherently superior or more significant simply because they themselves were born Jews. Sidney Hook recalled that "we took ourselves for granted as Jews and were concerned with the Jewish question primarily as a political one."[4] To them, Judeocentrism in any form was repugnant. If one chose to write for a Jewish magazine or about Jewish issues, one did so only from the perspective of the interconnection of the fate of all humanity.

The particular kind of universalism to which these young Jewish intellectuals were drawn as they encountered Marxism is best exemplified in the twentieth century by such revolutionary internationalists of Jewish origin as Rosa Luxemburg, Leon Trotsky, and Deutscher himself, who sought to overthrow the existing social order in order to construct a world culture that drew the best from all people from every class, ethnic group, and continent. Such an aspiration differs quite markedly from assimilationism or accommodationism, which means adapting to or even imitating features of the dominant culture of one's society. In its ideal form, internationalism can also be distinguished from the variant of universalism (sometimes called, pejoratively, "national nihilism") that demands total abandonment or only perfunctory recognition of one's ethnic identity; this abandonment might be a virtue, perhaps, if one comes from a dominant group, but it is potentially a form of self-denial if one comes from a persecuted race or nationality, as in the case of Afro-Americans or a colonized people. The universalist-internationalist perspective, fraught as it is with many difficulties, often remains more an aspiration than a goal concretely achieved. For the group that was to become the New York intellectuals, it did not come clearly into focus until the early years of the Great Depression, when the combination of sudden social dislocation and the rediscovery of Marxist theory exposed the limitations of the cultural pluralist doctrine.

Cultural pluralism, the product of American Progressivism's response to eastern and southern European immigrants, had a special meaning for Jewish Americans at that time. In the century following the French Revolution, Jews in western Europe seemed to have the possibility of assimilation within their grasp, while those in the east faced persecution, oppression, and isolation. Massive Jewish immigration to the United States, however, reinforced the concept of cultural pluralism that was vigorously put forward and defended by Horace Kallen, Randolph Bourne, and other liberal and radical intellectuals just before World War I.

As a theory, cultural pluralism suffers, as John Higham has noted, from "chronic indistinctness"; in fact, two ostensibly contradictory theses are embraced in the work of Kallen and Bourne.[5] While cultural pluralism was opposed to assimilation and the concept of the "melting pot," it was equally opposed to cultural and ethnic parochialism, positing as an alternative the future achievement of cosmopolitan values, including the absence of narrow loyalties and provincial prejudices, as well as a willingness to borrow from all cultures to achieve the richest blend. The precise relationship between these two desiderata unfortunately was never probed. Further, the doctrine was predicated upon a situation of stability and steady economic growth in which all groups shared equally. It did not take into account the possibility that in a class society certain cultures become the instrument of political and economic domination, while others are expressions of sectors of the population possessing few resources to promote their values.

Even before the turn of the century, the pluralist doctrine, advocating the development by different groups of their own cultures within the confines of a common civilization, had been articulated by such advocates as William James. Kallen's version came to fruition in the optimistic atmosphere of the Progressive era, which also produced John Dewey's instrumentalist philosophy, the liberal historical scholarship of Charles and Mary Beard, Lincoln Steffens's muckraking journalism, and Herbert Croly's *New Republic*. Bourne's views were partly motivated by his opposition to the national chauvinism that he saw engendered by the onset of World War I.

The anti-assimilationist aspect of cultural pluralism is emphasized in Kallen's famous description of society as an orchestra with multiple ethnic groups serving as various instruments in order to "make up a symphony of civilizations."[6] The antiparochialist and cosmopolitan facets were developed by Randolph Bourne who, in accord with Kallen's perspectives, praised some Zionist Jews for their ability to incorporate into their outlook the latest advances in science and other areas of knowledge. Bourne excoriated the melting pot thesis, which he took to be a mere euphemism for assimilation to the dominant Anglo-Saxon culture, arguing instead for what he termed a "spiritual welding," which, rather than diluting humanity to a single strain, would instead create a rich and powerful blend.[7]

The *Menorah Journal* was the main Jewish publication that promoted this particular combination of anti-assimilationism and cosmopolitanism. Horace Kallen was a founder of the Menorah Society, and one of Bourne's most famous polemics against the melting pot thesis appeared in the *Menorah Journal* in 1916.[8] The vital atmosphere created by combining cultural pluralism and the cosmopolitan ideal attracted such diverse sponsors as Henry Hurwitz (the *Menorah Journal*'s official editor throughout its existence), Harry Wolfson, Adolph Oko, and Waldo Frank in their efforts to create a place for the Jewish intellectual and Jewish culture in modern society. The first Menorah Society had been formed at Harvard University in a 1906 response to the ostracism and insecurity experienced by Jewish students. Nine years later, Hurwitz published the first issue of the *Menorah Journal*. The new magazine promoted a nonsectarian and academic humanist spirit, which aspired to cultivate respect for the Jewish past while also responding to the American present.[9]

The Menorah Society, which was eighty chapters strong by 1920, was animated by the temper of Hurwitz's publication and its search for a more positive definition of Jewry in America. The journal's program of developing a Jewish humanism led directly to the formation of a Jewish intellectual vanguard that aimed to create a Jewish cultural renaissance within the framework of cultural pluralism. Early on there were signs that the *Menorah Journal* could not entirely escape the ethnocentric bias in American culture. The magazine's strategy, as Robert Alter has since noted, was to "validate Jewish cultural phenomena by assimilating them to Western analogues."[10]

PORTRAIT: ELLIOT COHEN

Into this movement, in its inchoate stages, came the unique and catalytic personality of Elliot Ettleson Cohen. Born in Des Moines, Iowa, in 1899, Cohen was reared in Mobile, Alabama. His father, Henry Cohen, had remained in Russia to become a rabbi when his family immigrated to the United States. Later, to escape serving in the czar's army, he crossed the ocean by himself at the age of twenty. Elliot's mother, Rose Ettleson, also came from eastern Europe. Her family settled in Texacali, Texas. Beginning his career as a peddler, Henry Cohen soon opened a clothing store in Tama, Alabama, near Mobile, and met his future wife at a cousin's home while on a buying trip to Chicago.

Elliot Cohen was a prodigy from birth. At the age of two or three he could pick up a newspaper and read the headlines. By then his head was already as big as his father's, and it remained large in proportion to his body throughout his life. As a young man of medium height, graced with a fine smile and sparkling eyes, he also had a quick and nasty temper. Once a man outside of his father's clothing store began to beat a horse, and Elliot terrified his family by the violence with which he rushed out the door to stop him.[11]

At the age of fifteen he enrolled at Yale, graduating with a brilliant record at eighteen having specialized in English literature and philosophy. Believing that it was impossible for him to obtain a university appointment, open to few Jews in the liberal arts at that time, he passed several years at Yale's graduate school and then looked elsewhere for a profession.[12] He had been president of the Menorah Society at Yale, and he had won an intercollegiate essay contest with an article critical of American rabbis' lack of knowledge about contemporary Jewish life. Hence it came as no surprise when in October 1923 his first contribution to the *Menorah Journal* was a report on the New York summer school program that reflected the fundamental cultural perspective that would become Cohen's hallmark.

In interpreting the Menorah movement's stated goal, the seeking of the place of the Jew in the modern world, Cohen argued that the Jew be treated not in isolation but as part of the life of humanity as a whole. He emphasized that the Jew was dependent on the same social, economic, and psychological forces that conditioned the lives of other people. Thus, he concluded, knowledge about the Jew was of value for all human self-understanding and advancement. The terminology of cultural pluralism was evident in his plea that Jewish history should be studied "for the light it is sure to lend to those pressing problems of adjustment among all self-conscious racial, national, and cultural minorities in the modern state."[13]

Yet Cohen was a complex if not contradictory person; such high seriousness represented only one facet of his personality. Within a year he began writing monthly humor columns, first called "Notes for a Modern History of the Jews" and later "An Elder of Zion." Here he mainly attempted to recreate the satirical, debunking style of H. L. Mencken's *American Mercury* by presenting a cacophony of quotations, marginal annotations, and news items depicting Jews in all walks of life, including gangsters, athletes, eccentrics, and civil libertarians. Lionel Trilling, one of the *Menorah Journal*'s assistant editors, recalled afterward that "when it came to the Jewish present, we undertook to normalize it by suggesting that it was not only as respectable as the present of any other group but also as foolish, vulgar, complicated, impossible and promising."[14]

Even though these early writings expressed Cohen's distinctive temperament, his paramount influence on the *Menorah Journal* came not through his own literary contributions. Trilling later recalled Cohen as a Socratic personality who "conversed endlessly, his talk being a sort of enormously enlightened gossip—about persons, books, baseball players and football plays, manners, morals, comedians ... clergymen ... colleges, the social sciences, philanthropy and social work." Cohen felt that he had gained special benefits from his Alabama upbringing and "was proud of his knowledge of an American life that wasn't easily available to young Jewish intellectuals, and he cherished his feeling for the unregenerate commonplaces of ordinary experience."[15] Cohen also had severe difficulty sustaining his own writing, which prompted a tendency to use the literary endeavors of others as surrogates. Although judged by Trilling and others to be a great editor and teacher, Cohen so compulsively devoted himself to improving the *Menorah Journal* contributions that some of the writers found it necessary to withdraw from the strangling embrace of his tutelage in self-protection.

In the latter 1920s and at the very beginning of the next decade, Cohen's influence on the *Menorah Journal* was at its zenith. It was during this period that a small but lively band of talented young writers coalesced into a distinct coterie inspired largely by Cohen's personality and cultural sensibilities. In fact, the intellectuals grouped around the *Menorah Journal* might best be understood as an elite carefully selected by Cohen, the creator and molder of the group. Most had been Columbia students: Lionel Trilling (b. 1905) had earned his B.A. and M.A. at Columbia and then taught for a year at the University of Wisconsin before returning to work on his doctorate in English; Herbert Solow (b. 1903) worked as a journalist; Clifton Fadiman (b. 1904) had published widely and was teaching English at Ethical Cultural High School; Henry Rosenthal (b. 1906) was enrolled at the Jewish Theological Seminary; Tess Slesinger (b. 1905) was a short-story writer and a reviewer for several New York newspapers; Anita Brenner (b. 1905) was a specialist in Mexican art who had done graduate work at Columbia; Felix Morrow (b. 1906), formerly editor of the *Arch* at Washington Square College of New York University, was studying philosophy at Columbia. Also published by Cohen were Louis Berg (b. 1906), a Russian-born journalist who held various jobs, and Albert Halper (b. 1904), who was just beginning his career as a novelist. The group's influence through friendships and acquaintances reached out beyond these *Menorah Journal* contributors.

Through his elucidation of the *Menorah Journal*'s literary-cultural mission, Cohen provided a theoretical framework and vista that helped fertilize the literary imaginations of these young intellectuals. Trilling remembered his college days "as an effort to discover some social entity to which I could give the credence of my senses, as it were, and with which I could be in some relation." He felt that he had "no ground upon which to rear an imagination of society" until he came under Cohen's influence.[16] Felix Morrow recalled that Cohen had the ability to attract young intellectuals who were not at all drawn to things Jewish. Instead of proselytizing, he simply offered them an opportunity to write and publish in a prestigious journal, thereby creating "the simulacrum of a movement of young Jewish writers."[17] Later, they found out they had set down roots in the Jewish experience, although in a way that kept most distanced from official Jewish institutions and conventional religious practices.

PORTRAIT: LIONEL TRILLING

Lionel Mordecai Trilling never identified himself as having been a cultural pluralist in his youth, but he was closely associated with Elliot Cohen's *Menorah Journal*. He grew up in an orthodox home, first in Far Rockaway and then in upper Manhattan, where his family kept a kosher household. His bar mitzvah was an elaborate affair that included a service at the Jewish Theological Seminary (for which he was prepared by Max Kadushin, a disciple of Mordecai

Kaplan), followed by an original speech given before the family circle.[18] In later life he wrote explicitly about his Jewish identity on four or five occasions, twice referring to the pleasurable recollections he had of his Jewish rearing. On one occasion he noted that his parents, "although orthodox in the form of their religion . . . had a strong impulse to take part in the general life and to want it for me."[19]

Trilling nevertheless was acutely sensitive to the way in which society attempted to exclude Jews. From early childhood on, he felt a strong emotional reaction every time he saw the word "Jew" in writing. In his personal notebook for 1928 he wrote: "Being a Jew is like walking in the wind or swimming: you are touched at all points and conscious everywhere."[20] Consequently he decided to fight enforced exclusion through participation in a literary movement that he later called "the literature of self-realization," which he identified with the novelist and critic Ludwig Lewisohn. The movement presented a critique of the "sin" of "escaping" one's Jewish heritage. Trilling wrote in 1966 that during the 1920s he had felt a special antagonism toward groups such as the Ethical Culture Society, which he saw as a haven for genteel German Jews who were proud of their high degree of acculturation.[21]

His posture toward his Jewish upbringing and the Jewish community nonetheless is the subject of some debate. Those critical of Trilling for lacking a sufficient identification with Judaism frequently cite his 1944 statement in the *Contemporary Jewish Record*: "As the Jewish community now exists, it can give no sustenance to the American artist or intellectual who is born a Jew. . . . I know of writers who have used their Jewish experience as the subject of excellent work; I know of no writer in English who has added a micromillimetre to his stature by 'realizing his Jewishness.' "[22]

A more balanced summary of Trilling's views appeared in a memoir of *Commentary* critic Robert Warshow, who died in 1955 at the age of thirty-seven. Trilling wrote that Warshow's life resembled his own in that he "acknowledged, and with pleasure, the effect that a Jewish rearing had had upon his temperament and mind, and he was aware of, and perhaps surprised by, his sense of connection with Jews everywhere—and [yet he] found that the impulses of his intellectual life were anything but Jewish, and that the chief objects of his thought were anything but Jewish."[23]

The tragic themes animating some of Trilling's work, and the periods of depression recorded in his notebooks, are indicative of an occasionally tormented state of mind about which little is known. However, one psychologist personally acquainted with Trilling has drawn attention to the possible impact of the traumatic experience undergone by Trilling's father at the time of the father's bar mitzvah.[24] David W. Trilling was the descendant of a distinguished rabbi of Bialystok and a precocious child destined by his parents for the rabbinate. For unexplained reasons he broke down in the midst of his reading of the haftarah. His parents, embarrassed and humiliated, shipped him, against his will, to the United States. Thereafter he had the unpleasant task of receiving relatives as they arrived from abroad, each of whom painfully reminded him of the way he had shamed his family.

David Trilling subsequently married a strong, ambitious woman, Fannie Cohen, who had been born in England. Fannie had long dreamed that their son, Lionel, would receive a Ph.D. from Oxford, and when Columbia University officials refused to admit Lionel as an undergraduate because of a deficiency in mathematics, she personally convinced them to reverse their decision. Meanwhile, David Trilling assumed the manners of a gentleman and became something of a dandy, but failure continued to pursue him. First, he abandoned his trade as a custom tailor to become a wholesale furrier, so that his son could say that his father was a manufacturer rather than a workman. Then, at the start of the Great Depression, he began to produce expensive raccoon coats for chauffeurs, even though open cars were beginning to go out of fashion. His poor judgment on this matter cost him everything, and so it fell upon Lionel to support his parents while he was still a struggling graduate student.

The father's anguish apparently generated a fear of failure in the son that was occasionally paralyzing. Although he graduated from Columbia in 1925 and received a master's degree in 1926, Lionel could not bring himself to complete his doctoral dissertation on Matthew Arnold. More than twelve years dragged by during which several chapters were rejected by his adviser until, spurred on by a struggle to retain his teaching position at Columbia, he finally finished the dissertation which was published as a subsidized book.

In several short stories that he wrote for the *Menorah Journal*, Trilling explores the negative feelings that acculturated Jews can have toward other Jews who are less removed from the shtetl or ghetto environment. In his 1925 story "Impediments," Trilling uses the first-person narrative to probe the mind of an assimilated Jewish college student repelled by another Jew who is "too much of my own race."[25] In "Chapter for a Fashionable Jewish Novel," published in 1926, Trilling presents several scenes in which two Anglophilic young Jewish women, Janet and Julia, exhibit virtual anti-

Semitic revulsion against the more "common" eastern European immigrant Jews of New York.[26]

These stories reflect a remarkable honesty on Trilling's part in confronting the conflicts experienced by young Jewish intellectuals in the 1920s. A year before his death he wrote that "to speak of the *Menorah Journal* as a response to 'isolation' isn't nearly enough— you must make the reader aware of the shame that young middle-class Jews felt; self-hatred was the word that later came into vogue but shame is simpler and better."[27]

Do these barely dramatized confessional stories reflect a transcendence of feelings of shame on Trilling's part or a sense of guilt stemming from a suppressed desire to escape his Jewish past? The purpose of this early fiction was simply to depict the existence of such psychological conflicts among Jews in the hope that an awareness of them would lead to greater understanding. Trilling's overall participation in the *Menorah Journal*, however, was within the boundaries of the cultural pluralist and cosmopolitan perspectives associated with Kallen and Bourne. What is pronounced in Trilling's writing at this time is a desire to divest the treatment of Jewish subject matter of any form of parochialism or chauvinism. His discussions of Jewish novels, including those by Ludwig Lewisohn, were usually harsh and his criticisms were aimed at the narrow horizons of the authors. In 1929 he wrote that "only when the Jewish problem is included in a rich sweep of life, a life which would be important and momentous even without the problem of Jewishness, but a life to which the problem of Jewishness adds further import and moment, will a good Jewish novel have been written and something said about the problem."[28]

Trilling's youthful opposition to parochialism also comes to the fore in his last fictional contribution to the magazine, "Notes on a Departure." In a significant episode the protagonist—a young Jewish teacher in a middle western community—admits that he intentionally cuts himself off and isolates himself from participating as fully as possible in the world around him by cultivating an excessive Jewish self-consciousness:

> Once he had held that the town was going to make him do things he must not do. It sought to include him in a life into which he must not go. To prevent this he made use of a hitherto useless fact. He had said, "I am a Jew," and immediately he was free. He had felt himself the embodiment of an antique and separate race . . . and was unable to partake of what he thought [was] the danger that lay in the town and university.

He had made a companion of the solitude he had gained, gazed fondly and admiringly at it; he had made an exorcizing charm of it and when he touched it the town became harmless.[29]

This passage, reminiscent of the style of Henry James, may provide a clue to Trilling's rejection of the Lewisohn movement, which occurred about that time, and his later remark that Lewisohn's kind of literature made "easier the sin of 'adjustment' on a wholly neurotic basis. It fostered a willingness to accept exclusion and even to intensify it, a willingness to be provincial and parochial."[30] After Trilling left the *Menorah Journal* in 1931, he never again established official connections with Jewish institutions or organizations. Throughout the rest of his life he maintained that even though his Jewish identity had influenced his intellect and temperament, he was unable to pinpoint any Jewish ideas that had inspired him and that he did not regard himself as a specifically "Jewish writer."[31]

PORTRAIT: HERBERT SOLOW

Not all of the young intellectuals around Cohen shared his feelings about the vitality of the contemporary Jewish experience. For example, Herbert Solow, a Columbia graduate who became assistant editor of the journal in 1928, wrote to Cohen a year later, when he became a contributing editor: "Being a Jew might, in my case, have evolved from the category of unpleasant facts in which I placed it in my early youth, into the category of utterly irrelevant facts. That it achieved interest and significance for me is solely due to the *Menorah Journal.* . . . once I met the journal my interest was deeply stirred."[32]

Unfortunately, the details of Solow's upbringing are obscure. Thus it is difficult to conjecture about the significant causes of his negative response to Jewish identity before becoming associated with the *Menorah Journal.* All that is known is that both of his parents were Jewish and that no intermarriages had occurred before his generation. While in high school Solow attended religious training classes on Sundays and he may have been bar mitzvahed.[33] After college, his life and activities become well documented, and they seem not unlike many of the experiences of others in Cohen's *Menorah* circle.

Herbert Sidney Solow was born in Manhattan in 1903. His father, Dr. L. J. Solow, was a successful dentist who had emigrated from

Russia; his mother was born in New York of French and German ancestry. He attended P.S. 6 and De Witt Clinton High School, entering Columbia College in September 1920. There he majored in history and literature, graduating in June 1924 as a member of Phi Beta Kappa with a B.A. cum laude. The following year he studied journalism at Columbia, and, in June 1925, received a B. Litt. ("*cum grano salis*," he once quipped).[34]

During his Columbia years, Solow was a tall, slender, slightly stooped, reddish-haired youth with bored brown eyes, who talked with a drawl. He befriended Whittaker Chambers during his freshman year, worked on the college paper *Spectator*, and belonged to a circle of precocious Jewish students. One of Solow's teachers, Mark Van Doren, provided a portrait of Solow in "Jewish Students I Have Known," a 1927 article for the *Menorah Journal*. Not classifying Solow among the scholars, like Meyer Schapiro, Van Doren placed him instead, with Lionel Trilling, in a group "lazier than these, though no less intelligent and certainly no less interesting."

Van Doren's memoir reveals a young Solow of exceptional ability, who exuded a melancholia in his speech and bearing:

It was not a bitter irony, for nothing mattered enough [to Solow] to make him bitter—or so I thought. It was rather a disposition which he had to find that one thing in the universe balanced another, and that all things cancelled out to make a zero. To go in one direction or another would be to lose something of one's poise here and now; so one might merely stand and gaze, and none too gaily smile. The first intimation I had that [Solow] was not amused but tortured by the state of his mind was when he showed me an essay in which he maintained that nothing which could happen could hurt—and drew a picture of a young man looking on indolently while someone took a knife and slit the veins of his wrist. Something did hurt, I knew then.

Van Doren also recorded an important change that came over Solow as he found a calling in journalism during the late 1920s:

Some years later [Solow] visited me after a year in Europe, and his face was gray all over with the news of some personal calamity—connected with love, perhaps—that he never revealed. Another year of looking on and thinking, and word came to me that [Solow] had talked of suicide. Still another year and he found a position as a literary critic on a New York review. Now controversies engage him; he does research for remarkably well-informed articles; he is proud and busy; and I hear he does not speculate about speculation or about suicide.[35]

Van Doren concluded that Solow eventually transcended his melancholic inertia and emerged as a dedicated polemical journalist. The former student is portrayed as having become transformed from a cynical nihilist to a fighter for high principles. Yet there remains a contrary opinion as to whether Solow really changed into a poised individual who had overcome the debilitating agonies of his student years.

In Tess Slesinger's *The Unpossessed* (1934), a briefly popular roman à clef about Eliot Cohen and his bohemian-radical circle, the character suggestive of Solow, Miles Flinders, is depicted as still fundamentally a prisoner of psychological compulsions. Slesinger married Solow in June 1927 at the Ethical Culture Society's meeting hall on Central Park West. In the early 1930s she left her husband and his circle of friends, dedicating her novel to them because its contents explained the reasons for her departure. The analogy Slesinger uses to convey Flinders-Solow's gloomy disposition is that of Calvinism, and she attributes to him a New England ancestry with a harsh, Puritanical outlook that makes him suspicious of all joy, beauty, and optimism. The fictional Solow is depicted as a purist in Marxist politics, especially ruthless in judgments of himself and his associates.

Intellectual brilliance, a tortured emotional life, and high political ideals—these elements characterized the Solow emergent in the late 1920s. Yet even though the periodic recurrence of severe depression and his choleric moods were well known to his friends, they did not let these problems interfere with their respect for his political judgment. In later years Solow described himself as a neurotic whose sense of inadequacy and guilt had inhibited his day-to-day functioning. His friend Felix Morrow, however, thought that Solow's depressions could not be attributed in the main to neurotic traits and would have been treated by antidepressant drugs if they had been available at that time.[36] In general, the recollections of Morrow, Sidney Hook, and other of Solow's friends are quite at odds with Tess Slesinger's fictional account of her husband's psychological malady as the determinant of his highly principled politics.[37]

To understand this discrepancy, it should be kept in mind that Slesinger wrote *The Unpossessed* after both a personal and political break with her husband. Shortly afterward she moved to Hollywood, remarried, and, during the Popular Front period, adapted to the politics of the Communist Party orientation. The bitterness of Slesinger's breakup with Solow may well have colored her portrait of Miles Flinders as a compulsive fanatic who transfers his psychological frustrations onto his politics (Marxism having replaced his grandfather's Puritan God). Such a portrayal is also in harmony with the theme of *The Unpossessed*, which describes a group of would-be radical intellectuals whose political efficacy is negated by their psychological maladies. Sidney Hook acerbically argued that Slesinger simply lacked the political acumen to offer a fair account of the *Menorah* group's politics:

> She never understood a word about the political discussions that raged around her. . . . Her book shows that. There is no coherent presentation of any political idea in it—and it has always amazed me to find people giving it political significance. . . . Tess could talk about Virginia Woolf, Jane Austen, some of the characters in Dostoyevski—not Ivan Karamazov— but the political isms were something her "obsessed husband and his odd friends" were concerned about—a concern which affected her life. She ended up hating them. . . . Tess caught the psychological mood of some of Herbert's friends but she was a political innocent until the day of her death.[38]

In remarks published at the time of his death, another novelist, Eleanor Clark, offered a strikingly different description of the young Solow from the one found in Slesinger's novel. Soon after graduating from Vassar in 1934, one year behind Mary McCarthy, Clark met Solow at the home of Margaret De Silver. She recalled that Solow was a man who suffered from intense inner conflicts but never used politics as a means of resolving them. She does somewhat echo Slesinger in describing him as having a "strong streak of the Old Testament," although this is in reference to her recollection of Solow as a man who lived by his beliefs and was always engaged in full-time work for them, whether or not he received remuneration. While Solow's brilliance was well known in the New York intellectual community and he had held good jobs, Clark recalled that he consciously rejected a life of security, was lean and ravaged-looking, went years without buying a new suit, and lived in borrowed apartments and wretched abodes during the 1930s.[39]

Solow's experience with the *Menorah Journal* was crucial in shaping his outlook, as it was for the entire coterie who came under Cohen's influence. From his early youth Solow had taken no particular interest in his Jewish origin. He passed five years at Columbia without having contact with the campus chapter of the Menorah Society, with which the magazine was associated. But once he encountered the *Menorah Journal*, he felt his interests deeply stirred. He came to see that a strong point of the publication was its ability to make the concept of Jewishness significant to a young Jew educated in American schools. Furthermore, Cohen's unusual editorial abilities taught Solow how to write in a way that he found more valuable than all of his college courses.[40]

But Solow's interest in Judaism was never theological—and, like others in Cohen's group, especially Morrow, he excelled mainly when he wrote against the Jewish establishment. Consequently, a constant tension developed between the Cohen-Solow inspired staff of the *Menorah Journal*, and the *Menorah Journal*'s board of directors led by Henry Hurwitz. The friction rapidly sparked a crisis when Solow initiated a series of articles critical of Zionism. Felix Morrow recalls that Solow, although genuinely independent, was then "in the sphere of influence of the Communist International and especially on colonial questions" and that the Zionists had never encountered a critic of Solow's caliber. Most important, Solow "appeared as it were from within—in a Jewish magazine—and his criticisms were therefore all the more telling. The Solow articles on Zionism were the first real indication of where our group was going."[41]

In a statement published at the time of Solow's death, Sidney Hook recalled the significance of Solow's polemic against Zionism. He remembered first meeting Solow at a conference called by the *Menorah Journal* in the spring of 1930 and presided over by Cohen, who then sported a magnificent black beard. After an address by the Zionist Schmarya Levine, Hook asked an innocent question about the human rights of Palestinian Arabs. This threw Levine into a rage and the meeting into pandemonium. Solow then and later defended Hook, for whom the episode marked Solow's beginning as a "member of the permanent opposition."[42]

Actually, Solow had attended the Sixteenth Zionist Congress held in Zurich in the fall of 1929 and had sent the *Menorah Journal* two articles harshly critical of everything that he encountered. Then he went to Palestine, at that time a mandate of Great Britain, as a special correspondent for the *Menorah Journal* and also on behalf of the Jewish Telegraphic Agency. Shortly thereafter Solow's attitude toward Zionism underwent a dramatic transformation from an ambivalent left-wing critic of the main Zionist current to an outright opponent.

By late November Solow had become too angered by what he had seen in Palestine to complete his promised articles. He felt morally disgusted by what he called "black Jewish chauvinism of the most repulsive kind," which he believed had resulted in an unacceptable policy toward Arabs and had even caused the 1929 riots that stemmed from a violent clash at the Wailing Wall in Jerusalem. Solow concluded that many of the Jews in Palestine were behaving like the worst anti-Semites in America. He repudiated the position he had held before; he had merely suspected that the Zionist leaders were corrupt, but he was still bound by such a firm sense of solidarity with Jews that his mind had been closed to the situation of the Arabs. He returned to New York a firm anti-Zionist.

Once back in the United States Solow wrote a second pair of articles for the *Menorah Journal*, this time attacking Zionism straight on. But it should be noted that, despite the shrewdness of the exposé contained in "The Realities of Zionism" and "Camouflaging the Zionist Realities," Solow tended to be long on criticism and short on alternatives. He convincingly demonstrated errors made by Zionists who either depended on British imperialism or looked to support from the rising Arab middle classes. His warning against looking for solutions from the very social forces that caused oppression was prophetic. But his own solution stopped there. Clearly he was gravitating toward the kind of answers that Marxism provides, but he was not yet ready to embrace Marxism openly and fully.[43] Both he and Hook, with whom he now began associating, had considerable sympathy for the ideas of the rabbi and educator Judah L. Magnes, who advocated a binational state in Palestine.[44]

Solow's anti-Zionist articles came at the very end of the association between Elliot Cohen's group and the *Menorah Journal*. Cohen and Solow agreed to solicit responses to Solow's article from the Zionist community and planned a special issue containing the responses as well as a rebuttal by Solow. But Solow and Hurwitz quarreled bitterly about the content of both the rebuttal and Hurwitz's introduction. Solow threatened to resign from the journal's staff and finally, in October 1931, followed through on his threat, despite the fact that the special issue on Zionism did appear.[45]

FROM CULTURAL PLURALISM TO
REVOLUTIONARY INTERNATIONALISM

The departure of Cohen, Solow, Morrow, and several others from the *Menorah Journal* marked the political turning point for the group. But it was not unexpected; it had been anticipated since the stock market crash of 1929. By that time Solow and Felix Morrow, at least, were beginning to think of themselves as Marxists. Subsequently, the former *Menorah* group was drawn quite logically in the direction of the Communist Party, which appeared to provide the answers to the social and political problems that increasingly preoccupied the young writers. But they did not approach the party in prostrate awe. While new to Marxism, they had their own history as a group, their own high standards of intellectual achievement, and their own principles of integrity and fair play.

In a certain sense it was the conceptual categories advanced and reinforced by Cohen that became the foundation of the *Menorah* intellectuals' grappling with Marxist politics. At Cohen's funeral in 1966, Trilling pointed out that he and others in his circle had gained a "complex and vivid idea of culture and society" from Cohen, whose own mind "was dominated by his sense of the subtle interrelationships that exist between the seemingly disparate parts of a culture, and between the commonplaces of daily life and the most highly developed works of the human mind."[46]

The vanguard sensibility emanating from the *Menorah Journal* could hardly remain static as the 1920s gave way to the 1930s. The group's nonreligious, sociological attempt to understand the role of Jews in modern society led directly to considerations of class and politics. This intellectual process, galvanized into a desire for political action by the advent of the depression, propelled the group (united by a self-concept as a vanguard of nonreligious Jewish humanism) decisively to the left. George Novack, a friend of Cohen, Solow, Morrow, and the Trillings, recalled that they were motivated by the conviction that "the socialist revolution and its extension held out the only realistic hope of saving the Jews, among others, from destruction." They thought that the cultural and religious heritage of the Jewish people that might have been essential to its past survival in the diaspora and the ghetto "contained very little that was usable and capable of further development once we learned about the internationalism of scientific socialism."[47]

Why did revolutionary internationalism come to dominate the thinking of the New York intellectuals in the early 1930s, and how did it replace the influence of cultural pluralism on Cohen, Trilling, and the other members of the *Menorah* group? First, even though the revolutionary internationalism of that era repudiated adherence to particularistic traditions and cultures, it shared with cultural pluralism a hostility to assimilation by the dominant culture.[48] Capitalist society was seen as the creator of a false consciousness with false values that had to be countered by socialist-internationalist consciousness and values. Second, revolutionary international-ism shared with cultural pluralism a "cosmopolitan ideal" of sorts, although the means proposed for its attainment were different. Fur-ther, a stream of revolutionary leaders from Marx to the Bolsheviks personified this ideal.

With these two components, hostility to assimilation and a cos-mopolitan ideal, as a bridge, it is not difficult to see how the New York intellectuals moved from cultural pluralism to revolutionary internationalism under the impact of the Great Depression. As a theory, cultural pluralism presupposed a relatively stable if not static society; it was not designed to cope with intense class con-flict and economic collapse. Cultural pluralism came of age during the Progressive era and was linked to a liberal view of the prospects for democratic capitalism. When the depression began, Cohen's *Menorah* group abandoned the cultural pluralist perspective; it ap-peared insufficient from the vantage point of their intense radical-ization after the stock market crash.

The *Menorah* group became pro-working class and began to iden-tify the outlook of the magazine with that of the middle class. In his 1931 letter of resignation as contributing editor of the *Menorah Journal*, Solow accused Hurwitz of obstructing the work of Cohen because Hurwitz allegedly wanted to make the publication into the organ of "small manufacturers, tradesmen, professionals and execu-tives with comfortable but 'modest' incomes." Moreover, Solow regarded the magazine's program of "Jewish education" as the pro-gram of the middle class, arguing that such a program was inade-quate to meet the needs of the "suffering masses (especially East European)."[49]

From the perspective of revolutionary internationalism, the pre-vailing culture could only be transcended, and the cosmopolitan ideal realized, through the abolition of class society. In this process the decisive role was assigned to the industrial proletariat. For the revolutionary internationalist, the responsibility of the intellectual became to advance the interest of the working class, and, hence, the search for the place of Jewish culture in modern society lost its special urgency and unique significance.

The pattern of radicalization among Jewish intellectuals in the United States appears to be halfway between the eastern European and western European models. In Russia and Poland, where anti-Semitism was the official state policy, and the majority of Jews tended to be workers and paupers, there was a massive movement of Jewish intellectuals into labor, revolutionary, and socialist move-ments of all types. In England and France, where anti-Semitism was not official and where there had been a considerable integration of Jews into the middle and upper classes since the eighteenth and nineteenth centuries, the Jewish intelligentsia tended to be liberal, conformist, and, at best, moderately reformist; radical intellectuals were relatively exceptional.

In the United States, the *Menorah Journal* writers and their contemporaries (usually second-generation immigrants) were neither outcasts, as were the east Europeans, nor deeply integrated into the existing society and its established values, as were the English and French Jewish intelligentsia. The interwar years in the United States were marked by potentially radicalizing factors, such as the existence of a substantial Jewish working class and the persistence of a virulent anti-Semitism. Thus all wings of the radical movement in the United States experienced a considerable influx of Jewish intellectuals in the 1930s. Then during the 1940s and after—with the decrease in the Jewish working class, the greater possibilities of upward mobility because of the postwar economic boom, the withering of anti-Semitism in the face of the information about Nazi atrocities, and the conservatizing pull of Zionism—all wings of the radical movement experienced a comparable depletion. In short, there was a high degree of correlation between factors such as the ups and downs of anti-Semitism and economic mobility, and the ups and downs of rebelliousness among the Jewish intelligentsia; the different ideological currents (communism, social democracy, anarchism, etc.) available to the Jewish intelligentsia modulated these movements to the left and right but were not in and of themselves the causal factors, nor did any one (for example, Trotskyism) evidence a greater attraction for Jews than any other.

CHAPTER 2

Dissident Communists

I believe that communist principles are more important than communist organizations, for they enable us to judge the theory and practice of existing communist organizations in their light.

—Sidney Hook,
"Why I Am a
Communist," 1934[1]

· ·

THE *MENORAH* GROUP MOVES LEFT

The 1930s radicalization of American intellectuals was adumbrated and anticipated in the late 1920s. Its matrix was a growing disillusionment with what Elliot Cohen referred to in an essay as the Jazz "Age of Brass."[2] Underlying political discontent was dramatically manifested by the fervent involvement of John Dos Passos and other writers in the Sacco-Vanzetti defense campaign. This preparatory process was, of course, reflected as well in the pages of the *Menorah Journal*, guided by Cohen, whose broad cultural outlook served as a natural gateway to social consciousness and political radicalism, even before Cohen and the members of his circle began their collaboration with the Communist Party. In the early 1920s, for example, Louis Fischer, then the European correspondent for the *New York Evening Post*, submitted contributions to the journal that praised the economic situation of Jews in the Soviet Union.[3]

Besides Fischer, other *Menorah Journal* contributors also became, for a time, sympathizers or members of the Communist movement. These included the novelists and poets Edwin Seaver, Isidor Schneider, Stanley Burnshaw, and Kenneth Fearing; the artist and art critic Louis Lozowick; the journalist A. B. Magil; and the German writer Lion Feuchtwanger. In 1927 Maurice Hindus, in a prophetic study called "The Jew as Radical," argued that Jews had a predisposition to radicalism that stemmed from their ancient heritage, a predisposition that could be stimulated to action by certain conditions. In 1930, Mike Gold, probably the most prominent Communist writer of his time, published a chapter from his forthcoming *Jews without Money* (1930) in the pages of the *Menorah Journal*.[4]

The *Menorah* group's metamorphosis during the pre- and early depression years is recorded in the memoirs of Albert Halper, who encountered the New York coterie at the beginning of his career as a novelist. In 1929, Halper, freshly arrived from Chicago with one story already accepted for publication by Marianne Moore's *Dial*, traveled the regular circuit of small magazines and left-wing agit-prop theater meetings and attended a few John Reed Club sessions. His visit to the *Menorah Journal* office found him discussing politics with Cohen. But Cohen, projecting an aura of great personal integrity, did most of the talking—about the stock market crash, the necessity of economic changes, the *New Masses*, and the *Daily Worker*. Halper recounted the direct transformation of Cohen's liberalism into radicalism in the early 1930s, and the resultant friction with Henry Hurwitz. Cohen aspired to have his own magazine with full control of its editorial policy.[5]

Gradually, the core of the *Menorah* group gravitated toward the Communist Party and its auxiliary organizations. Among the most capable and committed of the group was Felix Morrow. Born Felix Mayorwitz on 3 June 1906 in New York City, he was the son of eastern European Jewish immigrants who ran a small grocery store. Although his family came from a Hasidic tradition, at the age of fifteen Morrow's father had fled in disillusionment from the House of the Chortkow Rebbe where his own father was a Gabe (a manager of the affairs of a Hasidic rabbi). Morrow's parents both became socialists in the United States, but his mother remained religious. Consequently, Morrow had a traditional Jewish education in addition to joining the Junior Circle of the Young People's Socialist League and attending activities at the Brownsville Labor Lyceum.

At sixteen he became a reporter for the *Brooklyn Daily Times* and shortly thereafter began working his way through New York University as a reporter for the *Brooklyn Daily Eagle*. As a philosophy major Morrow became close to the department head, Philip Wheelwright, who one day asked him to come along to meet a boat carrying a new instructor from Oxford who turned out to be James Burnham. Morrow also audited Sidney Hook's first class on Marxism at the university and edited the school newspaper, the *Arch*. One morning, he went to the *Menorah Journal* office to take Cohen's secretary, a high school friend, out to lunch. Cohen seized on him, as he did almost any bright student, and began suggesting topics on which Morrow might write. At the time, Morrow reluctantly accepted the notion of dealing with Jewish material for the sake of publishing in a prestigious magazine.[6]

Three of his longest polemical articles demonstrated his use of Jewish subject matter as a springboard to broader concerns. "The Yiddish Theatre in Transition" scored the Yiddish theater's trends toward an imitation of popular American theater.[7] In "Religion and the Good Life," Morrow lambasted the belief, expressed by Walter Lippmann in *A Preface to Morals* (1929), that there is a dependent relationship between the influence of religion and the prevalence of morality. Morrow explained instead that morality is a social relationship, therefore the dynamic of Judaism stems from its being more an ethical tradition than a religion.[8] Finally, in "Higher Learning on Washington Square: Some Notes on New York University," Morrow's political side waxed explicit as he joined his remarks about discrimination against Jewish teachers to observations about racism against blacks, noting the shift in interests on the campus from literary concerns to Communist ideology.[9]

In 1928 Morrow graduated from New York University and began graduate study in the Philosophy Department at Columbia University pursuing a special interest in religion. When he enrolled a friend told him that "you'll go farther with a neutral name," so Mayorwitz matriculated as "Morrow." He also continued his journalistic activities, contributing to the *New York World* and *American*, while simultaneously writing for literary publications such as the *Symposium*, edited by Wheelwright and Burnham, and the *Menorah Journal*.[10] He had entered Columbia with the fantasy of going back to New York University to teach philosophy; however, he was quickly disenchanted when he learned that John Dewey had left the department. When Hook asked him if he was really "ready to put in all those years on Kant," he began to feel rudderless. In 1931 Morrow applied for membership in the Communist Party; Israel Amter, the New York district organizer, told him to consider himself a party member but that he would be more valuable as a secret member—so secret, in fact, that Amter would personally hold Morrow's application in his desk.

In the Communist Party Morrow found clear direction for the first time. During 1930–31 he traveled around the country extensively as a reporter for the *New Masses* and *Daily Worker* under the pseudonym "George Cooper." His accounts of the political struggles in which party workers in various cities were engaged were later translated into Russian and published in book form as *Life in the United States in This Depression* (1933). Alexander Trachtenberg, head of International Publishers, the party's press, tried to get Morrow to visit the Soviet Union, tempting him with the huge sum of rubles he had earned from royalties on the book. But Morrow showed no interest, preferring instead to undertake a series of articles for the *New Masses* on the "Bonus Army" (concerning World War I veterans demanding financial relief), the "Hunger March" (concerning unemployed Ford auto workers in Detroit), and other struggles.[11] He also gave courses on American history at a Communist school, participated in the party's speakers' bureau, and assisted Joseph Freeman on the *New Masses*.

In the summer of 1931, four couples from the *Menorah* circle shared a millionaire's lodge that they had managed to rent for $800. Included were Morrow and Fadiman and their wives; Norman Warren, a former student in architecture at New York University, who had contributed a review to the *Menorah Journal*, and Rose Warren, who had grown up in the same neighborhood as Morrow and Meyer Schapiro; and Elinor Rice, a future novelist and biographer, who had graduated from Barnard in 1923 and became a close friend of Diana Trilling, and her husband, George Novack, a Harvard-educated young advertising executive in the publishing field.

During the summer months Morrow was much interested in a strike in Paterson, New Jersey, in which a Communist-led union was participating. The others listened as Morrow pressed them to become Communists. At one point Fadiman declared: "If what Felix says is true, we'll have to change the whole course of our lives!"[12] A year later, in the fall of 1932, Fadiman's article "How I Came to Communism" was published in a *New Masses* symposium. But the change may not have been quite so dramatic, since the article said little more than that the author was moving leftward. Morrow suspected that Whittaker Chambers, a classmate of Fadiman's who was then editing the magazine, so titled the article as a practical joke.[13]

Nonetheless, the *Menorah* writers and their associated friends were becoming a small presence in the *New Masses*. John McDonald, a recently arrived young writer from Detroit, who had quickly become fast friends with Herbert Solow after hearing him speak at a John Reed Club meeting, contributed a review of Liam O'Flaherty's *Skerret* in December 1932.[14] Articles by Anita Brenner and Norman Warren appeared in February 1933.[15] In May 1933 Louis Berg reported in the *New Masses* on recent events in the Scottsboro case, and Meyer Levin, who occasionally contributed to the *Menorah Journal*, reviewed one of his own books.[16] Sidney Hook and James Rorty, who soon became politically linked to the *Menorah* group, were among those who offered statements on the struggle against fascism in the April 1933 issue.[17]

Solow, however, was the key political activist in the group and by this time had become acquainted with Sidney Hook, a former member of a pro-Communist student group who was now leading a current of intellectuals who believed they could change the policies of the Communist Party by friendly criticism. Hook's group was aware of the factional struggles then occurring in the Communist International, and Hook later recalled that most of the people under his influence had had some sympathy for Leon Trotsky in the early 1930s.[18]

NEW ALLIES: SIDNEY HOOK, JAMES RORTY, CHARLES RUMFORD WALKER

Sidney Hook was born on 20 December 1902 in New York City, the son of Isaac and Jenny Halpern Hook. He grew up in the Williamsburg section of Brooklyn where he was exposed to considerable left-wing propaganda and activity. As a student at Boys High School he defended Marxism against his teachers and adamantly supported the Socialist Party's revolutionary internationalist position during World War I. In the fall of 1919, when he was a sixteen-year-old freshman, he helped organize a Social Problems Club at the City College of New York. Comprised of Socialists and Communists united in their vehement support of the Soviet Union, the group met secretly to discuss revolutionary ideas.[19]

Several precocious undergraduate essays published in *Open Court*, a monthly magazine "devoted to the Science of Religion, the Religion of Science, and the Extension of the Religious Parliament Idea," announced a theme that remained constant in Hook's political writing for the next fifteen years: the pragmatic necessity of social revolution. His article repudiating "The Philosophy of Non-Resistance" declared that "when Bertrand Russell abandons his faith in the necessity for armed insurrection on the ground that violence may destroy 'the priceless heritage of civilization,' is he not called upon to show that the inevitable wars generated by the present industrial system are less devastating in their ravages, less destructive to art and beauty than any social revolution can be?" A few sentences later Hook concluded that, although pacifism has its place, "the danger to society arises when the pragmatic criterion is not retained, when those modes of conflict which are adapted to specific situations are reified above the dialectical flow of natural and social forces."[20] His witty "Philosophical Dialogue," published a few months later, pursued the relationship between absolute values and practical necessity in a debate between "Universalis" and "Pragmaticus."[21] Under the growing influence of his teacher, Morris Cohen, Hook's interests became almost entirely redirected toward scholarly matters. By the time he graduated, his left-wing activism had evaporated, although his pro-Communist sympathies remained.

A brilliant student, Hook received the Ward Medal for Logic and at graduation a Certificate of Merit in Philosophy. After obtaining his B.S. in 1923, he began teaching in the public schools. A year later he married a woman who lived a block away from the Hook family. A former social worker, she was also a loyal member of William Z. Foster's faction in the Communist Party, occasionally performing secretarial work at party headquarters.[22] Through her Hook kept in touch with internal party life. He came to know a number of members including Joseph Freeman and Mike Gold, and he assisted the party in various publishing matters under the direction of Alexander Trachtenberg.

In 1926 Hook received an M.A. in philosophy and a Ph.D. in 1927, both from Columbia. His dissertation, directed by John Dewey, was quickly published as *The Metaphysics of Pragmatism* (1927), and he was hired as an instructor at New York University. At the same time, his ongoing interest in communism was demonstrated by projects such as the party's publication of his translation (with David Kvitko) of Volume 13 of Lenin's *Collected Works* (1927) and a two-part essay on Lenin's *Materialism and Empirio-Criticism* (published in English in 1927), which appeared in the *Journal of Philosophy*. In the essay he introduced another theme that would recur in his later work: the failure of contemporary Marxists to accurately represent Marxism because they misunderstood its partisan and scientific aspects. His essay prompted a series of sharp exchanges with Max Eastman, another student of Dewey specializing in Marxism, that would rage throughout the early 1930s.[23]

Short in stature with a high forehead, sharp features, round spectacles, and a dark mustache, Hook had extraordinary energy. Garrulous and aggressive, his speaking and writing combined relentless "logic-chopping" with a street-brawler's willingness to jump into a fray at the slightest provocation. Determined to establish himself as the foremost expert on Marxism in the United States, he treated the doctrine with the scholarly sophistication that it deserved. He especially worked to restore its revolutionary content which had been earlier excised by social democratic scholars. In 1928 he won a Guggenheim Fellowship to study abroad, and he and his wife visited the University of Munich during the summer. That fall they settled in Berlin where he attended the lectures given by Karl Korsch, among others. When his Guggenheim award ran out in June 1928, he was granted a renewal to do research on the "Young Hegelians" at the Marx-Engels Institute. During this time Hook first became aware of the seriousness of the persecution of the Trotskyists in the Soviet Union, but he was not yet drawn to Trotsky politically.[24]

Upon his return to the United States, Hook was introduced to Herbert Solow by Felix Morrow. Solow was in transit from militant liberalism to Communism, and Hook assisted the process. Within a year Solow declared himself to be a full-blown professional revolutionist and even demanded that Tess Slesinger, his wife, decorate their Washington Heights apartment with red curtains. By now Solow had come to exercise a strong political influence on Elliot Cohen, who tended to follow him, albeit protestingly. They would often quarrel and make up like a husband and wife. But in a more general sense Solow was incapable of leadership, despite his enormous gift for analysis and his prosecuting attorney's drive to expose and indict. Alvin Johnson, who employed Solow for a short time on the *Encyclopedia of Social Sciences*, referred to him as "Mordecai with the uplifted finger." But choleric and uncontrollable moods plagued Solow. Although he professed to be above jealousy, he seethed with anger at Slesinger's flirtations and occasional infidelities. Later he would alternately curse his friend Hook as a centrist and then ask to serve as Hook's "lieutenant" in the latter's struggle to save the Communist Party from Stalinism. On other occasions he made embarrassingly ultraleft pronouncements such as declaring that the European working class should march on Moscow in order to save the Bolshevik revolution from corruption. At least once he mysteriously faltered and attenuated his political line in an important debate.[25]

In the fall of 1931, while involved in a study of the history and theory of the Communist movement, Solow decided to look up Whittaker Chambers whom he had seen only sporadically since their Columbia University days.[26] This was followed by a period of collaboration with the Communist movement in connection with the student movement. For example, in April 1932, Solow published a letter in the *Nation* on behalf of the National Alumni Association urging support for and defense of the Communist-led National Student League delegation which had been threatened with mob violence while investigating conditions in the Kentucky coal fields. When Chambers became editor of the *New Masses* later that spring, he asked Solow to contribute an analysis of the student radicalization. As late as December 1933, Solow, together with Hook, organized a citywide Conference on Student Rights.[27]

In the summer of 1932 Solow traveled to Germany and the Soviet Union. Before returning the the United States, he visited Leon Trotsky, then in exile on the Turkish island of Prinkipo. Solow had favorably reviewed Trotsky's *The Real Situation in Russia* (1928) in the *New York Evening Post* and no doubt had heard about the plight of the Left Opposition from Hook.[28] But probably the main motivation for Solow's visit to Prinkipo was the one that had inspired his trip to Palestine: he felt a personal need to thoroughly analyze all sides of a question from a firsthand experience.

Having been appalled by what he encountered during his visit to the Soviet Union, Solow now wanted to know even more facts about the situation. Later he would state that his entire life was affected by Trotsky's unique forecasts of the tragic drift of world affairs, including Stalin's malignant role. He also reminisced that he was struck by Trotsky's literary brilliance and romantic personality, although from the onset he was skeptical of Trotsky's program that called for a political revolution that would sweep out Stalin's bureaucratic dictatorship while retaining nationalized property in the Soviet Union.[29] However, a transcript of their conversation preserved among Trotsky's papers reveals a somewhat hyper-revolutionary Solow trying to prove that the Communist Party had already been transformed into a social patriotic organization and urging that a Fourth International be founded as soon as possible. He also discussed with Trotsky the "group of intellectuals" he was assembling, and Trotsky recommended that he weed them out through a discussion of concrete political issues, such as those presented in recently published documents on the Chinese revolution.[30]

Returning to the United States in the fall of 1932, Solow contacted the leaders of the American Trotskyist movement, James P. Cannon and Max Shachtman, although this connection was not known to everyone in Solow's circle. Hook and Meyer Schapiro later recalled that at the time Solow was eager to become a "professional revolutionary." He insisted that Communist intellectuals must devote themselves full time to revolutionary work and leave their libraries and laboratories for a life commitment to the cause.[31]

Solow concentrated his efforts on winning pro-Communist intellectuals to Trotskyism by working among them and gradually raising political questions that would expose to them the ways in which the official Communist Party fell short of its Marxist principles. In such efforts, Solow influenced others besides his circle of friends from the *Menorah* group. He came in especially close contact with two other writers, James Rorty and Charles Rumford Walker, in the process of building the two most important organizations of revolutionary intellectuals that existed during the early 1930s: the National Committee for the Defense of Political Prisoners and the League of Professionals. (The John Reed Clubs were oriented toward new and unknown writers from the working class, although Solow, Hook, Schapiro, and other professionals attended some meetings.)

James Hancock Rorty was born on 30 March 1890 in Middletown, New York, the son of Richard McKay Rorty and Octavia Churchill Rorty.[32] His father, a political refugee from Donegal in Ireland, had fought the British and continued to maintain his Fenian associations while running a small grocery store. The son absorbed socialist and anarchist ideas quite naturally as he began to pursue a variety of journalistic and literary activities. Graduating from Tufts College in 1913, he was initiated into the advertising business in New York. He volunteered as a private in the Ambulance Service of the U.S. Army during World War I. Serving as a stretcher-bearer on the Argonne front, he earned the Distinguished Service Cross, but the experience turned him into a militant pacifist.

A short, trim man with delicate features and a gentle personality, Rorty moved to San Francisco after his World War II service to begin dual careers as an advertising executive and an experimental poet. He wrote in a free verse style that occasionally recalled Whitman and at times approached the quality of Carl Sandburg and Edgar Lee Masters. Usually his poems were topical. He attempted to communicate to a wide audience his response to the social and cultural forces threatening his survival and development. In 1922 he won the *Nation* poetry prize for "When We Dead Awaken," and two years later he issued a small volume of poetry called *What Michael Said to the Census Taker* (1924).

In 1925 he left California and later in the year joined the staff of the *New Masses*, which was then close to but not yet controlled by the Communist Party. Somewhat of an eclectic anarchist, Rorty actually felt closer to the Socialist Party. He earned $50 a week and collaborated with fellow editors Egmont Arens, Joseph Freeman (who had received a $27,000 grant for the publication from the Garland Fund), Hugo Gellert, Mike Gold, and John Sloan. But a bitter controversy erupted on the editorial board after Rorty had arranged for the publication of Robinson Jeffers's "Apology for Bad Dreams." Several of the editors regarded the work as reactionary, and Rorty was soon back in advertising at three times his *New Masses* salary. In 1926 he published a second volume of poetry, *Children of the Sun*, and the following year was arrested in Boston for participating in a protest against the impending execution of Sacco and Vanzetti. In 1928 he was divorced from his first wife, Mary Lambin, and married Winifred Rauschenbusch, daughter of Walter Rauschenbusch, a well-known Christian socialist. A son, Richard, was born in October 1931, the year that Rorty decided to make a second attempt at collaborating with the Communist Party.

Charles Rumford Walker was born on 31 July 1893 in Concord, New Hampshire, the scion of the Congregationalist minister who had originally settled the region.[33] On his mother's side he was connected with the Wentworths, from whose family came the last royal governor of the colony. His father was a kindly physician who had the habit of not collecting bills from his patients. Charles had an unusually happy childhood in which his two main interests were literature and technology. From an early age he aspired to be a writer and was fascinated by languages, excelling in Greek in high school, but he also achieved local notoriety for his construction of miniature passenger balloons. Eventually he combined the two preoccupations by establishing a printing press and a local newspaper, the *Daily Messenger*. He set his own type and his equipment occupied the entire third floor of the family's red brick house, which shook threateningly whenever the paper went to press. The *Daily Messenger* had such a large following that Charles kept it going from afar after he left Concord to attend preparatory school at Exeter.

At Yale, from which he graduated in 1916, he was editor of the *Yale Literary Magazine* and began a lifelong friendship with Edmund Wilson, his counterpart at Princeton. His other college friends included Archibald MacLeish, Phelps Putnam, Stephen Vincent Benét, and Thornton Wilder. With the advent of World War I, Walker was caught up in the patriotic fervor. He enlisted and went first to the Plattsburgh training camp and then to the regular army where he was assigned to the artillery, but he fell ill during transit across the Atlantic and was hospitalized until after the armistice had been signed.

Walker had never thought of himself as a radical, but, coming out of the army, he felt as if his life had been turned upside down. Consequently, he pledged himself to learn about the real nature of the society in which he lived, beginning with the steel industry, since steel seemed basic to American life. Nearly six feet tall with very blond hair, fair skin, and piercing blue eyes, Walker was healthy, strong, and adventurous. He hopped a train to Pittsburgh where he had heard that Jones and Laughlin was hiring. For a while he worked as a third helper on an open hearth and then in the brass mills. He had originally intended to use his firsthand experience to assist him in making a career in American industry, but a political turning point came during the depression of 1921 when he took a job in the personnel office of a firm in the copper industry. He found that he was unable to represent company interests to the families of laid-off workers, so he quit and went to New York to seek employment with labor reform organizations.

In 1922, he published *Steel, the Diary of a Furnace Worker*, and, after a stint as an assistant editor at the *Atlantic Monthly* in Boston, he traveled abroad to write *Bread and Fire* (1927), a novel about his experiences in Pittsburgh and among the reform organizations in New York. Back in Boston in 1928, he met and married Adelaide George, a Wyoming-born actress and member of the Boston Repertory Stock Company. Following the marriage his political interests temporarily flagged, so he began a book of short stories published as *Our Gods Are Not Born* (1930) and set about raising a family. By the spring of 1931 Walker was so far removed from politics that he decided to pursue his childhood fascination with travel balloons by wangling an assignment from *Colliers* to go on a thirty-day balloon trip. Upon his return, he discovered that Adelaide was doing volunteer work for the Communist-led Unemployed Council, and that autumn they went together to Kentucky to work for the Dreiser Committee of the National Committee for the Defense of Political Prisoners (NCDPP).

THE NATIONAL COMMITTEE FOR THE DEFENSE OF POLITICAL PRISONERS (NCDPP) AND THE LEAGUE OF PROFESSIONALS

The National Committee for the Defense of Political Prisoners was founded in June 1931 by intellectuals, writers, and artists as an adjunct to the International Labor Defense (ILD), led by the Communist Party. According to Malcolm Cowley, it originated at a meeting held that spring at the apartment of Theodore Dreiser who declared that "the time is ripe for American intellectuals to render some service to the American worker." Actually, Dreiser had been collaborating rather closely with Joe Pass, a Communist Party organizer, and through their joint efforts the NCDPP came into existence.[34] According to an announcement in the *New Masses*, the organization aimed to respond to racist, industrial, and political persecutions. Theodore Dreiser was the chairman, Lincoln Steffens the treasurer; among others mentioned as endorsers were John Dos Passos, Suzanne La Follette, Franz Boas, Floyd Dell, Waldo Frank, and Josephine Herbst.[35] But Elliot Cohen and other former *Menorah Journal* writers and their friends quickly became the main administrators of the NCDPP. Cohen became executive secretary with Adelaide Walker as his assistant, and Diana Rubin, an aspiring singer who had married Lionel Trilling in 1929, worked in the NCDPP office as secretary of the Prisoners' Relief Committee.[36] The NCDPP sponsored two now-famous tours of writers to investigate conditions in Harlan County, Kentucky. The Walkers organized the second, but could not go themselves because they were still under indictment for "criminal syndicalism" for their participation on the first tour. The NCDPP was also active in the Scottsboro and Angelo Herndon defense cases and published several pamphlets including *Kentucky Miners Speak* (1931) and Cohen's *The Yellow Dog Contract* (1932).[37]

Cohen himself had begun to develop a bit of a following on the Columbia University campus at this time. Among his circle was Davis Herron, son of George D. Herron, the famed Social Gospel minister and professor of Applied Christianity at Grinnell College. Davis Herron was born and raised in Florence, coming to the United States to attend Columbia. There he befriended Cohen's younger brother, Mandel, and Rob Hall, a friend of the Cohen family from Alabama who later became a Communist official. Also in the circle was Meyer ("Abe") Girschick, a mathematician already close to Trotskyism while en route to a position as a statistician in the Department of Agriculture. Cohen's coterie, some of whom had attended Columbia classes given by Corliss Lamont and who had also been activists in the Communist-led National Student League, held meetings at his house. It was there that Herron encountered Cohen's sister, Elsa-Ruth, home on vacation from Radcliffe. In 1933 Davis visited the Soviet Union with Girschick, and on his return trip to the United States he met with Trotsky in Prinkipo, where he proposed that a magazine sympathetic to the Left Opposition be initiated in the United States.[38] The following year he and Elsa-Ruth were married.

In the spring of 1932 Cohen decided to organize a protest of intellectuals against President Hoover's brutal treatment of the Bonus March veterans in Washington, D.C. He asked Rorty to stop by the NCDPP office in the same building that housed the International Labor Defense offices at the corner of Broadway and 10th Street. Rorty was at once struck by Cohen's appearance: "[T]he heavy melancholy of the long Greco-like facial mask . . . the suffering that looked out of his brilliant brown eyes. His hair was black and his face unlined. Yet he looked already like a biblical patriarch, prematurely aged."[39] Cohen frankly told Rorty that the NCDPP was a Communist front but one that defended non-Communist victims. He convinced Rorty to join Waldo Frank and Sherwood Anderson in what turned out to be an aborted attempt to meet with President Hoover.[40] Shortly after, Cohen contacted Rorty again and this time proposed that Rorty become secretary of a "League of Professional Groups for Foster and Ford," the Communist presidential and vice-presidential candidates. Soon Rorty was ensconced in an office in the same building on East 13th Street that housed the Communist Party, with Helen Schneider, wife of the Communist poet Isidor Schneider, as his secretary.

By the time the campaign was launched Rorty had collected some fifty well-known names for the league's letterhead, including Sherwood Anderson, Newton Arvin, Erskine Caldwell, Robert Cantwell, Lewis Corey, Malcolm Cowley, Kyle Crichton, Countee Cullen, H. W. L. Dana, John Dos Passos, Waldo Frank, Horace Gregory, Granville Hicks, Sidney Hook, Sidney Howard, Langston Hughes, Matthew Josephson, Alfred Kreymborg, Lincoln Steffens, Charles R. Walker, and Edmund Wilson. The league also distributed forty thousand copies of the manifesto *Culture and the Crisis* (1932), jointly written by Corey, Cowley, Rorty, Hook, and Josephson, and five thousand copies of a leaflet called "Architects and the Crisis." On 30 October 1930 the league sponsored a public meeting at Cooper Union featuring Earl Browder, Waldo Frank, Cowley, and Rorty; two thousand people attended and another two thousand were turned away for lack of space, although a goodly portion of the attendance consisted of rank-and-file party activists. Members of the league also filled about thirty speaking engagements during the campaign, which was but a fraction of the total requests for speakers.[41]

Following the election, an attempt was made to retain the organization as simply the "League of Professionals." An ambitious program of educational activities was discussed, including publication of pamphlets and a new magazine. A lecture series on "Culture and Capitalism," which was organized by Rorty and John McDonald, was held in a large room over Chaffard's French Restaurant on 7th Avenue near 23rd Street. Featured speakers included Hook on philosophy and Meyer Schapiro on art. But the party quickly began to crack down on the independence of the intellectuals, some of whom began to use these occasions to criticize the Communist line that designated all Socialist parties as "social fascist." This analysis served as the justification for the party's use of the "United Front from Below" tactic, which meant trying to reach the Socialist ranks by violently denouncing their leadership. Another area of criticism was the party's advocacy of dual unionism, which meant the construction of "revolutionary" trade unions as rivals to the American Federation of Labor (AFL). A third disagreement was with the party's slogan, "Self-determination for the Black Belt," which was based on the belief that there already existed an independent Afro-American nation in states with a heavy concentration of black sharecroppers. These criticisms were met with jeers from party intellectuals and their allies present at the discussions. Then, in the middle of these disputes, a brutally harsh criticism of Hook's philosophical views appeared in the party theoretical organ, the *Communist*. Next, the final text of a league pamphlet written by Lewis Corey vanished after Rorty had turned it over to the party for inspection. Corey, whose real name was Louis Fraina, had for some time been regarded with suspicion by the Communists because of his activities as a leader of the party in the early 1920s.[42]

The acrimony came to a head following Hitler's seizure of power in Germany. An emergency meeting of the league was called at which Solow put forward a motion that the league initiate a united front of the entire left against the advance of nazism. This was the Trotskyist line, sharply contrasting with the Communists' view that the main danger was not fascism but "social fascism," i.e., social democracy. The motion passed, but, when Rorty led a delegation to the party offices to report the decision, Clarence Hathaway, editor of the *Daily Worker* and a member of the party's Politburo, refused to consider the proposal on the grounds that "Solow is a Trotskyist." Rorty never called another meeting of the league and it simply faded away.[43]

The NCDPP met a parallel fate in which Solow played a catalytic role as well. During late 1932 and early 1933 he discussed politics intensely with all activists with whom he came in contact. Now separated from Slesinger, he held court at his Greenwich Village apartment. The explosion in the NCDPP finally occurred at a 28 April 1933 meeting. As with the crisis in the league, the proximity of this date to Hitler's coming to power is important; but it is also important to consider other aspects of the conflict to recognize that, while the necessity of struggling against fascism was paramount, the dissidents were not solely concerned with that issue nor were they moving away from communism. If exclusive concern with German fascism had been the case, one might be led to the erroneous conclusion that the group had approached the Communist Party seeking an ally against fascism—a position more characteristic of the liberals who would be drawn into the Communists' Popular Front organizations after 1935 and again during World War II. But in 1933, with only a few exceptions, the intellectuals were dissident communists, not liberal fellow travelers or Socialists. Many, in fact, were like the Trillings, whom Morrow and Novack remembered as being ardent Leninists and Hook recalled as being disdainful of liberals and Socialists.[44]

The dissidents offered an explanation for their walkout from the explosive 28 April meeting in a letter dated 8 May 1933, which was signed by Berg, Brenner, Novack, Cohen, Rubin [Diana Trilling], Rice, and Solow. The letter is written from the perspective of individuals who considered themselves partisans in the revolutionary working-class movement against capitalism, but who also had specific criticisms of certain tactics of the major force within that movement, the Communist Party. The letter addressed two major issues: a proposal by Solow and Rorty to organize a united front of all organizations claiming to be antifascist and a resolution by Solow and Cohen calling upon the International Labor Defense to dissociate itself from certain racist statements made by Samuel Liebowitz, the ILD attorney in the Scottsboro case, who had stressed the alleged ignorance and inferiority of the black defendants.

Faced with a fusillade of abuse from party members and supporters, particularly directed at Solow, to the effect that such proposals were acts of counterrevolutionary sabotage, the group stated that it had come to doubt the possibility of free discussion for "loyal members" of the NCDPP such as themselves. Further, they denied that they had any connection with the Communist League of America (the Trotskyist organization), which was probably true for most of them who knew little about Trotskyism at that point except that it was a bad word in the Communist Party's lexicon.[45]

Solow, however, had lied, for there is no doubt that he was consciously trying to move his circle toward Trotskyism. By September 1933 he had already persuaded Novack to donate money to the Communist League of America after hearing the Trotskyist leaders James P. Cannon and Max Shachtman—and the Mexican muralist Diego Rivera—proclaim the need for a new International when

they spoke at Irving Plaza.[46] Felix Morrow had been secretly reading the Trotskyist newspaper, the *Militant*, for some time. Novack
clearly recalled Solow as the person most responsible for influencing him toward the Trotskyists, and he believed that this was probably the case with Morrow as well. Before Solow began to work on
him, Novack had hardly given the Trotsky-Stalin dispute any serious consideration.[47] Solow's political activity complemented the
Trotskyist newspaper, the *Militant*, which also predicted that the
campaign against "social fascism" in Germany would bring disaster, and exposed errors made by the Communist Party in its Scottsboro defense work.

Finally, on 16 February 1934 Solow's hard work bore real fruit.
The Communist Party, carrying out its line against "social fascism," violently disrupted a Socialist Party rally at Madison Square
Garden organized to protest the Austrian chancellor Dolfus's armed
attack on workers' houses in Vienna, which were mainly occupied
by Austrian Social Democrats. The dissident intellectuals were outraged. Immediately afterward Cohen and John McDonald composed
a letter of protest and, with the aggressive help of Rorty and others,
gathered twenty-five signatures of writers, intellectuals, and journalists. The open letter articulated three features of left-wing anti-
Stalinism that made it politically compatible with certain aspects
of Trotskyism: (1) it reaffirmed the partisanship of the signers for
the movement of the working class and against capitalism in its
fascist and imperialist manifestations; (2) it severely criticized the
disruptive tactics of the Communists that tended to produce the
opposite of their professed goals; (3) it rejected the reformism of the
social democracy which, the signers charged, had tended to tolerate
rather than struggle against the fascist advances and which had suspicious ties to the status quo as well. The signers were Louis Berg,
Will Gruen, Elinor Rice, Robert Ford, James Rorty, Diana Rubin,
Louis Grudin, Anita Brenner, Felix Morrow, Elliot E. Cohen, George
Novack, Lionel Trilling, Meyer Schapiro, John Dos Passos, Clifton
Fadiman, John McDonald, Edmund Wilson, John Chamberlain,
Margaret de Silver, George D. Herron, Meyer Girschick, Gilbert C.
Converse, Samuel Middlebrook, Robert Morss Lovett, and John
Henry Hammond, Jr.[48]

The *New Masses* responded by singling out John Dos Passos and
urging him to free himself from the "queer company" of the other
signers, many of whom were believed to be troublemakers. The
New Masses editors began their response with a didactic treatise on
the "United Front from Below" strategy and ended by praising Dos
Passos's past activities. The editors also denounced Fadiman for

having a "ritzy" office (he was an editor at Simon and Schuster), Chamberlain for hiding in the sanctuary of the *New York Times* (he was daily book reviewer for the *Times*), and Berg, Cohen, Brenner, and Edmund Wilson for having "scarcely a nodding acquaintance with the masses." They dressed their contempt for the remaining signatories in metaphor:

> As to the rest, those vacillating intellectuals who overnight have become metamorphosed from their academic cocoons into revolutionary butterflies, flit dizzyingly from Zionism to internationalism, from Lovestoneism to Trotskyism and Musteism. When the crucial moment comes they will no doubt flee in an attempt to save their beautiful multicolored wings from the fire.[49]

In the 20 March issue of the *New Masses*, a letter of response from Anita Brenner was printed, although others from Berg and Novack were not. In her letter Brenner emphasized that individuals, not a group, had signed the open letter. She argued that the signers had all been active sympathizers of the revolutionary movement and therefore were justified in raising criticisms, and she polemicized against the "United Front from Below" policy, the disruptive effects of which she claimed to have personally witnessed in Spain.[50] In a full-page answer to Brenner, the editors of the *New Masses* justified their previous position while making certain tactical adjustments. This time they affirmed that the Communist Party would be quite pleased to receive the cooperation of some of the open letter's signers such as Robert Morss Lovett, Meyer Schapiro, and John Chamberlain. Others, however, were in a different category:

> Edmund Wilson has formed an unholy alliance with the "shady" Max Eastman [already known as a partisan of Trotsky] and the still "shadier" [V.F.] Calverton [editor of *Modern Monthly*, an independent Marxist journal] and Hook. James Rorty is a member of the so-called American Workers Party [just formed by A. J. Muste], an organization which at the present time is trying to split the ranks of the working class.

As for Brenner and the others, the editors promised that the question of their sincerity would be probed in a future article.[51]

The promise was fulfilled in a *New Masses* editorial of 27 March entitled "Unintelligent Fanaticism." In it the editors sneered at the vacillating records of such intellectuals as Upton Sinclair, Theodore Dreiser, and Sherwood Anderson, who had moved from anticapitalism to pro-Rooseveltism in the recent period. The editors admitted that, in its own "eagerness for allies from all disaffected sections of society," the *New Masses* had often erred in being "insufficiently discriminating" and too ready to hail the tenuous leftward steps of prominent intellectuals, who often turned out to be detrimental to the movement. Many of the signers of the open letter were only lesser-known examples of this dangerously deceptive type:

> On a microscopic scale we see the same class laws operating in the case of some of the signers of the Open Letter to the Communist Party protesting the Madison Square Garden events. We refer to the Gruens, the Grudins, the Girschicks, and particularly to the erstwhile *Menorah Journal* group— these loop-de-loopers from Zionism to "internationalism": the Brenners, the Cohens, the Bergs, the Novacks, the Trillings, the Morrows, the Rubins. . . . They now imagine themselves to be Trotzkyites, hence the declared enemies of the Communist Party use them for what they are worth. (It is rather significant that individuals like Sidney Hook and Herbert Solow, their intimates, who have already declared themselves Trotzkyites or Nationalist "Communists" [a reference to the American Workers Party], desisted from signing the letter.)

According to the *New Masses* editors, the above noted individuals were unhappy with capitalism yet unwilling to make sacrifices, so they ultimately had to turn to creating an unreal brand of revolutionary politics of their own. Referring to a letter that they had received from Dos Passos, confirming his sympathy for the open-letter protest, the editors of the *New Masses* acknowledged that he too had succumbed to the disease—although they expressed the hope that, like Maxim Gorky, Dos Passos might eventually return to the revolutionary fold. In the meantime, they optimistically concluded that, with the world in revolution and the American Communist Party recruiting at the rate of 1,500 members a month, the vacillations of a small group of intellectuals should not be taken too seriously.[52]

The editorial was reinforced by a letter from Isidor Schneider, who had once contributed to the *Menorah Journal* but was now a leading Communist writer. Schneider charged that the core of the signers of the open letter had originally come to the workers' movement with an elitist attitude. They had by and large spent less than a year on the periphery of the movement, then raised criticisms in the NCDPP and quit the organization when it was pointed out that these criticisms resembled those of the Trotskyists. Now they had set about organizing a rival committee, the Non-Partisan Labor Defense, which could only have a splitting effect.[53]

While the more activist-oriented of the dissident communists—Solow, Morrow, Novack, Hook, Berg, and Walker—did become involved in new revolutionary socialist organizations, Lionel Trilling's evolution left its mark in several magazines, including the *Modern Monthly*, V. F. Calverton's independent Marxist journal. In the 1920s, Trilling had warned the Jewish novelist against parochialism; in 1931 he urged the left-wing novelist to "make at least part of his function to be a propagandist for political decency and against obscurantism if he is to continue to have any function at all."[54] In the early 1930s, during which he came as close as he ever would to collaborating with a self-proclaimed Marxist organization, Trilling had become painfully aware of the contradictions, antinomies, and dilemmas faced by himself and his associates:

> Today, when so many of our middle-class intellectuals are swinging left, it is well to remember that the position of the bourgeois intellectual in any proletarian movement has always been an anomalous and precarious one. However sincere he may be, the mind of the intellectual is apt to be overlaid with conflicting values so that it is impossible for him to be sure of his position; having so many values, he is likely to betray one to defend others. In this dilemma the recognition of his own training and nature can be his only safeguard against confusion and eventual missteps.[55]

THE INTELLECTUAL DISEASE

"*The Unpossessed*," Murray Kempton wrote twenty years after the open letter protesting the disruption of the Madison Square Garden rally, "is almost our only surviving document on a group of intellectuals who were drawn to the Communists early in the thirties and left them very soon."[56] Tess Slesinger's impressive novel published in early 1934 achieved immediate notoriety, especially in New York City.[57] Nevertheless, her satirical roman à clef about the *Menorah Journal* group managed also to lend itself to misrepresentation. In retrospect the novel is limited; it captures, through imaginative portraits, only certain facets of the *Menorah* group and its preoccupations. Yet, unlike many pro-Communist literary efforts that attempted to use "art as a weapon," Slesinger's synthesis of innovative literary techniques, psychological insight, and quasi-political themes is spontaneous and penetrating.

Slesinger was born in 1905; her father was a small businessman in the garment trade and her mother was a social-welfare worker who became a lay analyst.[58] Slesinger attended Ethical Culture High School and Swarthmore College and graduated from the Columbia School of Journalism in 1927. Subsequently, she became assistant fashion editor of the *New York Herald Tribune* and assistant literary editor of the *New York Evening Post*. In June 1928 she married Herbert Solow and through him entered Elliot Cohen's circle. Soon she was contributing reviews, quite often about books that dealt with problems of contemporary marriage, to the *Menorah Journal*. In March 1930 the *Menorah Journal* published her first short story and a second appeared a year later.[59]

In the early 1930s, following her divorce from Solow, she achieved some prominence with the publication of the short story "Missis Flinders" in the December 1932 issue of *Story Magazine*. Based on her own experience of having an abortion at the insistence of her husband, it may have been the first story to address that theme that appeared in a general-circulation magazine. In response to requests that she expand the story into a novel, Slesinger eventually incorporated "Missis Flinders" as the closing chapter of *The Unpossessed*. Publication of *The Unpossessed*, according to Lionel Trilling, was an act of passing judgment upon and separation from the very "contemporaries" to whom the book was dedicated.[60] It appeared in print not long after the 1934 open-letter controversy.

Slesinger soon left New York for Hollywood where she wrote screenplays for movies such as *The Good Earth* (released in 1937) and *A Tree Grows in Brooklyn* (released in 1945). In the mid-1930s she published a collection of short stories, *Time: The Present* (1935). She married Hollywood producer Frank Davis and became a supporter of the Communist Party during the Popular Front period. Her name would appear on the famous letter denouncing the John Dewey Commission's investigation of the Moscow trials, which her former husband, Solow, would be so instrumental in initiating. She also endorsed the call to the Communist-initiated Third American Writers' Congress (1939).[61] Although she never stopped being pro-Soviet Union, she became significantly disillusioned with the Soviets at the news of the Hitler-Stalin Pact later that year. She may even have enjoyed a partial reconciliation with several of her old New York friends before her death from cancer in 1945 at the age of thirty-nine.[62]

When *The Unpossessed* appeared, it was instantly reviewed by the *New Masses*. Philip Rahv, a young Communist poet, gleefully seized on the character "Comrade Fisher," who was supposed to be a member of a band of pro-Trotskyist agents attempting to "bore from within" by manipulating a group of Communist fellow travelers. Fisher, Rahv wrote, is "kneaded out of the same mud-pile as those insufferably clever young men, veterans of the Zionist Salvation Army, who are now writing articles for liberal weeklies on the strategy and tactics of the world revolution and the villainy of Stalin." Still, Rahv concluded, Slesinger's book was not without faults, for it did not present a "disciplined orientation" for radicalized intellectuals. In other words, the absence of an explicit call in the novel for intellectuals to join the Communist Party suggested that the author was not totally unsympathetic to the characters she was condemning.[63]

In the fall of 1934 Edwin Seaver, another pro-Communist writer, reviewed the novel in the *Menorah Journal*, which had changed from a monthly to a quarterly and had been appearing irregularly after Cohen left it at the beginning of 1932. Seaver pulled no punches in identifying Slesinger's frustrated intellectuals as the dissidents of the open-letter controversy. Arguing that the novel was, in fact, already somewhat dated, Seaver dissected the character strongly suggestive of Elliot Cohen:

> If he were strictly contemporary, Miss Slesinger, your Bruno Leonard would not be concerned with the immortal mission of the intellect; nowadays he would be taking fits because Stalin is not radical enough for his sudden conversion, because the Comintern is too petit-bourgeois for his Kosher tastes. Each Bruno Leonard in search of the aesthetic and philosophical grail has become a little Trotsky in search of a fourth international.

The situation has changed, Seaver explained, and the Bruno Leonards deserve even harsher treatment because the only real choice facing humanity is life with the revolutionary movement (namely, the Communist Party), or death at the hands of the fascists. The Bruno Leonard type, Seaver concluded, is still "crazy as a bedbug," but the Freudian-oriented bedbugs of the past have become the Trotskyist intellectuals of today.[64]

The Unpossessed is a highly original novel. Slesinger adapts some of the modernist techniques of Joyce, Proust, and the early Hemingway to her purposes, but the book is also shaped by her close reading of Katherine Mansfield, Dorothy Parker, and Virginia Woolf. *The Unpossessed* anticipates both Saul Bellow's novels about frustrated Jewish intellectuals such as *Herzog* (1964) and Mary McCarthy's political satires such as *The Oasis* (1949). At the same time, it is reminiscent of earlier American works by and about radical intellectuals, especially Max Eastman's *Venture* (1927) and Edmund Wilson's *I Thought of Daisy* (1929). As in those two novels, personal (more precisely, sexual) and political themes run together in *The Unpossessed*, overlapping, intertwined, and often infused with intentional ambiguity. For example, in *The Unpossessed* the conception and ultimate abortion of Margaret Flinder's baby and the evolution of Bruno Leonard's magazine run parallel. The contemporary reader will undoubtedly focus on the embryonic feminism implicit in the novel, while Slesinger's dominant, although not entirely separable, intention was to depict the "problem" of the radicalized intellectual disaffected from capitalist society and in search of a bond with common people and a more natural existence. This "problem" constitutes another close thematic tie to *Venture* and *I Thought of Daisy*. The disalienation that Eastman's Jo Hancock finds in the woods with his Russian proletarian beauty and that Edmund Wilson's narrator seeks in the chorus girl of *I Thought of Daisy* Margaret Flinders hopes to locate through motherhood, and her male characters aspire to achieve through their association with the working-class movement.

In each of the three novels the unifying character is derived largely from the author's own personality and experiences, although *The Unpossessed* may be somewhat differentiated in that a secondary character, Elizabeth Leonard, appears to embody certain important aspects of the author as well. A recent essay by Janet Sharistanian has convincingly demonstrated that Margaret suggests certain aspects of Slesinger's life in the early 1930s while Elizabeth embodies her "flapper" experiences in the 1920s.[65] This splitting of a single consciousness into characters embodying its contradictory elements might be extended into other areas as well. The depiction of Elizabeth as Jewish and Margaret as non-Jewish may be indicative of Slesinger's partial assimilation, which stands in contrast to Bruno's affirmation of his Jewishness even as he seeks to identify with the international working class.

These novels are also admirable in that they demonstrate the unabashed and frankly honest self-scrutiny particularly characteristic of the bohemian-radical intellectuals whose basic intellectual formation occurred prior to the domination of the movement by the Communist-led writers. In Slesinger's case, her literary sensibilities were strong enough to resist the oversimplified good-versus-evil treatment of intellectuals typified by Mike Gold's *The Hollow Men* (1941) and Isidor Schneider's *The Judas Time* (1946), both of which were also directed against those New York intellectuals who comprised the anti-Stalinist left.

Like its predecessors, Slesinger's novel is rooted in the actuality of the historic moment: *Venture* is thematically situated in the Golden Age of pre–World War I radicalism; *I Thought of Daisy* reflects the discomfort of the 1920s; and *The Unpossessed* exudes the disorientation of the early depression. Slesinger's work communicates the pain and contradictions of the intellectuals trained and informed by the environment of the 1920s as they struggled to relate to the new realities and demands of the 1930s. *Venture, I Thought of Daisy,* and *The Unpossessed* are all romans à clef; but Slesinger's novel is closer to Wilson's as a study of a specific milieu that produced distinct character types. Both novels illustrate how radical intellectuals have employed the novel as a tool in the search for truth and the moral meaning of the lives and actions of their associates.

At least one attempt has been made to connect each major character in *The Unpossessed* with its "real life" counterpart from the *Menorah Journal* group. In *Part of Our Time* (1955), Murray Kempton accurately identifies Bruno Leonard with Elliot Cohen and Miles Flinders with Herbert Solow but incorrectly equates Jeffrey Blake with Lionel Trilling. Actually, Blake very clearly suggests Max Eastman, with whom Slesinger had an affair at the time.[66] Yet *The Unpossessed* cannot be fully understood in terms of such analogues. Unlike Edmund Wilson's Hugo Bamman, for example, who obviously resembles John Dos Passos, the characters in *The Unpossessed* are essentially composites designed to express a variety of themes emanating from the milieu engaged in the NCDPP and the League of Professionals.

Solow was scarcely the Irish Catholic with the New England Calvinist temperament that Miles is, yet that particular aspect of the fictionalized persona serves as an effective vehicle for capturing the gloomy disposition and intense, almost monomaniacal, quest for lofty principles that has been associated with Solow in memoirs by his contemporaries. Jeffrey Blake suggests several other writers besides Eastman: Blake's superficial notion of himself as a fellow-traveling Marxist intellectual recalls Clifton Fadiman; when Blake is criticized for including a "racy demonstration chapter" in one of his novels, Albert Halper, the author of *Union Square* (1933), comes to mind; and Blake's preoccupation with sexual mystique suggests V. F. Calverton, for whom Slesinger did some secretarial work.

The most important characteristic assigned to the intellectuals in *The Unpossessed* as a group is that they are sterile. They are sterile because of the social patterns, values, and life-styles that they have established for themselves. The major manifestation of their sterility is portended in Slesinger's title: Dostoyevski's *The Possessed* is reversed to *The Unpossessed*, suggesting "uncommitted." Slesinger portrays a group whose convictions are more rhetorical than real. Bruno Leonard's concluding monologue about the uselessness of diseased intellectuals to the revolutionary movement reflects Slesinger's basic view: "My friends and I are sick men—if we are not already dead."[67]

Bruno Leonard, the Jewish professor of English, endlessly brooding over his Jewishness and its impact on his intellect, ceaselessly tormented by a writer's block, is the high priest of *The Unpossessed*. He is the mentor of a campus-based group of militant, self-righteous young Communists known as the Black Sheep. But Bruno's coterie of friends are also his students and he is their teacher in the arts of life, wit, sex, and politics. Bruno's most important male intimates are Miles and Jeffrey, who had been radical pacifists with Bruno on the same campus, suggestive of Columbia, twelve years earlier. Bruno, the valedictorian, remained there to teach, while Miles took a low-paying office job and Jeffrey penned a series of light-weight novels. They are reunited in a scheme to publish a revolutionary magazine.

In addition to Miles and Jeffrey and their wives, Margaret Flinders and Norah Blake, Bruno acts as a teacher to two other characters. One is his cousin, Elizabeth Leonard, an artist living in Paris when the novel opens. Bruno had used his influence to liberate her from a boring conventional life and put her on what she calls a "fast express" of bohemian living and "chain loving." The other is Emmett Merle, the sheltered and miserable son of a wealthy family. Emmett's relation to Bruno allows Slesinger to probe the homosexual aspects of Bruno's personality and his role as a teacher. But perhaps more significant is Bruno's function as a surrogate parent. Although Emmett is in rebellion, he still needs a role model. Bruno's problem, or perhaps his virtue, is that he is aware of his inability to serve Emmett in that capacity.

The Unpossessed, with its narrative structured around aspects of marriage, friendship, and adultery, is above all a study of group dynamics. Woven in and around the story of Bruno, his magazine, his friends and his students, is a subplot of the failing marriage of Margaret and Miles. One facet of their problem is bound up in Miles's deteriorating sense of self-esteem because he earns less money than his wife. But Slesinger also employs the relationship to evoke an eternal, almost mystical dialectic of male and female relations, one that turns on the notion that a man and woman, as ideal lovers, create a third entity. Yet Miles cannot give himself wholly to this synthesis in a way that Margaret can. He fears drowning if he relinquishes himself totally, believing that he must retain a part of himself, his restlessness, as private and secretive. Women, Margaret concludes, are perceived by men as rivals to the world of action. Whether Slesinger was parodying this romanticized stereotype or endorsing it is not altogether clear.

Miles resents Margaret's desire for complacent happiness, her belief that lovers can achieve sufficiency through "each other." He associates her talk of happiness with his stern Uncle Daniel's remark that "pigs are happy." Miles is opposed to Margaret's having a baby, a fairly common attitude among radical intellectuals of the time.[68] He sees childbirth as a capitulation to bourgeois society, an acceptance of it and a sellout of his own principles. Deeply pessimistic, Miles resents Margaret's hopefulness about the future, characterizing it as "balmy."

Margaret, in contrast, embodies a variety of feminine themes. She is oppressed in her subservience to Miles, as well as by her own guilt, because she cannot satisfy him. All she can offer is comfort, which only irritates him. She and Norah Blake also seem to embody mystical female qualities; they are more natural and less self-contrived than the male characters, or even Elizabeth Leonard who lives "like a man."

Desiring to realize herself in a less artificial world, especially through the act of childbirth, Margaret especially resents the ersatz culture of the group. She is particularly contemptuous of the way they surround themselves with German newspapers and Russian movies when, in fact, she herself has rarely ventured from New York City. Margaret aspires to be one of the ordinary people, whose simplicity is represented in minor characters such as Mr. Papenmeyer, with his children and his *Verstand*, and Arturo Tresca, a musician also full of love for his wife and children. Norah epitomizes the Lawrentian ideal of a woman: raised in the country, she has maintained the simplicity of childhood, which Margaret with her urban upbringing has lost; she has become the open, comfortable port to which the womanizer Blake returns safely after each of his frequent voyages.

The molding of character by social environment was a common theme in the literature of the 1930s. In *The Unpossessed* the atmosphere of the 1920s and the closed character of the small intellectual clique conditioned Leonard's group so that its members could not effectively relate to concerns of ordinary people or even fulfill their own aspirations. The members of the group were political only in drawing rooms and at parties and as such had only a parasitic relation to the class struggle.

The formative years of several of the characters—Miles, Margaret, Bruno, Elizabeth, and Norah—are analyzed as well. Miles, who is most intensely scrutinized, was reared in the austere, morose environment of a New England farm, one that might have been created by Eugene O'Neill. There, rocks abounded in the fields, and punishment and suffering were accepted as ineluctable features of life. Miles, now in his thirties, remains suspicious of his wife's "rose colored" expectations and aspirations, and he perceives any sign of political compromise as inviting gangrenous corruption. To Margaret, Miles seems a tortured saint; his Marxism, which she regards as merely crude economics, is perceived by her as a product of his fatalistic religious temperament. She calls it his "new God."[69]

Spurred on by his Calvinistic compulsions Miles is driven to seek complete purity, condemning the petit-bourgeois deviations of his associates. He is repelled by the proposal that the revolutionary magazine be funded with money raised through a dance sponsored by a decadent businessman. He is also punctilious about describing his views as "communist" rather than "socialist," although he himself is not a member of the party. Miles's high and ascetic personal standards are measured against an incident in his youth when his Uncle Daniel—his parental surrogate for a weak father and a beautiful (therefore evil) mother—unflinchingly shoots the family dog because it killed a neighbor's chickens. It was not necessary to shoot the dog, yet it seemed a natural act because it corresponded to the harsh world outlook of his culture. When he carried out the execution, Uncle Daniel became deified in the eyes of Miles: "Miles knew well that day that there was something bigger in men than themselves, that could drive them to do what alone they never would have dared."[70] Later Daniel falls ill, and Miles begins to wish for his death. When his wish comes true, Miles's encompassing sense of guilt is fully formed.

Thus in *The Unpossessed* we have an attempt to portray the *Menorah* group during the years 1932 and 1933, with its cliquish and cultist and insular features, its combination of witty rhetoric (provided by Bruno) and bottled-up fanaticism (embodied in Miles), both of which lead nowhere. Yet, as Lionel Trilling emphasized in his criticism of Murray Kempton's too literal interpretation of the book, the essentially apolitical nature of Slesinger's fictional group divests the portrait of its verisimilitude. The attraction of Bruno's coterie to a vague abstraction of the Communist Party and the manipulation of Jeffrey Blake by Ruth Fisher scarcely convey the actual evolution of the *Menorah* group. Trilling emphasized that "any member of the group would have been able to explain his disillusionment [with Stalinism] by a precise enumeration of the errors and failures of the Party, both at home and abroad."[71]

In this respect, then, the novel contains more invention than fact and Kempton erred in presenting it, as he did in *Part of Our Time*, as bitter reality. Slesinger, like any satirist, relied upon an exaggeration of certain tendencies in her satiric objects, which was done at the expense of achieving a truly rounded portrait of the *Menorah* group. Slesinger did, however, provide some penetrating insights into the social relations of the group, especially their attitudes toward marriage, children, sex, and how the various personalities coped with the radical movement during the depression. But the resulting novel was predominantly psychological. Its realism is mixed: the atmosphere of the depression, the conformist rebellion of the Black Sheep, the contradictions and pretensions of Bruno's group, are all captured through little incidents, scenes, and scenarios. Yet the novel provides no sense at all of the *Menorah* circle as a highly politicized, dynamic group whose members would eventually go anywhere or accomplish anything. One would not know from reading *The Unpossessed* that this was a group that would carry the stamp of its unique politicization for decades and ultimately leave its imprint upon the cultural establishment of New York. If anything, Slesinger's novel predicts that it is the Black Sheep who, breaking with Bruno at the end, will become the vital force in society.

The failure of *The Unpossessed* to portray the political essence of the group cannot be divorced from the fact that Tess Slesinger herself chose to follow a very different political course from that of her earlier associates. It is not clear, however, whether at the time that she wrote *The Unpossessed* Slesinger had become a partisan of the Communists, and, accordingly, offered the book to them as a club to use against their intellectual opponents. Possibly her real attitude was expressed in a letter that Michael Blankfort, who in the early 1930s had been associated with V. F. Calverton's *Modern Monthly*, wrote to *Commentary* thirty-two years later:

. . . Tess Slesinger was profoundly dismayed and sickened by the political storms breaking across the days of our lives. It is difficult today, as Trilling remarks about similar events, to understand how bloody and cruel were the internecine wars of the 30s among the Stalinists, Trotskyists, Lovestoneites, et al. . . . the wars were catastrophic enough to cause sensitive artists like Tess Slesinger to run away from them, from New York, and even from writing itself, in order to avoid the deadly accusations of treachery and the awful turning away of one friend from another because of something said about the latest theses from the Comintern.[72]

This attitude, if indeed it was Slesinger's, may account for certain ambiguities in the book, especially the incident where Bruno, in arguing with the weak Jeffrey who wishes to placate the Communist Party at all costs, declares that he "won't print lies."[73] The implication seems to be that there is a higher integrity combined with Bruno's hyperintellectualism than one finds in the mentality of those who were more subordinate to the party. Inspired by a vision of the first truly human culture described by Leon Trotsky at the end of *Literature and Revolution*, Bruno is also subject to a disease of skepticism that undermines his confidence in this vision even as he considers it. The ability to honestly confront his own weaknesses and to understand that his psychological maladies corrupt his political aspirations renders Bruno far more attractive than any of the other leading characters.

Still, all the central characters in *The Unpossessed* suffer from an affliction that prevents them from acting out their convictions. The source of Bruno's affliction is a compulsion to travel endlessly and narcissistically into the recesses of his own mind which has "a hundred impulses balanced evenly."[74] Jeffrey's stems from personal opportunism, and Miles's results from the transference of the personal guilt he feels to political engagements. In Slesinger's portrait they are all victims of emotional disorders associated with their intellects, rather than diabolical counterrevolutionaries.

To the extent that individuals play a decisive role in creating movements, the evolution of the *Menorah* group began with Elliot Cohen's search for the role of the Jew in the modern world and the broad human, cultural, and social sympathies Cohen fostered. Heightened by the fierce political acuity and activism of Herbert Solow, the group moved, with the onset of the depression, toward the Communist vortex of the radical movement. From there most were impelled toward Trotskyism.

It is not surprising that Trotsky, who incarnated internationalism and cosmopolitanism, the Jew who had shattered the manacles of religious identity and who strove to merge himself with the forces of the world revolution in every country and culture, should for a period become their rallying point. Although these same intellectuals would later come to see, and fixate upon, an authoritarian side to Trotsky, at the moment they were strongly attracted by the moral appeal in the writer and activist who transcended intellectual and physical strictures, led a revolution, directed the Red Army, suffered exile and persecution, and simultaneously fought against the corruption of his life's work. For the later members of the *Partisan Review* group, literary conflicts and a refusal to relinquish modernism exacerbated their increasing distrust of the Communists prior to their public break with the party. But for the *Menorah* group, the Stalinized Marxism of the Communist Party—its dogmatism and dread of criticism, its sectarianism in practice, its authoritarianism—was from the very beginning of their collaboration incompatible with their burning intellectual vivacity. Their initial rejection of Stalinism was not by any means a repudiation of communism, and for a number of years afterward they had hopes of revivifying an authentic revolutionary Marxism.

To call *The Unpossessed* a "document" of this group in the early 1930s, as Murray Kempton did, is far from accurate. Although an important stream of literature in the 1930s was, in fact, documentary, and many novels used documentary techniques, *The Unpossessed* is not a documentary in any sense. Like the radical-bohemian novels of Max Eastman and Edmund Wilson, it is not even a political tract. Rather it is a satire of the moment and an inquiry of sorts into the dialectic of human emotions and thought, an examination of the nature of a specific group of intellectuals and their relationship to the conflicts and issues of their time.

CHAPTER 3

Radical
Modernists

> What distinguished
> *Partisan Review* from
> the *New Masses* was
> our struggle to free
> revolutionary litera-
> ture from domination
> by the immediate
> strategy of a political
> party.
>
> —William Phillips
> and Philip Rahv,
> Letter to the
> *New Masses*, 1937[1]

. . . .

IN DEFENSE OF LITERATURE

In the fourth decade of this century, a generation of young American writers and literary critics began to turn from immersion in the
experimental forms and esoteric sensibilities of the years following
World War I to the politico-literary activism of the early 1930s. Yet
this move from what we now call literary modernism was a far less
sweeping and unqualified process than might appear from our vista
in the 1980s; simply put, the achievements of the 1920s were considerable and could not be ignored. The disillusioned exiles and
aesthetes of the postwar decades had technically revolutionized and
deepened the thematic internationalization of American literature.
The disciples of Pound, Eliot, Joyce, and Stein, despite the apolitical
and sometimes reactionary social views of some of their modernist
masters, established themselves against twentieth-century materialism and commercialism as an avant-garde in literary protest. To
most writers galvanized into political activity by the 1929 stock-
market crash and subsequent depression, the legacy of Eliot and
others appeared insufficient. Yet to certain of the newly radicalized
literary intellectuals, the 1920s were viewed as an important component of a cultural tradition that required assimilation.

It was in part their preoccupation with the literary productions
of the previous decade—its innovations in technique and sensi-

bility, its Europeanization of American culture, its absorption with the estrangement of the intelligentsia—that distinguished William Phillips and Philip Rahv from most of the young writers attracted to the Communist Party's literary wing and its John Reed Clubs. This preoccupation would later account significantly for the development of *Partisan Review*, when the two editors broke with the Communist Party after assessing historical events in the Soviet Union, Spain, and Germany, and after witnessing the failure of the proletarian cultural movement. At the end of 1937 Phillips and Rahv emerged as the leading editors of an independent Marxist, but anti-Stalinist literary journal, whose mark on American intellectual and cultural development remains evident today.

Rahv was born Ivan Greenberg at Kupin in the Russian Ukraine, the second of three sons.[2] His mother was an ardent Zionist and the family ran a struggling dry-goods store in a Jewish ghetto surrounded by peasants. When Greenberg was eight his father moved to Providence, Rhode Island, where he worked as a house-to-house peddler to raise money to bring his wife and children to the United States. At the time of the October Revolution, the family shop was expropriated, and the Greenbergs fled to Austria, remaining there for two years before reuniting in Providence. But several years later most of the family moved to Palestine where Greenberg's father opened a small cement factory. After that venture failed, the fourteen-year-old Ivan returned to the United States by himself. There he finally mastered English, which he added to the Russian, German, Yiddish, Hebrew, and French he had already acquired. For the rest of his life, however, he spoke with a noticeable east European accent and was regarded as "less assimilated" into American culture than those Jewish-American writers of his circle who had been born in the United States.

An autodidact who never graduated from high school, Greenberg found his first work writing advertising copy for a firm in Oregon, while giving Hebrew lessons on the side. His spare hours were passed in the public library where he pored over the classics of literature, history, and philosophy. When the depression came he lost his job and moved eastward, spending six months penniless in Chicago in 1930 before arriving in New York where he stood in breadlines and slept on park benches. In 1932, living in dirt and poverty and eking out a few pennies as a *melamed*, teaching elementary Hebrew by rote, he was taken to a John Reed Club meeting by Nathan Adler, an aspiring writer. Soon after, he joined the Communist Party and took the party name "Rahv," meaning "rabbi" in Hebrew.

In the party, Rahv became secretary of the monthly magazine *Prolit Folio*, sponsored by the Revolutionary Writers Federation that was affiliated with the International Union of Revolutionary Writers. He published reviews in the *Daily Worker* and *New Masses*, joined the Rebel Poets group, and wrote and translated left-wing poetry. The wholeheartedness with which he gave himself to the revolutionary excesses of the party in the early 1930s is illuminated by his 1932 "Open Letter to Young Writers" in the *Rebel Poet*. In an apocalyptic style characteristic of the time, Rahv heralded the brilliance of Marxian analysis while excoriating the decadence of bourgeois culture. Observing that for writers there are no "neutral subjects," he drew the conclusion that the writer's only choice is between prostitution and revolution.[3]

William Phillips was also the son of Jewish emigrants from Russia. His father, who had changed his name from Litvinsky, was trained as a lawyer but was unable to sustain a practice.[4] The son, born 14 November 1907, grew up in poverty and attended the City College of New York during the late 1920s. Inspired by the ironic skepticism of his teacher Morris Raphael Cohen and the literary experiments of T. S. Eliot, he pursued graduate studies at New York University and Columbia University, teaching part-time to support himself.

At the beginning of the Great Depression, Phillips's circle of bohemian-literary friends gravitated toward the Communist Party. By 1932 he was a convinced Communist, submitting an article called "*Class*-ical Culture" to the party's theoretical review. No less fervent in tone and style than Rahv's "Open Letter," Phillips's contribution was more party-oriented, replete with denunciations of the "social fascism" of the Socialists and declarations of fidelity to the "*real* leaders" of the working class, "the Communist parties in every country."[5] Phillips, who chose the party name "Wallace Phelps," differed from Rahv in that he tried for a brief time to pursue a traditional academic career concurrent with his Marxist commitment. Hence, in the same month in which he made his debut in the *Communist*, an essay in the *Symposium* appeared under his own name entitled "Categories for Criticism," in which he tentatively presented the case for Marxist aesthetics in conventional critical vocabulary.[6]

Phillips and Rahv first met in the New York chapter of the John Reed Club, and, in 1933, together with other members, they conceived a plan for their own magazine. With the support and assistance of established Communist cultural leaders like Joseph Freeman and Mike Gold, the new journal was launched with $800 raised through a lecture by the British Marxist John Strachey.[7] Recollections conflict as to who did what in initiating the magazine, but early editorials indicate an agreement that the *Partisan Review* would concentrate primarily on literary and cultural questions, leaving the *New Masses* free to turn increasingly to political matters.

From the journal's inception, the articles written by Phillips and Rahv showed greater subtlety and sophistication than had been evident in their earlier Communist writings. They generally pursued three objectives: a desire that proletarian fiction and criticism should incorporate certain aspects of the literary achievements of the 1920s; an opposition to schematic, sectarian, and reductive applications of Marxism; and a concern with developing a full Marxist aesthetic that acknowledged the special needs of radical intellectuals. In articles such as "Criticism" by Phillips and Rahv and in "A Season in Heaven" by Rahv, the editors positively assessed T. S. Eliot's writings. The *Partisan Review* critics maintained that despite evidence of Eliot's royalist sympathies, his writing expressed criticisms of contemporary life that transcended his political views, an approach that recalls Marx and Engels's treatment of Balzac, and Lenin's of Tolstoy.[8]

Phillips's "Three Generations," which discussed trends in American literary tradition and their impact on the new generation of left-wing writers, lauded Eliot for his technical proficiency. Searching for a "usable past," Phillips noted that the only successful school of American writers had been the movement analogous to that of Zola in French literature: the realist-naturalist tradition of Dreiser, Anderson, Lewis, Robinson, and Sandburg. The "Lost Generation" writers who rejected this heritage were in turn rejected by the older, radical writers, Joseph Freeman, Mike Gold, and Joshua Kunitz. "Nevertheless," Phillips concluded, "the spirit of the twenties is part of our heritage, and many of the younger revolutionary generation are acutely conscious of this."[9]

The campaign by Rahv and Phillips against mechanically applied Marxism, to which they assigned Lenin's epithet of "leftism," was a hallmark of their criticism. Of course, both gave allegiance to the Communist International's call for a consciously proletarian literature and art. They also believed in building an organized movement of anticapitalist and pro-Soviet intellectuals. "The profile of the Bolshevik is emerging in America," they said, "heroic battles are developing new human types and relations are budding in and around the Communist Party."[10] As revolutionaries they asserted that the writer's assimilation of this new material could not occur by passive observation but only through active participation in the working-class struggle. The task was to guard the revolutionary aims and direction of the budding revolutionary cultural movement: "The critic is the ideologist of the literary movement, and any ideologist, as Lenin pointed out, 'is worthy of that name only when he marches ahead of the spontaneous movement, points out the real road, and when he is able, ahead of all others, to solve all the theoretical, political and tactical questions which the "material elements" of the movement spontaneously encounter. It is necessary to be critical of it [the movement], to point out its dangers and defects and to aspire to *elevate* spontaneity to consciousness.' "[11]

These early articles constitute a valuable catalog of the dangers of a mechanical and sectarian application of Marxist theory to writing and criticism. In 1934 Phillips and Rahv asserted that the most widespread error in leftism occurs when "zeal to steep literature overnight in the program of Communism results in . . . sloganized and inorganic writing." To view the writer's goal as merely "discovering" the class struggle for the reader was to renege on one's creative responsibility, which is to assimilate the political context imaginatively. Literature, they affirmed, was not so much a medium of abstract conceptualization as one "steeped in sensory experience" requiring the transformation of the class struggle into "images of physical life."[12]

One year later Phillips and Rahv echoed the same points in a jointly written discussion article on the eve of the 1935 American Writers' Congress, a major national gathering initiated by the Communist Party. In the article they took issue with a long list of Communist literary shibboleths. Ironically, the Congress would mark the beginning of the party's new "respectable" political turn to the right, which would result in the jettisoning of the proletarian cultural orientation altogether. Among other criticisms, Phillips and Rahv questioned the slogan "Art as a Weapon," because the weapon's range was limited to those susceptible to art. Using Faulkner and Proust as examples, they challenged the equation of a nonproletarian attitude on the part of individual writers with the ideological perspective of the bourgeoisie. They concluded that "revolutionary literature is not the literature of a sect, like surrealism or objectivism; it is the product of an emerging civilization, and will contain the wealth and diversity which any cultural range offers."[13]

The search for a truly Marxist aesthetic concerned Phillips and Rahv throughout the 1930s; they never accepted the slogans of the Communist International as sufficient guides for revolutionary writers and critics. Early in 1935, attempting to apply Marxist dialectics to critical theory, Phillips discussed the relationship of literary form and content. Examining the views of Plato, Plotinus, Kant, Hegel, Croce, and Dewey, Phillips argued that any separation of form and content was simply false. Hamlet's soliloquy, he noted, is banal in its content but achieves aesthetic cogency through its integration in a literary form. Phillips cited the writings of Sidney Hook and Robert Cantwell as representative of contemporary misunderstandings of this dialectical unity.[14] Likewise, in a review of Joseph Wood Krutch's *The Modern Temper*, Rahv related historical materialism to the theory of tragedy, concluding that the modern recrudescence of tragedy had a material basis in the heroic struggle of the industrial working class.[15]

Despite their evolving critique of the Communist Party's exploitation of the proletarian literary movement, Phillips and Rahv remained an integral part of that movement until the demise of the original *Partisan Review* in the fall of 1936. Their criticisms of leftism were balanced with warnings against the "right danger," that is, writers who "seek to assimilate the Joyce-Eliot sensibility without a clear revolutionary purpose."[16] The *Partisan Review* also contained denunciations of renegades, as well as subtle accolades for Communist leaders. Rahv and Phillips wrote as if they anticipated an imminent renaissance of proletarian writers and literature: "This last year has seen a quickening in the growth of revolutionary literature in America. The maturing of labor struggles and the increase of Communist influence have given the impetus and created a receptive atmosphere for this literature. As was to be expected, the novel—which is the major literary form of today— has taken the lead. Cantwell, Rollins, Conroy and Armstrong have steered fiction into proletarian patterns of struggle."[17]

By the beginning of 1935 a switch in Communist Party policy was becoming apparent. Not only had the expected proletarian cultural renaissance failed to materialize, but the Communist International was at the point of a historic political jettisoning of its ultrarevolutionary Third Period policies of 1928–33. After the disastrous consolidation of Hitlerism, facilitated by the Communists' refusal to seek unity in action with the German Social Democrats against the Brown Shirts, the party began to seek a defensive rapprochement with liberal and "progressive" capitalist forces. The John Reed Clubs, founded as organizations of workers and proletarianized intellectuals who were openly anticapitalist and partisans of the Soviet Union, were peremptorily liquidated by the party in favor of formations like the American Writers' Congress and the League of American Writers that had a wider appeal to the liberals among the academics, commercial authors, and literati. As Malcolm Cowley has recounted, the Comintern's literary and political turnabout went hand in hand: "Dimitrov called for the People's Front on August 2, 1935, which was some months after the [American Writers'] Congress. But the premonitory rumblings of the People's Front were already spreading over the world."[18]

Even before the American Writers' Congress was held, most of the John Reed Clubs had been dissolved, which effectually eliminated much of the material support for *Partisan Review* and its copublications. With the demise of the John Reed Clubs, the *Partisan Review* became organizationally independent, although it still remained under the guidance of its three main editors: Phillips and Rahv, who then worked for the Federal Writers Project, and Alan Calmer, who was employed by International Publishers. The journal drifted in the direction of the new League of American Writers, which from the 1935 congress until late 1936 considered making its organ *Partisan Review*. Failing to get organizational support, Rahv and Phillips faced financial difficulties and in early 1936 decided to merge *Partisan Review* with Jack Conroy's publication, *Anvil*.[19] When the *Partisan Review* and *Anvil* were forced to close down altogether at the end of 1936, Rahv and Phillips continued their search for the reason why the proletarian cultural movement had failed. They were particularly concerned with the Communist Party's authoritarian interventions in the movement.

The two-year interlude between the first and second American Writers' congresses (1935 and 1937) proved to be the turning point for Phillips and Rahv. By the time of the second congress, the Communist Party policy had undergone such a complete transformation that not only had the proletarian literary movement been abandoned but, in accordance with the new Popular Front strategy of alliances with "progressive" capitalism, the party's cultural leaders even hailed literary patriotism, the new nationalism of Van Wyck Brooks, and the culture industry of Hollywood. On both literary and political grounds, Rahv and Phillips were appalled. The outrageous Moscow trials (1936–38) were commencing, and, simultaneously, reports emanated from Spain that the Communists had crushed the Workers Party of Marxist Unification (POUM), a dissident Marxist organization, and other left-wing forces.[20]

Thus Phillips and Rahv arrived at a new assessment of the relationship between revolutionary politics and radical literature. Above all, they concluded that writers and critics must be free of all partisan political and organizational pressure. Yet they also felt that they had been duped by the appealing simplicity of the notion that writers must ally themselves with the revolutionary working class. As a substitute for a genuine aesthetic, this abstract call for an alliance tended to merge politics and literature; it equated the personal views of a writer formed amidst specific circumstances with historical class objectives, and it led to the evaluation of a writer's merit and achievements and relation to the working class on the basis of his or her support for the policies of a particular Marxist party. In an analysis offered by Rahv in 1940, he concluded that "within the brief space of a few years the term 'proletarian literature' was transformed into a euphemism for a Communist Party literature which tenaciously upheld a factional faith identifying the party with the working class, Stalinism with Marxism and the Soviet Union with socialism."[21] But if Rahv and Phillips were the most articulate in their criticisms of party policy and defenses of the legacy of the 1920s, they were hardly alone. Their disaffection with the party and their project of reconstituting the *Partisan Review* as an independent communist organ coincided with the political evolution of several other writers and critics.

OTHER DISSIDENT WRITERS AND CRITICS ON THE LEFT: JAMES T. FARRELL, F. W. DUPEE, EDMUND WILSON

James T. Farrell was born into a working-class Irish-American family in Chicago on 27 February 1904. His father was a teamster and his mother worked as a domestic servant. The Farrells were so poor that when James was three, he had to be turned over to the care of middle-class relatives. He financed several years in the University of Chicago by working as a gas-station attendant and in other assorted jobs but quit before graduating in order to become a writer. In 1931 he eloped to Paris with Dorothy Butler, writing industriously while they lived in poverty. The next year he settled permanently in New York City, experiencing a change in fortune when his first novel, *Young Lonigan* (1932), was published by the Vanguard Press. This was followed by *Gas-House McGinty* in 1933, and *The Young Manhood of Studs Lonigan* and *Calico Shoes and Other Stories* in 1934. In 1935 the appearance of *Judgment Day* completed the *Studs Lonigan* trilogy, which left Farrell firmly established as a major figure in American letters.[22]

Although Farrell had read socialist classics and was attracted to radicalism during the late 1920s in Chicago and in 1931 when he was in Paris, he did not become actively involved with the organized left until he moved to New York City. As a supporter of the Communist Party from 1932 to 1935, Farrell wrote for various party publications and collaborated in a number of party activities until he became affected by many of the same political and literary questions that had caused the *Menorah* group and the *Partisan Review* editors to reaffirm communism as an antidote to Stalinism. Although personal considerations required that he proceed with caution—his companion at the time, Hortense Alden, feared that her acting career would be damaged if they openly opposed the party—he finally issued *A Note on Literary Criticism* in the spring of 1936.[23] A Marxist polemic against the political manipulation of literary judgments as practiced by the Communist Party, the theoretical underpinnings of the book are consistent with Trotsky's views expressed in *Literature and Revolution* (1923). Farrell had discussed a draft of the work with George Novack, by then a committed Trotskyist, when they were together at Yaddo, a retreat for writers and artists in Saratoga Springs, New York.

In his own work Farrell did not attempt to write "Marxist novels," although he was greatly influenced by Marx and his books have many political implications. Still, although Farrell did not draw inspiration for his fiction from reading *Das Kapital*, he was an authentic artist whose vision of the world was enriched and enhanced by his assimilation of socialist theory. No accurate assessment of Farrell can ignore the fact that a major source of his desire to write was his rebellion against what he called the "biological tragedy" of humanity—the corrosiveness of time and the inevitability of death. On the other hand, complementing this concern was his rebellion against what he called the "social tragedy" created by class society, which can be overcome through education and political action.[24]

The *Studs Lonigan* trilogy itself is consecrated to revealing how American culture prevents humanity from achieving its fullest expression which will be most clearly realized through the abolition of class society. The spiritual godfathers of the trilogy were members of the English faculty at the University of Chicago who strongly encouraged Farrell: James Weber Linn and Robert Morss Lovett. They saw the vast literary potential in a character called "Studs," whom Farrell had first created in a short story by the same name. However, as Farrell developed the story into three novels over the next several years, against the setting of the Great Depression, he began to see Studs as not just a character but also as a social manifestation.

The broader historical significance of the trilogy may not be immediately apparent because it is written in the cliché-ridden idiom of the protagonist who has roots in a specific Chicago South Side neighborhood. However, the tragic destiny that overwhelms Studs is bound up in the course of America's social and economic development from the Woodrow Wilson years to the Great Depression. Studs's fall in the third volume, *Judgment Day*, provides an opportunity for Farrell to pass judgment not merely on Lonigan but on American capitalist society. The book as a whole dramatizes the failure of cultural myth as a program of action.

For example, as the characters live through the boom years of the 1920s, Studs and his family and friends remain true believers in the myths of American society propagated by the schools, businesses, churches, and other institutions. These myths cohere in what is commonly referred to as the American dream: a belief that the democratic capitalism of the United States permits all those who have sufficient ambition and ability to become whatever they wish. Consequently, when the Great Depression hits, not only the economic but also the spiritual foundations of Farrell's characters' lives are demolished. Feelings of profound dislocation are displayed at the end of *Judgment Day* in the ruminations of Studs's father, Paddy Lonigan: "It was neither right nor fair. He could not see why all these troubles must come to him. What had he done? He wanted to know. Here he was, a man who had always done his duties. Hadn't he earned his place in the world by hard work? Hadn't he always provided for his family to the best of his abilities, tried to be a good husband and a good father, a true Catholic, and a real American?"[25]

As a foil to Studs and the Lonigan family, Farrell offers glimpses of the growing consciousness of the rebel Danny O'Neill, who decides to work his way through the university while employed as a gas-station attendant. O'Neill begins to break with the false consciousness perpetrated by his society, especially with the myth of Christianity: "He conceived of the world, the environment he had known all his life, as lies. He realized that all his education in Catholic schools, all he had heard and absorbed, had been lies. . . . An exultant feeling swept him. God was a lie. God was dead. God was a mouldering corpse within his mind. And God had been the center of everything in his mind. All his past was now like so many maggots on the mouldering corpse of God within his mind."[26]

Studs Lonigan dies of heart failure at the end of *Judgment Day*, but in part his illness has a social basis—for his health was damaged during the Prohibition era by the consumption of large quantities of cheap bootleg liquor, which he used to anesthetize himself against the pain of the disappointments in his life. The final passages of *Judgment Day* are rich with symbolically evocative episodes. As Studs lies in his sickroom near the end, he experiences a deathbed fantasy. Before him appear many figures who, like the characters in a medieval pageant, represent not only various aspects of his life but also objectify the false religious and cultural codes and attitudes he has adopted. Immediately thereafter occur two more episodes. While his mother listens without comprehension to the Latin incantations of the priest giving extreme unction to Studs, Paddy Lonigan witnesses a Communist-led demonstration against unemployment in which banners bearing slogans calling for revolutionary political action are visible. Even though Farrell never lectures his readers on political doctrine, the significance of the juxtaposition is obvious.

Farrell's eagerness for knowledge, a personality trait matched only by his irascibility, was forged in rebellion against the cultural poverty of his boyhood on the South Side of Chicago. His reading began with and remained rooted in the social thought of the American pragmatists, the novels of the realists and naturalists, and the historical and class outlook of the European Marxists. Consequently, his critical thought, expressed in a plethora of reviews and essays, largely probes the social basis of human experience—of morality, psychology, aesthetics, and of the concepts of time and the historical process. His political convictions informed all his literary projects; ever since the 1920s he viewed the re-creation of the world of his experiences through art as an act of social redemption. In this endeavor he sought to include no propaganda in his work; he simply ascribed to his role as an artist the task of preserving the memory and dignifying the lives of common people by revealing the nature of their experiences in American society.

If Farrell's boyhood struggles predisposed him to radicalism, there was nothing particular in the background of Frederick Wilcox Dupee that led to his leftward development during the 1930s. Born 25 June 1904, also on the South Side of Chicago, he grew up in small towns in Illinois. His father had to move about in search of better business connections as the family fortune declined.[27] His Huguenot descent meant much to him as a youth; it was a way of differentiating his family from other small-town families that he thought were boring. In fact, with his jaunty demeanor, wry face, and flashing blue eyes, quite a few of his friends thought that he looked French.

He attended first the University of Illinois, then the University of Chicago, and finally Yale, from which his father had graduated. At Yale he joined the Elizabethan Club, and, with his friends Dwight Macdonald and Wilder Hobson, immersed himself in Spengler, Proust, Joyce, James, Sherwood Anderson, and Irving Babbitt. After graduation he spent two years teaching at Bowdoin College before deciding to become a writer and begin traveling around the United States. In late 1929 he and Macdonald initiated a bimonthly literary magazine published in New York, the *Miscellany*, which ran from March 1930 until March 1931. Dupee contributed stories to the magazine before it folded. At the same time he wrote a number of reviews for the *Symposium* that suggested that he had an antiradical bias: at one point he denounced John Dos Passos's left-wing writings as "bogus modernism," and at another he suggested that Edmund Wilson's blend of Communist politics with his modernist sensibilities brought ill consequences.[28]

Dupee next went to Mexico, living in small towns and on the beaches, surviving on a small income of $87 a month augmented by payments for occasional travel articles that he wrote and sold. Unable to finish a novel, he fell into a deep depression during which he contemplated suicide. When he emerged from his despair, he had formed a new identity as a literary critic and a new political consciousness based upon what he had learned about the Mexican Revolution.[29]

Returning to the United States in the mid-1930s, he went immediately to New York City where he discovered that all his former literary friends—including Dwight Macdonald, James Burnham, and Robert Cantwell—had become radicals. Cantwell directed him to the Communist Party with a warning that writers should probably refrain from joining the party. Despite such admonitions, Dupee joined at once and accepted an assignment working on the waterfront with longshoremen. Whereas most writers in the party lived in Greenwich Village and did little more than arrange cultural events and pass out leaflets, Dupee was anxious to be more active, to be more than just an armchair revolutionary. His major effort involved assisting an attempt to build a rank-and-file caucus in the International Longshoreman's Association. After a month he was made educational director of the party unit in the union, which gave him a chance to study Marxism, but he continued to distribute *Shape Up*, the rank-and-file paper, on the docks in the early morning cold. He also participated in a militant anti-Nazi protest aboard the SS *Bremen*, a German luxury liner.

Soon a friend took Dupee to the *New Masses* offices, and, when Isidor Schneider was called to Europe, Dupee was asked to replace him as literary editor. He started work in February 1936. That summer both the Spanish Civil War and the Moscow trials began. As his disillusionment increased, various people began efforts to influence him: James Burnham, an acquaintance from the *Miscellany* and *Symposium* days, began phoning him at the office to call his attention to the criminal absurdity of the trials. Newton Arvin and Horace Gregory, on the other hand, pressured him to stay on.[30] Philip Rahv walked into the office one day and shortly thereafter introduced him to William Phillips.

When Rahv and Phillips first broached the idea of Dupee's joining them in relaunching the *Partisan Review* on an independent basis, Dupee still felt bound to the party. After a while, however, he remained at the *New Masses* only because Rahv and Phillips thought that it was a good tactical move to have him stay there until publication of the new magazine was announced, thereby making his resignation more dramatic. However, conflicts at the *New Masses* continued to increase so that Dupee felt he could not stay any longer. Shortly after the start of the Moscow trials, Theodore Draper, called "The Commissar" behind his back by the staff, marched into the office and began reciting the names of people the *New Masses* had to "get," beginning with Herbert Solow. Dupee was soon assigned a list of members of the American Committee for the Defense of Leon Trotsky to contact in order to persuade them to resign from the committee. His first call was to a young writer named Mary McCarthy, who howled with laughter, convincing him to abandon his efforts. He also requested permission from the party to criticize the design of a new Soviet monument in memory of the October Revolution, but permission was refused. Finally, at the urging of Burnham, Dupee read Trotsky's *History of the Russian Revolution* (1932–33) and found that Trotsky's implicit criticism of Stalin's usurpation of the promise of the revolution provided a political focus for his various misgivings about the party. One day at the office he turned to his young assistant, Samuel Sillen, and said, "You know, I really can't take any more of this." He said good-bye to Joseph Freeman, the editor, and walked out with a folder of letters documenting some of the conflicts he had endured. One pertained to a campaign in opposition to his publication of Rahv's harsh review of Steinbeck's *Of Mice and Men* (1937) on the grounds that Steinbeck was moving toward the left. Shortly after, Dupee received a formal expulsion notice from the party, based upon the charge that he had tried to make the *New Masses* "a forum for attacks on the Soviet Union."

It was not only young and upcoming writers such as Farrell and

Dupee who became convinced that authentic Marxism had to be defended against vulgarization. Edmund Wilson, born in 1895, had inherited a deeply rooted antagonism toward capitalism's business ethic and commercial mentality from his family, whose ties to the professional stratum of the middle class reached back over a century to preindustrial days. Wilson was also acutely conscious of the thwarted idealism of his father, a brilliant but maladjusted lawyer.[31] The son initially expressed his alienation from bourgeois society when, after graduating from Princeton, he joined the army in the hope of forcing a change in his life. Returning from service in France in 1919, he wrote on cultural matters for *Vanity Fair*, *Liberator*, *Dial*, and *Bookman*. Eventually he became literary editor of the *New Republic* and remained associated with the magazine until 1940 when he resigned over the publisher's prowar stance. The execution of Sacco and Vanzetti, which he wrote about in "The Men from Rumpelmayer's," provided the first specific focus to his personal disquiet.[32] In 1929, the Gastonia, North Carolina, textile strike finally jarred Wilson from his perch as a spectator.

During the post–World War I years, Wilson forged a historico-literary method that sharply differentiates him from other critics of his generation. From Hippolyte Taine's *History of English Literature* (1864), which Wilson had read at the age of fifteen, he derived a view of literary schools as forces in a larger social drama. He employed a synoptic style, summarizing plots and biographies, and his forthright approach delved directly to the social core of a literary problem. If he occasionally forsook critical subtlety, it was to focus on a writer or gain perspective on a literary trend. Never awed by the oblique, obscure, or elitist literary schools, Wilson became known in some respects as a popularizer who rendered recondite modernist writers—such as Joyce, Proust, and Eliot—more accessible to the uninformed reader.[33]

The bulk of Wilson's writing in the 1920s appeared as short review articles. He also wrote several volumes of mediocre plays, poems, and dialogues, and one important novel, *I Thought of Daisy* (1929), perhaps the most definitive portrait of Greenwich Village bohemia at that time. Wilson's first mature book-length critical work, *Axel's Castle* (1931), explicitly revealed the social orientation for which he would be hailed as a "conscience" by F. Scott Fitzgerald, Alfred Kazin, and others. Inspired by Alfred North Whitehead's *Science and the Modern World* (1925), Wilson argued that the modern symbolist movement in literature—represented by writers such as Yeats, Valery, Proust, Joyce, and Stein—was essentially a second wave of reaction against the advance of science and industry in the wake of the nineteenth-century romanticists.

Begun in 1926, *Axel's Castle* is a sympathetic but critical exposition of the isolation from an unsympathetic society that underlay writings of the symbolist mode. Modern symbolism, Wilson maintained, expressed the retreat of artists from an encroaching reality into endless psychological explorations and mythical worlds. *Axel's Castle* reflected the crosscurrents of social and personal change during the years in which it was written; consequently it embodied an uncertainty of viewpoint that would be found again in *To the Finland Station* (1940). Wilson so convincingly communicated the acute sensibilities of the symbolist writers that his ultimate criticisms were largely undermined. Yet there is no doubt that Wilson meant to reject symbolism in favor of a more serviceable life of reason and humanizing art.

Wilson's radicalization in the 1930s was profound, although his active involvement in Communist and other left-wing activities was brief and without depth. In 1931 he rejected liberal progressivism for communism. Then, after an episodic collaboration with the Communist Party, he endorsed A. J. Muste's American Workers Party. By 1933, however, he had abjured association with organized movements and for the remainder of the decade he devoted himself to a study of the ideas of communism.

Wilson's public declaration of the bankruptcy of reformism that appeared in the *New Republic* in 1931 was an important event. In "An Appeal to Progressives," he criticized the recently deceased founder of the *New Republic*, Herbert Croly. In *The Promise of American Life* (1909), Croly had ascribed the evils of American society to the default of the postrevolutionary Jeffersonians who had appropriated the Hamiltonian program of conservatism under a guise of false rhetoric. Lumping Croly with a whole panoply of liberal-progressive ideologues—John Dewey, Charles Beard, Walter Lippmann, and Stuart Chase—Wilson declared that all were sincere but were hopelessly tied to capitalism. Reformism was an inadequate response to the present economic and moral crisis, Wilson asserted, and he argued that American radicals "must take Communism away from the Communists." This slogan meant that, because Progressives disagreed with the tactics of the official Communist Party, they were obligated to unanimously announce that their own goal was likewise "the ownership by the government of the means of production."[34] Wilson followed his appeal with a cross-country pilgrimage to ascertain the state of the nation in

1931. He contributed a series of articles to the *New Republic* that ultimately became the depression chronicle, *The American Jitters* (1931). These articles disclosed an intensification of Wilson's animus against American capitalism and a growing sympathy for the American Communist Party and the Soviet Union.

Wilson's personal observations in the penultimate chapter of *The American Jitters*, however, revealed an unmistakably moralistic and psychological interpretation of socialism. While he believed that Marx's predictions were being empirically verified, he disparaged the scientific claims of Marxism. Marx, "like the other great Jewish prophets," had the ability to look "searchingly into one's heart." Wilson explained that the real laws of capitalist production "are merely the instinctive workings of human acquisitiveness, selfishness, and self-deception."[35] Wilson also espoused an ideological identification with the Enlightenment of preindustrial capitalism: "I believe in progress as the eighteenth-century people did. . . . I do not, however, believe in progress in the sense in which the nineteenth-century capitalists used the word . . . a conception entirely different from the visions of the earlier philosophers, who had not foreseen that the rising middle class would be able to seize upon machinery as a powerful instrument for human exploitation."[36]

In February 1932 Wilson, who was not by temperament a person of action, joined the NCDPP delegation to investigate the miners' strike in Harlan County, Kentucky. In October his name appeared as a supporter of the League of Professionals for Foster and Ford. However, Wilson never felt comfortable with the kind of literary criticism that he read in the *New Masses*. He mulled over the vast gulf between the quality of Lenin's ideas—"the mind of Lenin was one of the sharpest lenses through which human thought has ever looked"—and those of the American Communists and soon came to the opinion that he was being misused by the party.[37] He began a brief liaison with V. F. Calverton's *Modern Monthly* and A. J. Muste's American Workers Party before turning exclusively to theoretical inquiry for the remainder of the decade.[38] Among Wilson's various heresies at the time was an unbounded admiration for Leon Trotsky's literary achievements and his preservation of Marxist principles that Wilson celebrated in a two-part essay in the *New Republic*.[39]

THE APPEAL OF TROTSKYISM

With the literary and political rebellion of the *Partisan Review* editors and their growing association with Farrell, Dupee, and Wilson, the influence of Trotskyism began to extend beyond the small circle of dissident communists in the NCDPP and League of Professionals. Among other themes, Trotsky was now writing about the Moscow trials, exposing their fraudulent content with the greatest force and authority, thereby himself becoming an indispensable component of the burgeoning movement of anti-Stalinist left-wing intellectuals. In addition, Trotsky had a special appeal to radicalized literati that stemmed from his literary, historical, and polemical achievements which had earned him authentic credentials as a first-rate writer and theorist. One biographer, Baruch Knei-Paz, observed that, as an integral facet of Trotsky's personality, "there emerged, almost from the outset, a seemingly compulsive inclination toward the world of ideas, and of intellectual preoccupations in general." In a powerful study of Trotsky's literary method, Norman Geras observes that, even in Trotsky's early writings, "the techniques and inspirations of creative literature inform . . . his activities as historian and journalist, revolutionary theoretician and polemicist."[40]

Even more, his intellectual and literary predilections blended harmoniously with his extraordinary career of revolutionary activism, which included his service as the president of the Petrograd Soviet in 1905, as the director of the military committee that organized the October uprising, as the Soviet Union's first commissar of foreign affairs, and as the commander of the Red Army. Throughout these many years of dangerous and vigorous activity, Trotsky's imagination, independence of thought, rebellious spirit, and literary productivity never declined. "With full, almost naive conviction Trotsky believed in the creative possibilities of the word," wrote Irving Howe many decades later,

> but he believed not as most Western intellectuals have: not in some ironic or contemplative or symbolic way. The common distinction between word and deed Trotsky scorned as a sign of philistinism, worthy—he might have added—of liberal professors and literary dilettantes. He regarded his outpouring of brilliant composition as the natural privilege of a thinking man, but more urgently, as the necessary work of a Marxist leader who has pledged his life to socialism. The heritage of the Russian writers of the nineteenth century is stamped upon

his books, for he took from them the assumption that to write is to engage in a serious political act, a gesture toward the redemption or recreation of man.[41]

Throughout his life Trotsky developed a set of distinctive ideas about literature and culture. Like many leading revolutionaries, he approached cultural matters with the same passionate intensity that characterized his study of politics. As late as 1935 he wrote that "politics and literature constitute in essence the contents of my personal life."[42] His essays collected in *Problems of Everyday Life* (1924) present theoretical arguments explaining why the mastery and critical assimilation of all existing culture is the central task of the proletarian revolution. In his literary criticism, Trotsky, who was much inspired by the Russian radical critic Vissarion Belinsky, focused on the social aspects of literature, but he rigorously differentiated between his assessments of the political views of an author and his judgments of the artistic quality of a work. *Literature and Revolution* (1923) and many subsequent essays demonstrate that Trotsky had no patience with critics who claimed that a certain political ideology might automatically enhance an aesthetic work or guarantee a more profound and sensitive exploration of life through the imagination.[43] Just as Marx admired the monarchist Balzac more than many socialist writers of his day, so Trotsky lauded the art of Pushkin, Gogol, and Tolstoy, whose political outlooks might be characterized as mystical and even reactionary. Above all, Trotsky had always been aware of a consanguinity of temperament between the rebel artist and the social radical. Cultural and political heretics were potentially bonded by their refusal to accommodate to the status quo. In 1938 Trotsky wrote that "generally speaking, art is the expression of man's need for a harmonious and complete life, that is to say, his need for those major benefits of which a society of classes has deprived him. That is why a protest against reality, either conscious or unconscious, active or passive, optimistic or pessimistic, always forms part of a really creative work."[44]

Trotsky devoted extensive correspondence during the 1930s to the question of the significance of American intellectuals for a small revolutionary workers' party. The main tendency of intellectuals, once radicalized, was to gravitate toward the Communist parties that were the official representatives of the Soviet regime because, among other attractions, they offered a strong material alternative to capitalist literary institutions, including numerous left-wing magazines, the possibility of being published in the Soviet

Union or participating in international lecture tours, and an audience of respectable size. Trotsky was brutally harsh in his assessment of pro-Communist intellectuals:

> A whole generation of "leftist" intelligentsia has turned its eyes for the last ten or fifteen years to the East and bound its lot in varying degrees, to a victorious revolution, if not to a victorious proletariat. Now, this is by no means one and the same thing. In the victorious revolution there is not only the revolution, but there is also the new privileged stratum which raises itself on the shoulders of the revolution. In reality, the "leftist" intelligentsia has tried to change masters.[45]

Trotsky therefore urged that his followers exercise special precautionary measures when assimilating former Communist intellectuals: "if it is a matter of a young intellectual who has been in our movement, that's another thing; a worker is also another thing; but an intellectual with an education gained in a Stalinist party, that's a dangerous element for us."[46]

From the onset, Trotsky pressed American radical intellectuals and writers who had become disillusioned with Stalinist communism to strive for theoretical and political clarity. He believed that a recurring problem among these intellectuals was their tendency to mistake the opinions of bureaucratized Communist parties for authentic Leninist practice. The once-burned intellectuals frequently concluded that collaboration with any Marxist party would result in a repetition of their being manipulated and suppressed as they were by the Communists. Consequently, they tended to stay aloof from identification with parties, sustaining, as best they could, a general anti-Stalinist radicalism. As early as 1932, Trotsky criticized the limitations of this standpoint in a letter to V. F. Calverton, who was beginning to open the pages of the *Modern Monthly* to a discussion of Trotskyist ideas:

> A Marxist who, for one secondary consideration or another, does not draw his conclusions to the end betrays Marxism. To pretend to ignore the different Communist factions, so as not to become involved and compromise oneself, signifies ignoring that activity which, through all the contradictions, consolidates the vanguard of the class; it signifies covering oneself with the abstraction of the revolution, as with a shield, from the blows and bruises of the real revolutionary process.

Still, Trotsky held that a uniquely promising situation existed among American intellectuals, although, paradoxically, he believed that it was partly determined by what he called "the political back-wardness of the United States, technologically the most advanced country in the world." The basis for this contention of backward-ness was that the United States "lagged behind in the domain of socialist theory." It also lacked the potent socialist traditions and mass radical organizations that existed in Europe. But Trotsky's analysis was, ultimately, overoptimistic about the prospects of a revolutionary movement. He held that the very same factors that caused political retardation prepared the way for a great leap for-ward: "The great transoceanic 'porridge' is unquestioningly begin-ning to boil," wrote Trotsky to Calverton, "the breaking point in the development of American capitalism will unavoidably provoke a blossoming of critical and generalizing thought, and it may be that we are not very far from the time when the theoretical center of the international revolution is transferred to New York. . . . Be-fore the American Marxist open truly colossal, breathtaking per-spectives."[47]

The relative weakness of working-class political traditions and organizations in the United States helped account for the fact that so many of the most advanced and independent-minded intellectu-als gave serious consideration to the miniscule and isolated Trots-kyist organization. The political weight of the Communist and So-cialist parties in the United States was not insignificant, but it was not so overwhelming as in many European countries. However, after the success of the Popular Front and the exponential growth of the American Communist Party in numbers and influence, which was capped only by the onset of World War II, the stream of intellec-tuals toward Trotskyism virtually ceased.

What helped to distinguish the Trotskyist-influenced critics, es-pecially those who would rally around the reorganized *Partisan Re-view*, and what exacerbated their relations with the Communists, was their willingness to openly blend Marxism with an aggressive sympathy for the modernist themes and techniques of the 1920s, exemplified by T. S. Eliot. In contrast, the official Communist atti-tude was expressed by Mike Gold: "[In] the Twenties the young poets followed T. S. Eliot. Eliot was to the poetry of the boom period what Mencken had been to its prose; both were anti-people, and fascist-minded, and both were washed away like rotten piers in the flood of new insights and new demands that the depression brought to American writers."[48]

Gold's reductive viewpoint epitomized the vulgarization of Marx-ism in the sphere of literary criticism that so exercised the *Partisan Review* editors. Rahv and Phillips held that new forms and stages of class society can produce new forms of art, most famously demonstrated by the rise of the novel, that became a generalized literary form only with the rise of bourgeois society. But they also agreed with Marx and Engels that art has substantial residual value, that it did not necessarily have to change its forms dramatically or render its earlier achievements obsolete with every new conjuncture in class relations. The poetry of Eliot, in fact, owed an important debt to artistic achievements that had been realized prior to the boom period, namely, the revolt against gentility as well as the Imagist experiments. Eliot's writings were certainly not "washed away" by the 1930s.

Gold also attached a political label, "fascist-minded," to the poetry of Eliot, claiming that when the modernist writers radicalized they rejected their former mentors because of their politics. This subordination of art to politics was characteristic of many Communist Party critics throughout both the Third Period and Popular Front phases of its cultural activity during the 1930s. It is reflected in Gold's judgment of Nathanael West, a Communist Party sympathizer who wrote *Miss Lonelyhearts* (1933): "His writing seemed to me to be symbolic rather than realistic and that was, to me, the supreme crime."[49] Symbolic form is judged criminal. To be sure, many Communist writers employed modernist techniques, and others privately held views similar to those of Phillips and Rahv, but it was the open endorsement of modernism as a viable heritage for communists that gave *Partisan Review* its special stamp.

Yet the theory and practice of the leading *Partisan Review* writers must be judged a partial achievement at best. Their Marxist critique of modernism never went beyond a few illuminating insights, unlike the brilliant work of such European contemporaries as Walter Benjamin, Theodor Adorno, and Georg Lukács.[50] In fact, there were elements of elitism inscribed in *Partisan Review's* project from its inception. It overreacted to vulgarized Marxism by assigning high culture its virtually exclusive center of interest and was rather selective in the modernist writers it promoted. This approach, of course, contradicted Trotsky's views. His well-known opposition to a theory of proletarian culture as an official policy of the Soviet Union did not stem from a lack of interest in creative activity among workers or literary depictions of working-class life. Rather, Trotsky held that the dictatorship of the proletariat was intended to be a transitional and exceptional phase; its goal was to construct a classless society and a socialist culture.

Moreover, from the point of view of the overall development of American literature, it can now be seen that even the most clumsy and forced attempts of some of the pro-Communist writers to bring the experiences of the oppressed and the outcast to the printed pages had a historic significance that the post-1936 *Partisan Review* editors failed to appreciate. Some aspects of certain "proletarian" novels are noteworthy on purely literary grounds as well, such as the vivid depiction of work experience pervading Jack Conroy's *The Disinherited* (1933) and the forms of oppression among plebeian and working-class women described by Tillie Olsen and later published as *Yonondio: From the Thirties* (1974). It is possible to recognize such accomplishments without indulging in a policy of celebrating a writer's book simply because he or she adheres to a certain political line or comes from a certain class background.

What ultimately vindicates the cultural perspective championed by *Partisan Review* is not so much the specific judgments that the editors made about the works of the time, as it was the fact that so many of the finest books of the decade embodied the magazine's spirit of openness to modernism and its radical political commitment: *U.S.A* (1932–38), *Call It Sleep* (1935), *Let Us Now Praise Famous Men* (1941), and *Day of the Locust* (1939). The fusion of these two elements is also evident in the work of Farrell, an early contributor to *Partisan Review*, who admired Marcel Proust as well as Marx and Lenin. *Gas-House McGinty* (1933), for example, was the highly experimental first volume of an intended trilogy about the Wagon Call Department of the Amalgamated Express Company in Chicago as it evolved under the successive direction of four chief dispatchers. It was originally titled "The Madhouse" and described as "a Romance of Commerce and Service."[51] The structure of the novel is designed to reflect the flow of internal pressures felt by the company workers. The success of his *Studs Lonigan* trilogy (1932–35) is related to Farrell's attempts to find new modes of communicating the spiritual desolation of his characters. The influence of Joyce is evident in Farrell's use of dreams, interior monologues, and "snap-shot" episodes.

Some cultural historians have oversimplified the antagonism that immediately flared up between *Partisan Review* and the Communist Party in 1937, offering an explanation centered mainly on the editors' decision to heavily emphasize modernist literature. The first issue of the reorganized magazine included poetry by Wallace Stevens and James Agee, fiction by Delmore Schwartz, an essay on Flaubert by Edmund Wilson, and a review of Kafka's fiction by Dupee. However, the *Partisan Review*'s attraction to modernism per se was scarcely sufficient to cause the Communists to launch a literary attack of the magnitude that they mounted against the *Par-*

tisan Review's editors. Muriel Rukeyser, Horace Gregory, Malcolm Cowley, Kenneth Burke, Kenneth Fearing, Henry Roth, and Nathanael West all had been influenced by modernism, nonetheless they had been courted by the party at different points in the 1930s. More decisive for the party was the political direction in which a writer was moving. After 1935, only liberalism and Popular Front communism were acceptable political postures; Trotskyism, anarchism, and even the left-wing socialists were not tolerated.

The Communists attempted to mobilize their literary resources to isolate the new magazine because Phillips, Rahv, and their circle had set themselves up as a rival center of revolutionary thought and an alternative pole of attraction for non-Stalinist Marxism among intellectuals. Even worse, the Trotskyists and Trotsky himself were welcomed as legitimate participants in the discussions that emanated from the new rival center. Consequently, the editors were assaulted with a fusillade of invective. The appearance of the new *Partisan Review* prompted a rash of articles in the *New Masses* and *Daily Worker* headlined variously as "Falsely Labeled Goods," "A Literary Snake Sheds His Skin for Trotsky," "Trotskyist Schemers Exposed," and "No Quarter to Trotskyists—Literary or Otherwise." V. J. Jerome, the Communist Party's "commissar of culture," wrote that the *Partisan Review* editors were "of the same ilk that murdered Kirov, that turned the guns on the backs of Loyalist civilians in Spain and betrayed the army's front lines, that have been caught red-handed in plots with the Gestapo and Japanese militarists to dismember the Soviet Union."[52] By the mid-1930s, it was apparent that the core of the anti-Stalinist left intellectuals no longer could be characterized as simply modernists; their attraction to Trotskyism was far more decisive and would become clearer as they began to initiate their own literary and political activities.

PART II

Revolutionary Intellectuals

CHAPTER 4

Philosophers and Revolutionists

Under thirty a revolutionist, thereafter a scoundrel.

—Popular French Saying[1]

. . . .

THE NON-PARTISAN LABOR DEFENSE COMMITTEE (NPLD) AND THE AMERICAN WORKERS PARTY

The internationalist Jewish intellectuals and fellow dissidents broke with the Communist Party in 1933–34, and the radical modernists became alienated from the party at the beginning of the Moscow trials in 1936. Yet these two rebellions should not be confused with rifts that occurred later in the decade. These separations occurred early in their participants' engagement with radicalism, at a time when revolutionary prospects still seemed promising. The CIO was emerging as a major force in American society; fascism had not yet triumphed in Spain; and the full scope of the purges in the Soviet Union under Stalin was not yet apparent. Consequently, most of the rebels, rather than calling communism itself into question, began to seek out revolutionary alternatives to the Communist Party.

At the same time, an important process of differentiation had begun between those intellectuals who were willing to make a serious, long-term organizational commitment to revolutionary politics and those whose engagement with Marxism was becoming subordinated to the pursuit of their personal and professional lives. Of course, the two extremes—embarking upon a lifelong full-time commitment to revolutionary politics as opposed to maintaining no organizational connection with the movement—were rarely evident. Much more common were variations and intermediate combinations. One such pattern began with an intellectual assuming a purist, hypercritical, and usually ultraleft stance toward the existing radical movement, followed by a startling rejection of socialist politics altogether. Another entailed an intellectual's announcement of differences with Marxist philosophy in order to justify an essentially literary association with the socialist movement. Still, one can find occasional examples of purists who overcame their ultraleftism, as well as heretical philosophers who devoted many years to building a Marxist party.

Many of those who were drawn to activism during the early 1930s considered three particular organizations on the left to be anticapitalist, revolutionary, and non-Stalinist: the American Workers Party (AWP), an indigenous revolutionary organization, led by A. J. Muste; the Communist Party Opposition (CPO), or Bukharinists, led by Jay Lovestone; and the Communist League of America (CLA), Trotskyists, led by James P. Cannon and Max Shachtman. The most prominent of the dissident communists gravitated toward the Muste group, the most loosely structured of the three. Sidney Hook, for example, was one of the central organizers of the AWP and the author of its revolutionary program. Also affiliated with the AWP were James Burnham, who taught with Hook in the Department of Philosophy at New York University, James Rorty, V. F. Calverton, and Edmund Wilson. The Lovestone group would eventually attract only Lewis Corey, who was essentially a secret member from 1937 to 1939, although the founders of the CPO in 1929 included such talented intellectuals as Will Herberg and Bertram D. Wolfe. By December 1934, those who had joined the CLA included Herbert Solow, Felix Morrow, George Novack, and John McDonald, while allies of the Trotskyists included Elliot Cohen, Elinor Rice, Anita Brenner (who occasionally wrote for the Trotskyist newspaper under the name "Jean Mendez"), Louis Berg, and Diana Rubin (her husband, Lionel Trilling, was a sympathizer but remained more distant).[2]

In addition to the personal charisma of Trotsky and the power of his critique of Stalinism, three other factors may have helped to consolidate the alliance of the younger and more activist intellectuals with the CLA. In the first place, the intellectuals' break with the Communists was enthusiastically welcomed by the Troskyists. Second, during the summer of 1934 the CLA led the famed Minneapolis Teamster strikes, thereby establishing itself as a legitimate force in the American labor movement. Third, partly as a result of the success of the Minneapolis strikes, the AWP began to express an interest in fusing with the CLA.[3] The mechanism by which the first wave of "Trotskyist intellectuals" began their collaboration with the CLA was through the construction of an alternative to the National Committee for the Defense of Political Prisoners (NCDPP) called the Non-Partisan Labor Defense (NPLD).

When the *New Masses* denounced the February 1934 open letter of the dissident intellectuals, the Trotskyist newspaper, the *Militant*, responded aggressively by publishing an article called "The Intellectual Revolt against Stalinist Hooliganism." Although the *Militant* claimed, falsely, that none of the signers had as yet drawn Trotskyist conclusions from their criticisms, the revolt was nonetheless assessed as significant. The Trotskyists emphasized that among the signers of the open letter were a number of bonafide activists, including Elliot Cohen, former secretary of the NCDPP; George Novack, secretary of the Prisoners' Book Committee; Diana Rubin, former secretary of the Prisoners' Relief Committee; and James Rorty, former secretary of the League of Professionals as well as a founding editor of the *New Masses*. The *Militant* offered to provide space for a public discussion with these dissidents on the tactics of the United Front.[4]

In the 17 March 1934 issue an anonymous article—whose author was probably Solow—was attributed to a signer of the open letter. Explaining that the protest of the twenty-five was just the first overt product of the ferment then in process among intellectuals close to the Communists, Solow reviewed the conflicts in the NCDPP and League of Professionals, claiming that at least thirty more individuals agreed with the open letter and that many had been influenced by Trotsky's writings on the United Front.[5]

A week later a second unsigned article written by Solow presented a "Program for Intellectuals" that included guidelines for their relation to a revolutionary movement. He began by emphasizing that it would be incorrect for the CLA to encourage all radical intellectuals to join its ranks; the purpose of a revolutionary party was to unite those whose primary interest was organizing a social revolution. Accordingly, most intellectuals could be more effective as allies or sympathizers of such a party, with a program of their own activities to carry out. On the other hand, Solow believed it would be a mistake for intellectuals to organize as a separate, autonomous entity, since they comprised a social layer with certain weaknesses and might well end up transmitting and reinforcing the political liabilities of the middle class. He concluded that the proper place for intellectuals was in mass organizations where they could collaborate with both workers and a revolutionary party. Among the most fruitful areas of activity was labor defense because it provided opportunity for intellectuals to participate in a meaningful fashion, using their exceptional talents in valuable capacities such as writing and fund-raising.[6]

Of course, for some members of the *Menorah* group, Solow's articles were already dated. Novack and Morrow had already joined the CLA, and Solow himself, while not officially a member, had galvanized the others into establishing a new organization: the Non-Partisan Labor Defense. Since the origin of the conflict in the NCDPP revolved around whether or not to establish a genuine United Front, the NPLD was not simply a liberal civil-rights organization. In an official letter to Roger Baldwin of the American Civil Liberties Union, Solow explained that the NPLD's program called for a struggle against capitalist oppression. Its national executive board consisted of Anita Brenner, Louis Berg, Elliot Cohen, Elsie Gluck, Martha Gruening, Sidney Hook, Albert Margolies, Felix Morrow, George Novack, Abraham Schneider, Herbert Solow, Thomas Stamm, Carlo Tresca, and Adelaide Walker.[7]

The NPLD's first case involved Antonio Bellussi, an Italian anti-fascist follower of Carlo Tresca. Arrested for heckling a fascist meeting, he was threatened with deportation to Italy where he was likely to be imprisoned.[8] A Bellussi Anti-Fascist Dinner committee was established to raise funds. Elinor Rice was designated treasurer. Solow was scheduled to give the NPLD fund-raising speech following the dinner, but, on the day of the event, the Trotskyist leader James P. Cannon informed Novack that Solow was simply incapable of speaking and that Novack would have to take his place. This sudden inability to speak was characteristic of the psychological problems that plagued Solow, which resulted in his often assuming a behind-the-scenes role while Novack and Morrow did most of the public speaking at the other NPLD activities that followed. These included mass meetings in support of striking workers in Minneapolis and Toledo, actions against the impending deportation from Holland of four young left-wing German refugees, and a demonstration against a pro-Hitler rally held in Madison Square Garden at which some of the demonstrators were arrested.[9]

During 1934 and 1935 Solow combined his journalistic and political activities. At the start of 1934 he published a critique in the *Nation* of the response of German writers to the new fascist regime.[10] In February, he reported on the New York hotel-workers strike of which Trotskyists were the leaders.[11] During the summer of 1934 Solow traveled to Minneapolis to edit the *Organizer*, the paper of Teamsters Local 544 which, led by the CLA, was engaged in a series of historic strikes. Strike leader Farrell Dobbs, a Trotskyist, was listed as editor on the paper's masthead, but it was initially Max Shachtman, and later Solow, who actually put the paper out and wrote most of the articles that appeared in it. Under difficult conditions—virtual civil war in the streets of Minneapolis amidst an intense red-baiting campaign directed especially against "outside agitators"—Solow so impressed the workers with his courage and efficiency that they made him an honorary member of the union.[12] Solow also wrote about the Minneapolis strike in the *Nation*, beginning with a piece called "Class War in Minneapolis" and continuing with a series of articles and letters that appeared throughout the fall of 1934.[13]

Returning to New York, Solow and John McDonald formally joined the CLA in December 1934, although Solow had been functioning as a de facto member for at least a year. Their decision to join came partly in anticipation of the fusion of the AWP and the CLA that occurred only a few weeks later. The fusion process had been under way since the spring of 1934 when the AWP sponsored a series of conferences in New York to discuss its program. Solow, Morrow, and Novack had been asked by the CLA leaders to help accelerate the process of fusion through their close personal and professional ties with various intellectuals in the AWP, including Hook, Rorty, Burnham, and Calverton. The fusion itself was proclaimed by the Trotskyists as a historic alliance of grass-roots activists (from the AWP, which had recently led the Toledo Auto-Lite strike) with revolutionary Marxist theorists (from the CLA). The new organization was called the Workers Party of the United States (WPUS) and its paper the *New Militant*. But of the intellectuals associated with the AWP, only Burnham chose to establish firm ties to the new party. Hook and Calverton were kept on the rolls for a period but never attended any meetings. Rorty intended to switch his membership from the AWP to the WPUS, but then decided that, as a journalist who was frequently on the road investigating strikes and workers' struggles, it would be best for tactical reasons to become an "independent."[14]

At the beginning of 1935, Solow flew to California to serve as secretary of the National Sacramento Appeal Committee, a branch of the NPLD established to assist in an important trial. The main defendant was Norman Mini, a recent convert to Trotskyism and a militant young leader of agricultural workers who had been indicted under the state Criminal Syndicalism Law. Members of the Communist Party were also on trial, which made the situation exceedingly complex. Solow pushed himself to the limit organizing the legal defense, raising funds, writing for the *New Militant* (under the party pseudonym "Harry Strang") and the *Nation*, as well as authoring the NPLD pamphlet, *Union-Smashing in Sacramento: The Truth about the Criminal Syndicalism Trial* (1935). But Solow also ran into difficulties with the Political Committee of the WPUS, which censured him for allegedly stirring up members of the San Francisco branch against the national leadership and for hiring Chicago attorney Albert Goldman, who had resigned from the CLA the previous November to join the Socialist Party. Solow refuted the charges in great detail by mail. The tone of Solow's defense of his actions seemed surprisingly good-humored, but the episode revealed a streak of individualism on his part that was scarcely compatible with the party discipline the Trotskyists aspired to establish.[15]

PARTY FACTIONALISM AND THE "FRENCH TURN"

When Solow returned to the East Coast, he found that a major dispute had broken out in the fledgling WPUS concerning the party's future posture toward the Socialist Party. A minority tendency, led by Cannon and Shachtman, argued that greater attention should be paid to developments in the Socialist Party's left wing. They were opposed by a variety of internal groups, the most important of which was led by Hugo Oehler, a former Communist Party district organizer who had joined the CLA in 1930. Another group, led by A. J. Muste, believed that Cannon and Shachtman's proposal was only a gambit to prepare the WPUS ranks to enter the Socialist Party, which was what the Trotskyists in France had done. Oehler believed that such an entry, known as the "French Turn," would be a violation of revolutionary principle, a capitulation to reformism. Muste also feared accommodation with the reformists, but additionally was unhappy about the possibility of abandoning his newly formed organization and uncomfortable with the ethical aspects of entry.[16] As the Cannon-Shachtman position began to gain support, the Oehler opposition grew more adamant and started to publish its own newsletter, thereby raising the possibility of being expelled for indiscipline. Morrow and Novack quickly sided with Cannon and Shachtman, but Solow and McDonald held a position somewhere between Oehler's and Muste's. Solow failed to show up at the meeting where the vote to expel the Oehler group was taken, while McDonald identified himself with the expelled group and met briefly with them afterward. However, neither McDonald nor Solow ever joined another Marxist organization.[17]

Several faction fights had already occurred in the Trotskyist movement before the one concerning the "French Turn." One of the most important had resulted in the expulsion of B. J. Field.[18] Born Max Gould in New York City in 1903, Field had graduated from Columbia University. Shortly after, he and his wife, Esther, moved to Europe for several years, where he became fluent in French and German. He returned to New York and embarked upon a successful career on Wall Street as a petroleum analyst. After the stock-market crash he rapidly moved to the political left and applied to join the CLA.

Of medium height, slightly stocky, and swarthy with jet-black hair and a mustache, Field was brilliant but erratic. He was a good speaker, although he tended to talk above the heads of most workers. In the CLA he organized private study groups in his home, later remembered by his young disciple Paul Jacobs for its legendary book and record collections. When the New York branch of the CLA insisted that such educational activities should be brought under its direction, Field refused to cooperate, which led to his and Esther's expulsion in 1932. Field then journeyed directly to appeal to Trotsky in Constantinople, making such a strong impression on Trotsky with his writings on the capitalist economy, which he knew intimately from firsthand experience, that Trotsky persuaded the CLA to take him back into membership after a period of collaboration.

The New York Hotel Strike broke out in January 1934. Because of his facility with languages Field was assigned by the CLA to assist in the strike because French chefs, who knew little English, were playing an important role. He was soon propelled into leadership of the strike along with Aristodimos Kaldis, a Greek-born Trotskyist waiter who later became a famous landscape artist.[19] Once more Field refused to collaborate with the CLA, and once more he was expelled.[20] This time Field and Kaldis organized their own group, the League for a Revolutionary Party, which briefly found some supporters among a group of precocious Columbia students, including the future philosopher Morton G. White and the military analyst Albert Wohlstetter. Although Field's Canadian affiliate, led by the journalist William Krehm, grew at one point to more than a hundred strong and became more significant than the official Trotskyist organization in Canada, the American group dwindled, surviving for only a few years until it fell apart. After being expelled from his own organization, Field was offered a job in a prosperous California real estate firm run by the attorney Nat Mendelsohn, a former follower, and ultimately disappeared from the political scene.

Thus the CLA leadership had compromised with but had not completely bent to Trotsky, who obviously had had great hopes for a person as extraordinarily talented as Field. Therefore it is surprising that most scholars argue that Cannon and Shachtman were mechanically following orders from Trotsky in their subsequent support of the "French Turn."[21] That Trotsky supported the tactic of entry and carried the highest authority with Cannon and Shachtman is beyond question, but Trotsky's history of stormy relations with his followers around the world suggests there is no reason why Cannon and Shachtman could not have opposed him if they thought that the entry strategy was untenable. To the contrary, their willingness to implement the "French Turn" strategy in the United States exemplified a flexibility and practical sense that distinguished them, at least in this particular instance, from the rigid sectarianism, organizational fetishism, and purism characteristic of the growing number of ex-Trotskyist splinter groups that had appeared on the scene. These split-offs included not only the Field and Oehler groups, but also the followers of Albert Weisbord (a Harvard graduate who led the 1926 Passaic textile strike) and George Spiro (who called himself "Marlen," after Marx and Lenin). Several letters written to Trotsky by Harold Isaacs, then a young party intellectual, testify to considerable skill and organizational evenhandedness on the part of Cannon and Shachtman during the dispute over entry into the Socialist Party.

Isaacs, born 13 September 1910 in New York City, graduated from Columbia University in 1930.[22] Taking a job as a reporter for the *China Press* in Shanghai and Peking, he befriended a South African journalist, C. Frank Glass, who was sympathetic to Trotskyism but had been collaborating with the Chinese Communists through his association with the writer Agnes Smedley. A facile writer with a sharp mind, Isaacs was an adventurous sort and soon he established further connections with Trotskyists during an investigation of a rebellion in the Kuomintang. After being introduced to Smedley, he was able to obtain funds from the Communist Party to establish an English-language paper called *China Forum*, which he edited for two years. He then issued a public statement, "I Break with the Chinese Stalinists," and returned to the United States, where he joined the WPUS, but found himself opposed to the entry proposal.[23] His letters to Trotsky from early February to early March 1934 describe his about-face regarding Cannon and Shachtman's positions. In particular, his detailed praise for their objectivity, their fairness in treating internal opponents, and their nonfactional style of leadership, adds at least another perception of this important turning point in the relationship of New York intellectuals to the Trotskyist organization.[24] Isaacs, who used the pseudonym "H. F. Roberts," would remain loyal to Cannon until the end of 1940. When the Trotskyist newspaper *Socialist Appeal* was launched in late 1937, Isaacs was for several years its real editor—organizing the staff, assigning articles, and editing most of the contributions—despite Max Shachtman's name on the masthead. In 1938 he published his classic *The Tragedy of the Chinese Revolution*, with an introduction by Trotsky, who had also helped formulate its thesis. Discouraged by the assassination of Trotsky and the onset of World War II, Isaacs began a new career as a *Newsweek* editor and correspondent in 1943. In 1951 *The Tragedy of the Chinese Revolution* was reissued with Trotsky's introduction deleted and the revolutionary Marxist conclusions expunged. That same year Isaacs inaugurated a successful academic career at Harvard University, the New School for Social Research, and the Massachusetts Institute of Technology, from which he retired as a professor of political science in 1976.

John McDonald, on the other hand, concluded that the struggle had revealed the actual degeneracy of the two Trotskyist leaders. He later claimed that he and Solow had differentiated themselves from the Oehler group by opposing entry on "democratic" grounds; they believed that "the Trotskyists' intention to dissolve and re-form themselves inside the Socialist Party formed a poor model for a future society."[25] But Sidney Lens, an AWP member who had joined the Oehler group and later a well-known radical writer and activist, recalled in his autobiography that Solow and McDonald had supported Oehler. Moreover, Solow sent a letter to Margaret De Silver a few months later suggesting criticisms of Cannon and Shachtman that clearly parallel those of Oehler.[26]

Accusing the *New Militant* of "left-wing Thomasism," Solow complained that the WPUS had already made concessions to the Socialists by not criticizing Socialist Party leader Jack Altman when he praised trade unionist David Dubinsky for supporting Roosevelt instead of the Socialist presidential candidate. In addition, Solow castigated the Trotskyists and Felix Morrow in particular for not dissociating themselves and the Tampa Committee of the NPLD from a statement by Norman Thomas proclaiming that the Tampa Committee was opposed to all violence and favored "the American tradition of fair play." Solow concluded that the Trotskyists really did plan to abandon their revolutionary politics and adapt

to the Social Democracy, citing these incidents as dishonest maneuvers designed to pave the way. He was certain that NPLD would
soon be sacrificed by the Trotskyists as well.[27]

In the subsequent conflict over the NPLD, it is difficult to judge
whether or how much each succeeding stage was conspiratorially
plotted in advance. George Novack later recalled that the Trotskyists had never intended to come out in favor of abandoning the
NPLD, which Solow continued to lead even after he left the WPUS.
But it soon became apparent that the Socialist Party regarded the
NPLD as a Trotskyist front which stood as a roadblock to entry
into the Socialist Party. This stance precipitated an intense and bitter struggle in mid-1936 between the Trotskyists in the NPLD, especially Morrow and Novack, and most of the members of the former *Menorah* group. In the end the Trotskyists entered the Socialist
Party, and the Workers Defense League was established as a replacement for the NPLD. The 1936 struggle took a significant toll on the
Trotskyist membership, which had risen from one hundred in 1929
to two hundred in 1932 to 429 just before the fusion with the AWP.
After the fusion, the membership of the WPUS was seven hundred,
but it had dropped to between five and six hundred at the time of
the entry into the Socialist Party.[28]

Novack wrote most of the new Worker Defense League's program. As the NPLD faded, Solow and his circle—exclusive of Hook,
who had enthusiastically supported and worked with the WPUS in
effecting the entry—became very bitter toward the Trotskyist leadership. Novack and his wife, Elinor Rice, were on opposing sides in
the fight, and a personal crisis ensued that eventually led to the end
of their marriage. Still, a personal attraction to Trotsky and some of
his political ideas persisted so that, when the Moscow purge trials
began a few months later, Solow and several of the others would
find a means of again working with the Trotskyists, although with
constant suspicion and at a greater distance.[29] In fine, the dispute
over entry into the Socialist Party and abandonment of the NPLD
became the vehicle by which many of the early anti-Stalinist revolutionary intellectuals could justify withdrawing from organizational responsibility to the anti-Stalinist communist movement
while still maintaining their quasi-Trotskyist ideas in the abstract.

In addition to their activity on behalf of the NPLD, members of
the *Menorah* group left a record of their Trotskyist sympathies in a
number of publications. Elliot Cohen wrote a defense of Trotsky in
the *Nation* in 1934, responding to an attack on the exiled revolutionary by Louis Fischer. In "Stalin Buries the Revolution—Prematurely," Cohen argued that Trotsky had proven himself to be the

greatest defender of the Russian Revolution by opposing Stalin's dictatorship. He concluded by describing Trotskyism as synonymous with "international communism" and particularly praised the Trotskyists for their construction of authentic united fronts.[30] Under the pseudonyms "David Ernst" and "Thomas Cotten" he took a similar orthodox stance in reviewing several books by Max Eastman in the *New International*, the journal established by the Trotskyists in 1934. Yet a few months later all of his associations with Trotskyism simply vanished, having been subsumed by his personal and professional life. In the late 1920s, Cohen had married a politically radical elementary school teacher from New Haven who was attending Columbia Teacher's College part-time. The Cohens decided to have a child in the early 1930s, and Elliot began a ten-year stint at the Federation of Jewish Philanthropies, where he made valuable friendships with several leaders in the Jewish community who would later help him launch *Commentary*.[31]

Another publication in which former members of the *Menorah* group left a record of their views was V. F. Calverton's *Modern Monthly*, which in some respects was a predecessor of the post-1937 *Partisan Review*. Born George Goetz in Baltimore on 25 June 1900, Calverton transferred his allegiance from Lutheranism to socialism while working his way through Johns Hopkins University.[32] After a brief membership in the Socialist Labor Party, he began teaching in the junior high schools in Baltimore and in 1928 published the first issue of the *Modern Quarterly* (originally to have been called the *Radical Quarterly*), for which he adopted his pseudonym, although his friends continued to call him "George." The journal reflected Calverton's personal blend of interests in Marxism, psychology, literature, history, anthropology, sociology, medicine, Afro-American culture, and sex. These interests were also expressed in a series of books written by Calverton including *The Newer Spirit* (1925), *Sex Expression in Literature* (1926), and *The Liberation of American Literature* (1931), which on occasion reflected Calverton's tendency to popularize and to vulgarize Marxism as well as a looseness about borrowing material. Plump with a dark mustache, Calverton wore his black hair in a sort of ring around his great high forehead. He was about five feet ten inches tall and a heavy pipe and cigar smoker. A fast talker and a furious worker, he could write away on his typewriter while the room was full of noisy guests.

Remaining close to the Communist Party from 1926 through 1932, he lived in New York four days a week, working for publishing houses, lecturing, and writing reviews. He regularly contributed to the magazine section of the Saturday *Daily Worker* and visited the Soviet Union in July 1927. He held frequent parties in his studio apartment where both Communist and non-Communist intellectuals came together to discuss and argue politics. Although Calverton claimed to support Stalin against Trotsky and hid whatever criticisms he had of the Soviet Union, the Communists were becoming suspicious of his refusal to join the party and his constant emphasis on "Americanizing" their strategy and tactics. Believing that Calverton's work and activities in some manner gave support to the ideas of the Trotskyists and other dissidents who were becoming too independent, both the party and the Communist International itself printed a series of articles attacking him as a fascist in 1932–33.[33] As a result, Calverton opened his pages to articles by Trotskyists and Lovestoneites and then joined the AWP. Among the dissident communist intellectuals who wrote for the *Modern Quarterly*, which became known as the *Modern Monthly* from 1933 until 1938, were Lionel Trilling, Felix Morrow, James Rorty, Herbert Solow, Louis Berg, Elliot Cohen, Anita Brenner, and Lewis Corey. At various times Edmund Wilson, Max Eastman, and Sidney Hook served on the editorial board, the last two notable for the philosophical controversy they initiated among the left.[34]

Calverton much craved acceptance as a major intellectual and was bitterly disappointed by his lack of recognition when he died suddenly in 1940 at the age of forty.

THE EASTMAN HERESIES

Many of the tensions between making a serious commitment to a Marxist organization and maintaining a purely literary association with Marxism are typified by the career of Max Eastman.[35] It was never easy to discern whether or to what extent Eastman should be taken seriously. A lucid, witty, and prolific writer, he could pen a masterful polemic one moment and seem to miss the point entirely the next. An erratic activist who had risked his life and career at various points, he also had earned a reputation as a playboy. While in the Soviet Union at the onset of the 1920s, for example, he became so engrossed in pursuing a liberated love life and nude swimming that the fatal factional struggle at the Communist International's Fourth Congress virtually receded into a dim background. A report on Eastman sent to Trotsky during the late 1920s by a member of the Russian Left Opposition insisted that he was by no means a communist, just a typical radical intellectual superficially excited about the Russian Revolution, who maintained very loose ties to Trotskyism. Yet in a private letter to Trotsky in 1933, Eastman bragged that "I supported every step taken by the Bolshevik party and by you and Lenin from the seizure of power and the dissolution of the Constituent Assembly (horrible as it was to all other American editors) to the condemnation of the Social Revolutionaries. I was for six years alone in America in supporting the Left Opposition. I *was* the Left Opposition."[36]

Born in 1883 as the son of two ministers, Eastman had departed sharply from the religion and sexual repression dominant in his culture to become a bohemian iconoclast and political radical in Greenwich Village. Influenced by his strong and independent mother, he campaigned for women's suffrage, birth control, and sexual and artistic freedom. He assumed editorship of the *Masses* in 1912, and, with his friend John Reed, supported the left wing of the Socialist Party and the Russian Revolution. During World War I he was threatened by lynch mobs for his antiwar agitation, and in 1918 he and the other editors of the *Masses* were twice tried under the Espionage Act.

In 1919 Eastman was catapulted to fame as an outstanding agitator opposed to allied military operations against the newly founded Soviet state. This prominence came from Eastman's dramatic revelation of the contents of secret letters, purloined from the under secretary of state, to an audience described by the *New York Times* as "6,000 shouting Reds at Madison Square Garden."[37] Six years later Eastman gained an international reputation as well. After a sojourn in the Soviet Union from 1922 to 1924, he released to the world press the contents of Lenin's last two letters to the Bolshevik Party, which became known as the "Suppressed Testament." In this explosive document the dying leader of the Russian Revolution called for Stalin's removal from his post as party secretary and praised Trotsky as the most able member of the central committee. Quickly Eastman became known as the Western world's foremost champion of Trotsky in the crucial factional struggle then convulsing the Communist Party of the Soviet Union. This reputation was reinforced by Eastman's publication of *Since Lenin Died* (1925), a political analysis, and the biography, *Leon Trotsky: Portrait of a Youth* (1926).

In 1928 the German-born Marxist Ludwig Lore introduced Eastman to a Russian member of the International Left Opposition named Eleazer Solntstev, who was working at the Soviet Embassy in New York. Lore had already been expelled from the American Communist Party on charges of Trotskyism, based mainly on the fact that he had associated with Trotsky during Trotsky's brief stay in New York in 1917. A circle was initiated that included Max and Eliena Eastman (his Russian-born wife, the sister of Justice Commissar Nikolai Krylenko), Solntstev, and Antoinette Konikow, a socialist doctor from Boston who had formed the first Trotskyist group in the United States, the Independent Communist League.[38]

Although Eastman was unwilling to assume organizational responsibilities, Solntstev persuaded him to translate and publish some documents of the Russian Opposition. They appeared as *The Real Situation in Russia* (1928). Shortly after the publication of the volume, the man known as the foremost radical in the United States was isolated by the Communists and transformed into a pariah. The American public viewed Eastman as a dangerous revolutionary, while the Communists denounced him as a "Trotskyite disrupter." In the 1930s Stalin personally defamed Eastman as a "Gangster of the Pen," and during the Moscow trials the *Daily Worker* published a story slandering him as a "British agent."[39]

From his rural home in Croton, New York, Eastman continued to support the cause of Trotskyism until the mid-1930s. He gave financial support (the proceeds of *The Real Situation in Russia* were used to launch the *Militant* newspaper), produced a magnificent translation of Trotsky's *History of the Russian Revolution* (1932–33), and published a searing indictment of the Stalinists' cultural policy called *Artists in Uniform* (1934). Daniel Eastman, his son from an earlier marriage to Ida Rauh, was a member of the Trotskyist party for a few years in the mid-1930s.

However, in books and left-wing journals, including the Trotskyists' *New International*, Eastman argued that Marxism was an unscientific philosophy requiring the purgation of its religious elements, especially the Hegelian dialectic. On several occasions Trotsky expressed dismay over Eastman's rejection of dialectical and historical materialism, suspecting that it might be the precursor of a political break. Consequently, Trotsky urged his American followers to undertake a thorough critique of American philosophy, and especially of the influence of John Dewey.[40]

Eastman's relations with Trotsky had not always gone smoothly. They first became acquainted when Eastman was in the Soviet Union for a year and nine months during 1922–24. When Eastman made references to Stalin's suppression of Lenin's "Last Testament" in *Since Lenin Died*, Trotsky was forced for tactical reasons to repudiate Eastman, later writing him a letter of apology.[41] Nine years after their initial meeting, the Eastmans became more intimate with Trotsky when they spent twelve days with him at Prinkipo, the Turkish island to which he had been exiled. They passed the days fishing and in casual conversation. Trotsky even proposed that they collaborate in writing a drama about the American Civil War, combining Trotsky's firsthand military experience and Eastman's imaginative powers. Then they had an unpleasant quarrel over Eastman's handling of an article on Stalin, during which Trotsky insinuated that Eastman was incompetent and indicated that he would replace Eastman as his literary agent.

Nevertheless, Trotsky was anxious for the Eastmans to stay on for a few more months and seemed to be unaware of the developing tensions. But Eastman had come to the view that no real meeting of minds could take place, and the Eastmans left Prinkipo with some unpleasant memories. Eastman felt that Trotsky lacked the "gift of mutuality," by dominating in any intellectual interchange. He was also appalled by the drab condition of Trotsky's home, concluding that Trotsky only appreciated art when it appeared in books.[42]

But the only differences of any importance to Trotsky were those in the area of Marxist philosophy, which Eastman had expressed as early as 1916 in the *Masses*. Indeed, Eastman's admiration for Lenin had been partly based on the conviction that Lenin, like himself, was not a "true believer" in dialectical materialism. Thus he was surprised to discover how seriously Marxism was taken in post-revolutionary Russia. With typical aplomb, he took it upon himself to make a contribution to the revolution by explaining Marxism's fallacies. Feeling something like a Connecticut Yankee in King Arthur's court, Eastman marched into the Marx-Engels Institute to do the research that resulted in his book, *Marx, Lenin and the Science of Revolution* (1926).

At the time Eastman merely thought certain ideological elements of Marxism were impeding the revolution, which had basically made an auspicious beginning. A decade and a half later he would rewrite the book as *Marxism: Is It a Science?* (1940), in which, instead of counterposing Lenin's practicality to Marx's religion, he would find strong links between Stalinist tyranny and Leninist precepts. He would reduce Lenin's contribution from having engineered an epoch-making revolution to providing a strategy for the seizure of power by an elite.

Eastman's criticisms of Marxism were dispersed through a variety of essays and reviews and developed at length in the two aforementioned books and *The Last Stand of Dialectical Materialism* (1934), a polemic against Sidney Hook's *Toward the Understanding of Karl Marx* (1933). In his works Eastman advanced the argument that Marxism was not truly scientific but metaphysical and religious: "Marxism was a step from Utopian socialism to a socialist religion, a scheme for convincing the believer that the universe itself is producing a better society and that he has only to fall in properly with the general movement of the universe."[43] Eastman agreed with Engels's explanation that Marx had turned the Hegelian system on its head by rooting the dialectical method in material reality. However, Eastman claimed that Marx had erred in positing an "animistic materialism," a world of matter moving inexorably on its own, like a robot, toward ultimate perfection. Eastman charged Marx with having substituted this concept for Hegel's notion of idealistic reason which also moved of its own accord toward ultimate perfection. Marx, like Hegel, was a German Romantic who committed the mistake of projecting his own subjective desire for socialism onto the machinations of reality. To Eastman, "it was Marx and not history that was determined to produce a social revolution."[44] Therefore, a true follower of Marx must have faith in a self-acting world.

Eastman asserted that Marx contradicted his own beliefs by actively intervening in social strife and his stated desire not to be a philosopher by actually writing philosophy. Eastman felt that Marx had made an important contribution in his discovery of the class struggle, a discovery that Eastman equated with Darwin's achievements, but he argued that the scientific must be extracted from religious nonsense. Eastman attributed Lenin's success to his flexibility in ignoring Marx's fatalism, whether or not Lenin would admit it.

Eastman's views had a considerable impact on Edmund Wilson, who argued a similar position in his chapter "The Myth of the Dialectic" in *To the Finland Station* (1940) and acknowledged a personal debt to *Marxism: Is It a Science?*. George Lichtheim's harsh estimation of this aspect of Eastman's work, however, seems closer to the truth: "[Eastman's] reflections on Marx, Lenin, Communism . . . are not merely trite; they are trite in a peculiarly amateurish sort of way. It is regrettably evident that in all the years when he preached the doctrine he later came to renounce, he really had no notion of what he was talking about."[45]

Among the many who locked horns with Eastman during the 1930s were Louis Boudin, Waldo Frank, Sidney Hook, and James Burnham. All were astounded by Eastman's claim that Marx had posited a theory of "animistic materialism" that maintained in a mechanical manner that socialism was inevitable. Burnham, for example, argued in the *New International* that, although they described history as operating according to scientific laws, Marx and

Engels never contended that social development was completely self-acting and self-operating. What Marx argued was that the wills of individual humans are not decisive factors; history provides a general context for and defines the scope and limitations of human action. While it is true that Marx and Engels saw direction in history, they did not inscribe their moral preferences into its laws of development. Rather, they saw such a historical development in terms of the growth of the means of production. Marxists base their projections for action and social change on their understanding of reality. It was, in fact, the utopian socialists against whom Marx polemicized, who posed an abstract moral idea as a goal. It was not Marx who read his own subjective views into history but rather those who advocated medieval and agrarian solutions. And here, it was not a question of whether these ideas were morally wrong, Burnham asserted, but rather that they were impossible to realize.[46]

All of Eastman's detractors, and even his admirer Edmund Wilson, noted many methodological weaknesses in his critique of Marxism—Eastman, they claimed, focused on abstractions, phrases, and concepts torn from time and context. Moreover, he exaggerated the role of individual quirks, padding his ad hominem attacks with unscholarly insinuations, such as in his claim that Marx spent years in the British Museum because he was compelled to accumulate evidence to prove his previously assembled "religious" convictions.[47]

Hook and Burnham attributed Eastman's much-emphasized "inevitability" theory to the epigones, not the originators, of Marxism. They argued that expectations for socialist transformation were and remained based on the real development of production and that the probability of revolution continues to be high if partisans of the working class act effectively and with sufficient resolve. Burnham enumerated the objective conditions for socialist transformation that had begun to emerge in Marx's time and continued to obtain to the present. They included such features as the centralization of industry; the increasing level of technology; the socialization of labor; the occurrence of extremes of economic dislocation and social unrest; the fact that socialization remained the only way that the full powers of production generated under capitalism could be realized; and the continuing existence of individuals and organizations who desired a social transformation, since productive forces by themselves could not accomplish such a change.[48]

The venomous language exchanged in the Eastman-Hook debates as well as between Eastman and other opponents parallels the language found in the most vituperative factional fights within Marxist organizations. This suggests that, whatever kept most of these intellectuals aloof from party commitment, it could hardly have been a revulsion against abusive polemics. After describing Eastman's views as "pluralistic pragmatism," Waldo Frank denounced him for "philosophic opportunism."[49] Hook ridiculed Eastman's "emasculated instrumentalism."[50] Ironically, only Burnham refrained from such excesses. He emphasized that Eastman rendered a service to revolutionists by attacking various unfortunate distortions of Marxism; what was regrettable was that Eastman erred in attributing those very distortions to Marx himself.[51]

The dilemma of the Trotskyists in dealing with Eastman's contributions was exemplified by their attitude toward his *Artists in Uniform* (1934), in which he once again offered an irritating combination of positions they found alternately agreeable and abhorrent. Elliot Cohen wrote in the *New International* that Eastman's arguments always seemed to boil down to his own little hobbyhorse and not much else. He thought that Eastman went too far in his acceptance of the autonomy of art: to be against all restrictive uniforms is one thing, but Eastman was advocating total nudity! In a subsequent review of *Art and the Life of Action* (1934), Cohen agreed that Eastman was correct in arguing for artistic independence of revolutionaries from any parties, but wrong in suggesting that art was self-justified and self-maintaining. He noted that when Eastman asserted that the sole end of art was to heighten consciousness, he was not talking about art as a reality but about some intangible essence of art that he had concocted. Eastman was simply disorienting himself in imputing a single function, evocation of awareness, to art. From the Marxist point of view, art has as many functions as might arise. Cohen concluded that perhaps Eastman had allowed himself to be provoked into overreacting by the vulgar Marxist excesses of writers such as Mike Gold. But what distressed Cohen was that the implications of Eastman's stark opposition of art, identified with expression, to science, identified with control, might theoretically lead in a totalitarian direction—that is, it seemed to justify the separating out from the rest of society a leadership fixated on practical control.[52]

MARXISM AND PRAGMATISM

The Eastman debates typified an important aspect of the intellectual life of the anti-Stalinist left of the early 1930s, animated first by conflicts about Marxist philosophy and later by disputes over the relationship of Leninism to Stalinism and the social nature of the postrevolutionary society in the Soviet Union. The philosophical exchanges were fiercely conducted by skilled polemicists with boundless confidence and interminable arguments; but in the end they may not have been as productive as they seemed at the onset. Unlike the dispute with the Communists over "proletarian culture" and modernism, the philosophical altercations, although they raised many important issues, failed to advance theory or provide a legacy that could be assimilated by future generations, with the one possible exception of the writing of Sidney Hook in the early 1930s. Certainly none of the defenders of classical Marxism developed their arguments into a book or article that enjoyed widespread currency on the left, then or now; by and large their efforts were restricted to a restatement of basic principles.

One of the best defenders of classical Marxism was Rubin Gotesky, a young philosophy instructor at Long Island University, who wrote a three-part critique of Hook's *Toward the Understanding of Karl Marx* that was published in the *New International*.[53] The essay is remarkable for its lucid and sophisticated restatement of the methodological tenets and doctrinal conclusions of classical Marxist philosophy. Born in Poland in 1906, Gotesky was the son of a labor organizer and joined the Communist Party in New York.[54] Discovered reading a book by Trotsky in a library, he was expelled for Trotskyism and joined the CLA in 1931. Yet only two years after completing his thoughtful defense of Marxist principles, Gotesky left the Trotskyists and returned to graduate school at New York University to pursue his doctorate. In a pattern that would become all too familiar, he retained from his Trotskyist experience only an admiration for Trotsky's "capacity to see what was and is rotten in actual socialist [*sic*] states."[55] In 1940, when the New York City Board of Higher Education held hearings following the Rapp-Coudert investigation of Communist professors, Gotesky testified for the prosecutors at every single trial as an "expert witness" on the question of the Communist Party's advocacy of force and violence to overthrow the government.

As for the critics of Marxist orthodoxy, at a certain point they simply reached an impasse—their attempt to "modernize" Marxism had become transformed into a full-scale repudiation of the Marxist doctrine and method. Ten years later not a single one of the modernizers or critics of classical Marxism, and scarcely more than a handful of its defenders, could still be classified as a "Marxist" in any meaningful sense of the term. What had transpired, despite its auspicious beginnings, proved to be an embarrassing disruption of the development of Marxist thought in the United States that would leave the indigenous radical movement almost wholly dependent on European thought for stimulation and inspiration in future decades.

The problem was not that the participants in the debate had meager intellectual resources or were especially ill-informed, particularly compared with those who made pronouncements on philosophical matters for the official Communist movement, such as V. J. Jerome and Earl Browder. More decisive was that the Marxist culture in which such debates might have flourished was impoverished in the United States because of the same complex historical factors that had retarded working-class self-organization and consciousness.[56] In Marxist philosophy there had been no influential American progenitor of the caliber of Plekhanov in Russia or Labriola in Italy; only the curious figure of William English Walling, whose superficial attempt to combine Marxism and pragmatism was a harbinger of the debates that occurred during the depression years.

A complicating factor was that some of the modernizers and critics of classical Marxism in the 1930s were themselves undergoing personal transformations because of rapidly changing events even as they launched their polemics. Consequently, various philosophical positions might inadvertently become instruments of political differentiation, or, more likely, rationales for maintaining arm's-length relationships with the organized left or abstaining and/or withdrawing from it. What appeared to be a penetrating philosophical insight one moment might become justifiably suspect the next, as a theoretican's overall position was reworked to rationalize a political shift. Such shifts were almost always to the right although occasionally they were preceded by a brief spurt of left-wing purity.

Max Eastman and Sidney Hook were the best-known exemplars of this phenomenon. Rather than arguing their positions within the organized left, they used their philosophical differences to distance themselves from it, creating a syndrome in which philosophical heresy became virtually synonymous with political elitism and apostasy. This resulted in an unfortunate situation that prevailed throughout the 1930s and after, during which a polarization occurred between the "orthodox" and the "heterodox." Virtually all questioning of classical Marxist precepts became suspect as a sign of impending deradicalization, and little development of historial materialism took place. It was understandable that an attempt to bypass rather than critically assimilate new philosophical challenges had occurred within the official Communist movement, which by this time was uncritically accepting the increasingly os-sified politico-cultural pronouncements emanating from Moscow. That such a crude bifurcation between orthodoxy and heterodoxy should have replicated itself, albeit in a milder form, in the anti-Stalinist left, was unnecessary. After all, it was not foreordained that the Trotskyists and other anti-Stalinist Marxists should be in-capable of philosophical development, especially since this sterile polarization did not repeat itself in France and elsewhere where conditions were different.

Hook's *Toward the Understanding of Karl Marx* is something of an exception to this generalization because certain aspects of Hook's discourse bear the influence of Georg Lukács's early philo-sophical work. But these may be evidenced more in its creative spirit than in its philosophical substance. To be sure, key passages reveal a vaguely Lukácsian appreciation of reification. Certainly Hook's interpretation of Lenin as the modern manifestation of the essence of Marxism by virtue of his activism and undogmatic ap-proach to social revolution echoes Lukács, although perhaps more the Lukács of *Lenin* (1924) than of *History and Class Conscious-ness* (1923). What meager references Hook makes to the "organiza-tional question" seem to be, like those of the young Lukács, more in the spirit of what Marcel Liebman calls "libertarian Leninism" or Luxemburgianism than in the tradition of Zinoviev's "Bolshe-vization" project or Stalinist theory and practice.[57]

However, the only substantial parallel between Hook and Lu-kács may be in Hook's consideration of revisionism and reformism, in which he seems to repeat certain themes of Lukács's chapter, "What Is Orthodox Marxism?" One should not be misled, however, by two odd twists in Hook's argument. Lukács states that he is an "orthodox" Marxist, but he clarifies this to mean that orthodoxy inheres in the method of dialectics, which contrasts dramatically with the fatalism, revisionism, and reformism of the Bernstein-Kautsky school. Hook, on the other hand, declares that he is *not* an orthodox Marxist for essentially the same reason. He identifies orthodoxy with dogmatism, declaring Marx himself *un*orthodox.

Both affirm allegiance to a praxis-oriented revolutionary commu-nism, with Lenin as the model for a creative application of the ur-doctrine and social democratic reformism as the epitome of self-serving corruption. Where the two sharply depart is in Hook's effort to present Marxism as being compatible with John Dewey's prag-matist instrumentalism. Hook begins by reiterating Lukács's claim that the method of Marxism can be detached from its conclusions. But Hook's purpose was to formulate a complex argument that

Marxism is "scientific" while not a "science" per se. For Hook, Marxism, though class-based and partisan, could be "scientific" insofar as its method approached, or presaged, Dewey's instrumentalism, which Hook considered the epistemological formulation of the scientific method. On the other hand, Hook asserted, "science" itself was classless. This argument is compelling in that science cannot be regarded as class-bound in the same sense as political ideology; dubious, however, is the view of science as authentically classless. Certainly, the social sciences are inevitably bound up in a class viewpoint, conscious or not. In regard to the natural sciences, it is, on the one hand, untenable to talk of "proletarian biology" or "bourgeois astronomy"; on the other hand, it is questionable to view natural science as wholly apart from historical determination by the structure of the social formation in which scientists carry out their work.[58] Moreover, one might even distinguish the content of scientific claims from the status of its aims or methods—rejecting the claim that science is a purely objective *method*, but accepting the truth of scientific theories.

That Hook was trying to straddle two horses is crucial to understanding the nature of his book, as well as its relation to *History and Class Consciousness*, its reception by the Communist and other left-wing press, and, indeed, Hook's future evolution. In *History and Class Consciousness* Lukács was largely attempting to create intellectual space in order to function within the confines of the Communist movement, which at the time was just beginning the process of ossification that would eventually overwhelm it. In contrast, Hook was trying to sustain his dual position as virtually the only Marxist professor in the United States and a close ally of the Communist Party, to which he had been bonded by the pro-Communist activities of his college days, his first marriage to a devout member of William Z. Foster's faction of the party, and periods of collaboration with the party on literary, intellectual, and electoral activities.

Hook, it seems, was ready to make considerable compromises to maintain a modus vivendi with the Communists, but he would not entirely abandon his intellectual independence. In the preface to *Towards the Understanding of Karl Marx*, he deftly balances an acknowledgment of his debt to Karl Korsch and Lukács with a comparable amount of criticism, thereby providing some degree of protective distance between himself and the two heretics. After his philosophical ideas came under attack by V. J. Jerome in the official party publication, the *Communist*, Hook fought vigorously to maintain his legitimacy as a loyal intellectual ally of the Commu-

nist movement. He even agreed to private meetings with party officials to examine his ideas.[59]

Only when the Communist Party definitely rejected Hook—because of a combination of political suspicion (Hook, along with
Eastman and journalist Quincy Howe, had defended Leon Trotsky's
right to asylum in 1932), a longing for philosophical uniformity,
and a probable jealousy on the part of the Communist theoretician
Jerome, who felt overshadowed by Hook's relative brilliance, and
fear on the part of party leader Earl Browder, who was threatened by
Hook's independence—did Hook emerge with a new political orientation that roughly parallelled Trotsky's International Left Opposition. Shortly thereafter he helped organize A. J. Muste's American
Workers Party and steered it toward fusion with the Communist
League of America.

Hook's decision not to join the new party came as a surprise. In
the negotiations for the fusion that began in early 1934, Hook was
adamant in insisting that the only differences he had with the official Trotskyists were over tactical matters, such as the most effective choice of language to convince people to become communists;
he was even in favor of working to build the Fourth International
(which had as yet to be founded). It is possible that tensions between his roles as a revolutionary politician and a bourgeois academic were a factor in his decision to pull back from organizational commitment. Earlier Hook had been the object of a fierce
red-baiting campaign by the Hearst newspapers. He was being considered for promotion to associate professor and was even offered
the chairmanship of the Philosophy Department at New York University in 1934.[60] Of course, he may have already had some political doubts, but, if so, his other actions suggested that any disagreements that he had with the new party were minimal. Just a year
later Hook closely collaborated with the Trotskyist leaders Cannon
and Shachtman against his former friends and comrades Herbert
Solow and A. J. Muste to facilitate a fusion of the Workers Party of
the United States with the Socialist Party. In 1936 he signed a joint
statement with members of the Trotskyist faction in the Socialist
Party endorsing Norman Thomas for president on a revolutionary
socialist basis.[61]

In order to understand Sidney Hook's contribution to Marxist
philosophy, it is crucial to understand the precise terrain of the
debates about Marxism and its relation to epistemology and science that raged within the anti-Stalinist left during the 1930s.
A historic struggle was fought on this terrain over the legacy of
Marx and Engels, a struggle for the appropriation of their legacy

by different methodologies representing divergent currents within the broad socialist movement. If the original writings of Marx and Engels were as one—devoid of inconsistencies, contradictions, and ambiguities—perhaps there would have been a lesser need for the kind of debates that occurred. But even if fully consistent, the theories of Marx and Engels would still require continuous refinement or correction precisely because they seem so plausible to many; the greater the relevance, the more richly and subtly elaborated must be the doctrine. And since Marxism also demands further development in light of new experience, it embodies tensions of the sort that often sparked provocative and relevant debates.

For the anti-Stalinist left in the 1930s, as well as for some of its predecessors and successors, a central tension was felt between what might be called Marxism's "scientific" and its "activist" (sometimes referred to as "praxis") component. The tension— which is more complex than simply dichotomous—might be suggested in a passage from Marx's 1859 "Preface to a Critique of Political Economy":

> In considering such [social] transformations, a distinction should be made between the material transformation of the economic conditions of production, *which can be determined with the precision of natural science,* and in the legal, political, religious, aesthetic or philosophic—in short, ideological forms in which *men become conscious of this conflict and fight it out.* (Emphasis added)[62]

The first group of underscored words could be interpreted as emphasizing the "scientific" element in Marx; he borrowed and developed techniques from existing scientific method in applying his social analysis, and he viewed history and nature as proceeding according to certain laws. The second group of underlined words could be understood as emphasizing the "activist" element in Marx; the view that the human agency, that is, human will or human actions, are critical to the consummation of historical change. No doubt there are other tensions present in Marx's work as well, but this apparent one constitutes perhaps the most crucial one for the 1930s dispute. It was in light of their training with John Dewey that Hook and Eastman aspired to resolve what they saw as a tension.

The work of the classical Marxists—Marx, Engels, Lenin, Trotsky, and Luxemburg—held the two elements in dialectically interconnected balance, the subjective will, itself objectively conditioned, having a variety of options within the limitations of an objectively conditioned reality. In contrast, the so-called official Marxism of the established Socialist and Communist movements —the Second International under Bernstein and Kautsky, and the Third International under Stalin—often presented Marxism in a highly reductionist manner. It is not so much that the Social Democrats and the Communists developed the "scientific" side while quashing the activist side. Rather, in their own ways each truncated Marxism: the Second International, under the influence of Kautsky's reformism, reduced politics to economic determinism, predicting an inevitable overthrow of capitalism as the next historic stage. The Third International alternately emphasized human will or scientific fatalism, depending on the political exigencies of the Communist Party of the Soviet Union in different periods. The truncated version of Marxism of the Second and Third International is usually referred to as "economism" or "vulgar Marxism."

In retrospect, it can also be seen that such efforts of the American modernizers of Marxism as Hook and Eastman were part of a phenomenon in Western Marxism that arose, first with the young Georg Lukács and Karl Korsch, in response to the ossification of the Second and Third Internationals. In their individual ways, what Eastman and Hook shared with so many others, then and now, was a vulgar "anti-Engelsism," although it should be noted that the young Lukács's criticisms were actually not "vulgar." Both Eastman and Hook attributed to Engels a mechanical materialism, a reductive determinism, a crude epistemology, and an aspiration to transform Marxism into a naturalistic metaphysical system by positing a dialectic of nature. The difference between Eastman and Hook was that the former insisted that Marx and Engels were as one in this pseudo-scientific approach, while the latter, in contrast, drew a sharp line between the two and claimed to find the seeds of a pragmatic approach in Marx's activism. Hook's solution was to improve Marxism by infusing it with experimental pragmatism, while Eastman sought to replace it with "social engineering."[63]

Sebastiano Timpanaro describes this phenomenon well: "The downgrading of Engels implies a particular mode of understanding Marxism today. During the twentieth century, each time that a particular intellectual current has taken the upper hand in bourgeois culture—be it empirio-criticism, Bergsonism, Croceanism, phenomenology, neo-positivism, or structuralism—certain Marxists have attempted to 'interpret' Marx's thought in such a way as to make it as homogeneous as possible with the predominant philosophy."[64] Thus Eastman gutted Marxism of its philosophical apparatus entirely, saving only the strategy of class struggle which he justified on empirical-scientific grounds. Hook discovered that, liberated from the naive and simplistic Engels, Marxism had the capacity to assimilate without distorting the essence of even the most recent development in modern bourgeois philosophy: John Dewey's instrumentalism. Hook also disputed Eastman's claim that Marx had anticipated Freud's theories of repression, the unconscious, and rationalization, while both Hook and Eastman affirmed in the name of a pragmatist conception of experimental science that Lenin was free of the major vices of past Marxist theory and practice. Thus they declared themselves to be true revolutionary Leninists whose mission was to save the existing Marxist parties that were certain to succumb to reformism if they embraced the fatalistic (positivist) interpretation of Marx over its voluntaristic (activist or pragmatic) variant. Hook especially held this view even though the ties between these philosophical and political stances are more probably familiar associations than genuine conceptual links.

Fifty years later, much more is known about the Marx and Engels relationship in light of subsequent scholarship and the publication of hitherto unknown manuscripts. This body of knowledge challenges the tenability of the view, voiced by Eastman and popular among theoreticians of the Second and Third Internationals, that completely subsumes Engels in Marx and thereby, regardless of intentions, diminishes Engels's creative individuality as a thinker. Among other unique contributions, Engels's work on the origins of women's oppression opened up the whole field of socialist feminism within the context of historical materialism, and Engels wrote explicitly on the semiautonomy and historical efficacy of ideologies.

While Engels is also noteworthy for having paid greater attention than Marx to the natural setting in which humanity creates its history, he was certainly erroneous if he held that physics and biology offer paradigms for explaining social behavior, a view that Hook attributed to Engels and one that Eastman assigned to both pioneers of scientific socialism. To do so is nothing less than constructing a very crude "physicalism" blind to humanity's ability to act upon and transform its natural and cultural environment in an extraordinary number of ways. A more convincing materialist approach that seems more consistent with the general method of Marx and Engels would be for socialists to present laws about social processes presupposing that they might resemble those at work in the physical world but which are not reducible to such laws of nature. Moreover, at this stage in the development of humanity's powers, and also due to the dialectical essence of the subject/object relationship in history and society, it would be unjustified to claim that the propositions of Marxism carry the same relative certainty as do those of the physical and biological sciences.

Despite its questionable manner in which it divides the natural and the social world, Hook's *Toward the Understanding of Karl Marx* should be recognized as a breakthrough in the development of Marxism in the United States. The centerpiece of the book, Hook's trenchant criticism of the theory and practice of social democracy, remains powerful and convincing, as do his criticisms of reductive materialism and his exposition of the Marxist theory of the state. But, ironically, both the strengths and weaknesses of the book stem from Hook's emphasis on the dynamic, activist Marx. This approach liberates the reader from the concept of automatic fatalism, but it simultaneously opens a gateway to pragmatism—an interpretation different from Marxism's emphasis on becoming familiar with patterns or laws of class struggle as the foremost task for those who want to change the world.

In the end it is important to recognize not only the ambiguities of the "praxis" approach to Marxism (the term "praxis" can have quite different meanings; often it means saying very little about science and materialism), but of the particular approach Hook took to criticizing the Marxism of the Second International. Hook aimed to underscore the link between vulgar materialism and social democratic reformism, and his book provided an implicit warning that the Third International might follow a similar course.

In conclusion, the self-proclaimed orthodox defenders of Marxism in the United States in the 1930s were not really able to come to grips with the current of thought represented by Hook and other pragmatist and praxis-oriented philosophers. Unable to assimilate its positive features and counterpose a richer doctrine, the orthodox defenders simply sought to restate classical Marxist philosophical principles and bypass Hook's critique, or, in the case of the Communists, to refute only vulgar caricatures of his argument. Yet Hook's discussion of the problems existing between "science" and "praxis" enlarged the terrain of American Marxism. Hook may not have resolved these problems, but, with the possible exception of some earlier passages in works by Louis Boudin and Louis Fraina, he was the first to offer a full exegesis of them. The dialectical transcendence or sublation (in the Hegelian sense of *Aufhebung*) of this debate is the sine qua non for the revival of Marxist theory and practice in the United States.

CHAPTER 5

The Moscow Trials

> But it is not only the old Bolsheviks who are on trial [in Moscow]—we too, all of us, are in the prisoners' dock. These are trials of the mind and of the human spirit. Their meanings encompass the age.
>
> —Philip Rahv, "Trials of the Mind," 1938[1]

. . . .

THE AMERICAN COMMITTEE FOR THE DEFENSE OF LEON TROTSKY

A decisive event that simultaneously consolidated the anti-Stalinist left while setting the stage for its disintegration was the Moscow trials which began in 1936. These four trials were extraordinary for a number of reasons. First, the men and women who were placed in the prisoner's dock and charged with treachery, sabotage, and espionage against the Soviet state included virtually all of the living leaders of the Russian Revolution, with the exception of Joseph Stalin, the behind-the-scenes organizer of the trials. Although he was in exile, charges were also brought against Stalin's arch adversary, Leon Trotsky. Second, the accused, who were publicly tried in Moscow, abjectly confessed guilt to the charges against them and some even begged to be punished. Third, the trials were accompanied by a mass purge that affected all of Soviet society. In addition to those coerced into performing the show-trials, it is estimated that literally millions of workers, peasants, party members, intellectuals, military officers, and government officials were arrested and executed by administrative order.[2]

While today the Moscow trials are regarded throughout the world as a horrendous frame-up, at the time many American intellectuals were confused about what they meant and failed to defend their victims. One cause of their confusion was the existence of a widespread sympathy for the Soviet Union in the middle and late 1930s.[3] In this instance these intellectuals, none of whom thought of themselves as "Stalinists," were moved more by feeling than by careful analysis. In the eyes of many liberals and radicals, Stalin, after 1935, had made a reasonable and practical turn in issuing his call for a "Popular Front" against the fascist powers. Only a few months before the first Moscow trials Hitler had begun to remilitarize the Rhineland. In France the Communists, liberals, and Socialists had formed a victorious electoral coalition led by Léon Blum. In Spain the Communists were fighting side by side with the Republicans against Franco's fascists, and it seemed as if any open denunciation of the trials might disrupt the antifascist alliances. "It is always a temptation to believe the best about one's allies," Malcolm Cowley recalled years later in a memoir discussing his own refusal to condemn the trials, "or at least to conceal their crimes from oneself in order to maintain a precarious sincerity when one is forced, as a matter of policy, to deny in public the existence of those crimes."[4]

But even among those who were not inclined to actively block the disclosure of the truth for pragmatic political reasons, other obstacles contributed to their silence and perplexity. Some of the liberals sympathetic to Stalinist Russia had worked out complicated rationales that enabled them to tolerate undemocratic judicial procedures and other drastic measures in the Soviet Union, ones that they would find totally unacceptable in the United States. There were those who argued that authoritarian rule was in harmony with Russian culture and traditions; others believed that such methods were necessary if the illiterate peoples of the underdeveloped nations were to be dragged into the modern world. Lincoln Steffens, often cited as representative of this particular type of liberal known as the "fellow traveler," wrote: "I am for them to the last drop, I am a patriot of Russia; the Future is there. . . . But I don't want to live there."[5]

Trotsky excoriated the fellow-traveler mentality from a Marxist point of view. He asserted that the increase in friendship toward the Soviet Union under Stalin's rule reflected "the reconciliation of bourgeois liberalism with the bureaucracy which had strangled the October Revolution." He further noted that "the more extensive the privileges of the new leading stratum [of the Soviets] became, and the more conservative it grew in defense of its privileges—the greater became the number of its friends among the bourgeois intellectuals and the liberals, snobs who keep up the vogue of the day.

The inspirers of this state of mind became Walter Duranty [Moscow correspondent for the *New York Times*] and Louis Fischer [European correspondent for the *Nation*], downright sycophants of the Soviet oligarchy."[6]

Still another factor that disoriented liberal intellectuals was their fear of confronting a truth that was likely to be profoundly disturbing. James T. Farrell recalled in a memoir of the Moscow trials that "if the official verdict of the trials were true . . . the co-workers of Lenin and the leaders of the Bolshevik Revolution must be considered as one of the worst gangs of scoundrels in history; if the trials were a frame-up, then the leaders of Soviet Russia were perpetrating one of the most monstrous frame-ups in all history. An outstanding and humane American, known for his anti-Communism and utter honesty, wrote to me, stating that while he saw the justice of this question, he hated to face it."[7]

It was not long after the demise of the NPLD that many of the same individuals who had been active in the organization came together again through the establishment of the American Committee for the Defense of Leon Trotsky. The administrative personnel of the committee was largely, although not exclusively, comprised of Trotskyists (represented by George Novack, Felix Morrow, Pearl Kluger, and Martin Abern) and the same group of intellectuals around Herbert Solow who had broken with the American Trotskyists over the latter's abandonment of the NPLD. Each current operated autonomously inside the Trotsky Defense Committee, with each maintaining its own ideas, although the two groups were largely compatible in this endeavor. In October 1936 the Trotskyists, who by that time had collectively joined the Socialist Party, sent James Burnham, Max Shachtman, and George Novack to confer with Socialist Party leaders Devere Allen and Norman Thomas at the party's national committee meeting in Philadelphia to gain their support for the Trotsky Defense Committee. In the meantime, Solow and the others were working with Sidney Hook, who would eventually serve as the link to John Dewey's involvement in the special Commission of Inquiry into the Charges Against Leon Trotsky in the Moscow Trials.[8]

Nevertheless, suspicions remained despite the collaboration. The Trotskyist members did not function as individuals; rather, they represented the views of their political current. Perhaps an element of intrigue marked Solow's group as well, which tended to act as an informal caucus, but this did not prevent Solow from becoming a firm supporter of the committee. When Trotsky, in Mexico, sent a letter to New York in early 1937 to urge the rapid establishment of the Commission of Inquiry, Solow obtained $5,000 from Margaret De Silver to support the effort. In a running debate by mail with Lewis Mumford, Waldo Frank, Tom Mooney, and others, Solow argued on behalf of the project, even reaching the breaking point with his old college friend Clifton Fadiman, who refused to cooperate with Solow in certain related matters.[9]

Solow deserves much of the credit for the success of the American Committee, which was an especially significant achievement in light of the difficulty that similar projects encountered in other countries. On 1 March 1937 Solow received a letter from Pierre Naville, the French intellectual who was then a Trotskyist leader, reporting on the struggles that were going on in the French committee, a weak body that had attracted little collaboration from intellectuals other than André Breton, Victor Serge, and, clandestinely, André Gide. Naville proposed that the American Committee designate itself as the central international coordinating body.[10]

The centerpiece of the Trotsky Defense Committee's activities was undoubtedly the Dewey Commission of Inquiry into the Charges Against Leon Trotsky in the Moscow Trials. For eight days in Coyoacan, Mexico, Trotsky gave testimony to and was interrogated by an investigating committee of prominent intellectuals led by John Dewey. Dewey's enthusiasm for the event was expressed in a letter he later sent Max Eastman: "You were right about one thing—if it wasn't exactly a 'good time,' it was the most interesting single intellectual experience of my life."[11] Dewey was seventy-eight years old at the time. The commission's hearings presented the only significant opportunity that Trotsky had to defend himself in the court of world opinion against Stalin's accusations of sabotage and espionage. The Commission of Inquiry had an aura of high drama that a socially conscious poet, playwright, or novelist might invent, or about which an imaginative historian might dream. "It is a shame that you are not here to attend the hearings," wrote James T. Farrell, an observer, in a letter to a friend on the penultimate day of the proceedings. "It is a spectacle to see, a spectacle rare in history. Imagine Robespierre or Cromwell under such circumstances. Well, this is more, because neither Cromwell nor Robespierre had the intellectual breadth that Trotsky has."[12]

The formation of the commission itself was an act of determination in the face of apathy and even aggressive hostility on the part of a sizable component of the New York intellectual milieu in which it was initiated. Indeed, just a few days after his return from Mexico, Dewey delivered an address at New York City's Mecca Temple in which he issued a strong indictment of the "systematic and organized effort made to prevent the investigation which is now successfully taking place."[13]

Farrell was a member of the Executive Committee of the Trotsky Defense Committee, the organization formed to secure asylum for Trotsky and enable him to have a hearing. Accordingly, he participated in the selection of the members of the Dewey commission. He later recalled that the committee simply chose "people who we assumed had some integrity and reputation."[14] An ability to stand up against the predominant opinion among the left intelligentsia turned out to be the decisive quality required to conquer the forces that began to exert pressures designed to sabotage the inquiry. This pressure manifested itself most forcibly through the periphery of the Communist Party, which of course heralded the verdict reached in the Moscow trials, but it was also reflected in the organs of liberal opinion, the *New Republic* and the *Nation*. An "Open Letter to American Liberals" was issued that attacked the work of the commission. Among its eighty-eight signers were Heywood Broun, Malcolm Cowley, Theodore Dreiser, Lillian Hellman, Rockwell Kent, Max Lerner, Robert Morss Lovett, Robert S. Lynd, Carey McWilliams, Dorothy Parker, Henry Roth, Paul Sweezy, Lillian Wald, Max Weber, and Nathanael West.[15]

But when Dewey agreed to head the commission and to travel to Mexico to interview Trotsky, who was not permitted to enter the United States, the commission had found a chairman who personified to the highest degree the requisite integrity. "Scarcely anyone knows the intensity and variety of pressures he had to withstand," wrote Sidney Hook at the time of Dewey's death, "not least of all from the members of his immediate family, some of whom feared he might be killed in the excitable political milieu of Mexico City .... The simple truth of the matter is that Dewey made up his mind irrevocably [to go] only after he became aware of the efforts and far-flung stratagems of the Communist Party to *prevent* him from going."[16]

THE HEARINGS IN MEXICO

In New York City on Friday, 2 April 1937, Dewey, Farrell, and a small party of commissioners and staff boarded the Sunshine Special en route to Mexico City via St. Louis. Meanwhile, technical staff provided by the Trotsky Defense Committee had arrived at the home of the renowned Mexican muralist Diego Rivera and his companion Frida Kahlo, where the investigative proceedings were to take place. Solow was the central organizer of all the American citizens present; he assisted with the legal and technical arrangements as well as serving as chief contact with the office of the Trotsky Defense Committee in New York. Because he had broken with the American Trotskyist organization over the "French Turn," Solow and Trotsky apparently spent a good part of the time before the hearings in heated debate. On 2 April he reported to Margaret De Silver, "The old man [Trotsky] continues in character. I have had two violent fights with him and expect another tomorrow. At the same time he breaks his heart about one professor John Martin who was banged up in an auto accident on his way to visit the old man. The two of them had never met, but the old man takes responsibility for the accident to one who was about to visit him, and he asks five times a day for the guy's health. And he works on and on, turning out grand stuff. He is incredible."[17]

Also present were John McDonald, who helped with the physical preparation of materials, and his wife, Dorothy Eisner, who did several paintings during the hearings. They stayed for a time at the residence of Mrs. Robert Latham George, the mother of Adelaide Walker. Charles Walker took charge of relations with the press. In addition to the technical staff, the arrival of the commissioners from the United States was awaited by a number of Trotsky's political followers, who constituted his personal staff or who had some other function during the forthcoming hearings. The personal staff included a three-man secretariat: a Czech Trotskyist named Jan Frankel, who was shortly to become the first husband of novelist Eleanor Clark; Jean van Heijenoort, later professor of philosophy at Brandeis University; and Bernard Wolfe, a former Yale student.

Wolfe was born in New Haven, Connecticut, on 28 August 1915.[18] His father, Robert Wolfe, was a Russian Jewish immigrant who attempted a career as a violinist and director of synagogue choir groups but eventually became a factory foreman. His mother, Ida Gordon, was from a wealthy Jewish family in Poland but had rebelled to join a Tolstoy study circle. At the age of fourteen she went to work in a sweatshop to earn money to come to the United States, joining her sister in New Haven. In the 1920s, Wolfe's parents prospered; there was a socialist atmosphere in the home and a sympathy for workers' struggles. But during the 1930s Robert Wolfe's plant moved to another city, and he fell into a deep depression that eventually required institutionalization. Ida Wolfe struggled to survive in poverty by running a small neighborhood store.

Their sons, Albert and Bernard, were deeply impressed by these tragic events and turned to radical politics. Bernard also began reading Freud.

In 1931 Bernard entered Yale University as a premedical student at the age of sixteen. At about the same time, Albert, an unskilled worker, came under the influence of a high school friend, Morris Gandleman, whose father had been a founder of the Communist Party in Connecticut and was later expelled as a Trotskyist. Bernard soon began seeing the Gandlemans as well. He rapidly became convinced of the correctness of Trotsky's outlook and threw himself into political work at the same time that he pursued an honors course in psychology in preparation for a career in psychiatry. In the Trotskyist movement Bernard assumed the name "Ben Hardee," and Albert became "Al Hardee."

An activist in the antiwar and unemployed movements, Wolfe found himself isolated at Yale because the other New Haven Trotskyists were all workers and off campus, and the Communist youth group was the dominant force among the students. When he attended a convention of the National Student League at Vassar, Wolfe attempted to speak from the floor but was beaten up and thrown out by the Communists. Finally, he broke out of isolation at Yale when he gained the sympathy of Arthur Mizener, a young radical professor who later became famous for his biography of F. Scott Fitzgerald, *The Far Side of Paradise* (1951). Mizener was an enthusiast of Trotsky's *History of the Russian Revolution*, and, under Wolfe's influence, he contributed to the *New International*.

After receiving his B.A. degree in June 1935, Wolfe briefly attended Yale graduate school but abandoned his plans to become a psychiatrist. For a while he directed the College of Women Trade Unionists at Bryn Mawr. In the fall of 1936 he moved to New York to assist with literary work for the Trotskyist movement. There he met Felix Morrow, one of the Trotskyists assigned to organize the American Committee for the Defense of Leon Trotsky, which secured asylum for Trotsky in Mexico and attempted to permit him a hearing to refute the fraudulent charges leveled against him in the Moscow purge trials. Morrow explained that Trotsky's secretarial staff in Coyoacan was weak in the English language and that Wolfe's knowledge of French would be of great value as a common language among the secretariat if he could raise the money to join the Trotsky household. Wolfe immediately contacted Mizener who helped him obtain the necessary funds.

Wolfe stayed in Mexico from January until August 1937. Returning to New Haven and then New York in the fall, he continued to write for the Trotskyist press for another ten months until he began to drift off into Greenwich Village bohemia. By 1939, both he and Albert were out of the Trotskyist movement, and Anäis Nin and Henry Miller got him a job producing a dozen pornographic novels at a dollar a page. In 1972 he published an autobiography, *Memoirs of a Not Altogether Shy Pornographer*, describing this phase of his life. In the mid-1940s he coauthored a minor classic, *Really the Blues* (1946) with Milton "Mezz" Mezzrow, the biography of a Jewish jazz musician who adopted the music, language, and many of the attitudes of Afro-Americans. Following psychoanalysis in 1950 with Dr. Edmund Bergler, proponent of the concept of "psychic masochism," Wolfe published a series of psychological novels that culminated in *The Great Prince Died* (1959; reissued in 1975 under the title *Trotsky Dead*). The thesis of the novel is that Trotsky, called Victor Rostov, had unconsciously assisted in his own assassination because of guilt over his role in the 1921 suppression of the uprising at Kronstadt naval base. Wolfe subsequently moved to Hollywood where he continued to write novels and screenplays until his death in 1985.

Two additional Trotskyists arrived on the Sunshine Special to join Wolfe and the others in Coyoacan: Pearl Kluger, who assumed a secretarial role, and George Novack, the secretary of the Trotsky Defense Committee. Finally, there were two more Trotskyists who came in from Chicago: Albert Glotzer, a founding member of the Communist League of America, who served as verbatim reporter for the proceedings, and labor lawyer Albert Goldman, who was Trotsky's attorney during the interrogation.

In addition to Dewey, the commissioners included Bejamin Stolberg, who was born in Munich in 1892 and immigrated to the United States in 1908.[19] After graduating from Harvard University and pursuing further studies at the University of Chicago, Stolberg became a labor journalist and moved to New York in the mid-1920s. An enchanting conversationalist who lacked the drive to realize his talents in a substantial manner, Stolberg developed a friendship with David Dubinsky of the International Ladies Garment Workers Union and had considerable influence on intellectuals including Sinclair Lewis and Dorothy Thompson. In 1933 he read and reviewed Trotsky's *History of the Russian Revolution* for the *Nation*. He developed an admiration for Trotsky but never became a political disciple. With him was Suzanne La Follette, the niece of U.S. Senator Robert La Follette, Sr., who had been a journalist and then art critic for the *Nation*. Under the influence of Alfred Jay Nock's extreme individualism, she edited the *New Free-*

man for several years. She, too, was more taken with Trotsky's personal brilliance than his political views.[20] The fourth commissioner was Otto Ruehle, a prominent German Marxist and biographer of Marx, then in exile from Hitler.

The most controversial commissioner was Carleton Beals, author of many books on Latin America, who drove down to Mexico City from Los Angeles with his wife. By the end of the hearings, relations were not at all cordial between Beals and virtually everyone else. In the opinion of Dewey and the other commissioners, Beals took advantage of the hearings to ask some improper questions that had no bearing on the charges raised during the Moscow trials, questions that might have jeopardized Trotsky's status as an exile in Mexico. Beals claimed, for example, to have special information that Trotsky had sent Michael Borodin as his emissary to foment revolution in Mexico seventeen years earlier. This was especially provocative in light of the fact that Trotsky had been permitted into Mexico on the promise that he would not attempt to intervene in Mexican affairs. In the midst of the hearings, Beals resigned from the commission, denouncing it as biased in favor of Trotsky.[21]

One of the additional tasks with which those not directly involved in the hearings assisted was the physical defense of the Rivera villa where the hearings were held. "There was the anxiety that the Stalinists might raid the hearings," recalled McDonald. "Some of us were pressed into service as armed guards, among our duties, but Buster Keaton-like, I had so much trouble with my gun that I had to turn it in."[22] On another occasion Charles Walker armed himself to accompany Trotsky into town.[23] Farrell helped for a while building barricades to buttress the wall behind Trotsky's desk, until it began to affect his sinuses. Later, after the hearings were over and Trotsky had gone on a vacation to Cuernavaca, Farrell took over the guard of Trotsky's papers from Bernard Wolfe, sitting on a table with pistols in holsters, bullets strung across his shoulders and chest, and a machine gun in his hand.[24]

Tensions ran high among the small group. At one point a fist fight broke out between John McDonald and Albert Goldman.[25] In another incident, Solow, McDonald, and Wolfe were taking a break, sitting on a table smoking with their legs dangling. Trotsky, who was known to be obsessive about orderliness and intolerant of cigarette smoke, came into the room and asked for a translation that had been in preparation. When Wolfe said he would have it completed in just a few moments, Trotsky, irritated, slammed the glass door behind him, breaking a pane as he left.[26]

Tension existed between the Trotskyists and the non-Trotskyists as well. For example, Stolberg and La Follette had objected to George Novack's going on the train from New York City to Mexico City, believing that the mere presence of a known Trotskyist on the scene could compromise the impartiality of the commission; Dewey, however, seemed unconcerned, and Novack usually took pains to be discreet and avoided acting as a spokesman for the Trotsky Defense Committee. After arriving in Mexico, Novack discussed the problem with Trotsky who concluded that a concession would have to be made. Novack thereafter stayed in a separate residence and remained somewhat apart from the central organization of the hearings. As a gesture of friendliness, Trotsky later invited Novack into his study to help him improve a draft of his eloquent summary speech. Novack recalled that Trotsky had some difficulty describing Dewey in precise terms. After scratching out several alternatives, Trotsky characterized him as "the personification of genuine American idealism . . . a man of unshakable moral authority . . . who by virtue of his age should have the right to remain outside the skirmishes in the political arena."[27]

The train arrived in Mexico City on Tuesday morning, 6 April, and that evening Dewey reported his initial impressions to Robbie Lowitz, his future wife:

> We have had a fairly busy day with consultations with one another and with the press and with Trotsky's lawyer [Albert Goldman]. I'll begin with him; he is a Chicago socialist, and makes a good impression on me of both quick intelligence and good practical judgment. He says that in Trotsky's interest as well as in our own we must lean over backward whenever necessary in order to be fair. Trotsky has consented to be guided entirely by the ideas of the Commission as to the management of the hearings. Not that I think that he had much difficulty in convincing Trotsky but that Trotsky is used to the Continental method [in] which there is much more opportunity for speeches and less questions and answers to them.[28]

On Saturday, 10 April, the hearings officially began with a powerful statement by Dewey condemning the refusal of many countries to grant asylum to Trotsky so that he could have an opportunity to defend himself against the charges of the Stalinist regime: "This Commission, like many millions of workers of city and country, of hand and brain, believes that no man should be condemned without a chance to defend himself. It desires at the outset . . . to congratulate the Mexican government on its broad interpretation of the meaning of political democracy which makes our meeting possible."[29] Later that day Solow described to Margaret De Silver some of the events that had occurred in the charged setting, made even more electric by Frida Kahlo's beauty and the presence of Diego Rivera surrounded by a delegation of Mexican trade unionists:

> Dewey's opener was a honey. Goldman spoke 30 minutes, outlined what LDT's [Trotsky's] side means to prove. . . . In the meantime millions of photographers, quite a few union delegates present, LDT brilliant as can be, shifting from one language to another . . . Finerty [legal counsel for the commission, who had also been the defender of Sacco and Vanzetti, and Tom Mooney] turning up late for the second session, me translating Ruehle's questions and Trotsky working me out of a job translating his answers to them by giving them first in German and then English, Dewey like tart cider asking the best questions of all.

Solow went on to describe some of Trotsky's comments and personal reactions:

> Oh, I can't tell the story tonight, but it went off O.K., although I imagine the unfriendly press will twist many a thing against us. Here are a few cracks:
> Goldman: Were you a tailor in New York?
> Trotsky: Unfortunately I never learned a productive trade.
> Dewey: Is Vishinsky [the Soviet prosecutor] quoting correctly when he says Lenin in 1904 called you a phrasemonger?
> Trotsky: I think I recognize Lenin's style.
> The political stuff was old dope to me and we didn't get to brass tacks (Romm, Hotel Bristol, etc. [referring to some of the blatantly falsified testimony against Trotsky]) today so the real high spot was at the start when Goldman was asking the usual formal opening questions. When he got to Trotsky's family and children, and finally to the daughter who committed suicide, the old man couldn't take it. His face twitched before he replied, and when he did his eyes were visibly wet and red. There is only one thing lacking, and that is a Stalinist attorney to do the cross examining. I'd give a foot to have Brodsky [a well-known Communist lawyer] here and an arm to have Vishinsky here. They'd end up giving both feet and both arms to get out alive.[30]

Glotzer, who had experience in the legal process, also believed it would have been preferable if Communist representatives had been present and an adversarial proceeding ensued. Yet he insisted that the testimony showed that the commissioners asked sharp questions; they did not simply accept anything Trotsky said without corroboration from written documents.

Once the sensational hearings were under way, the excitement mounted each day. On Thursday, 15 April, Dewey reported: "Yesterday was the most interesting day yet. 'Truth, justice, humanity' and all the rest of the reasons for coming are receding into the background before the bare overpowering interest of the man and what he has to say."[31] On Friday Farrell wrote to Margaret Marshall, book-review editor for the *Nation*: "Trotsky has utterly demolished the macabre fables of the Moscow Trials for any human being who is susceptible to reason and who does not require that his opinions be manufactured for him by persons thousands of miles across the sea. He has presented documentary evidence which creates more than a reasonable doubt [about the charges against him]. He has built up a logical case, and despite the fact that he has gone on answering questions almost six hours a day since Saturday, his testimony holds together like a most amazing piece of logic."[32]

Trotsky's closing speech, in which he dealt with the historical context of the frame-up trials, the nature of Stalinism, and his whole life story, provided a fitting climax. Glotzer recalled that he spoke "with great passion and his voice and speech were alternately inflected with rising and lowering power, depending on matters treated. The voice was on the high side but clear and strong and captivating." Trotsky sat throughout the summation, although he would have preferred to stand and pace and gesture. Under the table at which he sat, his hands and forearms were in constant motion. When he finished, the audience burst out in spontaneous applause.[33]

Following additional hearings in New York conducted by an affiliated body in Paris, the commission's verdict that Trotsky was innocent of all charges was made public in December 1937. Both the verbatim transcript of Trotsky's testimony and the commission's deliberations were published as *The Case of Leon Trotsky* (1937) and *Not Guilty* (1938).

MARXIST CULTURAL RENAISSANCE

The most important cultural impact of the Moscow trials involved the evolution of the *Partisan Review* in the late 1930s. The connection between *Partisan Review* editors Phillips and Rahv with Trotsky, and to a lesser extent with his followers in the United States, was largely confined to the province of ideas. Their private correspondence with Trotsky indicates far more agreement with him than they publicly acknowledged, although they failed to establish a relationship with the Trotskyist movement, other than that of teaching a few classes for the Trotskyist organization and meeting with its leaders on occasion. However, one editor of the revamped publication, Dwight Macdonald, would make a stronger commitment and join the Trotskyists in the fall of 1939.

Born in New York City on 24 March 1906, Macdonald was descended from two generations of lawyers.[34] After graduating from Phillips Exeter in 1924, he followed in his father's footsteps by going to Yale University where he became a film enthusiast. This was not surprising since his father's law firm had a number of motion picture companies as clients. With his friends F. W. Dupee and George L. K. Morris, Macdonald took over *Yale Lit*. After graduation in 1928 he worked for a while at Macy's department store in New York, trying to save money in order to write, and then he attempted to establish an intellectual community on a farm in Ohio owned by his friend Dinsmore Wheeler. Soon he was back in New York where another Yale friend, Wilder Hobson, got him an interview that led to his becoming the first editorial employee of the newly founded *Fortune*. At the same time, he, Morris, and Dupee initiated the *Miscellany*, and he wrote on film for the *Symposium*.[35]

With the advent of the depression, many of the staff members at *Fortune* began to move left politically, coming into conflict with the publisher. In late 1934 Macdonald married Nancy Rodman, a left-wing mathematics major and Phi Beta Kappa from Vassar (1932), whose brother, Selden Rodman (Yale 1931), was editor of *Common Sense*. By the mid-1930s, Macdonald was reading Marx and had become a fellow traveler of the Communist Party, collaborating with the party in founding the *Time-Life* unit of the Newspaper Guild. In 1936, having accumulated some savings from his $10,000-a-year salary, which were added to Nancy's income from a trust fund, he wrote a provocative series of articles on U.S. Steel and resigned from *Fortune* after his work was bowdlerized.

Soon after, his relationship with the Communist Party came into question as the Moscow trials began. In a long letter to the *New Republic*, only part of which was published, Macdonald aggressively challenged Malcolm Cowley's defense of the trials. Subsequently, Dupee introduced Macdonald to Phillips and Rahv. Not only did they induce him to break with the party but they persuaded him to join the editorial board of the newly reorganized *Partisan Review.*[36]

The fifth member of the new editorial board—along with Phillips, Rahv, Dupee, Macdonald, and Morris, the magazine's financial mainstay—was Mary McCarthy. Born in Seattle on 21 June 1912, she devoted her Vassar years to literary activities with her friends Elizabeth Bishop, Muriel Rukeyser, and Eleanor Clark.[37] Newly married in 1933, her actor-husband brought her into contact with Communist circles in New York. Soon she was marching in May Day parades and attending fund-raisers for the *New Masses.* She came close to joining the party when she separated from her husband in the summer of 1936. At the time she was writing reviews for the *Nation* and the *New Republic,* working part-time as Benjamin Stolberg's typist and research assistant, and beginning a job as editor at Covici Friede, a left-wing publishing house. At a cocktail party in honor of the legendary cartoonist Art Young, she found herself agreeing with James T. Farrell that Trotsky deserved a hearing. Soon after, her name was listed on the letterhead of literature published by the American Committee for the Defense of Leon Trotsky. Irritated at attempts by friends to force her off the committee, she began to take an interest in the case and concluded that the Moscow trials were fraudulent. Soon she was seeing Farrell and Hortense Alden, and through them she came to know Philip Rahv with whom she began to live in the summer of 1937. When *Partisan Review* was relaunched that December, McCarthy was listed as an editor in charge of theater reviews, a token assignment she would later insist was due to her once having been married to an actor.

Before the June 1937 American Writers' Congress, the ever-cautious Phillips and Rahv had not publicly revealed any disaffection from the Communist Party, let alone sympathy for Trotsky. They attended the party's literary criticism workshop together with Macdonald, McCarthy, Dupee, and Clark. Granville Hicks, the leading Communist Party critic who was chairing the session, stood helplessly by as Rahv delivered an eloquent discourse on the history of freedom and human thought. Macdonald discussed Trotsky's prose style, emphasizing that its brilliance must be acknowledged even by those who did not agree with Trotsky's politics.[38] When the new *Partisan Review* was launched, Phillips and Rahv endeavored to develop a number of Trotsky's literary and political ideas.

In March 1938, for example, Phillips turned to Trotsky for assistance in clarifying the historical record regarding the aesthetic views of Marx and Engels. After recapitulating their essential contributions—their description of the laws governing the cultural superstructure, their tributes to various writers, and their warnings against economic determinism—Phillips cited Trotsky as the only major Marxist leader who had written authentic literary criticism. Trotsky, Phillips contended, was outstanding in that he "not only saw in literature a mirror of society but was acutely conscious of those qualities which, taken together, make up the social vision of a work of art." Phillips then summarized and praised Trotsky's analysis of postrevolutionary Soviet culture and his explanation of how the shifting social forces were refracted through the texture of literary work. More important to Phillips, however, was Trotsky's "polemic against those critics who were impatient with history and wanted to establish by decree a proletarian art." Phillips concluded with tributes to Trotsky's amplitude and his variety of insights. He also explained Trotsky's approach to the nature of the artistic element using Eliot as an example: "Is not the autumnal sensibility of Eliot a kind of comment on the state of society?"[39]

Rahv, too, considered Trotsky's *Literature and Revolution* in the summer of 1939 when he surveyed the literary record of an eventful decade. But on the whole his commentary demonstrated how far Rahv had evolved from his once vivid confidence in a proletarian literary renaissance. He noted that while, during the early part of the decade, the immersion of young writers in political action had played a liberating role, now, on the eve of a new world war, with the Communist Party behaving more patriotically than even the Democrats, the political movement was rapidly retrogressing in the direction of a "new gentility." The intellectual or artist who wished to remain faithful to truth must now stand alone guided only by his or her conscience:

> If a sufficiently organized, active and broad revolutionary movement existed, it might assimilate the artist by opening to him its own avenue of experience; but in the absence of such a movement all he can do is utilize the possibilities of individual and group secession from, and protest against, the dominant values of our time. Needless to say this does not imply a return to a philosophy of individualism. It means that all we have left to go on now is individual integrity—the probing conscience, the will to repulse and assail the forces released by a corrupt reality.

Concerned with how best to maintain the integrity of the intellectual, Rahv was clearly moving away from the classical Marxist view of the central role of the international working class. The importance of Trotsky for Rahv was not the latter's reaffirmation of authentic Marxism-Leninism with a corresponding mandate to organize the vanguard of the proletariat for the coming struggle for power. Trotsky seemed more important to Rahv for his other insights. Affirming that a study of the "special role and changing status of the intellectual" is crucial to any "social examination" of modern writing, Rahv concluded that "Trotsky is, I believe, the only Marxist critic who develops his analysis of writers and literary trends largely around this concept. . . . But Trotsky does not credit this factor with sufficient power."[40]

Thus for a time the *Partisan Review*, as its political position emerged through Rahv's essays, considered the impending World War II from a heterodox perspective. The magazine accepted classical Marxist analysis, as reaffirmed by Trotsky, particularly in its critique of capitalism and the way that Trotsky explained the degeneration of the Russian Revolution. Moreover, in 1938 the editors even applied a Marxist analysis to the coming war itself: "The exigencies of imperialist rivalries makes [*sic*] a new world war inevitable, especially since, with the degeneration of the Comintern, the threat of revolutionary action has been definitely withdrawn. . . . The war, even if the 'democrats' win, will not solve a fundamental problem of society. . . . Only unalterable opposition to capitalism, only utilization of the imperialist war for revolutionary ends, opens any prospect to humanity and its culture."[41] Yet the *Partisan Review* presented no corresponding working-class program of action to prevent the war; its great concern seemed to be that the forthcoming interimperialist maelstrom would constitute a terrible test for the morality and culture of intellectuals.

Several documents reveal Trotsky's attitude toward the *Partisan Review* group, after it publicly broke with the Communist Party in 1937. In a letter to editorial board member Dwight Macdonald, Trotsky expressed his fear that the *Partisan Review* was tending to hide behind the abstract banners of "independence" and "freedom," rather than using these concepts as means of ideological struggle. He also suggested that, in the face of the coming social crisis, the journal might well transform itself into a "small cultural monastery, guarding itself from the outside world by skepticism, agnosticism, and respectability."[42]

In his essay "Art and Politics in Our Epoch," published in the *Partisan Review* only a few months later, Trotsky offered a perspective for revolutionary artists and writers challenged by the dual obstacles of capitalism and the Soviet Thermidor: "Generally speaking, art is an expression of man's need for a harmonious and complete life, that is to say, his need for those major benefits of which a class society has deprived him. That is why a protest against reality, either conscious or unconscious, active or passive, optimistic or pessimistic, always forms part of a really creative piece of work. Every new tendency in art has begun with a rebellion." Trotsky buttressed his thesis by pointing to the paths—from aesthetic revolt to acceptance in the bourgeois academies—that were taken by classicism, romanticism, realism, naturalism, symbolism, impressionism, cubism, and futurism. However, whether this pattern would continue depended on the stability of bourgeois society. Trotsky asserted that in its decline capitalism was no longer capable of absorbing the rebellion of new tendencies in art: "Hence new tendencies take on a more and more violent character, alternating between hope and despair. The artistic schools of the last few decades—cubism, futurism, dadaism, surrealism—follow each other without reaching a complete development. Art, which is the most complex part of culture, the most sensitive and at the same time the least protected, suffers most from the decay of bourgeois society." Since, from the Marxist viewpoint, art is in itself insufficiently independent to overcome social crises or even to defend itself, such tasks require a social transformation, and "the function of art in our epoch is determined by its relation to the revolution."

According to Trotsky, many leftists made the mistake of only supporting the victorious Soviet revolution, thereby giving fealty to the new privileged stratum of the Stalinist bureaucracy instead of declaring their allegiance to the international working class. Furthermore, they failed to perceive how the fate of Soviet art testified to the character of art's relation to revolution. Following the October Revolution in 1917, Soviet art underwent a great liberation. But after the rise and consolidation of Stalin's bureaucratic regime, artistic quality greatly deteriorated. Even courtly art, Trotsky noted, although based on idealization, avoided the outright falsification that had so opprobriously marred Soviet art, especially as exemplified by the careers of Vsevolod Ivanov and Alexei Tolstoy, and in the falsification of the events of the revolution in cultural artifacts. In contrast, Trotsky held up the work of Mexican artist Diego Rivera, whose frescoes still drew inspiration from the true spirit of the October Revolution.

The impending social crisis generated by the coming war, Trotsky argued, demanded a response from dissident artists and intellectuals. Referring to an attack on Trotskyism in a letter recently published in the *Partisan Review*, Trotsky emphasized that one must not fear smallness and isolation, for "not a single progressive idea has begun with a 'mass base.'" This condition obtained for art as well as for politics. Trotsky declared that artists should support the revolutionary vanguard of the working class, the Trotskyist Fourth International, but he simultaneously emphasized how necessary it was to oppose supervision of art by any party, whether it be Stalinist or Trotskyist: "The ideological base of the conflict between the Fourth and Third Internationals is the profound disagreement not only on the tasks of the party but in general on the entire material and spiritual life of mankind." He concluded his essay with the ringing appeal for the independence of art within the revolutionary process:

> Art, like science, not only does not seek orders, but by its very essence, cannot tolerate them. Artistic creation has its own laws—even when it consciously serves a social movement. Truly intellectual creation is incompatible with lies, hypocrisy and the spirit of conformity. Art can become a strong ally of revolution only insofar as it remains faithful to itself. Poets, painters, sculptors and musicians will themselves find their own approach and methods, if the struggle for freedom of the oppressed classes and peoples scatters the clouds of skepticism and of pessimism which cover the horizon of mankind.[43]

Later in the autumn of 1938 the *Partisan Review* published "Manifesto: Towards a Free Revolutionary Art," which, although signed by Rivera and the French surrealist André Breton, was written by Trotsky and Breton. This declaration repeated the sentiments expressed in "Art and Politics in Our Epoch," emphasizing that the artist "is the natural ally of revolution." It called for the formation of an International Federation of Independent Revolutionary Art. In the winter of 1939, the *Partisan Review* printed a letter from Trotsky to Breton, in which he traced the deterioration of André Malraux's work as he changed from an adventuristic but truthful champion of the colonial revolution to an apologist for Stalinism: "The struggle for revolutionary ideas in art must begin again with the struggle for artistic *truth*, not in terms of any single school, but in terms of *the immutable faith of the artist in his own inner self*. Without this there is no art. 'You shall not lie!'—that is the formula of salvation." The new organization of revolutionary artists, Trotsky elaborated, should not be an aesthetic or political school, but rather it should "oxidize the atmosphere in which artists breathe and create," for under present conditions of impending social cataclysm, "truly independent creation cannot but be revolutionary by its very nature."[44]

The appearance of Trotsky's articles and programmatic statements in the *Partisan Review* did not by any means indicate that Phillips and Rahv completely agreed with his views. The journal, by its very nature, was open to a variety of radical political opinions. Nevertheless there was a definite confluence of sentiment on many questions. In the summer of 1939 the names of all of the magazine's editors appeared as supporters of the newly formed League for Cultural Freedom and Socialism. The views articulated in the league's programmatic statement corresponded to those expressed by Trotsky in previous articles, and the organization was intended to be the American affiliate of the International Federation of Independent Revolutionary Art. Among the league's sponsors were intellectuals publicly known as members of the American Trotskyist organization, including James Burnham, Dwight Macdonald (the league's acting secretary), Sherry Mangan (a New England poet and journalist living in Paris who under the pseudonym "Sean Niall" contributed the "Paris Letter" column to *Partisan Review*), George Novack, Harry Roskolenko (a New York poet), and John Wheelwright (a New England poet).

But a gap still remained between the Trotskyists who were political activists and Rahv and Phillips, and it would widen considerably during the next few years. The Trotskyists themselves quite prophetically predicted the divergence in an editorial in their paper *Socialist Appeal*, which was launched as they were being expelled from the Socialist Party in the fall of 1937, just in time to greet the newly reorganized *Partisan Review*. The editorial, written by George Novack under direction of the editorial board, congratulated the magazine for its break with the Communist Party and its repudiation of the Stalinist method of judging literature by political line. But the Trotskyists disputed some of the formulations employed by the new journal in its first editorial in December 1937, formulations which implied that the editors might be overreacting to organized politics in general because of their experience with the Communists.

The *Partisan Review*, the *Socialist Appeal*'s editorial noted, called for independence not just in art but in politics as well. For the Trotskyists, as for all classical Marxists, political independence or nonpartisanship was impossible in a social environment divided by warring classes, where one's every act contained political implications and consequences, including even one's personal desire for neutrality. To the contrary, the *Socialist Appeal* argued, the lesson to be learned from the experience with Stalinism was not that *all* relations with political parties are inherently deleterious to art but that only certain ones are. The negative influence of the Communist Party on radical intellectuals and literature did not spring from the party's role as a revolutionary Leninist vanguard, but precisely from its opposite function as a bureaucratic instrument of the Thermidorean reaction in the Soviet Union. As a corrective, the Trotskyists recommended that the *Partisan Review* establish a friendly collaboration with their revolutionary party and that the magazine aggressively expose the Stalinists as "a pack of conscienceless scoundrels in the service of the great corrupter and destroyer of the socialist revolution." The new *Partisan Review*, the *Socialist Appeal* asserted, had made a good beginning, but in order to thrive as a genuine revolutionary force it must not only maintain its own art as independent, it must actually link up with the working-class movement. "In avowing itself hospitable, experimental, democratic, the *Partisan Review* has set its foot on the right road. But it is not enough to have a broad circumference; it is equally necessary to have an ideological and political center from which all the rest logically radiates."[45]

THE AMBIGUITIES OF ANTI-STALINISM

Although the Moscow trials confirmed Trotsky's analysis of the malaise that had overtaken the international Communist movement, they also sapped the confidence of many militants who were hoping to build a revolutionary socialist movement. One symptom of this trend was the widespread discussion of "ends and means" among independent leftists in the late 1930s. In June 1938 Trotsky published "Their Morals and Ours" in the Trotskyist journal *New International*, defending the concept that "the end justifies the means," with the caveat that some means contradict certain ends. John Dewey endorsed the essence of Trotsky's argument in the August issue of the same magazine, but insisted that Trotsky violated his own precepts by giving priority to class struggle as a law of social transformation. When a similar discussion was held in the journal *Common Sense*, virtually every participant with the exception of Sidney Hook agreed with Selden Rodman's claim that the root cause of the Stalinist terror was "Marxist absolutism and its dependence on violence." Thus many anti-Stalinists were moving toward a view that communism itself was "amoral."[46]

Herbert Solow, to take another example, had not yet renounced his Trotskyist politics, but he appeared to be incapable of establishing an ongoing collaboration with the American Trotskyist movement. Throughout the hearings in Coyoacan, he and Trotsky argued steadily, wagging "their fingers in each other's noses."[47] Still, in a 12 June 1937 letter to Harold Isaacs, Trotsky reported that Solow had raised the question of starting a magazine with himself as editor that would involve Walker, Farrell, Eastman, Stolberg, and La Follette. Trotsky was not unsympathetic to the idea, but at the same time he feared that the authentic Trotskyists might be treated as "poor relatives" in such a venture. He thought that perhaps the Trotskyists' first responsibility was to develop their own new theoretical magazine to replace the *New International*, which had been abandoned during their entry into the Socialist Party. Once having done that, they could possibly form a coalition with left-wing anti-Stalinist elements.[48]

The following year, in March 1938, the Trotskyist leaders of the newly formed Socialist Workers Party held a discussion with Trotsky in Mexico about their relations with American intellectuals in common political defense work. Solow's name was often mentioned. Trotsky's attitude toward Solow by then had become somewhat cynical, and he remarked that "our excellent friend Solow will see that he remains a political celibate." Meanwhile, Solow heard from an unnamed source that Trotsky had also referred to him as "a decent chap but a mercurial dilettante." Trotsky's opinion was that the American Trotskyists should not attempt to rely upon or maneuver with vacillating intellectuals but should strive to build a solid political defense organization of their own that would attract the best of minds, including Solow's.[49]

The fall of 1937 found Solow frequently in the company of Sidney Hook. He learned from Hook that his college friends Meyer Schapiro and Whittaker Chambers were talking and that Chambers was getting "fed up" with Stalinism. One night in February, Chambers rang Solow's doorbell and they discussed the latter's political dilemma. For the next few months Solow urged Chambers to openly break with the Communist underground by making a public statement so as to prevent his being whisked away in secret, as other secret agents had been.[50]

In March and April, Solow still seemed to be in political harmony with the revolutionary elements on the anti-Stalinist left. He contributed to the "Ripostes" section of the *Partisan Review* several humorous pieces on the Communists' rapid changes in attitude toward various writers.[51] At the same time, under the pseudonym

"Junius," he wrote a series of articles for the *Socialist Appeal* about the possible political implications of the disappearance in the Soviet Union of a former Soviet agent named Rubens.[52] But he also published an article on the Rubens case in the virulently anti-communist *New Leader*, which perhaps foreshadowed a change in his political orientation. Then he published two articles in late 1939 which unveiled a new Solow, completely bereft of any pro-socialist convictions while fully retaining an obsessive anti-Stalinism. Both appeared in the *American Mercury*, which had come under the editorship of Eugene Lyons. Lyons, born in 1899 in Uzlian, Russia, grew up in New York City. As a radical journalist, he returned to the Soviet Union for six years, serving as a correspondent for the United Press.[53] Toward the mid-1930s he came back to the United States where he published a classic of disillusionment, *Assignment in Utopia* (1937). After some episodic collaboration with the Trotskyists in connection with their publishing projects, Lyons turned wholeheartedly to a career as an anticommunist journalist.

Solow's first piece for *American Mercury*, "Stalin's American Passport Mill," provided a more thorough update on Rubens's disappearance, which Solow theorized might be part of a Soviet plan to stage a new Moscow trial, at which Rubens and his wife would "confess" to being anti-Soviet reactionaries in league with the Trotskyists and anti-Stalinist intellectuals in the United States.[54] His second essay, "Stalin's Great American Hoax: The League for Peace and Democracy," was a blunt exposé of how the Communists established and manipulated this Popular Front organization, originally known as the League Against War and Fascism. Solow documented the party's methods of control and how it had purged all officials who fell out of step with the Stalinist line. Most peculiar, from a socialist point of view, was the reason that Solow gave for opposing a government witch-hunt of the league in the tradition of A. Mitchell Palmer's 1919 "Red Scare" raids. Instead of pointing out that such an investigation would result in the suppression of the rights of everyone involved in the struggle for social change, Solow warned that it would crown the league with a martyr's halo, which would catalyze support for the organization among its liberal constituency.[55] This line of argument is characteristic of the type of "criticisms" of U.S. government repression that the New York intellectuals would develop during the Cold War period under the spurious claim that such "criticisms" proved their independence from the excesses of the witch-hunt.

In addition to writing the two articles for the *American Mercury*, Solow investigated the disappearance of Juliet Stuart Poyntz, a former teacher at Barnard College, who had vanished from the American Woman's Club in New York City in June 1937. Poyntz had played a prominent role in American Communism until 1934, when she began carrying out assignments for the Communist International. Solow had unearthed evidence that Poyntz had been in the process of withdrawing from the party at the time that she disappeared, and he suspected foul play.[56]

What the two articles and the related Poyntz investigation reveal is how the anti-Stalinist component of Solow's political outlook was beginning to become detached from his socialist and anticapitalist views, a decisive process that would lead him to become an outright anticommunist and anti-Marxist. From the Trotskyists' perspective, as well as from the viewpoint of a more revolutionary-minded Solow of an earlier period, one could not object to exposing the sham of the Communists' front organizations, nor would one have opposed publicizing the Stalinist terrorist apparatus. Indeed, an authentic socialist had the duty to expose the nature of Stalinism. Nevertheless, such exposures would have been regarded by socialists as just one small facet of a general political struggle against Stalinism, a struggle the major expression of which would have been the creation of a movement to win the working class to a genuine revolutionary socialist program. To the Trotskyists, Solow appeared to be placing an undue emphasis on the Communist underground apparatus and elevating anti-Stalinist propaganda above advocating a larger anticapitalist program; this raised the danger of becoming dependent on capitalism as the primary weapon against Stalinism.[57]

No doubt the assassination of Trotsky in August 1940 by an agent of Stalin's secret police reinforced Solow's new course. Since they had remained aloof from organizational ties, many anti-Stalinist Marxist intellectuals were bonded to Trotskyism through attachment to Trotsky himself. That year Solow had become an assistant to the president of the New School for Social Research, Dr. Alvin Johnson, in which capacity he administered a $1 million fund provided by the Rockefeller Foundation and other funding agencies to rescue scientists, scholars, and intellectuals from Hitler-dominated regions. Solow also became an unpaid occasional operative for the Office of Strategic Services (the forerunner of the Central Intelligence Agency) in mid-Manhattan, providing information on Communist activity.[58] On 11 January 1943 Solow's longtime friend, Carlo Tresca, was gunned down in New York as he left the Fifth Avenue offices of *Il Martello*, the anti-fascist Italian-language journal that he edited. Once more Solow found himself immersed in research as he sought to uncover possible motivations for the assassination. He suspected that the fascists, the Stalinists, or the Mafia could have murdered Tresca, but the case was never solved.[59]

Later in 1943 Solow made contact with T. S. Matthews of the Luce publishing empire, and within a short time he became a contributing editor for *Time*, writing mainly on education, business, political, and technological topics. In 1945 he moved permanently over to *Fortune*, where his special interests involved him in extensive travel, most often to Africa and Latin America, covering international politics. For the next twenty years, as he rose to an honored position on the magazine, Solow would retain only the vaguest connections to New York intellectual life, dying of a heart attack on Thanksgiving Day, 1964.

Charles and Adelaide Walker experienced a similar, if less pronounced, evolution.[60] In 1933 they had fallen under Solow's influence, but their efforts to keep afloat the Theatre Union, a Marxist drama group of Communist and Socialist forces, caused them to refrain from signing the 1934 open letter. That same year they visited the Soviet Union carrying party-provided letters of introduction to various Soviet cultural luminaries, including Sergei Eisenstein. On their journey back to the United States, through an arrangement made by Solow, they met Trotsky's son Leon Sedov in Paris.

The Walkers were much liked by the Communists because they were activists and also because Walker, due to his age, experience, and personal presence, gave the impression of being a sensible radical, thoughtful and open. Thus when Solow led them in the direction of the Trotskyists, they were warmly welcomed as well. On the eve of the Walkers' departure for Minneapolis in 1935 to do research for what would become the classic account of the Trotskyist-led 1934 teamster strikes, *American City* (1936), James P. Cannon and James Burnham urged them to join the Trotskyist organization. They demurred, partly because of tactical reasons advantageous to their research. However, once in Minneapolis they became so enthusiastic about the three Trotskyist Dunne brothers that they were eager to join but could not bring themselves to ask for membership. Their first doubts about Trotskyism came a year later in Mexico during the Commission of Inquiry hearings, when they began to wonder whether the Soviet Union would have been significantly different had Trotsky's policies prevailed. In 1938 they moved to Cape Cod to coauthor a book clarifying their views about Marxism, Stalinism, and Trotskyism. No sooner did they begin work than they discovered that their views were evolving even as they wrote. Progress on the book was stymied because of their uncertainty about where they stood. They began to run out of money, so when their friend Russell Davenport offered Adelaide a job at *Fortune* magazine, she accepted. By 1940 they no longer considered themselves to be revolutionaries. Politically they stood somewhere between Norman Thomas and Franklin Roosevelt. Just a year or so later, Adelaide found herself working with great enthusiasm for the industrialist Wendell Willkie, the 1940 Republican presidential candidate and a leading spokesman of business interests opposed to the New Deal. Charles, in the meantime, returned to the Episcopalian faith and accepted a position as assistant secretary of Yale University. In the years before his death in 1974, he also returned to his youthful love of classical languages, preparing many translations of Sophocles and other Greek dramatists for publication.

Another example of a post-Moscow trial defection was the particularly abrupt about-face of the novelist Charles Yale Harrison. Born in Philadelphia in 1899, Harrison was a newspaperman who enlisted in the Royal Montreal Regiment in the early days of World War I. He returned home a radical and drifted toward the Communist Party for which he served as a contributing editor of *New Masses*, directed the party's agitation on behalf of Sacco and Vanzetti, and helped to found the John Reed Clubs. His 1930 antiwar novel, *Generals Die in Bed*, became a best-seller and caused a storm of controversy among conservative critics, turning him into a hero of the left. But when Trotsky's daughter, Zina, committed suicide in 1933, Harrison broke publicly with the party to become a sympathizer of the Trotskyists.[61]

In the summer of 1936 Harrison conceived the idea of writing a popularization of Trotsky's ideas and traveled to Oslo for a personal interview. Prevented by the Norwegian government from arranging a meeting, Harrison returned to the United States pledging in a letter to Trotsky that he would redouble his efforts to "plead your cause and the cause of revolutionary socialism before my colleagues in the literary circles, in the universities and before the youth."[62] In 1938 he published an anti-Stalinist satire, *Meet Me at the Barricades*, which Bernard Wolfe enthusiastically commended in a letter to Trotsky.[63] By 1939, however, Harrison had left New York radical circles for a government post in Washington and was so hostile to the Trotskyists that Shachtman and Burnham publicly attacked him as a renegade and opportunist in the *New International*.[64]

The ambiguous nature of anti-Stalinism was also evidenced in the short and sad story of the *Marxist Quarterly*, probably the most distinguished socialist theoretical journal ever published in the United States.[65] In 1936 a group of Communist sympathizers at Harvard asked Lewis Corey to join with them in establishing a left journal, initially called the *American Marxist Review* and later *Science and Society*. Corey instead proposed to found a Marxist journal that would involve a variety of revolutionary tendencies and convinced Corliss Lamont, at the time a critical supporter of the Communists, to provide funding for the venture. Corey assembled representatives from the Trotskyists, James Burnham and George Novack; from the Lovestone group, Will Herberg and Bertram D. Wolfe; and from the left-wing Socialist and independent milieu, including Louis Hacker, Francis Henson, Sidney Hook, Meyer Schapiro, Sterling Spero, and Herbert Zam. The Communists, as expected, declined to participate. To resolve a personality conflict, Corey, a short, dark-haired, soft-spoken man, became the journal's managing editor while Hacker assumed the post of the president of the "American Marxist Association," which sponsored the journal.

The first issue included an inspiring editorial that posed two challenges. The first was directed "to the forces of disorder, bewilderment and reaction. . . . We believe that it is possible to analyze scientifically the complex subject matter of society from a definite point of view without sacrificing the richness of the material considered, without ignoring difficulties, without bogging down in a mass of unrelated descriptive correlations which comprises so much of American social science." The second was directed "to Marxists themselves. Too much Marxist writing, especially in America, consists of mere doctrinal exegesis that is wholly discreditable to Marxism. Too often a mistaken sense of organizational loyalty is given precedence over the weight of evidence and truth. With all too few exceptions, Marxist writing is not rooted in American history, conditions and problems. The whole of American life needs to be explored by Marxist scholarship." The statement concluded with a boast that, despite tactical differences among the editors, they were unified by "a spirit of free enquiry guided only by fundamental theory and their intellectual conscience, a confidence in scientific research as the means by which new truths can be won, and a willingness to learn."[66]

However, a crisis erupted immediately after the appearance of the first issue. The Trotskyists became wholly absorbed in fighting the Moscow trials frame-up, while the Lovestoneites and Lamont defended the trials. Burnham, Novack, and the Socialist Zam resigned from the editorial board. Two more issues appeared, but when Nikolai Bukharin, the Lovestone group's mentor, was tried, convicted, and executed, the Lovestoneites and Lamont bitterly split and Lamont withdrew his financial support on the grounds that the publication was moving in an "anti-Soviet" direction.

Both Corey and the Lovestone group were indeed moving precipitously to the right. In 1940, the former would renounce Marxism and become a bitter anticommunist, while the latter abandoned their organization to eventually become conservative ideologues of considerable influence in intellectual circles and the organized labor movement.[67]

Louis Hacker's evolution was quite similar. Born in 1899 in New York City, the son of Austrian immigrants who worked in the sweatshops, he intermittently studied history at Columbia University, receiving a B.A. in 1922 and an M.A. in 1923.[68] After spending the 1920s working for the *New International Encyclopedia* and the *New International Year Book*, he began to write a series of left-oriented books on American history modeled after Charles Beard's work, including an influential Marxist study called *The Farmer Is Doomed* (1933). During a stint as head of the Historical Project of the Works Progress Administration, Hacker brought in Solow, Morrow, McDonald, and Corey as co-workers, and in the process developed close ties to the anti-Stalinist left. He also became the inspirational figure for a promising but unfulfilled attempt by Novack, Morrow, and others to revise the contributions of the Progressive historians, such as Beard and Vernon Parrington, from a Marxist perspective. Hacker's political writing expressed the need for "the building of a revolutionary party" and "the conversion of the imperialist war into civil war." He called upon workers to use "mass power to free themselves from a system of production—the profit system—which was every day proving that it had outlived its usefulness."[69] Yet only two years after the demise of the *Marxist Quarterly*, he published *The Triumph of American Capitalism* (1940). Here he presented a class-struggle analysis of American history up to 1900, but then he proclaimed that the New Deal was overcoming all manifestations of inegalitarianism and economic insecurity, thereby proving "that capitalism was a success." James Burnham, nearing his own last gasp as a revolutionist, criticized the book in the *Partisan Review*, ironically titling the review, "God Bless America."[70]

Certainly the most complete political turnabout of the late 1930s was that of Max Eastman. At the start of the decade his views had been firmly pro-Bolshevik. In *Artists in Uniform* (1934) he fully embraced revolutionary socialism, his only caveat being that revolutionists must find ways of preventing a replication of the Stalinist malaise when they extended the socialist revolution to other countries. But following publication of the book his doubts became so strong that for two years he remained silent on the Soviet Union, abandoning his pro-Soviet lectures. Then, in 1936, under the impact of the first Moscow trial, he wrote an article for *Harper's* called "The End of Socialism in Russia," in which he reversed his previous opinion.[71] The defects of the Soviet system now outweighed its economic gains. In *Stalin's Russia and the Crisis in Socialism* (1940), Eastman explained that he no longer saw Stalinism as the enemy of Leninism but as its logical product. He then rewrote *Marx, Lenin and the Science of Revolution* (1926) as *Marxism: Is It a Science?* (1940) in order to bring the book into accord with his new outlook.

One year later, in 1941, at a cocktail party, Eastman told those present that he had become completely antisocialist in orientation.[72] He became a roving editor for the *Reader's Digest* and also served for a short time as a member of the editorial board of the *New Leader*, but only because he agreed with its anticommunist views. Eastman always had a tendency to consider human instincts as a force sufficiently potent to transcend environmental material factors.[73] This view now became central to his argument against socialism and in defense of capitalism:

> Another mistake of the Socialists was to imagine that there might be brotherly peace in a free society—a settlement, that is, of all head-on conflicts of interest, all caste and class struggles. That might happen in heaven, but on earth men will always divide into groups with conflicting interests.... The task of the social idealist is not to suppress these groupings, or try to reconcile them, but to keep them in a state of equilibrium—never to let any one of them get out of hand.[74]

An earlier Eastman, of course, would have seen the fundamental absurdity in believing that as a law of nature humanity must divide into slave master and slave, feudal lord and serf, or industrial profiteer and exploited laborer, let alone that "equilibrium" between oppressed and oppressor must be sustained in the name of "social idealism." But such banalities now became the stock-in-trade of his popular journalism. In a special article written for the *Reader's Digest* in 1941, Eastman declared that Lenin failed in the Soviet Union, just as Robert Owen had failed in the United States, not for historical-material reasons but because both designed experiments that fundamentally ignored humanity's competitive instincts. Moreover, he contended, a classless society would sim-

ply be a bore.[75] Having jettisoned all support for socialist internationalism, Eastman's anticommunism soon mushroomed into virtual paranoia.[76]

Mary McCarthy's short story, "Portrait of an Intellectual as a Yale
Man," collected in *The Company She Keeps* (1942), captures an
element of the opportunism, or, at least the glibness, that pervaded such turnabouts. The protagonist, the journalist Jim Barnett,
is a composite recalling James Burnham in name, resembling John
Chamberlain in body, and probably drawn from Dwight Macdonald,
Herbert Solow, and various other anti-Stalinist radical intellectuals
of the 1930s in career. After graduation from Yale, Barnett takes a
position on the *Liberal*, a weekly journal of opinion suggestive of
the *Nation* or the *New Republic*. There he simultaneously dabbles
in radical politics and has an affair with a young woman, Meg, who
had been isolated by her fellow-traveling colleagues because of her
defense of Trotsky at the time of the Moscow trials. Barnett is characterized by his pragmatism (he abhors systems) and a remarkable
ability to combine personal success with the repeated assertions of
his integrity. For example, he resigns from the *Liberal* staff in protest over Meg's treatment, but he had actually been looking for a
good excuse to move on to a new career. In the end, Barnett's real
mediocrity is exposed. He becomes a staff writer for *Destiny*, a
magazine resembling *Fortune*, his intellectual promise unfulfilled
and his radicalism as well as his feelings for Meg suppressed because they remind him of his own failings.

Certainly there is an element of authenticity in Barnett, yet the
engagement with radicalism of many intellectuals may have operated on several levels at once. Part of their experience is captured
not just in Barnett but also in Meg, who is ostracized for her views
and who is genuinely motivated by moral concerns. But, as in virtually all fiction about radical intellectuals of the 1930s, the substance of political thought is absent. Barnett is simply incapable of
the literary productions and active political commitment of a Burnham, a Macdonald, or a Solow. In regard to intellectual qualities,
McCarthy may have intended instead to depict John Chamberlain
or even Clifton Fadiman, who, despite greater public recognition, in
no sense had the theoretical abilities or sense of commitment to be
central to the formation and development of the anti-Stalinist left.

TWILIGHT OF THE THIRTIES

Anti-Stalinism in and of itself had a dual nature. It allowed the possibility of either a return to classical Marxism or a sharp turn to the right, depending on individual circumstance and the complexity of the context in which an individual became an anti-Stalinist. More common among the New York intellectuals in the late 1930s, however, was an attempt to rethink Marxism in some original way. Occasionally such an attempt only delayed but did not prevent a conservative course of development, but in other instances it shifted one's radicalism onto a new terrain. Edmund Wilson's *To the Finland Station* (1940) reflects just such a development.

Throughout the years spent researching and writing his magnum opus on socialist thought, Wilson's political views were in transition. The Mosow trials proved to be a turning point. In *Travels in Two Democracies* (1936), Wilson expressed guarded criticisms of the Soviet bureaucracy, although he did not hesitate to attack the American Communists in a more direct manner. In *The Triple Thinkers* (1938), Wilson explicitly denounced international Stalinism as a perversion of Marxism. But by the time he had completed *To the Finland Station*, he was prepared to call the whole progressive significance of the Russian Revolution into question.

Wilson joined the American Committee for the Defense of Leon Trotsky in 1936. Although he greatly admired Trotsky and in *To the Finland Station* he would restore Trotsky to his rightful place as Lenin's staunchest collaborator, Wilson made little differentiation between the organized expressions of the international communist movement in the 1930s. In his view the Communists, the Trotskyists, and the Lovestone group were all mechanical imitations of a dogmatic brand of politics appropriate only to Russian conditions. In 1937 he wrote: "As for the Trotskyists, they are often more intelligent [than the Communists], and they are freer to think and say what they think. But they suffer, also, from the Russian defects in being the obverse of the Stalinist coin. They, too, tend to turn everything into a factional issue and are likely to proceed to a literary discussion with all the polemics of a party unmasking."[77]

Wilson devoted more than six years to writing *To the Finland Station* and read more than a thousand books, including Michelet's twenty-seven volume *Histoire de France* (1833–67). In addition, he learned Russian and German in order to read the Marxist classics in the original. He also spent six months in the Soviet Union where he nearly died of scarlet fever.[78]

His efforts resulted in *To the Finland Station*, which has earned a permanent reputation as one of the most outstanding collective biographies of this century.[79] Wilson approached his subject with both the strengths and weaknesses of a literary critic and an imaginative writer. Most noteworthy was his presentation of the nineteenth- and twentieth-century socialist movement as a class-conditioned development and his vivid portraits of its leaders. The work was also unusual in its treatment of the literary styles of the principal communist theoreticians, an approach that brings to mind the writing of the German Marxist biographer Franz Mehring. Moreover, as a skillful popularizer and experienced exegete, Wilson brought many pivotal historical problems of the socialist movement to the present as contemporary burning issues.

To the Finland Station aspires to probe the central sources of Marxism and Bolshevism from the perspective that a revolutionist is one who aims to consciously intervene in the historical process but can do so only by understanding its laws. Wilson's study begins with an examination of the life and work of the French scholar Jules Michelet (1789–1894). He describes Michelet's discovery of the work of Giovanni Battista Vico, the Italian author of *Principles of a New Science* (1795). Vico was one of the first to reject the view of history as biography or as a god-directed process, preferring instead to search for its patterns of development. Michelet assimilated Vico's project and linked it to the impulse of the ideals of the French Revolution. Michelet's work is described by Wilson, who with masterful artistic skill, employs a poetic use of myth and symbols to capture and concretize abstract ideas: "Michelet succeeds in dominating history like Odysseus wrestling with Proteus, by seizing it and holding onto it through all its variety and metamorphoses."[80] Yet, as the revolutionary impetus passed from the bourgeoisie to the proletariat in the nineteenth century, historians who followed Michelet proved unable to enlarge his accomplishments. The conservative French scholars Joseph Ernest Renan (1823–92) and Hippolyte Taine (1828–93) retained aspects of Michelet's achievement, yet the dynamic thrust of their writing progressively disintegrated. Finally, the skeptical, superficial Anatole France emerged, embodying the dimming of the Enlightenment spirit altogether. "With his dressing gown, his slippers and his Larousse," he reduced the plight of humankind "to the level of entertaining conversation."[81]

The second section of *To the Finland Station* returns to the French Revolution and traces the more advanced line of thought that followed upon its achievements and limitations, the socialist movement as developed through the contributions of Gracchus Babeuf, Duc de Saint-Simon, Charles Fourier, Robert Owen, and Prosper Enfantin, among others. This phase of his study culminates in an examination of the utopian movement that flourished in the United States during the 1830s and 1840s.

The young Marx, whose portrait is most lovingly drawn by Wilson, is presented as an idealistic and romantic poet. His early lyrics disclose an affinity for the myth of Prometheus, while the depths of his consciousness are haunted by a Luciferian temperament. Wilson recalls the close relationship between the young Marx and his father Heinrich as the rebellious student follows a reckless course at the University of Bonn, which climaxes in a duel in 1836. Then, at the University of Berlin, Marx undergoes a transformation and becomes fascinated by Hegelian philosophy, the major intellectual preoccupation of the times. With much enthusiasm and a paucity of evidence, Wilson also roots Marx in the Judaic tradition, contending that he was on the path to becoming the great secular rabbi of his day—"the pride and independence, the conviction of moral superiority, which gave his [Marx's] life its heroic dignity, seems to go back to the great days of Israel."[82]

After the reactionary wave of the 1830s in Germany ruled out an academic career, Marx began writing for the *Rheinische Zeitung*, which eventually led to his crossing paths with the young Frederick Engels. Together they would perform "the thought of all great thinkers in summing up an immense accumulation of knowledge, in combining many streams of speculation, and in endowing a new point of view with more vivid and compelling life."[83]

The political and intellectual peregrination of Marx and Engels is but a prelude to Wilson's finale, in which Lenin and Trotsky bring the Marxist tradition to culmination in the twentieth century. Wilson's account terminates just prior to the Revolution of 1917, when Lenin having arrived at the Finland Station stands "on the eve of the moment when for the first time in the human exploit the key of a philosophy of history was to fit an historical lock."[84]

Wilson's anti-Stalinism had led him to a firsthand reexamination of the Marxist-Leninist tradition, but he chose to divest the tradition of its scientific basis in order to laud its moral vision. Stemming from his own inveterate alienation, Wilson felt a compatibility with the personalities of intellectual exiles such as Marx and Trotsky; accordingly, he evidenced a greater sympathy for the men than for their ideas. *To the Finland Station* is pivotally concerned with personalities and relationships, and Wilson often becomes idiosyncratic when he departs from his narrative in order to theorize.

His disdain for the scientific foundation of Marxism and his preoccupation with personalities often results in a distorted approach to various of his subjects, such as his paying far too much attention to the fascinating but rather unimportant Prosper Enfantin. It is also evidenced in his reiteration of Eastman's claim that "from the moment that they [Marx and Engels] admitted the dialectic into their semi-materialist system, they had admitted an element of mysticism."[85] But Wilson went even further than Eastman in his attempt to discredit dialectics by tracing the Hegelian triad (thesis/antithesis/synthesis) to its alleged origins in Christianity, and, before that, to symbols deriving from the male sex organs. Hegelian dialectics, Wilson claimed, has nothing to do with Plato's dialectics, which was a method of arriving at the truth by reconciling two opposite statements. Hegel's dialectics was rather a vehicle for bedevilment and oversimplification which polarized phenomena into antagonists and protagonists.

Engels was equally condemned by Wilson for deriving examples of the laws of dialectics directly from Hegel's *Logic* (1812–16). The dialectic was not a method of thought derived from objective reality but merely a rationalization of a wish. Marx desired the victory of the proletariat and therefore set up a mechanical theoretical construct that guaranteed such an outcome. Similarly, Wilson argued, the labor theory of value has no scientific basis; it was yet another result of Marx's projecting his own desires onto reality: "Karl Marx, who was not only on the side of the worker but wanted to see him inherit the earth, asserted that all value was created by labor."[86]

Wilson's inability to grasp complex totalities and his recourse to simplistic theories (such as charging Marx with psychological projection) was not restricted to his consideration of Marxism. *To the Finland Station* also provides a very meager analysis of the ideology of the Enlightenment, which is at the center of the book's first section. Even with his enormous talents, Wilson seems to have suffered from the hyperspecialization of the society in which he was educated, which locks even its professional intellectuals and most creative artists in a constrictive division of labor. Despite his aspirations toward developing a consistent historical methodology, Wilson rarely transcends his preoccupation with personalities and surface phenomena, although his imaginative insights can often lend an aura of brilliance to his work. Wilson located the source of the victorious October Revolution in the "historical imagination" rather than in the necessities of the class struggle and the comprehension of the laws of social change. This was no small error. The central claim of Marxists to political relevance is an ability to grasp the general trends of history and to project requisite means for intervening in its processes.

Wilson, following Eastman, showed little interest in Hegel, and *To the Finland Station* is deformed as a consequence. In a study intended to probe the theoretical roots of the Bolsheviks' success, Michelet is allotted disproportionate space (five chapters), while Hegel is not only maligned but barely even discussed. In assessing influences on the development of Marx's thought, Hegel rather than Michelet unquestionably deserves center stage. Moreover, far more attention should have been devoted to Feuerbach and the young Hegelians, Bruno Bauer, Moses Hess, and Max Stirner. The theory that led to the Russian Revolution was not produced simply by the transmission of moral fervor and historical imagination from one thinker to the next but through the elaboration of a program and outlook determined by scientific methods. Most important, that program was informed by a critical synthesis of classical German philosophy, French socialism, and English political economy. German philosophy and English political economy are clearly slighted in Wilson's study, apparently because of his antipathy to both the dialectical method and the labor theory of value.

It is not surprising that Wilson's rejection of dialectics is accompanied by a glib dismissal of the labor theory of value. The dialectical method was necessary to Marx's defense of the theory that labor is the source of all value. Moreover, Marx traced the development of the contradictions of capitalism to their roots in the dual nature of labor—a duality that he called "concrete" and "abstract," which stood at the very heart of the capitalist economic system. The point is that Marx might not have been able to penetrate the mysteries of capitalism without employing the dialectical method, a method that is based upon the recognition of the contradictory essence of all things and a study of their modes of development. This dismissal of the Hegelian component of Marxism may be part of the reason why the attempts of Eastman and Wilson to "modernize" Marxism simultaneously embodied strong anti-Marxist implications that unfolded progressively during the demoralization and disillusionment of the radical intellectuals during the late 1930s, although in Wilson's case it led to an eccentric leftism.

The literary and political peregrination of the *Partisan Review* from 1934 to 1939 also reflects an attempt by its editors to resolve various problems in a creative manner at the same time that the magazine abandoned certain aspects of classical Marxism. Often this contradiction was expressed through literary criticism. For example, even though the editors originally held that the modernist aesthetic advances of the 1920s were ambiguous, by 1939 Rahv began to assess them as having been overwhelmingly positive. Modern literature, he affirmed, essentially involves a dispute with the modern world. To a large degree the modern artist's introversion and privacy are necessary for survival under capitalism, because only in this way can artists defy commodity fetishism and "remain the masters instead of the victims of their products." Considering the evolution and character of the Popular Front alliance of Communist and liberal writers and their return to literary patriotism, Rahv concluded: "In view of what has happened, is it not clear that the older tradition was a thousand times more 'progressive'—if that is to be our criterion—was infinitely more disinterested, infinitely more sensitive to the actual conditions of human existence, than the shallow political writings of our latter days?"[87]

Such a view, which flourished at the decade's end, was decidedly influenced by the ambiguous impact of the Moscow trials; the *Partisan Review*'s break with Stalinism probably also implied more of a repudiation of certain aspects of Marxism than was immediately apparent at that time, even to Rahv and Phillips themselves. That the trials were a watershed for the entire decade was nowhere more eloquently revealed than in Rahv's essay "Trials of the Mind." The trials called into question the whole significance of the Soviet experiment, which had been such a powerful factor in motivating American writers to become part of the communist movement. They also had served as a trial and a test for various aspects of classical Marxist theory, and Trotsky had arisen as the great defender of Marxism-Leninism against the epigones in Moscow.

But for Rahv the trials had special significance for intellectuals—both for those who were on trial in Moscow and for those in the United States, many of whom remained silent throughout the duration. Rahv frankly admitted that despite his early questioning of Communist Party policy he was surprised and shaken by the trials, this "massacre of the firstborn of the October Revolution." Rahv's beliefs were threatened far beyond his loss of faith in the Soviet Union: "We were not prepared for defeat. The future had our confidence, which we granted freely, sustained by the tradition of Marxism. In that tradition we saw the marriage of science and humanism. But now, amidst all these ferocious surprises, who has the strength to reaffirm his beliefs, to transcend the feeling that he has been duped? One is afraid of one's fear. Will it soon become so precise as to exclude hope?"[88] Thus a process of doubt and skepticism had begun. For Rahv the trials had undermined the classical model of proletarian revolution altogether, hence his preoccupation with the alienated literary intellectual, which had always been present, reemerged stronger than ever. It had, in fact, become central in his transitory attraction to Trotsky.

Although the *Partisan Review* editors were never really Trotskyists, Trotsky's influence on them was substantial. It was scarcely a passing fad or symbol, as one recent historian has implied.[89] In 1973, F. W. Dupee reminisced that "there's no question that Leon Trotsky definitely influenced me more than any American did. Many liberal-radical intellectuals in the 1930s worshipped FDR, but I never did."[90] But Trotsky's influence was incomplete, and Phillips and Rahv in particular relied upon their own independent critical thought, reinforced by their negative experience with Stalinism, to keep their distance.

Trotsky and his ideas were a vehicle by which radical intellectuals like Phillips and Rahv, whose primary concern was literary inquiry rather than constructing political organizations, could break with Stalinism and still remain for a while within the Marxist left. Trotsky's incisive critique of Stalinism broadened their horizons far beyond their own personal experience with the Communist Party's subordination of literary judgments to political expediency. As they followed Trotsky's analysis of political events, their own modes of thought and analysis undoubtedly were affected by his polemical sharpness and historical breadth.

And above all, Trotsky personally incarnated the ideal of the revolutionary intellectual in excoriating the exploitation of capitalism, warning against the tragic degeneration of the Russian Revolution, and standing alone in Coyoacan before the world, defiant of the Kremlin's executioners. But in the view of the editors of the *Partisan Review*, Trotsky ultimately failed to build a viable political movement and paid for his failure with his life. After his death, and the start of World War II, the editors' journey away from the original goals of the 1937 reorganized *Partisan Review* was more direct and unimpeded.

CHAPTER 6

Cannonites and Shachtmanites

Men's vices, it has long been known, are for the most part bound up with their virtues.

—Lenin[1]

. . . .

PARTY LEADERS AND PARTY POLITICS

James P. Cannon (1890–1974) and Max Shachtman (1904–72) were two of the most able and important Marxists active during the Great Depression, despite the small size of the organizations that they co-led from 1928 to 1940. The American Trotskyist movement had an impact on virtually an entire generation of New York-based intellectuals, a surprising number of whom held membership in its organizations and youth groups. It also managed to break out of the confines of internal theoretical debate, playing a significant role in several major unions such as the Teamsters and the United Auto Workers, and it organized at least one major mobilization against domestic fascists in the late 1930s. Unfortunately, in recent times historians who have had little firsthand knowledge of the problems inherent in constructing a socialist organization have tended to ridicule the two founders of American Trotskyism. Cannon and Shachtman have been caricatured in score-settling autobiographies written by several spiteful ex-followers and tragically misrepresented by a number of self-proclaimed disciples.[2]

Serious, capable men, neither Cannon nor Shachtman were without their political flaws or defects of character. But the records of their organizations during the 1930s and for several decades afterward—built and sustained without the backing of any government, the support of any substantial group of union officials or "establishment" luminaries, or the financial assistance of more than a handful of maverick businessmen—testify to the power of their ideas

Herbert Solow, Albert Goldman, John McDonald, and Leon Trotsky during the hearings of the John Dewey Commission of Inquiry into the Charges Against Leon Trotsky in the Moscow Trials, Coyoacan, Mexico, 1937. (Courtesy of Cassandra Johnson)

Three snapshots from the Dewey Commission hearings. Top left: Herbert Solow and Leon Trotsky. Top right: Herbert Solow, Leon Trotsky, and John McDonald. Bottom right: John Dewey, Albert Goldman, Herbert Solow, John McDonald, and Dorothy Eisner. (Courtesy of Cassandra Johnson)

Herbert Solow. A politically astute and
charismatic journalist, Solow was a
Trotskyist in the early 1930s and later
became a respected member of the
editorial board of Fortune magazine.
(Sylvia Salmi Collection)

Herbert Solow. (Sylvia Salmi Collection)

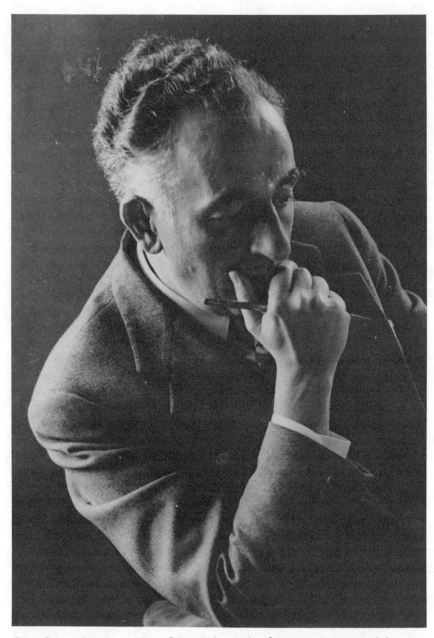

Elliot Cohen. A brilliant editor, Cohen led a circle of young writers toward the Communist Party when he was managing editor of the Menorah Journal *in the late 1920s, then toward virulent anticommunism when he founded* Commentary *in the 1940s. (Sylvia Salmi Collection)*

Tess Slesinger. Married to Herbert Solow in the late 1920s, Slesinger was author of the 1934 novel The Unpossessed, *which satirized the flirtation of the* Menorah Journal *writers with Communism. (Peter Davis Collection)*

John McDonald. A close friend of Herbert Solow, McDonald joined him in the journey from Trotskyism to Fortune *magazine. (Sylvia Salmi Collection)*

James Rorty. A poet and left-wing journalist in the 1930s, Rorty wrote scripts on "The Communist War Against Religion" for the Voice of America in the early 1950s. (University of Oregon Library)

James Rorty. (University of Oregon Library)

Felix Morrow. A protégé of Elliot Cohen in the 1920s, Morrow became a leading Trotskyist who was sent to prison under the Smith Act in the 1940s; in the 1950s and 1960s he consummated a new career as a highly successful publisher of mysticism and the occult. (Sylvia Salmi Collection)

Lionel Trilling. A member of Cohen's Menorah Journal circle in the 1920s, Trilling passed through phases of sympathy for Communism and Trotskyism before establishing his reputation as one of the foremost literary scholars in the United States. (Sylvia Salmi Collection)

Sidney Hook. A prolific writer and indefatigable polemicist, New York University philosophy professor Hook devoted much of the 1930s to an effort to build an alternative revolutionary communist movement to the official Communist Party. (Sylvia Salmi Collection)

Davis Herron. The painter was the son of a famous Social Gospel minister and the brother-in-law of Elliot Cohen. In the early 1930s he was active in radical politics on the Columbia University campus and in 1933 visited Trotsky in Prinkipo. (Sylvia Salmi Collection)

Carlo Tresca and Margaret de Silver. Tresca, an Italian-American anarchist who was assassinated in 1943, and de Silver, widow of the founder of the American Civil Liberties Union, were intimates of Herbert Solow and others in the anti-Stalinist left. (Photograph by Harry de Silver, Sylvia Salmi Collection)

William Phillips. A young writer who supported the Communist Party until 1936, Phillips collaborated closely with Philip Rahv in transforming Partisan Review into the main literary organ of the anti-Stalinist left. (Boston University Photo Service)

Max Eastman. A poet and journalist, Eastman was an early proponent of Trotskyism in the United States. (Sylvia Salmi Collection)

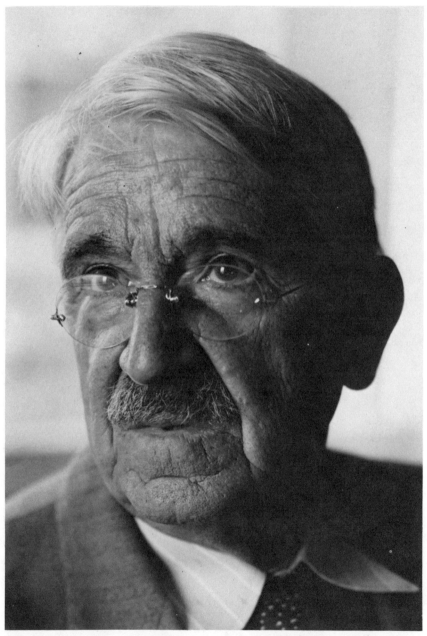

John Dewey. The most eminent philosopher in the United States, seventy-eight-year-old Dewey traveled to Mexico in 1937 to investigate the charges against Leon Trotsky in the Moscow trials. (Sylvia Salmi Collection)

Eleanor Clark. As a young writer in New York, the novelist met Herbert Solow in 1934 and in 1937 married Jan Frankel, Trotsky's secretary. (Sylvia Salmi Collection)

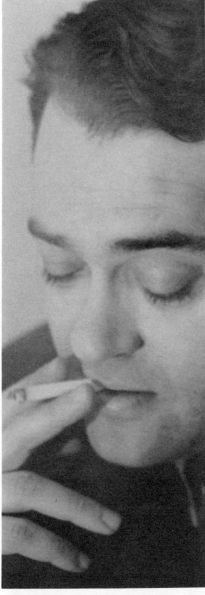

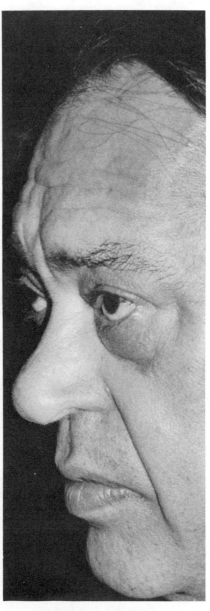

Philip Rahv. Rahv was the dynamic force behind Partisan Review, *which in the late 1930s promoted quasi-Trotskyist politics and a sympathy for literary modernism. (Betty Rahv Collection)*

Philip Rahv. (Photograph by Peter Diamadopolis, Betty Rahv Collection)

Mary McCarthy. McCarthy satirized members of the anti-Stalinist left in some of her novels and stories. (Sylvia Salmi Collection)

Charles Rumford Walker. From a patrician background, Walker was a journalist, novelist, and playwright who worked closely with the Communists and then the Trotskyists in the 1930s. (Sylvia Salmi Collection)

John Dos Passos. The novelist had many friends and associates in the anti-Stalinist left. (Sylvia Salmi Collection)

Edmund Wilson. The literary critic was a strong admirer of Trotsky in the 1930s but developed his own eclectic brand of radical politics. (Sylvia Salmi Collection)

Dwight Macdonald. An enormously gifted editor and journalist, Macdonald made the transition from Trotskyism to anarcho-pacifism in the 1940s. (Sylvia Salmi Collection)

James T. Farrell. The novelist supported the Communist Party until 1936 and then became an independent Trotskyist until the late 1940s. (Vanguard Press)

James T. Farrell. (Photograph by Charles Gekler, Vanguard Press)

Harvey Swados. The novelist was a Trotskyist in his youth and remained an independent radical until his death in 1972. (Photograph by James Salter, University of Massachusetts Library)

and their personal commitment to building a revolutionary socialist movement against overwhelming odds.

The two typified certain virtues of the Trotskyist movement, virtues shared by many of its secondary leaders and rank and file.
Cannon was an educated worker, with a good understanding of the
practical side of Marxism, a passion for organizational stability
and continuity, and a feeling for the reality of the working class
in the United States.[3] Shachtman was a revolutionary intellectual
from a plebeian background who had attended college for only a
few months (he referred to himself modestly as a "semi-skilled intellectual"). Attracted to theory, he had a colorful personality and a
flair for witty, incisive prose.[4] Both were superb orators in their
respective genres: Cannon as the popularizer of basic socialist concepts and guardian of his party's historical heritage, Shachtman as
the dazzling elocutionist, who soared through historical analogies
and political parallels, replete with quotations from the Marxist
masters. Throughout the 1930s, despite episodic feuds and mutual
suspicions, they formed an attractive team. In the decades after
their political split in the spring of 1940, the former stood fast to
his principles in a world where imminent Marxist predictions were
refuted by events or realized in unexpected ways, while the latter
progressively abandoned the convictions of his youth and political
insights of his middle years, becoming by the 1960s one of the very
"renegades" from revolutionism that he had so colorfully excoriated for years.

Cannon and Shachtman closely collaborated from the early 1920s
through their expulsion from the Communist Party in 1928, and
again throughout the 1930s, despite a near rupture in their relationship in 1932–33. In the fall of 1939, a dispute erupted in the Trotskyist organization, the Socialist Workers Party, which divided the
party into factions led respectively by Cannon and Shachtman. The
dispute involved questions relating to actions taken by the Soviet
Union in eastern Europe and also touched on internal organizational policies and practices, questions about which almost always accompany a major factional struggle. The membership of the
Trotskyists had risen to 1,520 in 1938, after the group had been
purged from the Socialist Party, and then it dropped to 1,095 in
1940, on the eve of the break between Cannon and Shachtman. In
1942, Cannon's Socialist Workers Party was at 645, and Shachtman's Workers Party was a few hundred less.[5]

In retrospect, it is clear that the real core of the 1939–40 controversy was the famous "Russian Question," that is, the class nature

of the Soviet Union. A year later Shachtman would embrace the position, initially advocated by his ally James Burnham, that a new class had come to power in the Soviet Union. Shachtman first considered the new "bureaucratic collectivist" system an improvement over capitalism, worthy of defense if assaulted from the outside, but he changed his mind after Hitler's invasion of the Soviet Union in June 1941, concluding that there was nothing worth defending in the new social order.[6] Cannon held to Trotsky's view that the Soviet Union had abolished capitalism but was blocked in its transition to socialism by the development of a bureaucratic "caste," which had established a totalitarian system of political rule much like that of the Nazis.[7] Since, unlike a class, a caste is not intrinsic to the social, structure, Trotsky made a distinction between the Soviet Union's nationalized economy, which ought to be defended and democratized, and its political regime, which required total extirpation. In the spring of 1940, Shachtman's faction split from the Socialist Workers Party to form the Workers Party, which changed its name to the Independent Socialist League in 1949 and dissolved into the Socialist Party in 1959.

Trotsky supported Cannon during the dispute, but even earlier, when interparty feuding of 1931–33 had led Trotsky to condemn both Cannon and Shachtman for "sharpening the struggle by means of impermissible organizational methods and by poisoned polemics," it was clear that he regarded Cannon as the representative of the stable proletarian base essential to the core of a Marxist party. Shachtman, for all his brilliance and personal charm, was regarded by Trotsky as a potentially unstable intellectual much like the German Trotskyist Kurt Landau and the French Trotskyist Pierre Naville, both of whom had created many problems for Trotsky.[8] Trotsky complained in 1931, for example, that Shachtman tended to be "guided . . . more by personal and journalistic sympathies than by fundamental political considerations."[9] Although Trotsky also gave Cannon a few knocks, he generally respected Cannon's tactical advice, and even deferred to his policies when it came to organizational matters, confining his disagreements to private conversations and letters.[10]

Within certain limitations, Cannon and Shachtman's personal capacities for leadership crucially affected the course their movements took, both during the time they functioned in a unified party and after their bitter separation in 1940. Therefore, information about their lives and salient personal characteristics may add a previously neglected dimension to an understanding of the numerous political disputes that filled the pages of documents, newspapers, and journals and that rang through party headquarters and halls during preconvention and convention debates of the political movement most central to the formation of the anti-Stalinist left. Although Cannon and Shachtman both had politically committed fathers and apolitical, religious mothers, and each in his youth developed a fondness for literature, they had little in common in appearance, temperament, and styles of leadership.

PORTRAIT: JAMES P. CANNON

When Cannon emerged as a midwestern leader of the pro-Bolshevik wing of the Socialist Party in 1917, he was still a gangling young man of medium height with light-brown hair, blue eyes, large ears and nose, and a heavy chin. As a leader of the Communist Party in the 1920s, he became known as a superb orator, an accomplished writer, a shrewd politician, and an American radical with vital links to earlier indigenous movements. Fifteen years later, as one of the two central leaders of the Trotskyist movement, he had grown stocky, with iron-gray hair that would become a thick, white, leonine mane by the 1950s. His body, still sturdy, had just begun to go soft, and his shoulders had acquired a slight stoop, although he retained a dignified and confident stance throughout his life. His right thumb was missing, presumably from a work-related accident in his youth.

A complex, often misunderstood man, Cannon elicited undesired adulation from some and unwarranted suspicion from others. He began a novel in his youth, wrote skillful sonnets, sang beautifully in a mellow voice, and drew upon his extraordinary memory to recite lengthy poems by Kipling and Bryant in informal company. His vices included a tendency to self-indulgence and a predisposition to procrastination. His theoretical knowledge was essentially confined to the basics of Marxism. He was a haphazard administrator, and he was capable of raging factional diatribes in a movement notorious for vitriolic polemics. Yet his self-indulgent lassitude evaporated at the first sign of a genuine party crisis, as if he had been conserving his energy in order to see the important struggles through to the end. Most significantly, he had an enviable ability to inspire talented young men and women from diverse backgrounds to devote their lives to socialism rather than conventional careers, thereby creating a nucleus of party cadres that he was able to sustain over many decades.

Some saw Cannon as the embodiment of the jovial Irish stereotype: round face, ruddy complexion, a twinkle in his eye, a gift for gab, a ready wit invariably armed with a few new jokes to tell when he got together with friends to drink and talk. Others perceived him as a stony, rude, and moody person whose physiognomy expressed inner bitterness, a man unable to manage more than a wintry smile, who projected, even in his greetings, a heavy preoccupation. To some extent Cannon's psychology will always remain a mystery, not because he was given to masks or poses, but because, like so many other socialist workers of his generation, he never revealed his inner life, believing that it was irrelevant or harmful to dwell on one's personal problems. There are several aspects of his life about which little is known. Among these are his relationship with his mother, who died in 1904 when he was fourteen and whose devout Catholicism may have influenced him to consider himself a "Christian Socialist" as late as 1911; his marriage at the age of seventeen to his thirty-year-old high school teacher, Lista Makimson; and the causes and nature of his addiction to alcohol, broken only later in life, that was so pronounced during the 1920s that some called his circle in the Communist Party (which included William F. Dunne, Clarence Hathaway, and Thomas J. O'Flaherty) "the drinking faction."

His leadership abilities were indisputable. His devotion both to his youthful vision of socialism and to the Trotskyist movement was complete. He stuck to his small outcast party by choice, for there is little doubt that his skills would have enabled him to find a comfortable position in the union bureaucracy if he had so desired. Cannon instilled in his followers a confidence in his ability to lead despite the many defeats that they suffered. Although possessed of a somewhat anarchistic personality and imbued with a plebeian anger against the injustices produced by the prevailing social order, Cannon disciplined himself in the mold of Lenin to create a team of party leaders, expertly balancing off their talents and defects.

Speaking quietly in a lecture style, with a ringing tenor voice and a Kansas-Missouri border twang, Cannon had a distinctive habit of raising his tone a bit on the second or third word of a sentence. With straightforward but colorful language he could render a complex situation clear and simple. His commanding personal presence could not help but inspire imitators, and more than one young disciple would fold his thumb into his palm when giving a public talk, unconsciously replicating the gestures that Cannon made with his thumbless right hand. But for all of Cannon's pride and self-esteem, flatterers only irked him; he preferred his authority to derive from his ideas, not his personal charisma.

Born in Rosedale, Kansas, on 11 February 1890, Cannon was the son of Irish immigrants raised in England. One grandfather had been a cabinetmaker and the other a tailor. His father, John, was a spindlemaker until a machine process eliminated his skilled trade. In the 1880s, Cannon's family immigrated first to Rhode Island and then moved to Rosedale after his father's brother Jim landed a job in a rolling mill there. When the mill failed, it was converted into a foundry where John Cannon worked as a laborer.

The Cannons were steeped in the Irish nationalist tradition of Robert Emmet; John Cannon successively identified with the Knights of Labor, the Populists, the Bryanites, and finally the socialists for whom he sold subscriptions to the *Appeal to Reason* as a member of the "Appeal Army." His son Jim went to work in a Swift meat-packing house at the age of twelve. At sixteen, Jim was propelled into Socialist Party politics by the famed Haywood-Pettibone-Moyer labor defense case. Uplifted by radical ideals and desiring some knowledge of culture, he entered the local high school when it was built a year later, despite the derisive laughter of his pool-hall buddies. When he was given the part of Marc Antony in a school performance of Shakespeare's *Julius Caesar*, his oratorical abilities caused a sensation in Rosedale. Local Democrats talked of his becoming a prominent lawyer or politician, but, before graduation, his predilection toward radical politics led him to become a traveling organizer for the Industrial Workers of the World (IWW) and a follower of Vincent St. John. At twenty-one, after hearing several lectures by Arthur M. Lewis on "social and organic evolution," the former altar boy abandoned the last vestiges of his religion.

Very active in the IWW from 1911 to 1913, Cannon left his role as a traveling organizer to become one of the "home guard" following his marriage. After the Russian Revolution he rejoined the Socialist Party and resumed his political activity, although he also took night courses at Kansas City Law School while holding down a full-time office job during the day. When his comrade, Earl Browder, was arrested for antiwar agitation and sent to prison, he left Cannon to assume the editorship of *Workers World*, a socialist newspaper published in Kansas City. Soon afterward Cannon himself was arrested for activities in support of a local miners strike. Quickly he rose to become a leading figure in the Socialist Party's left wing. Following the 1919 split in the Socialist Party, he joined the Communist Labor Party led by John Reed and Benjamin Gitlow, and, when the United Communist Party was formed in the spring of 1920, he was elected to its central committee and assigned as organizer of the party's St. Louis–Southern Illinois district. Toward the end of 1920 he moved to Cleveland to edit the *Toiler*, a party organ, and in 1921 he transferred to New York City to participate in the party's top leadership body. He lived for five or six months with Robert Minor, the *Masses* cartoonist who was married to Mary Heaton Vorse, until his wife Lista and their two children were able to join him. It was Vorse, a professional journalist, who taught him how to organize materials for speeches and articles, but for the most part his speaking, debating, and writing skills were self-taught from the time of his high school days.

After participating in an internal struggle to create a legal party as a means of ending the underground existence of the Communist movement, Cannon was elected chairman of the national committee of the Workers Party, the new above-ground organization. In 1922–23 he served on the Presidium of the Communist International in Moscow, and between 1925 and 1928 he headed the International Labor Defense, in which capacity he raised money and publicized the cases of the Centralia prisoners, Tom Mooney and Warren Billings, and the McNamara brothers. He also organized the International Labor Defense's Sacco-Vanzetti defense campaign. During these years Cannon's group of followers, including Max Shachtman and Martin Abern, formed a bloc with William Z. Foster's group against the faction led by Charles Ruthenberg and Jay Lovestone. The two factions quarreled over such issues as the party's attitude toward a labor party, trade union strategy and tactics, the location of the national office, and the nature and composition of the party leadership. During that time Cannon left Lista and began living with Rose Karsner (1890–1968), a Romanian-born party worker whose maiden name was Greenburg. A small, indefatigably energetic woman, Karsner brought stability to Cannon's life and greatly promoted his welfare. She had served as a secretary for Max Eastman's *Masses* magazine and had been married to David Karsner, a journalist and biographer of Eugene V. Debs. The Karsners were such good friends with Walt Whitman's secretary, Horace Traubel, that they named their daughter "Walta" in honor of Whitman.

During the summer of 1928 Cannon attended the Sixth World Congress of the Communist International where he received a translation of Trotsky's "Criticism of the Draft Program of the Communist International." Captivated by the program of Trotsky's Left Opposition, Cannon and his followers were expelled from the American Communist Party in October for circulating Trotsky's views. With Shachtman and Martin Abern he began publishing the

Militant newspaper immediately and founded the Communist League of America (Left Opposition) (CLA) in mid-1929. The CLA had only a hundred members at first, but it doubled its size over the next several years and began publishing a theoretical magazine, the *New International*, in 1934.

Shortly after he had been expelled from the Communist Party, Cannon entered one of the most difficult periods of his life. His wife, Lista, fell ill and died, leaving Cannon and Rose to care for two more children. Having no income or financial security, Cannon accepted David Karsner's assistance in securing a job in the circulation department of the *New York Tribune*. His drinking increased. At the same time, unflattering stories began to circulate within the newly founded Trotskyist organization that Cannon desired to retire from politics and go into the hotel business with his brother in the Midwest, that he was hostile to the younger members and opposed political initiatives, that he was kept in power by a group of "handraisers" from the party's Minneapolis branch who showed up at party plenums to vote with Cannon but never expressed their own opinions, that National Committee members who lived outside New York could not participate in shaping party policy because they never received important information and were always presented with faits accomplis, and that Cannon was contemptuous of intellectuals, antitheoretical, lazy, and opportunist. These accusations fueled a factional struggle between Cannon and his two chief lieutenants, Shachtman and Abern, which kept the party continuously at the point of a split until 1933. Then the fortunes of the Trotskyist movement began to improve. For the next six years, Cannon, Shachtman, and Abern constituted a leadership team, with Cannon continuing to hold positions as national secretary of the party and editor of the *Militant*. He later served as a delegate to the founding conference of the Fourth International in 1938 and as a member of the International Executive Committee of the Fourth International.

Cannon's admirers were adamantly pro-Cannon and his detractors equally anti-Cannon. Hence it is difficult to assess the real basis of the litany of charges against him, charges that would be frequently repeated for decades by his political opponents. At the least, the accusations seem to have been grossly exaggerated in the hothouse atmosphere of the tiny Trotskyist movement, comprised of a few hundred men and women who were hypersensitive to any signs of bureaucracy and highly conscious of the need for theoretical clarity. The claim, for example, that Cannon had contempt for intellectuals seems to be only partly true: he had a contempt for those he called "playboy intellectuals" or "dilettante intellectuals," individuals he took to be dabblers slumming in the proletarian movement. But there is evidence that Cannon held in high esteem those he considered to be undivided in their allegiance, who had cut their ties with their middle- or upper-class background to reshape their lives in service to the working-class movement. It may be accurate, as some of his critics claimed, that a few of Cannon's followers sought to conceal their own New York Jewish intellectual backgrounds by talking out of the sides of their mouths, as they imagined tough proletarians talked; but it is not clear that Cannon was responsible for that kind of behavior. It also seems likely that Cannon was noticeably uncomfortable around anyone whose dress, behavior, or speech might be associated with manners of the elite classes. This may be an excusable attitude for a worker-revolutionary, but it did mean that, if one were an intellectual, one might have felt the burden of convincing Cannon that he or she had not been brainwashed by the class enemy. Perhaps a different attitude might have enabled Cannon to maintain better relations with some of the writers attracted to the Trotskyist movement, but many of his fears and misgivings turned out to be justified. During the late 1930s and the 1940s, he witnessed a stampede to the right, a full retreat from revolutionary politics, by virtually an entire generation of intellectuals who had swung to the left in the years following 1929.

PORTRAIT: MAX SHACHTMAN

If Cannon's personality evoked varied reactions, Shachtman seems to have been much more widely regarded as a pleasant person. Few failed to admire his crackling wit, polemical style, sense of irony, robust humor, and exceptional political acumen. Five feet nine inches tall and stocky, Shachtman had jet-black hair, a thin mustache, full lips, and dark brown eyes whose penetrating gaze was perhaps his most distinctive facial feature. His tendency to paunchiness increased with age but halted in the 1950s when he suffered a coronary thrombosis. By then his hair had thinned to the point of baldness. Occasionally, like Trotsky, he sported a goatee.

A facile writer, his breezy style and razor-sharp wit animated his polemical sallies, which were grounded in an exceptional knowledge of the history of the Marxist movement. On the platform he was a devastating speaker and debater, over the years demolishing opponents ranging from Earl Browder to Alexander Kerensky. His voice was rather high-pitched, sometimes rising to a screech, but ordinarily of resonant timbre. Many remembered his passionate, resounding orations, which often lasted for hours. For some, Shachtman's extraordinary speaking style recalled a Beethoven symphony: he began slowly, building in soft whispers, and then burst forth, with powerful resonance, filling the room with a spine-tingling crescendo. For others, his sarcasm, humor, ad hominem attacks, forceful logic, and deep emotional sincerity provided high entertainment.

Shachtman's humor was notorious. He could tell stories that lasted fifteen minutes yet were still funny. Energetic and gregarious, always ready with an off-color anecdote, Shachtman sometimes prolonged a one-liner to the breaking point while savoring the dramatic moments made possible by his Yiddish accent. One exchange illustrating the vulgar side of his humor occurred amidst a 1934 debate with CLA member Tom Stamm over the proper way to relate to the new forces from Muste's American Worker's Party, with whom the CLA was fusing. Shachtman, urging moderation, pointed out that the new organization about to be born was "like a baby that has to be nursed." "Yes," Stamm replied, "but nursed at the left breast of revolutionary Marxism and not at the right breast of conciliationism and centrism." To this Shachtman retorted that he certainly favored nursing at the proper breast, "but at a breast and not at an organ of the body that's designed for other functions."[11]

There were some, however, who felt that Shachtman had cold, odd, or even light-minded sides as well. Other than his longtime associate, Albert Glotzer, few knew him intimately. Cannon welcomed Shachtman to his home many times, but Shachtman never reciprocated. Notorious for not returning borrowed books, he could be maddeningly irresponsible—not keeping appointments or completing articles by deadlines. He tended to rush to the office and dash off an article for the party's newspaper or fulfill some other assignment at the very last minute. In the mid-1930s he first broached the idea of writing a full-scale history of the Third International. Although he researched the subject throughout the 1960s, and even signed a contract with a publisher, nothing came of the project but unpublishable notes found after his death.

Shachtman's biography resembles those of many other New York Jewish radicals of his generation. He was born in Russia on 10 September 1904. To escape military servitude, his father had immigrated to the United States shortly after Max's birth. His wife and son joined him eight months later. They first lived on the Lower

East Side, then on the Upper East Side, and finally in East Harlem on 100th Street between First and Second avenues. Shachtman's father was a men's tailor and an activist in the Journeymen's Tailor's Union for many years. Before World War I he supported the Socialist Party and read the *Jewish Daily Forward*; afterward, he became pro-Communist and read the *Freiheit*.

Formed by his family and environment, as a teenager Max considered himself a socialist, but he was not especially interested in politics. While attending De Witt Clinton High School in the Bronx, he had some contact with the Young Peoples Socialist League, the youth group of the Socialist Party. He did well in mathematics, but his favorite subject was history. He came under the influence of Dr. Abraham Lefkowitz, a notorious dissenter suspected of pacifism during 1917–18, and later a leader of the teacher's union. Shachtman got a subtle infusion of socialism from Lefkowitz's classes and began to check out books from the library of the Socialist Party's Rand School of Social Science. In 1920, at sixteen, he entered the City College of New York. By that time his parents had acquired a bit of money and wanted him to become a professional; instead, he soon dropped out of college to become a full-time participant in the radical movement.

Attending public meetings at "Trotsky Square," at the north end of Central Park at 110th Street and Fifth Avenue, he tried to make contact with the underground Communist Party. When that failed, he allowed himself to be recruited by Alexander Trachtenberg, who worked at the Rand School library, into the Workers Council, a communist group that was trying to induce the Socialist Party to affiliate with the Third International. Shortly thereafter the Workers Council gave up the project and fused with the Communist Party. Shachtman joined the party, but not the youth group. However, he soon became fast friends with the youth leader Martin Abern.

Born Martin Abramowitz in 1898 in Romania, Abern had grown up in Minneapolis. He joined the IWW and the Young Peoples Socialist League at fifteen and then became a star football player at the University of Minnesota. Refusing to serve in the military during World War I on political grounds, Abern was expelled from college and imprisoned for six months. In 1920 he was elected as the youngest member of the Central Committee of the underground convention held to unite the Communist Labor Party and the Communist Party, and he was soon sent to Chicago as the national secretary of the Young Workers League.[12] A few years later, Shachtman, then nineteen and assisting Louis Engdahl on the

Daily Worker, readily accepted Abern's invitation to join him in Chicago to help put out the *Young Worker*. Shachtman spent a year in Chicago, living in the back room of the youth group's national office.

In 1923 he attended the Fifth Plenum of the Communist International in Moscow, secretly bringing back money to assist the youth organization. His own wages, when he received them, were $10 a week. In 1927 he attended the Seventh Plenum of the Comintern. But during the mid-1920s, after returning to New York City, he worked mainly with the International Labor Defense. With Cannon, whom he regarded as a model, Shachtman addressed scores of meetings in support of Sacco and Vanzetti and wrote a pamphlet on the case as well. As its editor, he turned the International Labor Defense publication *Labor Defender* into the first left-wing pictorial magazine in the United States. He also occasionally put out the *Daily Worker* when the other staff members were away.

Shachtman was well read in literature, writing in the *Liberator* on James Joyce and other literary matters with extreme confidence.[13] Although he continued to admire such Russian writers as Tolstoy and Chekhov, he became so absorbed in social theory that he virtually stopped reading fiction. During the mid-1920s he became something of a bibliophile and a collector of the classics of socialism. He also began doing translations. He was fluent in French and German, knew Yiddish well, and had a passing knowledge of Spanish. In the Trotskyist movement, Shachtman served as the principal editor of *New International* from its founding in 1934. His book *Behind the Moscow Trial: The Greatest Frameup in History* (1936) was among the first to present the facts about the purge of the Bolshevik leaders. In January 1937 Shachtman and George Novack drove to Mexico to greet Trotsky and his wife upon his arrival in Tampico, and in 1938 Shachtman presided over the founding conference of the Fourth International in Paris.

JAMES BURNHAM: FROM NEO-THOMISM TO TROTSKYISM

The intellectuals among the anti-Stalinist left during the 1930s were largely comprised of writers, scholars, and artists who either belonged to or were otherwise connected to the movement led by James P. Cannon and Max Shachtman. Some, including James T. Farrell and Meyer Schapiro, never joined but may have been closer in thought and outlook than Dwight Macdonald, who was briefly a member. Those who held membership came from diverse backgrounds and performed different roles. Those from New York City were mainly middle class or working class in origin. Many were either at the outset of careers or had been temporarily blocked in their chosen professions by the depression.

A notable exception was James Burnham, the son of a British-born executive of the Burlington Railroad, who held a B.A. from Princeton and an M.A. from Oxford. He was a member of the faculty at New York University, where he taught in the Philosophy Department. He had earned a national reputation as coeditor of the *Symposium* and coauthor of a much admired textbook, *Introduction to Philosophical Analysis* (1932).[14] Born in 1905 in Chicago, his parents were devout Roman Catholics. His brother, Philip, later became editor of the Catholic magazine *Commonweal*, and Burnham was an ardent believer until the middle of his Princeton years. He then became a literary neo-Thomist, studying with Father Martin C. D'Arcy at Oxford where he developed special interests in medieval and Thomistic philosophy. At the onset of the Great Depression, he was torn by incongruous sentiments. Propelled leftward by the economic crisis, he started reading Marx while living in the south of France during the summer of 1930; yet that same autumn he and Philip Wheelwright initiated the *Symposium* modeled after T. S. Eliot's *Criterion*.

The magazine became a forum through which Burnham tried to resolve the conflicts that plagued his intellect and emotions. The result was often confusing because, despite a calm, cool, personal presence, he asserted opinions in writing with great certainty, suggesting a maturity, wisdom, and experience far beyond his twenty-five years. At the same time, he was desperately in need of a system on which he could anchor his authoritative judgments. While his old system was crumbling, he floundered as he tried to construct a firm position that could reconcile his contradictory impulses.

Burnham's initial contributions to the *Symposium* reveal a burgeoning modernist literary sensibility that would flicker brightly several more times during the 1930s and then fade out. At the beginning of 1931, for example, he published a subtle and prophetic defense of Faulkner, followed by a favorable review of Denis Saurat's *Literature and the Occult Tradition* (1930), which endorsed poetry as the highest mode of self-knowledge.[15] Ten months later Burnham's attention was riveted on Max Eastman's translation of the first volume of Trotsky's *The History of the Russian Revolution* (1932): "Reading this remarkable book was an exciting experience; and it left me with the impression of understanding very clearly those events of which it claims to be an accurate record and a valid explanation." In a tone suggestive of a conversion experience, Burnham enthusiastically devoted his lengthy review to explicating Trotsky's cogent and enchanting method. Beginning with a thoughtful exposition of Trotsky's prose, the review flowed inexorably to the conclusion that "Trotsky's style cannot be separated from his view of history." Finally Burnham asserted that Trotsky's method should be called "dialectical materialism" in distinction to "historical materialism." Trotsky's Marxism, he noted, rather than analogizing history to the physical processes, paid greater attention to the role of the individual and the "inner necessity" of the historical process.[16] Burnham's last words constituted a cautious prediction of an American revolution during his lifetime, a revolution that would parallel October 1917 in form but not in content.

Just six months later, Burnham wrote a strange polemic called "Marxism and Aesthetics." Although he credited Marxism with some general insights into the social basis of art, he ascribed to Marxist literary criticism the very excesses and mechanistic approach that he had praised Trotsky for surpassing. Then he veered back toward religious idealism, concluding that "because I believe that Marxism is, in the last analysis, false, false in this sense— inhuman in offering an order of values not acceptable to man nor in keeping with man's nature—I do not rest my hopes for art in any esthetics it can give birth to."[17] Six more months passed and Burnham and his coeditor Wheelwright were considering politics again, this time more seriously than before, having issued their "Thirteen Propositions" on the crisis of American capitalism. Although its first several pages were taken up with caveats about how the world is far more complex than Marxists recognize, their conclusion was anticapitalist, revolutionary (in a very literal sense: they called for a "seizure of political power"), and collectivist. Moreover, they argued that the Communist Party should be written off for political and spiritual failings; a much greater sensitivity to the social reality of the United States was required, as well as an inculcation of moral values "in the tradition of western civilization."[18] Responding to criticisms of the "Thirteen Propositions" in a subsequent issue, including a charge by the *New Masses* that they were "fascist," Burnham offered some considerable modifications of his views. Not only did he wish to clarify that his admonitions against the Communists were directed only at the American Party and in no way were aimed at the Soviet Union, but he wanted to make it clear that he had really only meant to denounce certain *tactics* of the American Party. Moreover, his views had further evolved: "Now I should no longer 'denounce' at all. I still believe that most of the charges are substantially correct, but I believe also that they should be offered in such a way that the Party will be supported, not hindered; and I now understand better the objective difficulties against which the leaders strive."[19] This spurt forward in his radicalization seems to have been partly inspired by his observation of a miners' strike in southern Illinois.[20]

It seems rather remarkable that, having just announced his fidelity to the Communist Party, Burnham would be engaged only a month or two later in organizing the American Workers Party, a clear rival to the Communists. But at this point he seems to have fallen substantially under the influence of his colleague Sidney Hook. He read Hook's *Toward the Understanding of Karl Marx* and appeared to replicate the stages of Hook's relationship with the Communists, albeit in telescoped form. Indeed, his review of Ralph Fox's biography of Lenin submitted to the *New Masses* in late 1933 appeared in January 1934. All doubts and caveats now gone, Burnham declared Lenin "the chief political leader of all time" and embraced the dialectical materialist method as the only theory capable of explaining the "relation of the . . . leader to history."[21]

Burnham threw himself into the American Workers Party with great energy. Abandoning the *Symposium*, he assumed the post of the American Workers Party's national secretary and contributed a regular column to its paper, *Labor Action*. When Hook began to urge that the AWP fuse with the Trotskyists, Burnham, too, became an ardent advocate of fusion, and, when the Workers Party of the United States was formed, he took on the position of coeditor (with Shachtman) of the new organization's theoretical magazine, the *New International*. To the Trotskyist movement he brought some special qualities: a breadth of cultural knowledge, a writing style free of Marxist clichés, an aura of objectivity and impartiality, and a fresh perspective on indigenous political issues. Tall, thin, bespectacled, conservatively dressed, and a good speaker, Burnham however, displayed little warmth in personal relations. He was liked by the young party members and admired by Shachtman, but he kept aloof from the rank and file. An excellent teacher, he was asked one summer to give classes on socialism to the Trotskyists in Minneapolis but refused to give up his vacation in Connecticut. He lived at Sutton Place in New York City and would occasionally attend political committee meetings in a tuxedo because he had just come from or was en route to cocktails at the Rockefellers or at the home of some other wealthy family with whom he was friends.

Burnham wrote prolifically for the Trotskyist press, sometimes under the party name "John West" (he was also known as "Kelvin"), and played a leadership role in the organization from the start, although he resisted all proposals to leave his teaching position at New York University to become a full-time party functionary. When the Trotskyists entered the Socialist Party and Cannon moved to San Francisco for a year, Burnham and Shachtman led the Trotskyist faction from New York. After the Socialist Workers Party was founded at the end of 1937, Burnham, Shachtman, and Cannon formed its three-person secretariat, in charge of the party's day-to-day affairs. Burnham's polemical specialty was attacking reformism, whether it be the social democrats' policies regarding war, the construction of a nonrevolutionary labor party, or the Communists' new "People's Front" orientation which he lambasted in a particularly lucid pamphlet.[22] Occasionally he turned to literary criticism, reflected in his balanced assessment of Hemingway's *To Have and Have Not* (1938).

Two of Burnham's most impressive contributions were his rebuttals to Max Eastman, written in 1935 and 1938. Eastman had polemicized first against Marxist philosophy and then against Trotsky's interpretation of the results of the degeneration of the Russian Revolution. It was thus ironic that Burnham himself had serious doubts about dialectical materialism and was on the verge of launching a full-scale repudiation of Trotsky's analysis of the social nature of the Soviet Union.[23] Possessed of a classical kind of religious temperament, Burnham was in private tormented by uncertainty, but in public he could marshal a powerful, utterly logical case, as long as the basic tenets of his system retained some plausibility. Between late 1937 and 1940, however, Burnham's new system began to unravel, just as his old one had disintegrated between 1930 and 1933. Once more he was caught up in a sequence of embarrassing contradictions and rapid turnabouts until, in the mid-1940s, he settled upon a vulgar anticommunist ideology that would sustain his increasingly banal writings for the next forty years.

The central theoretical issue that prompted Burnham to forge a halting yet relentless move to the right was Trotsky's theory of the class nature of the Soviet Union. In the wake of the Moscow trials, a primary concern for the entire anti-Stalinist left intelligentsia was whether or not the Soviet Union remained a transitional society, however impeded in its progress—that is, a postcapitalist society that was originally en route to socialism under Lenin, but retrogressing under Stalin's totalitarian rule (in Trotsky's awkward terminology, "a degenerated workers' state"). If so, the Soviet Union still warranted a dual approach on the part of revolutionaries, one of support for certain features of its economic system against an assault by capitalist or fascist states, combined with an unremitting opposition to its political regime. If this approach did not obtain, then how should the Soviet Union be characterized, and what would be the political implications of that characterization if the Soviet Union were attacked—and for the prospects for socialism in general if the Soviet Union were to be something other than an impeded transitional society?

Trotsky's theory eventually would prove to be lacking in several important respects. For example, he regarded the bureaucratic ruling caste as a temporary, unstable phenomenon and was certain that it would not survive World War II. He also held the view that, because they were under the tutelage of the Soviet party, Communist parties in other countries were no longer capable, except under the most extraordinary circumstances, of abolishing capitalist societies. The problem before Marxists during the late 1930s was not only to recognize such potential weaknesses in Trotsky's theory but to realize that any alternative theories would have to be substantial theoretical achievements, not simply a reflection of despair over conjunctural events.

In the weeks prior to the founding convention of the Socialist Workers Party at the end of 1937, several intellectuals in the Trotskyist movement repudiated Trotsky's view of the Soviet Union, declaring that, if attacked, the Soviet Union merited no support whatsoever. Among them were Harry Roskolenko and Max Geltman, close friends who had combined bohemian, cultural, and political activities since the late 1920s. Roskolenko had been born Harry Roskolenkier in New York in 1907, the thirteenth of fourteen children, eight of whom died before his parents left the Ukraine.[24] He went to work in a factory at the age of nine and at thirteen shipped out as a seaman on an oil tanker bound for Mexico. In 1929 he was assigned by the Trotskyists to enter the Communist Party, where he lasted about a year and won ten new members to Trotskyism. Subsequently he devoted himself to literature, contributing poems (sometimes under the name "Ross") to the Trotskyist youth paper, the *Young Spartacus*, and even to the *Northwest Organizer*, when he visited Minneapolis during the 1934 strikes. Geltman, whose party name was "Glee," was born in 1906. A Communist in the 1920s, he wrote for the *Daily Worker* and founded a radical theater group, the "Pro Lab." A younger brother, Emanuel Geltman, also joined the Trotskyists, and an older brother joined and remained a Communist until 1956.[25] Others who agreed with Roskolenko and Geltman included Max Eastman's son, Daniel, and Attilio Salemme. Salemme walked out of the SWP right after the convention, and the rest departed over the next year. Those associated with Roskolenko and Geltman held a few discussions in a small restaurant, then went their separate ways. Roskolenko later published three autobiographies, a few volumes of poetry, a number of other books under various pseudonyms, and several travelogues recounting his adventures in various parts of the world. Geltman worked as a stage manager, and, moving ever further to the right, raised funds for the Irgun and wrote for the *National Review*. Daniel Eastman was sentenced to a conscientious objectors' camp during World War II, and Salemme became a respected painter.

As in 1933, when Sidney Hook became Burnham's stepping stone to Trotskyism, Burnham required an original theorist to provide him with a perspective that could facilitate his new period of transition. He found one in Joseph Friedman, who was born in 1910 and became a socialist at the age of fourteen. Friedman led the Communist youth movement at City College during the late 1920s and was expelled for Trotskyism in December 1928.[26] A founder of the CLA, Friedman, who used the party name "Joseph Carter," had been a special antagonist of Cannon, particularly on organizational matters, since the early 1930s. A short, thin, energetic man who usually smoked a pipe, Friedman read a few pages of Lenin every day and educated his comrades in a Socratic manner. He supported himself during most of his life by working as a clerk in a radical bookstore. For some time he had been developing a theory that the Soviet Union was neither a workers' state nor a capitalist state, an idea that he first formulated after reading Rudolph Hilferding, but one that would also come into circulation through a book called *The Bureaucratization of the World* (1939) by the Italian ex-Communist Bruno Rizzi.[27] At the December 1937 SWP convention, Friedman and Burnham differentiated themselves from Geltman and Salemme by submitting a minority proposal that challenged Trotsky's theory but which agreed with him that the Soviet Union should be defended against external attacks.[28] They also joined forces with Hal Draper, a New York City high school teacher, to present a counterresolution on what organizational principles the new party should adopt. Draper, who was born in Brooklyn in 1914, received his B.A. from Brooklyn College in 1934. He had been elected national secretary of the Young Peoples Socialist League, the youth organization of the Socialist Party, when the majority of the organization voted to ally with the Trotskyists in the fall of 1937.

After some minor concessions, the counterresolution on organizational principles was withdrawn, but Burnham had expressed many concerns about the nature of party discipline in a long letter to Trotsky several weeks earlier. Cannon and Shachtman, he complained, tended to favor a conception of the party that Gregory Zinoviev had tried to impose upon the Third International—a concept that described the party as an organization with "two disciplines," in which the leaders kept their real views and disagreements hidden from the membership. Burnham further contended that Cannon's fanatical belief that the majority's policies represented true Bolshevism meant that even small disagreements became transformed into major factional struggles because of his view that just one deviation would inevitably lead to complete revisionism. Burnham insisted nonetheless that he supported the concept of party discipline; in fact, he had advocated expelling Geltman for disloyal behavior months before the convention. But what he feared was that the current trend would culminate in a situation in which members might be excluded simply for their *views*, which put them in the situation of either having to recant their opinions or leave the party.[29] Less than two years later Burnham and Friedman would join forces with Shachtman and convince almost a majority of the SWP to support their positions on these two issues—the inadequacy of Trotsky's characterization of the Soviet Union and the nature of the party's regime—although Burnham himself had come to the verge of repudiating Marxism altogether.

SCHISM

The debate between Cannon, on one side, and Shachtman and Burnham, on the other, about what kind of party should be built, should not be downplayed, even if the dispute over the Soviet Union was the dominant issue that divided the two political currents that would become known as the "Cannonites" and the "Shachtmanites." Charges of bureaucratic abuse permeated the Marxist movement back to the time of Marx himself, when Bakunin accused him of maintaining a dictatorship over the First International. The pioneer American communists charged the right wing of the Socialist Party with using undemocratic methods against the left wing in 1919, when a minority expelled the pro-Bolshevik majority. The Trotskyists, of course, made similar accusations against the Communist Party when they were expelled in 1928, and Weisbord, Field, and Oehler likewise all claimed that the

Cannon-Shachtman leadership of the Trotskyists was undemocratic during the early 1930s. Thus it is not surprising that the Shacht-man-Burnham minority, which comprised about 40 percent of the party as well as virtually the entire youth group, should charge the Cannon majority with bureaucratic practices prior to the 1940 split.

It should be recalled, however, that Burnham had raised similar criticisms against *both* Cannon and Shachtman in 1937. Even before then, a virulent hatred of "Cannonism," which occasionally touched Shachtman because of his collaboration with Cannon, had been expressed by many longtime members including Joseph Friedman, Nathan Gould, Martin Abern, and Albert Glotzer, who all joined the Shachtman-Burnham opposition. On the other hand, for many years Cannon had regarded such types as Friedman as "petit-bourgeois" elements disruptive of the functioning of a proletarian party. During the 1939–40 struggle, Trotsky agreed that Cannon's faction was more proletarian in composition than Shachtman's, which Trotsky also characterized as "petit-bourgeois." This was certainly true in the general sense that the thoroughly working-class branch in Minneapolis completely agreed with Cannon while the more middle-class branch in New York supported Shachtman, but it was hardly accurate in every instance. Moreover, determining the value of one's political analysis according to his or her class background or occupation was as open to abuse in interparty struggles as it was in left-wing literary debates over aesthetic value. Even from a Marxist point of view, a group with a proletarian social composition is not guaranteed a political orientation that best expresses the interests of the working class. More convincing was Trotsky's association of certain of the views held by several leaders of the Shachtman faction with a generalized drift of middle-class intellectuals to the right, a phenomenon that Shachtman and Burnham themselves analyzed in their powerful essay, "Intellectuals in Retreat."[30] Indeed, ideological commerce between Shachtman and intellectuals in the anti-Stalinist left during and after the 1930s was probably more extensive than can be documented by specific texts and testimonies; to some extent Shachtman was the intellectual guru of the non-Communist radical intelligentsia, a good part of which read his *New International* and *Labor Action* in the 1940s and who in some cases borrowed and then individually developed his ideas.

The Cannon faction's assessment of its differences with the Burnham-Shachtman minority over organizational policy was summarized after the split: "The Socialist Workers Party wants an integrated, homogeneous party, based upon a common program and common methods of thought and work. The Workers Party [the name of the new organization led by Shachtman] wants an organization of diverse tendencies, a federation of factions where any anti-Marxist innovation is assured a friendly hearing."[31] Comparing the organizational practices of the Socialist Workers Party and the Workers Party, Albert Goldman, who defected from the Cannonites to the Shachtmanites in 1945, wrote that the latter "believe that it is best to avoid the creation of factions but we consider that the best method of preventing the creation of factions is to offer such freedom of discussion that serious comrades will think a long time before organizing a faction."[32] As in much of the debate that raged between the two sides against the backdrop of the early months of World War II, both positions had their strengths and weaknesses.

To some degree Shachtman's position was more in accordance with the practice of Lenin's party than Cannon's. The Bolshevik Party, which was considered a model by both Cannon and Shachtman, was a battleground of different tendencies and factions which issued their own public newspapers, at least before the civil war. Cannon's view, by his own admission, entailed a special interpretation of Leninist principles as applied to conditions in the United States. His approach to party organization was based on his first-hand experience with the paralyzing factionalism of the Communists during the 1920s and the Trotskyists in the early 1930s. He correctly believed that it was dangerous to give party members the impression that it was healthy or normal to rush to form a faction without recognizing the serious threat to party unity and efficiency such a step might entail. Cannon was deathly afraid of his party's becoming a "talkshop" rather than an instrument of action. He believed that the construction of factions, while constitutionally permissible, almost always brought a party to the point of a crisis that could lead to a split.

Shachtman's open acceptance of factions as an integral part of the internal life of a party was probably based more on a recognition of reality than on a desire for factional strife. The heterogeneity of the working class, in the sense of both life experience and levels of consciousness, as well as the political and intellectual limitations of any single leadership team, made it probable that differences of more than a passing importance would arise in a Marxist party. It followed, for Shachtman, that individuals with important differences would have to develop mechanisms that could facilitate collaboration. But Shachtman quickly found that he, too, had to draw the line somewhere, and when he did so during the first year of

his own party's existence, he was then accused by Dwight Macdonald, Philip Selznick, Irving Kristol, Seymour Martin Lipset, and
other oppositionists, of reinstituting "Cannonite" bureaucratic
methods. According to Martin Glaberman, a follower of C. L. R.
James, who was twice in the Socialist Workers Party for a total of
six years and once in the Workers Party for an equal length of time,
the Shachtman group was somewhat more democratic than the
Cannon group, but the difference was not qualitative.[33]

Concerned that the repressive conditions of impending war
would threaten his party's organizational continuity, Cannon
tended to assign the "centralist" component of democratic centralism a higher priority than did Shachtman. But Shachtman's claim
that Cannon intended to construct a "monolithic party" (a slogan
of Zinoviev's "Bolshevization" campaign of the early 1920s, which
Cannon had endorsed at the time) was unfounded. Cannon's objection to Shachtman's concept was not based on his opposition to
allowing a range of views within the party but to the form that the
expression of those views might take, especially under the pressures of war. Despite Cannon's well-deserved reputation for organizational stringency, he did offer several concessions to Shachtman's
faction at the postconvention plenum of the SWP held in the spring
of 1940: the Shachtman minority could publish its documents in
the party press; an internal written discussion could continue in a
bulletin jointly edited by both factions; and the minority faction
would be allowed to participate in the party leadership without
prejudice, as long as it refrained from publicly presenting the minority views without authorization. Cannon, of course, refused to
allow the minority to publish its own organ as the Bolsheviks had
done. In a small organization (comprised of approximately one
thousand members) with very limited resources, such a practice
might have led to the very paralysis that Cannon most feared. If
Shachtman and Burnham did have any real justification for leaving
the SWP, it must have been their deep-seated conviction that the
Cannon faction was simply not trustworthy and would not carry
out the spirit of the conciliatory proposals.

Cannon's concept of "an integrated, homogeneous party, based
upon a common program and common methods of thought and
work"—an admirable model for a smoothly humming political machine—was abstract and therefore conducive to different interpretations. Who determines what falls within or without the pale of
"common program" and "common methods"? Commonality can
be defined broadly or narrowly. It would be very difficult to draw up
precise guidelines that would prevent a leadership, either by mis-

take or malice, from deciding that some particular position was "incompatible" with their definition of the "common program and methods." If by "common program" Cannon meant agreement on broad political matters such as the Trotsky's Theory of Permanent Revolution or his view of the class nature of the Soviet Union, then there would have been no basis for the original rupture with the Weisbord, Field, or Oehler groups. But if the notion of a "common program" is taken to mean the current interpretation of such broad theories as codified in the most recent party convention resolutions, there is a danger that anyone who opposed the majority's resolutions might be accused of having a program (or method) insufficiently in "common" with the majority's positions. Indeed, it is possible that Cannon's particular attitude toward factions—formally recognizing their legality while predicting that irresolvable conflicts would ensue from them—could create a chilling atmosphere scarcely conducive to internal discussion. The creation of a faction might be perceived as tantamount to announcing a forthcoming split. Members might hesitate to organize even a "current" opposed to the party leadership for fear that such a current might be accused of "inevitably" leading to the formation of a faction that would "inevitably" precipitate a split. Nevertheless, the growth and survival of Cannon's party, while Shachtman's declined and collapsed, suggests that Cannon's powerful leadership qualities overcame whatever the potential problems were endemic in his approach. Shachtman's organization, despite its relative looseness, was unable to avoid a steady stream of splits and defections, although it should be noted that the majority of these were by individuals and groups who were abandoning a revolutionary perspective.

It thus appears that no juridical formula in itself can insure intraparty democracy by guaranteeing not only the right of members to freely debate different policies but also the ability of the organization to implement the decisions approved by its majority. Such factors as the quality of party leaders, the degree of the membership's political consciousness, and the objective political situation in which the party functions are probably more decisive, even though both constitutional guarantees protecting dissent and mechanisms for implementing policy after a decision has been made are absolutely necessary.

If Leninist organizational concepts proved to be open to a wide variety of interpretations, one might think that the question of political theory at the heart of the Cannon-Shachtman debate—the social nature of the Soviet Union—might be resolved with greater certainty in light of available empirical evidence. Had a genuinely new bureaucratic *class* come to power in the Soviet Union, or was it still a postcapitalist society impeded in its transition toward socialism—in Trotsky's terminology, a "degenerated workers' state"?

In the early 1930s Trotskyists such as Yvan Craipeau and Hugo Urbans had raised the issue of whether and if so to what extent the Soviet Union was a progressive new social order. The same debate had erupted in the American Trotskyist movement following the publication of contributions to the internal party discussion by Geltman, Burnham, and Friedman in late 1937 and by the Shachtman-Burnham minority in 1939–40. Partisans of all sides in the dispute tended to dismiss the interpretations of their opponents as ridiculous, anti-Marxist, and religious. However, such characterizations were conventional in intraparty polemic. The actual level of discussion was quite high; many of the contributions to the party bulletin were more cogently written than scholarly essays on the subject by academicians.

Trotsky himself set the tone for the debate by publishing the most forceful and coherent exposition of the question. His argument, set forth in his book *The Revolution Betrayed* (1937) and in various articles collected later in *In Defense of Marxism* (1941), derived logically from his earlier views. He had devoted a major portion of the last seventeen years of his life to fighting "Stalinism," which he defined as the political expression of a bureaucratic caste that had come to rule the Soviet Union. He conceived of this caste as a parasitic social layer that played no essential role in the context of the new property relations and forms of production established by the October Revolution. Trotsky frequently wrote about the "dual nature" of the Soviet Union and of the bureaucracy, by which he meant its contradictory character. On the one hand, the Soviet economy was based on nationalized property relations that had been established by the revolution. Trotsky believed that these nationalizations, which had been brought about by a massive, democratic workers' upheaval, were the Soviet Union's most progressive feature. If the Soviet social formation were attacked from without, the bureaucracy would most likely mobilize to defend it. On the other hand, the Stalinist bureaucracy had usurped from the workers all political power, thereby constituting a reactionary political and ideological current that was capable of functioning in a counterrevolutionary manner in the international socialist movement.

The Hitler-Stalin Pact followed by the Soviet Union's invasion of Poland and Finland in 1939–40 brought to a head the debate in the

American Trotskyist movement over this issue. Shachtman did not at the time offer an opinion on the nature of the Soviet Union, but, after the SWP split in 1940, he adopted a version of Burnham and Friedman's theory of "bureaucratic collectivism," which he modified several times during and after World War II.

In his much-debated analysis of the war, Trotsky had carefully distinguished between the reactionary aims and actions of the Soviet bureaucracy and what he considered to be the revolutionary significance of the transformation of property relations in the territories newly occupied by its armed forces. Trotsky's method had certain analogies with Marx's analysis of the French Revolution in its Napoleonic phase. Although Napoleon's dictatorship was politically counterrevolutionary vis-à-vis the original aims of the revolution, the march of his troops through Europe overturned existing feudal property relations, thereby helping to create the preconditions for the emergence of a more advanced bourgeois order. The central issue, as Trotsky and Cannon and their supporters saw it in 1939–40 was the question, Had or had not the Stalinist bureaucracy rolled back the conquests of the October Revolution in the realm of production? Because Trotsky believed that the Stalinist bureaucracy had *not* done this, he advocated the use of the slogan "Defend the Soviet Union," because he was opposed to the imperialist powers intervening in the Soviet Union to reinstate capitalist property relations. By the formula "Defend the Soviet Union," Trotsky also meant that the Russian working masses should pursue an intransigent political opposition to the Stalinist bureaucracy and its policies, which he believed disarmed the Soviet workers, rendering them more vulnerable to assault by the fascist powers and betrayal by the imperialist "allies."

The problem for the contemporary student of these historical debates is that the Soviet Union, perhaps even more than other social formations, is so complex that it is enormously difficult for a single theory, especially one formulated forty years ago in a relatively condensed manner, to explain every facet of its dynamic satisfactorily. Trotsky himself admitted at one point that the theory that held that the Soviet Union was "state capitalist" could admirably explain certain specific features of the Soviet Union. He also thought the "bureaucratic collectivist" interpretation might have some plausibility if his prediction of global revolution were not realized in the postwar period.[34] In fact, virtually every serious, well-researched, or nuanced interpretation seems to make some useful point about the nature of the Soviet Union or of Stalinism, regardless of whether the interpretation is advanced under the aegis of the theory of state capitalism, bureaucratic collectivism, or Trotsky's postcapitalist state in transition. However, the weight of contemporary scholarship—in particular, the monumental studies of the Soviet Union by Isaac Deutscher and E. H. Carr—seem to support Trotsky's "transitional" analysis as the best guide to an *overall* assessment of the Soviet Union. Moreover, adherents of the transitional-society approach, such as the Belgian Marxist Ernest Mandel, have been most successful in outlining laws of motion (economic, social, and political) peculiar to that society.

It should be noted, however, that Deutscher, as well as several others who shared his perspective, did not necessarily reach the same political conclusions as did Trotsky. Indeed, it has not been uncommon for those who agreed with Trotsky's "degenerated workers' state" theory to develop illusions about the Soviet Union, which led them to reject several of his most important conclusions: that "defense" of the Soviet Union meant only the defense of certain of the Soviet Union's residual economic features from outside attack; that the need to fight the totalitarian Stalinist bureaucracy was so exigent that it should have been sustained even while the Soviet Union was at war; that new seizures of territory by the Soviet Union should be opposed; and that one must subordinate the whole question of defense of the Soviet Union to the needs of the international socialist movement.[35] Without such qualifications, Trotsky's theory might be interpreted in such a way as to justify rather than oppose Stalinism; for example, by arguing that this or that oppressive action by the Soviet Union was necessary to defend the nationalized economy against the restoration of capitalism. Trotsky's "degenerated workers' state" theory is also problematic because its terminology can be confusing; workers have no political power whatsoever in the Soviet "workers' state." In addition, certain aspects of Trotsky's theory have never been fully developed, such as his implication that the Soviet Union was moving backward toward a restoration of capitalism as early as the mid-1930s.[36]

Burnham and Shachtman, in contrast, had failed to see any lasting progressive effects of many accomplishments of the October Revolution because of the eventual loss of political power by the workers, and this approach seems to have had an extraordinarily disorienting effect on many would-be revolutionary socialists. Burnham himself provides a dramatic example of one such outcome. At the end of the faction fight in 1940 he attended the meeting which launched the new Workers Party and then dropped a letter off with the secretary at the Workers Party headquarters to resign from the party. In the letter he stated that he really had not been a Marxist for some time and that he had no confidence in the organization he had just founded.[37] Within a year he published *The Managerial Revolution* (1941), which offered the thesis that various forms of a new postcapitalist "managerial society" now existed in the Soviet Union, in Hitler's Germany, and in the United States as embodied in Roosevelt's New Deal. The "managerial revolution" was the trend of the future. The postwar world, Burnham predicted, would be divided among the victors: Germany, Japan, and United States. Following this imaginative flight, in his essay "Lenin's Heir," that appeared in the *Partisan Review* in 1945, Burnham proclaimed the very view he had refuted so many times—that Leninism had created Stalinism. Soon after, he was advocating that the Western powers launch a preventive atomic war against the Soviet Union.[38]

Shachtman would follow a less extreme but similar course, although more slowly and painfully, and without ever openly abandoning Marxism. Near the end of his life he even invoked "Marxist" arguments to buttress his support of Richard Nixon in 1972.[39] First Shachtman modified his theory, then his politics. A year after he founded the Workers Party, Shachtman declared that the Soviet Union was a new class society but one more advanced than capitalism and worthy of defense if attacked. In this instance he was countering not only Trotsky's theory but also the view that the Soviet Union was "state capitalist," promoted by a tendency in his own organization led by C. L. R. James, a West Indian who had become a Trotskyist in England where he wrote *World Revolution* (1937). In 1938 James published *The Black Jacobins* and moved to the United States. Called "Nello," short for "Lionel," one of his middle names, he wrote under the pseudonym "J. R. Johnson" and was over six feet tall, slim, athletic, and unbelievably handsome. A speaker who could rival Shachtman and Cannon, James enthralled audiences for hours with no notes, no podium, and without hesitating on a single word.

When the Soviet Union was attacked by Germany in June 1941, Shachtman altered his views. He now argued against defending the Soviet Union on the grounds that the Soviet Union, then allied with England, was merely a partisan belligerent in an international war between two imperialisms. By the late 1940s Shachtman had declared that bureaucratic collectivism was the very barbarism that revolutionaries such as Rosa Luxemburg had warned about if the socialist revolution failed to spread. It was probably this particular analysis more than the general hypothesis about a "new class" in the Soviet Union that led him, by 1960, to give "critical support" to capitalism and imperialism as the only means of fighting the spread of the new "barbarism."

In this context Shachtman's call for revolutionary socialists to establish a "Third Camp" took on a new significance. The term had been briefly used by the Socialist Workers Party to mean a refusal to support neither the Stalinist leadership nor the capitalist powers but only genuinely independent struggles of workers and poor peasants throughout the world. In the framework of the theory of bureaucratic collectivism, however, especially its latter manifestations, the possibility of a Third Camp of any kind became illusory. The imperialist countries drove their victims into collaboration with Stalinist regimes, who doled out aid for their own reasons, thus intertwining independent nationalist movements with various shades of Stalinism. Thus the concept of a Third Camp had the potential for becoming redefined in unrealistic terms, with some of Shachtman's followers implicitly demanding that revolutionaries in the dependent nations refuse assistance from their only available ally. For Shachtman and many of his followers, the whole concept collapsed in the face of the real world of political struggle by the late 1950s.

Shachtman finally conceived a strategy for "realignment," which counseled socialists to enter the Democratic Party where they could coalesce with those within the party who were interested in fighting for "democracy." Within a short time, however, he gravitated to the right wing of the Democratic Party. He supported the Bay of Pigs invasion of Cuba, America's intervention in South Vietnam, and the decision to bomb North Vietnam, making a mockery of his onetime boast that "I will support American imperialism when hair grows on the palm of my hand!" In the 1960s he drew close to George Meany, the conservative president of the American Federation of Labor–Congress of Industrial Organization (AFL-CIO), and became an informal but important consultant to I. W. Abel and Albert Shanker as well as to such influential Democrats as Henry Jackson and Hubert Humphrey. Only a few of his followers who broke with him in 1960 remained militantly anticapitalist. In the 1972 Democratic Party primaries, those led by Michael Harrington and Irving Howe supported McGovern, but those still loyal to Shachtman backed Jackson. In the November election, Shachtman led the Socialist Party–Social Democratic Federation grouping that gave tacit support to Richard Nixon. Such a course was by no means preordained, but it was a degeneration from Shachtman's earlier practices that may well have been facilitated by Shachtman's "new class" theory of the Soviet Union. In the end, Shachtman had come to the same position as the *New Leader*, only it took him many decades longer.

Why was this the case? Unlike many others on the anti-Stalinist left who were primarily writers, philosophers, or intellectuals within the context of established institutions, Shachtman throughout the 1940s and 1950s remained the outstanding recognized leader of an organized political tendency. The existence of such an organization, as well as Shachtman's decades-long commitment to working-class socialism, was a check on the acceptance of right-wing conclusions, even for a decade after the formulation of his very disorienting "Stalinism is barbarism" thesis. It is reasonable to speculate that, even in its poorly organized, demoralized, and rightward drifting state in the 1950s, Shachtman's Independent Socialist League created a context for a voluntary but very real political and intellectual discipline. As long as the Independent Socialist League continued, those who aspired to shift their allegiance in the direction of supporting the "democratic" imperialist foreign policy of the United States had to break from the organization. Once the organized political tendency ceased to exist, the speed with which Shachtman moved to the far right of social democracy appalled not only many of his associates but even those who had previously left his group.

Thus the schism that tore apart the SWP in 1939–40 had a broader significance than might have seemed the case at the time. The positions of Shachtman and Burnham, despite the sincerity of their followers and the usefulness of some of the political points they made about various aspects of the Soviet Union and the application of Leninism to conditions in the United States, tended to parallel the evolution of the deradicalizing anti-Stalinist left as a whole. Of all the intellectuals grouped in or around the Socialist Workers Party in 1940, with the exception of a handful who remained members such as Harold Isaacs, Felix Morrow, George Novack, and Joseph Vanzler, only James T. Farrell and Meyer Schapiro agreed with Cannon and Trotsky on the issues in dispute. By 1946 only Novack and Vanzler still agreed with Cannon. The others, if they retained any socialist convictions, felt closer to the Shachtman-Burnham position on the Soviet Union, and in various ways and at different rates were traveling the same general trajectory to the right.

CHAPTER 7

The Second Imperialist War

The point is that Western imperialism as a whole, whether in its totalitarian or its "democratic" manifestations, is no longer able to serve the cause of human progress.

—A. J. Muste, 1941[1]

. . . .

THE ENIGMA OF WORLD WAR II

During and after World War II most of the New York intellectuals abandoned the revolutionary pro-working-class perspective they had earlier defended. For many, signs of their later transformation first appeared in a startling reversal of one of the most fundamental political positions they previously had held, namely, that capitalist America's entrance into World War II would not be to defend democracy or to fight fascism on principle but to attain domination of the world's economy. Until 1939 many of the New York intellectuals argued that, when the inevitable world war broke out, it would have to be politically opposed as an imperialist war. The international working class, oppressed minorities, and colonial nations all should be urged to continue their struggles for a socialist world, regardless of the war, and to eradicate fascism, permanently, by eliminating its capitalist roots.

In April 1936, for example, Sidney Hook had debated Popular Front supporter Ludwig Lore in the pages of the *Modern Monthly* on the issue of whether to support the League of Nations's sanctions against Italy for its invasion of Ethiopia. Hook argued that these sanctions would simply serve as an instrument in the hands of the great capitalist powers, England and France, to strengthen their imperialist grip over their newer rivals. Hook adamantly argued that the United States, France, and England should not be portrayed as good or progressive in contrast with such rival capitalist powers as Italy and Germany because such a comparison would obscure the imperialist economic foundation that they had in common. "Notice that bourgeois democratic France is doing in Indo-China, bourgeois democratic Belgium is doing in the Congo, bourgeois democratic England is doing in Egypt precisely the same thing which Italy wants to do in Ethiopia," admonished Hook.

Hook also insisted that it was false to depict the coming war as a "choice between fascism and bourgeois democracy." He argued that "politically, economically and culturally the real choice is between *socialism* and fascism. Those who look for a lesser evil to escape the struggle for socialism will always find one at hand, relegating socialism ... to the land of pipe dreams." Hook maintained that the primary enemy of any oppressed class is its own ruling class: "From the point of view of the working class any measure which strengthens the military arm of the state power weakens the workers in their struggle for socialism. Was this not the lesson of the social democratic debacle in Germany [in 1914] where the socialists voted military appropriations as 'defense' against the enemies of *Kultur* ... only to discover that the military machine would countenance no socialist agitation, and was used most ruthlessly against the working-class?" Hook concluded his polemic with a memorable prophecy: "Those who are diverting the labor movement from the struggle for socialism to a support for nationalist sanctions and imperialist war may live to see the suicidal consequences of their policy, i.e., the destruction of the militant working class movement."[2]

Just four years later many of the New York intellectuals carried out precisely what Hook had explicitly characterized as a "suicidal" policy. Under the pressure of popular support for the war they lost sight of its overriding class character as an interimperialist conflict, thereby ironically emulating the Communist party's Popular Front politics. To them the war was reducible to but one of its facets—a war against fascism. The monster of British imperialism —once described as the brutal master of India, much of Africa and the Mideast, and as "perfidious Albion," betrayer of the Spanish Republic—had been entirely supplanted by the image of the heroic England of the Battle of Britain.

But the reasons for the prowar positions taken by many of the New York intellectuals (among the exceptions for various reasons were Edmund Wilson, Mary McCarthy, Clement Greenberg, Meyer Schapiro, Dwight Macdonald, and James T. Farrell) have to be located to some extent in the material reality of the times, which was marked by mass pressure to conform to the government's propaganda campaign in support of the war. Much has been written about the pressure on intellectuals to conform during the postwar McCarthy period, but less often discussed is the similar kind of pressure Washington exerted during World War II.

World War II was an immensely popular war. The entire American left, with the exception of minuscule groups of pacifists and Trotskyists, enthusiastically supported it.[3] After all, the revelations of fascist atrocities were hideous beyond belief; the Jewish people were being exterminated. After Germany attacked the Soviet Union in June 1941, the issue of the very survival of the Soviet Union loomed large for those who felt that it still retained some progressive features. Radicals, above all, understood that in conflicts in the real world there is no room for fence-sitters; either one fought fascism in the concrete—that is, militarily—or one did not. These were all very powerful arguments for not simply or routinely viewing World War II, from a Leninist or Luxemburgian point of view, as a rerun of World War I.

Yet to change one's characterization of the essence of the war from that of a fundamentally interimperialist conflict to a fundamentally antifascist struggle had a logic of its own. In retrospect, there is evidence that even those who decided to give the war no more than "critical" support were unable to act in any meaningful way to sustain working-class militancy and antiracist struggles at home, or to support (even if only through propaganda and education) movements for national liberation in such colonies as India. In practice, political support for the war meant that one must subordinate the interests of the working class to those of business and government. Advocates of this position thus succumbed to the same myth of a "sacred union" based on a supraclass "national unity" that had discredited and virtually destroyed the Second International at the advent of World War I.

The clearest evidence that declaring one's political support for the American government's war effort meant calling off the struggle for socialism and placing the campaign for the liberation of oppressed minorities on the back burner can be seen in the actions of the Communist Party. After briefly opposing the war during the one-year Hitler-Stalin Pact, the Communists dubbed all wartime strikes as "treacherous." They applauded the government's imprisonment of the leaders of the Socialist Workers Party under the Smith ("Gag") Act. They denounced the "Double V" campaign of Afro-Americans for civil rights at home as well as victory abroad as disruptive. They called Norman Thomas an "accomplice of fascism" because of his concern with civil liberties on the home front, as in the case of his criticism of the internment of the 110,000 Japanese-American citizens. And they opposed the movement for national independence of people in the colonies of the Allies.[4]

That World War II posed enormous complications for traditional Marxist analyses must be acknowledged at the outset. Trotsky's own writings on the subject show considerable evolution and development through the late 1930s, especially during the last few months before his death.[5] In an 1938 article, "Lenin and Imperialist War," written in 1938, Trotsky advocated in the event of war the traditional internationalist position of "defeatism," which he defined as "a parallel struggle by the workers of each country against their own imperialism, as their primary and most immediate enemy." However, he also pointed out that fascism, the "most consistent expression" of imperialism, had taken on "a far sharper and more graphic character."[6] A few months later, responding to Palestinian Trotskyists who held that such a "defeatist" policy was inapplicable to bourgeois democratic countries at war with fascist regimes, Trotsky again defended the traditional position: "Defeatism is . . . conducting an irreconcilable revolutionary struggle against one's own bourgeoisie as the main enemy, without being deterred by the fact that this struggle may result in the defeat of one's own government; *given a revolutionary movement* the defeat of one's own government is a lesser evil."[7] Trotsky of course knew that the horrendous conditions for millions within Nazi Germany differed qualitatively from the situation in the Western bourgeois democracies, but he always evaluated societies from the viewpoint of the most oppressed sectors of the population, which included colonial peoples: "In the long run the imperialists are distinguished from one another in form—not in essence. German imperialism, deprived of colonies, puts on the fearful mask of fascism with its saberteeth protruding. British imperialism, gorged, because it possesses immense colonies, hides its saberteeth behind a mask of democracy. But this democracy exists only for the metropolitan center."[8]

A few weeks after the start of World War II, Trotsky wrote an unpublished article that tried to come to grips with the reality that revolutionary movements did *not* exist, at least as a viable alternative, in any of the bourgeois democracies. He proposed a two-stage program for the struggle against fascism: "We Bolsheviks also want to defend democracy, but not the kind that is run by sixty uncrowned kings [a reference to Ferdinand Lundberg's popular 1937 study of the American ruling class, *America's Sixty Families*]. First, let's sweep our democracy clean of capitalist magnates, then we will defend it to the last drop of blood." But a few paragraphs later he affirmed that, as long as revolutionaries were not strong enough to reorganize society on their own, they should participate militarily in the war against fascism: "This war is not our war. The responsibility for it lies squarely on the capitalists. But so long as we are still not strong enough to overthrow them and must fight in the ranks of their army, we are obliged to learn to use arms as well as possible."[9] In June 1940, at the time of the German invasion of France, he again modified his position for revolutionaries: "I will not sabotage the war. I will be the best soldier just as I was the best and most skilled worker in the factory. At the same time I will try to convince you [nonrevolutionary soldiers] that we should change our society. In court my fellow-worker would say, 'He said that he would be a disciplined soldier, that he wouldn't provoke rebellions. All he asked for was the right to give his opinion.' "[10] Finally, in an unfinished essay on which he was working at the time of his assassination two months later, he elevated such insights to a clear theoretical statement:

> The present war, as we have stated on more than one occasion, is a continuation of the last war. But a continuation does not signify a repetition. As a general rule, a continuation signifies a development, a deepening, a sharpening. Our policy, the policy of the revolutionary proletariat toward the second imperialist war, is a continuation of the policy during the last imperialist war, primarily under Lenin's leadership. . . . In this case, too, a continuation signifies a development, a deepening and a sharpening.[11]

James P. Cannon is generally regarded, by admirers and detractors alike, as a party-builder, rather than an original Marxist theoretician. Nevertheless, he responded to Trotsky's last recommendations with considerable creativity by applying classical Leninist positions to the specific conditions in the United States. In doing so he formulated what may have been the most reasonable position that revolutionary internationalists in the United States could take, given the complex realities of World War II. In a speech delivered in September 1940, Cannon acknowledged that the policies that the Socialist Workers Party had pursued before the outbreak of war in Europe were now inadequate: "We didn't visualize, nobody visualized, a world situation in which whole countries would be conquered by fascist armies. The workers don't want to be conquered by foreign invaders, above all by the fascists. They require a program of military struggle against foreign invaders which assures their class independence. That is the gist of the problem." More specifically, he rejected the two-stage theory that Trotsky had previously advocated ("the workers will first overthrow the bourgeoisie at home and then they will take care of the invaders"), because "the workers did not make the revolution in time." Instead, Cannon argued that it was now imperative that "the two tasks must be telescoped and carried out simultaneously."[12]

In a series of articles that appeared in the Socialist Workers Party newspaper, the *Militant*, Albert Goldman tried to popularize this approach. For example, in early 1941 he explained that it was untrue that the SWP did not care whether Hitler or Great Britain won the war and that the SWP certainly did not advocate the defeat of the United States. Hitler should be regarded as "the greatest enemy of the working class," he wrote, therefore it was the SWP's policy that "all those we influence must go to war and do what they are told by the capitalists." Furthermore, "we would not prevent war materials being shipped to fight Germany and Japan." Nevertheless, the SWP was fundamentally opposed to the policy of the U.S. government: "They want to protect interests; we want to transform the war into a real war for democracy." In this context "revolutionary defeatism" meant that the SWP would publish anti-imperialist propaganda and continue to wage the class struggle in the United States on behalf of the rights of workers and minorities. If a strike or antiracist struggle began to negatively affect the war effort, the blame should not be placed on the workers but rather on the capitalists, who had the resources to meet just demands. The SWP ultimately preferred that the working class should take over conduct of the war on a socialist basis, which would greatly increase the chances of victory. The rapid defeat of France clearly illustrated the inability of the bourgeoisie to lead the fight effectively.[13]

Whatever its limitations, such a policy had the virtue of neither remaining aloof from the real struggle against fascism nor abandoning revolutionary internationalist ideology and its tradition of working-class independence, as the Communist and Socialist parties had done. Goldman's statement that Hitler was the main enemy was meant to be taken seriously because American Trotskyists actually participated in the war. They understood the immediate urgency to fight against fascism, despite the refusal to give their political support to the war. The most obvious flaws in the SWP's argument were its frequent subsidiary predictions that the United States, after entering the war, would itself become totalitarian, and that liberal capitalism was simply incapable of defeating the fascist powers, even in the short run.[14]

In comparison, Shachtman's Workers Party, which had different assessments of the roles that China and the Soviet Union would play in the war, seemed considerably disoriented at the outbreak of hostilities in Europe. At first it advocated draft resistance, then, in practice, its posture toward military service was similar to the course proposed by Cannon and Albert Goldman of the SWP, even to the point of expelling draft dodgers. Shachtman's argument, however, was that a worker must go to war along with the rest of his or her class to share its experiences. In the *New International* Shachtman ridiculed Cannon's statement (while mocking Cannon personally for his lacking "the elementary equipment" to discuss fundamental theoretical questions) about "telescoping" the anticapitalist and antifascist struggles. In consonance with the Workers Party view that the SWP was moving to the right, Shachtman called Cannon's policy "a concession to social patriotism."[15] In mid-1942, Irving Howe, one of the Workers Party's most prolific journalists, defended the two-stage defeatist approach: "We are in favor of the defeat of fascism. We believe, however, that an indispensable prerequisite for that defeat is the establishment of workers' and farmers' governments in the Allied countries, which, by freeing the colonial people now enslaved by the Allied imperialist powers and extending the hand of socialist brotherhood to the German workers oppressed by Hitler, can alone effectively fight a revolutionary war to smash all forms of fascism."[16] Among the New York intellectuals, discussion over what approach socialists should take toward the war was much less substantial because only a handful still considered themselves as revolutionary internationalists. Nonetheless, the question was discussed in the pages of the *Partisan Review*.

DWIGHT MACDONALD: FROM TROTSKYISM TO ANARCHO-PACIFISM

By his own admission, Sidney Hook played a central role in persuading the *Partisan Review* editors Philip Rahv and William Phillips to revise their revolutionary internationalist position on war, a position that had been intrinsic to the magazine's outlook since its inception.[17] During the fall of 1939 a statement entitled "War Is the Issue!" was prepared by the League for Cultural Freedom and Socialism and endorsed by all the *Partisan Review* editors and a large number of its regular contributors. The statement insisted that, should the United States enter the war, "every branch of our culture would be set back for decades." The signers proclaimed that the duty of American intellectuals was to give "conscious and organized expression" to the antiwar sentiments of "the great majority of the American people." The statement's political orientation was essentially the same as the "defeatist" view advocated by the Trotskyists before 1940:

> We loathe and abominate fascism as the chief enemy of all culture, all real democracy, all social progress. But the last war showed only too clearly that we can have no faith in imperialist crusades to bring freedom to any people. Our entry into the war under the slogan of "Stop Hitler!" would actually result in the immediate introduction of totalitarianism over here. Only the German people can free themselves of the fascist yoke. The American masses can best help them by fighting *at home* to keep their own liberties.[18]

Less than two years after this firm pronouncement, two editorials appeared in the *Partisan Review*, implying the beginning of a process of differentiation among the editors. The first, "Notes on a Strange War," was signed by Dwight Macdonald, who had just completed a twenty-month sojourn as a member of the SWP and then the WP and who now considered himself to be an independent Trotskyist. His evolution had been rapid, much as it had been between 1935 and 1937 when he quickly passed from liberalism through Communism to Trotskyism.

Macdonald's organized association with the Trotskyists began after he joined the American Committee for the Defense of Leon Trotsky. He had initiated a correspondence with Trotsky during the summer of 1937 on behalf of the then reorganizing *Partisan Review*.[19] James Burnham, whom he had known from his association with the *Symposium*, encouraged Macdonald to write for the *New International*.[20] He made his debut during the summer of 1938 in characteristic fashion: he contributed the first of what would become a regular column called "They, the People," blasting the lack of response of the government and liberals to depression problems from a revolutionary point of view. In the same issue, he submitted a letter to the editors sharply criticizing an article by Trotsky defending the Bolshevik suppression of the revolt at Kronstadt naval base in March 1921. Macdonald characterized Trotsky's article as "disappointing and embarrassing."[21]

In the article Trotsky had connected the Kronstadt rebels with the future rise of the Stalinist bureaucracy, insisting that both represented groupings that had given in to the demands of the peasantry against the interests of the proletariat. The peasants had been angered by the Bolshevik's policy of "war communism" that had been necessitated by the civil war. They were especially upset by the requisitioning of their products, and they wanted to accumulate their own material goods. Examining the situation sociologically, Trotsky argued that the best elements among the original Kronstadters, the devoted proletarian communists, had gone off to fight in the civil war. Those who remained at the base were sailors with peasant ties who believed they were only on temporary assignment. Apart from whether or not it was necessary to use violence to crush the Kronstadt rebellion, Trotsky's analysis of what they represented politically was based on a class interpretation of their social origin, ties, and outlook.[22] Trotsky's essay was followed by a scholarly work by John G. Wright, who answered the claim that the Bolsheviks had provoked the Kronstadters into revolting against the government. The rebels' call on 1 March for "free elections" had been a reasonable one, but two days later they demanded "Soviets without Communists," which was a direct threat to the new Soviet society since the Communists were the stable force leading it. Wright contended that nothing significant had happened between 1 March and 3 March except attempts by the Bolsheviks to appease the Kronstadters. Thus he concluded that their first slogan was merely a tactic designed to garner broader sympathy, while the second expressed the real counterrevolutionary essence of the situation.[23]

Unfortunately Macdonald's letter failed to present an alternative analysis of the Kronstadt episode; he mainly objected to Trotsky's tone and raised hypothetical questions about the relationship between the policies of Lenin and Trotsky and those of Stalin. He missed the real weakness of the essay, which was that Trotsky's sociological analysis had little to do with what the Bolsheviks ought to have or have not done under the precise circumstances. The editors, Shachtman and Burnham, defended Trotsky's tone but did little to advance the discussion.[24] To a certain extent the discussion of Kronstadt, which during the mid to late 1930s became a hotly debated topic throughout the anti-Stalinist left, was not conducive to advancement.

The real underlying issue was the relationship of Leninism to Stalinism. Chronologically there is no doubt that the act of repression by the Bolsheviks at Kronstadt in 1921 was a forerunner of later acts of repression under Stalin. But was the essence of the repression the same, and did the former necessarily lead to the latter? There are only two ways that one might resolve the meaning of Kronstadt with any certainty. One would be to have knowledge of the "real" motives of the Bolshevik leaders at the time; the other would be to have indisputable knowledge of the "real" motives of the rebels and the exact nature of the events that occurred. Neither seems possible at this late date. But it is certainly arguable that the violent assault on Kronstadt was Trotsky's greatest blunder (Lenin had little to do with it; Zinoviev gave the orders; Trotsky, while not a participant, accepted political responsibility) and that his persistent defense of the action actually gave credence to those who saw Bolshevism as the parent of Stalinism.

The importance of the debate is captured in the following observation by Princeton political scientist Stephen Cohen: "Tell me your interpretation of the relationship between Bolshevism and Stalinism, and I will tell you how you will interpret almost all of significance that happened in between."[25] In other words, for those who see Bolshevism as the cause of Stalinism, Kronstadt provides an early example of totalitarian rule; for those who see Stalinism as the negation of Bolshevism it was either a "tragic necessity," as Trotsky put it, or an error in judgment, as Sidney Hook persuasively argued in early 1938:

> Lenin and Trotsky were indisputably guilty of harshness and brutality—as were the leaders of civil war and revolution in every country in the world (Cromwell, Sherman, etc.). This is important in evaluating the validity of revolutions and the nature of revolutionary process. But it is a far cry from this to the crimes of which Stalin has been guilty. Lenin and Trotsky justified themselves on the ground that they were only meeting harshness and cruelty on the other side—a greater harshness and cruelty. Sometimes they were clearly mistaken, e.g., at Kronstadt where I believe the differences could have been peacefully negotiated. Each case must be judged on its own merits. But only those who are opposed to any use of violence at any time by any side—like genuine Christians and Tolstoyans—have a right to a blanket condemnation of Lenin and Trotsky.[26]

In December Macdonald began contributing to the *Socialist Appeal* as well, with the same mix of praise and criticism.[27] By February 1939 he had his own column first called "Off the Record," which after April became "Sparks in the News."[28] One noticeable feature of these columns was Macdonald's lack of modesty. For example, in his 13 June 1938 column he devoted considerable space to discussing a letter he had sent to *Time* magazine and to plugging his *New International* column.[29] In the 11 July issue he explained to his readers that, although he has not yet decided to join, he had attended the recent SWP convention where he was disturbed by the sessions starting late and by the anti-New York and anti-intellectual attitudes expressed by some of the delegates.[30]

However, following the Hitler-Stalin Pact and the invasion of Poland by Germany and the Soviet Union, Macdonald felt he had a responsibility to join the SWP. He scheduled a meeting with Cannon, who suggested that he might not be a party type and accordingly might play a more valuable role as an independent. Macdonald, suspecting that Cannon was aware of his affinity for the burgeoning Shachtman-Burnham faction, became more determined to join. Once admitted, Macdonald behaved responsibly. He took on the assignment of secretary of the SWP campaign committee, which was running Max Shachtman and Lyman Paine, a former award-winning architect, for New York City Council, and he taught a class at the SWP's Marxist School on "The War Deal." In the factional debate itself, Macdonald, who assumed the party name "James Joyce," mainly read contributions to the discussion and listened. Close to six feet tall, slightly overweight, with a goatee and often sporting a blue workshirt, Macdonald had a distinctive appearance. Despite personal charm, Macdonald was not a good speaker. He spoke only once during the debate and, although he wrote several documents supporting the minority, they decided to publish only one because of his newness to the movement.[31]

With the launching of the Workers Party, Macdonald threw himself into political activity with even more enthusiasm than before; in fact, he was so bitter against the Cannon faction that he had refused to join with them in singing the "Internationale" at the close of the SWP convention. He edited the first two issues of *Labor Action*, the paper of the Workers Party, and did all the technical work for the first two issues of *New International*, of which the minority had retained control after the split. If he was depressed by Burnham's sudden departure, he may well have been inspired by Shachtman's pronouncement in the first issue of *Labor Action*: "We propose to build a party of a new kind in the American revolutionary movement: disciplined yet democratic, thoroughly internationalist yet oriented primarily not toward Russia but toward the struggle in this country, and, above all, steadfast in the fight against both warring imperialist camps and for the world-wide victory of the masses in the Third Camp."[32] Macdonald's columns and articles, as well as conspicuous advertisements for his contributions to the *Partisan Review*, appeared prominently in *Labor Action*. He filled the pages of the WP's *Internal Discussion Bulletin* and the

New International with his theoretical criticisms of the party's line.

Those of his criticisms that primarily centered on Germany tended to parallel not only those of Burnham but also those of liberals who denied the capitalist origins of fascism by insisting that it was based upon a "new class." Ironically, WP leader Albert Glotzer rebutted Macdonald's argument by claiming that he focused on "indecisive phenomena" to reach this conclusion, which was the same argument made by Trotsky in refuting the theory of a "new class" as it applied to the Soviet Union.[33] By November 1940 Macdonald's political differences were augmented by organizational grievances as well: he charged that C. L. R. James, the West Indian leader of the WP, was using his editorials in the newspaper to attack him. In turn the WP leadership charged that Macdonald was using his *Partisan Review* articles to attack the WP and demanded that Macdonald discuss his outside literary work with them.[34]

By the spring of 1941 Macdonald's charges against the WP leadership had escalated. He claimed that, without a hearing, the WP leadership had banned him from all editorial responsibilities, had denied him a reasonable amount of space to present his views in the party publications, and had been treating him as "a factional opponent; at worst, a sort of fifth-columnist from the camp of the bourgeoisie." In short, he charged that the WP leadership was now closely approximating the Cannon regime in the SWP, in which those who disagree with the leadership become "second class citizens." Finally, Macdonald offered an explanation for this development: the desertion of Burnham, combined with the unanticipated Nazi conquest of France, coming right after the split, had thrown a "great scare" into the WP leadership, causing it to retreat into "orthodoxy" and abandon everything that it had learned during the faction fight in the SWP.[35]

The WP leaders responded in kind, with a litany of charges of their own: that Macdonald had too great a sense of self-importance, conceiving of his individual relationship to the WP as that of one organization to another; that Macdonald was well aware that the WP intended to be a democratic-centralist organization, because he had witnessed a dispute between Shachtman and Burnham on the eve of the split in which it was decided that the "orthodox" positions were to be maintained; and that Macdonald wanted to be recognized as some sort of "privileged aristocrat" in the WP, free to publicly attack the party's views on the nature of fascism. While the WP leaders were hesitant to interfere with Macdonald's work on the *Partisan Review*, because they had no desire to advance a line on cultural and aesthetic matters, they thought that Macdonald's main orientation should be "to tear the hide off the renegade and backsliding 'radical intellectuals.'" Instead, Macdonald excluded the WP point of view from a *Partisan Review* symposium on the nature of fascism, and, after being criticized, announced that he was not going to write or speak for the WP, or let his name be used by the WP, until he could have things his own way.[36] Thus ended Macdonald's association with the Workers Party.

At that time, however, Trotsky's influence remained strong, as can be seen by Macdonald's assessment of Trotsky in the *Partisan Review* a few months after his assassination: "Trotsky was the one man still living whose name and prestige could have become a rallying point for a mass revolution in almost any part of the world, and especially in Russia. And even more important, as long as he lived, there was a center of revolutionary Marxist consciousness in the world, a voice which could not be frightened or corrupted into silence." Macdonald compared his feelings toward Trotsky to a parent-child relationship: "[H]e was a father to many of us in the sense that he taught us our political alphabet and first defined for us the problems to be solved, so that even when, in the manner of sons, we came to reject the parental ideas, our very rejection was in the terms he taught us." Trotsky's most significant flaw, Macdonald maintained, was that "he was a great political thinker in the sense that he took a given body of doctrine, the revolutionary Marxism of the pre-1914 period, and used it to interpret events with the greatest realism and penetration. But he was apparently incapable of examining the instrument itself, of scrutinizing with empirical skepticism the given doctrine." Specifically, "he never conceived of more than two alternatives in the Soviet Union: either progress to socialism or retrogression to capitalism."[37]

Though feeling perhaps orphaned by Trotsky's death, Macdonald, despite his common political background with Burnham, understood at once the real political direction in which the latter was headed; he sharply disassociated himself from *The Managerial Revolution* in early 1942 in a critique that predicted the right-wing direction that Burnham would soon take:

> Burnham's thesis seems to me to create at least three highly dangerous illusions: 1) by presenting the "new order" in specifically managerial-productive terms and playing down the role of the dictators, it makes it appear desirable from the standpoint of materialistic progress; 2) it greatly exaggerates the strength, the internal consistency, and the conscious plan-

ning of these totalitarian systems; 3) by presenting fascism as historically inevitable . . . and by underestimating the subjective, I venture even to say moral factors working on the other side, Burnham's theory paralyzes the will to fight for a more desirable alternative.[38]

When the debate about World War II began in the *Partisan Review* in mid-1940, Macdonald, despite his lack of party affiliation, acted as if the magazine would simply continue the quasi-Trotskyist positions adopted at its founding in 1937. His first statement on the war included an ungainly preface that presented a number of personal opinions and theories, but his conclusion remained "defeatist" in the sense that he called for "revolutionary action against the warmakers."[39]

The issue also featured an incisive but ambiguous statement by Rahv, "What Is Living and What Is Dead," originally intended to be part of a symposium on Marxism that highlighted Trotsky and others.[40] A skilled polemicist, Rahv began by differentiating himself from both "revisionists" and "diehards," then turned to a consideration of the "crisis in Marxism" provoked by the triumph of the "counter-revolution" in the Soviet Union. He concluded that while the predictions of Marxism about the ills of bourgeois society had been validated, its predictions regarding the potential of the working class as a force willing to and capable of acting to reconstruct society should, in the least, be reexamined. So scrutinized, too, should be the forms of party organization revolutionists had advocated to lead and direct the working class. He concluded with an evenhanded discussion of Marxist methodology. On the one hand, he dismissed dialectics as an unscientific but useful "source of metaphors relating to the ideas of change and transformation." Yet he also criticized the anti-Leninist writings of Max Eastman and Lewis Corey as examples of "ideological determinism" because they attributed the growth of Stalinism to its Bolshevik origins rather than to multiple historic factors. Rahv himself declared his own belief in the need to revise Marxism in order to renew and reinvigorate it; but he saw this need as being qualitatively different from the work of a "panicky fugitive" from radicalism, such as Corey, who used Marx and Lenin as "scapegoats" for the horrors of Stalinism.[41]

Rahv's article made no reference at all to World War II, but two months later it became clear that a schism had been developing among the editors. In the November–December issue Macdonald and editorial board member Clement Greenberg published "Ten

Propositions on the War." Greenberg, an aspiring artist and art critic, had been born in 1910 in the Bronx, where his father, a small shopkeeper, had become a successful manufacturer of metal goods.[42] Greenberg attended the Art Students League in 1924–25, and, a few years after graduating from Syracuse University in 1930, he obtained a job as a clerk for the Civil Service Commission. He had worked for the United States Customs Service in New York since 1937 and began contributing to the *Partisan Review* after a letter he wrote to Dwight Macdonald was expanded into his famous essay "*Avant-garde* and *Kitsch.*" His thesis was that avant-garde literature drove society forward and evaded exploitation as propaganda, while kitsch (mass culture) was easily manipulated. In 1940 he became an editor. One of his brothers, Sol, was a member of the WP, and the antiwar statement Clement Greenberg coauthored with Macdonald indicated that he, too, was much influenced by the Shachtman group. The basic critique of the prowar position resembled that of the WP. But it overemphasized two erroneous beliefs, namely, that entrance of the United States into the war would bring something close to domestic fascism and that Germany and Italy could only be defeated by workers' governments. Moreover, a description of how to combine the fight against fascism with the fight against capitalism nowhere appeared.[43]

Rahv responded with "10 Propositions and 8 Errors," a powerful polemic with an aura of practicality that was lacking in Greenberg and Macdonald's piece. Criticizing the two for their apocalyptic vision of the socialist revolution as being "just around the corner" and imperialism as "tottering on the edge of the abyss," Rahv insisted that each country conquered by fascism was thereby removed entirely from the arena of potential revolutionary action, thus virtually excluding the possibility of a socialist alternative: "Now we have reached the stage where the war will either be won by the combined might of the Anglo-American imperialism and Stalin's Red Army, or else it won't be won at all; and the military defeat of Germany remains the indispensable precondition of any progressive action in the future." In subsequent paragraphs he responded convincingly to the arguments that Roosevelt himself would introduce fascist measures to carry out the war and that the imperialist Allies were incapable of defeating Hitler.

Rahv's views were expressed from an ostensible "revolutionary Marxist" perspective; he wrote that "life is running so low in the revolutionary movement that only a top to bottom transformation, on a world scale, of our entire moral and political environment can possibly bring about its recovery. In the meantime let us not lull

ourselves with illusions about the war-aims of the bourgeois democracies on the one hand, or about the ability of the workers to
fulfill the Marxist prophecies on the other."[44]

In a brief rebuttal, Greenberg and Macdonald accurately pointed
out that, in the long run, ill consequences might follow from abandoning an independent working-class strategy in favor of relying on
Roosevelt and Churchill to lead the war against fascism, but they
also made the mistake of reiterating their own weakest point: "We
think a military victory can be achieved by the Allies only as the
result of profound changes in their present social structure, and
that these changes will add up to either fascism or socialism."[45]
Among other peculiarities, Greenberg and Macdonald did not foresee the Soviet Union's playing an important role in the war against
Hitler, possibly because the two of them subscribed to a version
of the "bureaucratic collectivist" theory that minimized the economic and social advances that had occurred in the Soviet Union
since Stalin's triumph.

Immediately following the bombing of Pearl Harbor and the entrance of the United States into the war, the five editors jointly
signed a statement declaring that, because of their differences,
"*Partisan Review* can have no editorial line on the war." Pointing
out that their magazine "cannot undertake to present the kind of
programmatic guidance one expects of a political party," they affirmed that their main task was to preserve "cultural values against
all types of coercion and repression." In this context, they assured
the readers that they would in the future still "give space to radical
. . . analysis of social issues and the war."[46]

Macdonald defended his views in two more essays, but by the
summer of 1943 a split was well under way.[47] The editors agreed
that if Rahv and Phillips could find independent support for the
magazine, they would assume full control and Macdonald would
resign (Greenberg, in the meantime, had been drafted); if not, the
magazine would be turned over to Macdonald. As it turned out,
Rahv and Phillips came up with an "angel," the wife of a high-
ranking military officer who insisted that the magazine withdraw
even further from political affairs.[48] The parting of the editors was
nearly as bitter as an interparty split. Although there was no brawl
over control of the headquarters, Dwight and Nancy Macdonald
conducted a sit-in until they were given a copy of the *Partisan Review*'s mailing list. Rahv threatened to call the police, and the
whole episode was followed by a nasty exchange in the letters
column.[49]

The only satisfaction Macdonald may have gained from the affair was that he was allowed to choose his successor on the editorial board. He selected Delmore Schwartz. Born in New York City in 1910, Schwartz had attended the University of Wisconsin but showed no interest in radicalism until he enrolled at New York University where he took courses from Sidney Hook.[50] While a graduate student at Harvard, he came under some suspicion for allegedly holding Trotskyist views, and he associated with the poet John Wheelwright, a flamboyant Trotskyist of Brahmin origins.

Schwartz had been identified with the *Partisan Review* since its reincarnation in 1937 and was the most immediately successful of the group in the literary world. Like Macdonald, Schwartz considered himself to be an anti-Stalinist Marxist, close to Trotsky. While he retained his revolutionary internationalist views during World War II, unlike Macdonald, who saw himself as a political leader, if not a one-man political party, Schwartz reserved his authoritative judgments for literary matters and was more or less content to be a fellow traveler of the Marxist wing of the *Partisan Review* circle, at least through the 1940s. In a letter responding to the more aggressive Macdonald who had asked Schwartz to speak out forthrightly against U.S. policy during the war, Schwartz stated that intellectuals were themselves impotent as the initiators of political action, especially during times of national crisis. He argued that intellectuals ought to present themselves as defenders of "culture and truth," advancing to a more overt "political stand when such a one is made possible by the movements of the well-known masses."[51]

Yet even as he dashed off lectures about the evils of private property and the fundamental sickness of American culture, which he mailed to R. P. Blackmur and others, Schwartz was filled with an awareness of the limitations of revolutionary politics as an "adequate philosophy of life."[52] This was one of the reasons that as a youth Schwartz had conjoined seemingly disparate figures such as T. S. Eliot and Trotsky, regarding each as complementary to and corrective of the other. If the sensibility of Eliot, in isolation, shaded off into reaction and anti-Semitism, Trotsky's logical purity, without countervailing tendencies, might evolve into the revolutionary madness depicted in Dostoyevski's *The Possessed*. In letters he called his "logic-chopping" philosophy professor Sidney Hook (referred to by Schwartz on occasion as "Sidney Chop") a prime example of one who lacked the salutary tensions that might result from a proper marriage of Marxism and modernism—Hook's alleged contempt for the "sacred art of poetry" horrified Schwartz.[53] Thus Schwartz was altogether too Hamlet-like to continue Macdonald's views on the war question. As the decade went on, increasing signs of Schwartz's mental instability became evident: his poetic and analytical powers deteriorated; he became more and more obsessed with job security and economic survival; and he tended to fixate on the petty jealousies of the literary life.

Macdonald went on to found *Politics* in 1944, which ran for forty-two issues. At its peak the circulation reached five thousand, and Macdonald was periodically able to convene public discussions of two to three hundred people under the aegis of the magazine. Although a one-person operation, the magazine attracted considerable support from an impressive array of writers and intellectuals who later became quite prominent, including C. Wright Mills, Daniel Bell, Hannah Arendt, Lewis Coser, Paul Goodman, and the young Irving Howe, who sometimes wrote under the name "Theodore Dryden." With these and others, Macdonald continued to debate problems in revolutionary strategy and theory until the use of the atomic bomb in 1945 threw into question for him "the whole Marxist conception of socialism as the great crown of scientific progress."[54] During these years both he and Mary McCarthy fell under the influence of Nicola Chiaromonte, an Italian-born writer who spent the war years in the United States. Chiaromonte advocated a kind of utopian socialism and was a close friend of Albert Camus.[55] Soon Macdonald came to regard himself as an anarcho-pacifist, a phase that lasted until 1949, a year after he gave up *Politics*. The Soviet blockade of Berlin convinced him that, without American military might as a countervailance, millions of people would be "betrayed" to the Soviet Union.[56] Subsequently his interest in politics diminished considerably, and in 1951 he began a fifteen-year career as a staff writer for the *New Yorker*.

MEYER SCHAPIRO: SOCIALIST INTERNATIONALIST

Of the several articles in the *Partisan Review* that addressed the question of the war, the most sensational was the debate between Sidney Hook and Meyer Schapiro that was published in 1943. The exchange grew out of a series of articles that Hook had begun on "The New Failure of Nerve." In the first article, Hook seemed to be mainly defending science and reason against the growth of religious and nonrational ideas in the work of Reinhold Niebuhr in the United States and several of his counterparts in Europe.[57] But in a second essay, "The Failure of the Left," Hook declared that scientific thinking could only be demonstrated by giving support to U.S.

government policy in World War II; he merged left critics of the war and revolutionary internationalists with the antirationalists, arguing that they shared a common "utopianism."

Hook's article was more than simply a defense of a prowar position, which was in itself a bit surprising but hardly implausible in the face of the Nazi threat. It also testified to his reconciliation with forces he had once so vigorously urged others to oppose, and it represented a repudiation of the very values by which he had lived his own life since World War I. Hook's thesis was that the appearance of a current of thought among liberal intellectuals who were struggling "to break out of our time of troubles by a faith that would serve sinners, but *also* lead to a better social order" had its parallel in the radical left: "For in its own way the political left shows just as definite a failure of nerve as the more numerous and conservative groups to which it aspires to give leadership. In virtue of its pretentious claims, its failure is even less excusable."

Hook's attack was undoubtedly directed against his one-time allies, the Trotskyists of both the SWP and the WP as well as against a few unaffiliated intellectuals such as James T. Farrell. The Communist Party was dismissed as irrelevant to the discussion because it was "little more than the American section of the G.P.U." Hook by now was regularly characterizing everyone on the left in the same kind of vulgar, dehumanizing language with which he himself had been traduced in the early 1930s by such Communist functionaries as Earl Browder and V. J. Jerome. The Trotskyists—Hook said he would not specifically name the groups because one (the SWP) was "currently being subject to unjust and foolish prosecution by the government"—should be characterized as "Platonic Revolutionists": "They worship a system of Ideas originally projected as instruments of social action. Historical experience, having long since been impolite enough to reveal the inadequacy of these Ideas, is no longer regarded as capable of exercising a veto power over them. And so they have become transformed into shining fetishes valid in their own right." In Hook's view the Trotskyists' position on the war was tantamount to "political insanity": the SWP's recently modified strategy of fighting for socialism and against fascism simultaneously should be considered "normal madness," while the WP's two-stage proposal for fighting U.S. capitalism first and fascism second was "psychopathic." Even more ludicrous were "Bohemian revolutionists" without any party commitment such as Dwight Macdonald, who made similar declarations but did little to further their views other than write for the *Partisan Review*. He briefly mentioned the Socialist Party, which, since Pearl Harbor, had been carrying out a prowar line in practice despite vague reservations on the part of Norman Thomas.

In elaborating his own views, Hook, like Rahv before him, evinced considerable skill in justifying his new orientation in a way that seemed as consistent as possible with his former Marxist values. In noticeably subdued language, he criticized right-wing socialists and liberals in the Roosevelt camp who had begun to overlook "the objective oppositions between those who are for the moment companions-in-arms"—the workers and the capitalists. Thinking of the future, he warned that "a socialist and labor movement which ideologically disarms itself when it cooperates with its opponents for a specific task, may find itself terribly disadvantaged after a purely military victory." Hook offered four recommendations to prevent this from happening: he urged socialists to continue to work for an independent labor party; to develop specific policies of their own as to how best to prosecute the war instead of rallying around Roosevelt; to resist the temptation to believe that defeating Hitler will be "a final solution to problems that were unsolved when he came to power"; and to fight the illusion that under Roosevelt the United States was in a "drift toward collectivism," thereby justifying all increases in Roosevelt's personal power. Hook observed that Roosevelt might be replaced by someone who would really turn the New Deal in a totalitarian direction, such as Vice-President Henry Wallace, who was an ardent admirer of the Soviet Union. Hook concluded by proposing that socialists support efforts to conduct the war as democratically as possible by establishing "war councils" of workers and consumers, but he simultaneously insisted that authority and respect would come during the postwar period only to those who took the lead in supporting the war effort, even as "ideological drum majors."[58]

Hook's essay was subjected to a long and detailed rebuttal by Meyer Schapiro, but at Hook's recommendation Schapiro used the pseudonym "David Merian" to protect his job at Columbia, a university notorious for having dismissed dissident faculty during World War I.[59] Meyer (originally "Meir") Schapiro had been born in Shavly, Lithuania, in 1904. His family moved to the United States in 1907, and he became a naturalized citizen in 1914.[60] His father, Nathan Menachem Schapiro, a bookkeeper in Lithuania who became a small businessman in the United States, had an orthodox Jewish upbringing but broke with religion when quite young. He had become interested in science and socialist ideas through the Jewish Socialist Bund before he left eastern Europe. As one who read constantly and widely, the elder Schapiro subscribed to the *Forward* and to the *New York Call* in New York. But his wife, Fanny Adelman, was pious and insisted that her children receive a traditional Jewish education. Eventually the two compromised by sending Meyer to a modern Hebrew school instead of a *cheder* (which emphasized teaching Hebrew by drill and repetition). Extraordinarily precocious, Schapiro learned to speak Hebrew rapidly and soon read much of the Bible in Hebrew. Although he never believed in God, he had early assimilated and retained for the rest of his life a fascination with religious concepts as expressed in history and art. He began drawing in elementary school and subsequently enrolled in evening art classes with John Sloan at the Hebrew Educational Settlement House.

Although Hebrew education and art were his main intellectual interests during his first sixteen years, Schapiro also absorbed radical politics at the Brownsville Labor Lyceum. He joined the Young Peoples Socialist League while at Boys High School in Brooklyn, where he excelled in mathematics and Latin. Although he and Felix Morrow were from the same neighborhood, they did not meet until 1920 when Morrow was invited to a party to observe a young genius with a photographic memory: the prodigy turned out to be Schapiro who performed for the guests. They continued to see each other episodically during the 1920s. Enrolling at Columbia University at the age of sixteen on a Regents State scholarship, awarded for intellectual merit, Schapiro studied with John Dewey and Franz Boas, although by special arrangement he also took drawing classes at the National Academy of Design. He received a B.A. in philosophy and art with honors in 1924, and, after being rejected by Princeton University for graduate study probably because of Princeton's anti-Semitism, he continued at Columbia for his doctorate where he specialized in the late antique and early medieval periods. A two-year Carnegie Corporation fellowship enabled him to travel for sixteen months in the Near East, Italy, Greece, Spain, and France during 1926 and 1927, and it supported him for a year while he wrote his doctoral dissertation. Returning to the United States in the late summer of 1927, he resumed a relationship with Lillian Milgram, the sister of his best friend from Brownsville; she had been a Barnard student before going on to medical school at New York University. They were married in 1928, the same year in which he completed his dissertation, "The Romanesque Sculpture of Mosaic," and soon he began a lectureship at Columbia on a one-year renewable contract at $50 a week.[61] His dissertation was presented in 1929 and it was published in the *Art Bulletin* in 1931, although he did not bother to deposit the required copies with the university until 1936, which is the date on his diploma.

Thus Schapiro began a lifelong career at Columbia. Although popular among his students, his popularity stemmed from the excitement that he inspired in his lectures, for he was often too busy to devote much personal attention to the students. He also elicited considerable resentment from many faculty members, not only because of his revolutionary politics and his Jewish background, but because of his unrestrained expression of opinions, his outspokenness, his contentiousness, and his persistency in argument. He was not promoted to associate professor until 1948. With Greenwich Village artists, however, his relations were quite the opposite; he enjoyed the company of bohemians and maintained close friendships with such disparate individuals as Whittaker Chambers and Delmore Schwartz. These associations, however, were in marked contrast to his own stable, industrious life.

In many ways Schapiro's political evolution paralleled that of Felix Morrow, except that Schapiro kept organized politics at arm's length and never joined a party or made a full-time commitment to the movement. What may have differentiated Schapiro from others who also remained aloof and may have allowed his revolutionary Marxist convictions to persist much longer was not a lack of seriousness or conviction. Schapiro was primarily devoted to something he thought more substantial than the transient realm of politics. From an early age he became committed to a concept of culture based on art, as if art were an eternal realm continuously being added to but which remained constant despite the vicissitudes of politics. Schapiro's vision was permanently fixed on this realm of art. As a kind of extension of that vision, he was a socialist in the sense that he wished well for humankind and believed that the preservation and extension of the artistic realm might best be achieved through socialism.

Through his college friendship with Lionel Trilling he was marginally connected to the *Menorah* group, and, in the early 1930s, he felt torn between a desire to commit himself wholeheartedly by joining the Communist Party and a desire to do his own work. He felt incapable of adding party responsibilities to his scholarship and teaching. He chose the latter course but retained a respect for those who chose the former. Although he was out of the city when the *Culture and Crisis* manifesto was prepared, he circulated a similar statement among architects. He also became active in the John Reed Clubs through which he published a pamphlet on public housing and was an active member of the League of Professionals.[62]

During the late 1920s Schapiro, as a friend of Chambers, followed the factional struggle in the Communist Party and, like Chambers, felt sympathy for the Lovestone group that was expelled in 1929. But also like Chambers, who went back to the Communists, Schapiro, too, felt that he could not trust the Lovestone group and that the Communist Party was the center of the movement. Although he had signed the open letter of protest in 1934, he retained strong ties to the party. In 1935 he assisted the party in gathering various kinds of information, and in 1936 he addressed the First American Artists Congress, established as part of the Popular Front. In his paper, "The Social Bases of Art," he rejected pure individualism and argued that artists should ally with the revolutionary working class.[63] Still, when the November elections came, he followed the Trotskyists' advice and voted for the Socialist Party's candidates.

From then on he worked diversely in the anti-Stalinist left. He spent a year in a key editorial role on the *Marxist Quarterly*, remaining even after the Trotskyists left. He endorsed the American Committee for the Defense of Leon Trotsky, wrote for the new *Partisan Review*, and joined the League for Cultural Freedom and Socialism. He remained a member of the American Artists Congress until the 1939 Hitler-Stalin Pact when he led a split that established the Federation of Modern Painters and Sculptors.[64] Amidst all of these activities he retained and developed his heterodox cultural beliefs: he found artistic freedom within the traditionalist restrictions of Romanesque art, and he argued that abstract expressionist art reflected the antibourgeois rebellion of the artist while simultaneously eliciting a sense of freedom from the responsive observer.[65] During the 1939–40 fight in the SWP, he followed the discussion closely, sensing that Cannon and Trotsky were more correct.

Schapiro's rebuttal to Hook, "The Nerve of Sidney Hook," however, was sui generis. It was written according to the dictates of his own perspective. Conceding no ground, he began by challenging Hook's interpretation of the term "failure of nerve," first used by Gilbert Murray to argue that the decline of rationalism in the Hellenistic age "was connected with a loss of interest in civil responsibilities and political life." On the one hand, Schapiro argued, the term made no sense when applied to Trotskyists, who were simply carrying out, in modulated form, their prewar analysis in spite of enormous pressures to change their views. On the other, when railing against unambiguously irrationalist trends, Hook had brought together too many disparate phenomena, forgetting that "the irrationalist content of contemporary arts, their motifs of anxiety and exasperation, the sympathy with the tormented, suffering, psychotic, primitive, infantile and magical, and the violent hostility to social life, and even to science, include a valid criticism of existing institutions and make us more deeply aware of the inner world of the self." Schapiro suggested that Hook was merely using the term as "a convenient label with which to discredit opponents," primarily the Trotskyists. "He taxes with failure of nerve individuals who have courageously maintained, at the risk of persecution, the same unpopular views about the war that they held before it began. At the same time he is silent about those who have abandoned the camp of socialism for a shallow and palpably false doctrine of a new managerial society." An important point of Schapiro's argument was that Hook himself had undergone a tremendous change of perspective without admitting or explaining it, and he cited a series of statements made by Hook between the fall of 1939 and 1943 to demonstrate Hook's turnabout.

Schapiro was a genuine independent, but a classical Marxist nonetheless, struggling to keep a Leninist view alive under difficult conditions. Of course, his advocacy of a working-class war against Hitler was the advocacy of a war that did not exist, even in embryo; yet the social activist must always advocate policies not yet extant for the purpose of trying to bring them into being. The conundrum of Leninism in World War II is whether such a class war was possible or would have been effective under any plausible set of circumstances. In any event, Schapiro and the other Leninists accurately predicted that the victorious allies would reestablish the same type of social formations that had originally caused the rise of fascism. They also pointed out that the "critical supporters" of the war were incapable of making significant criticisms (other than anti-Soviet ones) because serious support to a war effort by one's own nation paralyzes criticism.

Schapiro continued his allegiance to revolutionary Marxism throughout the 1940s and into the early 1950s, when he quietly shifted to left-wing social democracy. A supporter of the Workers Party and the Independent Socialist League in those years, he followed their publications and participated in a sharp debate with James T. Farrell over the political nature of the film *Open City* in the *New International*.[66] He maintained friendships with party members as well as with some lapsed Trotskyists—such as Louis and Sarah Jacobs—no longer in organizations. When James Kutcher, a member of the Socialist Workers Party who had lost both legs fighting in World War II, was fired in 1948 from his Veterans Administration position, Schapiro joined the political defense committee and participated in raising funds.[67] On 27 February 1949 Schapiro addressed a public meeting sponsored by the Independent Socialist League on "Art and the State," at which he defended the liberating impact of the Russian Revolution on the arts and also the Bolshevik cultural policies of the Lenin period.[68] As late as 1956, Schapiro addressed an Independent Socialist League forum on the Hungarian revolt.

At the time *Dissent* was founded he joined the board of sponsors and adhered to its independent radicalism until the 1960s, although he rarely contributed articles to the magazine.[69] Then, like some of the other *Dissent* sponsors, he responded negatively to the excesses of the New Left by which time he had also developed a strong attachment to Israel. Still, he never railed against the non-Stalinist left, nor did he explicitly repudiate Marxism, as did *Dissent* editor Howe. By the time his fame as an art historian had come to national attention in the late 1970s and early 1980s, his political past was so vague and obscured that the most complete biographical study of Schapiro erroneously depicted him as having moved from Communism in 1932 to the Socialist Party in 1936. This interpretation was based on Schapiro's vote for Norman Thomas that year, but support for Thomas was merely the official Trotskyist policy in connection with its temporary entry into the Socialist Party. The biography omitted entirely the fact that Schapiro considered himself a revolutionary Leninist in opposition to social democracy at least until the late 1940s.[70]

THE POLITICS OF LITERARY CRITICISM

Many of the New York intellectuals came to dismiss the reality of American imperialism during the late 1940s and the 1950s. This was due to the abandonment of their anti-imperialist position during World War II, coupled with the beginning of the Cold War and the failure of the postwar upsurge of the working class to sustain itself. Their new view was explicitly articulated in 1948 by Philip Rahv who contended that "American 'imperialism' is the bogey of people who have not yet succeeded in getting rid of their Stalinist hangover."[71]

In various forms most of the other New York intellectuals also came to embrace the very supraclass theories they had once rejected. They did so by reorganizing their thought around a cluster of key terms that began to appear increasingly in their writing: "modulation," "variousness," "skeptical realism," "moral realism," "the

imagination of disaster," "the end of ideology," and, in the arena
of political polemic, "liberal anticommunism" and "anti-anticommunism." All of these coinages were utilized to convince the intellectuals as well as their audiences that they had moved forward
rather than backward. Yet most of their "new" views about the
sociological character of the Soviet Union and the "straight-line
thesis" that Leninism automaticaly leads to Stalinism had been
stated decades earlier by the Mensheviks and other opponents of
the October Revolution. Moreover, the particular political programs they espoused for the reform of capitalism scarcely went beyond the reforms of the New Deal that they had long been accustomed to criticize from the left.

It is clear that the intellectuals' new views had not evolved in
isolation from changes in their social status. In the absence of a
viable and militant working-class pole, the intellectuals had gravitated toward the seats of power in bourgeois society. Equally important, the unprecedented economic prosperity of postwar America
had provided enormous opportunities for them to pursue careers in
the universities and in publishing, especially with the impeccable
anticommunist credentials that they had earned through their activities in the American Committee for Cultural Freedom. Even
their cultural interests became more American-centered as Rahv,
Trilling, and Dupee devoted themselves to promoting Henry James
as a home-grown modernist, while Greenberg and Harold Rosenberg secured their positions as the foremost defenders of the New
York school of abstract expressionism.

Still, the scars of alienation from American culture in the 1920s
and 1930s ran deep among those of the New York intellectuals with
profound literary sensibilities. Not all felt themselves at ease in the
new social setting. Several carried on personal rebellions through
their literary criticism. In some instances the political pressures of
the time brought peculiar results, as in the case of Philip Rahv,
who abandoned his efforts to advance a Marxist aesthetic for a dubious attachment to high modernism as the salvation of the radical
intellectual.

Rahv's whole approach to cultural modernism had always had an
ambiguous relation to Marxism, as can be seen through a comparison of his work with that of Georg Lukács, perhaps the most systematic of the Marxist critics of modernism. According to Lukács,
literature of the capitalist epoch had reached its zenith in the age of
"classical realism" (represented by the novels of Balzac and Sir Walter Scott) because writing during that period was animated by a
historical consciousness linked to the French Revolution. After

1848, however, literature had declined into "naturalism" (represented by Zola and Flaubert) in which a static, ahistorical, superficial apprehension of reality comes to mar artistic perception. Lukács's view is that modernism is a further development of naturalism, wherein an ahistorical perception of reality becomes fetishized, the distorted and subjective vision of the artist replaces objective reality, and an exaggerated preoccupation with form and technique becomes the prevailing principle of creativity.[72]

Like Lukács, Rahv prized historical insight into the nature of an epoch. Yet instead of discussing the relevance of historical materialism as a guide to understanding the social matrix in which a work of art is conceived, Rahv chose to discuss historical consciousness in the way that Nietzsche did—as "virtually a new faculty of the mind, a sixth sense."[73] Consequently there is no systematic methodology, Marxist or otherwise, present in Rahv's writings. His critical preoccupation with the ironies and tensions in modernist literature makes him a strange cousin to the school of New Criticism that began to dominate American literary criticism in the late 1940s and 1950s.

Rahv's treatment of modernism in his essay "Twilight of the Thirties," written in 1939, provides a good example of the peculiar political and philosophical direction in which one can go when one's "Marxist" interpretation of social process is more dependent on a "sixth sense" than on historical materialism. Rahv accurately argues against a mechanical attribution of the labels "bourgeois" and "proletarian" to particular schools and works of literature because they do not take into account all the factors that mediate the class origins of an artist and a work of art itself. Trotsky, he points out, analyzed the symbolist schools that flourished in Russia before the October Revolution by situating them amidst the "special role and changing status of the intellectuals" that obtained at that time.

Departing from Trotsky's analysis, Rahv then presents his own view that a central feature of modernist culture was its perception that art does not derive its value from its relation to society but that it has value "in itself." Rahv believed that even though this perception was inaccurate, it tended, under certain conditions, to encourage "the creation of moral and aesthetic values running counter to and often violently critical of the bourgeois spirit." Therefore, radicals should have an interest in supporting modernist culture because it encourages and requires the detachment of intellectuals from bourgeois society: "From *René* [by Chateaubriand] to *The Waste Land*, what is modern literature if not a vindictive, neurotic, and continually renewed dispute with the modern world?"

Further, Rahv argued that modernist literature, despite its weaknesses, was clearly superior to literature that either adapted itself to the capitalist marketplace or to the left-wing literary movement during the 1930s, which, Rahv believed, had placed itself abjectly at the service of the Communist Party. Writing at the very outset of World War II, Rahv announced that he had decided to take his stand with modernism mainly out of pessimism: "If a sufficiently organic, active, and broad revolutionary movement existed, it might assimilate the artist by opening to him its own avenue of experience; but in the absence of such a movement all he can do is utilize the possibilities of individual and group secession from, and protest against, the dominant values of our time."[74]

Thus Rahv's approach to modernism begins with a legitimate criticism of vulgar Marxist aesthetics but ends up by defining the role of the vanguard intellectual in supraclass terms, as a self-exiled "outsider," alienated and *angst*-ridden. If he and his fellow intellectuals had actually remained faithful to the program of "secession from, and protest against, the dominant values of our time," they would have ended up very differently. But the actual result was that Rahv's modernism became a mechanism for negation, for abstention and withdrawal, in regard to left-wing movements. Ultimately this version of modernism may even have provided justification for a form of cultural elitism that served as a barrier to those intellectuals who once wished to participate in the struggles of the oppressed classes.

Whatever enthusiasm the American Trotskyist movement may have had for the *Partisan Review*, it was not derived from any special attachment to modernism. In *Literature and Revolution* and elsewhere Trotsky had articulated a position, generally accepted by his political disciples, that it was dangerous to endorse any particular school or style above others and that all literary movements had dualistic tendencies. Even though Trotsky was renowned for his polemics against the "proletarian culture" movement that sought official sanction in the Soviet Union, he always had a special interest in and sensitivity to literature by workers or about working-class life.

In the United States the most important creative artist significantly influenced by Trotskyism was James T. Farrell. Although his critical writings of the 1930s and 1940s defended modernist writers against narrow-minded "philistines" of both the right and the left, he was also very concerned with fostering nonelitist literature that communicated the life experiences of the plebeian classes. This did not mean, however, that Farrell exaggerated the merit of a literary work because of the virtue of its political line or the class origin of the author. Farrell, in fact, held that the "Lost Generation" decade of the 1920s had produced a greater number of extraordinary works of literature than had the radical writers of the 1930s. On the other hand, he believed that the writers of the Great Depression decade, despite certain deformities due to the influence of Stalinism, had made unparalleled advances in terms of bringing characters, perceptions, and experiences of men and women from the working classes into the pages of American literature.[75]

In his well-known essay, "Proletarian Literature: A Political Autopsy," written in 1940, Rahv barely acknowledged this achievement. By the 1940s he had essentially transformed the *Partisan Review* into an organ of modernist high culture at the expense of other literary schools, most notably realism and naturalism.[76] Twenty years later, Rahv still adhered to this view despite the fact that modernism had lost much of its capacity as a vehicle of intellectual rebellion, especially in light of its close association with the conservative New Criticism, largely based on modernist texts. Delmore Schwartz noted the phenomenon of the incorporation of modernism in a 1958 address at the Library of Congress:

> ... the revolution in poetic taste which was inspired by the criticism of T. S. Eliot ... has established itself in power so completely that it is taken for granted not only in poetry and in the criticism of poetry, but in the teaching of literature.
>
> Once a literary and poetic revolution has established itself, it is no longer revolutionary, but something very different from what it was when it had to struggle for recognition and assert itself against the opposition of established literary authority.[77]

Confronted with what he regarded as the vulgar "new sensibility" of the counterculture of the 1960s, Rahv once more affirmed the alienated modernist as a role model for dissident intellectuals and was unable to appreciate such new, exciting, and positive developments as the growth of literature depicting the life experiences of blacks, Chicanos, and Native American Indians; challenging the sexual oppression of class society; or illuminating the rise of liberation movements in the Third World. Ironically, as Rahv drew back into a dubious mode of rebellion, a renewed interest was just emerging in the work of Marxist cultural theoreticians such as Georg Lukács and Walter Benjamin.

If the New York intellectuals initiated and won the good fight to liberate modernist culture from vulgar political coding, they were less successful in their efforts to develop a relationship between Marxism and modernism, other than housing both in the same journal for five or six years. Despite the gloss of theory that appears in the writings of the group, it is difficult to locate a sustained and consistent theoretical statement about the origins and political significance of modernism that justifies their dogged valorization of the genre above all others. Their writings never seriously answered the question of whether modernism is an authentic antibourgeois tendency or, in fact, a decadent phase in bourgeois culture. Nor did they offer a cogent explanation as to whether modernism is to be defined primarily by its experimental form or by its ideological content—or by some complex relation of the two.

By the 1940s, the New York intellectuals were partisans of more than just literary modernism; with the rise to prominence of the writings of Harold Rosenberg and Clement Greenberg, the group became known as the primary champion of artistic modernism as well. Born in New York City in 1906, Rosenberg attended City College in 1923–24 and graduated with a law degree from St. Lawrence University in 1927. By the early 1930s he was contributing to the *Symposium* on literary criticism.[78] In the mid-1930s he wrote for the *New Masses* and the first *Partisan Review* but was soon drawn to anti-Stalinist Marxism, although a brother, David, was an active member of the Communist Party. During 1938–42 he was national art editor of the *American Guides* series produced by the Works Projects Administration (WPA), and during World War II he worked in the Office of War Information as deputy chief of the domestic radio bureau. His first *Partisan Review* contributions were mainly poems and literary essays, but later he began to focus on abstract expressionism in the 1940s. In these years he and Greenberg developed the critical apparatus for rendering the new art form accessible to analytical discussion, although two earlier essays by Meyer Schapiro had pioneered the terrain.[79] Rosenberg and Greenberg differed about the importance of tradition and the significance of the painting process, but in the end their writing became so devoid of Marxism that they are now held responsible by some critics for the institutionalization of abstract expressionism in a form that blunted the very critical edge they once celebrated. By the end of the 1940s, the new style had become transformed from what originally appeared to be a vehicle of antibourgeois revolutionary consciousness to the "ornamental decoration of established society."[80]

The incomplete character of the cultural theory of the New York intellectuals is also revealed in their one-sided critique of mass culture. The writings of Dwight Macdonald, who was almost the only member of the group who deigned to talk about the subject at length and to propose a theory, present an analysis that more or less parallels the Frankfurt School view of the "culture industry" as a one-way, monolithic medium of indoctrination: "Mass culture is imposed from above. It is fabricated by technicians hired by businessmen; its audiences are passive consumers, their participation limited to the choice between buying and not buying. The Lords of *kitsch*, in short, exploit the cultural needs of the masses in order to make a profit and/or to maintain their class rule."[81]

As Jurgen Habermas and others have pointed out, this type of interpretation fails to take into account that the messages of mass culture are ultimately dependent on the way in which they are assimilated by the viewer, reader, or listener, who can respond critically as well as passively.[82] Moreover, other theorists have pointed to evidence of an emancipatory potential in mass culture through the expression of popular sentiments, longings, and hopes.[83] By and large, Macdonald's point of view was shared by those of the group gripped by modernism, who also saw "mass culture" as the vehicle by which Stalinism manipulated public opinion through the medium of the Popular Front.

The primary statement of opposition from within the anti-Stalinist left appeared in James T. Farrell's pamphlet, *The Fate of Writing in America* (1945). Farrell simply rejected the bifurcation between high culture and low culture, and other variants of the categories, as a viable method of analysis. Instead, he proposed the concept of the "commercialization of culture." Farrell perceived this commercialization as creating a struggle between the desire of the artist to present an authentic vision of the world and the desire of filmmakers and publishers to make art marketable. Marketability was achieved by adapting to what filmmakers and publishers believed to be the taste of the masses, and they achieved this marketability by using methods of standardization and repetition and by promoting already-established authors rather than new and innovative ones.[84]

During the 1940s, Edmund Wilson began to march to the beat of a drummer entirely different from that of the *Partisan Review* editors and their coterie of contributors. Wilson had been among the few who opposed World War II, although from an isolationist rather than a Trotskyist perspective. At its outbreak he simply turned in upon himself, contemplating the same problems that had concerned him during the 1920s. His major critical work of the war years, *The Wound and the Bow* (1941), elaborated on a theme from *I Thought of Daisy*—that creative genius and personal maladjustment are intertwined. In 1946, Wilson released a sexually explicit collection of short stories, *Memoirs of Hecate County*. The book sold 50,000 copies in four months before it was declared obscene by a Court of Special Session and banned. After the war he toured the ruined cities of Europe, writing a series of articles that became *Europe Without Baedeker* (1947).

By this time Wilson had altogether abandoned the search for the historical, moral imagination that he had begun in *To the Finland Station* and that he sought in such figures as John Jay Chapman and in his own father. As World War II was supplanted by the Cold War, the New Criticism with its focus on textual analysis came to power in the universities, and Wilson's critical credentials were subjected to a barrage of attacks, forcing him toward the periphery of American letters throughout most of the 1950s.

In 1958 Wilson received a notice to appear before the Internal Revenue Service to explain his failure to file income-tax returns between 1946 and 1953. This futile protest, which one admirer likened to the Copperhead resistance, netted him a fine with interest of $60,000, which Wilson, who frequently made as little as $2,000 a year during these difficult times, was unable to pay.[85] He responded with a controversial indictment of the U.S. government, *The Cold War and the Income Tax* (1963). A moralistic tract with some reactionary implications, the book described the United States as "self-intoxicated, homicidal and menacing."[86] Wilson charged the government with committing many crimes ranging from executing the Rosenbergs to conducting biological warfare. He declared, "I have finally come to feel that this country, whether or not I continue to live in it, is no longer any place for me."[87] This declaration was actually the capstone of a long-since consummated process. In the 1950s Wilson had begun to spend an increasing amount of time in Talcottville, New York, in his old family home, which his father, Edmund Wilson, Sr., had used as a retreat after he began suffering from mental illness in his early thirties. At the same age, Edmund Wilson, Jr., had also suffered a severe nervous breakdown.

Wilson no longer concerned himself with the central political or cultural questions of American life. His best work centered around his family, himself, and the American past. His literary criticism discussed little-known or insignificant writers, while he ignored the most important contemporary writers: Albert Camus, Samuel Beckett, Jean Genet, Albert Moravia, Günter Grass, the work of the later Faulkner, Saul Bellow, the French *nouveau roman*, and others. Cloistered in his "pocket of the past," as he called Talcottville, Wilson increasingly resembled a modern Nathaniel Hawthorne, rejecting the beliefs of his ancestors yet eternally ensnared by their conflicts. *Patriotic Gore* (1962), despite its literary merits, carried Wilson's search for his roots in the American past almost into the realm of absurdity, with its idealization of Alexander Stephens, vice-president of the Confederacy under Jefferson Davis, and the antebellum South.

In the spring of 1965, Wilson's name appeared with six hundred writers, editors, painters, sculptors, and actors on a full-page advertisement entitled "End Your Silence," published in the Sunday *New York Times*.[88] The text denounced the interference of the U.S. government in the affairs of Vietnam and the Dominican Republic. Yet this protest was only a faint echo of Wilson's revolutionary socialist past. He had already traveled to the outer reaches of individualism. He now promulgated a mélange of ideas that combined pacifism with a view of war as a product of biological determinism.[89]

Wilson's literary reputation, however, was significantly restored during the 1960s. Despite his crotchety antagonism toward the universities and his rancorous attacks on government bureaucracy, Wilson was again read in academe and was awarded several honors. In old age he was hallowed as a Diogenes of American letters by some, while others regarded him as a literary curmudgeon. With the resurgence of social consciousness in the 1960s and 1970s, it appeared that Wilson might be remembered not so much for his enervating works of disillusionment and frustration as for the three masterpieces of the Red Decade: *Axel's Castle*, *The American Jitters*, and *To the Finland Station*.

Refusing for eccentric reasons to permit the insertion of a pacemaker to assist his heart, Wilson died in the spring of 1972. An echo reverberated from his revolutionary past even as the sand was being shoveled over his ashes in the grave at Wellfleet on Cape Cod. The funeral oration was delivered by Charles Rumford Walker, a comrade of those many battles that Wilson fought long ago as a Communist sympathizer, as a partisan of the anti-Stalinist left, and as a literary radical who sought to direct his scholarship and cultural sensibility in service to the humane cause of social emancipation.[90]

CHAPTER 8

The New York Intellectuals in Fiction

All through life, mind
limps after reality.

—Leon Trotsky,
*Literature and
Revolution*[1]

. . . .

LITERATURE AND IDEOLOGY

By the end of World War II the deradicalized New York intellectuals
had established a distinct tradition in culture and politics. They
had entered the mid-1930s as dissident revolutionaries influenced
by Leon Trotsky; as universalists and internationalists in spite of
(or, perhaps in some cases, because of) the Jewish backgrounds of
many; and as partisans of modernism, which they had embraced as
an avant-garde cultural rebellion against the whole of bourgeois society. By the later 1940s, they had moved politically (and uneven-
ly) away from their distinctive current of communism toward an
equally distinctive current of anticommunism, although a few who
had remained opposed to World War II—such as Irving Howe, Meyer
Schapiro, Mary McCarthy, Edmund Wilson, and Dwight Macdonald—did not become as deradicalized as the others. In cultural orientation they had drawn back from a perception of modernism as a
means of sweeping aside bourgeois falsehood and hypocrisy in alliance with the proletarian revolution. In fact, by the 1950s, the impact of avant-garde literature in America had been significantly
tamed. This change was due to the emergence of academic modernism at the center of the elite culture of the intellectual establishment, in the universities and in publishing circles, a development
in which some of the New York intellectuals themselves played an
important role.

The 1940s is in many ways the critical decade in the transformation of the New York intellectuals. Most of the writers advocated
the need for an individualistic regeneration different from their for-

mer program of social action based on a class analysis of society. However, as individuals their respective trajectories varied markedly. The evolution of writers such as Mary McCarthy and Edmund Wilson signified a genuine discouragement with what they considered to be outmoded Marxist strategies as they moved toward what would be a phase of erratic and personalized dissidence. The course of writers such as Lionel Trilling turned to what appeared to be individualism but was part of a larger project: the construction of a "New Liberalism" that enshrined anticommunism as one of its highest principles. In the 1950s the political practice of those who took Trilling's course would be reflected in part by the activities of the American Committee for Cultural Freedom. The fiction of these and other New York intellectuals written during the 1940s constitutes a literary record of their complex ideological migration.

Virtually all of the imaginative writing by the New York intellectuals is unambiguously political in its intent, a point sometimes missed by cultural historians. Some suggest that the New York intellectuals disdained the Communist Party's "proletarian" literature movement because of their desire to depoliticize art or else ingenuously accept at face value the many declamations of the New York intellectuals against the evils of ideology. Lionel Trilling states forthrightly in the 1975 introduction to his *The Middle of the Journey* (1947) that the book was largely intended as a political intervention: "From my first conception of it, my story was committed to history—it was to draw out some of the moral and intellectual implications of the powerful attraction to Communism felt by a considerable part of the American intellectual class during the Thirties and Forties."[2]

In addition, during the 1930s and after, several of the New York intellectuals claimed that imaginative literature might play a special role in exploring and validating political ideology. For example, in his influential 1939 essay, "Proletarian Literature: A Political Autopsy," Philip Rahv argued as follows:

> There are certain forms of demagogy, however, which a medium as palpable as faction—unless it degenerates to the level of pulp propaganda—excludes by its very nature. Thus the media of art, if only by that fact alone, prove their superior humanity to the media of politics. The kind of casuistry which may easily pass for truth within the pseudo-context of a political speech or editorial, will be exposed in all its emptiness once it is injected into the real context of a living experience,

such as the art of fiction strives to represent. The novel is the pre-eminent example of an experiential art; and to falsify the experiential terms in which it rationalizes itself is infinitely more difficult than to falsify abstract reasoning. Whereas politics summarizes social experience, the novel subjects it to empiric analysis.[3]

Rahv's argument—that the demands of representation are such that it is more difficult for authentic art to falsify life than it is for strictly "ideological" discourse to do so—appears to be a sophisticated Marxist literary formulation. Rahv alludes to Henry James as a genuine artist who achieves critical distance from propaganda by following the "law of art," which requires that ideas developed in imaginative literature of the first rank be vivified through the convincing recreation of human experience. This view of the literary medium is an early example of a similar view expressed by Lionel Trilling in his more well-known statement in *The Liberal Imagination* (1950) that "literature is the human activity that takes the fullest and most precise account of variousness, possibility, complexity, and difficulty."[4]

But Rahv and Trilling were not immune to the siren songs of Sidney Hook's Marxist-instrumentalist *Toward the Understanding of Karl Marx*, or, at least, to the cultural forces that shaped it and indeed permeated the whole of American radical thought. Underpinning their argument about the relationship between art and experience is a line of reasoning that engages rather simplistic, non-Marxist assumptions about ideology and epistemology that can only be called pragmatist. The crux of Rahv's statement counterposes what he perceives as the concrete and the abstract, the former embodied in the fictional grasp of experience and the latter inherent in the treacherous rationalism of political discourse. What renders this perspective essentially pragmatist is its suggestion that fiction's virtue derives from its necessary exclusion of "ideology," implicitly defined in the manner that pragmatists rather than Marxists would understand the term. Moreover, Rahv's statement refers almost directly back to a passage in John Dewey's *Art as Experience* (1934): "In the end, works of art are the only media of complete and unhindered communication between man and man that can occur in a world full of gulfs and walls that limit community of experience."[5] In other words, aesthetic experience is the paradigm of experience, experience freed from factors that would impede and thwart its development. Trilling's *The Experience of*

Literature (1967), a collection of fiction that he edited, reflected the continuity of this theme.

Pragmatists hold that ideology corrupts political discourse because it stems from abstract, deductive reasoning based on fixed and final principles and categories. That is, ideology is thought divorced from, and hence by its nature falsifying, social experience as really lived. Thus for Rahv, Trilling, and other New York intellectuals who came partly under the influence of pragmatism, great literature, inasmuch as it captures and expresses experience, simply cannot be "ideological." As a result, they never considered the argument that art might perform the function of critically distancing the reader from the inherent ideology of the text, which several European critics have come to regard as central to the Marxist aesthetic.

To be sure, Marxists have defined ideology variously, but the huge gulf in basic methodology between pragmatic and Marxist epistemology can be seen by contrasting Rahv's point of view with that of Terry Eagleton, a contemporary English Marxist who has written extensively on the relation between criticism and ideology. For Eagleton, experience is not reality divorced from ideology; rather, experience is precisely "ideology's homeland."[6] Eagleton claims that experience, properly speaking, connotes the way one senses, feels, or receives ordinary life activity; experience is another word for everyday consciousness, imbued with the norms and values of class society and its rulers.

This means that the hegemony of the social order is to some extent sustained with the assistance of the socially determined structure of perception by which, or through which, one receives and interprets ordinary events. And it is in this realm that ideology operates precisely to carry out the function described above. Inasmuch as a work of literature seizes upon, reshuffles, and depicts experience, it, too, resides in the realm of ideology. Thus Eagleton, as one exemplar of a Marxist critic, comes to precisely the opposite conclusion that Rahv and the pragmatists drew. Moreover, Eagleton proposes that superior artists—given how they are socially situated and how their unique ability senses and reenacts the complexity of history as it is "lived"—can reveal the fractures, faultlines, and contradictions of ideology as it historically dominates consciousness.

The above contrast is useful for understanding the enfeeblement of American Marxism at the hands of pragmatism. For the pragmatist, to depart from abstract reason and to settle in experience is to eschew ideology, avoid deception, and encounter the real—in fact, to approach scientific method and insight (as Rahv puts it, to "subject [life] to empiric analysis"). For the Marxist, to settle on the terrain of experience is to submerge oneself in the unexamined stuff of ideology. This distinction between pragmatism and Marxism may help inform, substantively and methodologically, the interpretation of literature produced by the New York intellectuals during the 1940s. Rahv's basic pragmatist differentiation between ideology and experience is reflected in his two influential essays of literary criticism, "Paleface and Redskin" (1939) and "The Cult of Experience in American Writing" (1940). In both Rahv calls for some sort of reconciliation between the writer of isolated ideas (a "Paleface," as Hawthorne), and the mindless celebrator of experience (a "Redskin," as Whitman).[7] Delmore Schwartz pursued the same theme in his late 1930s poem "Far Rockaway," in which he contrasts relaxed sunbathers (literally "redskins") at the shore with an alienated "novelist" on the boardwalk.[8]

If Eagleton's argument that art has the potential of liberating us from ideological illusion is correct, then the fiction of the New York intellectuals in the 1940s must be read with a sense of irony. The consistent theme of virtually every one of their important works of fiction published during and immediately after World War II proclaims the need for liberation from the ideologies of the radical movement, a process that they themselves were undergoing. As they moved from a position of support for social revolution to an endorsement of individual regeneration, they assaulted, with varying degrees of emphasis, both Marxism, which they considered to embody the myth of class struggle, and radical modernism, which they considered to incarnate the myth of the virtue of a total rebellion against a stultifying and hypocritical bourgeois society.

Paradoxically, the New York intellectuals' espousal of "skepticism" and "realism" and the self-proclaimed repudiation of Marxism by many must be understood as an aspect of the group's own emergent ideology. This ideology took the form of either a new variant of middle-class individualism or, more perniciously, a rationalization for the continued dominance of bourgeois society to which they had become reconciled. Proclaimers of a selective skepticism, they had produced nothing less than a sui generis ideology that seemed to suit the very institutions they had sought to abolish. Of course, on some issues they indeed became ruthlessly skeptical, particularly on those that involved radical social change. On other matters most were curiously conformist, especially on the foreign policy of the United States.

FROM ACQUIESCENCE TO ANTIRADICALISM

In *New York Jew* (1978) Alfred Kazin insightfully described Lionel Trilling as "the most successful leader of deradicalization" in the postwar era.[9] A good deal can be learned about Trilling's ideological and artistic evolution during the 1940s by examining two of his short stories that preceded *The Middle of the Journey*, although, in another context, these same stories might be analyzed for other themes and issues. "Of This Time, Of That Place," which appeared in the same issue of the *Partisan Review* as Sidney Hook's "The New Failure of Nerve," introduces what became for Trilling and most of his fellow writers a standard motif: the vicissitudes of a middle-aged person undergoing a profound change in values. The story concerns the unexpected decision of Joseph Howe, a former modernist poet turned English professor, to inform Dwight College's superficial and naive dean about the psychological problems of his most brilliant student, Ferdinand Tertan, even though Howe knows this will result in Tertan's dismissal from the college and his probable institutionalization. At the story's end, Howe, his arms linked with the dean en route to an academic procession, finds himself connected, by the dean's other arm, to a dishonest, opportunist student named Blackburn. Although Howe symbolically withdraws his arm, he had already decided to participate in the ceremony. Significantly, he has just been promoted to full professor and guaranteed a permanent position at the college.

The pivotal events in the story occur when, after concluding that Tertan has characteristics that conventional society would consider to be marks of "madness," Howe at first resolves that he will *not* bring Tertan to the attention of the administration and have him removed from school. Thus it is very much to his surprise that Howe finds himself, at the very next moment, requesting to see the dean in order to *report* Tertan: "[I]t would always be a landmark in his life that, at the very moment when he was rejecting the official way, he had been, without will or intention, so gladly drawn to it."[10] What can one conclude but that the story is a testament of acceptance of the once-abhorred society by the former rebel Joseph Howe? Morally, he has doubts about the "official way"; emotionally, he is relieved after he submits to the pressure to "do the right thing."

The importance of Howe's promotion, as well as his tenuous relation to Dwight College, seems to link the story to Diana Trilling's 1977 memoir of her husband, "Lionel Trilling, a Jew at Columbia," in which she describes his difficulties in achieving a secure academic post during the depression. In 1932 Trilling was appointed as an English instructor at Columbia, the same position held by Howe at Dwight College before he betrayed Tertan. However, Trilling nearly lost his position because of prejudice against him "as a Freudian, a Marxist, and a Jew." Finally, after Trilling published his doctoral dissertation on Matthew Arnold, Columbia President Nicholas Murray Butler decided in 1939 to promote him to assistant professor "under his summer powers."[11] Soon Trilling found that he had become substantially deradicalized.

If the anxieties surrounding Lionel's promotion as depicted by Diana Trilling in her 1977 memoir were in fact worked into "Of This Time, Of That Place," which was published two years after the events she describes, it is interesting to note that the prejudice directed against Trilling as a Jewish Freudian Marxist has been displaced by the prejudice Howe encounters because of his former connections with modernist poetry and his potential connection with the "mad" Tertan.

En route to a faculty dinner party, Howe discovers an article in a literary journal by an establishment critic denouncing his two books of poetry as mad, self-intoxicated, and irresponsible—words that might well describe Tertan. Later, Howe has an argument with his student Blackburn who, angry about the grade Howe had given him, threatens to tell the dean about the unfavorable article. Although Howe dramatically rebukes Blackburn for the threat, he later gives him a higher grade than he deserved, enabling Blackburn to receive the dean's praise for being the first member of his class to secure a job after graduation. Blackburn had also threatened to tell the dean that Howe had recommended the unstable Tertan for the college literary society, but by this time Howe had already betrayed Tertan.

The ideological thrust of the story advocates accepting the "official way" despite its imperfections. But Trilling so deftly understood the art of fiction that the reader is permitted to apprehend all the limitations and contradictions of such an acceptance while at the same time appreciating its attractiveness for the protagonist. From the beginning we learn that Howe has tired of the social and cultural rebellion of his youth: "At twenty-six, Joseph Howe had discovered that he was neither so well off nor so bohemian as he had once thought."[12] We observe how he becomes increasingly comfortable in the dull college environment, enjoying parties at faculty homes and even the silly ritual of cap-and-gown cermonies. Finally, a young woman, Hilda Aiken, begins to fall in love with Howe, and a conventional courtship seems imminent.

Trilling does nothing to make either the academic environment or the "official way" more interesting and attractive than they would be in real life; he clearly demonstrates that it is Howe himself who has changed and who is in the process of succumbing to the dull bourgeois world he once scorned. Even more impressive is the dignity that Trilling manages to assign to Tertan. In the closing scene the "mad" student stands apart from the others in the academic procession, but when Tertan merely glances at Howe standing arm-in-arm with the dean and with Blackburn, Howe feels so guilty that he drops the dean's arm.

Although secondary characters like Blackburn, the dean, and even Tertan are not fleshed out, they effectively embody the ambiguous forces acting upon Howe. Blackburn incarnates the real "insanity" of corruption and dishonesty that the "official way" gives free rein to in our society, and the dean functions as the well-meaning but obtuse arbiter who permits this sad state of affairs to exist. Tertan, however, is scarcely a personification of "madness," for Trilling imparts virtually nothing about the nature of his alleged illness and its causes. Instead, Tertan seems to be an incarnation of the true modernist hero of Howe's earlier period—passionately devoted to mind and truth, unqualifiedly hostile to a mundane, materialistic, sham world run by narrowly "scientific" principles, and expressing himself through a style of writing that is difficult and "disordered." Tertan's final comment is a scornful remark about "instruments of precision" in apparent reference to the camera Hilda is using to capture Howe's likeness. Trilling stated in a subsequent commentary that the "instruments of precision" may also have been intended to suggest Tertan's ironic judgment on the values of the society that had judged him abnormal.[13]

There is no "casuistry" in the story, no "abstract reasoning" about which Rahv was so concerned; the ambivalent world of Joseph Howe is vivified through his behavior and his progressive accommodation to the "official way." But the story is highly ideological nonetheless. Most striking is Trilling's semiconscious account of how the alienation of the nonconformist can serve to foster capitulation, a condition that the nonconformist accepts with resignation and by implication urges the reader to accept. Alienation in this context is not meant in the Marxist sense but in the manner in which it was discussed by the New York intellectuals in the 1940s: the painful, but purportedly salutary, sense of inevitably being compelled to remain apart, especially as experienced by the ex-radical and the secular Jew.[14]

In "Of This Time, Of That Place," Howe is uncomfortable at

every turn, never more than half committed to any alternative, always standing with one foot outside of a situation. As a modernist he had been alienated from the dominant culture, but he was alienated as well from his very stance of alienation. In accommodating to the "official way," he still recognizes that it is corruption, and he is even able to objectify his own behavior—to watch his own strange actions as if disembodied. And yet, in practice, he cooperates: his alienation yields an unexpected capitulation even though, from the pragmatic point of view, it produces a skepticism of abstract ideas and an immersion in concrete experience. Trilling regards this surprising outcome in a half-bemused, half-tragic manner. In his artistic practice, if not in his conscious theorizing, a part of Trilling may have indeed recognized that experience is "ideology's homeland" and thus a likely route to co-optation.

In contrast to this self-reflexive toying with his anti-ideological ideology, Trilling's 1946 story, "The Other Margaret," reveals an increasing blindness to his own ideological transgressions, one that works to the detriment of his artistic capacities. The story looses a highly loaded assault on the radical analysis of and solution to race and class oppression; indeed, one might even call it the first anti-affirmative action short story. There are two Margarets in "The Other Margaret." One is the thirteen-year-old daughter of Stephen Elwin, a publisher of scientific magazines; the other is the family's black maid.

Margaret the maid is hostile to her well-off employers, showing her resentment by "accidentally" breaking expensive things around the house. Margaret the daughter is under the influence of a "progressive" schoolteacher, Miss Hoxie. Thus the daughter protests that the maid Margaret cannot be blamed for what she does; as a black person she carries the burden of her race and class. In addition to constantly repeating that "society" is responsible for all bad behavior, the daughter Margaret also argues that blacks who are loyal, reliable, and courteous, like a former maid, Millie, have a "slave psychology."[15]

However, by the end of the story the daughter is exposed as a hypocrite who really, deep in her heart, does not accept her teacher's radical ideology; when the maid finally breaks something that the daughter truly values, a clay lamb that she had made as a gift for her mother, she bursts into tears and denounces the maid as having done it intentionally and thus as being personally responsible.

But neither Margaret forms the center of consciousness in the story. Once more, the protagonist is an adult approaching middle age who suddenly has undergone a change. The change in Stephen Elwin's attitude is described in a scene on a bus as he is returning home after purchasing a painting of a king by Rouault. He witnesses a nasty old conductor trick a little rich boy into missing his bus. The reader is told that Stephen's habit of mind is such that he would normally feel compassion for the conductor, a poor working man who had never had the advantages of the rich boy: "But now, strangely, although the habit was in force, it did not check his anger. It was bewildering that he should feel anger at a poor ignorant man, a working man. It was the first time in his life that he had ever felt so."[16]

Leaving aside the unlikely possibility that the middle-aged Elwin had never before felt anger toward a worker, it is important to recognize that the basis of his change in consciousness is bound up in his recollection, at several points, of Hazlitt's famous sentence, "No young man believes he shall ever die."[17] Just before the final conflict with the maid Margaret, this revelation comes to him as a flash of light: "It seemed to him—not suddenly, for it had been advancing in his mind for some hours now—that in the aspect of his knowledge of death, all men were equal in their responsibility. . . . Exemption was not given by age or youth, or sex, or color, or condition of life."[18]

Trilling's decision to present this banality as the portentous revelation of the story is an aesthetic and intellectual catastrophe. In what way can the observation that all are fated to die negate or even challenge the fact that different races and classes face substantially different kinds of obstacles in their struggle to survive or the fact that individual behavior cannot be fully assessed outside of its social context? What makes the inevitability of death a guide to conduct of any sort?

Trilling takes this non sequitur even further in the closing pages when Elwin concludes that his daughter for purely selfish reasons has needed to believe that society rather than individuals is responsible for bad behavior so that she herself would not have to feel guilty if she someday found herself committing an immoral act! Thus the story not only provides a partly Freudian critique of a political position, but it is also connected to Gerard Manley Hopkins's poem "Spring and Fall (To a Young Child)." The poem begins, "Margaret are you grieving / Over Goldengrove unleaving," and ends, "It is the blight man was born for, / It is Margaret you mourn for."

Trilling attempts to modulate the absurdity of this abstract position by having Elwin protest that what he really needs to communicate to his daughter is a "double truth," one that recognizes both social and individual responsibility for human behavior. But, for unexplained reasons, he lacks the ability to do this. This and other failings suggest that an atypical instance of rigidity on the part of Trilling has overwhelmed the method of his art so that, in spite of his caveat about "double truth," any reader who holds a more materialist view of the nature of social oppression is left dissatisfied. Why didn't Trilling at least attempt to suggest some of the concrete reasons for the maid Margaret's unruly behavior? Why are we denied all insight into the consciousness of the working class and of black characters, while every attempt is made to reveal the thoughts and feelings of the middle-class Elwins?

Finally, why is the "radical" point of view reduced to the repetition of simple phrases such as "we can't blame her" and "she's not responsible," and why is the only defender of this perspective a thirteen-year-old who bursts into tears after her clay lamb is broken? Is this a fair statement of the radical position? Is Trilling justified in claiming that the radical view is so devoid of complexity?

One possibility is that "The Other Margaret" may be partially intended as a response to Richard Wright's *Native Son* (1940), about a black youth who is tried and executed for two murders. The very title of Wright's book underscores the notion that the killer, Bigger Thomas, is a product of society, but a close reading of the text shows that Wright, a Communist Party member of the time, intentionally avoided the temptation to make Bigger into a mere victim of circumstance. There are two murders in the book. The first, of Mary Dalton, is accidental. Bigger inadvertently suffocates her when he fears he might be caught violating white society's taboo of being found in a white woman's bedroom in the middle of the night. The second, involving Bessie Mears, is a cold-blooded homicide committed in the hope of facilitating his flight from the police. Mr. Max, Bigger's Communist-supplied lawyer, does not plead for Bigger's freedom in his speech to the judge; he argues instead for a life sentence. Thus the most famous radical work of fiction of the time, whatever its weaknesses, certainly does not take the simplistic view of responsibility and oppression attributed to the daughter Margaret and her propagandistic schoolteacher, Miss Hoxie.

In 1946, James T. Farrell, who was still attempting to retain his revolutionary Marxist political position, published a brief comment on "The Other Margaret" in the *New International*, theoretical organ of the Workers Party, to which Farrell had recently switched allegiance after a dispute with the Socialist Workers Party. He praised the story's execution as "adroit" but charged Trilling with "tendentiousness" in his choice of characters and events and for the unfair ways in which Trilling presented the contending philosophies. Farrell concludes: "Thus, while we can recognize the skill with which this story is written, and while we can concede it the merit of producing a certain cultivated milieu of our time, we should realize that it is cleverly organized to present a reactionary moral view with insidious pervasiveness. I use the word reactionary here because Trilling's story establishes a conclusion concerning freedom and responsibility at the expense of those who most need to be free, and on the basis of citing relatively trivial incidents."[19]

Shortly afterward, Irving Howe, then a young leader of the Workers Party, made his debut in the *Partisan Review* by attacking Farrell's analysis: "[T]he story is not a thesis or an argument; it is, however imperfectly executed, a work of art. It is therefore concerned with and dipped in emotional ambiguity; it pictures a situation of conflict between ideas about race, class, and morality and deeply-imbued folk attitudes. Had it been Trilling's purpose to advance a thesis on morality, he would have written an essay. His purpose was rather to dramatize a situation."[20] Farrell may have misread a few minor aspects of the story, but Howe's protest augurs better as a defense of "Of This Time, Of That Place" than of "The Other Margaret."

From the beginning of the narrative, Stephen Elwin has been in search of wisdom. Wisdom and naiveté are continually counterposed throughout the story. Elwin purchases the portrait of the king by Rouault precisely because it suggests wisdom: "One could feel of him [the king] . . . that he had passed beyond ordinary matters of personality and was worthy of the crown he was wearing."[21] Neither a young soldier nor the daughter Margaret is able to appreciate the portrait and consequently they are shown to be naive.

The daughter Margaret is also shown to be foolish through her association with innocence as connoted by the clay lamb. "Why, darling," cries her mother when she spies the gift, "it looks just like you!"[22] A further episode reveals the daughter's naiveté: after self-righteously refusing to believe her mother's story about an underpaid worker who made an anti-Semitic remark, Margaret discredits herself by inadvertently making an anti-Semitic gesture.

Elwin, on the other hand, is continually the epitome of wisdom. It is he, after all, who purchases the portrait of the king. Moreover, after initially feeling that he behaved foolishly in becoming angry at the conductor on the bus going home, he has a revelation: "It then occurred to him to think that perhaps he had felt his anger not in despite of wisdom but because of it."[23] Finally, after his major confrontation with his daughter, we are told that he had "defeated his daughter" and that the daughter's continued defense of the maid Margaret was "stupid and obstinate."[24]

Where, then, is the ambiguity that Howe sees in "The Other Margaret"? Perhaps it lies only in the inability of Elwin to articulate his "double truth" at the end of the story. It certainly does not reside in the interaction between the two positions presented. But the implication is clear that with time and experience Elwin will have the courage to overcome his timorousness and act appropriately, that is, according to his new philosophy of death as an equalizer. Farrell's use of the term "reactionary" may have been too extreme, but Howe clearly failed to see the ominous implications of Trilling's assault on the "progressive" political position in light of the *zeitgeist* of the postwar period. He also missed the implications of Trilling's charge, via Elwin (there can be no doubt that the author and his character coincide in this instance), that the radical teacher had "corrupted" her student. The purge of left-wing teachers from the New York City school system had already begun, and a national witch-hunt of leftists in colleges and universities would soon follow. One might possibly argue that there are other more complicated elements in the story (for example, Lucy, the mother, seems to share an oversimplified version of Stephen Elwin's position), but one must conclude that the seven types of ambiguity depicted are mere window dressing for what is unambiguously a blatant assault on the left.

Howe seems to echo Rahv in his differentiation between a story (experience) and an argument (ideology); his view also seems to dovetail with Trilling's own praise of authentic literature as taking the "most precise account of variousness, possibility, complexity, and difficulty." But "The Other Margaret" *is* more an argumentative thesis than an ambiguous dramatization, which would be drenched in ideology anyway. It foreshadows the contention of Trilling's later book, *The Liberal Imagination*, that certain kinds of liberal and radical intellectuals (represented here not only by Miss Hoxie and her thirteen-year-old dupe, but by Elwin himself before his change in consciousness) easily fall prey to oversimplified social theory because of emotional rather than valid intellectual reasons. Many of the artistic problems of the story derive from Trilling's having gone too far in oversimplifying the oversimplification that he wants to refute. He was too zealous in honing his assault. Both Farrell and Howe were correct in pointing out that Trilling's skills of depiction in "The Other Margaret" are still considerable, and of course the story depicts much more than the political issues on which I have focused. But there is definite evidence that Trilling employed character and action in "The Other Margaret" that was based on political bias and polemical intent of a kind not found in "Of This Time, Of That Place."

POLITICS AND THE NOVEL

Trilling's stories dramatize a recurring theme in the World War II fiction produced by the New York intellectuals during the 1940s: a change in consciousness away from the ideologies of Marxism and radical modernism on the part of a central character with a left-wing or bohemian past. Several longer works published about the same time contain striking structural similarities: Edmund Wilson's *Memoirs of Hecate County* (1946), Trilling's *The Middle of the Journey* (1947), and Mary McCarthy's *The Oasis* (1949) all create imaginary semirural environments where the main characters, temporarily absent from or commuting to New York City, are confronted with a clash of carefully selected viewpoints. This structural motif allows these writers unusual freedom in dramatizing various arguments, but it also suggests that both the problems and solutions presented in fiction are often far removed from the life experiences of ordinary Americans—the working class, racial minorities, the urban masses.[25]

The texts are at least partially conscious of this phenomenon; this is also suggested by the fact that the terrain on which the leading characters have their revelation or "real experience" is itself somehow illusory, a rural idyll divorced from the social reality of struggle in the urban centers. Oddly enough, then, the "experience" in which the characters are educated is false and simplified. This confirms the contention of Eagleton and others that there is a high degree of half-conscious self-reflexivity in literary texts themselves. In other words, the narrative structures of the works of fiction manifest an inherent criticism of the works' own premises, which is that by immersing oneself in "experience" one can evade the deceptions and temptations of ideology. This would be an example of what Eagleton considers an "authentic art that can distance and critically reveal the very ideology being produced by the literary text."[26]

All three works include elements of the roman à clef, which suggests their insular character as well as the possibility that they might serve some sort of therapeutic function. Trilling acknowledged that his character Gifford Maxim is derived from his college classmate Whittaker Chambers; McCarthy is unmistakably clear in her portraits of her close associates Philip Rahv (as Will Taub) and Dwight Macdonald (as MacDougal MacDermott); Edmund Wilson's recently published notebooks reveal the autobiographical basis of his book, and the critic Sherman Paul has persuasively argued that Wilson's Sy Banks is based on Paul Rosenfeld and that the Milholland brothers express the views of Van Wyck Brooks and Archibald MacLeish during World War II.[27]

Finally, each book not only describes but *advocates* an "end of ideology"—a theme that surfaced in literature at least ten years before it was articulated by the sociologists Daniel Bell and Seymour Martin Lipset. In each instance, ideology is rejected primarily because of its inherent tendency to oversimplify. The common primary target in each book is the fallacy inherent in employing radical social theory, especially class analysis, as a means of changing society.

Edmund Wilson's nameless narrator in *Memoirs of Hecate County*, for example, is depicted in the pivotal story, "The Princess with the Golden Hair," as struggling with what appear to be class forces; each class is personified by a woman. Imogin Loomis, "The Princess," represents the attraction of the wealthy elite. In a probable parable of Marx's theory of commodity fetishism, the narrator is drawn to Imogin in the belief that her golden locks and aura must betoken inherent value; however, she is ultimately revealed to be a hollow sham, an illusion made possible by the reifications of bourgeois society. Anna, the waitress, is unabashedly proletarian, and Jo, an old girlfriend to whom the narrator returns at the story's end, represents the snug middle class—safely distanced from the deadly illusions of Imogin's world and the harsh realities of Anna's.

At the beginning of "The Princess," the narrator is close to making a commitment to Marxism. He has studied socialism in college and, with the advent of the depression, he starts reading the *Daily Worker*. But from his firsthand contact with Anna, he eventually learns that the abstractions of Marxism do not correspond to reality. The proletariat lacks class consciousness and is unfitted to its historical role:

> I felt I was merely embarrassing her [Anna] by consigning her to the category of a "working class." To tell her that the fur workers like her mother, the garment workers like her cousins, and the waitresses at Field's like herself were expected to dislodge their employers and the big figures she read about in the papers and to make themselves rulers of society—must

seem to her, I could see by her silence, to be thrusting on herself and her people a role for which she knew they were not fitted and for which I must know they were not—so that I soon began to feel silly and insincere.[28]

Wilson's story is anti-ideological, in the pragmatic sense, through its attack on abstract notions of the working class. From Anna, Wilson's narrator learns about the complexities of reality by immersion in concrete experience: "it was Anna who had made it possible for *me* to recreate the actuality; who had given me that life of the people which had before been but prices and wages, legislation and technical progress, that new Europe of the East Side and Brooklyn for which there was provided no guidebook."[29] Yet the immersion has been insufficient to constitute the basis for a completely new orientation; at the end the narrator simply returns to his prior state of alienation symbolized by Hecate County.

In *The Oasis*, Mary McCarthy's heroine is also momentarily doused in the sea of pragmatic experience and is likewise unable to substantiate a new orientation, returning at the end to the dreamworld of alienation. The structure of the novel is impressively worked out. McCarthy takes a relatively diverse group of individuals and isolates them in a utopian colony in Vermont. Within that group exist two factions, analogous to the divisions that grew out of the split in the *Partisan Review* over World War II. One consists of purists led by MacDougal Macdermott, who as pacifists believe that one improves society through moral example. The other consists of realists led by Will Taub, who have abandoned radicalism but have retained a sufficient amount of their "Marxism" to believe that humanity is shaped by historical development and by economic and class forces, and that isolated intellectuals can do little to change things in the face of present objective conditions. But the realists are willing to give the utopian experiment a chance, and they just barely have enough of the spirit of fair play to prevent them from intentionally trying to obstruct the experiment merely to prove their point.

What is most useful about the setting is that the characters operate within their self-created society; they are not directly bound by laws, police, the constricting environment of the city, regular jobs, and the immediate pressure of social convention. The purists are relatively free to establish their own moral codes and to make their own judgments. Into this environment McCarthy then introduces a series of symbolic tests as a means of gauging the response of each faction. Yet the pastoral setting, atypical for the United States in the mid-twentieth century, is problematic, thus making her story less convincing. Indeed, she never quite evades the sense that what happens is imaginary, in contrived conditions and a thin atmosphere. This may be one of the reasons that she described *The Oasis* as a *conte philosophique* rather than a novel. The book's strength is actually in its portraits of personalities, the depiction of intellectuals who are prideful and who overreact to and are obsessed by relatively small matters.[30]

The story is structured around three main tests to which the colony is subjected as a whole; there are also several subsidiary tests such as the series of events that seem to be testing the marriage of Katy Preston, a resident of the colony who tries to straddle the factions. The main tests all involve Joe Lockman. The first is a debate over whether Lockman, who arouses fear and suspicion from the start because of his atypical background, should be allowed to stay at the colony. As the owner of a leather factory and as an assimilated Jew, he feels less alienated from American society than the others. A movement to exclude Lockman from the colony begins after he accidentally surprises Taub with a gun. Taub, who likes to bully his opponents in argument, is exposed as a physical coward. Publicly shamed, Taub becomes determined to expel Joe as an alien among the utopians. For a moment the utopians are shown in an ugly light; in their elitist chauvinism against Joe and Eva Lockman, one can see the shadow of Nazi-like racial or ethnic hatred based on fear, jealousy, and the need for scapegoats. Fortunately, in the middle of the tense council meeting the utopians break out in laughter at the silliness of their situation, and the matter is dropped.

A second test involves the reaction of Katy Preston and others to Joe's spilling oil on the stove. A fire starts, breakfast is delayed, and people are angry. Because of the resentment already building against Joe, Katy's husband suggests that she should take the blame for the accident. Too cowardly to do this or to go ahead and blame Joe directly, she tries to indirectly blame Joe, perhaps the most selfish response of the three. Despite her high ideals, Katy is simply afraid to suffer the opprobrium of her friends.

The third test is the most dramatic. A family consisting of a man, woman, and child, who are described as poor farmers, come to pick berries on the colony's property. The colonists resent this but are incapable of communicating with ordinary people. Every strategy they use brings the opposite of intended results; for example, by being friendly and lenient, they embolden the intruders. Then, in a moment of panic and frustration they grab a gun loaded with blanks and force the poor farmers to leave the land—an act that may even associate the frustrated utopians with the Communists who forcibly drove the peasants off the land in the Soviet Union in the late 1920s. The point is that, despite their intentions and ideals, the utopians under certain conditions prove capable of committing any number of acts for which they have condemned others.

The confrontation with the poor farmers brings the colony to the brink of collapse; the members feel uncomfortable and Katy has a dream in which the members gradually depart. One is given the sense that, even though the colonists had successfully defended their territory, the doctrine of the purists was discredited: one cannot overcome social conditioning through individual moral example. As long as individuals live in a society with poor and upper classes that are estranged and fearful of each other—as long as some can afford to buy property while others are forced to steal food—individuals will be forced into certain patterns of behavior that involve violence or the threat of violence.

Yet the realists are not shown as victors, either. Katy, who seems to provide the moral touchstone for the book, ends up having a nasty exchange with Taub, who is equally bound up in the grip of abstract ideas, if of a different kind. It seems that neither faction can cope with Joe Lockman, who is involved in all three episodes. His name suggests John Locke, the ideologue of the American Revolution and Declaration of Independence. He is a small-time capitalist and his leather factory links him to the West and rugged individualism. Confronted with Joe as the symbol of American reality, both the realists and purists are shown to be in the grip of abstract ideas, too separated from experience to affect him, and by implication, the larger American social reality. At the end Katy retreats from both factions, escaping into sleep, again linked to her husband (whose motivations are always personal), as if to suggest that reality simply cannot be dealt with through abstract ideas.

Lionel Trilling originally conceived of *The Middle of the Journey* as a *nouvelle*, a very short novel with a high degree of thematic explicitness. His subject was to be the way death is perceived by middle-class intellectuals of the time. When the character Maxim, based upon Whittaker Chambers, came unbidden into the story, the book took on unexpected direction and eventually turned into a novel.[31] It seems significant that Trilling, who wrote virtually nothing about his revolutionary years in his essays, could not escape the subject in his major work of fiction. Once Trilling's imagination began to flow, an important relationship was established between the response of middle-class intellectuals to the reality of death, which they chose to either ignore or romanticize, and their response to the failure of utopian movements for social change. In both cases, ideology was shown to falsify experience.

Trilling's narrative occurs in the mid-1930s, just after the Moscow trials. The fellow-traveling Communist intellectuals at the center of his book are characterized by "an impassioned longing to believe."[32] They specifically wished to believe that the construction of a just and virtuous society was feasible, hence they were determined to credit the Soviet Union with having made a decisive step toward the establishment of such a society. To sustain this belief the fellow travelers only tolerated comments about the Soviet Union of a positive nature. Once a commitment to the belief had been made, it became almost impossible for any evidence to shake it. Those who offered such evidence were condemned as deficient in goodwill. If reality ever attempted to breach the believer's defenses, the contradictions between belief and reality were rationalized through the use of "dialectical logic."

The essential point was that Communist-oriented intellectuals of the time did not really have a political life. They refrained from political discourse and debate, thereby doing away with the defining elements of politics (opinion, contingency, conflicts of interests, clashes of will), regarding these as somehow repugnant to the vision of reason and virtue that would be the communist future. Trilling's polemical purpose in *The Middle of the Journey* was to bring to light this "clandestine negation" of the political life that Stalinism had fostered among intellectuals in the West.[33] To Trilling this negation was even more significant in its imperiously bitter refusal to consent to the conditioned nature of human experience. The novel is designed to engage a confrontation of ideology and reality; Maxim was intended to be a "reality principle" because he knew from personal experience the horror that lay beyond the glowing words of the Great Promise.

Trilling's protagonist, John Laskell, undergoes an enormous change in attitude during the course of the novel—similar to that experienced by Howe, Elwin, Wilson's nameless narrator, and Katy Preston—primarily in connection with a shift in his feelings toward Maxim. At the beginning, Laskell is convinced that Maxim is deluded in his believing that the party was trying to kill him; he refers to Maxim as absurd, even treacherous. Yet from the moment that Maxim leaves him at the country train station to meet his friends, the Crooms, Laskell begins to feel terrified, like Maxim, that "something untoward might happen."[34]

Laskell begins to subsconsciously reconsider his feelings about

Maxim as he observes his friends, the Crooms, trying to make excuses for the irresponsible behavior of Duck, their handyman. They always blame external factors rather than Duck himself. For example, when Duck gets drunk they insist that the cause is a constitutional weakness, not self-indulgence. They insist on viewing him as a tragic figure, unhappy in his present condition but capable of becoming something far better. Laskell, in contrast, wishes that the Crooms would become angry with Duck when he acts irresponsibly. Laskell's refusal to make excuses for Duck represents an important stage in his changing consciousness, for Duck is a symbol of undirected rebellion against society—in effect, an expression of modernist sensibility. Although the Crooms imagine Duck to be a worker, his biography resembles a character from a Faulkner novel: his grandfather was the richest senator from the state; his father lost money because of his weakness for speculating; Duck is unable to control his drinking. He directly recalls Faulkner's Popeye from *Sanctuary*—not only because of his cartoon name, but because, while the local women regard Duck as virile, he is sexually impotent.

The Crooms' blindness toward Duck is associated with their refusal to discuss Laskell's own brush with death during a recent illness. Although Laskell is anxious to discuss the episode with them, they seem to regard death as unnatural and continually evade the topic. This attitude is dramatized when Mickey, a child unspoiled by the falsification of reality, attempts to give Laskell a dead, moldy leaf as a gift. The nursemaid grabs the leaf and scrubs his hand while Nancy Croom attempts to substitute a fresh, green leaf, which Mickey rejects.

Soon after, Laskell's consciousness has completed its change: he realizes that Maxim is telling the truth. But recognizing that the new, fanatically religious and right-wing Maxim represents an ideology as false as that of the Crooms and his former self, he articulates a new outlook, one that is ostensibly beyond ideology: "An absolute freedom from responsibility—that much of a child none of us can be. An absolute responsibility—that much of a divine or metaphysical essence none of us is."[35] His friends respond with hostility to such ideas and are characterized as expressing "the anger of the masked will at the appearance of an idea in modulation."[36] Ideology not only falsifies the perception of reality, but it provides a mask of altruism occluding from sight the will to power.

Of all the novels and stories of the 1940s that express an ostensible rebellion against ideology in the name of experience, only *The Middle of the Journey* presents a hero and final perspective suggest-

ing that its author might play a leading role in directing intellectuals of subsequent decades. This contrasts with Saul Bellow's *Dangling Man* (1944), Isaac Rosenfeld's *Passage from Home* (1946), and
Eleanor Clark's *The Bitter Box* (1946), each written by an individual
formerly associated with the anti-Stalinist left. All depict a kind of
disillusionment with either radicalism or modernist/bohemian rebellion as the result of an immersion in experience; their protagonists, however, tend to be either younger or older than those of
Wilson, McCarthy, and Trilling, and these novels are set in an urban
locale.

Bellow, born in 1915 in Lachine, Quebec, and Rosenfeld, born in
1918 in Chicago, were part of a group of students won to Trotskyism at Chicago's Tuley High School during the early 1930s by Nathan Gould, a Trotskyist youth leader of legendary oratorical powers. Some had previously been members of the Young Communist
League.[37] Along with Oscar Tarcov, who later published the novel
Bravo My Monster (1950), Bellow and Rosenfeld formed a circle of
young, precocious literary-minded Trotskyists, who were active in
the Spartacus Youth League when it was the Trotskyist youth organization, the Young Peoples Socialist League during their sojourn in
the Socialist Party, and the Young Peoples Socialist League (Fourth
International) after the Trotskyists founded the Socialist Workers
Party.

Bellow and Rosenfeld enrolled at the University of Chicago in
1933 where they participated in the Trotskyist-run Socialist Club,
which published a sixteen-page printed magazine called *Soapbox*.
On the masthead was a quotation from William Randolph Hearst:
"Red Radicalism has planted a soapbox on every campus of America." At the university they organized "Cell Number Five" of the
Trotskyist youth group. Never regarded as political leaders, Bellow
and Rosenfeld were seen more as kibitzers and wits. At Trotskyist
social affairs, for example, they would take turns reciting Swin-
burne's poetry in various accents: Swedish, Polish, Jewish, Italian.
In 1935 Bellow transferred to Northwestern University where he
published his first short story. Called "The Hell It Can't," the story
won third prize in the student newspaper, the *Daily Northwestern*,
in February 1936. In the story, of which the title is drawn from
Sinclair Lewis's novel *It Can't Happen Here* (1935), Bellow graphi-
cally describes a beating administered by fascist thugs. In 1937, Bellow married Anita Goshkin, also a Trotskyist.

During the 1939–40 schism, Bellow and Rosenfeld were sympathetic to Shachtman, but they had begun to lose interest in radical
politics. Both moved to New York City in the early 1940s to launch

their literary careers, but Bellow soon severed all ties with the Workers Party, maintaining only a few personal friendships; Rosenfeld would occasionally speak at public forums on cultural subjects sponsored by the party. Their thorough disaffection with radical politics was distressing to their friend, David Bazelon, an aspiring midwestern writer who was then moving close to Trotskyism and contributing to *Politics*.

Although Bellow was considerably influenced intellectually by the anti-Stalinist left, surprisingly little of his Trotskyist experience worked its way into his fiction or memoirs. As noted, some of his college writing had political themes, and his second contribution to the *Partisan Review*, "The Mexican General," depicts the assassination of Trotsky from the point of view of Mexican police officials involved in the aftermath.[38] There are passing references to Trotskyism in other short stories as well as in *The Adventures of Augie March* (1953), which may derive its main character in part from Abraham Liebick, a gifted young Trotskyist from Chicago's Marshall High School who was killed while serving in the Navy's Medical Corps in the Pacific.[39] *Dangling Man* (1944) is about a restless young intellectual who joined the Communist Party in 1932 but broke away at the start of World War II, which approximates Bellow's relationship with the Trotskyists. While waiting to be drafted, the young man's disillusionment extends from radicalism to his circle of bohemian friends. At the end of the novel he has become skeptical of all the former values that he had acquired during his political and cultural rebellion. With bitter irony he submits to the experience of the majority of his generation by celebrating his last day as a civilian: "I am no longer to be held accountable for myself; I am grateful for that. I am in other hands, relieved of self-determination, freedom cancelled. Hurray for regular hours! And for the supervision of the spirit! Long live regimentation!"[40]

Rosenfeld wrote only one story, "The Party," reflective of his experiences in the Trotskyist movement. It is told through the eyes of someone different from himself, a full-time functionary who works in the party's printshop and draws cartoons for the party paper. The story presumably depicts the decline of the Workers Party during the mid-1940s, when he was no longer a member. In it Rosenfeld describes the peculiar mentality of a devout but self-abnegating member loyal to the forms of the movement—the rituals of party interventions and social affairs, the veneration of "old guard" leaders and the dynamics of faction struggle—even as its political content is lost. In this sense the story is simply a variation on the "end-of-ideology" motif. Rosenfeld's ideologues are brutally satirized because they remain impervious to experience.[41] *Passage from Home* has a more complex development, because, unlike "The Party," a change occurs in the outlook of the main character. Here Rosenfeld traces the awakening consciousness of fifteen-year-old Bernard Miller who leaves his father to live with his nonconformist aunt. Returning to his father at the end, Bernard's immersion in experience has taught him that the bohemian alternative to the alienation of conventional life is illusory, and he becomes resigned to his outsider status. Thus experience teaches that alienation is the permanent condition of humanity.

Eleanor Clark was born in 1913 in Los Angeles and raised in Roxbury, Connecticut.[42] Attending Vassar as a contemporary of Mary McCarthy, she met Herbert Solow in 1934 at the advent of her writing career in New York. She began to associate with the *Partisan Review* circle a year or so before the magazine was relaunched. In 1937, immediately after the Dewey Commission of Inquiry hearings in Mexico, Clark visited the Trotsky household and undertook the translations of some documents. Subsequently she married Jan Frankel, one of Trotsky's most important secretaries; her relationships with both Solow and Frankel, with some degree of invention, are blended together in Hannah Paltz's narrative of the Trotskyist "Ginko" in Chapter 4 of Clark's novel *Gloria Mundi* (1979). Returning to New York, Clark collaborated with the American Trotskyists and wrote Trotsky that she had applied for membership.[43] Frankel, who had joined her in the United States, began to drift away from Trotskyism at the time of the Cannon-Shachtman split, and their marriage dissolved. By 1943 Clark, no longer a radical, was employed by the Office of Strategic Services in Washington, D.C.

Clark's *The Bitter Box* (1946) traces the disillusionment with the Communist Party of a rather unimpressive bank clerk, John Temple, who in personal frustration one day quits his cloistered job to immerse himself in the experience of political activism. Although he achieves moral, social, and even spiritual comfort by devoting himself to party affairs, the underlying horror of his experience is revealed when he learns the fate of his friend Brand, who was "liquidated" because he knew too much about the party's underground activities. In this connection, Herbert Solow's relationship to Whittaker Chambers provided important background for Clark's novel, just as it did for *The Middle of the Journey*. Strangely, the novel is not directly political, even though it reflects in many other ways the anti-Stalinist experiences of the 1930s: the factional struggle between Brand's party and the opposition group (People's Will), whose leader is assassinated, suggests the Stalinist-Trotskyist conflict; the political turns and sudden changes in Brand's party's line suggest the "Third Period," Popular Front, and Hitler-Stalin Pact convolutions of the Communist Party; the party's newspaper, the *Word*, echoes the *Worker* (albeit with a religious twist), and the literary magazine *Everybody's* suggests the *New Masses*. But, as in Rosenfeld's "The Party," Clark creates as a center of consciousness a rather narrow mind subjected primarily to pressures and motivations other than those stemming from political theory.

A REVOLUTIONARY NOVELIST IN CRISIS

Until 1945 James T. Farrell was a dependable ally of the Socialist Workers Party. Except for Meyer Schapiro, Clement Greenberg, and Dwight Macdonald, he was virtually alone among the anti-Stalinist intellectuals in adhering to a revolutionary internationalist point of view during World War II. From 1941 to 1945 he served as chairman of the Civil Rights Defense Committee, which had been formed to defend the Trotskyist trade union militants in Minneapolis Teamster Local 544 and leaders of the SWP. These union militants and party leaders had been prosecuted as the first victims of the Smith "Gag" Act, which made it unlawful to advocate the overthrow of the U.S. government or to belong to any group advocating such an overthrow.

Farrell wrote and published fiction steadily during these years, arguing that there is an interdependency between the advancement of culture and the struggle for human liberation, although Farrell's fiction differed from that of John Dos Passos, who wrote explicitly political novels. Some of Farrell's work, such as his antifascist novelette *Tommy Gallagher's Crusade* (1939), dramatized important political issues, but his *Studs Lonigan* trilogy demonstrated that he was primarily a novelist of human character. Farrell was acutely sensitive to the psychological costs of living in a class society, and his conceptions of individual consciousness and social destiny were infused with a materialist outlook. This is most evident not only in the *Studs Lonigan* trilogy, but also in Farrell's second series, the O'Neill-O'Flaherty pentalogy: *A World I Never Made* (1936), *No Star Is Lost* (1938), *Father and Son* (1940), *My Days of Anger* (1943), and *The Face of Time* (1953). Although the pentalogy centers around the life of Danny O'Neill, Farrell preferred that the five books be called the "O'Neill-O'Flaherty series" because the main characters are derived from both families. Both the *Studs Lonigan* trilogy and also the O'Neill-O'Flaherty series, conceived about the same time and thematically interconnected, provide an exposé of the false consciousness created by the institutions of capitalist society. A third series, the Bernard Carr trilogy—consisting of *Bernard Clare* (1946), *The Road Between* (1949), and *Yet Other Waters* (1952)—evolved somewhat later but was still linked to the revolutionary Marxist period in Farrell's literary development.

The O'Neill-O'Flaherty series, comprising a sprawling 2,500 pages, suffers by comparison with the *Studs Lonigan* trilogy because its five units, read separately, lack cogency. Yet their cumulative effect is more potent and complex, and Danny O'Neill is a wholly unique creation. Studs Lonigan's humanity is only dimly perceived behind the warped values absorbed from his environment; his notions of evil, engendered by Father Gilhooley's sermons, are haunting and amorphous, and his daydreams of a better life, associated with his would-be childhood sweetheart, Lucy Scanlan, are vague and romantic. In contrast, Danny O'Neill, an autobiographical persona, is much more intelligent, thoughtful, and sensitive than Studs, and he moves, despite setbacks, unrelentingly toward victory over his environment. As Danny escapes the predestined roles prepared for him by his family and subculture, the skillful precision with which Farrell probes the processes of human consciousness demonstrates a literary debt to Joyce and Proust.

Using stream of consciousness and associational techniques, Farrell roots the emotional development of Danny in a childhood trauma when his parents, Jim and Liz O'Neill, turn him over to the care of his widowed grandmother, Mary O'Flaherty. Danny's mind and personality are thereafter subtly shaped by his interaction with the two families, one middle class and the other working class. The respective class differences in attitude and outlook are acutely dramatized by two of the central male characters: Danny's uncle, Al O'Flaherty, a shoe salesman, and Danny's father, Jim, a teamster. Al O'Flaherty worships conventionalized notions of education and culture, while Jim fears that Al will turn Danny into a soft "dude."

Chronologically, the pentalogy begins with *The Face of Time*, published last in 1953, which follows Danny's emergence into consciousness at the very time his grandfather, Tom O'Flaherty, is dying. It concludes with Danny's college years in *My Days of Anger* (1943), which emphasizes his renunciation of religion, his initial encounters with philosophy and modern literature, and his first eager steps as a writer. Of the five novels, only *A World I Never Made* achieved popular success, and this may have been partly due to a well-publicized trial in which Farrell was accused, and acquitted, of including obscenity in the novel. But the O'Neill-O'Flaherty series never attained the stature of the *Studs Lonigan* trilogy because it lacks the dramatic focus afforded by Studs Lonigan's violent eruption into young manhood followed by ill health and death. What is superior about the O'Neill-O'Flaherty series is its relentless detailing of the generational conflicts among big-city Irish-American families whose members are depicted in all of their intermediate stages of acculturation and economic advancement. Moreover, the series enjoys a distinct position: it is perhaps the definitive examination of the social basis of the emergent consciousness of an artist in the process of rebelling against the shackles of his lower-middle-class cultural heritage in order to redefine his own personality and objectives in Marxist terms.

Critics harshly accused Farrell of lacking a sophisticated literary technique, but Farrell never made excessive claims about his writing style. He stated that he wrote primarily from his unconscious, achieving characterization by intensely identifying with each of his fictional creations as he imaginatively recreated a world seen through their eyes. Although he admired the consummate craftsmanship of Henry James and James Joyce, he endeavored to achieve a "clear path" to his unconscious. Part of what Farrell meant was that he relied on his own imaginative resources in attempting to create the "body image" of each of his main characters. The notion of the "body image"—meaning the total sense of oneself, including the visceral—was assimilated by Farrell at the outset of his career from the Freudian psychiatrist Paul Schilder. Farrell saw a correlation between the work of Schilder and the views of William James, George Herbert Mead, and John Dewey, which argued that human character is a social product.[44] This approach to fiction required an intimate knowledge of the thoughts, emotions, and social circumstances of one's characters; and this is part of the reason why the bulk, although not the entirety, of Farrell's work centers around the experiences of his family and acquaintances in familiar Chicago and New York environments. Even in those works in which an autobiographical persona, usually Danny O'Neill or Eddie Ryan, is not the main character, he sometimes appears in a cameo role as if to facilitate the process of empathizing with the other characters.

The Bernard Carr trilogy—the name of the main character was changed from Bernard Clare to Bernard Carr after a libel suit was brought by a man named Bernard Clare—relies heavily on Farrell's personal experiences as do his earlier series, but it was intended to depict the process of political and moral corruption of writers in the 1930s. As the published version of the trilogy suggests, Farrell intended Carr to become a half-willing proponent of Stalinism and then fall victim to commercial corruption. But after eight years of writing, and with many false starts and a variety of projected conclusions, Farrell's original intention never materialized; Carr's future remains undetermined at the conclusion of the trilogy.

The reason that the original plan was aborted is bound up in the political crisis that overwhelmed Farrell during the late 1940s. In early drafts of the series, Danny O'Neill was to be introduced as a foil to Carr. O'Neill was to have appeared as a mature novelist of revolutionary Marxist but anti-Stalinist convictions. In a scene describing a radio debate between Carr and O'Neill that Farrell cut from the published version, O'Neill lambasted the self-serving and even reactionary political character of one of Carr's novels: "All of the agonizing, all of the frothy talk about his [Carr's] own sincerity, his own honesty, his discovery of what are called basic human values, is really a way for Mr. Carr to console himself, to console his hero, to permit his hero to accept the *status quo* and thereby to apologize for his hero's failure to overcome anything."[45]

The contrast between O'Neill and Carr was intended to expose Carr as an intellectual variant of Studs Lonigan—as someone incapable of an authentic rebellion against cultural conditioning and social pressures. Farrell decided to eliminate O'Neill from the final version of the book because he himself was beginning to lose confidence in revolutionary Marxist ideas. Instead, he closed the second volume of the trilogy on an ambiguous note. Then, at the close of the third volume he presented some tentative but optimistic suggestions for the future. The grounds for his cautious optimism were not so different from those obtained by Laskell at the end of *The Middle of the Journey*: Carr had first cast off the ideological blinders of the church, then rid himself of Stalinism; now he would be free to immerse himself in the experience of life.

This pragmatic theme is also indicated by an epigram from Heraclitus in the front of the book: "Into the same river you could not step twice, for other (and still other) waters are flowing." Toward the end of the novel the theme is dramatized in a striking scene when Bernard contrasts the abstractness of his book-learning with the reality of his own son: "I talk about the downfall of civilization, about the rise of Socialism, about human culture from Peking Man and Pithecanthropus *erectus* to *Mass Action* [the Communist literary publication], and I don't know a hell of a lot about a baby—my own baby, to be specific."[46] This change in focus took its toll on the quality and coherence of the trilogy. The change in the novel's political perspective also did violence to another important particular:

Carr's choice, unlike that of Farrell and his contemporaries, is always between Communism and anti-Communism; anti-Stalinist Marxism never appears as an option.

Farrell's political crisis was under way by 1944, at which time he began to follow the thinking of Albert Goldman and Felix Morrow, who led a tendency in the Socialist Workers Party. By 1948 Farrell had begun to issue crude anticommunist statements, establishing a political association with Sidney Hook that would last beyond the Cold War years. During the Cannon-Shachtman schism in 1939–40, Farrell at first had felt sympathy for Shachtman but then concluded "that there was validity in the slogan of defense of the USSR" even though he was somewhat uncertain about the Soviet Union's social character. He enjoyed good personal relations with many members of the Socialist Workers Party, including Cannon, Novack, Goldman, and Morrow, and threw himself into the work of the Civil Rights Defense Committee, which he saw as an independent activity through which he could make a special contribution.[47]

Nevertheless, when Goldman and Morrow began to develop a series of criticisms of the SWP leadership just before and during their imprisonment after being convicted of violating the Smith Act, Farrell was sympathetic. Goldman himself was an attractive and impressive figure. Born Albert Verblen of working-class parents in Chicago in 1897, Goldman graduated from Medhill High School and attended the University of Cincinnati while concurrently training to be a reform rabbi at Hebrew Union College.[48] During the summer of 1919, while working in the Dakota wheat fields, he came into contact with militant itinerant farmworkers and later that year joined the IWW. In 1920 he joined the Communist Party. For several years he worked as a journeyman tailor in the cloth-cutting trade, but in June 1923 entered the Northwestern University Law School, graduating with highest honors in 1925. From 1926 to 1933 he was a prominent attorney for the Communists' International Labor Defense. Following a visit to the Soviet Union in 1930 he began to be critical of the party and was finally expelled from it for Trotskyism in 1933.

Following his service as Trotsky's attorney during the Dewey Commission of Inquiry hearings, Goldman worked as counsel for Teamsters Local 574 in Minneapolis, resuming the post he had previously held during the 1934 strikes. In 1939 he moved to New York City to work full-time for the SWP at $15 a week. During the 1939–40 break with Shachtman, Goldman defended Cannon's position, but his tone was characteristically less harsh. In his articles for the Trotskyist press, and in popular educational lectures, Goldman established a reputation for expressing himself modestly and for being genuinely responsive to his opponents' arguments. In mid-1941 he was among the twenty-nine leaders and members of the SWP indicted in Minneapolis for allegedly violating the Smith Act; after a trial at which Goldman acted as defense counsel for those indicted, eighteen were convicted and Goldman received a sixteen-month sentence which he served at Sandstone Federal Prison in northern Minnesota.[49]

While in prison, Goldman and Morrow began to develop a series of increasingly harsh criticisms of the SWP leadership.[50] Their supporters never amounted to more than a few dozen, but they included several important figures, such as Jean van Heijenoort, a former mathematics student at the Sorbonne who had been Trotsky's chief assistant throughout much of his third exile and who served as secretary of the Fourth International, based in New York, during World War II. In addition, views analogous to Goldman and Morrow's were endorsed by a large minority among the French Trotskyists led by Yvan Craipeau; a majority of the British Trotskyists led by Jock Haston and Ted Grant; and virtually all of the exiled German Trotskyists.

In a familiar pattern that had unfolded in previous faction fights, the Goldman-Morrow tendency began with a central argument that had a good deal of truth to it. Their criticisms of the party's organizational practices, if correct, also seem justified. However, as the debate persisted and became more virulent, Goldman and Morrow began introducing a number of less tenable positions and taking desperate actions that undermined their claim as a loyal opposition. In the final stages of the factional struggle that they had begun in the name of defending true Trotskyism and Leninism against epigones, they rather quickly repudiated both and succumbed to the simplistic anticommunism they had fought for decades, which now dominated intellectual life in the United States.

Goldman and Morrow's strongest argument challenged Trotsky's somewhat catastrophic perspective that World War II would be followed by a wave of socialist revolutions in the major countries of western Europe, with Stalinism in the Soviet Union quickly eradicated either by an internal political revolution or an externally imposed capitalist restoration. Instead, Goldman and Morrow correctly foresaw that it would be necessary to struggle against an enlarged and politically enhanced Stalinist movement for decades. In contrast, Cannon and the majority of the SWP still adhered to Trotsky's original prediction, one that would not be realized, and they would continue to support it for a number of years. Yet the question remains as to whether Goldman and Morrow's predictions were actually based on a superior insight into the nature of the epoch; it is also possible that, in the process of losing their revolutionary convictions, they were merely projecting the existing, pessimistic situation of the mid-1940s into the future. Likewise, one can question whether the view of Cannon and his supporters simply entailed a dogmatic adherence to prewar predictions; those prewar predictions may have contained an important element of truth that Cannon should be credited for perceiving.

The course of postwar global history suggests that each position contained a mixture of subjective responses and insights into objective reality. Successful anticapitalist revolutions did occur, which undermined the stability of Western capitalism, but they occurred in China and Yugoslavia rather than in western Europe. Powerful working-class struggles did take place in several capitalist nations, as had been predicted, but for various reasons they did not result in an overturning of the social order. Cannon's perspective had to undergo considerable changes to adjust to this new world reality, and a certain dogmatism may have delayed his recognition and theorization of the changed situation longer than necessary. Still, Cannon and his followers in the Socialist Workers Party emerged from this difficult conjuncture with a balance between their anti-Stalinism and anticapitalism. Goldman and Morrow, on the other hand, became totally disoriented and drifted steadily to the right, with Farrell following not too far behind.

In 1945–46, as the faction fight entered into its penultimate stage, Goldman and Morrow proposed that the Socialist Workers Party reunify with the Workers Party. The proposal itself was not at all implausible, and, in fact, Cannon himself (albeit skeptically) would endorse it a year and a half later at the urging of leaders of the Fourth International. After all, Trotsky had argued that the split in 1940 was unnecessary and that supporters of his views could live with the followers of Shachtman-Burnham even if they were in a minority. By the mid-1940s it was clear that the Workers Party had not, as the Socialist Workers Party predicted, succumbed to social patriotism during World War II; if anything, the Workers Party's approach to the war was ultraleftist, although there were instances when such a position only prefaced a movement to the right. Goldman and Morrow, failing to win the Socialist Workers Party to a position favoring unity, began to openly collaborate with the Workers Party leadership, thereby jeopardizing their own membership in the Socialist Workers Party. Goldman, in fact, simply walked out of the Socialist Workers Party in May 1946 and joined the Workers

Party. Soon Jean van Heijenoort was working with the Workers Party. Then Lou Jacobs, known as a longtime Socialist Workers Party leader under the name "Jack Weber," and Sarah Jacobs, who had served as one of Trotsky's secretaries under the name "Sarah Weber," developed their own disagreements with the Socialist Workers Party and left to briefly collaborate with the Workers Party as well. Morrow was expelled from the Socialist Workers Party at its November 1946 convention on the grounds of engaging in unauthorized meetings with Shachtman, but by then he had become so discouraged that he never followed through on his commitment to join the Workers Party.

During the summer of 1945, Farrell had already begun associating more closely with the Workers Party. This turn was precipitated by an incident in which the Socialist Workers Party leaders refused to publish in the Socialist Workers Party journal, *Fourth International*, a letter by Farrell protesting what he believed to be the Socialist Workers Party's unneccessarily factional attitude toward the WP. Cannon then rather bluntly answered it in an article published in the Socialist Workers Party's *Internal Bulletin*.[51] As a copious contributor to the Workers Party magazine, *New International*, Farrell still appeared to be an ardent champion of revolutionary Marxism. He even looked askance at young party intellectuals such as Irving Howe, who seemed to be adapting to trends in culture that Farrell thought were conservatizing because they disparaged realism and naturalism in literature.[52] Yet in mid-1948 Farrell and Albert Goldman suddenly broke with the Workers Party and switched their allegiance to the Socialist Party. Only a few months earlier, Jean van Heijenoort had repudiated Marxism entirely.

In 1948 Farrell and Goldman jointly had taken exception to two positions of the Workers Party: they supported the Marshall Plan while the Workers Party opposed it; and they advocated endorsing Norman Thomas's presidential campaign while the Workers Party took the position that a protest vote for the Socialist Workers Party, Socialist Labor Party, or Socialist Party all were acceptable. In March 1948 Farrell suggested to Goldman in a letter that it was utopian to insist that the working class of Europe should struggle simultaneously against the forces of Stalinism and American imperialism. The former represented pure evil while the latter was an acceptable ally:

> The simple and blunt fact of the matter is that nothing stands in the way of the Stalinization of Europe but American power. The motives of the American capitalists in opposing

Stalinism are not your motives and they are not my motives. But for you and I, for thousands and millions of others, the question concerning Stalinism is a matter of actual survival. For the American capitalists, in effect, it's the same issue. It is for different reasons, but it is a question of survival. There is no fooling yourself about Stalinism. You either join it, support it, stay with it, or else it has only one statement to make to you: Death.

Trotskyism, Farrell contended, had simply failed to organize "a sufficient fighting force with which to meet Stalinism." In an ironic inversion of the Communists' Theory of Social Fascism, Farrell announced that the deluded theories of both the Socialist Workers Party and the Workers Party were objectively the same as those of Stalinism.[53]

Goldman responded by agreeing that supporting capitalism was the only way to stop Stalinism, but he wished to do everything possible to differentiate his motives from those of his would-be allies. "Only a fool or a Stalinist can be against the Marshall Plan," but, if he were a member of Congress, Goldman said that he would prefer to abstain rather than vote for the plan, unless his ballot proved to be the decisive one. He regretted having left the Socialist Party in 1937, and he dreamed of a new organization "uniting all the people who are for socialism [and] against capitalism and Stalinism into one propaganda organization. . . . Why should not I and you and Van [Heijenoort] and Felix [Morrow] and Max [Shachtman] and Sidney Hook belong to one organization in spite of all our differences?"[54]

Farrell was skeptical of both of these positions: for him, to support the Marshall Plan in practice yet refuse to give it a public endorsement implied a dangerous divorce between "feeling" and "formal ideas." Establishing a propaganda league to promote socialism was also a dubious effort because socialism had to present practical proposals, and all practical proposals at the moment might well "only lead to sectarianism." Farrell had come to believe that the Moscow trials should have been the turning point for the anti-Stalinist left. At that time, the true nature of Stalinism and the viability of democratic capitalism as the only means to fight it should have been recognized.[55] He was following the road that had been earlier traveled by Sidney Hook. In the 1950s Farrell would serve as chairman of the Committee for Cultural Freedom and in the 1960s he would become an ardent supporter of Hubert Humphrey and a harsh critic of the New Left. By the 1970s his views on such issues as affirmative action and Israel were hardly distinguishable from those of the neoconservative writers for *Commentary* and *The Public Interest.*

A 1954 essay in the *New Leader* called "Reflections at Fifty" gives some insight into the philosophical aspects of this change in views:

> When I first began to write I was full of indignation because of the sorrows of the world. I was angry because of cruelty, because of the exploitation of some men and women by others, because of the coldness with which some people manipulate others, because of dirt, ignorance, aggressiveness, and the other things which ruin and sadden human lives. . . . It is not possible at fifty to feel the indignation of one's youth. . . . Indignation has turned to a stoical feeling. I have come to see that pain and agony are part of the way it is in life.[56]

These sentiments are reminiscent of the ideas Ralph Waldo Emerson expressed in his essays "Compensation" and "Experience"; and it was also Emerson, the forerunner of such pragmatists as C. S. Peirce and William James, whom Farrell cited in a 1978 statement announcing his decision to join Social Democrats USA, the right wing of the American Social Democracy.[57] Although officially advocating socialism, the politics of this organization are hard to distinguish from those of traditional mainstream Democrats and Republicans.

This new mood, embryonic in Farrell's writings since the Bernard Carr trilogy was under way in the mid-1940s, grew steadily during a transition in his literary activities involving several false starts that lasted until October 1958. At that time he formally inaugurated his fourth and final series of books, "A Universe of Time." In content this series of a dozen published books is largely a ratification and extension of his lifelong plan "to create out of the life that I have seen, known, experienced, heard about, and imagined, a panoramic story of our days and years, a story which would continue through as many books as I would be able to write."[58] Many of the important characters in "A Universe of Time" had already appeared in earlier books, but now they were given new names—Danny O'Neill is called Edward Arthur Ryan, the O'Neills are the Ryans, and the O'Flahertys are called the Dunnes. Another difference is that the new series has a looser organizational conception and includes novels, a prose poem, and short stories that range over a broader, although ultimately interlinked, group of people, time periods, and locales.

A more decisive change, however, is that Farrell's new stoic philosophy of the 1950s is dominant in "A Universe of Time," manifested through the autumnal and mellow tone that has displaced the uncompromising anger of Farrell's earlier books. In the 1940s Farrell wrote that his fiction helped to forge a perspective necessary for a socialist future because his novels alerted readers to the "ideal of attaining the full stature of humanity."[59] In the 1950s he described "A Universe of Time" as "a relativistic panorama of our times" concerned with "man's creativity and his courageous acceptance of impermanence."[60] This new sense of acceptance is facilitated by the settings of most of this last group of books. The situations depicted are often insular and repressed in atmosphere. And the unifying character emerging from this, Eddie Ryan, is largely preoccupied with his own personal struggles between his emotional drives and the need for artistic self-discipline.

Five weeks before his death on 22 August 1979 Farrell completed a novel about a left-wing New York Jewish intellectual, *Sam Holman*, published posthumously in 1983. For those familiar with the inside history of New York radicalism in the 1930s, there was no doubt that the main character is based on the life of Herbert Solow, the brilliant organizer of the Dewey Commission of Inquiry, who eventually became one of the editors of *Fortune*. Moreover, in addition to Holman many other characters in the novel can be identified with New York leftists of the era, often by simply reversing the initial letters of their first and last names: Carl Winston is Whittaker Chambers; Saul Miklas is Meyer Schapiro; Tommy Stock is Clifton Fadiman; Norman Rosen is Felix Morrow; Oliver Hirsch is Elliot Cohen; Leroy Margolis is Max Lerner; Henry Smart is Sidney Hook; Ernest Milan is Max Eastman; Rita Moeller is Elinor Rice; Nobel Green is George Novack; Josephine Lawrence is Diana Trilling; Tommy Lawrence is Lionel Trilling; Frances Dunsky is Tess Slesinger; Carl Leon is Lewis Corey; Frank Y. Weathers is William Z. Foster; Donald Jolley is John McDonald; Henry Abelman is Albert Halper; A. M. Jillet is A. J. Muste; Charles Cleary is James P. Cannon; Bertram Jackson is James Burnham; Willard Endicott is Edmund Wilson; Kate Fieldstone is Freda Kirchway; Oscar Lacey is Liston Oak; Tracey Norren is Norman Thomas; and Edward A. Ryan is James T. Farrell.

Yet Farrell did not intend his portraits to be strictly biographical; they are constructed partly from memory, with considerable imaginative input. Holman, for example, receives a Ph.D. from Columbia University, which Solow never did. He also becomes involved in the Jewish-humanist publication *Modern Torah* while he is a radical, whereas Solow was assistant editor of the *Menorah Journal* years earlier and quit when he became an active Marxist. Eventually Holman joins the Communist Party, while Solow remained only an ally. In 1929 Holman, not yet a radical, travels abroad where he meets Henry Smart at the Marx-Engels Institute in Moscow and Ernest Milan while visiting Trotsky on the Turkish island of Prinkipo. In fact, Solow's trip to the Soviet Union was in 1932 when he was already pro-Communist and long after Hook had returned to the United States.

The theme of *Sam Holman* is indirectly related to that of the original plan for the Bernard Carr trilogy: the descent of genuine talent into mediocrity. Holman is among the most brilliant and respected of a brilliant group of young intellectuals, and he typifies their political trajectory from a revolutionary opposition to capitalism to a reconciliation with the status quo. But from first to last his achievements turn out to be disproportionately less than his promise once seemed to indicate.

Holman suffers a kind of rootlessness, an inability to locate the proper medium and vision through which to express his talents. Smart has his scholarly commitment to the field of philosophy and Miklas to art history, but Holman lives from day to day with little control over the direction of his life. This *luftmensch* quality is dramatized by a series of love affairs—including a first marriage that is little more than a long affair—that begin and end haphazardly. Reaching middle age, he stumbles into a second marriage as well as a comfortable job as a writer for *Empire*. In this more stable environment he is able to function productively for several decades but hardly at the level for which he once seemed destined.

The method of the book might easily lead to a misunderstanding of its point of view. Farrell's strategy in *Sam Holman*, as in most of his other works, is to use a minimum of authorial intrusion in order to depict the world through Holman's eyes with only occasional digressions into the minds of others. Thus the harsh judgments—for example, about the more committed leftists Rosen and Green—are those of the cynical Holman, not necessarily Farrell. We are pointedly reminded of this toward the end of the book when Holman muses with equal skepticism about the literary achievements of the Farrell persona, the almost-forgotten novelist Edward A. Ryan. Thus the somewhat hollow and disconnected atmosphere in the novel, as well as the shallow perceptions about various characters, are calculated to reflect defects in Holman's own emotional life.

Sam Holman is a serious attempt to tell at least part of the "personal truth" of what it was like to be a radical intellectual in the 1930s, thus in a certain sense resembling Harvey Swados's posthumous novel *Celebration* (1974). We are shown how men treat women; how personal and political ambitions are bound together; and how abstractions about social justice become substitutes for engagement in the real world. Yet the depiction of Holman would have been more convincing if we had also been given evidence of the quality of his intellect. Mary McCarthy's "Portrait of the intellectual as a Yale Man" more fully and effectively creates a radical intellectual of the time. Farrell's Holman, in contrast to her richly painted James Barnett, seems to have come from nowhere; the careful attention paid to the shaping forces of family and environment, so central to the vivification of Studs Lonigan and Danny O'Neill, are nearly absent. Not only do we know little of Holman's background, but we do not know much more about the reality of his presence other than that he sports a reddish-brown mustache and tends to be skeptical of the sincerity and intellect of almost every man he meets. The reasons for his astonishing sexual attractiveness to women are never explained. Moreover, the dialogue in *Sam Holman* suggests that Farrell found it difficult in his later years to vary the language and vocabulary of his characters within and among novels. This may be one of the reasons why some readers and critics fail to appreciate the true diversity of his oeuvre.

Although there has been a steady revival of interest since 1975 in Farrell's life and writing, his greatest impact was and probably will always be linked to his multifaceted role as a radical novelist and activist during the Great Depression and World War II years. An indication of renewed interest in him came at the time of the publication of his fiftieth book, *The Dunne Family* (1976). In celebration of this literary milestone, a "Salute to James T. Farrell" was held at the St. Regis Hotel in New York City. Norman Mailer, one of several prominent novelists who addressed the gathering, stated that Farrell's works had modified the sensibility of many writers of his generation and that Farrell's relentlessness in pursuing his literary goals in spite of all adversity should be a model for others to follow.[61] A second indication of a minor Farrell revival came on 7, 14, and 21 March 1979, when the National Broadcasting Company presented *Studs Lonigan* as a television miniseries that was seen by millions of viewers. Shortly afterward he received the Emerson-Thoreau award from the American Academy of Arts and Sciences.

But the brief spurt of interest in Farrell during the four years prior to his death will probably not alter his literary stature significantly. Three aspects of his work have been debated at length. While he was praised in the 1930s for his powers of observation and his bold use of American speech, he was accused early on of masquerading documentaries as novels and charged with being insufficiently selective in the experiences he depicted. In the 1940s some critics began to argue that he was a prisoner of the moribund school of naturalism; others claimed that he was a repetitious writer, clumsy, and devoid of grace and style.

The issue of Farrell's selectivity is a central one. Opinions range from that of Ann Douglas, who wrote in a eulogy that "Farrell's work constitutes the last important experiment to date in American literature with what can be viewed as deliberately unedited material," to that of Diana Trilling, who said that "the truth is that Farrell is a meticulous craftsman, choosing both incident and language with care and skill."[62] Trilling's assessment is more accurate, but the corollary is that the care and skill of selection must be guided by a clear and compelling vision that establishes priorities in the relationships revealed. During the first phase of Farrell's development, when he was animated by a Marxist anger at the manner in which class relations impeded human development, his vision was vividly sustained and focused on precise objectives. However, in the years leading up to "A Universe of Time," Farrell's anger dissipated into stoicism: a new vision had to be developed that made demands for which his technique was not always fully prepared.

The claim that Farrell was a simple environmental determinist or a prisoner of the putatively dated school of naturalism has largely been discredited. Farrell himself criticized the limitations of the naturalist perspective as early as his 1936 *A Note on Literary Criticism*: at that time he linked naturalism to mechanical materialism and accused it of fostering an expansive rather than an intensive approach to art. In 1964 Edgar Branch, Farrell's most reliable critic, published a convincing essay, "Freedom and Determinism in James T. Farrell's Fiction." Branch demonstrated that Farrell's "functional conception of the self" in his fiction was one that exhibited "a full pattern of human conduct . . . that accommodates freedom." Branch's conclusion that Farrell is a "critical realist" seems apt.[63]

Farrell's greatest weakness as a writer was that he failed to develop either sufficient consciousness about or a sophisticated theory of the uses of language in writing fiction beyond admirable but rather simple notions that language must serve the end of accurately recreating character and environment. There is no doubt that his heavy reliance on personal experience made Farrell's work appear redundant to many critics. In short, his prose failed to communicate to many readers the true diversity of the experiences he aspired to depict.

A famous man by the time he was thirty, Farrell's three decades from the mid-1940s to the mid-1970s witnessed a reversal of fortune; his survival as a writer became an ordeal. Hounded by censors in 1948 when Philadelphia police attempted to stop the sales of *Studs Lonigan*, sneered at by a herd of literary detractors, and harassed by publishers who did not find his books sufficiently marketable, he persisted in a curmudgeonly sort of rebellion and drifted into near obscurity. In the 1950s friends urged him to settle down to a teaching post, but he refused. Unwilling to let monetary considerations influence his writing and inhospitable to new cultural trends, he persisted in using his art idiosyncratically to tell the truth as he saw it. At one point he was evicted from his apartment for nonpayment of rent, and on another occasion financial desperation forced him to sell the movie rights to *Studs Lonigan* for a pittance. But he only became stronger in his belief that he must resist commercial forces. In 1961, at what was probably the nadir of his career, he publicly declared, "I began writing in my own way and I shall go on doing it. This is my first and last word on the subject."[64]

Future biographers will have to probe the psychological causes and artistic consequences of such single-minded determination, but Farrell himself justified his defiant pursuit of his own literary objectives in terms of social value. Quoting from Tolstoy's *What Is Art?* (1897–98), he explained that the purpose of his writing technique is to "infect [the reader] with feeling" so as to awaken the reader's mind to the social forces at work in shaping one's life.[65] "The most important thing that a person can do is teach," wrote Farrell at the outset of an essay, "The Value of Literature in Modern Society."[66] Farrell's ability to sustain a loyal readership in spite of decades of aggressive assault by critics suggests that his endeavor to transform his personal experiences into art resounded in the emotions and intellects of a significant audience.

PART III

The Great Retreat

CHAPTER 9

Apostates and True Believers

Tell him, in manhood,
he must still revere
The dreams of early
youth, nor ope the heart
Of heaven's all-tender flower
to canker-worms
  Of boasted reason,—
  nor be led astray
When, by the wisdom of
the dust, he hears
Enthusiasm, heavenly-
born, blasphemed.

—Schiller, *Don Carlos*[1]

. . . .

"RED FASCISM"

The particular variant of post–World War II social thought, in which many of the political and cultural ideas of the New York intellectuals became essentially hegemonic, was correctly characterized by Robert Booth Fowler as that of "believing skeptics," a selective kind of skepticism that is itself nothing less than ideology sui generis.[2] Not only was the notion of the "end of ideology" an ideological stance in its own right, but the supraclass values of "realism" and "modulation" vaunted by Lionel Trilling and others were equally deceptive. Despite the use of euphemisms (such as Dwight Macdonald's 1952 statement "I choose the West," all the more remarkable for one so adept at exposing the sham rhetoric of others), the program and perspectives of most of the New York intellectuals during the postwar era embodied support for capitalism, albeit with a sprinkling of criticism to salve their consciences.[3]

In 1967, Philip Rahv, who had suddenly become transformed back into a leftist, offered a trenchant critique of the role played by a sizable number of New York intellectuals in the American Committee for Cultural Freedom: "The people who accepted CIA subsidies without being clear in their minds as to what was involved are in many ways to be compared to the 'fellow-travelers' and 'stooges' of the 1930s, who supported Stalin's reading of Marxism and his murderous policies even as they spoke of the Russia he despotically ruled as a 'workers' paradise' and as a 'classless society.' But in contrast to the 'stooges' of yesterday, the 'stooges' of today are paid cash on the line for their various declarations."[4] True enough, affiliation with the American Committee for Cultural Freedom and its vision of an imperfect but non-imperialist United States could bring free trips abroad, subsidies for magazines, and executive jobs. Its 1954 budget, for example, totaled over $170,000 in grants from the Heritage Foundation ($41,000), the Farfield Foundation ($10,000), the Fleischmann Foundation ($40,000), and other institutions and individuals.[5] All that was required for a slice of the pie was a self-imposed blind spot when it came to U.S. intervention in Iran, Guatemala, and elsewhere, as well as an ability to minimize the pernicious antiradical witch-hunt in the United States.

Although distinct personal paths were followed, the rejection of an ideology explicitly based upon a Marxist analysis was eventually embraced by most of the New York intellectuals. It was scarcely coincidence that their shifts in perspective came to a head after World War II. Thus the transit of the New York intellectuals from revolutionary anti-Stalinism to a self-proclaimed "liberal anti-communism," with their corresponding shift in political allegiance, must be considered in a sociohistorical context. What remained most consistent in their ideological outlook in the postwar era was their virulent hostility to Stalinism, which increasingly became redefined to mean Leninism and ultimately any form of revolutionary Marxism. They seized on the fact that Leninism and Stalinism had a sequential relationship and certain superficial similarities, conveniently forgetting their earlier belief that the former was in essence a negation of the latter.

Furthermore, the intellectuals' rejection of Trotsky's dualistic conception of the Soviet Union as embodying a progressive socioeconomic structure presided over by an intolerably repressive regime may have facilitated the most debilitating misconception of the era. In the Cold War atmosphere the careful distinctions that the New York intellectuals had once made between criticizing Communism from the left and criticizing Communism from the right tended in some cases to dissolve into epithets that equated the Soviet Union with Nazi Germany: "Red Fascism," "Communazis," and the ambiguous term "totalitarianism."[6] "All evil was now to be attached to Communism," Alfred Kazin later wrote.[7] Several works by Arthur Koestler, George Orwell's *1984* (1949), and new editions of Aldous Huxley's *Brave New World* (1932) were popularly interpreted according to this anticommunist mood, and radical intellectuals themselves were drawn back to the demoralizing memory of the Moscow trials with their shocking confessions.

Into the charged atmosphere of this historical moment came Hannah Arendt's book *The Origins of Totalitarianism* (1951), which among intellectuals in New York may have performed a conservatizing role. Such an impact, however, was undoubtedly unintended by its author, a maverick thinker of considerable creativity who feared that the United States might itself move in a totalitarian direction under the impact of McCarthyism. Arendt's genuinely independent streak derived in part from a personal political history that deviated somewhat from the mainstream of the New York intellectuals; she had never passed through a Leninist phase, although she had partially assimilated the tradition of dissident communism through her husband, Heinrich Bluecher, a former Bukharinist.[8] Her German education and upbringing also distinguished her from the others, but it was from the New York intellectuals that she received her initial attention, support, and most lavish praise. In the late 1940s and 1950s she contributed to *Politics, Commentary,* and the *Partisan Review.* It was Kazin who first arranged for the publication of *The Origins of Totalitarianism* when her original publisher backed out of the contract. In reviewing the book, Mary McCarthy described Arendt's political acuity as "amazing," Kazin said that her thinking had a "moral grandeur," and Macdonald dubbed her "the most original and profound—therefore the most valuable—political theoretician of our times."[9]

The book represented a major departure from Marxism in its method. Its conflation of Stalinism and Hitlerism was developed without a comparison of class structures and economic systems, and it was based on the metaphysical assumption that the most appropriate measure for believing that the two social orders were a single genus was the degree of "radical evil" that they embodied. Thus the book could be read in such a way as to bolster the anticommunist hysteria of the 1950s, reinforcing the view that the Soviet Union was to be expected to behave as Nazi Germany had in the 1930s. Once this belief took hold among the New York intellectuals, it influenced how they perceived all other relevant information. Any ambiguous actions on the part of foreign or domestic Communists were taken as signifying a dangerous threat, whereas an observer with a more complex theoretical perspective might have seen other possible explanations. Like the apologists for the Soviet Union in the 1930s, the New York intellectuals began to perceive aspects of both the history of the Soviet Union and the nature of American capitalism in ways that were more conducive

to their new beliefs, ignoring facts that might have been dis-
comfiting.

Becoming firmly convinced that the Soviet Union would behave
as had Nazi Germany led to support of U.S. imperialism (recast as
"Western democracy" and "the free world") as the only practical
deterrent to Stalinism. Thus it became increasingly easier over a
period of time for many of the intellectuals to renege on their advocacy of progressive domestic legislation and eventually to turn
against all movements for fundamental change. This was especially
true among some who became pro-Zionist and who thus found
themselves allied with politicians who had right-wing domestic
views. In the 1960s quite a few of the New York intellectuals would
be distressed more by rebelling students, women, and blacks than
by the American government's slaughter of Vietnamese peasants
and its support of reactionary dictatorships around the world; some,
in fact, showed a real fear and loathing of the new militants precisely for the wrong reasons—because many of the students raised
intellectual challenges, refused blind obedience, and significantly
raised the country's moral and cultural level. In 1972 Sidney Hook,
Irving Kristol, Norman Podhoretz, and a number of other intellectuals voted for Richard Nixon as the "lesser evil" compared with
George McGovern, although they were registered Democrats. In
1980 and again in 1984 they supported Ronald Reagan.

If the admittedly complex phenomenon of World War II divested
the intellectuals of their internationalism, it was the postwar years
that wedded them ideologically to the social structure of which
they had once been so critical. In lockstep fashion they proclaimed
belief in the guilt of Alger Hiss and the Rosenbergs despite many
contradictions in the evidence and dubious procedures by the Federal Bureau of Investigation that have raised questions for decades.[10] They universally purged themselves of ideas at variance
with the ideology of Cold War liberalism, especially all forms of
Leninism, and in some cases may actually have blocked out from
memory the authentic nature of their past radical convictions.
Ironically, several of those who proclaimed faith in the freedoms of
the United States and scorned those who criticized the witch-hunt
as "alarmists" felt it tactically wise to misrepresent their political
histories in public statements—a tacit acknowledgment that there
was indeed an antiradical hysteria. Taking advantage of the general
public's ignorance of the different varieties of communism, they
claimed that they had been consistent anticommunists since the
early or mid-1930s, never mentioning the subsequent years during

which they had been independent communists decrying Stalinism for its adaptations to liberalism.

Such declarations were made, for example, when revelations about James Rorty's radical past caused him to lose his position as a script writer for the "Voice of America," where he specialized in sensational exposés of "The Communist War Against Religion."[11] In a 1951 letter to the Regional Loyalty Board of the United States Civil Service Commission, Rorty stated, "I have been fairly well-known for the past eighteen years as an active public enemy of the Communist Party. . . . I was never a member of the Communist Party or any of the Communist factions, or in any way affiliated with them."[12] It is true that, starting in 1933, he went into opposition to the Communist Party; but in 1934 he joined the American Workers Party, a revolutionary communist organization, and in 1935 he supported its fusion with the Communist League of America, refraining from membership for tactical reasons only. Despite his nonideological outlook and anarchist tendencies, Rorty's politics were essentially revolutionary communist for five years following the 1933 rupture with the National Committee for the Defense of Political Prisoners.

This blurring and then dissolving of the difference between revolutionary anti-Stalinism and simple anticommunism was a hallmark of the former radicals in the American Committee for Cultural Freedom, as can be demonstrated by three other examples. In a statement supporting Rorty, Sidney Hook attributed to himself a similar political biography: "I speak as one . . . who has been marshalling the efforts of all genuine liberal forces in the United States since 1933 to defend the structure of our freedoms from totalitarian attacks."[13] Yet until 1939, Hook's view was that the problem with the Communists was that they were insufficiently communist, having forsaken true revolutionary Leninist strategy for an alliance with liberalism; Hook had nothing but scorn and contempt for the reformism and liberalism of the Communist Party of the Popular Front years of the late 1930s. His primary allies and associates for most of that time were Trotskyists and other independent communists.

When Lewis Corey died in 1953, Sol Stein, executive director of the American Committee for Cultural Freedom, sent a letter of protest to the *New York Times*. He criticized its obituary stating that Corey "had helped to form the Communist Party in this country, but in recent years had turned against it." Stein claimed that the *Times* was "interpreting a twenty-year fight against Communism as something that happened in 'recent years.' "[14] Both the *Times* and Stein neglected the significance of Corey's dissident communist activity for six years after 1933, which included secret membership in the Lovestone group from 1937 to 1939.[15]

Finally, there was the bizarre episode of James T. Farrell's resignation as chairman of the American Committee for Cultural Freedom in 1956. From the onset, Farrell had been in the left wing of the committee. This position meant that he desired to decrease the domestic anti-Communist focus and pay greater attention to repressive aspects of McCarthyism. At the same time, he supported the American Committee's criticism of the Paris office for being too "cultural" and insufficiently "political" (viz., anti-Communist) in its activities abroad. In the spring and summer of 1956, however, he undertook a world tour on behalf of the committee and came to the conclusion that the approach of the Paris office did, in fact, more correctly correspond to the political situation in Europe and Asia. Yet, during a stopover in Turkey, he managed to get drunk and send a crude letter to the *Chicago Daily Tribune* with sentences such as the following: "Often I have criticized our Chicago and our America but we must stop taking as much as one insult from anybody in the world, we must apologize to no one for our country, and from here on in, we must not give one cent or one drop of the blood of our sons and nephews, unless it is for an honest and free partnership of free peoples."[16] Despite the vulgarity of the statement and its chauvinist overtones, it was in a certain sense still a "left" critique in that Farrell thought that the United States should not support social systems that were not really democratic merely for diplomatic reasons. Upon his return to New York he submitted his resignation by telegram, which a mortified executive committee gladly accepted. Since his official letter of explanation attacked the committee once more from the left, he also tried to bolster his anti-Stalinist credentials by referring to himself as having been "an active anti-Communist" since before 1936. As in the other cases, this formulation directly implied that there was no qualitative discrepancy between Farrell's revolutionary communism, which lasted until 1948, and the anticommunism he embraced only one or two years before the American Committee for Cultural Freedom was formed.[17]

No doubt the episode of political persecution at the "Voice of America" motivated Rorty to undertake the writing of *McCarthy and the Communists* (1954), sponsored by the American Committee for Cultural Freedom. Rorty, who now described himself as a "Taft Republican," collaborated on the project with Moshe Decter, the former political editor of the "Voice of America," who referred to himself as a "Stevenson Democrat." Their thesis was that, although McCarthy had performed a service in drawing attention to Communist agents who had sneaked into the Roosevelt administration, his sloppy methods had begun to hinder rather than aid the necessary purge of Communists.[18] The appearance of the book indicated a slight shift in the attitude of the American Committee toward McCarthy now that a substantial section of public opinion had been mobilized against him by other forces.

Earlier, in 1952, Farrell had demanded that a planning meeting for an American Committee for Cultural Freedom conference, "In Defense of Free Culture," adopt a resolution proclaiming that "the main job *in this country* is fighting McCarthyism." He insisted that domestic communism was no longer a threat and that "the most effective way of influencing European intellectuals is to show how we defend cultural freedom in our own country." Dwight Macdonald enthusiastically supported Farrell, and Richard Rovere indicated assent; but Sidney Hook, Daniel Bell, Clement Greenberg, William Phillips, F. W. Dupee, and the vast majority of others found various reasons to object.[19]

The conference was held at the Waldorf-Astoria Hotel on 29 March. According to notes taken by Macdonald, Rovere and Mary McCarthy spoke out against Joseph McCarthy at the morning session, but Max Eastman declared that the antiradical witch-hunt did not exist and insisted that any "unhappy incidents" were due to the failure of the liberals "to see the necessity of the main task," which was exposing Communists. In the afternoon session, James Wechsler of the *New York Post* proposed a resolution attacking McCarthy, but the chair, Lionel Trilling, ruled him out of order and promised that the American Committee for Cultural Freedom would discuss the matter in its appropriate bodies.[20] On 11 April, Macdonald and Rovere met with Bell and Kristol, but the latter two refused to support a general condemnation of McCarthy. They proposed instead that he be criticized for specific incidents such as his reference to Edmund Wilson's *Memoirs of Hecate County* as "pornographic and pro-Communist."[21]

Then, on 23 April, a meeting of the American Committee for Cultural Freedom was held at the Columbia Club. Since Farrell was not present, Macdonald spoke in favor of a general condemnation of the witch-hunt naming McCarthy, and Bell counterposed the idea of making specific criticisms when warranted. Elliot Cohen immediately objected to Macdonald's proposal on the grounds that it would detract from the anti-Communist campaign, and he was joined in various ways by William Phillips, Irving Kristol, Robert Warshow, Nathan Glazer, Sidney Hook, Herbert Solow, Sol Levitas, and most of the others. Macdonald's only vocal supporters were Arthur Schlesinger, Jr., Diana Trilling, James Wechsler, and Philip Rahv.[22]

In 1953, however, Hook published a letter in the *New York Times* declaring that McCarthy's reckless tactics objectively aided the Communists, and he urged "a national movement of men and women of all political parties to retire Senator McCarthy from public life."[23] When the book by Rorty and Decter appeared the following spring, Burnham, who had already been asked to leave the *Partisan Review* editorial board, led a walkout of the most conservative wing of the American Committee for Cultural Freedom. Beyond such belated, minor, and politically ambiguous actions, it is difficult to find any other evidence of anti-McCarthy activity by the New York intellectuals who had joined the American Committee for Cultural Freedom. A few who felt more strongly about the matter, such as Dwight Macdonald, handed in resignations.

Typical of efforts by the liberal elements of the American Committee who wanted only to modulate the witch-hunt was Lionel Trilling's participation in writing an ambiguous 1953 Columbia University policy statement on academic freedom. On the one hand, Trilling and the cosigners opposed federal investigations of American educational institutions as "unnecessary and harmful." On the other, they agreed that "membership in Communist organizations almost certainly implies a submission to an intellectual control which is entirely at variance with the principles of academic competence as we understand them."[24] Thus, while making a gentle and guarded case against the real practice of McCarthyism, the authors offered a powerful statement that implicitly bolstered the rationale for the McCarthyite campaign. It was as if they were doctors cautiously going on record against the surgical removal of a bodily growth, while loudly declaring the growth to be cancerous.

Of course, the issue of responding to the witch-hunt was complicated by the decision of the Communist Party and many of its allies to deny their views and present themselves as liberals. This allowed some of the anti-Stalinist intellectuals to self-righteously view the Communists and their fellow travelers as hypocrites, especially since the Communists had earlier supported the persecution of the Trotskyists under the same Smith Act now used against them. On the other hand, when the Independent Socialist League fought to get off the attorney general's list, and when the Socialist Workers Party launched an aggressive campaign in defense of the right of one of its own members, World War II veteran James Kutcher, to keep his job while maintaining his views, the American Committee for Cultural Freedom paid little attention. In fact, however much one might disagree with the tactic, one can understand the decision of the Communist victims to hide their views and affiliations because of the ferocity of the onslaught. In contrast, there was no excuse for the behavior of the Cold War liberals, who demonstrated only the ersatz quality of their "anti-Stalinism." After all, the more one feared and hated totalitarian rule in the Soviet Union, the more one should have opposed any replication in the United States. Yet these "anti-Stalinist" intellectuals showed an extraordinary tolerance toward those congressional committees that were menacing freedom of opinion and disregarding due process.

A few voices of left-wing resistance did come from a younger generation of anti-Stalinist radicals who participated in the 1952 *Partisan Review* symposium on "Our Country and Our Culture." Irving Howe, in his last months of membership in Max Shachtman's Independent Socialist League, affirmed that "Marxism seems to me the best available method for understanding and making history. . . . Even at its most dogmatic, it proposes a more realistic theory of society than the currently popular liberalism."[25] Norman Mailer, who, under the influence of his quasi-Trotskyist translator, Jean Malaquais, had moved in the late 1940s from a Popular Front Communism to a view of the United States and the Soviet Union as equivalently malignant forces, declared his alienation from the culture of his country.[26] C. Wright Mills, who had come close to the Workers Party during World War II and who had written his first book, *The New Men of Power* (1948), partly under Workers Party influence, frankly accused the *Partisan Review* editors of having betrayed their founding principles.[27] The one dissident voice among the older generation of intellectuals in the symposium was Philip Rahv's explicit assault on his own generation for succumbing to a process of "*embourgeoisement*." Clearly he had the center and right wings of the American Committee for Cultural Freedom in mind when he denounced

> some of the ex-radicals and ex-Marxists, who have gone so far in smoothly re-adapting themselves . . . as to be scarcely distinguishable from the common run of philistines. In their narrow world anti-Stalinism has become almost a professional stance. It has come to mean so much that it excludes nearly all other concerns and ideas, with the result that they are trying to turn anti-Stalinism into something which it can never

be: a total outlook on life, no less, or even a philosophy of history. Apparently some of them find it altogether easy to put up with the vicious antics of a political bum like Senator McCarthy, even as they grow more and more intolerant of any basic criticism of existing social arrangements.[28]

The evolution of Elliot Cohen's *Commentary* was yet another symptom of the transformation of the anti-Stalinist left into the New York intellectuals under the impact of Cold War anticommunist ideology. At the time of its founding in 1946, *Commentary* considered anti-Stalinist Leninists to be part of its intellectual community, frequently publishing feature articles by the Trotskyist Sherry Mangan as well as some essays and reviews by Workers Party member Irving Howe. Clement Greenberg was the central link to both men, although assistant editors Nathan Glazer and Robert Warshow agreed that the Shachtman group was an ally. Cohen was willing to tolerate this attitude, and Irving Kristol, another staff member, immersed in a return to Judaism, was simply unconcerned. By 1948 Mangan had essentially been purged as a regular contributor because of his refusal to give critical support to the "West." Later, when Howe launched *Dissent* magazine, partly to chart a path away from revolutionary socialist politics but also to challenge the conformist atmosphere of the early 1950s, Glazer wrote a sharp attack on its premier issue.

Cohen himself drew increasingly close to Sol Levitas, the influential editor of the *New Leader*, and functioned as a right-wing element in the American Committee for Cultural Freedom, only slightly less extreme than James Burnham. He also served as an unofficial adviser on Communism to executives at the Luce publications as well as to New York State officials. Yet his peculiar relation to Judaism persisted. Even during his radical years he took the unpopular position of defending the German-Jewish-American establishment, and after leaving the *Menorah Journal* he had worked as public relations director for the Federation of Jewish Philanthropies without ever becoming a Zionist. Indeed, it was anti-Zionism that was his main link to the American Jewish Committee, which sponsored *Commentary*, although Cohen's anti-Zionism stemmed from his original universalist perspective while the American Jewish Committee seemed to view Zionism as an expression of an east European Jewish nationalism that it did not share. Cohen's staff members also held non-Zionist positions: Glazer believed in a binational state in Palestine; Kristol's Judaism was confined to philosophical issues; and Warshow evidenced no special concern about the matter. When information about the Holocaust became public, Cohen appeared to be unaffected. Although Martin Buber once came to Cohen's home to discuss the situation in the Middle East, Cohen himself never traveled to Israel.[29]

Another indication of the disorientation of the anti-Stalinist left during the witch-hunt was its failure to rally to the cause of the Independent Socialist League's campaign to have its name removed from the attorney general's list of "subversive" organizations. When hearings were held on the issue in Washington, D.C., Shachtman was shocked that Hook refused to testify on behalf of the Independent Socialist League. In general, he found it difficult to get any intellectuals to testify. James T. Farrell refused to cooperate, probably because he was bitter about having been "used" by the Workers Party in the 1940s. C. Wright Mills refused to testify as well, apparently because he was hesitant to be identified publicly with a group still claiming to be Leninist and Trotskyist. Finally, Daniel Bell, Norman Thomas, and Dwight Macdonald were brought in to speak on behalf of the organization; all acted with considerable honor and integrity, although on the witness stand Macdonald insisted on raising his old grievance about one of his articles not having been published in its entirety. The main witness testifying to the organization's "subversion" was James Burnham, who reluctantly testified under government pressure. Arriving at the administrative hearing he proferred a friendly greeting to Shachtman, who responded with a brutal cold shoulder. Once on the witness stand, Burnham was forced by the Independent Socialist League's attorney, Joseph Rauh, to admit that he would lie in court if he felt it were his patriotic duty. This discredited the government's case and the Independent Socialist League's name was eventually removed from the list.[30]

The shift to the right was not confined to the founding generation of the New York intellectuals; younger writers, including some who had been Trotskyists, participated in what Mills called "The American Celebration."[31] Melvin J. Lasky, who was born the son of a manufacturer in New York in 1920, attended the City College of New York from 1935 to 1939, where he was known as a brilliant and ardent sympathizer of the Trotskyists. He continued his Trotskyist political activity during 1939–40 at the University of Michigan, where as a graduate student in history he attempted to reinterpret the Civil War era under the inspiration of Lenin and Trotsky, and in letters to Dwight Macdonald bemoaned the lapses from revolutionism of Hook and Rahv.[32] When he began graduate work at Columbia University in the fall of 1940, he was a supporter of the Workers Party. The following year, after World War II had begun in earnest, he found himself swayed by Sidney Hook's repudiation of the revolutionary internationalist position. Offered a job as literary editor of the *New Leader*, he accepted, although at first he and managing editor Daniel Bell considered themselves to be on the far left wing of social democracy.[33]

From 1943 until 1946 Lasky was in the United States Army, where he advanced to the rank of captain. Following the war he worked in Germany as a journalist, and in 1948 he was offered the job of running a United States-sponsored cultural magazine that was to be called *Der Monat*. After the Berlin blockade, a leading German Socialist proposed that Lasky invite writers who had been published in the magazine to attend an international conference to be funded by the West German and United States governments. The event became the first gathering of the Congress for Cultural Freedom, the international parent organization with which the American Committee for Cultural Freedom had an affiliation. The congress had simultaneously and independently been initiated in Paris by Michael Josselson (later identified as an agent for the Central Intelligence Agency), Nicholas Nabokov, Raymond Aron, Arthur Koestler, and Irving Brown (a former leader of the Lovestone group). In 1953 Lasky received a $275,000 grant from the Ford Foundation to open a publishing house for the purpose of publishing books sponsored by *Monat*, and *Monat* joined *Preuves*, *Encounter*, and *Tempo Presente* as journals affiliated with the Congress for Cultural Freedom. That same year, after reading a proposal from Macdonald and Mary McCarthy to launch a new journal called *Critic*, Lasky announced that he had repudiated the politics even of Stevensonian liberalism and wrote Macdonald that Mary McCarthy and Joseph McCarthy were "equally evil."[34]

A more complex evolution was that of Leslie Fiedler, who was not a resident of New York but who shared many common experiences with the younger adherents of the American Committee for Cultural Freedom. Born in 1917 in Newark, New Jersey, he switched from the Young Communist League to the Socialist Workers Party during his final year at New York University and became an organizer for the Socialist Workers Party while a graduate student at the University of Wisconsin. When the Workers Party was formed he was briefly a member, but at the end of 1941, halfway through the first year of his teaching job at Montana State University, he drifted away for nonideological reasons. A career and a family had changed the pattern of his life. At the start of the war he considered himself an independent Trotskyist, but by the 1950s he was writing virulent anticommunist essays so full of dubious psychologizing and calls for atonement by the entire left that Harold Rosenberg felt compelled to publish a lengthy rebuttal called "Couch Liberalism and the Guilty Past." Yet in the very year that Rosenberg's essay appeared Fiedler underwent a sharp change in his thinking, finding himself increasingly drawn to the Parrington tradition of indigenous American populism.[35] In the 1960s he embraced anarchism and became an enthusiastic proponent of the counterculture.

The kind of thinking that led the center and right wings of the American Committee for Cultural Freedom to equate cultural freedom with anticommunism appeared embryonically in its predecessor organization, the short-lived Committee for Cultural Freedom, launched by Sidney Hook in the late spring of 1939. Originally called The League Against Totalitarianism, it represented the first organized effort by New York intellectuals to separate anti-Stalinism from a revolutionary Marxist context. At that time, it was aggressively resisted by all the *Partisan Review* editors who, in alliance with Trotskyist writers and other radicals, gathered around the rival League for Cultural Freedom and Socialism. When the Trotskyist newspaper *Socialist Appeal* pointed out that Hook's committee "is silent on the question of socialism and social revolution," thereby giving its anti-Stalinism a "reactionary character," Hook's organization treated the allegation as a smear comparable to the *Daily Worker's* claim that the committee members were "agents of fascism."[36] The specialty of the committee, of course, was exposing "Communist front" organizations; thus, when World War II began and the Soviet Union emerged as an ally of the United States, the committee, whose leading members all supported the war, simply faded away.

Hook revived the committee when the Cold War was well under way, just after the 1949 Waldorf World Peace Conference, which was not actually a "peace" conference but a pro-Soviet gathering that attracted three thousand delegates, many of whom were Communists and fellow travelers. There were several attempts by anti-Stalinist intellectuals to counter the conference. Hook brought some of them together under the rubric Americans for Intellectual Freedom. With a $5,000 donation from David Dubinsky, the organizers took a hotel room as the center of operations. According to William Phillips, the central organizers were Arnold Beichman, a public relations director for an electrical workers' union who later became a professor of political science, and Merlyn S. Pitzele, a former Trotskyist who had become the labor editor of *Business Week*. The two men apparently launched a veritable disruption campaign against the Peace Conference that included the interception of mail and messages and the issuance of misleading statements in the name of the conference.[37] This temporary formation became the nucleus for the revamped American Committee for Cultural Freedom, organized shortly afterward.

THE PSYCHOLOGY OF APOSTASY

Throughout the history of the radical movement much vituperation has been aimed against those who have repudiated their former convictions. One is hesitant to join the chorus of shrill critics or, at least, to use the same terminology to describe the transformation of the New York intellectuals and a considerable portion of the anti-Stalinist left. Indeed, in a moving obituary for Max Shachtman, a former disciple, Julius Jacobson, still faithful to the revolutionary socialist cause and bitterly disappointed with the apostasy of his mentor, concluded with some anguish: "I tremble to use the word, renegade. But what term better describes a man who reneged on his earlier, most fundamental commitment to social justice? To say that he died, in any sense at all, a socialist, is to denude the word of all meaning, to deny the relevance and seriousness of what he taught us about socialism in years past."[38] The more extreme of the apostates tend to turn against their former convictions with a fanaticism that leads to the caricaturing of their own experiences and former beliefs; in the name of rebelling against leftist ideological dogmatism, they create a new world outlook as narrowly ideological and at least as dogmatic as the crudest adherents of the left ever achieved. Most apostates, however, present lesser manifestations and variations of this paradigm. Considerable attention has been devoted to analyzing the tergiversations of former Communists, but almost nothing analytical has been written about apostasy from anti-Stalinist revolutionary communism.[39]

The central document illuminating the experience of apostasy from anti-Stalinist Marxism is the powerful essay, "Intellectuals in Retreat," written in 1939 by the Trotskyist editors of the *New International*, James Burnham and Max Shachtman. With astonishing foresight they described the dynamic that would soon overwhelm their generation of intellectuals and, not long after, engulf themselves. The essay's essential argument is that the drift to the right—first, from revolutionary Marxism to social democracy, and then, for some, even beyond to pro-imperialism—is usually masked by a series of questionable grievances: criticisms of Marxist philosophy, most often based on a caricature of dialectical materialism as being too "fatalistic"; the inaccurate charge that Leninists advocate a one-party dictatorship, which was never true of Lenin; the claim that Leninist ideology inevitably produces Stalinism, which is a *real* example of fatalistic reasoning; objections to the harsh tone of Trotskyist polemics, even though many apostate intellectuals themselves never hesitated to accuse the Trotskyists of being crypto-Stalinists or even objectively fascists. Counterposed to these evils are a series of abstractions, devoid of precise content, about the need for "freedom" and "democracy." Finally, "the main intellectual disease from which these intellectuals suffer may be called Stalinophobia, or vulgar anti-Stalinism." This illness was caused "by the universal revulsion against Stalin's macabre system of frame-ups and purges. And the result has been less a product of cold social analysis than of mental shock, and where there is analysis, it is moral rather than scientific and political."[40]

The answers and alternatives to renegacy provided by Shachtman and Burnham were not as consistently convincing as the critique. As in earlier writings, they tended to be a bit evasive about the question of a one-party dictatorship, devoting most of their time to explaining why, under the specific conditions of the Russian Revolution, a one-party system unexpectedly came into being, instead of unambiguously declaring themselves in favor of a multiparty system.[41] The distinctions they made between Leninism and Stalinism were methodologically sound, but they failed to more directly address ways in which Lenin and Trotsky did, in fact, break in practice with their own theory of Soviet democracy. Nor did they acknowledge the specific errors that Lenin and Trotsky made during 1920–21 that contributed to the victory of Stalin's tyranny, namely, the exclusion of factions in the Communist Party; the banning of the Menshevik Party and various anarchist organizations; and the suppression of multiple slates in elections to the Soviets after the end of the civil war.[42] Nevertheless, their understanding of a basic feature of the psychology of apostasy—the inability to see or acknowledge the authentic nature of one's change—was sound, even if it was vitiated by shrill vituperation: "The foulness of Stalinism and imperialism can today breed only maggots; in particular it is impossible for *intellectuals* to avoid degeneration not merely of their characters as human beings but also of their minds if for any length of time they give their allegiance to these allied monsters of the lie."[43]

Burnham joined the maggots just a few years later, but Shachtman continued his self-righteous excommunications for almost two decades. Very often these were directed against comrades from his own organization whose only sin was that they tended to move more quickly toward social democracy than he did. Among the first members of the Workers Party to feel his wrath was a young sociology student, Philip Selznick, who used the party name "Sherman."[44] Born Philip Schachter in New Jersey in 1919, Selznick began attending the City College of New York in 1935 and joined the Trotskyist youth group, the Young People's Socialist League (Fourth International), just as it was departing from the Socialist Party. Soon he became the organizer of the "Joe Hill Unit" of the youth group, joining the Workers Party following the 1939–40 faction fight.

Selznick was attracted to the ideas of Dewey as well as Burnham and held some private meetings with the latter. Subsequently he organized a faction known as the "Shermanites" which considered itself "revolutionary anti-Bolshevik." Sherman also opposed the notion that Marxism should remain the official doctrine of the Workers Party and was taken to task for this view by Irving Howe in a formal debate. Among the ranks of the Shermanites were quite a few young intellectuals who would become prominent scholars and academics, including Gertrude Himmelfarb, historian; Seymour Martin Lipset, sociologist; Marvin Meyers, historian; Peter Rossi, sociologist; Martin Diamond, political scientist; Herbert Garfinkel, political scientist; Jeremiah Kaplan, founder of the Free Press; and Irving Kristol, neoconservative journalist. In their programmatic statement, "Defining a Tendency," the Shermanites accused the Shachtman leadership of employing "the same bureaucratic organizational methods as Cannon."

Under Shachtman's direction, the Political Committee of the Workers Party issued "Bolshevism and Democracy: On the Capitulation of the Sherman Group," which accused Selznick of various crimes: organizing a secret group during a time in which he claimed to have no differences with the Workers Party leadership; indoctrinating the group's members without the benefit of a full and democratic discussion in the Workers Party; and carrying on secret discussions with both the Socialist Party and with James Burnham. Although the Shermanites by then had already departed to join the Socialist Party, the Workers Party Political Committee nonetheless declared that its anti-Bolshevik views rendered them ipso facto "incompatible with party membership" and denounced them as "weaklings taking one pretext or another to escape the discipline of the revolutionary party in time of hardship." Shachtman, who had personally debated Selznick during one of the

Workers Party discussions, mocked the decision of these organizational purists to join the social democrats as "a very unappetizing ending—to join the 'party' of Norman Thomas and company. If there is one labor organization in the U.S. outside of the Communist Party which has a thoroughly undemocratic, totalitarian-Fuehrer regime, it is the Thomas organization." Shachtman insisted that, in the Socialist Party, the leaders did whatever they wished while young militants are "framed up and kicked out as the Trotskyists were a few years ago." Ten years later, after a revolutionary anti-Bolshevik period and then a return to liberalism, Selznick found an academic use for the ideas that germinated in his debate with Shachtman. At the height of the Cold War, the Rand Corporation published Selznick's *The Organizational Weapon: A Study of Bolshevik Strategy and Tactics* (1952), dedicated to two former Shermanites, Diamond and Garfinkel. Nevertheless, Selznick never moved all that far to the right. He even became a bit re-radicalized during the early 1960s, when he supported the Berkeley Free Speech movement on the opposing side of the barricade from Lipset, another ex-Shermanite who had become a well-known sociologist.

A second excommunication from the Workers Party for apostasy occurred during the late 1940s. When Albert Goldman submitted his resignation in the summer of 1948, the Political Committee simply described him as demoralized. But this was followed in early 1949 by the surprising resignation of Ernest Erber. Born in 1913 in Chicago, Erber had joined the Young People's Socialist League in 1931 and was elected its national chairman in 1935.[45] Tall with white-blond hair, Erber was soft-spoken, even-tempered, intelligent, and very popular among the young members, although he was not of the intellectual caliber of other young leaders such as Irving Howe. When Goldman had joined the Socialist Party on his own in 1934, he had begun to develop a relationship with Erber so that by the time of his reelection as national chairman in 1937, Erber enthusiastically led the majority of the youth organization to Trotskyism. A central leader of the Workers Party, Erber's defection was startling. He said that he resigned because he opposed Bolshevik policy, even though he had recently defended Bolshevism in a series of lectures sponsored by the Socialist Youth League, the youth affiliate of the Independent Socialist League. Probably Erber had been demoralized by the postwar situation in general, by the resignation of Goldman, and by the departure because of personal problems of his close personal and political friend, Nathan Gould.

In an utter rage, Shachtman responded in an article of 116 single-spaced pages called "Under the Banner of Marxism"; he dedicated it "in comradely solidarity to the delegates of our Fifth National Convention, and to all those who are unshaken and unshakable, who do not flinch and weaken." While not so professionally written, the essay was an extension of "Intellectuals in Retreat." It treated Erber and Goldman in much the same terms as Hook and Burnham. He called them the "I-was-a-political-idiot-but-now-I-am-smart school" because they seemed to think that the renunciation of earlier views made them more qualified, rather than less trustworthy, to serve as political guides in charting a new direction. Shachtman wondered how it had been possible for Erber to declare all previous defectors from Bolshevism victims of "class pressure," while insisting that his own change was due to authentic disagreements with the Workers Party program—of which he made no effort to inform the membership until after he left the organization.

Shachtman then answered Erber's charges with a long defense of the Bolsheviks' abolition of the Constituent Assembly following the revolution, insisting that "the composition of the Assembly, on the day it met, no longer corresponded even approximately to the political division in the country. The sentiments and aspirations of the masses had changed radically since the party lists for the assembly were first drawn up and after the voting had taken place. By its composition, we repeat, the Assembly was less representative than the Kerensky government in its heyday." But Shachtman's real concern in making such a lengthy case for the Bolsheviks' actions was that the defense of the legacy of the Russian Revolution "is the defense of authentic Marxism which is the defense of socialism."

According to Shachtman, most of Erber's complaints were merely an extension of those raised by earlier capitulators "to social imperialism via American chauvinism." He characterized Erber as "an Americanized Marxist. That is, an ex-Marxist cured of his socialism by shock-treatment from Stalinism and the softer touch of Rooseveltism." Erber was "cured of internationalism, too. Europe and Asia and their peoples don't exist for him." If they did, then Erber would surely have realized that it is the crimes of the imperialists that have driven the nationalist movements to accept Stalinism. Therefore, the best way to fight Stalinism is to abolish imperialism. Erber had also declared that the United States was on the verge of a war with the Soviet Union, a conflict in which the United States should be supported rather than weakened by those advocating a "Third Camp" position. Shachtman responded that "all that American imperialism can produce for the destruction of Stalinism is a military program"; but Stalinism, since it was a social system, must be replaced by a social system of a higher order if "reactionary consequences" are to be avoided. Allying with imperialism to defend "democracy" against either fascism or Stalinism made no sense because, as Rosa Luxemburg noted, "the fate of democracy is bound up in the socialist movement." In other words, only if the working class became independent of and hostile to the bourgeoisie could genuine democracy be sustained and extended.[46]

Actually, Shachtman was quite mistaken in equating Erber with Hook and Burnham; his quirky behavior on the eve of his departure was only a prelude to a long period of political silence during which he learned a skilled trade outside of the radical movement and started a family. A somewhat similar pattern occurred with Jean van Heijenoort, who, under the party names "Logan," "Gerland," and "Loris" had continued to collaborate with the Workers Party until late 1947. During that autumn, van Heijenoort held a number of political discussions with Meyer Schapiro in which he gave no sign that he had changed his views. Suddenly, he sent out invitations to about twenty people to hear him read a paper on the one hundredth anniversary of the *Communist Manifesto*. The gist of the paper was that, although Marx's predictions had seemed quite reasonable in 1848, they had turned out to be all wrong. Van Heijenoort explained that the political incapacity of the working class had been definitively proven to be an inherent and not a conjunctural weakness.

In a letter to Alfred Rosmer, an early but short-term member of the French Left Opposition who had lived in the United States during the war, Meyer Schapiro expressed shock that van Heijenoort's paper presented a very low level of analysis. Van Heijenoort had not carefully examined the subject presented in the paper but had coldly and haughtily claimed to have been let down by the working class. Schapiro was stunned not only by van Heijenoort's sad and in some ways unpleasant performance but also by the loud applause on the part of several supporters of Dwight Macdonald's *Politics* who were present. Shachtman was in attendance but he was too astounded to speak. Even more bizarre, in conversation afterward van Heijenoort insisted that his views really had not changed all that much. He suggested collaborating with Schapiro and others in publishing a new version of the *Marxist Quarterly*, a proposal that had been circulating among the remaining anti-Stalinist radical intellectuals. As it turned out, van Heijenoort chose as his last political act to publish his repudiation of Marxism in the *Partisan Review* under the pseudonym "Jean Vannier." He then vanished from the political arena to begin a new life as a professor of philosophy at Brandeis University.[47]

These instances of sudden and almost shameless *volte-faces* were only the latest in a long stream that stemmed back to the late 1930s. The Trotskyist movement was by no means unique in this phenomenon. Among the most extraordinary cases were those of Bertram D. Wolfe and Will Herberg, arch-theoreticians of the Lovestone group. A few weeks before the Lovestone organization disbanded in 1940, Wolfe appeared at a meeting to plead with the members not to change their Leninist-internationalist opposition to the coming war, as Lovestone himself had just done. In a moving voice he declared, "I have never supported imperialist war; I will never support an imperialist war; and I am breaking a lifelong friendship with Jay Lovestone over this issue because this war is no different from any other imperialist war." Yet within weeks, Wolfe's position became the same as Lovestone's.

Herberg was a man with a fantastic courtroomlike capacity to build up a case for any position he wanted. Yet with astonishing ease he showed himself just as capable as Lovestone and Wolfe of switching from one position to its opposite. A specialty of Herberg's was demolishing all arguments in favor of theology. When he discovered that Lovestone's young secretary, Edward Sagarin, was an agnostic, he marshaled such a barrage of evidence to demonstrate the nonexistence of God and the social evil of religion that Sagarin, fifty years later and a retired professor of criminology, could still feel the force of his logic. Yet Herberg himself went directly from militant atheism to wearing a yarmulke and praying, eventually establishing himself as one of America's leading theologians.[48]

Quirky behavior, political quiescence, and extraordinary turnabouts were among the least objectionable manifestations of apostasy exhibited by these defectors. Albert Goldman embarked on a course that veered between pathos and tragedy, while Felix Morrow's was worthy of performance by the Theater of the Absurd. At least a year before resigning from the Workers Party, Goldman had fallen into a political malaise. Unable to practice law because he had been disbarred, worried about supporting a young wife he had met and married during his Smith Act trial and a son born in November 1948, Goldman drove a taxicab for a while before accepting his brothers' generous offer to set him up as assistant manager of the Courtesy Car Service, a limousine taxicab company in Chicago. But business was so poor that Goldman himself had to do much of the driving. In these years Goldman underwent strange changes in personality and appearance. Formerly a hearty man, nearly six feet tall with brown hair, he now became extremely thin and even foppish in appearance. He declared himself a vegetarian, developed a cleanliness fetish, and insisted on boiling all his drinking water. Old friends found him hardly recognizable.

By 1950 he described himself as a "right-wing socialist" in a letter to *New Leader* editor Sol Levitas.[49] In 1951, his sister-in-law, while applying for a clearance to obtain a job with the Atomic Energy Commission, wrote AEC officials that "Mr. Goldman has contacts with the FBI and co-operates with them when they seek information about former Communists."[50] A year later Goldman himself gave testimony at an AEC security clearance hearing in order to assuage any doubts about his sister-in-law's loyalty. He confirmed that he had collaborated with the FBI, adding that "right now I would say that the agents of the FBI and Immigration Authority always come to me for help, not only with reference to particular individuals but with reference to a general attitude, for me to explain to them what the differences are between groups."[51] Declaring that he was now opposed to Marxism and the class struggle, Goldman claimed that he was still a socialist "on ethical grounds," explaining that "more and more I am going back, not to religion, but to the ethical concepts of Christ and the prophets. That is the basis of my present socialism." Still, he added, his anticommunism had become so strong that "if I were younger . . . I would gladly offer my services in Korea or especially in Europe where I could do some good fighting the Communists."[52] For the next four years Goldman struggled to obtain a pardon for his Smith Act conviction. After receiving the pardon, his license to practice law was restored in 1956, shortly before he was stricken with cancer. Once one of the best-known radical lawyers in the United States, he died in total obscurity in May 1960 in the Garden View Convalescent Home on Chicago's far north side.[53]

Felix Morrow remained a member of the Socialist Workers Party until the 1946 convention, vigorously fighting for his views.[54] In his final speech he declared, in what he thought at the moment was absolute sincerity, "You can't expel me; I'll live and die in the movement!" Party members in the audience saw that there were tears in his eyes. Yet ten minutes later, his expulsion approved, he was surprised to find himself tripping down the stairs of the convention hall with the greatest sense of glee and freedom. Reneging on his commitment to join the Workers Party, he also resisted Schapiro's proposal that he edit a new version of the *Marxist Quarterly*. Morrow then threw himself into a job at Schocken Books, a publishing house, that Schapiro and Elliot Cohen had helped him obtain. With the activist skills learned in the Trotskyist movement, he had no difficulty in becoming Schocken's vice-president by the end of the year. To celebrate his newfound sense of freedom, he and a female friend gave an operatic concert at the home of his brother-in-law, the theatrical lawyer William Fitelson, who had contributed financially to the *Partisan Review* and would later support *Dissent*. Originally trained in opera, Morrow had not performed in more than twenty years. It was also at the Fitelson home that he met the twenty-three-year-old woman who became his third wife.

Soon Morrow became even more immersed in Cold War anti-communist activity than was Goldman. Although he insisted that he only informed on Communists, he found it difficult to draw the line. Files obtained under the Freedom of Information Act disclosed that he may have given some information about the Socialist Workers Party as well.[55] In addition, he began collaborating with the Central Intelligence Agency as an unpaid consultant on various literary projects, including an aborted effort to smuggle Russian-language editions of *Dr. Zhivago* into the Soviet Union. With the advent of the Vietnam War, Morrow began to have doubts about the Cold War ideology to which he had been so passionately devoted, but he rejected a return to radicalism. Instead, he busied himself with the publishing house he had started in 1956 while also working as a sales representative and consultant to a half-dozen other publishers, usually earning $50,000 to $60,000 a year.

The publishing company, called University Books, specialized in the occult and was central to the boom in that field in the 1960s. Morrow was at first drawn to the occult when he handled the arrangements for the publication of the book *Flying Saucers Have Landed* (1953) in the United States and began reading *Fate* magazine. He believed that something in his Hasidic background linked him with the subject. Consequently he decided to start his own Mystic Arts Book Society, and he wrote introductions to a number of the books that he published. Since he only halfheartedly believed in the occult, he invented a persona, John C. Wilson, for his occultist literary endeavors and never wrote under his own name. But the stress between the two sides of his personality—Morrow the materialist and Wilson the mystic—brought the whole project to an end in 1966. At that time he took a big gamble by expanding his book club to include soft erotica, spending a fortune on a promotional campaign to secure new members and stretching himself far beyond his means. In addition, he concluded that Timothy Leary, whose books and whose journal, *Psychedelic Review*, Morrow had been publishing, was unbalanced from overuse of LSD. As a consequence of this stress, Morrow suffered a severe mental breakdown and was forced to sell his entire business to the Lyle Stuart publishing house at a great loss.

In the late 1950s Morrow encountered Elliot Cohen, his old mentor, at a New York subway station, en route to the *Commentary* office. Although Morrow knew that Cohen had suffered periods of deep depression since the 1920s, he was unaware that Cohen's mental health had so deteriorated that he rarely showed up at work. In the few minutes they stood on the street corner Cohen said to Morrow, "Do you know somebody who needs an office boy?" Morrow responded, "Why? Does your boy want some additional work or something?" Cohen answered, "No, I mean *me!*" Morrow was preoccupied with business worries, so he dismissed the peculiar remark. On 29 May 1959 he opened the *New York Times* and read that Cohen had committed suicide by placing a plastic bag over his head and tying it closed with a string.

Around 1968 Morrow attended a convention of humanistic psychologists where he heard a lecture-demonstration by Ira Progoff, a former Jungian who specialized in a method of encouraging personal growth through the use of an intensive journal. In the late 1940s Morrow had undergone psychoanalysis five days a week for five years with Paul Federnn and Leci Fessler. Then, after religious feelings began to surface, he had been a disciple of Georges Ivanovitch Gurdjieff from 1956 to 1966. Now he became a full-time publicist for Progoff, working at Dialogue House in New York, until a methodological schism developed between the two and Morrow established his own practice. In the late 1970s he read Michael Harrington's *The Twilight of Capitalism* (1976), which, much to his own surprise, convinced him that he must return to his socialist roots. Subsequently he joined the Democratic Socialist Organizing Committee, now known as the Democratic Socialists of America. In the 1980s, he divided his time between working as a consultant for the Internal Revenue Service on the fair-market value of literary properties and spending his weekends at a spiritual community called Center for the Living Force.

The transformations of Erber, van Heijenoort, Goldman, Morrow, and others were not due to the "original sin" of having been infected with Trotskyism, anti-Stalinism, or any other particular ideology; on a generational level, the changes were rooted in the postwar situation of economic boom, upward mobility, the failure of revolutions in western Europe, and the advent of the international Cold War and domestic McCarthyism. Moreover, the fear of harassment by the Federal Bureau of Investigation and the resulting isolation should not be underestimated; suspect intellectuals as well as union militants were shunned by their fellow workers. On May Day 1953, the Independent Socialist League held its traditional rally in New York City, and the leaders were stunned to find only fifty members and twenty-five sympathizers in attendance.

Apostasy takes its most notorious form when a former communist makes a career out of anticommunism. Sometimes this happened without conscious forethought. Alfred Kazin has written of many former New York intellectuals that "the Cold War and McCarthy era needed them, raised them, publicized them."[56] The most successful professional anticommunist was Sidney Hook. Indeed, Hook will probably be remembered more for his career as an anticommunist than for his contributions to philosophy; *Heresy, Yes—Conspiracy, No* (1953), in which he used liberal arguments to legitimize the essence of the witch-hunt, gave him a new lease on life as a leading intellectual. First as a leftist, then as a Cold War liberal, and finally as a neoconservative, Hook gained his authority by writing books and articles that rationalized to intellectuals the larger social trends in which he and others were caught up.

For example, fifteen years after he published *Toward the Understanding of Karl Marx* during the height of the Great Depression, Hook wrote a second introduction to Marx's thought that was much more appropriate to the changed political climate. Moreover, the new book itself, appearing under the title *Marx and the Marxists* (1955), contains dramatic alterations of Hook's earlier point of view that are never acknowledged. This time Marx, instead of being presented as *un*orthodox, is depicted as the *fount* of all orthodoxy, although the term still lacked the positive connotation that it had for Georg Lukács. To the "born again" Hook, Marx's writings are orthodox because he believes that socialism is a logical stage that must and can only follow advanced capitalism—a position shared by the reformists, who now replace Lenin (described here, with other Bolsheviks, as a deviant) in the line of direct descent. This leads Hook to such inaccuracies as claiming that Trotsky concocted the theory of "uneven and combined development" to justify the Bolsheviks' allegedly premature seizure of power in 1917, even though the concept of "uneven and combined development" is implicit in Marx's writings and was clearly a component of Trotsky's Theory of Permanent Revolution as it was first articulated in 1905.

Hook conveniently omitted a central argument that had originally appeared in *Toward the Understanding of Karl Marx*, an argument that held that the primary test of an authentic Marxist is an understanding that the state must be abolished because it is an instrument of the oppressing class. Also present is Hook's assertion that in 1917 Lenin had led a coup, even though this view contradicts his contention in *Toward an Understanding of Karl Marx* that revolutions cannot be made by groups but are the results of a historical process. Thus it seems that by 1955 Hook either held the view that no revolution had been made in the Soviet Union, or that a coup is synonymous with a revolution. According to Hook, authentic socialism should now be understood as being simply a current of liberalism, a notion that ironically paralleled the Popular Front thesis, once ridiculed by Hook, that communism was but a more militant current of liberalism.[57]

The psychology of apostasy is nicely illustrated by Hook's utter reversal of his previous assessment of Leninism which led him to misconstrue the record of Lenin's views. In a carefully documented critique of Hook's view of civil liberties during the 1950s, two young members of the Independent Socialist League (the new name for the Workers Party after 1949), Gordon Haskell and Julius Jacobson, examined the quotations from Lenin that Hook had used to prove the case he presented in *Heresy, Yes—Conspiracy, No*. Hook had asserted that Lenin's doctrines provided the basis for an international communist conspiracy. In each instance Hook simply deleted, sometimes even without ellipses, the specific context of the quotation, which enabled him to attribute a very different meaning to the respective passage. For example, Lenin wrote that revolutionists must use subterfuge in the trade unions *if their democratic rights are proscribed*. Hook simply deleted the part of the quotation that referred to the proscription of rights, thus bolstering his theme that, for Lenin, conspiracy was a way of life. Or when Lenin wrote that revolutionaries should operate in larger organizations in secret groups *if they faced the threat of arrest or deportation*, Hook again deleted the qualifying clause. It is especially ironic that such methods were used by Hook, who was totally dedicated to exposing the "Big Lie" of the Communists.[58]

During the early 1930s, when Hook ardently believed that "no tinkering with capitalism will enable us to avoid the evils of war, cyclical depression, and cultural perversion inherent in the existing social relations of production," he had interpreted Lenin very differently, considering him to be the greatest defender of the democratic process.[59] As a young faculty member at New York University in 1932, Hook had reviewed Lenin's manifesto of organizational principles, *What Is to Be Done?*, in the *American Journal of Sociology*, calling it "one of the landmarks in the social and intellectual history of Russia in recent times." In a tone just as cocksure and self-confident as the one that marked his *New York Times Magazine* articles twenty years later that "exposed" pro-Communist professors as conspirators, Hook insisted that Lenin's strategy of revolution was based not on deception but on "the causal efficacy of class-*consciousness* in accelerating social change."[60] In a review of the first volume of *The History of the Russian Revolution* that same year, he had even criticized Trotsky for not describing the full democratic nature of the Leninist party: "the . . . independent initiative of its rank and file, the freedom of criticism which prevailed even at crucial moments."[61]

How is it possible, then, that in 1955, Hook could say of Lenin that "as a Marxist theoretician he was comparatively undistinguished," or that he ruthlessly ran a "small group . . . poised to strike against the democratic regime which followed the collapse of absolutism," or that when "Lenin sometimes characterized the structure of the party as one of 'democratic centralism,' it actually meant that the exercise, degree, and occasion of democratic activity on the part of the membership was determined by the central source—the bureaucratic and self-perpetuating directors of a military machine"?[62] Since there is no reason to believe that Hook is intentionally dishonest, one must attribute such extraordinary lapses to the Stalinophobic fanaticism that overtook his generation, causing genuine memory lapses in those instances when historic facts conflicted with the ideological needs of the Cold War. As Hook himself observed in another context, "It is an elementary truth of the psychology of perception that what a man sees depends upon his beliefs and expectations."[63] In looking back at the communist movement that he had once known so well, virtually as an insider, Hook failed to realize how his new opinions had shaped his new conclusions. He became a victim of the familiar phenomenon of perceiving all information as independent confirmations of his viewpoint, while not realizing that his highly emotional bias against communism had preselected the information about Lenin and other radical matters that he now used to buttress his new theorizations.

Another clue to the process of Hook's apostasy was his insistence that his switch from revolutionary to reformist socialism (referred to as "democratic socialism" to avoid the stigma of "social democracy," against which Hook had railed so often), was based on changes that had occurred in the world and not in him personally. In his contribution to the 1952 symposium, "Our Country and Our Culture," he presented the most persuasive case for the new politics of his generation. History, he argued, had simply limited its choice to only two possibilities, that is, "between endorsing a sys-tem of total terror [the Soviet Union] and *critically* supporting our own imperfect democratic culture with all its promises and dan-gers."[64] Once he advanced beyond this rhetoric, however, it be-came clear that his talk of "imperfect democratic culture" was an ideological mystification: without evidence, he declared that the economy of the United States should be recognized as "mixed." He also claimed that the U.S. working class enjoys "more bread and freedom than anywhere else in the world"—as if this generalization might give comfort to large segments of the American working class who were excluded from the fruits of postwar prosperity, or the workers of dependent nations whose economic stagnation was part of the price of the U.S. domestic achievement.

Although Hook insisted that criticisms of American life were still appropriate, he warned that such criticisms ought be made "without forgetting for a moment the total threat which Commu-nism poses to the life of the free mind."[65] This implied that "free minds" existed in American culture but might be suddenly lost if one gave aid and comfort to the enemy; the logic of this position is to eschew far-reaching criticisms of the United States on the grounds that one is objectively aiding the enemy. Hook simply had no use for the more plausible argument that a rapacious American capitalism not only brings a relative prosperity and freedom to some sectors at the expense of others, but that it aids the stability and expansion of Stalinist regimes by failing to offer an attractive alternative to movements for social change throughout the world.

Above all, Hook would never acknowledge that the change in his views could be explained by social pressures brought on him and his generation in addition to the postwar prosperity that resulted in a loss of ability to view the world from the class perspective of the oppressed. To the contrary, his method of analysis, and those of the other neoconservatives for whom he would become a guiding spirit in the 1970s, was to perceive a reversal in the pressure, to insist that he was always going against the stream and taking great risks, as he had genuinely done in the early 1930s when he first came out in support of Marxism and then broke with the Communists from the left.

At the onset of World War II, for example, Hook claimed that he was virtually alone in standing up for reason, resisting combined pressures from the left and from the new irrationalists, both of which were retreating into utopian fantasies. During the postwar witch-hunt he fantasized that he and a few stalwart colleagues were standing almost alone defending the right of liberal "heresy" against Communist conspirators on the left and irresponsible Mc-Carthyites (irresponsible because they were bungling the job of fighting Communism with their excesses) on the right. In each case Hook was actually finding social democratic reasons for adapting to the tide of opinion while depicting himself as "out of step." In the same manner, the leader of the younger generation of deradicalized intellectuals, Norman Podhoretz, would claim to be "breaking ranks" when he joined the Reagan parade in the 1980s.

Social democracy, the variant of socialism that functions within the framework of capitalist institutions rather than counterposing a program of workers' self-management to capitalism, was sufficiently flexible to be invoked by Hook in his revolutionary anti-imperialist phase of the late 1930s as well as in his pro-Reagan phase of the 1980s. His claim of adherence to social democracy, manifested in recent years in his membership in Social Democrats U.S.A., the only socialist organization he ever joined after his sojourn in the American Workers Party, allows him to reassure the residue of his younger self: "I never went over to the class enemy; I remained a socialist to the end." It constitutes the ideological shield that he has erected around himself, perhaps in order to appease his conscience and justify his political transmogrification since the late 1930s. Nevertheless, it is hard to consider Social Democrats U.S.A. an authentic part even of the social democratic movement today. The organization does have ties to labor officials and supports a welfare state up to a point, but in its ideology and politics it is indistinguishable from the neoconservatives with whom it seeks a dialogue.

As late as the summer of 1985, Hook coauthored an ostensibly Marxist essay, " 'Bashing' the Raj: Truth or Propaganda," in response to recent films and books critical of British rule in India.[66] Basing himself on some of Marx's 1853 writings, Hook not only repudiated the "common cause" he had felt with the Indian fighters for national independence in the 1930s, but he insisted that colonial rule was less harmful than the independence movement. His conclusion was that this continues to be the case in Africa and Asia and that anticolonial sentiments actually aid Soviet expansion by weakening U.S. hegemony over the Third World. Thus forty-five years after he lost all plausible claim to being a Marxist, he still maintains that he is the only authentic interpreter of Marx's "complexity" and Marx's awareness of the "tragic dimension in history."

THE IRON CAGE OF ORTHODOXY

The decline of the American left after World War II took its toll in all progressive quarters, causing a narrowing of outlook and a retreat to rigid, sometimes paranoid, thinking. The handful of intellectuals who survived the difficult postwar years, who remained generally independent of and militantly opposed to both Stalinism and Cold War imperialism, were scarred in ways that were different from the apostates but were scarred nonetheless. In a certain sense the evolution of Shachtman's group is easiest to understand. Some time after it split from the Socialist Workers Party in 1940, the Workers Party began a process of social democratization. This was heatedly denied by its leaders and members for nearly twenty years, but it is hardly questionable today.[67]

At what point the WP actually became social democratic is quite another question. The Socialist Workers Party's 1940 predictions about the social patriotic course on which the Workers Party was embarked were premature. As late as 1947 the orthodox Trotskyists of the SWP were willing to consider a merger with the WP, and the WP came close to gaining admission to the Fourth International as fraternal members. Shachtman, however, was trailing down the path trod by the deradicalizing intellectuals, albeit reluctantly. By the late 1960s, at the latest, his path had conjoined with Sidney Hook's, although he apparently failed to confront the profound nature of his change and made almost no references in writing to the contrast between his previous and his new views. Those former WP members who had accepted the turn to social democracy, but not the right-wing variant embraced by Shachtman, formed the Democratic Socialist Organizing Committee (later, the Democratic Socialists of America) led by Michael Harrington and Irving Howe. Those who still adhered to the revolutionary convictions that Shachtman had once held broke with him in 1960. Several formed the Independent Socialist Clubs (later, the International Socialists) while others began the journal *New Politics*.

The evolution of the orthodox Trotskyists of the Socialist Workers Party is somewhat more difficult to grasp. Emerging from World War II, the Trotskyists faced an inevitable crisis because their prewar short-term predictions failed to materialize. Contrary to expectations, no wave of successful revolutions occurred in the major European capitalist countries, and Stalinism had become stronger than ever. Moreover, U.S. capitalism thrived in its new role as a major world power. Goldman and Morrow fixated on these developments, thereby missing a larger picture which arguably confirmed several of Trotsky's longer-term predictions, namely, that there *was* a rise in revolutionary working-class struggles in western Europe; that there *were* overturns of the social systems in eastern Europe and China (to be followed by social overturns in North Korea, North Vietnam, and Cuba during the next decade); and that the continued success of U.S. capitalism would have to be contingent on its efficacy in dominating economically underdeveloped countries. Short-term predictions were never meant to be taken as certain but were intended rather as successive approximations necessary to guide political action; thus there were no objective factors in the postwar period that mandated an abandonment of the basic Marxist perspective, although subjective factors abounded. What was needed was a readjustment of Marxism in light of a new world reality, especially a means of analyzing the phenomenon of Stalinism, the major system for which Trotsky's predictions were most amiss.

The persistence of Stalinist rule in the Soviet Union was in itself not the main problem. After all, a transitional society is not obliged to appear or disappear according to any rigid chronological formulas. Plausible reasons for the survival of the bureaucratic Stalinist regime were legion, including the failure of new revolutionary leaderships to provide positive alternatives in western Europe. Whether Stalinist systems were aberrations, as Trotsky theorized, or inevitable (which would demand a new conceptual framework) might not be definitively answered until an anticapitalist revolution occurred in an industrialized country with a sizable working class. What was more threatening to the traditional Trotskyist worldview was the apparent social transformations that had occurred in China, Yugoslavia, and other states of eastern Europe for which Communist parties and the Soviet Union claimed credit. In none of these cases did the social transformations follow the classical model of the Russian Revolution. Moreover, those who had led the transformations were decidedly non-Trotskyist.

Thus the orthodox Trotskyists of the SWP and the Fourth International (with which the SWP had only a fraternal relationship because of U.S. legislation prohibiting international political affiliations) were faced with a fundamental problem. Trotsky had theorized that only an authentic Fourth Internationalist party, consciously based on the International's Transitional Program (the founding programmatic document, written in 1938), could lead a social transformation, except under a rare set of circumstances in which a non-Trotskyist leadership might be forced to carry out a revolution against its will.[68] Faced with this contradiction between theory and reality, the Trotskyists were posed with four alternatives: they could abandon building the Fourth International and organizations such as the SWP; they could correct, update, and adjust Marxism and Trotskyism in light of the unexpected phenomena; they could attempt to demonstrate how all the post–World War II social transformations actually *did* occur according to Trotsky's pre–1940 perspectives; or they could deny that authentic revolutions had occurred in the aforementioned countries.

The majority of the orthodox Trotskyists in the SWP began in the late 1940s with the fourth position, that is, they denied that what had occurred in China and eastern Europe were authentic social transformations. By the early 1950s, they had moved painfully to the third position, that is, they admitted that social transformations had indeed occurred but asserted that they had occurred against the conscious intentions of the Stalinists who led them. The fact that the SWP began with the fourth alternative and moved slowly toward the third shows an admirable caution that was far superior to impressionistic theorizing. Such caution may have been partly responsible for their survival during the difficult World War II and Cold War years. But the fact that they stopped at the third alternative without progressing to the second suggests that they feared to stray too far from formulas of Trotsky even when, as in this instance, material reality called for a more rigorous analysis. Thus the SWP developed, and for twenty-five years would continue to defend, the view that Communist parties with origins in the Stalinist movement were incapable of consciously leading anticapitalist revolts. Like the parent Soviet regime, which was, in fact, opposed to social transformations that might upset the world balance of power or pose an attractive alternative model to the totalitarian system that prevailed within the Soviet Union, such parties were characterized by the SWP as "counter-revolutionary." What had really happened, in their view, was that in China, eastern Europe, North Korea, and, later, in North Vietnam, mass upheavals of one sort or another had pushed these Communist leaderships much further than they had wanted to go; what Trotsky had theorized as a rare exception became the norm. But the orthodox Trotskyists of the SWP failed to comprehend the dynamic of these mass upheavals because the realities challenged orthodox Trotskyist doctrine.

In the rest of the world Trotskyist movement, sentiment leaned toward the second alternative and concluded that Communist parties of China and Yugoslavia were not "Stalinist" in the same sense as was the Soviet party. Such parties *were* capable of leading social transformations, even if they were incapable of constructing postcapitalist societies without bureaucratic deformations. This meant a less epicentric conception of the role of Trotskyism in world politics but an important role, nevertheless.

Because of these different perspectives and because of divergent tactical proposals flowing from them—such as the recommendation of the majority of European Fourth International leaders that Trotskyists enter Socialist and Communist parties in certain countries—there ensued a fierce debate in the Fourth International that climaxed in late 1953. In the SWP, a tendency led by two founding members and important party leaders, Bert Cochran and George Clarke, agreed with the new positions of the Fourth International, although it gave these positions its own interpretation. Cochran had also differentiated himself several years earlier by opposing the SWP majority's support of the Walter Reuther faction in the United Auto Workers.

Cochran was born into a Jewish family in New York City in 1917. Trained as a pianist, he attended the University of Wisconsin before joining the Communist League of America in 1934.[69] From 1934 until 1939 he was an effective organizer in the United Auto Workers union, and beginning in 1939 he spent thirteen years as a full-time party functionary, writing (under the name "E. R. Frank"), editing, and serving in various administrative capacities. A dark, grinning man who balded early and who had a sly manner, Cochran was recognized as brilliant but self-centered. Clarke, born in 1913, was a founding member of the Communist League of America and had been a party functionary for many years.[70] The other main theoretical leader of the tendency was Harry Braverman (who used the party name "Harry Frankel"), born in 1920 in New York.[71] He had joined the Trotskyists in 1937 when they held the leadership of the Young Peoples Socialist League. Dropping out of Brooklyn College, Braverman became a coppersmith at the Brooklyn Navy Yard, then a steelworker in Youngstown, Ohio.

To the extent that the Cochran-Clarke tendency actually adhered to the political orientation then being developed by the leading European theoreticians of the Fourth International, they represented a necessary corrective to an orthodoxy that had proven incapable of assimilating major global changes. However, the extent of their adherence was always in doubt.[72] In any event, the SWP proved incapable of integrating both points of view, which at least in theory might have produced a balanced perspective. In the spring of 1953 James P. Cannon became convinced, on rather flimsy evidence, that the leaders of the Fourth International were using the Cochran-Clarke faction to engineer a split in the SWP. At the November

1953 plenum of the SWP, the party's National Committee indefinitely suspended members of the Cochran-Clarke faction because they had admittedly participated in a boycott of a meeting held in honor of the twenty-fifth anniversary of the SWP newspaper, the *Militant*. After this, all members of the SWP were required to denounce the faction members for boycotting the meeting; those who balked were expelled on the spot. No trials were held for either the leaders or members of the faction; the SWP majority claimed that by admitting participation in a boycott the faction members had eliminated the need for a trial.

The *Militant* articles announcing the expulsion constituted a nadir in sectarian bombast. A 16 November 1953 article blasted the boycott, which the Cochran-Clarke group had organized as a protest against their alleged exclusion from party life: "This treacherous, strikebreaking action constituted, in effect, an organized demonstration against the 25-year struggle of American Trotskyism, and, at the same time, an act of objective aid to the Stalinists who expelled the initiating nucleus in 1928."[73] Two weeks later an article by Joseph Hansen repeated this theme employing a curious mix of metaphors rather embarrassing for a labor-oriented newspaper: "Our anniversary meeting was in effect an SWP picket line.... By the boycott, the Cochranites crossed the picket line."[74] Isaac Deutscher, the Polish former Trotskyist then living in England who was believed by some to have inspired the new line of the Fourth International, was characterized in an editorial several weeks later as "the slick, sophisticated, 'non-Stalinist' apologist, capable of meeting strong skepticism with a well-polished but carefully loaded 'both sides of the question approach.'"[75] Unlike the Communists, the SWP had never had a policy of preventing its members from fraternizing with expelled members; but the use of the term "strikebreaker" was bound to effect similar results. Clearly the apostate intellectuals were not alone in succumbing both to paranoia and narrow ideological perceptions during the difficult 1950s.

At the same November plenum that purged the Cochran-Clarke group, the SWP also announced the formation of what was in effect a rival Fourth International, thus splitting the international Trotskyist movement for the next decade. However, some of Cannon's charges about the mixed political character of the expelled minority were soon confirmed. The Cochran-Clarke group walked out of the Fourth International six months later, at first because they felt pressure from the European leaders to initiate a reconciliation with the SWP, and later because they concluded that such an association was no longer relevant. Next, Clarke broke with Cochran and moved to Europe where he died a few years later in a car accident. For five years Cochran and Braverman published the *American Socialist*, a well-edited radical journal free of jargon and open to many fresh ideas. But the magazine and the organization that sponsored it, the Socialist Union, dissolved on the eve of the new radicalization of the 1960s. Cochran, who drifted in a political direction that was nonrevolutionary but hard to label, went on to write a half-dozen lively and thoughtful books such as *Adlai Stevenson: Patrician among Politicians* (1969), *Harry Truman and the Crisis Presidency* (1973), and *Labor and Communism: The Conflict That Shaped American Unions* (1977), and eventually became a senior associate of the Research Institute on International Change at Columbia University before his death in 1984. Braverman grew sympathetic to Maoism in the 1960s, became a leading editor at Grove Press, and then became the head of Monthly Review Books. His award-winning book, *Labor and Monopoly Capital*, was published in 1974.

Those intellectuals who remained members of the SWP made only a minor mark on American culture during the 1950s and later. The organization itself, of course, was in steady decline throughout the decade. The effects of postwar disorientation combined with the loss of many trade union cadre—not only through the expulsion of the Cochran group but also because the Trotskyist Teamsters in Minneapolis had been driven out of their jobs—were nearly devastating. In the 1940s, Socialist Workers Party membership had gone from 840 in 1944 to 1,470 in 1946. Then it dropped to 1,277 in 1948, 825 in 1950, 758 in 1952, and 480 after the break with the Cochran-Clarke group in 1954. The decline continued down to 434 in 1957 and 399 in 1959, then began to rise in the 1960s to four to five hundred and in the 1970s to well over a thousand.[76] Still, within the boundaries of such limited resources and an orthodox framework, a few intellectuals managed some achievements, and, as the radicalization of the 1960s began, the framework loosened considerably.

Unfortunately, the most learned of the orthodox Marxist intellectuals, Joseph Vanzler (better known by his party name, John G. Wright) died at the age of fifty-four in 1956, leaving behind a relatively small and scattered body of original material.[77] Born about 1902 in Samarkand, the burial place of Genghis Kahn in central Asia, Vanzler was the brilliant son of an aging rabbi and a fourteen-year-old girl. One of six Jews permitted to attend a Czarist school, Usick, as he was always called by his family and friends, had learned Latin, French, Greek, vernacular Russian, and Court Russian by the time he was eight.

In 1915, his mother fled with Usick to Boston, where another relative had previously moved, and married Max Cohen, who later became the successful owner of the Paramount Coat Company. In 1919 Usick entered Harvard to study chemistry. He left school in 1923, returned in 1925–26, and left again without receiving a degree. Subsequently Usick married Edith Konikow, daughter of the pioneer Boston Trotskyist Dr. Antoinette Konikow, and began a career in colloidal chemistry. Eventually he established his own successful business, manufacturing contraceptive jelly. Usick was learned in mathematics and science as well as in philosophy and literature. In the late 1920s he contributed a study of Greek culture to V. F. Calverton's *Modern Quarterly*.[78] In the early 1930s he helped to finance *Americana*, an irreverent, anarchistic magazine that was the brainchild of his friend Alexander King, the noted book illustrator and humorist.[79] During these years he lived in New York, associating with a bohemian circle that included the novelist Maxwell Bodenheim and the painter DeHirsh Margules. In 1933 the eccentric businessman decided to follow his wife and mother-in-law into the Trotskyist movement.

Usick was six feet tall, stocky, with long black hair, bushy eyebrows, a thick mustache, and a wide expressive mouth that often seemed twisted, as if he were thinking an ironic thought. When angered, he would tend to go overboard, using harsh and vituperative polemical language that contradicted his rather gentle nature. At first he made a bad impression on the party leaders. Although the articles he wrote for the *New International* were quite sophisticated, he had previously struck up an association with B. J. Field, and, in fact, had joined the Communist League of America in a frenzy in order to reform it. He was active with Field in the 1934 New York hotel strike, but the factional struggle between Field and the Cannon leadership that ensued had a strong impact on him. He began to feel incompetent as a political leader and decided that his skills and talents lay elsewhere. Transforming himself from an individualistic intellectual into a party worker, he devoted himself to giving classes on Marxist philosophy, serving on the editorial boards of the party's newspaper and magazines, translating writings by Trotsky, and drafting many of the party's political resolutions.

Although he had an odd and volatile personality, he differed markedly from most radical intellectuals in that he was not interested in eliciting personal recognition or being in the spotlight.

Most of his efforts were devoted to improving the work of others, although he produced quite a few meticulous articles on contemporary Soviet politics and the American economy as well as several on such diverse subjects as atomic energy and Feuerbach's philosophy. Utterly devoted to socialist revolution, he nonetheless abhorred violence and was motivated by a desire for an ordered world. His work habits were a bit bizarre. For extended periods he would sit in utter silence; then, usually at an odd hour such as midnight or 6:00 A.M., typing very rapidly with one finger, he would produce the final version of an article that he had been contemplating. The rewrites had all been done in his head.

Usick's last years were unexpectedly difficult. When his marriage broke up in the 1940s he turned his business over to his former wife. Remarried in the early 1950s, with a new baby and financially strapped, he fell ill with pneumonia and suffered a heart attack, which forced him to spend nearly two years convalescing before another heart attack killed him in the spring of 1956.

In addition to Vanzler, there were several others who did substantial and noteworthy intellectual work on behalf of the party. One was Joseph Hansen, born in 1910 in a small Mormon community in Utah. Hansen was drawn to Trotskyism by Earle Birney, the Canadian poet who was teaching at the University of Utah in the early 1930s, and for some years aspired to be a novelist.[80] From 1937 to 1940 he served as Trotsky's secretary in Mexico and thereafter primarily engaged in literary work for the Socialist Workers Party in New York. The author of long, meticulous polemics, Hansen had a tendency toward overconfidence and arrogance, but during the early 1960s he distinguished himself by producing a competent series of studies of the Cuban Revolution. To a considerable extent this work redeemed the orthodox Trotskyist position from its unconvincing interpretations of the Chinese and Yugoslavian revolutions.

Other party members produced literary work primarily on behalf of the Socialist Workers Party. George Breitman, born in 1916 in Newark and active in the Unemployed Leagues during the 1930s, wrote creatively on the political strategy of black liberation and undertook extensive and sustained research into the history of Trotskyism.[81] Evelyn Reed, born Evelyn Horwit in 1905 in New Jersey and trained as an artist in New York, published several books on the origins of women's oppression.[82] Laura Gray, born Laura Slobe in Chicago in 1910, had a brief career as an avant-garde painter influenced by Paul Klee, then devoted the last ten years of her short life to drawing naturalistic cartoons in the Boardman Robinson tradition for the *Militant*.[83]

Several others also contributed to party intellectual endeavors but had distinct careers before or after their association with the Socialist Workers Party. Duncan Ferguson, born in 1905 in China, was a successful sculptor and former chair of the art department at Louisiana State University who left his job in 1940 to become a party activist for the duration of his life.[84] George Perle, born in 1910 in Chicago, was a musician and composer influenced by Arnold Schoenberg and Alban Berg. A tall, wiry man with dark, unruly hair, he organized a chorus of Socialist Workers Party members and wrote on dialectics and music for the party journal under the name "George Saunders."[85] Paul N. Siegel, born in 1916 in New Jersey, received a doctorate from Harvard and contributed articles on literary themes under the name "Paul Shapiro" to various party publications in the late 1940s and 1950s.[86] After he was expelled with the Cochran-Clarke faction in 1953 he became a distinguished Shakespearean scholar. He rejoined the SWP in the 1970s but was expelled again in 1983. Yet another layer of Trotskyist intellectuals were in the environs of the party but never joined. Trent Hutter was the pseudonym of Peter Bloch, who was born in Germany of Sephardic Jewish parents. After studying in several European countries, he was a clandestine journalist for the anti-Nazi resistance in Belgium before arriving in the United States in 1949. For several years he contributed frequently to the Trotskyist press on popular culture, but in the early 1960s he abandoned Trotskyism to become an authority on Puerto Rican culture.[87] Richard Schank, a brilliant but highly eccentric psychologist, functioned as a free-lance Trotskyist for a time until he was arrested and imprisoned in Ohio in the 1940s for allegedly stealing ballot boxes during a union election.[88] Among the younger intellectuals in the SWP or its youth group in the 1950s and 1960s were several who would later, after leaving or being expelled, become distinguished during the rise of the New Left, including Staughton Lynd, James Petras, and Barbara Garson.

A good number of rising young scholars and artists passed through the ranks of the Workers Party during the 1940s (see chapter 10), but few became integrated into the organization or remained for any length of time. One of those who did was Noah Greenberg, who carried out devoted party work in the seamen's union for a number of years before becoming a world-famous specialist in medieval music. Others were Spencer Brown, a poet who was active in the teacher's union, and Jesse Cohen, an extraordinarily talented cartoonist, who was known in the Trotskyist movement as Joe Cohen and who signed his work "Carlo." In the late 1940s the novelist Calder Willingham had a brief flirtation with the

Shachtman group, encouraged by James T. Farrell whose review of *End as a Man* (1946) had given Willingham a national reputation. At one point Willingham paid Max Shachtman's plane fare down to Mexico, so that the two of them could visit Natalia Trotsky, but they quarreled en route and parted ways in Mexico City. In the 1970s, Hal Draper proved himself one of the foremost Marxist scholars in the world through the publication of his multivolume series *Karl Marx's Theory of Revolution*.[89]

In addition, a number of disciples of C. L. R. James made scholarly and theoretical contributions during and after the 1950s. This grouping, known as the "state capitalist tendency" because of its theory of the Soviet economy, first coalesced after James's arrival in the United States in 1938. In 1940 the state capitalists sided with Shachtman and became an organized tendency in the Workers Party until 1946; the tendency then returned to the Socialist Workers Party for five years before striking out on its own, with seventy members initiating the publication of *Correspondence* in 1951. The leading theoretician was Raya Dunayevskaya, a Russian immigrant who, under the name Rae Spiegel, had served as Trotsky's Russian-language secretary in the United States in 1937 and 1938. Using the party name Freddie Forrest, she wrote many articles on economic theory; later, as Dunayevskaya, she published *Marxism and Freedom* (1958) and *Philosophy and Revolution* (1973).

In 1955 Dunayevskaya had a falling out with James and established her own organization which published *News and Letters*. The remaining supporters of James included James Boggs, who published *The American Revolution: Pages from a Negro Worker's Notebook* (1963) and *Racism and the Class Struggle* (1970), and Martin Glaberman, author of *Wartime Strikes* (1980). But in 1961, Boggs broke with James, eventually establishing the National Organization for an American Revolution. Glaberman continued to promote James's ideas in *Facing Reality* for several years but disbanded his organization in the 1970s.[90] With the rise of the New Left, James's writings began to have considerable influence on many black and white activists, and his reputation continued to grow through the republication of several volumes of his work in the late 1970s and early 1980s. All of this came as a considerable surprise to many of James's former associates in the Workers Party, a number of whom had misjudged him as nothing more than an ultraleftist with the ability to inspire a small cult of followers.

Perhaps the Marxist scholar most successful at blending party intellectual work with literary production accessible to a broader public was George Novack, a close associate of Vanzler.[91] He had been born Yasef Mendel Novograbelsky in Boston in 1905. Novack's father soon simplified the family name for business reasons, and Novack himself anglicized his first and middle names when he began school. A bright, attractive high school student, with a trim figure, blond hair, and blue eyes, Novack was doted on by his mother to the extent that he desired nothing more than to escape her clutches. His father, who ran a Turkish bathhouse, was more easygoing and tolerant but gambled professionally and led an irregular life.

While at Harvard, Novack led an active social life in Jewish circles and devoured books on philosophy. His closest friend of those years, the poet Stanley Kunitz, recalled Novack as a thin and fairhaired young man with even, classical features. He seemed "better read and informed than other Harvard students on modern literature" and was congenial, socially at ease, and rather easygoing.[92] Yet an underlying restlessness, combining his disappointment with the elitist mode of teaching at Harvard and his need to get out from under his mother's jurisdiction, induced him to run away several times. Once he hitchhiked across the country and on another occasion he found a job in New York. He finally left Harvard without a degree in 1927 to launch a career in publishing and public relations. By 1928 he was working for a major lecture bureau in New York. He then moved to the advertising department of Doubleday and Company; finally he became advertising manager of E. P. Dutton, which had the largest advertising budget in the business. Well known among the younger publishing crowd, Novack might have gone on to become president of a publishing house, but the stock market crash reoriented his thinking entirely. By 1932 he had studied Marx and, under the influence of Herbert Solow, Elliot Cohen, the Trillings, and others from the *Menorah* circle, he became anxious to devote himself full-time to revolutionary political activity. After publishing a book of witticisms, *Who's Whoey* (1932), he began to free-lance. At times he was supported by his wife, Elinor Rice, who ran a bookshop.

As the 1930s progressed, Novack found himself progressively isolated from his associates, including Rice, who had begun breaking with the radical movement. In addition to serving as secretary of the American Committee for the Defense of Leon Trotsky, Novack's main accomplishment during these years was a steady stream of articles written for the Trotskyist press. These began in late 1934 with a series of polished and erudite critiques of non-Marxist theories of social change called "Passports to Utopia" and published under the pseudonym "John Marshall."[93] Then came a three-part study of the response of intellectuals to the Great Depression, still among the best work on the subject, and nearly a dozen essays interpreting aspects of American history from a Marxist point of view.[94] These historical essays, even if somewhat dated in the wake of subsequent research, provided a clear and striking perspective on the course of social development in the United States and bristled with excitement. They portended what might have been a major achievement. Novack, in fact, devoted the last part of the 1930s to original research for a projected three-volume history of the American civil war. Unfortunately, the first volume, focusing on the New York City antidraft riots, was rejected by many publishers and the manuscript of the other two volumes was lost in a fire.

When the conflict between Cannon and Shachtman began, Novack at first sympathized with Shachtman on the question of Soviet policy in eastern Europe. But as the debate deepened, he switched over to Cannon's side and undertook the task of defending dialectical materialism in the debates that ensued. Following the split, Novack gave a series of lectures on the subject that were collected and published in many editions, and, later, in several languages, as *Introduction to the Logic of Marxism* (1942). But the isolation of the 1940s and 1950s took its toll on much of Novack's work. The creative brilliance of his early writing was never fully replicated, although he wrote competently on a wide range of subjects and, whenever he turned to American history, the result was almost always an impressive blend of scholarly meticulousness with a creative application of theory. Yet Novack regarded his writings on Marxist philosophy as his paramount contribution, and most of these tended to be popularizations, similar to the efforts of Communist writers such as Ernst Thaelheimer and Maurice Cornforth. Novack competently defended orthodox Marxism albeit somewhat polemically, but he tended to repeat his major point (usually a defense of Engels), which, even if correct, resulted in a certain circularity of argument.

His culminating work, *Pragmatism versus Marxism: An Appraisal of John Dewey's Philosophy* (1975), however, presents an impressively systematic argument about how the two philosophies differ. The strength of the book is its attempt to situate pragmatism in American society. In opposition to the vulgar Marxist view that portrays pragmatism as an ideology of monopoly capitalism and a legitimator of imperialism, Novack argues that it is the work of human agents in a precise social setting:

The traits and tenets of a philosophical school reflect the psychology and sentiments of a specific set of people imbued with a definite collective will and animated by hopes, fears, sympathies, antipathies, and illusions of a specific kind. Their forms of consciousness, their passions, their inclinations have grown out of the social surroundings which molded them as individuals and conditioned their development in particular ways. These in turn form part of their total response to that environment.[95]

His conclusion—that pragmatism is the view of middle-class intellectuals—is perhaps incomplete, since features of pragmatism are shared by other social strata and the overall ideology of bourgeois society in general. But he provides a cogent demonstration of how Dewey's metaphysics, especially his conception of the indeterminacy of existence, facilitated the view that class struggle was incidental rather than endemic to capitalism.[96]

Under the impact of the radicalization of the 1960s, Novack was stimulated to undertake a major work, *Democracy and Revolution* (1971), which was a remarkable tour de force, demonstrating a stunning ability to cogently integrate large amounts of complicated data and to diligently assimilate a wide variety of political and historical texts. During these years Novack was indefatigable in his literary production, editorial work, and in the education of young Marxists of the new generation, enjoying considerable respect as one of the few revolutionary survivors of the 1930s left-wing intelligentsia.

But if the intellectuals drawn to orthodox Trotskyism could evidence genuine creativity under the impact of changed social conditions, the limitations of orthodoxy could reassert themselves in a time of crisis for the left. Novack, like Vanzler before him, had undergone a certain experience that convinced him that his appropriate arena of activity was as a technician of the revolutionary movement. He believed that there were boundaries of authority beyond which he could not step and still retain his position as a leading party intellectual. In 1953, during the political crisis that tore apart the Fourth International, Novack had been in Europe working on behalf of the SWP, and he developed a sympathy for the new line then being promulgated by the majority of the Fourth International and its central leader, Michael Raptis, who was more widely known under the party name "Pablo." Returning to the United States, Novack set out to persuade James P. Cannon that Pablo's ideas, while not fairly represented by the Cochran-Clarke faction, were correct.

Soon recognizing his inability to influence the situation, he fell into a deep depression, separated from his wife, and relocated to Los Angeles. After a failed suicide attempt he underwent psychoanalysis in which he came to see that the interparty conflict was analogous to a feud within a family, brother against father, and that isolation from the family was tantamount to death.[97]

Within a year Novack was on the road to recovery, but certain limits on his intellectual work had clearly been established. Preservation of his status as a respected party leader had become a psychological as well as a political necessity. In a certain sense he placed himself in confinement; his intellect and emotions could not be permitted to pass a certain point of disagreement with the party leadership. Thus twenty-five years later, when the SWP, in the hands of a new leadership comprised of former college students, began to renounce Trotskyism and purged almost all the surviving founders of the party, Novack remained tragically complicit by his silence.

If orthodox Trotskyism was imperfect in the way that it sustained an anti-Stalinist Marxism based on anticapitalist premises, at least it preserved the Marxist tradition in some form during the long postwar hiatus of radical activity in the United States. James P. Cannon's evolution provides a dramatic contrast to Max Shachtman's. After serving thirteen months of a sixteen-month prison sentence at the Sandstone Federal Penitentiary in 1944–45 for violation of the Smith Act, Cannon resumed his position as national secretary of the SWP. In 1954, after moving to Los Angeles, he became the party's national chairman and played an increasingly lesser role until his death in 1974. During these years the SWP published a number of his books, most of which were collections of letters and speeches.

Like Shachtman, Cannon at the end of his life was fully aware that the unanticipated persistence of Stalinism after World War II had made the issue of democracy more central than ever for socialists. Unlike Shachtman, however, he refused to embrace a conception of an abstract "democracy" devoid of precise social content, for he knew, as Shachtman had once known, that such a gambit was often the first step on a road that would lead to the abandonment of a Marxist program and practice altogether. Cannon left a testament of sorts in a letter written at the time of the Cuban Revolution, which he enthusiastically supported despite the fact that its leaders had not yet announced themselves as socialists. He affirmed his belief that "the fullest *democracy* in the transition period [to socialism], *institutionalized* by forms of organization which assure the participation and control of the working people at every stage of development, is an *indispensable* part of our program." He said that this is what "distinguishes us from and puts us in irreconcilable opposition to 'economic determinists' and totalitarians. It is the condition for the most efficient and rapid development of the new productive process [because a] planned economy will not automatically lead to a society of the free and equal."[98]

As a socialist leader, Cannon may have made episodic errors in one direction or another that allowed his political enemies to charge him with either "adapting to Stalinism" (the Workers Party point of view from 1940 onward), or succumbing to "vulgar anti-Stalinism" (the charge of Bert Cochran's faction in the early 1950s). In reality, however, an admitted "mortal fear of conciliation to Stalinism" rendered him immune from the first course, and his careful assimilation of the lessons learned through observation of the apostates from Marxism during and after the late 1930s kept him free of the second.[99] By and large, Cannon's small party managed to chart an honorable course through the difficult World War II and Cold War years avoiding the Scylla of Stalinism and the Charybdis of imperialism better than any other American radical group of its time.

A cogent analysis of the apostates from anti-Stalinist Marxism in the 1940s and 1950s has hitherto been blocked by two obfuscating perceptions. One depicts their retreat to previously discredited ideas, euphemistically renamed, as an advance to new ground; the other caricatures their recoil from an enormously difficult historical situation as a bald-faced "sellout." The first is a naive apology, the second a moralistic oversimplification. What is objectionable on the part of the New York intellectuals is not at all their rethinking of Marxism in the postwar era; such a rethinking was obviously required by the persistence of Stalinism, the restabilization of American capitalism, and the failure of the Trotskyist or any other revolutionary movement to grow in numbers. Rather, the behavior of the New York intellectuals is suspect because of the hastiness with which Marxism was entirely abandoned in the absence of a viable alternative theory of society; the falsification of past history so as to erase the revolutionary anti-Stalinist tradition; the blind spot exhibited in regard to U.S. imperialism; the dissipation of militant anger against domestic racism and class exploitation; and the gross insensitivity to the costs of the McCarthyite witch-hunt. Moreover, there is a direct line of continuity between many of the New York intellectuals engaged in the American Committee for Cultural Freedom and subsequent right-wing developments culminating in the neoconservative campaign of the 1970s against affirmative action and feminism, coupled with a new cultural elitism and a foreign policy somewhat to the right of Ronald Reagan. These are the aspects of the New York intellectuals' behavior in the 1950s that give credibility to Rahv's charge that the liberal anticommunism of the time was the ideological rationale for *embourgeoisement*.

The so-called true believers in Marxist or Trotskyist orthodoxy, on the other hand, insulated themselves from the pressures of the larger social reality through the protective shield of party life. Of course, those who left the orthodox fold—by choice, as in the case of the Shachtman group, or by expulsion, as with the Cochran group—failed miserably at building an organized movement to the left of social democracy. At best they left a legacy of books and publications requiring critical assimilation. Still, the alternative legacy of orthodoxy, while by no means a preposterous aberration of rational thought, is insufficient as a subtle and complex appreciation of the reality of late capitalism. The true disciples of Trotsky's prewar perspective maintained their revolutionary and anti-imperialist outlook, passing down an honorable record of struggle against domestic racism, class exploitation, and political repression. Yet those associated with the Socialist Workers Party produced theorizations of Stalinism and the prospects for social revolution with many schematic features. They waged bitter internal factional struggles that resulted in hyperbolic charges and countercharges and assumed a rather rigid attitude toward "orthodox Trotskyism" that only began to break down with the influx of new forces in the 1960s. The left-wing anti-Stalinist tradition suffered blows and underwent a disorientation in the 1950s from which it has never fully recovered. In short, anticommunism was the death of anti-Stalinism.

CHAPTER 10

The Cul-de-sac of Social Democracy

What would happen if
men remained faithful
to the ideals of their
youth?

—Pietro Spina in
   Ignazio Silone's
   Bread and Wine[1]

. . . .

PORTRAIT: IRVING HOWE

For the New York intellectuals, the consequences of Cold War anticommunism extend far beyond the 1950s. The transformation in ideology and political consciousness consolidated in the early 1950s definitively and perhaps permanently shifted the axis of anti-Stalinism from its revolutionary anticapitalist premise, creating a movement that discredited more than it assisted the far left. Indeed, the behavior of the bulk of the New York intellectuals in the 1950s undermined the validity of the whole anti-Stalinist current of thought and even somewhat redeemed the Communist, fellow-traveling, and progressive liberals who acted heroically by comparison.

After all, in the face of the political repression—the first real test for the generation that came of age in the 1930s—most of the anti-Stalinists not only denuded themselves of past radicalism but developed sophisticated rationalizations for tolerating the essence if not the precise McCarthyite form of the witch-hunt. Responsibility for the bulk of the resistance among intellectuals, as well as for antiracist and anti-imperialist political activity, was handed over to the Communists, fellow travelers, and progressive liberals. These women and men may have suffered persecution at the time, but they achieved near martyrdom in the eyes of the next generation of left-wing intellectuals. Ignorance on the part of 1960s New Leftists was not the sole reason that apologists for Stalinism such as Lillian Hellman, Paul Robeson, and the Hollywood Ten were resurrected as moral beacons; their rehabilitation was the logical by-product of the dismal record of all but a few of the founders of the intellectual anti-Stalinist left.

Factors such as political vision and sustained membership in socialist organizations seem to have been more important than age in determining whether or not one accommodated to the witch-hunt and the foreign policy it was intended to legitimize. Moreover, the course taken by most of the generation of radicalized students who had come to anti-Stalinist Marxism during the middle and the late 1930s parallels that of the founders. Those who held membership in or were closely allied with the Trotskyist movement in the New York and New Jersey area comprised an impressive range of future intellectuals: Irving Howe, literary critic and editor of *Dissent*; Melvin Tumin, sociologist and anthropologist; Lawrence Kradar, anthropologist; Martin Diamond, political scientist; Gertrude Himmelfarb, historian; I. Milton Sacks, political scientist; Morroe Berger, sociologist; Peter Rossi, sociologist; Seymour Martin Lipset, sociologist; Philip O. Selznick, sociologist; Leslie Fiedler, literary critic; Irving Kristol, journalist; and Melvin J. Lasky, editor of *Encounter*. Of this generation, almost none considered themselves as socialists of any variety after the Cold War began, and a fair number subsequently evolved considerably to the right. Among the exceptions was Irving Howe, perhaps the most significant and capable radical literary critic of our time.

That Howe was able to bring an element of socialist discourse into American literary and academic circles during the Cold War years testifies to his considerable intellectual resources and certain strengths of character. That he vehemently turned against the New Left of the 1960s and early 1970s, caricaturing its aims and activities, and even flirted briefly with the incipient neoconservatives and their campaign against the *New York Review of Books*, may be evidence of the limitations of the social democratic perspective that he chose as his political guide. Hardworking, an impressive literary craftsman, a critic of exceptional imaginative and intellectual powers, and a tireless fighter for his political views, Howe's inability to revitalize the anti-Stalinist left as more than an impotent wing of liberalism is due primarily to a self-defeating political strategy, not personal defects in morality or intelligence.

Howe was born Irving Horenstein in 1920, the son of immigrants who ran a small grocery store that went out of business during the Great Depression.[2] A socialist activist even before he entered the City College of New York, Howe gravitated quickly to the Trotskyist wing of the Young Peoples Socialist League, becoming one of its national leaders after it broke from the Socialist Party to become the youth group of the Socialist Workers Party. On the City College campus he was a main leader of the Trotskyist students, full of fiery rhetoric and eager for militant action not so different from some of the most extreme (but nonterrorist) elements of the New Left of the 1960s. During the Spanish Civil War he would jump up on the tables in the alcoves to give speeches.

A leaflet attacking the campus Reserve Officers Training Corps declared: "We must wipe it out. It is the organ of American imperialism in the college."[3] The major campaign of the Young Peoples Socialist League (Fourth International) was against the reformism of the Communist students who were insufficiently antiwar. In an open letter published in the *Campus*, the City College of New York student newspaper, Howe's group proclaimed: "The Stalinist leaders of the American Student Union are striving to lead the ASU along the road of their own social patriotism, and to the abandonment of militant struggle."[4] Shortly after, the group issued a leaflet warning, "Our main enemy is at home: American capitalism. FDR is trying to line up the working class for the next imperialist war—the second edition of 1914–18 may break out very soon."[5] In late 1937 Howe and his comrades published a longer manifesto called "Red Herrings from the Right," charging that the Communists wanted to turn the American Student Union "into a Roosevelt machine" and insisting that the only correct program against war "is the struggle for the revolutionary overthrow of the government, to set up a workers' government which can really ensure peace." They called upon City College students to help "build a new International" and "to continue the struggle for the principles of Lenin."[6] In 1938 they organized a "Strike against Imperialist War," which featured a rally with James Burnham and James T. Farrell and greetings from Sidney Hook.[7] To protest cuts in education, the group called for mass picket lines and sit-down strikes.[8] Howe himself edited a rough mimeographed publication called the *CCNY Red Book*, which denounced the university "as a striking example of the intellectual bankruptcy of the capitalist class."[9] He also wrote for and helped edit *Challenge of Youth*, the national newspaper of the Young Peoples Socialist League (Fourth International).

An immediate and admiring supporter of Max Shachtman during the 1939–40 dispute, Howe's journalistic talents were quickly recognized by the Workers Party leadership, and many saw him as Shachtman's most promising protégé. A few months after *Labor Action* was launched, Howe became the paper's managing editor, a post that he held until he was drafted into the army. Thereafter he contributed to the paper under the name R. Fahan. This seems to suggest *Rot Fahne (Red Flag)*, the name of Rosa Luxemburg's news-paper. But it also conveniently resembled one of his party names, R. Fangston, which he was dubbed by a comrade because he had some sharply pointed teeth that were later filed down, although Fangston also suggested his aggressive, polemical style. After his release from military service, a good part of which was spent reading in Alaska, he became a member of the editorial board under the name Irving Howe, which he had by now legally changed from Horenstein.

Howe's articles in *Labor Action*, which touched on a remarkable range of subjects, were marked by stridency and an occasional uto-pianism with religious overtones. For example, in an article about the use of poison gas during the war, he declared, "There is hope in the world of chaos and destruction, the star of socialism shines with constancy and promise. Not the ceaseless war, the chaotic postwar disintegration, the dictatorial brutality which capitalism promises, but the peace, the freedom, the human brotherhood which socialism alone can bring. That is our road."[10] Several years later, discussing the postwar situation in Europe, he declared, "If men would have a sense of dignity and purpose, a feeling that their lives are more than tribulation and suffering, they must fight for socialism. That is the path out of the desert."[11] Polemicizing against the reactionary Senator Theodore Bilbo from Mississippi, he urged, "Let us summon our hatred of injustice and let us burn the filth of Bilboism off the skin of the land. And then let us use the plenty and rich of this land to build a new society of peace and equality, of plenty for all, of the brotherhood of all men, where the children of tomorrow will play in the streets and the fields unaware of the deforming hatreds that now poison our lives."[12]

In the late 1940s Howe devoted considerable attention to expos-ing social democratic reformism in the United States as well as in Europe. Especially scandalous in his view was the failure of the French social democrats to demand the immediate removal of their armed forces from Indochina, which stood in a sorry contrast to the position of the Trotskyists in France:

> We have special reason to be proud of our French comrades—the Fourth International of the PCI [International Communist Party], who, without the slightest ambiguity, have come out in support of the Indo-Chinese people; who have demanded the complete withdrawal of French troops from Indo-China; and who . . . defied the Parisian police to demonstrate their soli-darity with their Indo-Chinese brothers in the streets of Paris. . . . We stand squarely by the side of the French Fourth Interna-

tional. They do not bow down before French imperialism; they rather defy it and send their brothers of Indo-China this message: We are with you in the struggle for independence; we are your brothers; we shall fight beside you against the Le Clercs, the Blums, and the Thorez's.

Howe concluded that in the behavior of the Socialist Léon Blum one sees "the true imperialist face of Social Democracy."[13] In a follow-up article some months later he again attacked the French social democrats: "the sight of these pious liberals, these democratic worthies who are so ready to read us lectures about 'Bolshevik amorality'—the sight, I say, of these liberals twisting themselves all over creation in the attempt to condone the French suppressions, is more than any socialist should be able to bear without anger."[14]

Howe also issued a lengthy criticism of an article written by his college classmate Daniel Bell in the late 1940s. In an issue of the journal *Modern Review*, Bell had proposed that socialists stop running independent election campaigns and strive to become the left wing of the Democratic Party on the grounds that such a policy was more "realistic." Howe, who in an earlier article had defined "realism" as "the first refuge of scoundrels," now defined it as a euphemism for "accepting the capitalist status quo." Howe asked, Can Bell be for "independent labor action" but not for a labor party? Bell believed socialists should work in the Democratic Party serving as "intellectual catalysts"; but to Howe this actually meant acting as "intellectual stooges" for the labor leaders, a "shameful" example of which had been already provided by Gus Tyler and Jay Lovestone. Such a policy, Howe insisted, would only serve the interests of the capitalist oppressors, who actually controlled the Democratic Party. In a closing paean to the Workers Party, Howe urged intellectuals to withstand the pressure to become "oppositionist liberals supporting the capitalist status quo" by having the "courage and wisdom" to struggle for "independent class action and the rebuilding of an independent socialist movement."[15]

Howe was an equally prolific contributor to *New International*, in which he devoted much attention to the politics of culture. Several of his essays presented an ongoing critique of the *Partisan Review* for backsliding on the revolutionary commitments of its founding editorial statement. In the early 1940s Howe focused on Rahv's reversal of his internationalist position on World War II.[16] During the late 1940s he dissected a rather astonishing *Partisan Review* editorial called "The Liberal Fifth Column," in which

American liberals were berated for being too soft on the Soviet Union and adoption of a more belligerent U.S. foreign policy was urged.

Howe pointed out that obsessive anti-Communism only obscures the question of which forces one should ally oneself with to wage the battle against Stalinism; it can "only render impossible an effective struggle against Stalinism—not to mention making hopeless any sort of positive aim." Howe explained that by rejecting "the method of analysis which characterizes the basic aspects of American foreign policy in class terms," the *Partisan Review* "has succumbed to *Stalinophobia*, a disease common among intellectuals who were once radicals; its major symptom is that regular tired feeling. *Stalinophobia* takes the form of bitter and quite justified denunciations of Stalinism without any corresponding effort to develop a sociological understanding of it. Hatred for Stalinism becomes an emotional block to its political analysis." Howe further identified the editorial with the "vulgar articles" published in the right-wing social democratic *New Leader*, "which always lead to support of one or another reactionary imperialism solely because of its conjunctural opposition to Russia."[17]

Between the summer of 1945 and the fall of 1947 Howe engaged in a complicated debate with fellow WP members over the work of Arthur Koestler. It began with a critical review by Peter Loumos of four books by Koestler.[18] Neil Weiss, a poet and WP member, wrote a letter protesting that Loumos had allowed political prejudice to interfere with an objective assessment.[19] Answering Weiss's letter, Howe agreed that Loumos had erred in "condemning Koestler because the main character of *Darkness at Noon*, Rubashov, is portrayed as a vacillating bureaucrat who capitulates to Stalinism rather than as an intransigent oppositionist." Howe then charged that Weiss was giving too much credit to Koestler's political criticisms of the Second and Third Internationals, especially as embodied in his essays, which had a value of "next to none." What was exciting about Koestler, what made him well worth reading, was his ability to brilliantly "*touch* the heart of the modern problem" (the growing complexity of world politics), "despite all those in the revolutionary movement whose minds still function as if it were 1920." Howe concluded by making a sharp distinction between the forms of expression in formal essays and in fiction. The former demanded scientific rigor, especially in the discussion of politics; but "the impressionism which I find intolerable in political analysis does have value in the novel or informal essay; it does, on a *different plane of communication,* provoke insights and touch sensitive areas of existence, which can be of subsequent help to political analysis."[20]

Eight months later there appeared a further exchange on the subject between Albert Glotzer, Shachtman's closest collaborator, and Howe. Glotzer insisted that Koestler should not really be judged as a novelist but as "a writer of fictionalized current events, or journalistic novels," thereby justifying Loumos's harsh critique. The meaning of the objection to Loumos by Weiss was therefore more serious than simply a "defense of literature" against vulgar Marxism; behind this pose, Glotzer contended that Weiss actually sympathized with many of Koestler's views. Thus he found it shocking that Howe had come to Weiss's defense. Apparently, in overreaction to Stalinist excesses, Howe was calling for a total separation of literature and politics, ignoring the fact that, even if literature had its semiautonomous sphere, the politico-social structure of society is what remains decisive in determining the nature of our lives. At the same time Glotzer pointed out that many of Howe's remarks on literature were themselves more political than literary—Howe's observation, for example, that "the world is no longer as simple as it was twenty-five years ago." In fact, Glotzer protested, "the world was not simple twenty-five years ago!" There were complex problems then, and the problems of today "are the extension of the unsolved problems of twenty-five years ago. . . . *What Howe fails to see is the continuity of the basic social problem and the continuity of its solution.*"[21] Howe's response was essentially that Glotzer seemed determined to narrowly judge literature, not by party line as did the Stalinists, but as if it were merely a convenient vehicle for political content.[22]

Other issues underlay this controversy, which expressed deeper problems and disagreements in the form of debates over literary criticism. To some extent Howe was already beginning to move toward his own sphere of cultural criticism. With publishing opportunities opening up to him in Elliot Cohen's new Jewish intellectual magazine, *Commentary,* and other journals, he naturally saw greater possibilities of exploration and discussion in the literary medium. Perhaps, too, he was reacting negatively against pressure from Max Shachtman to desist from a professional career as a writer, a career that Shachtman saw as a potential rival to party assignments such as the one he hoped that Howe would take as organizer of the Akron branch of the Workers Party. Moreover, since the early 1940s Howe had held the view that American literature must pass into a new phase of modernist sensibility, which resulted in a painful conflict with James T. Farrell, whose allegiance to literary realism was as ardent as was his openness to experimentation.[23]

Indeed, this early debate over Koestler foreshadows to some degree Howe's famous treatise on modernist literature, "The Culture of Modernism" (1970, revised version).[24] Throughout the Koestler debate and in the essay Howe asserted that unique forms of imaginative literature create a space free of political ideology. He contended that one must refrain from judging the political content of literature—especially literature of modernist sensibility—in the manner in which one judges straight political doctrine. This is certainly an improvement over the vulgar political coding of literary texts that had discredited the Communist literary movement. Yet, as in the case of Rahv, Howe's appraisal was partly based on a naive, pragmatist notion of "ideology" as formal political doctrine—and often only doctrine with which one disagreed—whereas he depicted authentic literature as an ideology-free realm of "experience." In a 1971 debate on "Literary Criticism and Literary Radicals," Howe endorsed the statement of the Austrian Marxist Ernst Fischer that art is "the triumph of reality over ideology," a formulation far too ingenuous.[25] Favoring a "social approach" to literary criticism but eschewing a social method, or any other kind of authentic method, neither Howe nor any of the New York intellectuals went beyond pragmatist simplicities to the knottier problems of literature and ideology. Twenty-five years after the Koestler debate, "The Culture of Modernism" presented a brilliant description of the modernist sensibility; but it did little more than suggest, without elaboration, a historical origin in romanticism, and it failed to address the highly relevant issue of the ideology of form.

His burgeoning talents opened to Howe in the late 1940s the possibility of developing an independent life as an intellectual. These talents had been nurtured by the skills he had acquired as a journalist for the Workers Party. They were also honed by the intensity of the party's intellectual atmosphere from which he absorbed several of the traits that would make him distinctive as a critic: a remarkable polemical dexterity, reminiscent of Shachtman's orations; a firsthand knowledge of the international socialist movement; and a politico-historical consciousness about the social basis of cultural activity. Moreover, his first publishing opportunities had come through the assistance of more established intellectuals in the Workers Party milieu—Farrell, Dwight Macdonald, and Clement Greenberg (employed at *Commentary*). Yet at this very moment he began to have intense doubts about his commitment to the party.

The bitter diatribes he then published against the complacency of former revolutionaries who had obtained secure jobs may well have been a symptom of his own inner turmoil. In the fall 1949 issue of *Anvil*, published by the New York Student Federation Against War, an organization that had been initiated by the Shachtman group, he urged students to "at least be willing to take chances with their lives and to commit themselves in their hopes and dreams," rather than "accept a living intellectual and moral death as the price of creature comfort." He further concluded that "the number of ex-radicals who are today comfortable labor bureaucrats—the kind who tell you that they too were once socialists (when they were young, you understand) or that they are still, in a sort of way, perhaps, socialists (but one must be practical, you understand)—is appalling, the mark of the suicide of a generation of Americans."[26]

Howe's disagreements with the Workers Party do not seem to have surfaced until late 1946; however, by 1948 they were full-blown at the same time that Goldman and Farrell were distancing themselves. In March 1946 Howe loyally defended the Workers Party in a strong polemic against C. L. R. James, the co-leader with Raya Dunayevskaya of those within the party who adhered to the "state capitalist" analysis of the Soviet Union. At this time, the James-Dunayevskaya group, known as the Johnson-Forrest Tendency, was moving toward a rapprochement with the Socialist Workers Party on the grounds that the Socialist Workers Party was more proletarian and revolutionary than the Workers Party. Howe accused James's formulations of being "an insult to the party for which we have worked the past six years," and he accused the Socialist Workers Party of cowardice during World War II by "playing ostrich in the unions" and for its theory of "telescoping" the struggle for socialism and the struggle against fascism.[27] But in September of 1946 Howe published a review of a translation of Trotsky's *The New Course*, which caused considerable protest from Workers Party members because it raised reservations about Trotsky's strategy in the struggle against Stalin without coming to definite conclusions. When he was additionally attacked in the *Internal Bulletin* for being too "hot-headed and impatient," and perhaps in need of consulting a psychologist, Howe responded bitterly that "those of us who have spent a good part of the last few years in writing polemics against Macdonald, Burnham, the editors of *Partisan Review*, and a number of other opponents of revolutionary

Marxism, tend to get a little annoyed when we are accused of anti-Marxism."[28]

In 1946 Howe had indeed launched a polemic against Macdonald in the pages of *Politics* magazine, which then employed Howe as a part-time assistant. Howe's line of argument was drawn from Burnham and Shachtman's "Intellectuals in Retreat": the "flight from Marxism of Macdonald and his friends" could be correlated to "the present period of reaction." However, these new backsliders persisted in deceiving themselves by constructing "rationalizations to withdraw from the struggle which continues to face humanity." Among the rationalizations that Howe refuted was the belief that the failure of the working class to transform society after World War II signified a permanent loss of its revolutionary potential, to which he replied: "The major social impulsions driving the working class to revolt persist; and the working classes of all countries do revolt. Sporadically, in disorganized and disoriented fashion, it is true, but they still revolt, even though doomed in the absence of revolutionary socialist leadership." Howe also claimed that Macdonald had caricatured Leninist party norms as "coercion," when, in fact, all that Leninism signified was "the discipline of a group of people who, voluntarily entering into certain associations from which they can just as freely withdraw, nonetheless believe that for a common purpose it is permissible to subordinate opinions on secondary matters in order to maintain continuous co-operation."[29]

Yet, at the same time, Howe published an essay in *Commentary* suggesting that some of his thought was elsewhere. Called "The Lost Young Intellectual: A Marginal Man, Twice Alienated," Howe presented a largely autobiographical portrait of the young secular Jew alienated from the past but a misfit in the present. Howe concluded that no solution to this rootlessness existed at present, although someday it might be solved "if an American society appears in which both the Jewish intellectual and his people, along with everyone else, can find integration, security, and acceptance."[30] Howe could not be expected to call upon the readership of *Commentary* to join the Workers Party, but the element of despair and passivity that pervaded the essay suggests that a second self coexisted in troubled tandem with the overconfident Howe of the *New International*, *Labor Action*, and *Politics*. Four years earlier he had written an article for the Workers Party on the "Jewish Question" that strongly insisted that "there is no such thing as 'the Jew'; there are rich and poor Jews, Jewish workers and Jewish bosses."[31] Both a class analysis, which Howe had so emphatically defended as the sine qua non of any intellectual discussion, and a revolutionary internationalist point of view, were muted, if not entirely missing, in the *Commentary* essay. What is most remarkable is that both Howes, the confident revolutionary and the twice-alienated marginal Jew, could present their cases with equal conviction, abundant evidence, and a well-crafted felicity of expression.

THE "SOCIALIST WING OF THE WEST"

Howe's political differences with the leadership of the Workers Party erupted in the spring of 1948. In a full-page article in *Labor Action* he reacted to the Stalinist takeover of Czechoslovakia with a flood of emotion. Beginning by announcing his "feeling of discouragement," he declared that "the world today is in far worse state than ten years ago when Hitler over-ran Europe." He concluded that "only the most sober realism, only, if you will, the most honest pessimism can possibly serve as a basis for a useful discussion." Perhaps he had intended his ending to be upbeat, but it was decisively undercut by his rhetoric: "That at the moment the war of atom bombs seems to be the more likely result of the current historical tragedy is, for this writer at least, too obvious to require reiteration. But it is not inevitable, it is not unavoidable. It is still possible for men to act! Perhaps then action can forestall the atom war; [or] perhaps it can only keep alive that spark of thought and hope, that flickery but still beautiful dream—with which those to follow us will try to rebuild from the ashes of the atoms. But even if it is the latter perspective which will be realized, to nourish and guard that spark is to us the most worthy and useful of dedications."[32] Protests abounded in letters to the paper, in the *Internal Bulletin*, and in private letters to Shachtman. While Howe remained a member of the party for another four and a half years, he was most certainly in a state of painful rethinking, and his literary contributions thereafter were confined mainly to the theoretical magazine.[33]

In early 1949 Howe's two closest associates, Stanley Plastrik (whose party names were "Sherman Stanley" and "Henry Judd," although he was also known as "Rajah" because of his fascination with India) and Emanuel Geltman (known as Emanuel Garrett), opposed Shachtman's analysis of the Marshall Plan, which they said had become more critical. They urged that the Workers Party adopt a policy of endorsing American economic aid to Europe but opposing military aid, which would be used for imperialist purposes.[34] Then, in January 1950, a year after the Workers Party had changed its name to the Independent Socialist League, Howe and Plastrik urged that the party transform *Labor Action* into a more "weighty and serious" paper. Finally, in October 1952, Howe and Plastrik submitted a long statement of resignation which began with the affirmation that "we are and intend to remain democratic social-ists. Our motive in leaving the ISL is a conviction that it has ceased to be useful for advancing the cause of democratic socialism or for providing a lively center in which its problems can be discussed."[35] The organization, in their view, was retreating to greater orthodoxy under the pressure of the times, which only made the situation worse:

> The 'third camp' concepts seem now to us meaningless. . . . There are not available, at the present juncture, those histori-cal energies which alone could activate a 'third camp'. . . . We are opposed to war. . . . But, as democratic socialists, our place is in the Western world, the democratic world, no matter how sharp our criticisms of its bourgeois leadership. The struggle between Stalinism and the West is not merely a struggle for the imperialist division of the world but, also, and in terms of consequences, more fundamentally a struggle between two ways of living: between democracy, however marred, and the most bestial totalitarianism ever known.

Insisting that they intended to be the "socialist wing of the West" but would "retain every right to criticize the bourgeois leadership for its policy vis-à-vis Stalinism," they concluded that "the major task of socialists today is to engage in sustained intellectual activity, mainly with the end of reorienting and reeducating ourselves."[36]

The response from Shachtman was predictable: "when two peo-ple like Howe and Judd [Plastrik] quit the organization, the act is a measure of the fierce pressures exerted upon individuals and move-ments alike by the objective circumstances of the present world situation." Strangely, Shachtman observed, Howe had been more active in recent weeks than ever before, speaking and writing in defense of Marxism, "but Howe's political instability is not a new thing and his present action is an expression of it." As for Plastrik, who at one time was a follower of B. J. Field, "since the end of the war, we have observed his evolution from the most hide-bound and terrifyingly 'orthodox' Marxist to a political chameleon." The major responsibility of the moment for revolutionaries is to maintain a socialist organization "to keep alive the great socialist traditions of the past and present for the coming generations." Anyone who abandons this duty "with a slick slogan like 'We Support the West' identifies himself with one of the imperialist powers or camps, and ceases to be, in the real sense of the word, a socialist."[37] Shachtman's response reflected the traditional view that leaving a socialist organization is tantamount to desertion of the cause. But complex personal elements may have been involved as well as the crucial political difference over "supporting the West." On the one hand, Howe had always been politically close to Shachtman and was taken by many to be his protégé. On the other, Howe's extraordinary literary productivity may have been a sore reminder to Shachtman of his own failings in that regard.

Despite the opposition of some leaders, Howe and Plastrik were invited to the New York membership meeting of the ISL to discuss their resignation. Howe was given forty-five minutes to present his views. Plastrik had originally declined to speak, but, after hearing the representative of the Independent Socialist League Political Committee, he demanded a rebuttal. In an undoubtedly partisan description of the meeting written by Glotzer, it was reported that Howe had accused the ISL leadership of using Cannonite methods in responding to his resignation and that he had charged the organization with impeding his literary activity. Howe's presentation was "undignified in its utterly subjective character, ungraceful in the material used, ungrateful in the failure of appreciation of what our movement has given him in more than a decade's membership."[38] When Howe, Plastrik, and Geltman began publishing *Dissent* magazine eighteen months later, Hal Draper printed a sharp criticism of it in *Labor Action*, charging the three editors with backsliding into liberalism. This was followed by a denial from Howe that was published in the next issue, but the ISL leadership went so far as to pass a motion forbidding members from contributing to *Dissent* without special permission.[39]

Howe did not leave the Independent Socialist League with the plan of starting *Dissent* as a rival publication to *New International* and *Labor Action*. The idea was suggested by the sociologist Lewis Coser at a meeting of former members and sympathizers of the Independent Socialist League. Although the core group—which included Howe's indispensable comrades, Plastrik and Geltman—saw themselves as Marxists and radicals to the left of social democracy, the central issue for the publication was dissenting from the McCarthyite atmosphere. Perhaps if Dwight Macdonald's *Politics* had continued, *Dissent* would never have come into existence.

Born in Germany, Coser had fled to France in 1933 where he participated in several radical groups, including a small Trotskyist organization named "The Spark" after Lenin's newspaper. As a wartime refugee in the United States, he wrote for *Politics* and Socialist Party publications under the name Louis Clair and for Workers Party publications under the name "Europicus." A letter announcing *Dissent* was prepared by Howe and issued under Meyer Schapiro's name. Financial contributions were held in escrow for one year and were to be returned if the project failed to get off the ground. Only two to three thousand copies of the first issue were projected, but it caused such a sensation that the editors had to reprint many thousands more.[40]

Part of the sensation was due to the bitter opposition of the *Commentary* circle. This opposition had already started to mobilize a few weeks earlier when Howe, at Philip Rahv's instigation, published "This Age of Conformity" in the *Partisan Review*. *Commentary* associate Robert Warshow submitted a long and peevish reply in the next issue, followed by Howe's rejoinder. The debate was a classic exchange between pro- and antiestablishment intellectuals. Howe had carefully charted a trend among intellectuals away from independent and critical thought and toward defense of the status quo. Warshow translated the political into the personal, claiming that Howe was a hypocrite for charging *Commentary* writers with impurity while he himself earned a living as a professor at Brandeis University and had worked for the Luce publications. As Howe noted, Warshow had simply trivialized the issues. The problem was not how intellectuals earn their living, a social necessity, but whether they devoted at least part of their skills to the political and cultural emancipation of humanity—whether they on some level acted to subvert, rather than merely adapt to, the conformist pressures of the institutions within which they work.[41]

If the Independent Socialist League leaders expected Howe to quickly follow the course of Eastman, Hook, and Burnham, they were quite mistaken. *Dissent* stayed distinctly to the left of the American Committee for Cultural Freedom and aimed a good deal of its fire at those Cold War liberals who complied with the antiradical witch-hunt, especially Sidney Hook and Irving Kristol. Even though the editors progressively rejected Bolshevism, they did not succumb to the Leninophobia characteristic of deradicalizing intellectuals of the time. *Dissent* was sharply critical of segregationist policies in the United States, and, much like Shachtman's Independent Socialist League, it assumed an attitude toward the labor movement favorable—in the end, too favorable—to the policies of Walter Reuther, the subject of Howe's first book, *Walter Reuther and the UAW* (1949), coauthored with Independent Socialist League leader B. J. Widick. Among *Dissent's* most glaring weaknesses was its two-dimensional caricature of the Communist movement.

The journal was consistent in defending on paper the democratic rights of party members, but its continual characterization of Communists as totalitarians and as essentially fascistlike had the effect of undermining action against concrete instances of repression. As Sidney Hook had done years earlier, the editors simply read the Communist parties out of the working-class movement. In the concluding chapter of *The American Communist Party: A Critical History* (1957), Howe presented with coauthor Lewis Coser a theoretical analysis of Stalinism that at least aspired to sophistication and complexity.[42] In practice, however, his view was more simplistically expressed in his 1957 controversy with A. J. Muste and Sidney Lens about the American Forum. Advocated by Muste and Lens, both contributing editors of *Dissent*, the American Forum was a means for organizing dialogue among the American left during the period of turmoil after Khrushchev's Twentieth Congress speech and the Hungarian revolt. Muste had declared himself an advocate of "revolutionary nonviolence" after his Trotskyist years, and Lens, a follower of Hugo Oehler until the early 1950s, had become known as a left-wing union official and author of books on labor, radicalism, and foreign policy that offered a "third camp" perspective.

On May Day 1957 Muste participated in a rally in New York City with representatives of the Socialist Workers Party, Communist Party, and other radicals. Howe was horrified that Muste and advocates of "democratic socialism" would share the platform with Communists, whose partners in Hungary had just repressed the student-worker uprising; and he was even more outraged that the Trotskyists would share the platform with the " 'comrades' of the executioners of Trotsky himself." From the viewpoint of political purism, Howe certainly had a point, but one wonders if the argument were a mere rhetorical ploy, since he never applied such stringent standards to himself. After all, as a "critical" supporter of the Democratic Party after 1952, Howe was not only sharing the platform with but assisting to power the "comrades" of lynchers in the South, bombers of Hiroshima, and strikebreakers throughout the country.

Subsequently Muste and Lens helped to organize the American Forum for Socialist Education with the same group of people who sponsored the May Day rally. Howe and other editors of *Dissent* refused to participate in this new organization primarily on the grounds that Communists were involved: "We regard the CP not as a radical group among other radical groups, but as an association of political enemies that has no place in the socialist community." In particular, Muste and Lens were to be criticized because this educational and discussion society lent "a helping hand to the Communist Party by providing it with a kind of privileged sanctuary and protective coloration."[43]

In his response, Muste acknowledged that two of the forty-member National Committee of the American Forum were Communist Party members. Still, he argued, the purpose of the forum was not to launch a new radical organization but simply to discuss and debate issues of socialist theory and practice. In this regard, the Communists had joined with the understanding that their views would be "subjected to the severest criticism." Howe, Norman Thomas, and others had been invited to join in order to participate in that debate. Moreover, Muste pointed out that Communist "monolithism" had broken down: many of the rebel students and workers in Hungary were themselves Communists; American Communists had openly denounced this repression in the *Daily Worker*; and Communists outside the Soviet bloc, such as Mao, were developing heretical positions. By participating in a discussion with Communists, one increased one's chances of influencing them. Finally, in terms of building a new radical movement, it was necessary to settle accounts with the historical differences represented by Communists, Socialists, and Trotskyists; to do that it was necessary to cease the "old type attacks on Stalinism" just as it was necessary to continue to oppose Stalinism itself.[44] The conflict between the members on the board of *Dissent* was so great, however, that when Lens submitted a piece on the same subject it was rejected. Lens then ceased to contribute and was asked to drop off the board by Howe; Muste resigned in an act of solidarity.[45]

Two years later Howe had a falling out with C. Wright Mills, a friend and political associate for the past decade. First, Howe published a harsh review of Mills's *The Causes of World War III* in the spring of 1959, accusing Mills's views on foreign policy of constituting "an accommodation not merely with Russia as a power but with Communist dictatorship as a form of society."[46] In the following issue, Mills asked Howe a pointed question: "Just how does your basic view of the world confrontation today differ from the line expressed by the work of Dulles-Adenauer? I suppose there are differences, but just how far do they extend?" Surprisingly, Howe completely sidestepped this accusation of "State Department socialism" and rebutted with the all-too-predictable charge that Mills was adapting to Stalinism.[47] If Howe was liberal or even radical on some issues, then his rigid, virtually right-wing social democratic views evidenced in the exchanges with Muste and Mills paved the way for *Dissent*'s position on the war in Vietnam.

Although he had demanded the immediate withdrawal of all troops during the French occupation, Howe defended the very stance he had once scorned when it came to the U.S. intervention in Indochina. In 1964 he stated that a pullout of U.S. troops would be "inhumane."[48] In 1966 he called simply for a "cease-fire" and went on to oppose antiwar actions in California that included civil disobedience because they challenged "the decisions of the democratically elected government."[49] That was a disturbingly weak argument, since (1) war had never been declared; (2) the population had voted overwhelmingly against escalation of the war by electing Lyndon B. Johnson in 1964; and (3) the same argument could be used to justify any action by an elected government of the United States, including genocide or nuclear holocaust. In early 1967 Walter Goldwater, a former SWP and WP member who had helped finance *Dissent*, wrote a letter criticizing Howe's policy and was bluntly told that "unilateral withdrawal is meaningless."[50]

By giving legitimacy to the American presence in Vietnam, Howe opened himself to the charge of actually defending U.S. imperialism, for he was granting the United States the right to determine the outcome of the struggle by interfering in the internal political life of the Vietnamese nation. While it is important that Howe had criticisms of the American role in Vietnam, such criticisms cannot be regarded as a substitute for opposing the U.S. presence in that country. By 1970, when the U.S. military effort was doing poorly and the demand for "immediate withdrawal" of U.S. troops had succeeded in winning the sentiment of the mainstream of the antiwar movement, Howe was insisting that he had always been "against the war in Vietnam." Julius Jacobson, one of Howe's sharpest critics, noted in response that this statement obscured the fact that Howe had "opted for the continued military presence in Vietnam even though he knew that this meant mass slaughter and devastation. That means support of the war no matter how critically, mournfully or reluctantly given."[51]

The weakness of Howe's new orientation was most obvious during the late 1960s. The bulk of Shachtman's organization had by then dissolved itself into the right wing of the Socialist Party. For a while Howe was reconciled with Shachtman; they collaborated on some literary projects, and Howe, Michael Harrington, and Shachtman functioned as a team in social democratic circles. Unfortunately, as the Vietnam War came to national attention in the mid-1960s, Shachtman revealed himself to be a "hawk" who considered the United States to be engaged in a progressive war against Stalinism. Consequently Howe and Harrington, who had a "negotiations" position, felt that they had to break with him, thus splitting the Socialist Party into two factions. Shachtman's group eventually became known as Social Democrats U.S.A. and grew to be a substantial force in the AFL-CIO. Such former associates of Shachtman as Donald Slaiman, Sam Fishman, and Tom Kahn would come to hold major organizational positions in the AFL-CIO; Carl Gershman, another associate in Social Democrats U.S.A., became Jeane Kirkpatrick's assistant at the United Nations in the 1980s. Shachtman himself gained influence over the black socialist Bayard Rustin, and together they established the A. Philip Randolph Institute, which allowed Shachtman to expand his role as a behind-the-scenes influence in labor circles. Ironically, Howe, who became a member of the Democratic Socialist Organizing Committee, now found himself being attacked from the right by the very comrades who had attacked him from the left a decade earlier when he had initiated *Dissent*. At first he was a cautious supporter of the New Left, but by the late 1960s his bitter denunciations clearly outweighed his commendations. To some extent his line of attack against the New Left was anticipated in an earlier essay, much reprinted, called "Authoritarians of the Left." Howe came to use this term in a way that had a disturbing resemblance to the manner in which the Communists had once used the opprobrium "social fascist," by which Howe meant that certain radicals may claim that they are for socialism but objectively they are authoritarians. Howe focused his attack on Marxist intellectuals such as Paul Sweezy and Paul Baran, but he reserved most of his vitriol for Isaac Deutscher, whom he disliked particularly.[52]

Howe claimed that, because they supported the Soviet Union's nationalization of its economy, Deutscher and the others were driven to apologize for Stalinist totalitarianism. Such an interpretation was obviously an outgrowth of the debates of the late 1930s and it suffered from the same inadequate method. It was indeed true that all three had, in varying degrees, made apologetic statements about the Soviet Union, but that was because of their erroneous political orientation, not merely because they discriminated between the nature of the social system and the political character of the Soviet regime. On the contrary, to reductively equate social structure and political regime led Howe to even more errors in his posture toward bureaucratized postcapitalist societies and left-wing political movements around the world. Specifically it led to the equally erroneous identification of a legitimate national liberation movement with its Communist or pro-Communist leadership. The end result led Howe to dismiss entirely the achievements of all anticapitalist revolutions because a certain normative stage of democracy had not been reached and to refuse to give his support to many struggles because of Communist participation or the acceptance of aid from the Soviet Union. Thus, when the New Left began to hold that the Cuban Revolution had brought significant social gains for the majority of its poor and that the Vietnamese people had the right to determine their own future, even if under National Liberation Front leadership, Howe lost all objectivity; for him, the New Left itself had become "authoritarian."

Since Howe dismissed both the Cuban Revolution and the National Liberation Front of Vietnam because of certain undemocratic features of the former and what he held to be the Stalinist features of the latter, he left no room for dialogue between him and the New Left. He ended up projecting the positions of a part of the New Left, which did in fact uncritically admire Castro and Ho Chi Minh, onto the movement as a whole. The anger Howe had once directed against imperialism and its social democratic and Stalinist apologists now became directed at those who had revived the revolutionary dreams of his own youth.

In especially poor taste were two articles by Howe in the *New York Times Magazine*, "The New 'Confrontation Politics' Is a Dangerous Game" (1968) and "Political Terrorism: Hysteria on the Left" (1970), luridly illustrated with photographs of bloody students (allegedly the victims of the New Left's own strategy) and of leaders of the terrorist fringe group "Weatherman."[53] The site of publication and the imbalance of the contents were guaranteed to make the articles seem nothing less than part of the general assault on the left rather than the fatherly guidance Howe may have intended. Although he had long ago abandoned revolutionary Marxism, Howe donned a proletarian mantle to criticize the young radicals for their middle-class backgrounds, and then a Bolshevik mantle to rebuke them for failing to follow Lenin's advice about retreat and compromise in *Leftwing Communism: An Infantile Disorder* (1920).

But the disoriented Howe surpassed even the misrepresentations of these essays in a 1971 article on the Op-Ed page of the *New York Times* called "The Campus Left and Israel." There he argued that, while Israel may be vulnerable to some criticism, the particular ones expressed by New Left academics stemmed from anti-Semitism and a favoring of dictatorial over democratic societies.[54]

Howe brought the same unfortunate perspective to bear on the women's liberation movement following the publication of Kate

Millett's *Sexual Politics* (1970), a pathbreaking indictment of patriarchal culture. Joining for his own reasons the general campaign to discredit the new feminism, Howe fired both barrels of his polemical guns in a piece called "The Middle-Class Mind of Kate Millett." It first appeared in *Harper's*, at that time under the executive editorship of Midge Decter, herself the author of an unrestrained blast against Millett's book in *Commentary*. Howe called Millett "a figment of the *Zeitgeist*, bearing the rough and careless marks of what is called higher education and exhibiting a talent for the delivery of gross simplicities in tones of leaden complexity." He then spoke on behalf of his working-class mother who, he insisted, was no more oppressed than his proletarian father. He concluded that "there are times when one feels the book was written by a female impersonator."[55]

On some issues, various New York intellectuals, including Macdonald and Mary McCarthy, who had long been on Howe's right were now on his left. Indeed, one can appreciate Howe's astonishment when in the 12 October 1967 issue of the *New York Review of Books*, Philip Rahv denounced him and Michael Harrington for excessive anti-Communism and reformism. In a letter of protest to the editor, Howe wrote, "And now, after nearly twenty years of painful circumspection, appears Philip Rahv, offering Michael Harrington and myself Little Lessons in Leninism. . . . Rip Van Winkle wakes up and fancies himself at the Smolny Institute." No stranger to the art of polemics, Rahv answered, "Irving Howe seems to be very angry. Too bad. Can it be that he is infuriated with them [the young people of the New Left], because they refuse to accept him as the *éminence grise* of American radicalism?" In a subsequent issue of the *New York Review of Books*, Dwight Macdonald denounced Howe's associate Michael Harrington for having deceived him into supporting a racist position on the Ocean Hill–Brownsville dispute between teachers and the black community.[56]

Although his motives may have been constructive, Howe seemed driven to repeat his basic error in considering every sector of the radical movement. By blowing out of proportion the excesses of the black movement, the women's movement, and the student movement, he created a fantasy world populated by middle-class, hedonistic political crazies. At the same time Howe seemed to be minimizing the corruption of the puppet regimes of the United States in Vietnam, and denying the oppressive policies of the Israeli government. He also fostered the same illusions about the extent to which leftists could shape the policies of the Democratic Party that he had previously refuted when they had been proposed by Daniel Bell two decades earlier.[57]

Was there any sense in which Howe was "standing fast," or had he undergone the same *embourgeoisement* for which he had so sharply rebuked his elders? Howe had initiated *Dissent* in 1954 on an ambiguous premise. He held that no viable socialist movement existed in the United States, but his objective was nevertheless to keep socialist ideas alive. In 1955 Howe had reaffirmed that "there are differences of a fundamental kind between liberals and socialists, differences which cannot be skimmed over and which are likely to become more, rather than less, significant with the passage of time." One difference cited was that socialists must describe U.S. foreign policy unambiguously as a function of the capitalist economic system. "*The ADA,*" he complained, "*was ready to challenge a good many manifestations of U.S. foreign policy, but never so much as to question its underlying assumptions*" (emphasis in original). Another was the liberals' erroneous identification with Roosevelt's New Deal, which had in fact been the incubator of many policies they now abhorred. A third was the liberals' desire to be "respectable," a form of compromise which they masked under the euphemism "responsible."[58]

Without ever theorizing or explaining the change, Howe spent the 1960s drifting across the boundary line he had carefully drawn. In his *New York Times Magazine* essay on "Confrontation Politics," he concluded by describing the Vietnam War simply as "a scandal and a disaster." In his subsequent writings about the 1930s, he retracted his onetime opposition to the New Deal. As early as 1964, *Dissent* was running an advertisement that proudly quoted *Time* magazine's description of Howe as "a responsible intellectual."[59] True, Howe remained a socialist, but in certain respects he had in fact redefined the meaning of socialism itself.

In the early 1950s Howe and his close collaborator Lewis Coser coauthored an essay called "Images of Socialism" in which they rejected the scientific arguments for the logical development of socialism as the stage of social organization that would replace advanced capitalism, positing instead an ethical vision. Socialists, of course, are for ethics, and a socialism without moral consciousness would be a horror; yet the divestment of a scientific approach from socialism, and the valorization of an autonomous discourse of ethics and morality, undermines the historico-causal basis of the argument for radical social change. Moral judgments are a poor substitute, for they tend to be subjective and relativistic, obscuring the objective reasons for the critique of capitalism and the necessity of its transformation. Over the years the call for this ethical socialism was replaced by the demand "to extend the welfare state," and eventually Howe, like Hook in the 1950s, came to identify true socialism as being essentially a militant wing of liberalism.[60] This shift was facilitated by the vagueness of the term "democratic socialism," to which Howe was able to attribute a different political content at each phase of his development.

From a far left viewpoint, it is tempting to argue that Howe's main contribution has been to provide socialist arguments for supporting capitalism, although that would be an unfair caricature. He has never been explicitly antiradical as was Sidney Hook, and he continues to make important contributions to socialist culture. In his worst moments he served as a kind of legitimator of deradicalization as did Lionel Trilling some decades earlier, meeting with some success. For example, neoconservatives of the 1980s such as Norman Podhoretz and right-wing "socialists" such as Tom Kahn and Carl Gershman were once at least somewhat under his influence, as was Michael Harrington, a veteran of the Shachtman organization during the 1950s, whose political course has paralleled Howe's while always remaining a few steps to the left. As once was the case with the *New Leader*, few of those integrated into the *Dissent* circle ever move toward or return to the left; their movement is almost invariably and steadily to the right, although sometimes much faster and further than Howe would prefer. In the 1980s *Dissent* no longer calls itself "socialist" or "radical"—it merely represents the views of the "democratic left." Neoconservatives Nathan Glazer and Hilton Kramer insist that Howe's differences with them are more rhetorical than real, and in areas such as affirmative action there may be some justice to this claim.[61] Howe has been partly captured by the very forces he himself set out to influence.

Still, during the late 1970s and early 1980s, the very time that Howe became a nationally known figure for *World of Our Fathers* (1976), he distinguished himself by offering strong resistance within the liberal community to the burgeoning neoconservative movement. His antifeminism all but disappeared, his attitude toward younger radicals (who were by now less numerous and less threatening) became more tolerant, and after 1982 he even spoke more critically of Israel. It should also be remembered that many of Howe's criticisms of the New Left—its failure to study history and theory, its insensitivity to the need to build a working-class base, its tendency to idealize individualistic rebellion rather than collec tive action, its cavalier attitude toward bourgeois democracy, its romanticization of Third World leaderships, its overestimation of the conjunctural prospects for revolutionary change in the United States—were largely accurate. It was Howe's lack of balance between negative and positive, his failure to consistently direct his main focus and anger at the real sources of oppression and violence, and his unwillingness to acknowledge the impotence of social democratic alternatives that justifiably deserved criticism.

The case of Irving Howe is quite different from that of Sidney Hook or, to point to an exact contemporary, Irving Kristol. He is far from a "renegade" in the classic sense. To the contrary, despite the lacunae in his memoirs, he has written of the past with a greater accuracy, fairness, and sensitivity than many others among the New York intellectuals. If he has exhibited moments of self-righteousness, he has also been frank about the psychological pain involved in his political journey, and his view of his own literary achievements is unnecessarily modest—especially in comparison with the braggadocio of Norman Podhoretz, whose achievements are incomparably inferior.

Despite the fact that Howe has progressively diluted the content of his socialism, no one has worked harder to keep the socialist idea alive in the liberal academic community. He has also kept open the discourse on such unfashionable topics as Leninism and the role of the working class. His personal failings seem to be those of his variant of socialism as well as quite human ones; the case against Howe is not at all ad hominem but centers on the limitations of an anti-Stalinist socialism that operates within instead of against the capitalist social order.

Howe's inveterate reformism—his insistence on proposing political solutions that only reinforce the systemic origins of the problems—has probably assisted the decline if not the demise of the anti-Stalinist left. His major theme for some years has been to define socialism "as an extension of democratic processes"; the formulation is ambiguous and not entirely erroneous, but in practice it has translated for Howe into a focus on building a left current within the Democratic Party.[62] Unfortunately, there is no evidence that such a strategy "extends" democracy; it more likely builds up and gives credibility to the ideology and institutions that undermine democracy by channeling the struggles of working people into efforts to elect millionaires to the House and Senate.

Howe's problem is that in basing his political strategy from within rather than without the institutions of the capitalist social order, he invariably ends up making that social order appear more tolerable and open to change than it actually is. Of course, Howe has no difficulty finding foils among radicals who exaggerate the domestic oppression in the United States or who oversimplify the road to social transformation. But a better antidote to those infantile leftists who lightly dismiss "bourgeois civil liberties" is not to exaggerate the significance of such hard-earned democratic rights; rather, socialists should defend socialism as a higher form of democracy than that which exists in the liberal-democratic bourgeois states. A higher form of democracy, however, is obtainable only through a democratically organized structural transformation. Unfortunately, such arguments fall beyond the pale of the social democratic vision.

PORTRAIT: HARVEY SWADOS

The problematical nature of the social democratic vision can also be seen in the political evolution of another committed and unusually talented veteran of Shachtman's party, the radical novelist and critic Harvey Swados. Swados was born in Buffalo, New York, in 1920 of a Russian-Jewish family.[63] He was tall, sturdy, and handsome, with wavy light-brown hair, regular features, and a ruddy complexion. His father, Aaron, was a physician, and his mother, Rebecca Bluestone, was a singer, pianist, and painter. Under the influence of his older sister, Felice, Swados joined the Young Communist League in high school and remained a member after he enrolled at the University of Michigan in 1936 at the age of sixteen. There, in his senior year, he met two graduate students from New York, Donald Slaiman and Melvin J. Lasky, who won Swados to Trotskyism. In letters to Felice's husband, Richard Hofstadter, with whom she had eloped to New York, Swados defended his new political views, just as Hofstadter was joining the Communist Party.[64]

Swados distinguished himself in literary affairs as well as in political activism at Michigan, winning the Hopwood Award for creative writing and publishing a story, "The Amateurs," in *The Best Short Stories of 1938*. Felice, too, had literary aspirations, and in 1941 she published *House of Fury*, a novel about women in a penal institution. After graduation, Swados returned to Buffalo to work with the Workers Party, using the party name "Dancers." There he got a job in an aircraft plant as a riveter and passed through a brief marriage. A year later, he moved to New York and worked in another aircraft plant in Long Island City. Drifting away from the Workers Party in about 1942, his organizational connection was far less than Irving Howe's, and in a certain sense Swados might be said to have been "with" but not truly "of" the Shachtman political tendency. He simultaneously began a lifelong friendship with C. Wright Mills, to whom he had been introduced by Hofstadter, and, in the following year, enlisted in the Merchant Marine where he was trained first as a seaman and then as a radio operator.

Between 1943 and 1945 Swados served as a radio operator on a number of ships which took him to the North Atlantic, the South Pacific, the Mediterranean, and the Carribean. In 1945 he was stunned by Felice's death of cancer at the age of twenty-nine. Returning to New York in 1946 he lived on his savings, married Bette Beller, and completed his first, unpublished novel. Between 1947 and 1955 Swados wrote furiously while supporting himself with a variety of part-time jobs augmented by unemployment compensation. Finally, in 1955 his first published novel appeared. *Out Went the Candle*, a story of his own generation during the 1940s, focused on the family of a Jewish businessman who becomes a war profiteer. Two years later Swados published *On the Line* (1957), a classic of radical fiction. Through eight detachable episodes, which stand as short stories, *On the Line* describes the lives of nine assembly-line workers in an automobile factory and the work process in capitalist America.

When it first appeared, only a small number of mostly forgotten books had been written on the work experience. But during the subsequent decades many social scientists corroborated Swados's literary theme that the rise of the American standard of living during the 1950s had failed to bring contentment to the American working class. Thus the novel's position, once considered "eccentric"—that a worker is oppressed because of his or her relationship to the means of production, regardless of wages or accessibility to commodities—became the concern of an increasing number of influential books, including Richard Sennet and Jonathan Cobb's *The Hidden Injuries of Class* (1973), Barbara Garson's *All the Livelong Day: The Meaning and Demeaning of Routine Work* (1975), Robert Pfeffer's *Working for Capitalism* (1979), and *Working* (1979), the popular collection of interviews by Studs Terkel. The subtitle of the best of these studies, Harry Braverman's *Labor and Monopoly Capital: The Degradation of Work in the 20th Century* (1974), clearly states the theme Swados sought to fictionalize in his novel.

At the time of its publication the few reviewers of *On the Line* who accorded it serious attention tended to celebrate the "authenticity" of Swados's depictions of assembly-line workers. Ironically, Swados's character portraits are partial and somewhat contrived, as if he sought to offset certain negative images of workers by going too far in the direction of "prettifying" them. Thus he fails to show the true range of responses to capitalist oppression. For example, none of the workers speaks the language one hears in factories and working-class bars, and there is no hint of wife-beating, very little racism, and no instances of escaping the pressures of the work routine through alcohol and drugs. The one heavy-drinking character, Harold, *controls* his alcoholism through submission to the work routine. Although Swados had other work experiences, the precise background for the book was a few months that he had spent as a finisher in an auto plant in New Jersey in 1956.

Rather than trying to validate the novel's worth through its "authenticity," the strengths and weaknesses of *On the Line* are more aptly disclosed through an examination of the way in which Swados used literary craft to express his political vision. For example, a remarkable feature of the book is that, probably more by intuition than conscious intent, Swados's vignettes of factory life dramatize the four characteristics of alienated labor elaborated by Marx's *Economic and Philosophic Manuscripts of 1844*. Marx's notion of the means by which workers are both alienated from and dominated by the products that they produce is depicted by Swados in two ways. Many of the workers show hostility and disrespect toward the cars they produce; yet, as is revealed in Swados's stories about Kevin and Pops, they also worship cars, with destructive consequences.

Concerning the second form of alienated labor, Marx wrote, "Alienation appears not only in the result, but also in the process of production and productive activity itself. The worker is not at home in his work which he views only as a means of satisfying other needs. It is an activity directed against himself, that is independent of him and does not belong to him."[65] Swados writes, "What troubled [Kevin] and nearly shook his faith was that his fellow workers were not merely indifferent, they were actively hostile to their surroundings and to what they did with their own hands: Their talk was continuously seasoned with contemptuous references to the factory, to their work, and to the lives they led. Almost everybody who discussed it with him hated the work and admitted frankly that the only incentive to return from one day to the next was the pay check."[66]

Swados suggests Marx's view of the alienation of workers from each other by not giving last names to his characters and by the awkwardness of their personal associations outside of the workplace: "Instead of learning names, we refer to the fellow with the bad teeth, or the guy with the blue coveralls. When I work next to a man for months and learn that his wife is being operated on for cancer of the breast and still don't know his name, it tells me something, not just about him and me, but about the half-connections that are all the factory allows you in the way of friendships."[67]

Finally, the fourth facet of alienated labor—alienation from society—is dramatized by a character disorder that appears in a number of workers: they begin to prefer the prisonlike factory to the external world. Pops, for example, is homeless outside the factory; Harold needs the total control of the rhythm of factory life to stop his drinking; and Orrin, the central character in the title story, derives his only sense of self-worth from the illusion that he is somehow indispensable to the factory operation.

On the Line incorporates a successful adaptation of traditional literary modes to a radical and working-class subject. The detachable episodes of psychological portraiture invoke, first of all, Sherwood Anderson's *Winesburg, Ohio* (1919), although echoes of Theodore Dreiser, John Dos Passos, and Upton Sinclair may also be detected. Swados's book, like Anderson's, falls somewhat short of the formal definition of the novel in its lack of a central character who undergoes a significant development. Still, *On the Line* is something more than a collection of stories because one can only grasp the basis for Swados's eight detachable episodes by stepping back and looking at the book as a whole. One can then see that the episodes are unified by the fact that workers must sell their labor power for wages in order to survive. Although workers develop an independent justification for being on the line, it is the money, certainly not pride in work or interest in fellow workers, that drew them there.

It is tempting to argue that the auto plant itself is the main character. Yet the factory, unlike the beastlike coal mine in Émile Zola's *Germinal* (1885), is insufficiently animated to serve such a central function; it is merely a steady, functioning machine that dominates, controls, and intrudes in the lives of the workers. What we have instead are dispersed *moments* of character development that aim toward changing the empathetic reader's political consciousness. One such moment is when the young Walter learns from the experienced Joe, a free-floating leftist, to respect the lives of his fellow workers and understand their entrapment. Another and more important moment is when the fifty-six-year-old Frank, returning to the line after decades in a small business that has just failed, overcomes his hostility to the United Auto Workers. He realizes that, in spite of the rough stuff the union pulled on him back in the 1930s and 1940s, its struggle was just and it represents the only hope for dignity at the present.

Of course, Frank does not appear until the end of the book, but the character change he undergoes is meant to be derivative of all the experiences that precede his entrance. For example, the novel begins with the stories of the most defeated characters—Leroy, whose goal of becoming an opera singer is destroyed by a plant accident; and Kevin, who flees the United States to return to a small town in Ireland when he discovers that the "American Dream" is only a sham. These stories might be seen as necessary prerequisites for understanding why Frank's reconciliation with the union in the end is so significant. The political concern of *On the Line* is survival *with* dignity, not fundamental change in one's life circumstances.

THE AMBIGUOUS LEGACY

In *On the Line* the politics of the artist's vision are sometimes a source of strength, but they are also responsible for certain weaknesses. Although he had remained adamantly "Third Camp" throughout the 1940s, by the 1950s Swados's early Marxist training was being overlayed with aspects of the social democratic perspective of limited reform. The extent of his deradicalization is revealed explicitly in *On the Line* in an exchange between the Communist leader of the union's opposition caucus and Joe, who evokes the class-conscious spirit of the 1930s. To the Communist's pro-Soviet propaganda, however, Joe can only counterpose a vague mix of anarchist-individualist radicalism. It is clear that neither character is intended to provide an alternative. Joe is even compared to the Native American Indians (he is called "the vanishing American"); that is, he represents the best of labor radicalism's past, but it is a past that one can only look to with nostalgia.

The real alternative is depicted at the end through the characters of Lou and the other "union boys" who save Frank's job and treat him with unexpected kindness and respect at the picnic of the United Auto Workers. Unless there is irony intended in this ending on the "little victory" of UAW fraternity, it would appear that Swados, pragmatist-fashion, is presenting us with the "experience" with which to counter the impotent ideology of the Communists and Joe. If so, it may well represent Swados's own "reconciliation with reality," but it is a view that is ideology-laden nonetheless.[68]

To revolutionary socialists still inspired by the heights of class consciousness once achieved by the American working class, Lou will seem somewhat of a Boy Scout, and the UAW's picnics and bingo games will seem very remote from the kind of political leadership necessary to solve the problems of capitalism.

Swados would move further to the left during the 1960s and sharply criticize the *Dissent* editors for being liberals masquerading as socialists. Yet the perspective of *On the Line* appears to be classic social democracy fostering an essentially uncritical endorsement of liberal labor leadership such as that of the Reuther brothers in the UAW, who at that time offered auto workers only piecemeal ameliorations and temporary job security.[69] Ironically, the result of such politics when transformed into literary characterization is perversely reminiscent of Soviet "socialist realism"; Lou is a cardboard figure, a two-dimensional "goody-goody," what the Stalinist cultural theoreticians once called a "positive hero."

This weakness, however, in no way negates the overriding power of the novel and its effective portrayal through the writer's craft of the nature of the industrial work process and of its human costs. Raymond Williams concludes *Marxism and Literature* (1976) with a provocative chapter called "Creative Practice" in which he attempts to offer categories for evaluating and classifying work by class-conscious artists. *On the Line* contrasts unfavorably with Nadine Gordimer's *Burger's Daughter* (1979), for example, in the sense that it fails to meet Williams's third and highest category, exhibiting "a struggle at the roots of the mind . . . confronting hegemony in the fibres of the self and in the hard practical substance of effective and continuing relations." But Williams's second category seems very well met: Swados's unique novel of the labor process deserves a special place in American literary history because it achieves the "embodiment and performance of known but excluded and subordinated experiences and relationships" in capitalist society.[70]

In the late 1950s Swados began a new career as a teacher of writing which took him to Sarah Lawrence, Iowa, San Francisco State, Columbia, and several other colleges before he accepted a professorship at the University of Massachusetts at Amherst in 1962. He published two novels, *False Coin* (1959) and *The Will* (1963), and two collections of stories, *Nights in the Gardens of Brooklyn* (1962) and *A Story for Teddy and Others* (1965), together with several anthologies, a biography of Estes Kefauver, and numerous journalistic articles and reviews, some of which were collected in *A Radical's America* (1962). Swados's work was admired, but his audience was small; in a certain sense he had yet to find his true subject, or to even come to grips with the complexities of his own psychology and family history. He also resented greatly the recommendation of some of his friends that he focus on journalism, although "The Myth of the Happy Worker" (1957) had achieved national attention, and "Why Resign from the Human Race?" (1959) was credited with inspiring the Peace Corps.[71]

In 1971 Swados published his most ambitious work, *Standing Fast*, which he intended to be the story of the radicalization and deradicalization of his generation. At first he had intended to call the book *Children of Our Time* and to focus on the most significant movement, the Communist movement, but soon he realized that he would have to draw primarily on his more intimate knowledge of the Workers Party. Thus the central characters in *Standing Fast* are a group of workers and intellectuals struggling to sustain and build a branch in Buffalo of an organization much like the Workers Party, starting in the early 1940s. Swados then pursues the political and private lives of these socialists and their recruits and sympathizers throughout World War II, the Bring the Troops Home Movement that came in its aftermath, the postwar labor upsurge, the McCarthyite reaction, the Hungarian revolt, the inception and development of the civil rights movement, the Cuban Revolution, and the assassination of John F. Kennedy.

The novel attempts to probe the meaning of the socialist movement of the 1930s and 1940s to the aging radicals as their convictions evanesce and they become increasingly integrated into the capitalist society that they once set out to overthrow. Swados's conclusion is pessimistic: the only purpose in life is to hold out or stand fast against inevitable despair and corruption as long as one possibly can. The narrative begins in 1940 at a street meeting just prior to the impending split in the Trotskyist movement and in broad outlines traces the history of the Workers Party with fidelity. The "New Party" is formed with its own paper, *New Labor*, and it survives for several years until it transforms itself into the New Socialist League and finally merges with the Socialist Party. Marty Dworkin, the New Party's dynamic leader, is a literary portrait of Max Shachtman, and other characters resemble figures from Shachtman's group. Many, of course, are composites. For example, in his journals Swados indicated that at one point he intended to create the character Norm by drawing upon aspects of himself, Irving Howe, and the liberal Richard Goodwin, a man for whom Swados had great contempt; and some of Norm's activities in the Philippines are based on the experiences of Swados's friend, Irving Sanes.[72]

The core cluster of radicals whose lives provide the thread for this lengthy novel spanning twenty-three years encompasses fourteen men and six women, although only eight of the men and none of the women are most prominently characterized. They include Fred, a radical English teacher who ends up involved in the rigged quiz show scandals of the Eisenhower era; Bill Zivic (in name and background suggestive of B. J. Widick), a militant auto worker from Akron who becomes a vote hustler for the Democratic Party; Big Boy Hull, a black steelworker who had broken with the Communist Party in the South because of its wartime policy of opposing the struggle for civil rights; and Norm, a soldier of fortune who leaves the movement early to become an independent radical journalist and then an international news correspondent. Besides Dworkin, the New Party leaders include Lewis Lorch, the organizational and financial expert who drifts away from politics to become a cultural entrepreneur; and Harry Sturm, the Buffalo branch's first organizer who becomes possessed by the idea that socialism can only be achieved by infiltrating and capturing the mass media.

The final sections of the novel largely focus on the children of the New Party group in whom many have invested the hopes once attached to their political commitments. One of these children is Paul, a moral idealist who is killed by a street gang in Harlem where he has gone to live and engage in social work. At Paul's funeral a single red rose arrives from Comrade Hoover, the retired Afro-American leader of the party who bears a strong resemblance to Ernest Rice McKinny, a leader of the Workers Party. The rose functions as a symbol of the concatenation between the generations of radicals. Meanwhile, Joe Link, a lifelong trade-union militant who seems a literary portrait of Workers Party activist Stan Weir, travels about the West Coast gathering material for a book that will explain the meaning of American labor radicalism to the youth of the 1960s, while Vito Brigante, a left-wing artist dying of stomach cancer, reaches for his sketchpad in an attempt to maintain the only activity that ultimately has given any meaning to his lonely existence. Another child of hope is Norm's son, Marlen, named for Marx and Lenin. After killing a female companion in a car accident, Marlen's nonchalant behavior confirms that he suffers from a mental illness that prevents him from feeling any guilt or responsibility. The final pages present a philosophy of simple stoicism. Paul's father, Irwin, is comforted by his cousin, Sy, with the advice that "the trick is to go on living even when you've found out what kind of world it really is." When Irwin bitterly protests that they wasted most of their lives in pursuit of unrealizable ideals, Sy shoots back, "I have nothing fancy to say. One way or another, we tried to keep an idea alive. There weren't enough of us, there never are. We were ridiculously wrong about a lot of things but who wasn't? And what idea did they keep alive, the others?"[73]

This pessimism about fidelity to youthful ideals and the possibility of fundamental social change, or even about the possibility of fulfillment through progeny, becomes a peculiar kind of optimism about the endurance of the human spirit in Swados's posthumously published *Celebration* (1974). The novel evolved from notebooks that conceived a central character who was an accomplished musician, then became an old man preparing a deathbed repudiation of the life of reason he had led. The end result was Swados's depiction of ninety-year-old Samuel Lumen as an embodiment of the tradition of American radicalism in the same sense that the life and character of Artemio Cruz embodies the historic experience of the Mexican middle class in Carlos Fuentes's *The Death of Artemio Cruz* (1962).[74] Features of Lumen's life are drawn from a variety of radical intellectuals who championed the cause of youthful rebellion and lived to an old age. In particular, Swados seems to have based the manipulative relationship between Lumen and Rog, his young radical secretary, on the gossip in liberal circles that Bertrand Russell in the 1960s was manipulated by his young leftist aide, Ralph Schoenman.[75]

The shocking central act in Lumen's sexually promiscuous life that torments him is the assault he made on his son's wife, Louise, who came to visit him while her husband was serving in World War II; the young Lumen is killed shortly afterward, and Louise gives birth to a child, Seth, most certainly the offspring of Sam Lumen and herself, just before she commits suicide. All reviewers of the novel evaded discussion of this pivotal event, either by neglecting it entirely or referring to it as a "seduction." What is misleading is that, although Lumen forces himself on the woman and she fights him vigorously, he only decides to go through with intercourse after determining that she is "wet between the thighs," indicating that she was aroused sexually. But this in no way mitigates the rape; Lumen is a highly attractive man, but it is not uncommon for a woman or a man to feel sexual stimulation without the intention of intercourse, which was clearly the case with Louise. Perhaps reviewers were reticent on this matter because they felt that Swados was vicariously confessing some dark secret about himself, too explosive to warrant discussion in reviews that usually amounted to obituaries for the recently deceased Swados. Although it is true that Swados's feelings toward his own father were psychologically complex, it is more likely that the episode was based on a story Swados may have heard about the violent manner in which a famous radical intellectual allegedly tried to force himself on his son's girlfriend.[76]

Lumen is celebrated as a hero of American culture and honored by the president of the United States despite his posture as part-rebel, part-hedonist. As a vision of the condition of the American intellectual left, *Celebration* has a ring of authenticity, but it offers little comfort. Swados, who was considerably more sympathetic to the New Left than was Irving Howe, surprisingly depicts the young radicals in the novel as devoid of serious ideas. At the time of the book's conception, he was in fact in a period of political confusion, exemplified by his activities in 1968. On the one hand, he criticized Irving Howe for having a point of view on the French student-worker uprising that was identical with the conservative one of the French Communist Party; on the other hand, he suddenly broke his longtime policy of refusing to support the Democrats.[77] This was followed by a brief period of collaboration with the McGovern-Shriver election campaign, and he even went to Sargent Shriver's home to work as a speech writer. Yet he walked out in bitter disillusionment after only a few weeks.[78] Like Samuel Lumen, he seems to have felt a deep alienation from the establishment as well as the left, Old and New. This was coupled with considerable frustration over the lack of success of *Standing Fast*, to which he had devoted enormous effort.

Swados died prematurely at the age of fifty in 1972 of an aneurism. He was, and most certainly would have remained, a committed socialist; he was to the end an intransigent, independent radical, immune to complacency and downright angry about social inequality. In his stance on the Vietnam War and in his friendship with C. Wright Mills, he placed himself considerably to the left of most of his former comrades, some of whom thought he was insufficiently critical of Communism. Still, if not a firm social democrat in the sense of Irving Howe, he had lost the revolutionary socialist vision that had guided him in the 1930s and 1940s, substituting the ambiguous *desideratum* of a welfare state based on a strong working-class movement. Thus his final political and cultural legacy, like Orwell's, remains suffused with ambiguity.

CHAPTER 11

The Bitter Fruits of Anticommunism

To bury Stalinism really means to revive the idea of socialism and to begin its construction all over again, a prospect as deadly for the aged leaders of "really existing socialism" as it is for the old capitalist masters.

—Daniel Singer, *The Road to Gdansk*, 1982[1]

. . . .

COLD WAR II

On 6 February 1982 the cultural critic, novelist, and filmmaker Susan Sontag addressed a mass meeting in New York City's Town Hall, which had been organized in support of the Polish *Solidarnosc* [Solidarity] movement. The distinctive feature of the meeting, according to its sponsors, was that a group of artists, intellectuals, and trade unionists would present statements in support of the Polish workers from a pro-working class, left perspective, which would distinguish their support of Polish *Solidarnosc* from that of President Ronald Reagan and other conservatives. Thus many of the speakers spent part of their time denouncing U.S. intervention in El Salvador and Nicaragua, the union-busting campaign of the Reagan administration against the air traffic controllers, and even Israeli policy toward Palestinians on the West Bank. It was in this anticapitalist context that most of the speakers proceeded to endorse Polish *Solidarnosc* as a more authentic expression of the socialist movement in Poland and the ideals promulgated by Marx and Engels than was the "communist" regime of Jaruzelski and his Soviet backers.

Sontag began by declaring her opposition to the U.S. government's war against the people of Central America, decrying Reagan as the "puppet master of the butchers in El Salvador." This was expected, for she had been known since the early 1960s as a sympathizer of the Cuban Revolution and had published in 1969 in *Ramparts* a laudatory article about Cuba's people and culture. Moreover, in the midst of the U.S. war against Vietnam she had traveled in protest to Hanoi; and in 1969 she had published a much-discussed book about her experiences called *Visit to Hanoi*, which caused some to label her a fellow traveler of the North Vietnamese. During the 1960s Sontag had supported the election campaigns of the Socialist Workers Party and had even met with party representatives to discuss the possibility of joining the party.[2]

However, she completely stunned most of those present with the balance of her speech:

> ... the principal lesson to be learned [in Poland] is the lesson of the failure of Communism, the utter villainy of the Communist system. ... We tried to distinguish *among* Communisms—for example, treating "Stalinism," which we disavowed, as if it were an aberration, and praising other regimes, outside of Europe, which had and have essentially the same character. ... Imagine, if you will, someone who read only *Reader's Digest* between 1950 and 1970, and someone in the same period who read only the *Nation* or the *New Statesman*. Which reader would have been better informed about the realities of Communism? The answer, I think, should give us pause. Can it be that our enemies were right? ... The similarities between the Polish military junta and right-wing dictatorships in Chile, Argentina and other South American countries are obvious. ... Communism is fascism—successful fascism, if you will. ... Communism is in itself a variant, the most successful variant, of fascism. Fascism with a human face.[3]

These remarks were not merely poor formulations of a more complex point of view but an apparently purposeful posture. In an interview with the *New York Times Book Review*, Sontag acknowledged that in preparing her remarks she "knew I would be booed and I would make some enemies there."[4] After offering her statement, she simply walked out of the meeting without waiting to hear the responses and, of course, without participating in the other manifestations of support for the Polish workers.

Sontag's remarks provided a field day for the press. They were reported in *Time*, the *New York Times*, the *Washington Post*, the

New York Post, the *Los Angeles Times*, the *San Francisco Chronicle*, the *Soho News*, the *Village Voice*, the *Nation*, and the *New Republic*, among other newspapers and journals, often accompanied by editorials in support of her words of wisdom. Her "defection" was especially welcomed by right-wing Cuban commentators on the radio stations in the "Little Havana" section of Miami.[5] No doubt such publicity, which made her more known among a broader public than ever before, accelerated the sales of her books in the conservative climate of the 1980s. A few months later she published a self-edited retrospective selection of her writings called *The Susan Sontag Reader*; *Visit to Hanoi* was not included in it.

What was notable about the response, however, was Sontag's failure to rally a substantial section of the left to her views. To the contrary, she received a wide range of rebuttals from other intellectuals who were not ready for a repeat of the early 1950s. For example, Garry Wills, a former conservative who had become radicalized in the 1960s, poked fun at her dramatic but obfuscating use of political terminology:

> Communism is fascism, according to Ms. Sontag. And, according to her, "the principal lesson to be learned from the Polish events is the lesson of the failure of communism." Then, since communism/fascism has failed, fascism is not successful in Poland, right? Wrong. Failed communism, it turns out, is really successful fascism: "Communism is in itself a variant, the most successful variant, of fascism." If both communism and fascism have succeeded, what has failed? Mainly Ms. Sontag's powers of analysis.[6]

An editorial in the *Nation* raised some questions about the quality of the information one might obtain by subscribing to *Reader's Digest*: "First, there is the helpful vocabulary. Communists, for example, are referred to as 'Red slave drivers and sadists,' and Soviet policy as 'the Kremlin's harvest of hate.' Second, there are bold forecasts, such as 'Why Red China Won't Break with Russia,' the title of a July 1957 article, and the repeated predictions of the imminent collapse of the Soviet empire."[7]

Also writing in the *Nation*, Philip Green was one of several who challenged Sontag's facile equation of Poland and other eastern European Stalinist regimes with Latin American dictatorships:

> These regimes (e.g., Chile's and Argentina's) are built around the violent suppression of organized labor. In Communist

Eastern Europe, on the other hand, the hypocritical Marxism of the ruling elite is an unremitting provocation, in constant danger of being taken seriously by the people. Thus, those regimes have generated three exhilaratingly promising revolts in twenty-five years, none of which was anti-socialist. . . . These revolts were also *successful* in their own (and our own) terms, in the sense that they could *only* be crushed by direct Soviet intervention or indirect Soviet threats—not by an allegedly "totalitarian" regime forever impervious to change.[8]

Philip Pochoda, a New York editor, commented on Sontag's equation of Communism with fascism: "Before succumbing to the Reaganite mentality of the *Reader's Digest* and Alexander Haig, we might at least consider that Auschwitz and Dachau were the triumph, the fulfillment, of *Mein Kampf*, whereas the Gulag and December 13 are the unspeakable, if all too common, travesties of the *Communist Manifesto*." In a closing reference to the editor of *Commentary*, Pochoda suggested that Sontag was in danger of becoming "Norman Podhoretz with a human face."[9] What also should have been added is that the partial truths contained in her talk were known to and publicized by the anti-Stalinist left fifty years earlier, which is why the content of her speech struck some observers as trivial, thoughtless, and pretentious.

Regardless of their other shortcomings, at least most of those who responded understood that one cannot effectively fight Stalinism by supporting capitalism and imperialism—any more than a trade unionist can struggle effectively against the bureaucratic or gangsterlike officials of his or her union by running to the bosses for help. This suggests that there are important differences between the Cold War atmosphere of the McCarthy period and the 1980s, which some radical critics are calling "Cold War II."[10] What the Sontag debate indicates is that, in the 1980s, the configuration of left and right forces among non-Communist intellectuals is considerably different from the early 1950s, when a rejection of Sontag's views by non-Communists would have been unthinkable. The present situation much more resembles the mid-1930s, a time marked by a considerable polarization between Marxist anti-Stalinists and reactionary anticommunists, when right-wing social democrats served as a bridge from the former to the latter. Although organizations and individuals involved use new political labels, the political perspectives are much the same.

In the 1950s the formerly radical New York intellectuals defended themselves against a conservative onslaught by attacking those further to their left, sometimes using the theory of "totalitarianism" to claim that the concepts "left" and "right" had lost their traditional meanings. Essentially they purged from the pale of respectability those adhering to ideas fundamentally at odds with Cold War liberal ideology, starting with all variants of Leninism. During the 1970s and 1980s, the dynamic of many leftists in transit toward social democracy is to criticize the left—which certainly needs criticism—not from a left position but from the right. This is true not only in the case of Sontag, even though she is still far removed from the neoconservatives, but also in the rightward migrations of two prominent historians: Allen Weinstein, author of *Perjury: The Hiss-Chambers Case* (1978), who regressed from liberalism to a position close to neoconservatism, and Ronald Radosh, coauthor of *The Rosenberg File* (1983), who abandoned first pro-Communism and then New Left radicalism for social democracy. In each instance, an investigation of the Hiss-Chambers and Rosenberg espionage cases, respectively, and the reexamination of the Cold War era undertaken in the political climate of the late 1970s, led to an encounter with dimensions of Stalinism (in particular, the underground apparatus) that the two scholars had neglected or minimized in their earlier studies of the cases. Both produced books reconvicting the accused and criticizing their left-wing supporters, largely on the basis of source material provided by the Federal Bureau of Investigation, of which they most likely would have been more skeptical a decade earlier.

The political transformation of David Horowitz is strongly reminiscent of the type of renegacy characteristic of the 1950s, in which an apostate misrepresents his or her past and fashions a new career out of denouncing his or her former comrades. In 1965 Horowitz published *The Free World Colossus*, a radical indictment of U.S. foreign policy that won high praise from longtime anti-Stalinist Dwight Macdonald.[11] In 1969 Horowitz published *Empire and Revolution*, which he dedicated to the former Trotskyist Isaac Deutscher, and two years later he edited a collection of essays in honor of Deutscher, *Isaac Deutscher: The Man and His Work* (1971). In 1973, in the preface to *The Fate of Midas*, a collection of his essays from *Ramparts* and other publications, Horowitz spoke of what a "lonely enterprise" it was to be a radical intellectual in the "present historical context."[12] The introduction that followed was primarily an intellectual memoir in which Horowitz recounted his break with the Old Left and his efforts to establish a radical foundation for a New Left. Having renounced Marxism in the wake of the Khrushchev revelations, he attempted in the early 1960s to work out a radical critique in his own terms. After a few years, he found himself returning to and reaffirming a critical Marxism with a fresh view and a more complex understanding that he wished to transmit to a New Left resistant to theory and thereby prone to repeat the mistakes of its predecessors.

Just six years after publishing this inspiring statement, Horowitz penned a revised autobiography that appeared in the *Nation* in which he described his radical career as a consistent whole. The strategy he used was the familiar one of omitting his radical anti-Stalinist phase. He referred to himself simply as having been "a soldier in an international class struggle" from his first May Day parade in 1949 until the mid-1970s, when he lapsed into inactivity.[13] He proceeded to indict the New Left for a "blind spot" in regard to the Soviet Union, even though he himself had been known among the New Left for his books and articles characterizing Stalinism as despotism, albeit from the Deutscherist view that the revolution had moved forward by barbarous means. In a letter responding to various criticisms, Horowitz insisted that he did "not repudiate nor regret thirty years in the radical movement," but only asked the left to exchange "its essentially religious longing for a socialist millennium for a more rational commitment to social change."[14]

Another six years went by and Horowitz, with his former *Ramparts* collaborator Peter Collier, published an essay in the *Washington Post* called "Goodbye to All That," in which he very explicitly sought to "repudiate" his left-wing past and in which he proclaimed himself a Reaganite. The essay attracted considerable attention and was reprinted by *Encounter*, by a neoconservative newsletter, and by newspapers around the world. This time, however, Horowitz "enhanced" his autobiography by including references to his onetime admiration for Kim Il Sung and the trashing of store windows, his fantasies of cop-killing, and his belief in imminent fascism—a record of ultraleftism which seems rather at odds with his political writings of the 1960s and early 1970s. In addition, this onetime defender of Deutscher's quasi-Trotskyist critique of the Soviet Union not only proclaimed agreement with Sontag's contention "that Communism is simply left-wing fascism" but even endorsed Reagan's religio-mystical characterization of the Soviet Union as the "evil empire."[15]

Horowitz, however, was joining, not initiating, a political current. The far-right terrain among intellectuals in the 1980s is already dominated by the "neoconservatives" (a term that essentially means recent converts from liberalism to conservatism). In contrast, closest to the anti-Stalinist left of the 1930s are those individuals and organizations vaguely grouped around a program of supporting *Solidarnosc*, exhibiting sympathy for the Nicaraguan revolution, and showing political independence from the Democratic and Republican parties. By and large the surviving members of the New York intellectuals have become the ideological leaders of the neoconservatives, a group that gained influence in the 1980s because of its ideological and material links to powerful trends in American business and government. Sidney Hook, who still calls himself a social democrat, remains the venerated founding father, and Irving Kristol and Norman Podhoretz are its central ideologists.

PORTRAIT: IRVING KRISTOL

Irving Kristol was born in 1920 in New York City, the son of a clothing subcontractor.[16] In 1936 he graduated from Boys High School in Brooklyn and entered the City College of New York. A Trotskyist sympathizer for some years, he deferred from joining the movement until the spring of 1940, when he graduated from college and the Workers Party was founded. He assumed the party name William Ferry (sometimes Irving Ferry), allegedly because during one of the debates between James P. Cannon and Max Shachtman, the former had referred to the City College Trotskyists such as Kristol and his friend Earl Raab as being "on the periphery [which he mispronounced 'perry-ferry'] of the movement." Raab, of course, became Perry.[17] A few months later, while working as a machinist's apprentice at the Brooklyn Navy Yard, Kristol joined the "Shermanites" in their departure from the Workers Party to enter the Socialist Party. The Shermanites made the change because they contended that Bolshevism was antirevolutionary, bureaucratic, totalitarian, and undemocratic. During his brief period in the Workers Party Kristol had developed a relationship with Dwight Macdonald and later wrote occasionally for *Politics*. In 1942 he accompanied his wife and comrade, Gertrude Himmelfarb, to Chicago where she began graduate study at the University of Chicago while he worked as a freight handler. He also served as an editor of *Enquiry*, the organ of the Shermanites, while he waited to be drafted.

Enquiry, published between 1942 and 1945, unambiguously called for a "social overturn" but insisted that its editors' "revolutionary outlook" was coupled with a thoroughgoing concern for the maintenance and extension of the practices and institutions of democracy. Denouncing "the bankruptcy of supporting the 'lesser evil' of compromise with the status quo," the editors added that "political support of the present war, organized by reactionary forces and deepening the totalitarian trend, will be found to be incompatible with a consistent fight for concrete democratic aims."[18] Among Kristol's most forceful essays was a critique of Sidney Hook's prowar position, which he attempted to discredit on the grounds that Hook had reduced all issues to the pragmatic goal of stopping Hitler immediately and by any means necessary: "In this near hysterical insistence upon the pressing military danger and in the complaint, 'mere theoretical carping,' we recognize not only a common academic reaction to events, but also an ominously familiar ideological weapon. It is the exact technique of the Communist-liberal coalition during the days of the Popular Front and collective security. One element is seized from its context as the receptacle of all political significance, and crucial political disagreements based on a broader perspective than 'licking the villain' are condemned as malicious and irresponsible criticism."[19] At the same time, Kristol was reading Reinhold Niebuhr and other neo-orthodox theologians of the period and was impressed by their critique of utopian doctrine.

Finally drafted in 1944, Kristol saw combat in France and Germany as an infantryman in the 12th Armored Division and was discharged in 1946 as a staff sargeant. While living in postwar England, where Himmelfarb was attending Cambridge University, Kristol, now substantially deradicalized, began contributing to *Commentary*. In 1947 he returned to New York to become the magazine's managing editor as it was becoming a major forum for anticommunist thought among intellectuals. This phase of Kristol's career began with a turn to religion and was climaxed with his famous statement in 1953 that "there is one thing the American people know about Senator McCarthy; he, like them, is unequivocally anti-Communist. About the spokesmen for American liberalism, they feel they know no such thing."[20]

He then returned to England to found and coedit the journal *Encounter*, sponsored by the Congress for Cultural Freedom, later revealed to have received funding from the Central Intelligence Agency. Kristol, together with associate Melvin Lasky, denied all knowledge of such funding, but his credibility among many liberals was permanently damaged.[21] After returning to the United States for a brief stint on the editorial staff of the *Reporter*, Kristol became the executive vice-president of Basic Books, a position he held for the next eight years. During this period, with Daniel Bell he founded the *Public Interest* and in 1969 became Henry R. Luce Professor of Urban Values at New York University.

Kristol would later claim that neoconservatism emerged in the late 1960s and early 1970s as the product of a new constellation of ideological forces, but his conservative politics in fact went back several decades and he personally embodied neoconservatism's continuity with Cold War liberalism. Thus the "consensus school" notion that Kristol and his associates are merely "inside-out Bolsheviks," behaving on the right as they once behaved on the left and always scornful of the middle road of liberalism, is an oversimplification. Personality traits may have remained the same, but there is simply no one style of "Bolshevik" behavior. Moreover, the neoconservatives who actually held membership in Leninist organizations were few and most did so briefly, either during or just after college. The American Committee for Cultural Freedom, of which Kristol became executive secretary and which was the first intellectual arena for the young Podhoretz, was a much more decisive determinant of the political values and organizing styles characteristic of the neoconservatives.

The leading neoconservative intellectuals had long sought ideological acceptance by the government. When this finally became possible through their links to the Nixon and then Reagan administrations, those leaders of the current who found this acceptable slightly modified their official political coloration to conform with the prevailing conservative sentiment, and their ranks soon followed suit. Thus there is a real continuity between Cold War liberalism and neoconservatism, both of which aspired to defend the same political system by different tactical means. The claim of a symmetry between their sojourns on the far left and the far right is not defensible, except insofar as Kristol and his colleagues aspired to be ideologues at all points in their evolution.

What had changed was the political climate of the middle and the late 1970s, which allowed Kristol and his contemporaries to openly call themselves conservatives, something they could not have dared to do before. Moreover, there was a declining cohesion of the New York intellectual community (as a result of the traumas of the 1960s), which limited its ability to continue to "impose" certain boundaries as acceptable political discourse. Claiming that the United States and the Western world suffered from a "crisis of authority" that is essentially cultural and that the American government is crippled by "overload" because it attempts to do too much domestically, the neoconservatives called for reducing the government and restabilizing the international order. Kristol has been closely associated with the Republican congressman from upstate New York, Jack Kemp, and the Arthur Laffer "supply side" school of economics.

There are, of course, important divergences within the neoconservative movement, and some neoconservatives were more reluctant than Kristol to accept the label when Michael Harrington first applied it. Daniel Bell, for example, had heralded the "end of ideology" in the West during the 1950s, and in 1965 had joined forces with Kristol to devote the *Public Interest* to practical problem-solving and to render social science knowledge useful to government policymakers. Yet he subsequently left the magazine and, like Hook, he continues to insist that he is a "socialist."[22] Public pronouncements, however, are not decisive in determining the authentic character and composition of a movement. For example, most neoconservatives insist that they support the "welfare state," even though a good number voted for Reagan, whose program amounted to dismantling it, and all claim to be against discrimination, even though most oppose strong affirmative action as a means of achieving equality for women and minorities.

Kristol's unique function has been to arm right-wing politicians and corporate executives with an ideological self-assurance that traditional conservatism could not provide. Through his connections with the American Enterprise Institute and the *Wall Street Journal*, and in lectures to business groups, Kristol makes his ideological services available for impressive fees. He has also established himself "at the center where the neo-boys' network interconnects," arranging positions for those who think as he does on editorial boards of journals and in universities.[23] At times Kristol expresses himself with power and eloquence, but he has also committed notorious gaffes which reveal a gross insensivity to the poor and the exploited. In 1960 he suggested that universal suffrage was a mistaken and potentially disastrous idea.[24] When questioned by the *New York Times Magazine* in 1981 about his support for federal cuts in school-lunch programs, he responded, "there's something to be said for parents making lunch. Kids shouldn't get used to the idea that life is one free lunch after another."[25] And when the Argentine newspaper publisher Jacobo Timerman published *Prisoner Without a Name, Cell Without a Number* (1981), a strong indictment of anti-Semitism and brutality in his homeland, Kristol responded by trying to link Timerman with a missing Jewish bank swindler who allegedly supported left-wing terrorists. He then charged Timerman's admirers in the United States with ignoring Communist violations of human rights.[26]

Kristol's political thought often seems banal. Patriotic in the narrow sense of romanticizing the U.S. past, his version of neoconservatism is based on a belief in a messianic "national destiny" for his country.[27] In a 1980 *Wall Street Journal* column entitled "Exorcizing the Nuclear Nightmare," he offered only one objection to using nuclear weapons against Cuba and Nicaragua: "the foreseeable revulsion of public opinion both at home and abroad."[28] His comments on Ronald Reagan's foreign policy invariably encourage the president to take greater military risks.

In a 1981 column, this lapsed revolutionary, an uncompromising nonconformist and resolute antimilitarist in his own youth, published a "Letter to the Pentagon." In it he deplored American soldiers who failed to stand properly at attention during the national anthem and urged the reinstitution of "proper military parades": "There is nothing like a parade to elicit respect for the military from the populace."[29] Although Kristol reminisced in his "Memoirs of a Trotskyist" that the 1940 debates between Cannon and Shachtman over the class nature of the Soviet Union were the paramount learning experience of his life, he resorts to the use of such vulgar characterizations as the "Soviet Mafia" and has recommended that Americans learn about the Soviet system by viewing *The Godfather* and *The Godfather, Part II*.[30]

PORTRAITS: NORMAN PODHORETZ AND MIDGE DECTER

Norman Podhoretz, second-in-command of the neoconservative ideologists, was born in 1930 in Brooklyn. A student of Lionel Trilling, he was not shaped by the anti-Stalinist left but by its eviscerated reincarnation as liberal anticommunism. First becoming associated with *Commentary* in 1955, he assumed the editorship in 1960, following the suicide of Elliot Cohen.[31] A left liberal who occasionally brushed up against the New Left for most of the decade, he published his autobiographical *Making It* in 1968 and startled some of his admirers with its frank admission that a lust for success was the motivating force in his life. This was followed by a steady drift to the right beginning in the late 1960s, which he described in the second installment of his autobiography, *Breaking Ranks* (1979). The turning points seem to have been the June 1967 Middle East war, which inspired a wave of chauvinism among the Jewish-American community, and the 1968 New York City teachers' strike, which pitted the black community against the heavily Jewish American Federation of Teachers.[32]

In the 1970s he concluded that the movement against the Vietnam War was a sign of American weakness and that participating in the campaign against nuclear weapons was an act of solidarity with the rulers of the Soviet Union. He then turned *Commentary* into a vigorous forum for denouncing busing to achieve integration, affirmative action, homosexual rights, and the Israeli peace movement. At one point *Commentary* even called for the United States to occupy Arab oil fields, and in another article it demanded restoration of the draft. In 1985 *Commentary* campaigned against corporate divestment from South Africa and misrepresented the antiapartheid movement as terrorist; several of its leading contributors also joined forces with the Reverend Sun Myung Moon to raise money for the reactionary Contras in Nicaragua.[33]

Perhaps Podhoretz's most startling pronouncement came in "The Culture of Appeasement," which appeared in the October 1977 issue of *Harper's*. Polemicizing against the decline of the military spirit in the United States, he unexpectedly introduced a discussion of "the central role homosexuality played in the entire rebellious ethos of the interwar period in England." Podhoretz claimed that many of the radicals who infected British culture with antipatriotic sentiments in the 1930s were homosexuals upset by the loss of potential male lovers in World War I. He then suggested that the same role was being played in our own culture by "such openly homosexual writers as Allen Ginsberg, James Baldwin, and Gore Vidal."[34] Another disturbing effort by Podhoretz to give intellectual respectability to the most extreme ad hominem accusations appeared in an October 1982 *Commentary* essay called *"J'Accuse"* in which he asserted that critics of the recent Israeli invasion of Lebanon and the mass killings at the Shatila and Sabra Palestinian refugee camps were actually motivated by anti-Semitism.[35] His 1982 book *Why We Were in Vietnam*—replete with factual errors, including a misleading synopsis of his own past positions—is a thinly veiled attempt to justify an aggressive U.S. policy of intervention in Central America.[36]

A consistent feature of Podhoretz's critique of his fellow intellectuals is the projection of his own motives onto others. The young Podhoretz was extraordinarily impressed when Lionel Trilling, "one of the most intelligent men in the world," remarked to him that that "everyone wants power. The only question is what kind."[37] This seems to have encouraged Podhoretz to explain the behavior of others in the same terms (power hungry) in which he now saw his own behavior. He argued that radical intellectuals in the 1930s capitulated to Marxism because they were then powerless in capitalist society and imagined that they would be leaders in a socialist order. In the 1960s, according to Podhoretz, radical students were motivated to protest by a combination of boredom and fear of being drafted rather than by a sincere belief in the values they espoused. Those intellectuals who supported them were driven by a desire to conform.

Even Trilling is accused by Podhoretz of ultimate cowardice for his refusal to endorse Podhoretz's "born again" conservatism. Since the 1950s Trilling had been tormented by a recognition that the "adversary culture"—the antibourgeois values that he and other New York intellectuals had promoted in the literature that they taught—might under certain conditions encourage rebellion against the very social order to which he was wedded. In 1968 Trilling's worst fears were realized when his own students at Columbia participated in the antiwar strike that shut down the campus and resulted in violent clashes with the police. Yet Trilling, as much as he abhorred the campus upheaval, could not bring himself to openly renounce the "adversary culture" in the same two-dimensional terms that Podhoretz proposed. Although Trilling claimed he was "fatigued," Podhoretz insisted that his former mentor was simply too cowardly to speak out against the vogue of the times.[38]

The central idea that emerges from *Breaking Ranks*, Podhoretz's testament of deradicalization, is that the New Left of the 1960s was analogous to the Stalinism of the 1930s; thus, by renouncing the New Left, Podhoretz is repeating the same heroic action of his predecessors who forged the anti-Stalinist left during the Great Depression decade. In order to defend this analogy, Podhoretz makes the fanciful assertion that the New Left (notorious for its anarchy) was dominated by a "party line" and was able to enforce a "reign of terror" against those who defected—although he can cite as evidence nothing more than a few personal cuts and unpleasant incidents at cocktail parties. The New Leftists differed from the Stalinists of the 1930s, argues Podhoretz, in that, as essentially a movement of intellectuals, they constituted a "new class" that has taken over the universities and the publishing, public service, and culture industries of the United States. Podhoretz's claim of victory for the New Left sets the stage for a strident and excessive epilogue, and in the final pages, Podhoretz issues a dire warning about the "plague" that has taken over our society, causing men to no longer act like men nor women like women.[39]

Like the former Communist Whittaker Chambers, Podhoretz feels guilty because he once contributed to the growth of this phenomenon, even though he had been naive as to its true character. But he has courageously decided to "break ranks" and issue a full confession to the public, naming names and issuing a warning to humanity that this sickness must be stamped out. Like Chambers's *Witness* (1952), which began with a "Foreword in the Form of a Letter to My Children," *Breaking Ranks* begins and ends with passages from "A Letter to My Son."

Podhoretz has been supported in his neoconservative crusade by his wife, Midge Decter. Together they form a formidable center to a network of right-wing publishing operations and committees. Decter's conservative ideas about women and the family began circulating at the same moment her husband explicitly moved to the right, suggesting that she is, in the least, the coarchitect of his new politics. Born Midge Rosenthal in St. Paul, Minnesota, in 1927, she studied at the University of Minnesota and the Jewish Theological Seminary of America before beginning a career as an editor variously at *Midstream, Commentary, Harper's, Saturday Review,* and Basic Books. Her first husband, Moshe Decter, was engaged by the American Committee for Cultural Freedom to coauthor *McCarthy and the Communists* (1954) with James Rorty.

In 1971 she published a collection of essays, *The Liberated Woman and Other Americans,* which were highly critical of the motives of the women's liberation movement. A second collection, *The New Chastity and Other Arguments Against Women's Liberation* (1972), openly argued that freedom of choice was a greater threat to women than their alleged oppression. A third book, *Liberal Parents, Radical Children* (1975), contended that liberal child-rearing practices of the 1960s and 1970s created a generation of self-indulgent and irresponsible youth. In February 1981 Decter announced that she had left Basic Books to work for the Committee for the Free World, an organization devoted to "the struggle for freedom." Some of the leaders of this new group—Sidney Hook, Leopold Labdez, Melvin Lasky, and Irving Kristol—are former participants of the Congress for Cultural Freedom. Perhaps mindful of the dangers of such a connection, a press release issued on behalf of the committee announced that "no money will be sought or accepted from any government or government agency." Yet nearly half of the committee's $125,000 in seed money came from foundations with close ties to the Central Intelligence Agency.[40]

In the 1950s and 1960s Lionel and Diana Trilling were frequently regarded as a team promoting similar anticommunist political ideas, with the important difference that Lionel tended to be reticent and even recondite, while Diana tended to be more direct and aggressive. Podhoretz and Decter seem to combine Diana's approach with a tendency to oversimplify and be abrasive. Podhoretz, for example, writes in defense of the "selfishness" of the "Yuppies," insisting that these "Young Upwardly Mobile Professionals" have become the object of satire by members of the leftist "new class" in retaliation for the Yuppies' wholly justifiable surrender to the bourgeois system they once opposed. The radicals who allegedly control American culture are "trying to make them feel guilty about betraying their old idealism. It is a strategy, in short, for shaming them back into the kinds of attitudes that nourish the political activism of the left."[41] Decter extends the same "look out for Number One" approach to the issue of Israeli–United States relations: "In a world full of ambiguities and puzzlements, one thing is absolutely easy both to define and locate: that is the Jewish interest. The continued security . . . of the Jews, worldwide, rests with a strong, vital, prosperous, self-confident United States."[42] Decter offers no explanation for the sudden disappearance of "ambiguity" or "puzzlement" in determining precisely what constitutes "Jewish interest," or authentic "security," or the means by which the United States might become "strong" and "prosperous." Nor does she feel the need to respond to the obvious fact that, if every interest group in the world puts its own religion, culture, race, or nation first, above all others, conflicts and wars will only intensify.

THE IDEOLOGISTS OF ANTIRADICALISM

Podhoretz and Decter seem unperturbed by the inability of their arguments to withstand careful scrutiny because, in fact, they are engaged in a serious fight for winning ideological hegemony. The method of debate they promote, and in which they train their following of young journalists and academicians, is candidly revealed in a September 1984 *Commentary* essay by Owen Harries, a Fellow at the Heritage Foundation. Harries's "A Primer for Polemicists" begins by citing Irving Kristol's call for neoconservatives to "own" the future by "determining the spirit of the age, the prevailing notions concerning what is possible, inevitable, desirable, permissible, and unspeakable." Harries presents a set of "rules" for achieving this end, the first of which is never to "confuse polemical exchanges with genuine intellectual debate." His other "guidelines" flow logically from this premise: develop a vocabulary inherently biased toward one's own values (Orwell called this "Newspeak"); concentrate on building up the morale of one's own supporters "in order to bind them more securely to the cause and make them more effective exponents of it"; feign "good sense, decency and fairness" as a tactic to win over the uncommitted; keep one's presentation on a low level and "when you have a good point to make, keep repeating it" because "success in ideological polemics is very much a matter of staying power and will"; and hold off on impugning the motives of your opponent until the *end* of the debate.[43]

The use of these strategies indicates that Podhoretz and Decter have no real interest in political and social theory and analysis. Podhoretz began as a promising literary critic, but, for unexplained reasons, became blocked in his work and wrote *Making It* as a substitute for a promised book-length literary study which he has yet to produce. Some of the neoconservatives, however, are considerably more talented, if less influential, and enjoy substantial reputations in diverse fields. For example, at the 1983 neoconservative conference on "Our Country and Our Culture" the historian Gertrude Himmelfarb presented a diatribe against the rise of "social history" in her profession; her presentation was particularly distressing in light of her appointment to the advisory board of the National Endowment for the Humanities, a critical source of funding for young scholars, many of whom work in social history.[44] Still, she produced a creditable study utilizing her anti-Marxist method in *The Idea of Poverty: England in the Early Industrial Age* (1984). Nathan Glazer, who at certain times has caricatured affirmative action as an illegal and un-American movement, is the coauthor of two books, *The Lonely Crowd* (1950) and *Beyond the Melting Pot* (1963), which are considered classics of descriptive sociology.[45] Daniel Bell, who keeps at arm's length from the worst excesses of the Podhoretz circle but has certain affinities with some of its premises, is a polymath whose theories of postindustrial society demand serious consideration. Along with Seymour Martin Lipset, he has been a major force in reshaping the scope and character of sociological thought in the United States. Glazer, Bell, and Lipset broke with Podhoretz over his uncritical support of the Israeli invasion of Lebanon in 1982.[46] This rupture suggests that the neoconservative movement may have been transcended, with Podhoretz and Kristol, moving more into the oribit of the traditional conservatism of the *National Review* and the others keeping a holding pattern for the present.

Hilton Kramer is an example of a burgeoning talent who seems to have been reborn in mid-career as the conservative judge of the American cultural left—which for him starts at the right center. Born in Gloucester, Massachusetts, in 1928, Kramer graduated from Syracuse University in 1950 and did postgraduate work in art in various eastern universities. A contributor to the *Partisan Review* and the *New Leader*, he was briefly editor of *Arts Magazine* and art editor of the *Nation* before spending nearly twenty years as the art news editor and art critic for the *New York Times*. Indications of Kramer's turn to the right first came in the mid-1970s with his remarks about sinister connections between homosexuality and radicalism. Even stronger was his 1976 article on the 1950s "blacklist," which caricatured the "revisionist" historians of U.S. foreign policy by attributing to them the view that the Soviet Union played a "benign" role in the postwar era, and which also depicted the "Hollywood Ten" as criminals instead of victims.[47]

In 1982 Kramer received a half million dollars from four corporation-connected foundations to initiate the *New Criterion*, named after T. S. Eliot's famous magazine. The *New Criterion* aims to identify the values of high culture with capitalist civilization, much as the *Partisan Review* sought to claim modernist culture for revolutionary socialism in the late 1930s. Like *Commentary*, the *New Criterion* adheres rigidly to a neoconservative line, publishes many of the same writers, and has the same "hit list" of left-leaning intellectuals. An obvious target is Irving Howe, who was accused by Kramer of evaluating novels sympathetically according to their degree of anticapitalism.[48] More surprising was the series of strained and rather unconvincing assaults by Kenneth Lynn and Lionel Abel against Alfred Kazin, published in late 1984.

Although Kazin is frequently identified as a leading New York intellectual, his evolution displays many uncharacteristic features. He was born in 1915 into a poor Jewish immigrant family in New York. His father, who had belonged to the Jewish-socialist Bund in Russia, joined the Socialist Party as an admirer of Eugene Debs.[49] But Kazin himself was profoundly moved by religion—first Christianity, later Judaism. As a student at the City College of New York and then an aspiring writer in New York City, Kazin was an armchair left-wing socialist, attracted to Marxist intellectuals but not to Marxism as a doctrine. Although he traveled for a while in the V. F. Calverton circle, he managed to stand apart from the internecine battles of the Stalinists and anti-Stalinists in the 1930s, regarding himself simply as "non-Stalinist," except for a brief time in 1936 when antifascism drove him close to the Communists. This disposition protected him from the excesses of the American Committee for Cultural Freedom in the 1950s; it may also have been the reason that he was drawn to Hannah Arendt, whose firsthand experience with fascism protected her from the exclusive obsession with Stalinism that dominated the milieu. Moreover, Kazin was differentiated by his fascination with American literature, in contrast to the Europocentrism of the *Partisan Review* group, and he was less inclined than almost all the other New York intellectuals to mobilize literary criticism as an adjunct in a broader political struggle. By the 1980s, Kazin had even abandoned his vague socialism, declaring himself merely a "radical" but one opposed to state control of industry and services beyond the boundaries reached by such countries as Sweden and Israel.

The *New Criterion* assaults were apparently in retaliation for Kazin's devastating 1983 *New York Review of Books* essay on "Our Country and Our Culture," the conference sponsored by the Committee for the Free World. Among other observations, Kazin ridiculed the *New Criterion*'s obsession with seeking out "anti-Americanism," usually exhibited when writers were critical of American business.[50] Thus it is no suprise that "anti-Americanism" is precisely the quality that Lynn and Abel discovered in Kazin's work. In a reconsideration of Kazin's masterwork, *On Native Grounds* (1940), Lynn faults it for its antibusiness bias, a not unusual perspective for criticism written against the backdrop of the Great Depression era.[51] From Lionel Abel, one would have expected a more subtle critique.

Born Lionel Abelson in 1910 in New York City, Abel was the son of a maverick rabbi. He attended St. John's University and the University of North Carolina before starting a career as a playwright, drama critic, and translator in New York City, with frequent visits to Paris.[52] His first wife, Sherry, was the sister of Albert Goldman, a connection that brought him close to Trotskyist circles. During the period of Trotskyist entry into the Socialist Party, Abel became a member and participated in the Trotskyist faction. Later he contributed to *New International*. During the 1950s he remained friendly to Shachtman's Independent Socialist League, and in the 1960s he was for a while a sponsor of *New Politics*, a left-wing publication in the Shachtman tradition, in which he attacked Irving Kristol as a secret conservative.[53] By the 1970s, however, Abel had signed up with the legions who were "breaking ranks." His brief against Kazin is party line, pure and simple; he claims that *An American Procession* (1984) proves Kazin to be a renegade from the pro-American literature attitudes of *On Native Grounds* (1940): "After twenty-five years of loving the American national character, Alfred

Kazin has decided to quarrel with it, and with those who represent it in our literature. . . . For he is no longer in love with the country whose coming to consciousness they represented for him in his first book."[54]

The *New Criterion's* most vicious campaign was waged against Noam Chomsky through the publication of a 1984 essay, "Censoring 20th-Century Culture," by the British linguist Geoffrey Sampson. Sampson was angry because the biographical entry he had written about Chomsky was removed by the publisher from a projected U.S. paperback edition of Alan Bullock's *20th-Century Culture*, which had already appeared in England, on the grounds that some of his claims about Chomsky were questionable. In his *New Criterion* article, Sampson repeated these claims, including the allegation that Chomsky endorsed "a book . . . that denied the historical reality of the Jewish holocaust" and that he repeated "polemics minimizing the Khmer Rouge atrocities in Cambodia." Moreover, Sampson insisted that Chomsky had succeeded in having the entry removed because he "threatened to initiate libel action" against the publisher.[55]

The *New Republic*, whose editor, Martin Peretz, had joined Kramer in helping to found the Committee for the Free World, repeated Sampson's allegations in a special editorial and concluded that "even in circles which had once revered him, Mr. Chomsky is now seen as a crank and an embarrassment. Shame on Lord Bullock [for eliminating the above charges from the Chomsky entry in the Book-of-the-Month Club paperback edition of the book] and shame on those in Harper and Row who countenance this cowardly complicity in keeping the truth about Mr. Chomsky from readers who would consult what purports to be an authoritative reference work."[56] Unfortunately, every one of Sampson's charges against Chomsky turned out to be false; yet both the *New Criterion* and the *New Republic* delayed publication of Chomsky's refutations for months, giving plenty of time for the falsehoods to circulate unchallenged.[57]

Whether articulated through the social criticism of Podhoretz's *Commentary* or the cultural criticism of Kramer's *New Criterion*, the ideological rhetoric of the neoconservatives masks a program that suggests that they have learned well at least one lesson from the Marxist incarnation of the New York intellectuals: that the social function of intellectuals is class-dependent. As radical young intellectuals, they chose to ally themselves with the working class and other movements for social change in an effort to restructure society for the benefit of all. As "mature" adults they took the opposite stance, and they hardly stop at trying to mobilize in defense of the status quo in the intellectual community but now aspire to become preeminent in the state and international spheres. Thus the 1980–81 "Report on Activities of the Committee for the Free World" describes how Executive Secretary Midge Decter "addressed an international gathering of military strategists from around the world, and sought to impress upon them that the critical defense to be mounted at this moment was in the field of propaganda. They were in full agreement and expressed much interest in the Committee and its work."[58] No doubt Decter had a few suggestions as to who might be engaged to carry out this propaganda.

In a period of cutbacks in social programs and layoffs for the poor, minorities, and working people in the United States, many of the neoconservatives began to "earn" substantial material rewards for their loyal services as publicists, legitimators, and ideologists of American expansionism, benignly renamed "democratic capitalism" by Michael Novak in his book *The Spirit of Democratic Capitalism* (1979).[59] The neoconservatives see their role as providing "moral" and "civilized" rationales for the exploitative activities of the American ruling elite, a task for which they receive large grants from such right-wing foundations as the American Enterprise Institute and the Heritage Foundation, and from various large corporations. With similar kinds of funding channeled through the Institute for Educational Affairs, they assist the publication of a network of some thirty conservative journals and newspapers on university campuses across the country, the most notorious of which has been the *Dartmouth Review*."[60] The Committee for the Free World issues a monthly newsletter, *Contentions*, which publishes a series of pamphlets by the "Orwell Press," holds national conferences, and jets its members around the world to confer with their counterparts in other "free world" countries.

This proliferation of corporation-funded projects recalls many of the same moral issues as did the dubious activities of the Congress for Cultural Freedom in the 1950s. In his 1967 article, "The CIA and the Intellectuals," Jason Epstein shrewdly pointed to the dangers inherent in the funding of ostensibly "independent" writers and scholars by the Central Intelligence Agency, the Ford Foundation, and other agencies that established

> an apparatus of intellectuals selected for their correct cold-war positions, as an alternative to what one might call a free intellectual market where ideology was presumed to count for less than individual talent and achievement, and where doubts

about established orthodoxies were taken to be the beginning of all inquiry. . . . [I]t was not a matter of buying off and subverting individual writers and scholars, but of setting up an arbitrary and factitious system of values by which academic personnel were advanced, magazine editors appointed, and scholars subsidized and published, not necessarily on their merits, though these were sometimes considerable, but because of their allegiances.[61]

Considerable amounts of money are involved in this effort to create a new intellectual elite. The Institute for Educational Affairs was initiated by Kristol in 1978 with $400,000 in grant funds from the John M. Olin, Smith Richardson, Scaife Family Charitable Trusts, and J. M. foundations. Soon seventy-four corporate patrons were involved and the total gifts for 1980 increased to $538,868. Although the average grant from a foundation is only about $12,000, the institute's role as a catalyst spurs gifts from other sources. A considerable amount of personnel exchange takes place among the institute's board, the higher echelons of corporations, and government agencies. Moreover, a number of former associates of student newspapers affiliated with the institute have found a home in the Reagan administration. The institute, with contributions as much as $25,000, has also financed several "scholarly" books presenting the neoconservative position on historical, social, and cultural issues.[62]

In his 1982 memoir, *The Truants*, the neoconservative writer and critic William Barrett invokes Delmore Schwartz and Philip Rahv as a warning to the reader about the terrible fate of alienated rebels who fail to appreciate the gifts their society has bestowed on them. Throughout Barrett's discussion of Schwartz, an impression is given that if the poet had rebelled less against the mainstream of American culture (if he had worked, for example, in an insurance office like Wallace Stevens), he might have found "more peace and in the end more time for his poetry."[63] Barrett's treatment of Rahv is even more important because Rahv is explicitly ridiculed as a prime example of an intellectual who fails to "grow up" and repudiate his radical past.

What galls Barrett most about Rahv is that the more secure Rahv became—in 1958 he was appointed professor at Brandeis University although he had never attended college—the more he openly returned to his leftist views. Truly this was a case of biting the hand that fed him: "He was like those children of affluence during the 1960s who found their middle-class advantages a further reason for hostility toward American society. Rahv, in fact, was one of those intellectuals of the 1950s who was preparing the way for the radical outbursts of the 1960s; and when these came, he was ready to receive them with open arms. All in all, it was to be a strange turn in the career of a man who had always been an outsider: hitherto, in the 1930s and 1940s, he had fought against the dominant trend, but now in the 1960s he had turned about and was running with the pack."[64] Hilton Kramer quoted the entire passage in the *New York Times Book Review,* calling it "quite the best thing in Barrett's book." Kramer is as incredulous as Barrett that "the more he [Rahv] prospered, the more violently did he denounce the system that had brought him success."[65]

Whatever one may conclude about Rahv, these remarks reveal much more about his adversaries, the contemporary neoconservatives. What is so reprehensible about self-made intellectuals, or for that matter disaffected members of the ruling elite, who ally themselves with working people and other social rebels in their struggle to construct a society in which all can enjoy the privileges presently enjoyed only by a few? Do Barrett and Kramer think that Rahv should have fallen on his knees before America's rulers in gratitude for having saved him from the pit of poverty and a life of meaningless work? Their views confirm that the neoconservatives have not completely abandoned their quondam Marxist analysis of the dynamic of capitalist society as a struggle of the haves against the have-nots. The difference, however, is that they have chosen to align themselves with the haves.

Marxism and Intellectuals in the United States

> For a privileged minority, Western democracy provides the leisure, the facilities, and the training to seek the truth hidden behind the veil of distortion and misrepresentation, ideology, and class interest through which the events of current history are presented to us. . . . It is the responsibility of intellectuals to speak the truth and expose lies.
>
> —Noam Chomsky, "The Responsibility of Intellectuals," 1967[1]

. . . .

What are the conclusions one might draw from the experiences described in the preceding chapters? This book argues that the collective history of the group that began as the anti-Stalinist left and was transformed into the New York intellectuals embodies many lessons for those interested in combining cultural, artistic, literary, and scholarly activity with a socialist political practice. Yet, even though the group was free of the political positions formally associated with official Soviet-type Communism, the anti-Stalinist left never reached in practice the potential ascribed to it in theory.

In this book I have tried to demonstrate that the obscured and often misrepresented switch from Marxist anti-Communism (authentic anti-Stalinism) to liberal anticommunism (bogus anti-Stalinism) was a crucial ideological factor in this failure. As Hannah Arendt observed in a public lecture in the late 1940s, "anti-Stalinism," a term that originated in the interior struggles of the Bolshevik Party, eventually became a catchall slogan in the United States to rally together diverse elements against radical social change. In this context, anti-Stalinism implies no reasoned approach to political philosophy. Pure and simple anti-Stalinists can, in fact, favor totalitarianism of other types; this contrasts dramatically with the political perspective of the nonconformist wing of the communist movement, which tended to be dominated by Trotskyism (and which was expressed in the 1930s by such intellectuals in the United States as Eastman, Hook, and Corey). Divorced from the context of a general anticapitalist and anti-imperialist outlook, anti-Stalinism can lead one to oppose something as basic as struggles by workers for higher wages if those struggles happen to be led by Communist-influenced unions.[2] As this book argues, the logic of pure and simple anti-Stalinism is to move its adherents toward an anticommunism that views the imperialist practices of the United States as a lesser evil in a world conflict of two "camps."

After precisely such an evolution took place, it became popular in the 1960s for some of those in the New Left to vilify the formerly radical New York intellectuals as sellouts, opportunists, and phonies. Although some may have deserved these epithets, ad hominem attacks are a poor substitute for the searching out of social and historical factors that encouraged the transformation of revolutionary intellectuals into an entirely different political species.

The ability of the anti-Stalinist left to sustain a revolutionary political outlook during the early and middle 1930s, despite their justified hostility to Stalinism, was partly dependent on events that inspired them to see the working class as a force for radical change. These include the heroic strikes of the 1930s—of dockworkers in San Francisco, truckers in Minneapolis, and auto workers in Michigan—as well as the rise of the CIO. The courage and idealism of the rank and file of the labor movement seemed to portend a new socialist order, while capitalism appeared impotent and decadent in the face of the crisis engendered by the Great Depression.

Momentous international events provided a further source of inspiration to the intellectuals—in particular, the Spanish Civil War and the activities of the Workers Party of Marxist Unification (POUM), the anarchists, and the Trotskyists in the face of both Francoism and Stalinism. It seemed possible that a revolutionary alternative to both the Stalinist bureaucracy of the Soviet Union and to Western capitalism might emerge in Europe. Trotsky was still alive, providing an authentic revolutionary voice that argued for the compatibility of communism and democracy and offered a critique of Stalinism from a Bolshevik point of view.

Most radical intellectuals did not have a secure niche within the American capitalist system. Only a few—James Burnham, Sidney Hook, Meyer Schapiro, and Lionel Trilling—held university appointments. Often the men were supported by their wives; several had jobs with the Works Project Administration from time to time; those who were students came from poor families and lived at home. They could not foresee their successful futures under existing social arrangements.

But by the end of World War II everything had changed. The very factors that had occasioned the development of the intellectuals into revolutionaries in the 1930s had dissipated. Moreover, they had abandoned their ties to those socialist groups that might have reinforced their original convictions. So by the time a resurgence of social and political struggle occurred in the 1960s, many of the intellectuals had become hardened apologists for American imperialism.

A few, however—Dwight Macdonald, Mary McCarthy, F. W. Dupee, and Philip Rahv—eventually broke free of their Cold War liberalism or political quiescence and moved unexpectedly back to the left, which demonstrated that deradicalization was not inevitable. Had the postwar labor upsurge sustained itself in the 1940s, at least some of the radical intellectuals would have remained on the left. In sum, the primary determinants in the deradicalization process were the political situation in the nation and the world in addition to the ascension of the intellectuals in status.

The lesson most knowledgeable commentators have drawn from the New York intellectuals' experience with Marxism is usually one or another variant of the argument advanced by Julian Benda in 1927 in his classic *The Treason of the Intellectuals*. Benda claimed that modern intellectuals, regardless of their particular views, had betrayed the cause of speculative thought to the interests of political passion and that they should and must remain free of all alignments with powerful social movements. This is essentially Daniel Aaron's conclusion in his recent study of Edmund Wilson's political trajectory during the 1930s: "He [Wilson] remained at the end of the decade what he had been at its beginning—the uncommitted and determinedly independent witness."[3]

No doubt this position might sound attractive to many intellectuals. Yet if one has gained nothing else from the preceding survey of the careers of the New York intellectuals, one ought to at least be alerted to the specious premise of Benda's thesis and of its modern variations. Was it not the very ideology of becoming "independent critical thinkers," indeed, intellectuals beyond the blinding grip of ideology itself, that became the chief means by which the New York intellectuals masked their shift in political allegiance? An axiom of Marxism, as well as of all other materialist philosophies, holds that total autonomy from the social institutions that shape lives and consciousness is a delusion, a myth that serves the ideological function of preserving the simulacrum of "free will" while sustaining the dominant institutions, social relations, and culture of the existing society.

Recently Raymond Williams powerfully argued this point in *Marxism and Literature* (1977). Williams theorizes that in a society riven by contending social forces, writers and intellectuals are always aligned with one force or another whether or not they understand or admit it. Therefore, it is preferable for a writer or intellectual to be committed—to make a conscious choice of alignment—rather than to be unconsciously aligned, that is, to play a role that one did not choose, or let oneself become regressively transformed by the very social institutions that one had originally set out to overturn.[4] This is more or less what Frederick Engels had in mind when he described the type of consciousness that would enable humanity to achieve freedom by recognizing necessity.[5] Appropriate action must be pursued with a full awareness of social reality. In the United States, conscious alignment might take the form of participation in counterinstitutions of capitalist society—trade unions, socialist political organizations, or women's, Third World, or community organizations that work for social liberation against the dominant political order.

The career of Philip Rahv provides an instructive example of an intellectual who sought to sustain a Marxism in isolation from counterinstitutions of any sort. Throughout the 1950s, except for one blast against McCarthy, Rahv was mostly silent on political matters. Then, in 1967, he tried to draw a sharp line between himself and the liberal anticommunists who, he said, had masked an accommodation to the status quo behind a self-righteous campaign against "Stalinist totalitarianism": "I was never a liberal anti-Communist or, for that matter, any other kind of liberal. When a small group of us broke away from the Communist movement in the late 1930s we did so because of our fundamental allegiance to democratic socialism; and substantially that is still my position today."[6]

A second public political stand that differentiated Rahv from other New York intellectuals was his political orientation toward the New Left, which he sought to educate in certain elementary ideas of Marxist tactics. In the pages of the *New York Review of Books* and in his own *Modern Occasions*, Rahv quoted Trotsky on the futility of individual terrorism ("the chemistry of high explosives cannot take the place of mass action"). Rahv pointed directly to a major weakness of the radical student movement of the 1960s: "it has failed to crystallize from within itself a guiding organization—one need not be afraid of naming it a centralized and disciplined party, for so far no one has ever invented a substitute for such a party—capable of engaging in daily and even pedestrian practical activity while keeping itself sufficiently alert on the ideological plane so as not to miss its historical opportunity when and if it arises."[7]

In the year or two before the latter article appeared, Rahv quarreled bitterly with William Phillips and the editorial board of the *Partisan Review*. According to a memoir by Mark Krupnick, Rahv believed that the others had capitulated to the "new sensibility"—a term associated with the counterculture of the 1960s and its emphasis on psychedelic drugs, rock music, pornography, science fiction, "happenings," and the ideas of Marshall McLuhan. Krupnick recalled that in Rahv's eyes, "*Partisan* read more like a pop magazine with each issue, with features on Burroughs, 'camp,' McLuhan's media, the Beatles, the new Mutants, and Protean Man. The editors weren't buying Charles Reich's 'greening of America,' but they weren't going to miss the train, either." So Rahv broke with the *Partisan Review* because "there was no center, no focus, no commitment," and he set out to lead the literary intelligentsia in a new direction with *Modern Occasions*.[8] Ultimately, this direction was not so new because the cultural values of the new magazine were those of classical modernism, and politically Rahv's shield of "independence" left him even more disconnected from the living movements and struggles in the 1960s and 1970s than he had been in the 1930s.

Modern Occasions was a failure and after its quick demise everything went steadily downhill for Rahv. A fire killed his second wife and destroyed his much-treasured library; his third marriage was disastrous; with his proclivity for quarrels, political and otherwise, he was isolated from most of his friends and the writers he had helped over the years. In his campaign against the counterculture Rahv became increasingly obsessed with literary vendettas, particularly against Leslie Fiedler and Norman Mailer, whom he regarded as archetypal hucksters, pandering to a mass audience in order to make a fast buck. According to Krupnick, Rahv fell into despair and depression about his failure to link up with young radicals and about the course of events in the United States in general. He drank excessively and depended on pills for innumerable ailments and violent "Timon-like rages."[9]

Rahv's elitist fixation on modernist culture was of a piece with his conception of an "independent and critical Marxism." In Rahv's hands Marxism even became an adjunct to modernism in the sense that he reshaped his political perspectives to justify the mood of despair and isolation that he cultivated after the 1930s. It was characteristic that Rahv titled his 1967 appreciation of Trotsky "The Great Outsider." He portrays the organizer of the Russian Revolution more as a heretic and a pariah than as a mass leader who devoted his intellectual powers to the living struggles of workers and poor peasants for social emancipation.[10]

The editors of a posthumous collection of Rahv's essays say that "in his last years . . . Rahv returned to many of his youthful Marxist-Leninist ideas."[11] This statement is problematic, even granting that the editors probably have a rather loose idea as to what constitutes "Marxism-Leninism." From the mid-1940s to the mid-1960s, the precise nature of Rahv's politics was one of the best-kept secrets in the world. However, Rahv's adaptability—"opportunism" is probably the more accurate word—did not suddenly appear in the Cold War years. From the beginning of his rupture with the Communist Party, Rahv prided himself on his ability to politically "maneuver." Maneuvering is, of course, a part of politics, and no one was more astute at strategical and tactical maneuvers than Lenin. But Rahv managed to free himself completely from Marxist principles that underlie and justify, as well as rule out, certain maneuvers. Krupnick aptly refers to him as a "disillusioned Leninist."

Rahv apparently favored a socialist revolution in the abstract and believed that such a social transformation would be impossible without the leadership of a Leninist party. He also believed, however, that no organization in existence had the potential for evolving into such a party. Such a combination of positions can be used as a rationale for abstention from participation in socialist political activity, and Rahv seems to have taken full advantage of this rationalization. Although he forcefully exposed the corruption of the ex-radical intelligentsia, he probably never appeared at a demonstration and may never have allowed his name to be used for any political advertisements during the 1960s and 1970s. After his death, the news that he had left his estate to the state of Israel came as a total surprise to political intimates of his last years, such as Noam Chomsky, to whom Rahv had never expressed an opinion about Israel.[12]

On the other hand, simplistic formulae about "choosing sides" or abstractions admonishing one to be for the working class or for unions or for women's liberation or for socialism do not solve the problem any better than a naive call to be "independent and uncommitted." As we have seen, deradicalizing intellectuals can delude themselves: a Sidney Hook, for example, can claim that he has never been an apostate from Marxism, only a genuine democratic socialist who has gone "beyond Marxism." It should never be forgotten that the professed aims of individuals, parties, groups, unions, and other organizations can be negated by their actual conduct.

It is also tragic but true that highly committed intellectuals who bind their fates to a particular Marxist party for many decades can become prisoners of that party should it veer off its original course by misleadership or the vicissitudes of history. Similarly, intellectuals who connect themselves to certain currents in the trade unions can become trapped in a false course should those currents undergo a bureaucratic transformation. I have argued, for example, that Irving Howe's variant of social democracy influenced him to forge links with counterinstitutions that were insufficiently "counter"; thus they deformed as much as they preserved his once revolutionary socialist consciousness. Howe began by attempting to win liberals to socialism and ended by becoming a political liberal with socialist ideals. Social democrats such as Howe and Harvey Swados may well be admirable individuals, but they have drifted far from and taken positions directly contradicting their original goals.

One must conclude, then, that intellectuals who make conscious political commitments cannot proceed according to abstract formulae that simply enjoin one to be "pro-union" or "pro-socialist." Their conscious choices must be informed by a certain degree of political acuity based on real experience, and the precise form of their commitment must be subject to a control—to a checking mechanism, a "critical consciousness," which is that element of autonomy that still functions within the limitations of socially determined existence.

Marxist intellectuals require a means of expressing an appropriate stance, one based on a knowledge of past experience—a stance that represents an alternative to the Julian Benda-inspired advocacy of an "uncommitted and determinedly independent witness." But it must be one that also avoids merely advocating intellectuals to "take sides"—although, to be sure, there are moments when intellectuals should rather quickly take sides, especially when those sides are clearly defined. The most appropriate stance would be one that is dialectical, that expresses the problematic aspects of both a willed commitment to a cause, a class, or a movement, and the retention of a critical consciousness—a "partisan but objective" stance, as it were. Perhaps the formulation "independence within a committed position" best expresses the tension that often marks the linkage of a self-reflexive consciousness with a willed commitment to a cause.

Radicalization and deradicalization have repeatedly occurred among Marxist intellectuals since the 1930s, although primarily during the early and late years of the Great Depression, the postwar era, and the 1960s. Certain patterns are now apparent. In the period of radicalization, Marxism, despite its defects, appears as the most useful analytical tool for interpreting the historical process and determining a course of action; the industrial working class appears strategically located as the central agent in the restructuring of capitalist society; and usually some recent upheaval in the economically underdeveloped world appears to be making remarkable social advances. In the period of deradicalization, the intellectuals in crisis invariably declare a "crisis of Marxism"; they disparage the capacities of the working class; and they declare that they have been "betrayed" by revolutions that have failed to achieve a normative version of "socialism." Given this history, intellectuals whose Marxism depends on a view of socialism as a steady, forward-moving process that can be achieved largely by urging adherence to a particular political party find themselves repeating this historical pattern, not learning from it. There is simply no panacea for solving the difficulties involved in sustaining during unpropitious times the four major components of Marxist political practice: a rigorously internationalist perspective; an uncompromising revolutionary vision of social transformation; activist affiliation with authentic counterinstitutions; and a determination to view the world from the standpoint of the oppressed groups in society.[13]

A veteran socialist once remarked to me that he thought it was harder to be an active Marxist in the 1980s than it was during the Great Depression because the left-wing movement has experienced so many disappointments in the last fifty years. After devoting considerable time to studying the checkered history of a segment of the Marxist intelligentsia in the United States, I would like to suggest that this observation needs to be balanced with the recognition that in the 1980s we have the distinct advantage of knowing far more about the problems and possibilities of fundamental social change than did our radical predecessors.

The advance of radical scholarship has brought to our attention a wide body of material unavailable to earlier generations. We can study the writings of the young Marx, the work of the Western Marxists, the acute analyses of heresiarchs of official Communism such as Trotsky and Bukharin, biographies and autobiographies of all sorts of American radicals—workers and intellectuals of both sexes, of all colors, and of many ethnic backgrounds. We can now look back over the seventy years that have elapsed since the Russian Revolution and assess for ourselves the meaning of various debates and the validity of policies, positions, and attitudes. We need to integrate this sort of theoretical consciousness about political strategy with careful empirical research into the experience of the previous generation of Marxists. In that way we will be able to advance the recovery of our radical heritage, to correct the political amnesia that has marred our legacy, and to redeem the promise of socialist intellectuals first augured in the writings of Marx and Engels.

Notes

. . . .

INTRODUCTION

1. Harold Rosenberg, *The Tradition of the New* (New York: McGraw-
Hill, 1965), p. 25.
2. *Toward an American Revolutionary Labor Movement: A Statement*

of Programmatic Orientation by the American Workers Party (New York: Published by the Provisional Organizing Committee of the American Workers Party, 1934), pp. 23–24.

3. Sidney Hook, "Why I Am a Communist: Communism without Dogmas, a Reply by Sidney Hook," *Modern Monthly* 8, no. 3 (April 1934): 165.

4. "Speakers Will Bare Hearst's Labor Record," *New Militant* 1, no. 8 (2 February 1935): 1, and "Mass Meeting Calls Hearst Labor Enemy," ibid. 1, no. 9 (9 February 1935): 1. See also Sidney Hook to AW, 4 February 1985.

5. Sidney Hook, *Heresy, Yes—Conspiracy, No* (New York: John Day, 1953), pp. 127 and 210.

6. Melvin J. Lasky to AW, 2 December 1982.

7. See the discussion of anticommunist ideology in Alan Wolfe's essay, "The Irony of Anti-Communism," in *Socialist Register 1984: The Uses of Anti-Communism*, ed. Ralph Miliband, John Saville, and Marcel Liebman, pp. 214–29 (London: Merlin Press, 1984).

8. Letter to the Editor from Sidney Hook and Arnold Beichman, *New York Times Book Review*, 25 March 1984, p. 26.

9. Clement Greenberg, "The Late Thirties in New York," *Art and Culture* (Boston: Beacon, 1961), p. 230.

10. Miliband, Saville, and Liebman, eds., *Socialist Register 1984: The Uses of Anti-Communism*, p. 1.

11. Some of these points were suggested in a letter from Ernest Erber to AW, 18 May 1984.

12. Some of the more helpful scholarly studies are Bert Cochran, "Intellectuals and the Cold War," in *Adlai Stevenson: Patrician among Politicians* (New York: Funk and Wagnalls, 1969), pp. 343–98; John Diggins, *Up from Communism: Conservative Odysseys in American Intellectual History* (New York: Harper and Row, 1975); James B. Gilbert, *Writers and Partisans: A History of Literary Radicalism in America* (New York: Wiley, 1968); David Hollinger, "Ethnic Diversity, Cosmopolitanism and the Emergence of the American Liberal Intelligentsia," *American Quarterly* 27 (May 1975): 133–51; Christopher Lasch, "The Cultural Cold War: A Short History of the Congress for Cultural Freedom," *The Agony of the American Left* (New York: Vintage, 1968), pp. 61–114; S. A. Longstaff, "The New York Family," *Queen's Quarterly* 83 (Winter 1976): 108–29; and Richard Pells, *The Liberal Mind in a Conservative Age: American Intellectuals in the 1940s and 1950s* (New York: Harper and Row, 1985).

The following is a partial list of the many books on individual figures: Elisabeth Young-Bruehl, *Hannah Arendt: For Love of the World* (New Haven: Yale University Press, 1982); Keith Opdahl, *The Novels of Saul Bellow: An Introduction* (University Park: Pennsylvania State University Press, 1967); William L. O'Neill, *The Last Romantic: A Life of Max Eastman* (New York: Oxford, 1978); Edgar Branch, *James T. Farrell* (New York: Twayne, 1971); Donald Kuspit, *Clement Greenberg: Art Critic* (Madison: University of Wisconsin Press, 1979); Doris Grumbach, *The Company She Kept: A Revealing Portrait of Mary McCarthy* (New York: Coward-Mc-

Cann, 1967); Stephen J. Whitfield, *A Critical American: The Politics of Dwight Macdonald* (Hamden, Conn.: Archon, 1984); James Atlas, *Delmore Schwartz: The Life of an American Poet* (New York: Farrar, Straus and Giroux, 1977); William Chace, *Lionel Trilling: Criticism and Politics* (Stanford: Stanford University Press, 1980); Leonard Kriegel, *Edmund Wilson* (Carbondale: Southern Illinois University Press, 1971); Carolyn Geduld, *Bernard Wolfe* (New York: Twayne, 1972).

13. Lionel Abel, *The Intellectual Follies: A Memoir of the Literary Venture in New York and Paris* (New York: Norton, 1984); William Barrett, *The Truants: Adventures among the Intellectuals* (New York: Doubleday, 1982); Daniel Bell, "First Love and Early Sorrows," *Partisan Review* 47, no. 4 (1981): 293–98; Leslie Fiedler, "Bergen Street: 1933," *Being Busted* (New York: Stein and Day, 1969), pp. 11–28; Albert Halper, *Good-Bye Union Square* (New York: Quadrangle, 1970); Michael Harrington, *Fragments of the Century: A Social Autobiography* (New York: Dutton, 1973); Sidney Hook, "Breaking with the Communists—a Memoir," *Commentary* 77, no. 2 (February 1984): 47–53; Irving Howe, *A Margin of Hope: An Intellectual Autobiography* (New York: Harcourt Brace Jovanovich, 1982); Irving Kristol, "Memoirs of a Trotskyist," *New York Times Magazine*, 23 January 1977, pp. 42–43, 50–51, 54–57; George Novack, "My Philosophical Itinerary: An Autobiographical Foreword," *Polemics in Marxist Philosophy* (New York: Monad, 1978), pp. 11–37; William Phillips, *A Partisan View: Five Decades of the Literary Life* (New York: Stein and Day, 1983); Harry Roskolenko, *When I Was Last on Cherry Street* (New York: Stein and Day, 1965); Diana Trilling, "Lionel Trilling: A Jew at Columbia," in *Speaking of Literature and Society*, ed. Diana Trilling, pp. 411–29 (New York: Harcourt Brace Jovanovich, 1980); Lionel Trilling, Afterword to *The Unpossessed* by Tess Slesinger (New York: Avon, 1966), pp. 311–33; Bernard Wolfe, *Memoirs of a Not Altogether Shy Pornographer* (New York: Doubleday, 1972).

14. *New York Times Book Review*, 17 February 1974, p. 1.

15. Representative works of this school are Paul Buhle, "Jews and American Communism: The Cultural Question," *Radical History Review*, no. 23 (Spring 1980): 9–36; Vivian Gornick, *The Romance of American Communism* (New York: Basic Books, 1977); Maurice Isserman, *Which Side Were You On?: The American Communist Party during the Second World War* (Middletown, Conn.: Wesleyan University Press, 1982); Mark Naison, *Communists in Harlem during the Great Depression* (Champaign: University of Illinois Press, 1983). For a critical response to some of these writings, see Alan M. Wald, "Remembering the Answers," *Nation* 233, no. 22 (26 December 1981): 708–11; "Writers Congresses and the C. P.," ibid. 234, no. 9 (6 March 1982): 258; and "C. P. Ups and Downs," ibid. 234, no. 23 (12 June 1982): 728–31.

16. See, for example, Terry A. Cooney's "Cosmopolitan Values and the Identification of Reaction: *Partisan Review* in the 1930s," *Journal of American History* 68, no. 3 (December 1981): 580–98, which depicts the political trajectory of the magazine's editors as evolving from pro-Commu-

nism prior to 1936 to "anti-Stalinism" after 1937, without clearly explaining that the specific content of their "anti-Stalinism" went through marked changes as well.

17. O'Neill, *A Better World*, pp. 75–97.

18. Pells, *The Liberal Mind in a Conservative Age*, pp. 76–83.

19. James Atlas, "The Changing World of the New York Intellectuals," *New York Times Magazine*, 25 August 1985, p. 22.

20. Alexander Bloom, "The New York Intellectuals: The Formation of the Community" (Ph.D. diss., Boston College, 1979), pp. 1–13. See also the critique of *Prodigal Sons* by AW in *American-Jewish History* 76, no. 1 (September 1986): 86–90.

21. James Burnham and Max Shachtman, "Intellectuals in Retreat," *New International* 5, no. 1 (January 1939): 3–21. Among those said to be "known to a considerable public" as "the Trotskyist intellectuals" are Sidney Hook, Edmund Wilson, Philip Rahv, and James T. Farrell.

22. Daniel Aaron, "The Treachery of Recollection: The Inner and Outer History," *Carleton Miscellany* 6, no. 3 (Summer 1965): 15.

23. Dwight Macdonald, "The Burnhamian Revolution," *Partisan Review* 9, no. 1 (January–February 1942): 77.

24. Floyd Dell to Max Eastman, 12 November 1953, Eastman Papers, LL. See also David Peck's documentation of the way recent memoirs and anthologies from the 1930s have been altered to accord with later judgments: "'The Orgy of Apology': The Recent Revaluation of Literature of the Thirties," *Science and Society* 32, no. 4 (Fall 1968): 371–82.

25. Emanuel Geltman expressed the view in a May 1981 interview in New York City that the Trotskyists suppressed Jewish identity, and Leslie Fiedler stated in a May 1981 interview in Buffalo that he "cheered" German victories when he was a young Trotskyist at the outset of World War II. However, Peter Seidman's *Socialists and the Fight against Anti-Semitism* (New York: Pathfinder, 1973) contains substantial documentation of Trotskyist activities against anti-Semitism in the 1930s. See also Irving Howe's comments on the records of Trotsky in the 1930s and the Workers Party in the 1940s vis-à-vis "the Jewish question," in *Commentary* 76, no. 3 (September 1983): 4–6.

26. Sidney Hook, "Remembering Whittaker Chambers," *Encounter* 46, no. 1 (January 1976): 78–89; Sidney Hook and Diana Trilling, "Remembering Whittaker Chambers: An Exchange between Diana Trilling and Sidney Hook," *Encounter* 46, no. 6 (June 1976): 94–96.

27. *Socialism in Our Time* (New York: Thomas and Nelson Independent Committee, 1936), p. 29.

28. W. Phelps, "*Class*-ical Culture," *Communist* 7, no. 1 (January 1933): 93–96.

29. This information was provided in a 29 January 1974 letter from James T. Farrell to AW, and it was confirmed in a 4 February 1985 letter from Sidney Hook to AW. Notice of Rahv's expulsion from the Communist Party appears in *Daily Worker*, 19 October 1937, p. 2.

30. Phillips, *A Partisan View*, p. 44.

31. Dwight Macdonald to Leon Trotsky, 23 August 1937, HL. See also Philip Rahv to Leon Trotsky, 1 March 1938, HL.

32. In the 4 February 1939 issue of *Socialist Appeal*, Phillips is listed on page four as speaking in a series at the Marxist School that featured leaders of the Socialist Workers Party in conjunction with the *Partisan Review*.

33. Phillips, *A Partisan View*, p. 51.

34. "Politics and *Partisan Review*," *Partisan Review* 4, no. 3 (February 1938): 62.

35. Barrett, *The Truants*, pp. 156–57.

36. A contemporary exposition and defense of Trotsky's concept is Michael Löwy's *The Politics of Combined and Uneven Development: The Theory of Permanent Revolution* (London: Verso, 1981).

37. Barrett, *The Truants*, p. 85.

38. Ibid., p. 210.

39. Michiko Kakutani, "An Inside 'Outsider' Recalls Postwar Intellectuals," *New York Times*, 24 May 1982, p. C3.

40. Barrett, *The Truants*, p. 8.

41. See Philip Rahv, "Proletarian Literature: A Political Autopsy," in *Essays on Literature and Politics, 1932–72*, ed. Arabel J. Porter and Andrew J. Dvosin, pp. 292–308 (Boston: Houghton Mifflin, 1978).

42. Barrett, *The Truants*, p. 77.

43. Ibid., pp. 87–88.

44. James Burnham, "Lenin's Heir," *Partisan Review* 12, no. 1 (Winter 1945): 61–72.

45. Midge Decter, "Socialism and Its Irresponsibilities: The Case of Irving Howe," *Commentary* 74, no. 6 (December 1982): 25–32.

46. George B. de Huszar, ed., *The Intellectuals* (Glencoe, Ill.: Free Press, 1960), pp. 52–80.

47. Michael Löwy, *Georg Lukács: From Romanticism to Bolshevism* (London: New Left Books, 1979), p. 15.

48. Antonio Gramsci, *Prison Notebooks* (New York: International, 1971), p. 9.

49. James Gilbert, "The Voice of Dissent from a Left Outsider," *In These Times*, 12–18 January 1983, p. 18.

CHAPTER I

1. Isaac Deutscher, *The Non-Jewish Jew and Other Essays* (New York: Oxford, 1968), p. 33.

2. A good synopsis of different views on the sources of Jewish radicalism is contained in Allen Guttman's *The Jewish Writer in America* (New York: Oxford, 1971), pp. 134–37. See also Lawrence H. Fuchs, "Sources of Jewish Internationalism and Liberalism," in *The Jews: Social Patterns of an American Group*, ed. Marshall Sklare, pp. 595–613 (New York: Free Press,

1958); Arthur Liebman, *Jews and the Left* (New York: Wiley, 1978); Jack Nusan Porter and Peter Dreier, "The Roots of Jewish Radicalism," *Jewish Radicalism* (New York: Grove, 1973), pp. xv–liv; Peter I. Rose, ed., *The Ghetto and Beyond* (New York: Random House, 1969); Stephen J. Whitfield, "The Legacy of Radicalism," *Jews in American Life and Thought* (Hamden, Conn.: Archon, 1984), pp. 73–96.

3. Isaac Deutscher, *The Non-Jewish Jew and Other Essays*, p. 27.

4. Sidney Hook to AW, 28 December 1978.

5. John Higham, *Send These to Me* (New York: Atheneum, 1975), p. 196.

6. Horace Kallen, "Democracy versus the Melting Pot," *Nation* 100 (1915): 191–94, 217–20. Allen Guttman discusses the possible influence of Kallen on Mordecai Kaplan and others in *The Jewish Writer in America*, pp. 93–100.

7. Randolph Bourne, "Transnational America," *Atlantic Monthly* 128 (July 1916): 86–97.

8. Randolph Bourne, "The Jew and Transnational America," *Menorah Journal* 2 (December 1916): 277–84. This was a speech to the Harvard Menorah Society.

9. The following provide useful background on the *Menorah Journal*: Robert Alter, "Epitaph for a Jewish Magazine," *Commentary* 39, no. 5 (1965): 51–55; Henry Hurwitz, [untitled foreword], *Menorah Journal* 14, no. 1 (1928): 1; Jenna Weissman Joseliet, "Without Ghettoism: A History of the Intercollegiate Menorah Association, 1906–1930," *American Jewish Archives* 30, no. 2 (November 1978): 133–54; Horace Kallen, "The Promise of the Menorah Idea," *Menorah Journal* 69, nos. 1–2 (1962): 9–12; Mark Krupnick, "The *Menorah Journal* Group and the Origins of Modern Jewish-American Radicalism," *Studies in Jewish-American Literature* 5, no. 2 (1979; joint issue with *Yiddish* 4, no. 1): 56–67; Norman Podhoretz, *Making It* (New York: Random House, 1967); Leo Schwartz, Foreword to *The Menorah Treasury* (Philadelpia: Jewish Publications Society, 1964), pp. vii–x; Lionel Trilling, Afterword to *The Unpossessed* by Tess Slesinger (New York: Avon, 1966); Alan M. Wald, "The *Menorah* Group Moves Left," *Jewish Social Studies* 38, nos. 3–4 (Summer–Fall 1976): 289–320. Henry Hurwitz (1886–1961) immigrated from Lithuania to Massachusetts and was educated at Harvard University where he helped found the first Menorah Society.

10. Robert Alter, "Epitaph for a Jewish Magazine," p. 52.

11. Author's telephone interview with Elsa-Ruth Cohen Herron, 5 November 1983, Truro, Cape Cod, Mass.

12. This point was emphasized by both Felix Morrow and Lionel Trilling in their comments on a draft version of the essay "The *Menorah* Group Moves Left" by AW.

13. Elliot Cohen, "The Menorah Summer School," *Menorah Journal* 9, no. 4 (October 1923): 339–45. In this report on school activities, Cohen refers to Kallen as one of the teachers.

14. Trilling, Afterword to *The Unpossessed*, p. 320.

15. Ibid., pp. 327–28.

16. Ibid., p. 313. Similar sentiments are expressed in a letter from Herbert Solow to Elliot Cohen, 23 December 1929, Solow Papers, HIL.

17. This was noted by Morrow on a draft of "The *Menorah* Group Moves Left" by AW.

18. Elinor Grumet, "The Apprenticeship of Lionel Trilling," *Prooftexts* 4, no. 2 (May 1984): 164.

19. Lionel Trilling, contribution to "Under Forty," *Contemporary Jewish Record* 7, no. 1 (February 1944): 15–17.

20. Lionel Trilling, "From the Notebooks of Lionel Trilling," *Partisan Review* 51, no. 4 and 52, no. 5 (Double Issue, Fall 1984 and Winter 1985): 496.

21. Trilling, Afterword to *The Unpossessed*, p. 316.

22. Trilling, "Under Forty," p. 17.

23. Lionel Trilling, Introduction to *The Immediate Experience* by Robert Warshow (New York: Atheneum, 1975), p. 14.

24. This and the following biographical facts are drawn mainly from Edward Joseph Shoben, Jr.'s *Lionel Trilling: Mind and Character* (New York: Ungar, 1981), pp. 11–14; and Diana Trilling, "Lionel Trilling: A Jew at Columbia," in *Speaking of Literature and Society*, ed. Diana Trilling, pp. 411–29 (New York: Harcourt Brace Jovanovich, 1980).

25. Lionel Trilling, "Impediments," *Menorah Journal* 11, no. 3 (June 1925): 286.

26. Ibid.

27. Lionel Trilling to AW, 10 June 1974.

28. Trilling, ed., *Speaking of Literature and Society*, p. 20.

29. Lionel Trilling, "Notes on a Departure," *Menorah Journal* 16, no. 5 (May 1925): 421–34.

30. Trilling, "Under Forty," p. 17.

31. Ibid., p. 15. For other discussions of Trilling's Jewish identity see Edward Alexander, "Lionel Trilling," *Midstream* 19, no. 3 (March 1983): 48–57; Thomas H. Samet, "The Social Imagination," in "The Problematic Self: Lionel Trilling and the Anxieties of the Modern" (Ph.D. diss., Brown University, 1980), pp. 1–43; Mark Shechner, "The Elusive Trilling," *Nation*, 17 September 1977, pp. 247–50, and ibid., 24 September 1977, pp. 278–80.

32. Herbert Solow to Elliot Cohen, 23 December 1929, Solow Papers, HIL.

33. Anne Solow to AW, 28 August 1978.

34. Interview with Sylvia Salmi, June 1975, Ajijic, Mexio. The details of Solow's college matriculation and graduation are contained in his Columbia College transcripts, copies of which are in Solow Papers, HIL.

35. Mark Van Doren, "Jewish Students I Have Known," *Menorah Journal* 13, no. 3 (June 1927): 264–68. The students in the article are unnamed, but in Mark Van Doren's 1958 autobiography he identified them as Henry Rosenthal, Clifton Fadiman, Meyer Schapiro, John Gassner, Louis Zukofsky, Herbert Solow, Lionel Trilling, and Charles Prager. See also Whittaker

Chambers, "Morningside," in *Cold Friday* (New York: Random House, 1964), pp. 91–144.

36. Felix Morrow to AW, 2 October 1975.

37. However, in a 24 December 1975 letter from Meyer Schapiro to AW, Schapiro emphasizes the importance of both *The Unpossessed* and Van Doren's recollection as valuable documents in relation to understanding Solow.

38. Sidney Hook to AW, 20 October 1975.

39. See Eleanor Clark's contribution to *Herbert Solow: Memorial Service at Community Church, November 30, 1964* (New York: Luce Foundation, 1964), and Eleanor Clark to AW, 13 August 1974.

40. Herbert Solow to Elliot Cohen, 23 December 1939, Solow Papers, HIL.

41. Felix Morrow to AW, 14 July 1975.

42. Sidney Hook, contribution to *Herbert Solow: Memorial Service*.

43. Solow's changing sentiments are recorded in two letters written in Jerusalem on 21 November 1929. One is addressed to Tess Slesinger and the other (never sent) to the editors of the *Menorah Journal*. The anti-Zionist *Menorah Journal* articles are "The Sixteenth Zionist Congress," 17, no. 1 (October 1929): 23–40; "The Era of the Agency Begins," 17, no. 2 (November 1929): 111–25; "The Realities of Zionism," 19, no. 2 (November–December 1930): 97–127; "Camouflaging Zionist Realities," 19, no. 3 (March 1931): 223–41.

44. Born in San Francisco in 1877, Magnes had achieved notoriety among American radicals for his militant opposition to World War I. Praised by pro-Bolshevik writers such as Max Eastman and Joseph Freeman, Magnes became sympathetic to the Russian Revolution during its early years. Arriving in Palestine in 1922, Magnes began to organize the Hebrew University, serving first as chancellor and then as president. During the time that Solow was briefly in Palestine (late 1929), Magnes had begun to achieve notoriety of a new kind. Sparked by the violence of 1929, he openly opposed official Zionist policy and began agitating for a binational cultural state in Palestine based on Arab-Jewish cooperation, joint ownership of the land, and the restriction of Jewish immigration. Although Solow's first encounter with Magnes erupted in a personal conflict—due probably to a misunderstanding by Magnes of Solow's motives in interviewing him—as late as the 1940s Solow remained attracted to Magnes's ideas and identified with the Ihud (Union) Association formed by Magnes in 1942. A summary of Magnes's political activities during World War I is contained in the chapter "The Pacifism of Judah L. Magnes" in Zosa Szajkowski, *Jews, Wars, and Communism* (New York: Ktav Publishing House, 1972), 1:79–102. Magnes's views on Palestine can be found in the following sources: Martin Buber, Judah L. Magnes, and Moses Smilansky, *Palestine: A Bi-National State* (New York: Ihud Publishing Association, 1946); Martin Buber, Judah L. Magnes, and E. Simon, *Towards Union in Palestine* (Westport, Conn.: Greenwood Press, 1972).

45. Solow wrote the Board of Directors informing them that Hurwitz was

trying to lead the magazine back to its conservative days before the advent of Cohen. He also charged Hurwitz with having spread the false story that Cohen had quit the *Menorah Journal* because he could not print material exclusively of his own viewpoint. See the following correspondence in the Solow Papers at HIL: Hurwitz to Solow, 18 June 1931; Solow to Hurwitz, 19 June 1931; Solow to Hurwitz, 21 June 1931; Hurwitz to Solow, 23 June 1931; Solow to Board of Directors, *Menorah Journal*, 12 October 1931; Hurwitz to Solow, 12 November 1931.

46. Lionel Trilling, "On the Death of a Friend," *Commentary* 29, no. 2 (1960): 94.

47. George Novack to AW, 24 December 1978.

48. It is true that many Marxists, especially before the Holocaust, referred to themselves as "assimilationists" or as advocating "assimilation," but they obviously could not have meant this in the sense of taking on the dominant Christian bourgeois culture. They believed, somewhat naively, that cultural, religious, ethnic, racial, and even sexual oppression and antagonisms among working people would be reduced by a linear growth of class consciousness in the industrial countries of the West.

49. Herbert Solow to Board of Directors, *Menorah Journal*, 12 October 1931, Solow Papers, HIL.

CHAPTER 2

1. Sidney Hook, "Why I Am a Communist: Communism without Dogmas, a Reply by Sidney Hook," *Modern Monthly* 8, no. 3 (April 1934): 143.

2. Elliot Cohen, "The Age of Brass," *Menorah Journal* 11, no. 5 (October 1925): 425–47. This remarkable essay not only decries the superficial Jewish culture of the Jazz Age, calling for a complete reconstruction of Jewish intellectual values, but also expresses considerable cynicism about World War I and shows some identification with Afro-Americans.

3. See Louis Fischer, "Under the Soviet Regime," *Menorah Journal* 10, no. 1 (February 1924): 21–32, and "Jews in the U.S.S.R.," ibid. 11, no. 2 (April 1925): 172–77.

4. Mike Gold, "Portrait of My Mother," *Menorah Journal* 18, no. 1 (January 1930): 59–70.

5. Albert Halper, *Good-bye Union Square* (Chicago: Quadrangle, 1970), pp. 26–32.

6. Felix Morrow to AW, 29 May 1974.

7. *Menorah Journal* 16, no. 4 (May 1929): 448–55.

8. Ibid. 28, no. 2 (February 1930): 97–117.

9. Ibid. 18, no. 4 (April 1939): 346–56.

10. According to an interview conducted with Felix Morrow at Princeton in the early 1950s (authenticated by and used with the permission of Morrow), it was his radical essays in the *Symposium* that first caught the attention of Joseph Freeman, who subsequently tried to recruit him to the Communist Party.

11. Author's interview with Felix Morrow, December 1980, New York City.

12. Author's interview with George Novack, September 1973, Oakland, Calif.

13. Noted by Morrow on a draft of the essay "The *Menorah* Group Moves Left."

14. *New Masses* 8, no. 5 (December 1932): 25.

15. Ibid., no. 7 (February 1933): 22, 28–29.

16. Ibid., no. 9 (May 1933): 28.

17. Ibid., no. 8 (April 1933): 25.

18. Sidney Hook to AW, 1 August 1974.

19. Ibid., 15 September 1984.

20. Sidney Hook, "The Philosophy of Non-Resistance," *Open Court* 36, no. 1 (January 1922): 5.

21. Sidney Hook, "A Philosophical Dialogue," ibid. 36, no. 10 (October 1922): 621–26.

22. Sidney Hook to AW, 15 September 1984.

23. Sidney Hook, "The Philosophy of Dialectical Materialism," *Journal of Philosophy* 25 (1 March 1928): 113–24, and ibid. 25 (15 March 1928): 141–55. The debate between Hook and Eastman begins with ibid. 25 (16 August 1928): 475–76 and ibid. 25 (15 March 1928): 587–88.

24. Sidney Hook to AW, 15 September 1984, and unpublished manuscript by Hook, "Encounter with Espionage."

25. Sidney Hook to AW, 20 October 1975, and Felix Morrow to AW, 2 October 1975.

26. This was recorded in a notarized 12 November 1938 memo on Whittaker Chambers in the Solow Papers, HIL.

27. Herbert Solow, "Modern Education," *Nation* 134, no. 3486 (27 April 1932): 518; Henry Storm (pseud. for Herbert Solow), "The Crisis on the Campus," *New Masses* 7, no. 2 (June 1932): 12–14; leaflet, "A Call to a City-wide Conference on Students' Rights," with the following note from Sidney Hook: "I helped Herbert Solow organize this in 1933."

28. *New York Evening Post*, 6 October 1928, p. 9.

29. Undated memo by Herbert Solow, Solow Papers, HIL.

30. "A Discussion with Herbert Solow," in *Writings of Leon Trotsky, 1929–33 (Supplement)*, ed. George Breitman, pp. 137–47 (New York: Pathfinder, 1979).

31. Meyer Schapiro to AW, 24 December 1975; Sidney Hook, "Breaking with the Communists," *Commentary* 77, no. 2 (February 1984): 49. George Novack confirms the ignorance about Trotskyism of most in the group in his obituary for Solow, "A Representative Figure Dies," *Militant*, 14 December 1964, p. 4: "I can recall a meeting of the dissident intellectuals at the climax of the internal dispute with the Communist Party, when most of those present indignantly repudiated any friendliness for the 'Trotskyites' and warned Herbert that, if he or anyone else had anything to do with such rascally renegades, 'we would never speak to him again.'"

32. Biographical material on Rorty has been assembled from rough drafts

of his autobiography, "It Has Happened Here," and other materials in the Rorty Papers, OL, as well as from an 18 August 1974 letter to AW from Winifred Rorty. There are also numerous biographical references to Rorty in *The Selected Letters of Robinson Jeffers*, ed. Ann N. Ridgeway (Baltimore: Johns Hopkins University Press, 1968). See also Daniel Pope, *"His Master's Voice*: James Rorty and Advertising Ethics," paper presented at the annual meeting of the Popular Culture Association, Toronto, Ontario, 1984.

33. Biographical information on Walker was provided by Adelaide Walker in a 28 May 1980 interview with the author at Cape Cod, Mass.

34. Malcolm Cowley, *The Dream of the Golden Mountains: Remembering the 1930s* (New York: Penguin, 1980), p. 57.

35. "Writers Form a Defense Committee," *New Masses* 7, no. 1 (June 1931): 22.

36. Unsigned article [probably by Herbert Solow], "The Intellectual Revolt against Stalinist Hooliganism," *Militant*, 10 March 1934, p. 4; Michiko Kakutani, "Diana Trilling, Pathfinder in Morality," *New York Times*, 16 November 1981, p. C13.

37. Cohen's pamphlet was reviewed by Grace Hutchins in *New Masses* 8, no. 1 (August 1932): 22.

38. Author's telephone interview with Davis Herron, November 1983, Truro, Cape Cod, Mass.; letter from Leon Trotsky to National Committee, Communist League of America, 2 October 1933.

39. Rorty, manuscript of "It Has Happened Here," Rorty Papers, OL.

40. Ibid.

41. Ibid.; see also Malcolm Cowley, *The Dream of the Golden Mountains*, pp. 15–16; Matthew Josephson, *Infidel in the Temple: A Memoir of the Nineteen-Thirties* (New York: Knopf, 1967), pp. 154–55; materials on League of Professionals in the Corey Papers, BL.

42. Rorty, manuscript of "It Has Happened Here," Rorty Papers, OL.

43. Ibid. For Cowley's version of the dissolution of the League, see *The Dream of the Golden Mountains*, pp. 124–26.

44. Author's interview with Felix Morrow, 29 December 1980, New York City; author's interview with George Novack, 5 August 1981, Oberlin, Ohio; Hook to AW, 15 December 1977.

45. These events are summarized from the author's interview with Felix Morrow, 29 December 1980, Princeton, N.J.; John McDonald to AW, 18 November 1974; letter of resignation to Joshua Kunitz, 8 May 1933; Joshua Kunitz to Albert Margolies, 19 May 1933; copy of resolution passed by meeting of National Committee of NCDPP on 28 April 1933; and Herbert Solow to Charles and Adelaide Walker, 16 May 1933. The last four items are in the Solow Papers, HIL.

46. George Novack, "Max Shachtman: A Political Portrait," *International Socialist Review* 34, no. 2 (February 1973): 26.

47. Author's interview with George Novack, August 1975, Oberlin, Ohio.

48. Letter to the *New Masses* 10, no. 10 (6 March 1934): 8–9.

49. "To John Dos Passos," ibid.

50. *New Masses* 10, no. 12 (20 March 1934): 21.

51. Editorial, "A United Front—with Whom?," ibid., p. 6.

52. Editorial, "Unintelligent Fanaticism," ibid. 10, no. 13 (27 March 1934): 6.

53. Isidor Schneider, "The Splitting Tactic," ibid., p. 24.

54. *Menorah Journal* 19, no. 4 (June 1931): 472.

55. *Modern Quarterly* 6, no. 2 (Summer 1932): 109.

56. Murray Kempton, *Part of Our Time* (New York: Delta, 1955), p. 122.

57. See the following reviews: J. Donald Adams, *New York Times*, 20 May 1934, p. 6; Robert Cantwell, *New Outlook*, no. 163 (June 1934): 53; Joseph Freeman, *Daily Worker*, 2 June 1934, p. 7; Lewis Gannett, *New York Herald Tribune*, 10 May 1934, p. 10; Horace Gregory, *New York Tribune Books*, 13 May 1934, p. 2; T. S. Matthews, *New Republic*, 23 May 1934, p. 52; Ferner Nuhn, *Nation* 138, no. 3594 (23 May 1934): 597–98; George Stevens, *Saturday Review of Literature* 10 (19 May 1934): 701.

58. Biographical information about Slesinger has been summarized from the following: Lionel Trilling, Afterword to *The Unpossessed* by Tess Slesinger (New York: Avon, 1966), pp. 311–33; Janet Sharistanian, Afterword to *The Unpossessed* by Tess Slesinger (Old Westbury, N.Y.: Feminist Press, 1984), pp. 359–86; Shirley Biagi, "Forgive Me for Dying," *Antioch Review* 35, nos. 2–3 (Spring–Summer 1977): 224–36; *Menorah Journal*, passim 1928–31; author's interview with Dorothy Eisner McDonald, June 1978, New York City.

59. "Mother to Dinner," *Menorah Journal* 18, no. 3 (March 1930): 221–34; "The Friedman's Annie," ibid. 19, no. 3 (March 1931): 242–60. Both were reprinted in her collection, *Time: The Present: A Book of Short Stories* (New York: Simon and Schuster, 1935), which was reissued as *On Being Told That Her Second Husband Has Taken His First Lover and Other Stories* (New York: Quadrangle, 1974).

60. Trilling, Afterword to *The Unpossessed*, p. 313.

61. Eugene Lyons, *The Red Decade* (New York: Bobbs-Merrill, 1941), pp. 254, 289, 291, 321.

62. Peter Davis to AW, 22 June 1977; Louis Berg to AW, 24 March 1976.

63. *New Masses* 11, no. 9 (September 1934): 26–27.

64. *Menorah Journal* 22, no. 3 (Autumn 1934): 189.

65. Sharistanian, Afterword to *The Unpossessed* (Feminist Press ed.), p. 377. See also Tess Slesinger's "Memoirs of an Ex-Flapper," *Vanity Fair* 43 (December 1934): 26–27, 74, 76.

66. Biagi, "Forgive Me for Dying," pp. 226–27.

67. *The Unpossessed*, p. 330.

68. Trilling, Afterword to *The Unpossessed*, p. 314.

69. *The Unpossessed*, p. 175.

70. Ibid., p. 53.

71. Trilling, Afterword to *The Unpossessed*, p. 328.

72. *Commentary* 42, no. 1 (July 1966): 16–17.

73. *The Unpossessed,* p. 122.
74. Ibid., p. 33.

CHAPTER 3

1. *New Masses* 25, no. 4 (19 October 1937): 21.
2. Biographical information on Philip Rahv has been assembled from the following: Andrew J. Dvosin, "Literature in a Political World: The Career and Writings of Philip Rahv" (Ph.D. diss., New York University, 1977); James B. Gilbert, *Writers and Partisans* (New York: Wiley, 1968); and Mary McCarthy, "Philip Rahv, 1908–1973," *New York Times Book Review,* 17 February 1974, sec. 7, pp. 1–2.
3. Philip Rahv, "An Open Letter to Young Writers," *Rebel Poet* 6 (September 1932): 4.
4. Biographical information on William Phillips is based primarily on William Phillips, *A Partisan View* (New York: Stein and Day, 1983), and author's interview with William Phillips, November 1973, New York City.
5. W. Phelps [pseud. of William Phillips], "*Class*-ical Culture," *Communist* 12, no. 1 (January 1933): 94. William Phillips was so close to the party in the early 1930s that many radical intellectuals believed he was a member. See James Burnham to Leon Trotsky, 30 April 1937, Trotsky Papers, HL.
6. William Phillips, "Categories for Criticism," *Symposium* 4, no. 1 (January 1933): 31–47.
7. "We propose to concentrate on creative and critical literature," states the first editorial in *Partisan Review* 1, no. 1 (February–March 1934): 2. See also William Phillips and Philip Rahv, "In Retrospect: Ten Years of *Partisan Review,*" *The Partisan Reader* (New York: Dial, 1946), p. 679.
8. Wallace Phelps and Philip Rahv, "Criticism," *Partisan Review* 2, no. 7 (April–May 1935); Philip Rahv, "A Season in Heaven," *Partisan Review and Anvil* 3, no. 5 (June 1936): 11–14.
9. Wallace Phelps, "Three Generations," *Partisan Review* 1, no. 4 (September–October 1934): 51.
10. Wallace Phelps and Philip Rahv, "Problems and Perspectives in Revolutionary Literature," *Partisan Review* 1, no. 3 (June–July 1934): 4.
11. Ibid., p. 5.
12. Ibid., pp. 5, 6.
13. Phelps and Rahv, "Criticism," p. 3.
14. Wallace Phelps, "Form and Content," *Partisan Review* 2, no. 6 (January–February 1935): 31–39. The theme of the relationship between form and content was a major preoccupation of Phillips. A provocative development of this issue appears in "Sensibility and Modern Poetry," *Dynamo* 1 (Summer 1934): 20–25.
15. Philip Rahv, "How the Wasteland Became a Flower Garden," *Partisan Review* 1, no. 4 (September–October 1934): 37–41.

16. Phelps, "Three Generations," p. 51.

17. Phelps and Rahv, "Problems and Perspectives," p. 3. In "How the Waste Land Became a Flower Garden," p. 38, Rahv describes Max Eastman as "politically degenerate and full of venom"; on p. 39, he cites Stalin, Dimitrov, and Thaelmann as heroes of the workers.

18. Malcolm Cowley, "Thirty Years Later: Memories of the First American Writers' Congress," *American Scholar* 35, no. 3 (Summer 1966): 497.

19. The merger is discussed in Mike Gold's article "Papa Anvil and Mother Partisan," *New Masses* 13, no. 6 (18 February 1936): 22–23.

20. Philip Rahv, "Two Years of Progress," *Partisan Review* 4, no. 3 (February 1938): 22–30.

21. Philip Rahv, "Proletarian Literature: A Political Autopsy," *Southern Review* 4 (1940): 617.

22. More detailed biographical information about Farrell can be found in Edgar M. Branch, *James T. Farrell* (New York: Twayne, 1971), and Alan M. Wald, *James T. Farrell: The Revolutionary Socialist Years* (New York: New York University Press, 1978).

23. James T. Farrell to AW, 5 November 1978. Between his arrival in New York City in 1932 and 1935, Farrell was frequently out of the city and too preoccupied with his writing career to pay much attention to the struggle between the Communist Party and the dissident intellectuals. When the League of Professionals for Foster and Ford was formed in 1932, he was so little known that no one thought to ask him to sign.

24. Ibid.

25. James T. Farrell, *Judgment Day* (New York: Avon, 1973), p. 424.

26. Ibid., p. 310. Some useful studies of the *Studs Lonigan* trilogy include Ann Douglas, "*Studs Lonigan* and the Failure of History in Mass Society," *American Quarterly* 29 (Fall 1977): 487–505; Henry Hopper Dyer, "James T. Farrell's Studs Lonigan and Danny O'Neill Novels" (Ph.D. diss., University of Pennsylvania, 1965); Blanche H. Gelfant, *The American City Novel* (Norman: University of Oklahoma Press, 1954), pp. 175–227; Josephine Herbst, "James T. Farrell's *Judgment Day*," *New Masses* 15 (25 May 1935): 25–26; Richard Mitchell, "*Studs Lonigan*: Research in Morality," *Centennial Review* 6 (Spring 1962): 202–14; Charles C. Walcutt, *American Literary Naturalism: A Divided Stream* (Minneapolis: University of Minnesota Press, 1956), pp. 240–57.

27. Biographical information has been assembled from an author's interview with F. W. Dupee, August 1973, Carmel, Calif., and from Mary McCarthy, "On F. W. Dupee (1904–1979)," *New York Review of Books*, 27 October 1983, pp. 19–20, 22.

28. Frederick Dupee, excerpt from letter, *Symposium* 3, no. 3 (July 1932): 386–87; review of *Axel's Castle*, ibid. 2, no. 2 (April 1931): 264–67.

29. James Burnham to Leon Trotsky, 30 April 1938, Trotsky Papers, HL.

30. Newton Arvin to F. W. Dupee, 8 June 1937, Dupee Papers, BL.

31. The essential biographical material was recorded by Wilson in "What I Believe," *Nation* 134, no. 3473 (27 January 1932): 95–98. It was reprinted

in *The American Jitters* (New York: Scribner's, 1932), pp. 304–13, but it was unfortunately omitted when these articles were reissued in *The American Earthquake* (New York: Doubleday, 1958).

32. Wilson, *The American Earthquake*, pp. 152–60.

33. Helpful estimates of Wilson's critical achievement include Frederick Crews, "Lesson of the Master," *New York Review of Books*, 25 November 1965, pp. 4–5; F. W. Dupee, "Wilson without Reputation," *New York Review of Books*, 7 November 1966, pp. 3–5; Stanley Edgar Hyman, *The Armed Vision* (New York: Knopf, 1948), pp. 19–48; Leonard Kriegel, *Edmund Wilson* (Carbondale: Southern Illinois University Press, 1971).

34. Edmund Wilson, "An Appeal to Progressives," *The Shores of Light* (New York: Vintage, 1952), p. 532.

35. Wilson, "What I Believe," pp. 96–97.

36. Ibid., p. 98.

37. Edmund Wilson, "The Literary Class War: II," *New Republic* 70, no. 910 (11 May 1932): 349. This second part of a longer article was deleted when Wilson reprinted the first part in *The Shores of Light*, pp. 534–39. Philip Rahv wrote a response to Wilson, also called "The Literary Class War," *New Masses* 8, no. 2 (August 1932): 7–10.

38. Useful information about Wilson's association with *Modern Monthly* and the American Workers Party can be found in Haim Genizi, "Edmund Wilson and the *Modern Monthly*, 1934–5: A Phase in Wilson's Radicalism," *Journal of American Studies* 7, no. 3 (December 1973): 301–19. Some additional details about Wilson's political activities in the early 1930s can be found in Edmund Wilson, *Letters on Literature and Politics, 1912–1972* (New York: Farrar, Straus and Giroux, 1977), and Edmund Wilson, *The Thirties* (New York: Farrar, Straus and Giroux, 1980). A fuller account is contained in Daniel Aaron, "Edmund Wilson's Political Decade," in *Literature at the Barricades: The American Writer in the 1930s*, ed. Ralph F. Bogardus and Fred Hobson, pp. 175–86 (University: University of Alabama Press, 1982).

39. Edmund Wilson, "Trotsky," *New Republic* 73 (4 January 1933): 207–9, and "Trotsky II," ibid. (11 January 1933): 235–38.

40. Baruch Knei-Paz, *The Social and Political Thought of Leon Trotsky* (Oxford: Oxford, 1978), p. 10; Norman Geras, "Literature of Revolution," *New Left Review*, nos. 113–14 (January–April 1979): 4.

41. Irving Howe, *Steady Work* (New York: Harcourt, Brace and World, 1966), p. 119. Howe's striking characterization of Trotsky's attitude toward writing appears in the essay, "Trotsky: The Costs of History," written as the introduction to *The Basic Writings of Trotsky* (New York: Random House, 1963), pp. 3–39. When Howe revised and expanded this essay as part of *Leon Trotsky* (New York: Viking, 1978), this section was dropped.

42. Quoted in Paul N. Siegel, *Leon Trotsky on Literature and Art* (New York: Pathfinder, 1970), p. 9.

43. The most useful collection of Trotsky's literary criticism is in Siegel's *Leon Trotsky on Literature and Art*. Most books about Trotsky refer to his

collaboration with the surrealist André Breton, but, as Jean van Heijenoort records in *With Trotsky in Exile* (Cambridge, Mass.: Harvard University Press, 1978), Trotsky's knowledge of and interest in surrealism were fairly limited, despite his openness to experimental art. Above all, he preferred to read French realistic novels.

44. Siegel, *Leon Trotsky on Literature and Art*, p. 104.

45. Ibid., p. 106.

46. Naomi Allen and George Breitman, eds., *Writings of Leon Trotsky* (New York: Pathfinder, 1937–38), pp. 114–15.

47. George Breitman and Sarah Lovell, eds., *Writings of Leon Trotsky [1932–33]* (New York: Pathfinder, 1973), p. 299.

48. Mike Gold, *The Hollow Men* (New York: International, 1941), p. 21.

49. Jay Martin, *Nathanael West: The Art of His Life* (New York: Hayden, 1971), p. 257.

50. A useful survey of European Marxist critiques of modernism is Eugene Lunn, *Marxism and Modernism: An Historical Study of Lukács, Brecht, Benjamin and Adorno* (Berkeley: University of California Press, 1982).

51. Branch, *James T. Farrell*, pp. 118–21, 163.

52. See the following: "Ripostes," *Partisan Review* 4, no. 1 (December 1937): 74; unsigned editorial, *New Masses* 24, no. 2 (14 September 1937): 9–10; Michael Gold, "A Literary Snake Sheds His Skin for Trotsky," *Daily Worker*, 12 October 1937, p. 7; unsigned article, "Trotskyist Schemers Exposed," ibid., 19 October 1937, p. 2; V. J. Jerome, "No Quarter to Trotskyists—Literary or Otherwise," ibid., p. 6. The "Trotzskyist Schemers Exposed" article announces that Rahv and Dupee have been expelled from the party and accuses them of providing "services to the fascists" by trying to depict Marxism as foreign. In V. J. Jerome's article, he also identifies James T. Farrell and Lionel Abel as Trotskyists.

CHAPTER 4

1. "Avant trente ans revolutionnaire, après canaille." Quoted by Trotsky in George Breitman and Sarah Lovell, eds., *Writings of Leon Trotsky [1932–33]* (New York: Pathfinder, 1972), p. 331.

2. Author's interview with George Novack, June 1976, New York City.

3. Additional details about the relations between the CLA and AWP can be found in James P. Cannon, *History of American Trotskyism* (New York: Pioneer, 1944), pp. 169–88.

4. *Militant*, 10 March 1934, p. 4.

5. Ibid., 17 March 1934, p. 3.

6. Ibid., 24 March 1934, p. 3.

7. Herbert Solow to Norman Thomas, 16 May 1934; Norman Thomas to Herbert Solow, 26 May 1934; Herbert Solow to Roger Baldwin, 13 Decem-

ber 1935; memorandum on discussion of labor defense, 25 September 1934; all in Solow Papers, HIL.

8. Articles and leaflets on the Belussi case are preserved in the Solow Papers, HIL.

9. The Solow Papers, HIL, contain the following: an undated NPLD leaflet announcing that Carlo Tresca, James Rorty, Bertram D. Wolfe, Arne Swabeck, and others will speak against the use of the National Guard against strikers in Minnesota and Toledo; an undated leaflet by NPLD protesting the deportation of four German refugees from Holland, and a *Militant* article on the protest; an article dated 19 May 1935 (publication not named) concerning an NPLD demonstration against a pro-Hitler rally at Madison Square Garden, plus a letter from Solow protesting the arrests made and an article from the *New York Post*, 21 June 1934, about Solow's protest of the treatment of the demonstrators at night court. See also the NPLD program in the *Militant*, 28 December 1935, p. 4, and "Summary of One Year of Non-Partisan Labor Defense," ibid., 30 November 1935, p. 3.

10. Herbert Solow, "German Writers Say 'Yes,'" *Nation* 138, no. 3576 (17 January 1934): 64–65.

11. Herbert Solow, "The New York Hotel Strike," *Nation* 138, no. 3582 (28 February 1934): 239–30.

12. Author's interview with Farrell Dobbs, December 1977, Berkeley, Calif. See also Cannon, *History of American Trotskyism*, pp. 154–55; Farrell Dobbs, *Teamster Rebellion* (New York: Monad, 1972), pp. 105–6; William Brown to Herbert Solow, 14 September 1934, designating Solow an honorary member of Teamster Local 544 and praising him for services during the strike, Solow Papers, HIL.

13. See the following by Herbert Solow in the *Nation*: "War in Minneapolis," 139, no. 3605 (8 August 1934): 160–61; "Unionism at Stake," 139, no. 3608 (29 August 1934): 241; "Father Haas," 139, no. 3612 (26 September 1934): 52; "Once Again: Western Unionism," 139, no. 3621 (28 November 1934): 622–23; "Class War in Minnesota," 139, no. 3625 (26 December 1934): 743–44.

14. See L. D., "Split Looms in Workers Party," *Workers Age* 4, no. 28 (13 July 1935): 5, and undated letter from James Rorty to A. J. Muste, Rorty Papers, OL.

15. See Political Committee to Barney [*sic*] Strang, 8 January 1935, and Harry Strang to Political Committee, 11 January 1935, in possession of the author.

16. See the discussion of Muste's attitude in Jo Ann Ooiman Robinson's *Abraham Went Out: A Biography of A. J. Muste* (Philadelphia, Pa.: Temple University Press, 1981), pp. 58–60. See also Harold Isaacs to Leon Trotsky, 6 February 1936, Trotsky Papers, HL, and George Novack, "A. J. Muste and American Trotskyism," *Liberation* 12, nos. 9–10 (September–October 1967): 21–23.

17. John McDonald to AW, 18 November 1974. See the interpretations of the faction fight presented by Sidney Lens, *Unrepentant Radical: An*

American Activist's Account of Five Turbulent Decades (Boston: Beacon, 1980), pp. 42–44; Constance Ashton Myers, *The Prophet's Army: Trotsky-ists in America, 1928–41* (Westport, Conn.: Greenwood, 1977), pp. 115–22; and Cannon, *History of American Trotskyism*, pp. 189–215.

18. Information on B. J. Field comes from the following sources: Cannon, *History of American Trotskyism*, pp. 126–33, 146, 191; Myers, *The Proph-et's Army*, pp. 63–65; Paul Jacobs, *Is Curly Jewish?: A Political Self-Portrait Illuminating Three Turbulent Decades of Social Revolt, 1935–1965* (New York: Atheneum, 1965), pp. 79, 93, 96, 103; George Breitman, ed., *Writings of Leon Trotsky: Supplement [1929–33]* (New York: Pathfinder, 1979), pp. 149, 150–61, 167; author's telephone interview with Jesse Simons, 8 June 1985, New York City; author's telephone interview with Leona Finestone, 10 June 1985, New York City; William Krehm to AW, undated; author's telephone interview with Edward Sard, 24 September 1983, New York City; untitled article by B. J. Field in *New International Bulletin* 1, no. 3 (January 1936): 34–38.

19. See obituary, "Aristodimos Kaldis, 79, Is Dead; Artist Noted for His Landscapes," *New York Times*, 3 May 1979, p. 25, and William Khrem to AW, undated.

20. James P. Cannon, *Speeches to the Party: The Revolutionary Perspec-tive and the Revolutionary Party* (New York: Pathfinder, 1973), pp. 84–86.

21. This is the thesis of the influential article by M. S. Venkataramani, "Leon Trotsky's Adventure in American Radical Politics, 1935–37," *Inter-national Review of Social History* 9, pt. 1 (1964): 2–46.

22. Information on Harold Isaacs comes from author's interview with C. Frank Glass, 5 April 1983, Los Angeles, Calif., and *Contemporary Authors*, New Revision Series (Detroit: Gale, 1982), p. 347.

23. Harold Isaacs, "I Break with the Chinese Stalinists," *New Interna-tional* 5, no. 4 (September–October 1934): 76–78.

24. Harold Isaacs to Leon Trotsky, 6 February 1936 and 4 March 1936, Trotsky Papers, HL.

25. John McDonald to AW, 18 November 1974.

26. Lens, *Unrepentant Radical*, p. 42.

27. Herbert Solow to Margaret De Silver, undated, Solow Papers, HIL.

28. George Breitman to AW, 17 July 1985.

29. Author's interview with George Novack, June 1978, New York City.

30. Elliot Cohen, "Stalin Buries the Revolution—Prematurely," *Nation* 138, no. 359 (9 May 1934): 527–29.

31. Author's telephone interview with Elsa-Ruth Herron, 5 November 1983, Truro, Cape Cod, Mass.; Sylvia Cohen to AW, 29 August 1977.

32. Biographical information about V. F. Calverton has been assembled from the following: Haim Genizi, "Victor Francis Calverton: Independent Radical" (Ph.D. diss., City University of New York, 1968); notebooks of C. Hartley Grattan, June 1957, courtesy of Michael Blankfort; Sidney Hook, "*Modern Quarterly*, a Chapter in American Radical History; V. F. Calver-ton and His Periodicals," *Labor History* 10, no. 2 (Spring 1974): 250–73; author's interview with Michael Blankfort, July 1982, Los Angeles, Calif.

33. The most substantial of these was David Ramsay and Alan Calmer, "The Marxism of V. F. Calverton," *New Masses* 7, no. 6 (June 1933): 9–27. Earlier there was a two-part series by A. Landy, "Cultural Compulsives or Calverton's New Caricature of Marxism," in the *Communist* 10, no. 9 (October 1931): 851–57, and ibid. 10, no. 10 (November 1931): 941–59.

34. Useful details about changes in the editorial board are contained in Haim Genizi, "Edmund Wilson and the *Modern Monthly*," *Journal of American Studies* 7, no. 3 (December 1973): 301–19.

35. The most substantial studies of Eastman are Milton Cantor, *Max Eastman* (New York: Twayne, 1970); John P. Diggins, *Up from Communism: Conservative Odysseys in American Intellectual History* (New York: Harper and Row, 1975), pp. 17–73, 201–32; Stanton Lloyd, "Max Eastman: An Intellectual Portrait," Harvard Honors Essay, 1965; William L. O'Neill, *The Last Romantic: A Life of Max Eastman* (New York: Oxford, 1978).

36. See E. Solntstev to Leon Trotsky, March or April 1928, and Max Eastman to Leon Trotsky, 24 February 1933, Trotsky Papers, HL.

37. Max Eastman, *Love and Revolution: My Journey through an Epoch* (New York: Random House, 1964), p. 154.

38. For further details on Konikow, see Dianne Feeley, "Antoinette Konikow: Marxist and Feminist," *International Socialist Review* 33, no. 1 (January 1972): 42–46.

39. Cited in O'Neill, *The Last Romantic*, p. 183.

40. George Novack, "Trotsky's Views on Dialectical Materialism," *Leon Trotsky: The Man and His Work* (New York: Merit, 1969), p. 94.

41. See Isaac Deutscher, *The Prophet Unarmed* (New York: Vintage, 1959), p. 295.

42. Max Eastman, *Great Companions: Critical Memoirs of Some Famous Friends* (New York: Farrar, Straus and Cudahy, 1959), p. 169.

43. Max Eastman, *Marx, Lenin and the Science of Revolution* (London: George Allen and Unwin, 1926), p. 26.

44. Ibid., p. 63.

45. George Lichtheim, "The Romance of Max Eastman," *New York Review of Books*, 14 January 1965, p. 8.

46. James Burnham, "Max Eastman's Straw Man," *New International* 2, no. 7 (December 1935): 220–25.

47. See Edmund Wilson's important assessment, "Max Eastman in 1941," *Classics and Commercials* (New York: Vintage, 1962), pp. 57–69.

48. Burnham, "Max Eastman's Straw Man," p. 223.

49. Waldo Frank, "Socialism and Value," *Modern Quarterly* 5, no. 4 (Winter 1930–31): 448–50.

50. Sidney Hook, "Marxism, Metaphysics, and Modern Science," ibid., pp. 388–94.

51. Burnham, "Max Eastman's Straw Man," p. 225.

52. David Ernst, book review in *New International* 1, no. 4 (July 1934): 26; Thomas Cotton, ibid. 1, 7 (December 1934): 158.

53. See the following by Ruben Gotesky in *New International*: "Marx-

ism: Science or Method?," 1, no. 6 (October 1934): 147–51; "Marxism: Science or Method: The Historical Limits of the Materialist Conception of History," 2, no. 3 (March 1935): 71–73; "Marxism: Science or Method? Part II," 2, no. 5 (May 1935): 106–9. Some of Gotesky's arguments had been presented by Trotsky in an earlier exchange with Hook. See Sidney Hook, "Marxism—Dogma or Method?," *Nation* 136, no. 3532 (15 March 1933): 284–85, and "Correspondence: Trotzky and Sidney Hook," ibid. 137, no. 3548 (5 July 1933): 18–19.

54. Information about Rubin Gotesky is from a 26 October 1974 letter from Rubin Gotesky to AW; an August 1981 interview with James Gotesky in Oberlin, Ohio; and Ellen Schrenker, *No Ivory Tower: McCarthyism and the Universities* (New York: Oxford, 1986), p. 94.

55. Rubin Gotesky to AW, 26 October 1974.

56. For a first-rate analysis of peculiar features in the development of the United States see Mike Davis, "Why the U.S. Working Class Is Different," *New Left Review*, no. 123 (September–October 1980): 3–44.

57. See Marcel Liebman, *Leninism under Lenin* (London: Merlin, 1975), pp. 113–212.

58. See the useful discussion by Howard Brick in "The Crisis of Evolutionary Socialism: Daniel Bell and the Rise of Modernist Sociology" (Ph.D. diss., University of Michigan, 1983), pp. 168–69.

59. V. J. Jerome, who had sat in on some classes taught by Hook at New York University, published his polemic called "Unmasking an American Revisionist of Marxism" in *Communist* 12, no. 1 (January 1933): 50–82. Hook wrote a response and it was published with an extensive commentary by Earl Browder in two parts as "The Revisionism of Sidney Hook," ibid., no. 2 (February 1933): 133–46, and no. 3 (March 1933): 285–300. Hook's meeting with party officials to discuss his philosophical ideas is described in a letter to AW of 26 November 1984.

60. For Hook's views at the time of the fusion negotiations, see "Discussions between American Workers Party and the Communist League of America (Opposition)," 26 February 1934, in the Martin Abern Papers, Archives of Labor History and Urban Affairs, Wayne State University, Detroit, Mich. In a letter to AW of 4 February 1984, Hook explains that he did not join the new party because he wanted more time to write and also because he was fed up with factional disputes.

61. See *Socialism in Our Time* (New York: Thomas and Nelson Independent Committee, 1936).

62. Robert C. Tucker, *The Marx-Engels Reader* (New York: Norton, 1978), p. 5.

63. See the discussion of the views of Hook and Eastman in O'Neill's *The Last Romantic*, pp. 142–47.

64. Sebastiano Timpanaro, *On Materialism* (London: New Left Books, 1975), pp. 73–74.

CHAPTER 5

1. Philip Rahv, "Trials of the Mind," *Partisan Review* 4, no. 5 (April 1938): 10.

2. The most detailed study of the Moscow purge trials is Robert Conquest, *The Great Purge Trials* (New York: Oxford, 1978).

3. For a thoughtful analysis of this phenomenon see Frank A. Warren, *Liberals and Communism: The "Red Decade" Revisited* (Bloomington: Indiana University Press, 1966).

4. Malcolm Cowley, *And I Worked at the Writer's Trade: Chapters of a Literary History, 1918–1978* (New York: Viking, 1978), pp. 50–51.

5. Quoted in David Caute, *The Fellow-Travelers: A Postscript to the Enlightenment* (New York: Macmillan, 1973), p. 168.

6. Naomi Allen and George Breitman, eds., *Writings of Leon Trotsky [1937–38]* (New York: Pathfinder, 1976), p. 277.

7. James T. Farrell, "Dewey in Mexico," *Reflections at Fifty* (New York: Vanguard, 1954), p. 104.

8. George Novack, "Max Shachtman: A Political Portrait," *International Socialist Review* 34, no. 2 (February 1937): 29.

9. Author's interview with George Novack, August 1975, Oberlin, Ohio. See also the following letters in the Solow Papers, HIL: Solow to Tom Mooney, 4 February 1937; Solow to Clifton Fadiman, 19 February 1937; Solow to Lewis Mumford, 10 February 1937; Mumford to Solow, 20 February 1937; Solow to Mumford, 24 February 1937; Mumford to Solow, 25 February 1937; Solow to Mooney, 2 March 1937; Mumford to Solow, 18 March 1937.

10. Pierre Naville to Herbert Solow, 1 March 1937, Solow Papers, HIL.

11. John Dewey to Max Eastman, 12 May 1937, Dewey Papers, LL.

12. James T. Farrell to Margaret Marshall, 16 April 1937, Farrell Papers, CPVP.

13. John Dewey, *Truth Is on the March* (New York: American Committee for the Defense of Leon Trotsky, 1937), p. 11.

14. Author's interview with James T. Farrell, May 1976, New York City.

15. Eugene Lyons, *The Red Decade* (New York: Bobbs-Merrill, 1941), pp. 252–55.

16. Sidney Hook, "Some Memories of John Dewey," *Commentary* 14 (September 1952): 247.

17. Herbert Solow to Margaret De Silver, 2 April 1937, Solow Papers, HIL.

18. The biographical information on Bernard Wolfe is from an author's interview with Wolfe, August 1974, Hollywood, Calif.

19. Information on Benjamin Stolberg is based on a June 1980 author's interview with Suzanne La Follette, Palo Alto, Calif., and "Memoirs of Benjamin Stolberg," in Stolberg Papers, BL.

20. Author's interview with Suzanne La Follette, June 1980, Palo Alto, Calif.

21. For further details, see Dewey, *Truth Is on the March*, pp. 8–9.

22. John McDonald to AW, 5 December 1976.

23. Author's interview with Adelaide Walker, June 1982, Cape Cod, Mass.

24. Author's interview with James T. Farrell, May 1976, New York City.

25. Author's interview with Albert Glotzer, June 1980, Edgartown, Cape Cod, Mass.

26. Bernard Wolfe to AW, 18 May 1977.

27. Author's interview with George Novack, June 1976, New York City; see also George Novack, "How the Moscow Trials Were Exposed," *International Socialist Review* (May 1977): 3–4, 10.

28. John Dewey to Robbie Lowitz, 6 April 1937, Dewey Papers, LL.

29. *The Case of Leon Trotsky: Report of the Hearings on the Charges Made against Him in the Moscow Trials* (New York: Merit, 1968), pp. 1–2.

30. Herbert Solow to Margaret de Silver, 10 April 1937, Solow Papers, HIL.

31. John Dewey to Robbie Lowitz, 15 April 1937, Dewey Papers, LL.

32. James T. Farrell to Margaret Marshall, 16 April 1937, Farrell Papers, CPVP.

33. Albert Glotzer to AW, 16 March 1977.

34. Biographical information on Dwight Macdonald is from the author's interview with Dwight Macdonald, May 1973, Buffalo, N.Y.; Dwight Macdonald, *Politics Past* (New York: Viking, 1970); Norman Levy, "The Radicalization of Dwight Macdonald," M.A. thesis, University of Wisconsin, 1966; Stephen J. Whitfield, *A Critical American: The Politics of Dwight Macdonald* (Hamden, Conn.: Archon, 1984).

35. Dwight Macdonald, "Notes on Hollywood Directors," *Symposium* 4, no. 2 (March 1929): 159–68.

36. Dwight Macdonald, "Trotsky and the Russian Trials," *New Republic* 91, no. 1172 (19 May 1937): 49–50; William Phillips, "How *Partisan Review* Began," *Commentary* 62 (December 1976): 45.

37. Biographical information on Mary McCarthy is from the author's interview with Mary McCarthy, May 1978, Paris, France; Mary McCarthy, *On the Contrary: Articles of Belief, 1946–1961* (New York: Noonday, 1962); Doris Grumbach, *The Company She Kept: A Revealing Portrait of Mary McCarthy* (New York: Coward McCann, 1967).

38. Author's interview with Dwight Macdonald, November 1973, Buffalo, N.Y.

39. William Phillips, "The Esthetic of the Founding Fathers," *Partisan Review* 4 (March 1938): 17, 19.

40. Philip Rahv, "Twilight of the Thirties," *Partisan Review* 5 (Summer 1939): 15, 11.

41. Rahv, "Trials of the Mind," p. 10.

42. Leon Trotsky, "The Future of *Partisan Review* : A Letter to Dwight Macdonald," in *Leon Trotsky on Literature and Art*, ed. Paul Siegel, pp. 101-3 (New York: Pathfinder, 1970).

43. Leon Trotsky, "Art and Politics in Our Epoch," ibid., pp. 105, 106, 112, 114.

44. Leon Trotsky, "Manifesto: Towards a Free Revolutionary Art," ibid., pp. 118, 124.

45. Editorial, *Socialist Appeal*, 4 December 1937, p. 7; author's interview with George Novack, October 1972, San Francisco, Calif.

46. The exchange between Dewey and Trotsky was reprinted in *Their Morals and Ours* (New York: Pathfinder, 1973). See also "Violence, For and Against," *Common Sense* 7, no. 1 (January 1938): 19–21.

47. John McDonald to AW, 18 November 1974.

48. Letter from Bernard Wolfe [Trotsky's secretary] to Harold Isaacs, 12 June 1937, copy in Cannon Papers, LSH.

49. "Discussion with Trotsky: II—Defense Organization and Attitude toward Intellectuals," in *Writings of Leon Trotsky [1937–38]*, ed. Naomi Allen and George Breitman, pp. 294–99 (New York: Pathfinder, 1976).

50. Notarized statement by Solow on relations with Chambers in Solow Papers, HIL. Trotsky's attitude in favor of giving public exposure to Soviet secret police defector Ignace Reiss may have influenced his approach.

51. *Partisan Review* 4, no. 4 (March 1938): 59–62, and ibid. 4, no. 5 (April 1938): 62–64.

52. Junius, "Moscow Admits 'Robinson' Held for Espionage," *Socialist Appeal*, 22 June 1938, pp. 1, 4; "Links Poyntz to 'Robinson' Spy Frame-up," ibid., 12 February 1938, pp. 1, 2; "Arrested Photographer Is Stalinist Sympathizer," ibid., 2 April 1938, p. 3; "Grand Jury Indicts Two in Rubens Mystery Case," ibid., 9 April 1938, p. 3.

53. See obituary, "Eugene Lyons, Reporter Turned Critic of Soviets," *Chicago Tribune*, 1 October 1985, p. 28.

54. Herbert Solow, "Stalin's American Passport Mill," *American Mercury* 47, no. 187 (July 1939): 302–9.

55. Herbert Solow, "Stalin's Great American Hoax," ibid. 47, no. 192 (December 1939): 394–402.

56. An unpublished manuscript called "Where Is Juliet Stuart Poyntz?" is in the Solow Papers, HIL, as well as undated articles from Carlo Tresca's *Il Martello* on the Poyntz case.

57. For a compelling analysis of the difference between revolutionary anti-Stalinism and reactionary anticommunism, see James P. Cannon, *American Stalinism and Anti-Stalinism* (New York: Pioneer, 1947).

58. This is noted in a memo in the Solow Papers, HIL. See also Herbert Solow, "Refugee Scholars in the United States," *American Scholar* 11, no. 3 (Summer 1942): 374–78.

59. Notes on the case and an undated brochure entitled *Who Killed Carlo Tresca?* (published by the Tresca Memorial Committee) are in the Solow Papers, HIL.

60. The following information is based on the author's interview with Adelaide Walker, May 1980, Cape Cod, Mass., and the chapter "Theatre Union. Theatre Is a Weapon," in Gerald Rabkin's *Drama and Commitment* (Bloomington: Indiana University Press, 1964), pp. 44–67.

61. Charles Yale Harrison to Leon Trotsky, 31 August 1936, Trotsky Papers, HL.

62. Ibid., 26 September 1936, ibid.

63. Bernard Wolfe to Leon Trotsky, undated, ibid.

64. James Burnham and Max Shachtman, "Intellectuals in Retreat," *New International* 5, no. 1 (January 1939): 4–22.

65. The information on *Marxist Quarterly* is based partly on Paul Buhle, "Louis C. Fraina, 1892–1953," M.A. thesis, University of Connecticut, 1968, pp. 93–97; and George Novack, "Radical Intellectuals in the 30s," *International Socialist Review* 29, no. 2 (March–April 1968): 30–31.

66. Editors, "Challenge," *Marxist Quarterly* 1, no. 1 (January–March 1937): 3–4.

67. See Buhle, "Louis C., Fraina," pp. 98–126, and Ronald Radosh, "Lovestone Diplomacy," *American Labor and United States Foreign Policy* (New York: Vintage, 1969), pp. 268–303.

68. The biographical information on Louis Hacker is based partly on Stanley Kunitz and Howard Haycraft, *Twentieth Century Authors* (New York: Wilson, 1942), pp. 593–94.

69. Quoted in John Melvin (pseud. for Melvin J. Lasky), "Intellectual in Defeat," *New International* 7, no. 1 (January 1941): 10–13.

70. James Burnham, "God Bless America," *Partisan Review* 7, no. 6 (November–December 1940): 479–81.

71. This was reprinted as a book, *The End of Socialism in Russia* (Boston: Little, Brown, 1937).

72. Max Eastman, *Reflections on the Failure of Socialism* (New York: Davin Adair, 1955), pp. 7–20.

73. Milton Cantor, *Max Eastman* (New York: Twayne, 1970), p. 48.

74. Eastman, *Reflections on the Failure of Socialism*, p. 37.

75. Cantor, *Max Eastman*, p. 161.

76. See William L. O'Neill, *The Last Romantic: A Life of Max Eastman* (New York: Oxford, 1978), pp. 231–36.

77. Edmund Wilson, "Communist Criticism," *Shores of Light* (New York: Vintage, 1952), p. 645.

78. These facts are recounted in Malcolm Cowley, "From the Finland Station," *Think Back on Us* (Carbondale: Southern Illinois University Press, 1967), pp. 178–84.

79. At the time of *To the Finland Station*'s publication, Sidney Hook announced: "I am acquainted with nothing in any language which equals the insight, the eloquence and essential justice of Wilson's biographical account of Marx," *New York Herald Tribune Books*, 29 September 1940, p. 5. Other laudatory assessments include Louis Hacker, "Distilled Disillusion," *Saturday Review of Literature* 5, no. 10 (October 1940): 11–12; V. S. Pritchett, "Edmund Wilson," *New Yorker* 48, no. 51 (23 December 1972): 75–78; Irving Howe, "Edmund Wilson: A Reexamination," *Nation* 167, no. 16 (16 October 1948): 430–33; Edward Feiss, "Art and Ideas," *Antioch Review* 1, no. 3 (September 1941): 356–67. A more critical discussion of the book is contained in Meyer Schapiro, "The Revolutionary Personality," *Partisan Review* 7, no. 6 (November–December 1940): 469.

80. Edmund Wilson, *To the Finland Station* (New York: Doubleday, Anchor Books, 1955), p. 47.

81. Ibid., p. 63.

82. Ibid., p. 118.

83. Ibid., p. 140.

84. Ibid., p. 467.

85. Ibid., pp. 188–89.

86. Ibid., p. 299.

87. Rahv, "Twilight of the Thirties," p. 14.

88. Rahv, "Trials of the Mind," p. 3.

89. Richard Pells, *Radical Visions and American Dreams* (New York: Harper and Row, 1974), p. 336.

90. Author's interview with F. W. Dupee, August 1973, Carmel, Calif.

CHAPTER 6

1. Quoted in Marcel Liebman, *Leninism under Lenin* (London: Merlin Press, 1975), p. 445.

2. The attitude toward Cannon in Constance Ashton Myers's *The Prophet's Army* (Westport, Conn.: Greenwood, 1977) is surprisingly biased. Harry Roskolenko's autobiography, *When I Was Last on Cherry Street* (New York: Stein and Day, 1965), is strongly partisan, but at least it is well written and witty; Bernard Wolfe's *Memoirs of a Not Altogether Shy Pornographer* (New York: Doubleday, 1972) retains the prejudice without the style. Radical groups in the United States such as the Spartacist League, which claims to be Trotskyist, and the Socialist Workers Party, which publishes Cannon's writings, have in recent years assumed political positions Cannon would have abhorred. The "Shachtmanite" tendencies represented today in the leading circles of Social Democrats U.S.A. and the AFL-CIO reflect only his final, conservative phase.

3. In addition to Cannon's own books, a few of the most important biographical sources about him are Les Evans, ed., *James P. Cannon as We Knew Him* (New York: Pathfinder, 1976); Theodore Draper, *The Roots of American Communism* (New York: Viking, 1957), and *American Communism and Soviet Russia* (New York: Viking, 1960). I have also drawn on the following: Milton Genecin to AW, 17 February 1984; Albert Glotzer to AW, 11 February 1984; Milton Zaslow to AW, 1 March 1984. In addition, I am grateful to Jeanne Morgan for providing me with a copy of her unpublished memoirs of Cannon and pages from her diary when she worked as his secretary.

4. The biographical information about Max Shachtman is partly based on the following: Julius Jacobson, "The Two Deaths of Max Shachtman," *New Politics* 10, no. 2 (Winter 1973): 96–99; Milton Alvin, "Max Shachtman, 1904–1972," *Militant*, 1 December 1972, p. 18; George Novack, "Max

Shachtman: A Political Portrait," *International Socialist Review* 34, no. 2 (February 1973): 26–29, 44; Stan Weir, "Requiem for Max Shachtman," *Radical America* 7, no. 1 (1973): 69–78; Milton Genecin to AW, 17 February 1984; Phyllis Jacobson to AW, 10 March 1984; Albert Glotzer to AW, 11 February 1984; author's interview with Emanuel Geltman, May 1981, New York City; Milton Zaslow to AW, 1 March 1984; Albert Glotzer, "Max Shachtman," *New America* 10, no. 22 (16 November 1972): 1, 4; Tom Kahn, "Max Shachtman: His Ideals and His Movement," ibid., p. 5; interview with Max Shachtman, Columbia University Oral History Project, Columbia University, New York, N.Y.

5. George Breitman to AW, 17 July 1985.

6. Tony Cliff, "The Theory of Bureaucratic Collectivism: A Critique," *Neither Washington nor Moscow: Essays on Revolutionary Socialism* (London: Bookmarks, 1982), pp. 87–88.

7. A typical quotation: ". . . in the USSR minus the social structure founded by the October Revolution would be a fascist regime." Leon Trotsky, *In Defense of Marxism* (New York: Pathfinder, 1973), p. 53.

8. George Breitman and Sarah Lovell, eds., *Writings of Leon Trotsky [1932–33]* (New York: Pathfinder, 1972), p. 126.

9. George Breitman and Sarah Lovell, eds., *Writings of Leon Trotsky [1930–31]* (New York: Pathfinder, 1973), p. 374.

10. In a June 1940 discussion with Trotsky on organizational questions, Cannon states the following: "I think that the party in the eyes of the leading militants should be considered as a military organization. The party forms should be much more considerably formalized in a deliberate form of hierarchical organization. A strict record of grades of authority in the party." In his response, Trotsky does not challenge these points directly but never discusses anything remotely like hierarchies and "grades of authority," emphasizing instead the relationship between internal democracy and discipline: " . . . it is necessary to create an elastic relationship between democracy and centralism. . . . To assimilate [large numbers of new members] can't be done by centralism. It is necessary to enlarge the democracy." Talking of Bolshevik Party functioning during the civil war, he says: "Even at the front we had closed party meetings, where all party members discussed with complete freedom, criticized orders, etc. But when we left the room, the orders became a strict discipline, for the breaking of which a commander could shoot." See Naomi Allen and George Breitman, eds., *Writings of Leon Trotsky [1939–40]* (New York: Pathfinder, 1973), pp. 286–87. An example of Trotsky's feeling that Cannon tended to be too factional can be found in a 6 December 1937 letter beginning: "The discussion regarding the nature of the USSR seems to us down here to be much sharper than is warranted and to possibly presage results out of proportion to the issues." Ibid., p. 87. In *The Struggle for Marxism in the United States: A History of American Trotskyism* (New York: Bulletin Books, 1971), pp. 60–62, Tim Wohlforth cites a number of letters from Trotsky to Cannon indicating that Cannon might be rushing too quickly toward a split.

11. Interview with Max Shachtman, Columbia University Oral History Project.

12. Unpublished biographical sketch of Martin Abern by Albert Glotzer.

13. See Max Shachtman, "James Joyce," *Liberator* 7, no. 6 (June 1924): 33; "Leonid Andreyev," ibid., no. 7 (July 1924): 30.

14. The biographical information on Burnham is based partly on the following: Benjamin G. Hoffman, "The Political Thought of James Burnham" (Ph.D. diss., University of Michigan, 1969); James Gilbert, *Designing the Industrial State* (Chicago: Quadrangle, 1972), pp. 266–84; John P. Diggins, *Up from Communism* (New York: Harper and Row, 1975), pp. 160–200, 303–42; author's interview with F. W. Dupee, July 1973, Carmel, Calif.; author's interview with B. J. Widick, September 1984, Ann Arbor, Mich.

15. James Burnham, "Trying to Say," *Symposium* 2, no. 1 (January 1931): 51–59; review of *Literature and Occult Tradition*, ibid., pp. 141–45.

16. James Burnham, review of *The History of the Russian Revolution*, ibid. 3, no. 2 (July 1932): 370–80.

17. James Burnham, "Marxism and Aesthetics," ibid. 4, no. 1 (January 1933): 3–29.

18. James Burnham and Philip Wheelwright, "Thirteen Propositions," ibid. 4, no. 2 (April 1933): 127–34.

19. James Burnham, "Comment," ibid. 4, no. 4 (October 1933): 403–13.

20. Author's interview with F. W. Dupee, August 1973, Carmel, Calif.

21. James Burnham, "His Place in History," *New Masses* 10, no. 4 (23 January 1934): 15.

22. James Burnham, "*War* by Norman Thomas," *New International* 2, no. 6 (December 1935): 240; James Burnham, "For a Revolutionary Socialist Party," *Socialist Appeal* 2, no. 7 (August 1936): 5–8; James Burnham, *The People's Front: The New Betrayal* (New York: Pioneer, 1937).

23. John West, "Max Eastman's Straw Man," *New International* 2, no. 7 (December 1935): 220–25; James Burnham, "Max Eastman as Scientist," ibid. 4, no. 6 (June 1938): 177–80.

24. The biographical information is based on the author's interview with Harry Roskolenko, June 1980, New York City.

25. The biographical information is based on the author's interview with Max Geldman (cousin of Max Geltman), April 1983, Los Angeles, Calif.; author's interview with Emanuel Garrett, May 1981, New York City; and obituary for Max Geltman, *New York Times*, 19 May 1984, p. 48.

26. The biographical information on Joseph Friedman is from *Militant*, 29 June 1929, p. 2; author's interview with B. J. Widick, September 1984, Ann Arbor, Mich.; and author's interview with Walter Goldwater, May 1981, New York City.

27. For additional information on Bruno Rizzi see Leon Trotsky, *In Defense of Marxism* (New York: Pathfinder, 1973), pp. x, xvi, 1, 4, 10, 11.

28. See "Amendment to Resolution on the Soviet Union," in *The Founding of the Socialist Workers Party: Minutes and Resolutions, 1938–39*, ed. George Breitman, pp. 141–45 (New York: Monad, 1982).

29. James Burnham to Leon Trotsky, 9 December 1937, Trotsky Papers, HL.

30. James Burnham and Max Shachtman, "Intellectuals in Retreat," *New International* 5, no. 1 (January 1939): 3–21.

31. [Socialist Workers Party's] *Internal Bulletin on "The Workers Party"* 7, no. 11 (1946): 26. The fullest explanation of Cannon's views on party organization and the conflict with Shachtman can be found in James P. Cannon, *The Struggle for a Proletarian Party* (New York: Pioneer, 1943).

32. Albert Goldman, "Unity—Will It Work?," *New International* 13, no. 4 (April 1947): 108.

33. See the following contributions to the Workers Party's *Internal Bulletins*: Philip Sherman et al., "Defining a Tendency" 2, no. 8 (April 1941): 4; letters from Dwight Macdonald, 2, no. 9 (May 1941): 4. Other information is from the author's interview with Martin Glaberman, September 1984, Detroit, Mich.

34. On state capitalist theory, Trotsky states in Allen and Breitman, eds., *Writings of Leon Trotsky [1937–38]*, p. 341: "We have rejected . . . this term, which while it does correctly characterize certain features of the Soviet state, nevertheless ignores its fundamental difference from capitalist states." In "The USSR in War," reprinted in *In Defense of Marxism*, Trotsky states the following about bureaucratic collectivist theory: "The inability of the proletariat to take into its hands the leadership of society [at the end of World War II] could actually lead under these conditions to the growth of a new exploiting class from the Bonapartist fascist bureaucracy," p. 9.

35. The following are characteristic remarks of Trotsky from *In Defense of Marxism* on these issues: "In the USSR the overthrow of the bureaucracy is indispensable for the preservation of state property. Only in this sense do we stand for the defense of the USSR," pp. 15–16; "The defense of the USSR is related to the world socialist revolution as a tactical task is related to a strategic one. A tactic is subordinated to a strategic goal and can in no case be in contradiction to the latter," pp. 17–18; "We were and remain against seizures of new territories by the Kremlin," p. 20; "*Our* defense of the USSR is carried out under the slogan 'For Socialism! For the World Revolution! Against Stalin!," p. 20.

36. In Allen and Breitman, eds., *Writings of Leon Trotsky [1937–38]*, p. 128, Trotsky states: "Twenty years after the revolution the Soviet state has become the most centralized, despotic, and bloodthirsty apparatus of coercion and compulsion. The evolution of the Soviet state therefore proceeds in complete contradiction to the principles of the Bolshevik program. The reason for it is to be found in this, that society, as has already been said, is evolving not toward socialism but toward the regeneration of social contradictions. Should the process continue in this direction, it must inevitably lead to the rebirth of classes, the liquidation of planned economy, and the restoration of capitalist property. The state regime will in that case inevitably become fascist."

37. James Burnham, "Letter of Resignation from the Workers Party," reprinted in Trotsky, *In Defense of Marxism*, Appendix T.

38. James Burnham, "Lenin's Heir," *Partisan Review* 12, no. 1 (Winter 1945): 61–72; James Burnham, "The Outcome," *The Struggle for the World* (New York: John Day, 1947), pp. 242–48.

39. Michael Harrington, *Fragments of the Century: A Social Autobiography* (New York: Dutton, 1973), p. 223.

CHAPTER 7

1. A. J. Muste, *The Essays of A. J. Muste* (New York: Bobbs-Merrill, 1967), p. 238.

2. Sidney Hook, "Against Sanctions," *Modern Quarterly* 10, no. 1 (April 1936): 15.

3. Howard Zinn, *A People's History of the United States* (New York: Harper and Row, 1980), p. 398.

4. See Irving Howe and Lewis Coser, *The American Communist Party: A Critical History* (New York: Praeger, 1957), pp. 387–436; and C. L. R. James, George Breitman, Edgar Keemer et al., *Fighting Racism in World War II* (New York: Monad, 1980), passim.

5. Isaac Deutscher makes a similar point in *The Prophet Outcast* (New York: Oxford, 1963), pp. 501–2.

6. Leon Trotsky, "Lenin and Imperialist War," in *Writings of Leon Trotsky [1938–39]*, ed. Naomi Allen and George Breitman, pp. 167–69 (New York: Pathfinder, 1974).

7. Leon Trotsky, "A Step toward Social Patriotism," in ibid., p. 209.

8. Leon Trotsky, "India Faced with Imperialist War," in *Writings of Leon Trotsky [1939–40]*, ed. Naomi Allen and George Breitman, p. 29 (New York: Pathfinder, 1973).

9. Leon Trotsky, "On the Question of Workers' Self-Defense," ibid., pp. 104–5.

10. Leon Trotsky, "Discussions with Trotsky," ibid., p. 258.

11. Leon Trotsky, "Bonapartism, Fascism, and War," ibid., p. 411.

12. James P. Cannon, "Summary Speech on the Proletarian Military Policy," *Socialist Appeal*, 26 October 1940, reprinted in *Revolutionary Strategy in the Fight against the Vietnam War* (New York: Education for Socialists Bulletin, 1975), p. 84.

13. Albert Goldman, *Militant*, 2 March 1941, p. 2.

14. For example, see Albert Goldman, "Differences between Imperialism? Yes, But Not Decisive," *Socialist Appeal*, 3 August 1940, p. 4.

15. See *New International* 7, no. 1 (July 1941): 3; and Milton Alvin, "On Shachtman's Answer to the Position of the SWP on Conscription, War, and Militarism," *Internal Bulletin* [of the Workers Party], no. 6 (January 1941): 6.

16. Irving Howe, "*Labor Action* Answers *California Eagle* Attack," *Labor Action*, 25 May 1942, p. 2.

17. Sidney Hook, "The Radical Comedians: Inside *Partisan Review*," *American Scholar* 54, no. 1 (Winter 1984–85): 45–61.

18. Statement of the League for Cultural Freedom and Socialism, "War Is the Issue!," *Partisan Review* 6, no. 5 (1939): 125–27.

19. Dwight Macdonald to Leon Trotsky, Summer 1937, Trotsky Papers, HL.

20. Author's interview with Dwight Macdonald, November 1973, Buffalo, N.Y.

21. V. I. Lenin and Leon Trotsky, *Kronstadt* (New York: Monad, 1979), p. 127.

22. Ibid., pp. 83–94.

23. Ibid., pp. 101–24.

24. Ibid., pp. 131–35.

25. Stephen Cohen, "Bolshevism and Stalinism," in *Stalinism: Essays in Historical Interpretation*, ed. Robert C. Tucker, p. 3 (New York: Norton, 1977).

26. Sidney Hook, "As a (Marxist) Professor Sees It," *Common Sense* 7, no. 1 (January 1938): 23.

27 Letter from Dwight Macdonald, *Socialist Appeal*, 10 December 1938, p. 4.

28. Dwight Macdonald, "Off the Record," ibid., 4 February 1939, p. 1; ibid., 14 February 1939, p. 4; ibid., 11 April 1939, p. 3.

29. Dwight Macdonald, "Sparks in the News," ibid., 13 June 1939, p. 3.

30. Ibid., 11 July 1939, p. 2.

31. Author's interview with Dwight Macdonald, November 1973, Buffalo, N.Y.; *Socialist Appeal*, 17 October 1939, p. 1; ibid., 3 November 1932, p. 2.

32. *Labor Action*, 26 April 1940, p. 2.

33. *New International* 7, no. 1 (January 1941): 49.

34. *Internal Bulletin* [of the Workers Party], no. 5 (November 1940): 1.

35. Ibid., no. 9 (May 1941): 4–9.

36. Ibid.

37. Dwight Macdonald, "Trotsky Is Dead," *Partisan Review* 7, no. 5 (September–October 1940): 339–53.

38. Dwight Macdonald, "The Burnhamian Revolution," ibid. 9, no. 1 (January–February 1942): 76–85.

39. Dwight Macdonald, "Notes on a Strange War," ibid. 7, no. 3 (May–June 1940): 170–75.

40. Leon Trotsky to Dwight Macdonald, 20 January 1938, Trotsky Papers, HL.

41. Philip Rahv, "What Is Living and What Is Dead?," *Partisan Review* 7, no. 3 (May–June 1940): 175–80.

42. Biographical information from author's Interview with Clement Greenberg, June 1980, New York City.

43. Clement Greenberg and Dwight Macdonald, "10 Propositions on the War," *Partisan Review* 8, no. 4 (July–August 1941): 271–78.

44. Philip Rahv, "10 Propositions and 8 Errors," ibid. no. 6 (November–December 1941): 499–506.

45. "Reply by Greenberg and Macdonald," ibid., 506–8.

46. "A Statement by the Editors," ibid., 9, no. 1 (January–February 1942): 2.

47. Dwight Macdonald, "The (American) People's Century," ibid. 9, no. 4 (July–August 1942): 294–310, and "Political Notes," ibid. 9, no. 6 (November–December 1942): 476–82.

48. S. A. Longstaff, "*Partisan Review* and the Second World War," *Salmagundi* 43 (Winter 1979): 108–29.

49. Michael Wreszin to AW, 3 March 1986.

50. The biographical information on Delmore Schwartz is from James Atlas, *Delmore Schwartz: The Life of an American Poet* (New York: Farrar, Straus and Giroux, 1977).

51. Robert Phillips, *Letters of Delmore Schwartz* (Princeton, N.J.: Ontario Review Press, 1984), pp. 132–33.

52. Ibid., p. 78.

53. Ibid., p. 168.

54. Dwight Macdonald, "Why I Am No Longer a Socialist," *Liberation* 3, no. 5 (May 1958): 4–7.

55. See Mary McCarthy's preface to Nicola Chiaromonte, *The Worm of Consciousness* (New York: Harvest, 1977), pp. xii–xvi.

56. Macdonald, "Why I Am No Longer a Socialist," p. 4–7.

57. Sidney Hook, "The New Failure of Nerve," *Partisan Review* 10, no. 1 (January–February 1943): 2–23.

58. Sidney Hook, "The Failure of the Left," ibid. 10, no. 2 (March–April 1943): 165–77.

59. Sidney Hook to AW, 12 August 1981.

60. The biographical information about Meyer Schapiro is based on the author's interview with Schapiro, June 1980, New York City; Schapiro to AW, 27 July 1974; Helen Epstein, "Meyer Schapiro: To Know and Make Known, Part I," *Art News* (May 1983): 60–85; "To Know and Make Known, Part II," ibid. (Summer 1983): 84–95; author's interview with Felix Morrow, May 1977, New York City.

61. Schapiro's dissertation has been reprinted in Meyer Schapiro, *Romanesque Art* (New York: George Braziller, 1977), pp. 131–264.

62. Sender Garlin, *Daily Worker*, 3 April 1934, p. 2.

63. Meyer Schapiro, "The Social Bases of Art," *First American Artists' Congress* (New York: American Artists' Congress, 1936), pp. 31–37.

64. Serge Guilbaut, *How New York Stole the Idea of Modern Art* (Chicago: University of Chicago Press, 1983), pp. 39–40.

65. For a typical expression of these views see Meyer Schapiro, "Recent Abstract Painting," *Modern Art* (New York: Braziller, 1978), pp. 213–26.

66. Meyer Schapiro, "A Note on 'The Open City': Some Comments on

Farrell's Review," *New International* 6, no. 12 (December 1946): 311–12.

67. James Kutcher, *The Case of the Legless Veteran* (New York: Pathfinder, 1973), p. 78.

68. *Labor Action*, 7 March 1949, pp. 1, 3.

69. Among Schapiro's few contributions were the very brief 1963 piece, "On David Siqueiros: A Dilemma for Artists," reprinted in Irving Howe, ed., *The Radical Imagination* (New York: New American Library, 1967), pp. 417–19, and an obituary for Alfred Rosmer, *Dissent* 12, 1 (Winter 1966): 75.

70. Epstein, "To Know and Make Known, Part II," p. 86.

71. Philip Rahv, "Disillusionment and Partial Answers," *Partisan Review* 15, no. 5 (May 1948): 522.

72. See Georg Lukács, *The Meaning of Contemporary Realism* (London: Merlin Press, 1963).

73. Quoted in Mark Krupnick, "He Never Learned to Swim," *New Review* (January 1936): 37.

74. Philip Rahv, *Essays on Literature and Politics*, ed. Arabel J. Porter and Andrew J. Dvosin, pp. 305-9 (Boston: Houghton Mifflin, 1978).

75. A good sampling of Farrell's views can be found in *Literature and Morality* (New York: Vanguard, 1947).

76. Rahv, *Essays on Literature and Politics*, pp. 293–304.

77. Delmore Schwartz, "The Present State of Poetry," *Literary Lectures* (Washington, D.C.: Library of Congress, 1973), p. 255.

78. See Harold Rosenberg, "*Seven Types of Ambiguity*," *Symposium* 1, no. 3 (July 1931): 413–19; "Myth and Poem," ibid. 2, no. 2 (April 1931): 179–91); "*Counter-Statement* and *The Human Parrot and Other Essays*," ibid. 3, no. 2 (January 1932): 116–22.

79. Schapiro, "The Social Bases of Art" and "The Nature of Abstract Art," *Marxist Quarterly* 1, no. 1 (January 1937): 77–98. For a useful discussion of the importance of these writings, see Frank Frascina, ed., *Pollock and After* (New York: Harper and Row, 1985), pp. 3–20.

80. Introduction to "Special Issue on Debates in Contemporary Culture," *Telos*, no. 62 (Winter 1984–85): 5. See also the excellent essay by James D. Herbert, "The Political Origins of Abstract Expressionist Art Criticism," ibid., pp. 178–86.

81. Dwight Macdonald, "A Theory of Mass Culture," in *Mass Culture: The Popular Arts in America*, ed. Bernard Rosenberg and David Manning White, p. 60 (Glencoe, Ill.: Free Press, 1957). The essay originally appeared in 1944 in *Politics* as "A Theory of Popular Culture," but in subsequent reprints he changed "popular culture" to "mass culture." For a comparative analysis of Macdonald's views, see Patrick Brantlinger, *Bread and Circuses* (Ithaca, N.Y.: Cornell University Press, 1983), pp. 200–203.

82. "Special Issue," *Telos*, p. 3.

83. Fredric Jameson, "Reification and Utopia in Mass Culture," *Social Text* 1, no. 1 (Winter 1979): 130–48.

84. This pamphlet was reprinted in *Literature and Morality*, pp. 35–78.

85. Jason Epstein, "Wilson's Amerika," *New York Review of Books*, 28

November 1963, pp. 9–11. During the Civil War the Copperheads were northerners who refused to support the war effort on the grounds that it was a violation of the American ideal of republican freedom.

86. Edmund Wilson, *The Cold War and the Income Tax* (New York: Signet, 1964), p. 128.

87. Ibid., p. 125.

88. *New York Times*, 27 June 1965, p. 28.

89. See Edmund Wilson's Introduction to *Patriotic Gore: Studies in the Literature of the American Civil War* (New York: Oxford, 1966), pp. ix–xxxii.

90. A description of the funeral is contained in Jason Epstein's "E. W.: 1895–1972," *New York Review of Books*, 20 July 1972, pp. 6–8.

CHAPTER 8

1. Leon Trotsky, *Literature and Revolution* (Ann Arbor: University of Michigan Press, 1960), p. 19.

2. Lionel Trilling, *The Middle of the Journey* (New York: Avon, 1975), p. vii.

3. Philip Rahv, *Essays on Literature and Politics*, ed. Arabel J. Porter and Andrew J. Dvosin, p. 303 (Boston: Houghton Mifflin, 1978).

4. Lionel Trilling, *The Liberal Imagination* (New York: Scribner's, 1976), p. xv.

5. John Dewey, *Art as Experience* (New York: Putnam, 1958), p. 105.

6. Terry Eagleton, *Criticism and Ideology* (London: New Left Books, 1976), p. 15.

7. Reprinted in Rahv, *Essays on Literature and Politics*, pp. 3–7, 8–24.

8. Delmore Schwartz, *Selected Poems: Summer Knowledge* (New Directions, 1969), p. 34.

9. Alfred Kazin, *New York Jew* (New York: Knopf, 1987), p. 192.

10. Lionel Trilling, *Of This Time, Of That Place and Other Stories* (New York: Harcourt Brace Jovanovich, 1979), p. 94. For interpretations of Trilling's fiction that respond to more diverse elements than I have space to consider in this chapter, see Robert Boyers's *Lionel Trilling: Negative Capability and the Wisdom of Avoidance* (Columbia: University of Missouri Press, 1977); William Chace, *Lionel Trilling: Criticism and Politics* (Stanford, Calif.; Stanford University Press, 1980); and Edward Shoben, *Lionel Trilling: Mind and Character* (New York: Ungar, 1981).

11. Reprinted in Lionel Trilling, *Speaking of Literature and Society* (New York: Harcourt Brace Jovanovich, 1980), pp. 411–29.

12. Trilling, *Of This Time, Of That Place*, p. 79.

13. Ibid., p. 115, and Lionel Trilling, *The Experience of Literature* (New York: Holt, 1967), p. 360.

14. For example, see Daniel Bell, "A Parable of Alienation," *Jewish Frontier* 13, no. 11 (November 1946): 12–19.

15. Trilling, *Of This Time, Of That Place*, p. 34.

16. Ibid., p. 19.

17. Ibid., p. 14.

18. Ibid., p. 33.

19. James T. Farrell, *Literature and Morality* (New York: Vanguard, 1946), p. 13.

20. Irving Howe, "The Critic Calcified," *Partisan Review* 14, no. 5 (September–October 1947): 550.

21. Trilling, *Of This Time, Of That Place*, p. 12.

22. Ibid., p. 31.

23. Ibid., p. 20.

24. Ibid., p. 35.

25. Of course, there are other works of fiction that concern the New York intellectuals from this time period that do not follow the pattern described. Two neglected ones are Michael Blankfort's *A Time to Live* (1943), which features characters largely based on Adelaide Walker, Charles Walker, and Herbert Solow; and Elinor Rice's *Mirror, Mirror* (1946), in which certain characters and episodes draw very indirectly upon her life in the 1930s.

26. Eagleton, *Criticism and Ideology*, p. 15.

27. See Sherman Paul, *Edmund Wilson* (Urbana: University of Illinois Press, 1967), pp. 160–61.

28. Edmund Wilson, *Memoirs of Hecate County* (Boston: Nonpareil, 1980), p. 220.

29. Ibid., p. 313.

30. Elizabeth Niebuhr, "Interview with Mary McCarthy," *Paris Review* 27 (Winter–Spring 1962): 58-94.

31. Trilling, *The Middle of the Journey*, p. xi.

32. Ibid., p. xviii.

33. Ibid., p. xx.

34. Ibid., p. 4.

35. Ibid., p. 301.

36. Ibid., p. 302.

37. The biographical information is partly from Ernest Erber to AW, 15 May 1984; author's telephone interview with Edith Tarcov, November 1983, New York City; author's interview with David Bazelon, May 1981, Buffalo, N.Y.; Albert Glotzer to AW, 7 April 1982.

38. Saul Bellow, "The Mexican General," *Partisan Review* 9, no. 3 (May–June 1942): 178-94.

39. Ernest Erber to AW, 15 May 1984.

40. Saul Bellow, *Dangling Man* (New York: Plume, 1974), p. 191.

41. Isaac Rosenfeld, *Alpha and Omega* (New York: Viking, 1966), pp. 122–52. See also the discussions of Rosenfeld in Mark Shechner, "Isaac Rosenfeld's World," *Partisan Review* 48, no. 4 (Fall 1976): 524–56; and Theodore Solotaroff, "The Spirit of Isaac Rosenfeld," *The Red Hot Vacuum* (New York: Atheneum, 1970), pp. 3–22.

42. The biographical information is from a letter from Eleanor Clark to AW, 13 August 1974.

43. Eleanor Clark to Leon Trotsky, Trotsky Papers, HL.

44. James T. Farrell, "Farrell Looks at His Writing," *Twentieth Century Literature* 22, no. 1 (February 1976): 13.

45. Unpublished manuscript in possession of AW.

46. James T. Farrell, *Yet Other Waters* (New York: Vanguard, 1952), p. 335.

47. James T. Farrell to Dwight Macdonald, 29 July 1945, Macdonald Papers, YL.

48. The biographical information on Albert Goldman is based partly on an unpublished biographical essay by Patrick Quinn; an unpublished biographical description by Albert Glotzer; and the author's interview with Sherry Abel, June 1978, New York City.

49. For further information on the case and for testimony by Cannon and Goldman, see James P. Cannon, *Socialism on Trial* (New York: Pathfinder, 1970), and Albert Goldman, *In Defense of Socialism* (New York: Pioneer), 1944).

50. The reconstruction of the faction fight is based on various issues of the *Internal Bulletin* [of the Socialist Workers Party] 1943–46; author's interview with Felix Morrow, November 1982, Ann Arbor, Mich.; James P. Cannon, *The Struggle for Socialism in the "American Century"* (New York: Pathfinder, 1977); and James P. Cannon, *Letters from Prison* (New York: Merit, 1978). See also Peter Jenkins, *Where Trotskyism Got Lost: World War Two and the Prospects for Revolution in Europe* (Nottingham, England: Spokesman, 1977).

51. See the detailed discussion of this episode in Alan M. Wald, *James T. Farrell: The Revolutionary Socialist Years* (New York: New York University Press, 1978), pp. 125–29.

52. James T. Farrell to AW, 1 May 1978.

53. James T. Farrell to Albert Goldman, 23 March 1948, Goldman Papers, WHS.

54. Albert Goldman to James T. Farrell, 16 April 1948, ibid.

55. James T. Farrell to Albert Goldman, 22 April 1948, ibid.

56. James T. Farrell, *Reflections at Fifty* (New York: Vanguard, 1954), pp. 61–62.

57. *New America* 15, no. 10 (December 1978): 10.

58. James T. Farrell, Introduction to *Judith and Other Stories* (New York: Doubleday, 1973), p. xi.

59. Robert Van Gelden, "An Interview with James T. Farrell," *New York Times Book Review*, 17 May 1942, p. 17.

60. Edgar M. Branch, *James T. Farrell* (New York: Twayne, 1971), pp. 139, 141.

61. George Novack to AW, 20 September 1976.

62. Ann Douglas, "James T. Farrell, the Artist as Militant," *Dissent* 27, no. 2 (Spring 1980): 216; Diana Trilling, *Reviewing the Forties* (New York: Harcourt Brace Jovanovich, 1978), p. 73.

63. Edgar M. Branch, "Freedom and Determinism in James T. Farrell's Fiction," in *Essays on Determinism in American Literature*, ed. Sydney J. Krause, pp. 62–85 (Kent, Ohio: Kent State University Press, 1984).

64. James T. Farrell, Introduction to *When Time Was Born* (New York: Horizon Press, 1961), p. 12.

65. James T. Farrell, *Literary Essays, 1954–1974* (Port Washington, N.Y.: Kennikat Press, 1976), p. 51.

66. Ibid., p. 50.

CHAPTER 9

1. The Marquis de Posa in Schiller's *Don Carlos*, 4.20.

2. Robert Booth Fowler, *Believing Skeptics: American Political Intellectuals, 1945–1964* (Westport, Conn.: Greenwood, 1978), p. 3.

3. Dwight Macdonald, "I Choose the West," *Politics Past* (New York: Viking, 1957), pp. 197–201.

4. Philip Rahv, *Essays on Literature and Politics*, ed. Arabel J. Porter and Andrew J. Dvosin (Boston: Houghton Mifflin, 1978), pp. 341–45.

5. Arnold Beichman to Harry Carman, 25 October 1954, American Committee for Cultural Freedom Papers, TL.

6. For a useful study of the development of this terminology, see Thomas R. Maddux, "Red Fascism, Brown Bolshevism," *American Historical Review* 75 (1969–70): 1046–64.

7. Alfred Kazin, *New York Jew* (New York: Knopf, 1978), p. 186.

8. Elisabeth Young-Bruehl, *For Love of the World* (New Haven: Yale University Press, 1984), pp. 127–28. Young-Bruehl mistakenly describes Heinrich Brandler, Bluecher's mentor, as a member of the Left Opposition.

9. Dwight Macdonald, "A New Theory of Totalitarianism," *New Leader* 34 (14 May 1941): 17. Kazin and McCarthy are quoted in Stephen Whitfield's *Into the Dark: Hannah Arendt and Totalitarianism* (Philadelphia: Temple University Press, 1982), p. 5.

10. David Hollinger's essay, "The Confidence Man," in *Reviews in American History* 7, no. 1 (March 1979): 134–41, is a fine analysis of the weaknesses in Allen Weinstein's *Perjury: The Hiss-Chambers Case* (New York: Knopf, 1978). The transcript of the debate, "Were the Rosenbergs Framed?" (New York: Nation Institute, 1983), summarizes many of the lingering problems in the government's case.

11. Rorty's scripts are among his papers, Rorty Papers, OL.

12. James Rorty to Andrew Clements, 2 August 1951, ibid.

13. Sidney Hook to Andrew Clements, 15 August 1951, ibid.

14. Sol Stein to *New York Times*, 14 October 1953, American Committee for Cultural Freedom Papers, TL.

15. Lewis Corey to Bertram D. Wolfe, 1 March 1952, Wolfe Papers, HIL; author's interview with Edward Sagarin, December 1983, New York City.

16. The text of Farrell's letter appears in a statement released to the *New York Times* by Diana Trilling on 29 August 1956, American Committee for Cultural Freedom Papers, TL. Farrell attributed the statement to inebria-

tion in an interview with the author, June 1977, New York City.

17. James T. Farrell to Norman Jacobs, 28 August 1956, ibid.

18. See the sharp critique of the book in Mary Sperling McAuliffe, *Crisis on the Left: Cold War Politics and American Liberals, 1947–1954* (Amherst: University of Massachusetts Press, 1978), pp. 125–26.

19. Minutes of Planning Conference of American Committee for Cultural Freedom, 1 March 1957, Corey Papers, BL.

20. Dwight Macdonald, "Notes on the Conference," 29 March 1952, Macdonald Papers, YL.

21. Dwight Macdonald, "Notes on Discussion, April 11," ibid.

22. Dwight Macdonald, "Notes on Meeting of American Committee for Cultural Freedom at the Columbia Club, " 23 April 1952, ibid.

23. Sidney Hook, letter to the *New York Times*, 8 May 1953, p. 24.

24. Lionel Trilling et al., "Statement on Academic Freedom," 1953, Central Administration files, Columbia University, New York, N.Y.

25. Statement by Irving Howe in [the pamphlet] *America and the Intellectuals: A Symposium, Partisan Review* ser. no. 4 (New York: *Partisan Review*, 1953), p. 43.

26. Statement by Norman Mailer in ibid., pp. 67–69. For additional information on Mailer's "Trotskyism," see William C. Pratt's "Mailer's *Barbary Shore* and His Quest for a Radical Politics," *Illinois Quarterly* 44 (Winter 1982): 48–56.

27. Statement by C. Wright Mills in *America and the Intellectuals*, pp. 75–79.

28. Statement by Philip Rahv in ibid., pp. 91–92.

29. Author's interview with Nathan Glazer, May 1981, Cambridge, Mass.; author's interview with Clement Greenberg, May 1981, New York City.

30. Author's interview with Albert Glotzer, June 1981, Martha's Vineyard, Mass.; author's interview with B. J. Widick, September 1984, Ann Arbor, Mich.

31. Irving Louis Horowitz, ed., *C. Wright Mills: Power, Politics and People* (New York: Ballantine, 1963), p. 603.

32. Melvin Lasky to Dwight Macdonald, 19 November 1939 and 29 March 1940, Macdonald Papers, YL.

33. Helga Hegewisch, ed., *Melvin J. Lasky: Encounter with a 60th Birthday* (London: Encounter, 1980), pp. 3–7; Melvin Lasky to AW, 2 December 1982.

34. Melvin Lasky to Dwight Macdonald, 27 March 1953 and 12 April 1967, Macdonald Papers, YL. Josselson is identified as a CIA agent in Peter Steinfels, *The Neoconservatives* (New York: Simon and Schuster, 1978), p. 83.

35. Author's interview with Leslie Fiedler, May 1982, Buffalo, N.Y. Some biographical information is contained in Leslie Fiedler, *Being Busted* (New York: Stein and Day, 1969). Fiedler's anti-Communist essays are collected in *An End to Innocence* (Boston: Beacon, 1955), pp. 3–90. Rosenberg's an-

swer is reprinted in *The Tradition of the New* (New York: Horizon Press, 1959), pp. 221–40.

36. *Committee for Cultural Freedom Bulletin* 1, no. 1 (15 October 1939): 4.

37. William Phillips, *A Partisan View* (New York: Stein and Day, 1983), pp. 148–49.

38. Julius Jacobson, "The Two Deaths of Max Shachtman," *New Politics* 10, no. 2 (Winter 1973): 99.

39. See the first-rate collection edited by Ralph Miliband, John Saville, and Marcel Liebman, *The Uses of Anti-Communism* (London: Merlin Press, 1984).

40. James Burnham and Max Shachtman, "Intellectuals in Retreat," *New International* 5, no. 1 (January 1939): 4–22.

41. See Max Shachtman's earlier essay, "Dictatorship of the Party or Proletariat," *New International* 1, no. 1 (July 1934): 9–11.

42. See the discussion by Ernest Mandel in *Revolutionary Marxism Today* (London: Verso, 1977), pp. 26–32.

43. Burnham and Shachtman, "Intellectuals in Retreat," p. 4.

44. The biographical information on Philip Selznick is based on the author's interview with Selznick, August 1982, Berkeley, Calif. See also the outstanding paper by Douglas G. Webb, "Philip Selznick and the New York Sociologists," presented at the annual meeting of the Canadian Historical Association, Toronto, 1982. Information on the Sherman group's activities in the Workers Party are from the [Workers Party] *Internal Bulletin* 9, no. 8 (April 1948).

45. Ernest Erbert to AW, 12 July 1984.

46. Max Shachtman, "Under the Banner of Marxism," [Workers Party] *Internal Bulletin* 4, no. 1, pt. 2 (1949). Erber's statement of resignation appears in ibid, pt. 1.

47. Meyer Schapiro to Alfred Rosmer, 8 December 1948, Rosmer Papers, MS; Jean Vannier, "A Century's Balance Sheet," *Partisan Review* 15, no. 3 (March 1948): 288–96.

48. Author's interview with Edward Sagarin, October 1983, New York City.

49. Albert Goldman to Sol Levitas, 4 February 1950, Goldman Papers, WHS. The information on Albert Goldman is from an unpublished essay by Patrick Quinn; author's interview with Sherry Abel, June 1976, New York City.

50. Betty Jacobson to A. Tamman, 4 December 1951, Goldman Papers, WHS.

51. Testimony of Security Clearance Hearing for Albert Goldman, 1952, ibid.

52. Ibid.

53. Quinn, "Albert Goldman," ibid.

54. The information on Felix Morrow is from the author's interviews in May 1973, New York City; October 1980, Ann Arbor, Mich.; December 1980, Ann Arbor, Mich.; February 1981, Ann Arbor, Mich.

55. The Federal Bureau of Investigation's files released under the Freedom of Information Act describe Morrow's providing information on the 1953 expulsion of the Cochran-Clarke group from the SWP.

56. Kazin, *New York Jew*, p. 185.

57. Sidney Hook, *Marx and the Marxists* (New York: Van Nostrand, 1955), pp. 82.

58. Gordon Haskell and Julius Falk, "Civil Liberties and the Cold War Philosopher," *New International* 19, no. 4 (July–August 1953): 184–227.

59. Sidney Hook, "Half-Baked Communism," *Nation* 134, no. 3492 (3 June 1932): 654.

60. Sidney Hook, review of *What Is to Be Done?*, *American Journal of Sociology* 38, no. 2 (September 1932): 315–17.

61. Sidney Hook, "An Epic of Revolution," *Saturday Review of Literature* 8, no. 32 (27 February 1932): 551.

62. Hook, *Marx and the Marxists*, pp. 75, 78.

63. George B. de Huszar, *The Intellectuals* (Glencoe, Ill.: Free Press, 1960), p. 359.

64. Ibid., p. 528.

65. Ibid.

66. Sidney Hook and Dennis King, " 'Bashing' the Raj," *New America*, July 1985, pp. 5–6.

67. See Irving Howe, *A Margin of Hope* (New York: Harcourt Brace Jovanovich, 1982), pp. 80–81.

68. Leon Trotsky, *The Transitional Program for Socialist Revolution* (New York: Pathfinder, 1973), p. 95. The oft-quoted sentence is: "However, one cannot categorically deny in advance the theoretical possibility that, under the influence of completely exceptional circumstances (war, defeat, financial crash, mass revolutionary pressure, etc.), the petty-bourgeois parties may go further than they themselves wish along the road to a break with the bourgeoisie."

69. The information on Bert Cochran is based on the author's interview with Cochran, June 1977, New York City; also, Milton Alvin, "Bert Cochran, Former Leader of SWP," *Socialist Action* 2, no. 7 (July 1984): 8.

70. The information on George Clarke is from the author's interview with Irving Beinin, October 1983, New York City.

71. The information on Harry Braverman is from George Breitman, "Harry Braverman: Marxist Author," *Militant*, 27 August 1976, p. 12.

72. The information on the 1953 political struggle is from the [Socialist Workers Party] *Internal Bulletin*, 1951–53; James P. Cannon, *Speeches to the Party* (New York: Pathfinder, 1973).

73. *Militant*, 16 November 1953, pp. 1, 3.

74. Ibid., 30 November 1953, p. 3.

75. Ibid., 25 January 1954, p. 3.

76. George Breitman to AW, 30 July 1985.

77. The biographical information on Joseph Vanzler is from the author's telephone interviews with Doris VanZleer, 29 December 1977 and 2 January 1978, Los Angeles, Calif.; obituary by Art Preis in the *Militant*, 2 July

1956, p. 1; George Novack, "Role of a Leading Marxist Scholar," ibid., 23 July 1976, p. 18; Harvard Records Office, Harvard University, Cambridge, Mass.

78. Joseph Vanzler, "An Introduction to the Social Basis of Grecian Art," *Modern Quarterly* 3, no. 4 (September–December 1926): 286–91.

79. King published a memoir of Vanzler in *Is There a Life After Birth?* (New York: Simon and Schuster, 1963), pp. 140–47.

80. Information on Joseph Hansen can be found in an obituary by George Novack in the *Militant*, 2 February 1979, pp. 8–9, 24. Information on Earle Birney is contained in Joseph Hansen, *The Abern Clique* (New York: Education for Socialists, 1972), pp. 3–5.

81. For example, see *How a Minority Can Change Society* (New York: Merit, 1965) and *The Last Year of Malcolm X* (New York: Merit, 1969).

82. See the obituary by Matilde Zimmerman in the *Militant*, 6 April 1979, pp. 26–27.

83. See the obituary in the *Militant*, 20 January 1958, pp. 1–2.

84. See the forthcoming essay by Alan Wald, "Sculptor on the Left," to appear in *Pembroke Magazine* in 1987.

85. Author's telephone interview with George Perle, September 1982.

86. Author's interview with Paul Siegel, August 1983, Oberlin, Ohio.

87. Peter Bloch to AW, 17 August 1983.

88. Author's interview with DeMila Jenner, June 1983, Benton, Calif.

89. Staughton Lynd to AW, 9 September 1980; author's interview with George Novack, August 1980, Oberlin, Ohio; Howe, *A Margin of Hope*, pp. 58–59; Spencer Brown to AW, 18 February 1982; Calder Willingham to AW, 12 October 1983.

90. Author's interview with Martin Glaberman, October 1984, Detroit, Mich. See also the Raya Dunayevskaya Papers in the Labor History Archives, Wayne State University, Detroit, Mich., and Kent Worcester, *C. L. R. James and the American Century* (San Juan, Puerto Rico: Documentos de Trabajo, 1984).

91. The biographical information on George Novack is based on a dozen interviews with Novack between 1974 and 1983; author's interview with Helen Hirschberg, June 1982, New York City; Harvard Records Office, Harvard University, Cambridge, Mass.

92. Author's interview with Stanley Kunitz, October 1983, Ann Arbor, Mich.

93. "Passports to Utopia," *New International* 1, no. 5 (November 1934): 115–17, and ibid. 1, no. 6 (December 1934): 145–47.

94 "Marxism and Intellectuals," ibid. 2, no. 7 (December 1935): 227–32; "American Intellectuals and the Crisis," ibid. 3, no. 2 (February 1936): 23–27; "The Intellectuals and the Crisis—II," ibid. 3, no. 6 (June 1936): 83–86.

95. George Novack, *Pragmatism versus Marxism* (New York: Pathfinder, 1975), p. 8.

96. See the thoughtful review by Milton Fisk in *Erkenntnis* 11 (1977): 269–73.

97. Author's interview with Dr. Robert Littman, July 1983, Los Angeles, Calif.

98. James P. Cannon to George Novack, 17 February 1961, George Novack Papers, New York City.

99. Les Evans, ed., *James P. Cannon As We Knew Him* (New York: Pathfinder, 1976), p. 253.

CHAPTER 10

1. Ignazio Silone, *Bread and Wine* (New York: Atheneum, 1962), p. 154.

2. The biographical information on Howe is from the following sources: Irving Howe, *A Margin of Hope* (New York: Harcourt Brace Jovanovich, 1982); author's interviews with Irving Howe, October 1978, Tuscaloosa, Ala.; B. J. Widick, October 1985 and March 1986, Ann Arbor, Mich.; Emanuel Geltman, May 1982, New York City; Julius and Phyllis Jacobson, May 1982, New York City; Albert Glotzer, June 1979, Cape Cod, Mass.

3. Leaflet in the archives of the library of the City University of New York, New York, N.Y.

4. Ibid.

5. Ibid.

6. Ibid.

7. Ibid.

8. Ibid.

9. Ibid.

10. Irving Howe, "Poison Gas," *Labor Action*, 18 May 1942, p. 4.

11. Irving Howe, "Terror," ibid., 3 August 1946, p. 5.

12. Irving Howe, "If Senator Bilbo Goes—Does the Bilbo System Remain?," ibid., 3 December 1946, p. 1.

13. Irving Howe, "Blum and Thorez Support Suppression of Indo-China," ibid., 6 January 1947, p. 3.

14. Irving Howe, "Paris, Saigon, New York," ibid., 27 January 1947, p. 4.

15. Irving Howe, "What Future for American Socialism?," ibid., 7 March 1949, p. 4.

16. Irving Howe, "The Dilemma of *Partisan Review*," *New International* 8, no. 2 (February 1942): 20–24; see also "The *Partisan Review* Controversy," ibid. 8, no. 3 (April 1942): 90–93.

17. Irving Howe, "How *Partisan Review* Goes to War," ibid. 13, no. 4 (April 1947): 109–11.

18. Peter Loumos, "Four Books by Koestler," ibid. 11, no. 8 (August 1945): 155–59.

19. Neil Weiss, Letter to the Editor, ibid. 11, no. 10 (October 1946): 250–51.

20. "A Reply by Irving Howe," ibid., pp. 251–52.

21. Albert Gates, "On the Significance of Koestler," ibid. 12, no. 7 (July 1947): 155–58.

22. "A Reply by Irving Howe," ibid., pp. 158–59.

23. For Howe's initial critique of Farrell and his view of modernism, see Irving Howe, "A Note on James T. Farrell," ibid. 8, no. 7 (July 1942): 182–84. Correspondence between Farrell and Howe in the Farrell Papers, CPVP, document the deterioration of relations.

24. Irving Howe, *Decline of the New* (New York: Harcourt, Brace and World, 1970), pp. 3–33.

25. Irving Howe, "Literary Criticism and Literary Radicals," *American Scholar* 4 (Winter 1971–72): 114.

26. Irving Howe, "Porkchoppers Prefabricated," *Anvil* (Fall 1949): 14–19.

27. Irving Howe, "On Comrade Johnson's American Resolution—or Soviets in the Sky," [Workers Party] *Internal Bulletin* 1, no. 9 (28 March 1946): 25–32.

28. Irving Howe, "A Note on Content with a Letter on Tone," ibid. 2, no. 7 (12 September 1947): 9–12.

29. Irving Howe, "The 13th Disciple," *Politics* 2, no. 10 (October 1946): 329–34.

30. Irving Howe, "The Lost Young Intellectual," *Commentary* 2, no. 4 (October 1946): 361–67.

31. Irving Howe, "The *Saturday Evening Post* Slanders the Jewish People," *Labor Action*, 5 April 1942, p. 4.

32. Irving Howe, "Observing the Events: Czechoslovakia," ibid., 8 March 1948, p. 4.

33. See *Labor Action*, 5 April 1948, p. 1; [Workers Party] *Internal Bulletin* 3, no. 2 (24 April 1948); E. R. McKinney to Max Shachtman, Shachtman Papers, TL.

34. [Workers Party] *Internal Bulletin* 3, no. 9 (14 January 1949): 30–32.

35. R. Fahan and H. Judd, "The New *Labor Action*," *Forum* (March 1951): 1–3.

36. "Statement of Resignation of Irving Howe and Henry Judd from the Independent Socialist League," ibid. (January 1953): 4.

37. Ibid., p. 5.

38. "Statement from the Political Committee on the Resignation of Irving Howe and Henry Judd," ibid., pp. 1–3; Albert Glotzer, "The New York Membership Meeting," ibid., pp. 8–9.

39. Hal Draper, "A New Magazine Presents Itself to the Socialist Public," *Labor Action*, 22 February 1954, p. 5; *Forum* (August 1954): 12.

40. Author's interview with Emanuel Geltman, May 1981, New York City.

41. See "This Age of Conformity: Protest and Rejoinder," *Partisan Review* 21, no. 2 (March–April 1954): 235–40.

42. Irving Howe and Lewis Coser, *The American Communist Party* (New York: Praeger, 1957), pp. 500–554. The book was originally undertaken with the collaboration of Julius Jacobson, a young leader of the Independent Socialist League, who did most of the primary research.

43. See Irving Howe and A. J. Muste, "Two Statements," *Dissent* 4, no. 3 (Summer 1957): 332–37.

44. Ibid.

45. Sidney Lens, *Unrepentant Radical* (Boston: Beacon, 1980), p. 222.

46. A. J. Muste and Irving Howe, "C. Wright Mills' Program: Two Views," *Dissent* 6, no. 2 (Spring 1959): 194.

47. "Irving Howe Replies," *Dissent* 6, no. 3 (Summer 1959): 298–301.

48. Irving Howe, "Last Chance in Vietnam," ibid. 11, no. 3 (Summer 1964): 3.

49. Irving Howe, "Cease Fire," ibid. 12, 1 (January–February 1966): 5–7.

50. Letter from Walter Goldwater and response by Irving Howe, ibid. 13, no. 1 (January–February 1967): 107–8.

51. "Julius Jacobson Replies," *New Politics* 9, no. 2 (Summer 1970): 98–99.

52. Irving Howe, "Authoritarians of the Left," *Steady Work* (New York: Harcourt, Brace & World, 1966), pp. 296–312.

53. Irving Howe, "The New 'Confrontation Politics' Is a Dangerous Game," *New York Times Magazine*, 20 October 1968, pp. 27–29, 133–39, and "Political Terrorism: Hysteria on the Left," ibid., 12 April 1970, pp. 25–27, 124–28.

54. Irving Howe, "The Campus Left and Israel," reprinted in *Israel, the Arabs, and the Middle East*, ed. Irving Howe and Carl Gershman, pp. 428–30 (New York: Bantam, 1972).

55. Irving Howe, "The Middle-Class Mind of Kate Millett," *The Critical Point* (New York: Horizon, 1973), pp. 203–32. See the effective critique by Phyllis Jacobson, "Kate Millett and Her Critics," *New Politics* 8, no. 4 (Fall 1970): 89–94.

56. Philip Rahv and Irving Howe, "An Exchange on the Left," *New York Review of Books*, 9 December 1965, p. 29; and Dwight Macdonald, "An Open Letter to Michael Harrington," ibid. 11, no. 10 (5 December 1968): 48–49.

57. See Howe's endorsement of Lyndon Johnson in *Dissent* 11, no. 4 (Autumn 1964): 380.

58. Irving Howe, "Liberalism: A Moral Crisis," ibid. 11, no. 2 (Spring 1955): 107–13.

59. Howe, "The New 'Confrontation Politics' Is a Dangerous Game," p. 139; Irving Howe, *Socialism and America* (New York: Harcourt Brace Jovanovich, 1985), pp. 49–86; see the inside jacket of *Dissent* 11, no. 2 (Spring 1964).

60. Howe, *Steady Work*, pp. 271–95; Irving Howe, "I'm Not a Marxist," *New York Times Book Review*, 20 October 1985, p. 11.

61. Hilton Kramer, "Professor Howe's Prescriptions," *New Criterion* 2, no. 8 (April 1984): 3; author's interview with Nathan Glazer, May 1981, Cambridge, Mass.

62. Howe, "I'm Not a Marxist," p. 11.

63. The biographical information on Harvey Swados is from the author's interviews with Betty Swados, May 1980, New York City; Irving Sanes, May 1980, Buffalo, N.Y.; Donald Slaiman, August 1980, Washington, D.C.

64. See the Swados-Hofstadter correspondence, Swados Papers, UMA.

65. Robert C. Tucker, ed., *The Marx-Engels Reader* (New York: Norton, 1978), p. 74.

66. Harvey Swados, *On the Line* (New York: Dell, 1978), p. 45.

67. Ibid., p. 75.

68. "Reconciliation with reality" was Georg Lukács's euphemism for his acceptance of the policies of the Third International after his opposition in the 1920s.

69. See the many letters from Swados to Howe in the Swados Papers, UMA.

70. Raymond Williams, *Marxism and Literature* (London: Oxford, 1977), p. 212.

71. The two essays are reprinted in Harvey Swados, *A Radical's America* (Boston: Little, Brown, 1962), pp. 111–20 and 328–38.

72. The notebook for *Standing Fast* is available in the Swados Papers, UMA; author's interview with Irving Sanes, May 1983, Buffalo, N.Y.

73. Harvey Swados, *Standing Fast* (New York: Doubleday, 1970), p. 648.

74. Author's interview with Irving Sanes, May 1981, Buffalo, N.Y.; Swados, Notebooks for "Celebration," which was published posthumously, Swados Papers, UMA.

75. Irving Howe makes this charge when attacking Schoenman for a critical review of his anthology, *Essential Works of Socialism* (1970) in *New Politics* 9, no. 2 (Summer 1970): 96. As a result of his agreement with Howe that Schoenman's criticisms were unjust, Swados (along with *Dissent* supporters Meyer Schapiro and Lionel Abel) removed his name as a sponsor of *New Politics*.

76. Harvey Swados, *Celebration* (New York: Simon and Schuster, 1975), p. 141; author's interview with Harry Roskolenko, June 1980, New York City.

77. See Harvey Swados to Irving Sanes, 18 November 1968, Swados Papers, UMA; and Harvey Swados, contribution to "Symposium: The Prospects for American Radicalism," *New Politics* 7, no. 2 (Spring 1968): 16.

78. Author's interview with Irving Sanes, May 1983, Buffalo, N.Y.

CHAPTER 11

1. Daniel Singer, *The Road to Gdansk* (New York: Monthly Review, 1982), p. 18.

2. See Susan Sontag, "Some Thoughts on the Right Way (For Us) to Love the Cuban Revolution," *Ramparts* 7, no. 11 (April 1969): 6–19; and author's interview with Leslie Evans, June 1984, Los Angeles, Calif.

3. Susan Sontag, "Communism and the Left," *Nation* 234, no. 8 (27 February 1982): 231. In regard to Sontag's talk and its aftermath, also see the thoughtful essay by Julius Jacobson, "Reflections on Fascism and Communism," in *Socialist Perspectives*, ed. Julius Jacobson and Phyllis Jacobson, pp. 119–54 (New York: Karz-Cohl, 1983).

4. Charles Ruas, "Susan Sontag: Past and Present," *New York Times Book Review*, 24 October 1982, p. 11.

5. *Nation* 234, no. 2 (27 March 1982): 370.

6. *Soho News*, 24 February–24 March 1982, p. 10.

7. *Nation* 234, no. 10 (13 March 1982): 292–93.

8. "Comments," in ibid., no. 8 (27 February 1982): 232.

9. Ibid., pp. 236–37.

10. See the article by Andrew Kopkind, "The Return of Cold War Liberalism," ibid. 236, no. 18 (23 April 1983): 1, 503–12, and the discussion in ibid. 236, no. 20 (21 May 1983): 624, 637, 641.

11. Macdonald's remarks are printed on the jacket of the book.

12. David Horowitz, *The Fate of Midas* (San Francisco: Ramparts, 1973), p. 7.

13. David Horowitz, "A Radical's Disenchantment," *Nation* 229, no. 19 (8 December 1979): 586.

14. David Horowitz, "Horowitz Replies," ibid. 230, no. 1 (5–12 January 1980): 20.

15. The article appeared in the 17 March 1985 issue of the *Washington Post Magazine* and was reprinted, among other places, in the May 1985 issue of *Contentions*, pp. 1–6.

16. The information on Irving Kristol is from the author's interview with Philip Selznick, August 1982, Berkeley, Calif., and from Douglas G. Webb's "Philip Selznick and the New York Sociologists," paper presented at the annual meeting of the Canadian Historical Association, Toronto, 1982.

17. Earl Raab to AW, 28 August 1985.

18. "Where We Stand," *Enquiry* 1, no. 1 (November 1942): 2.

19. William Ferry, "Other People's Nerve," ibid., no. 4 (May 1943): 3–6.

20. Irving Kristol, " 'Civil Liberties,' 1952—A Study in Confusion," *Commentary* 13, no. 3 (March 1953): 229.

21. See Peter Steinfels's chapter, "The *Encounter* Affair," *The Neoconservatives* (New York: Simon and Schuster, 1979), pp. 83–90.

22. Peter Steinfels's *The Neoconservatives* provides the best overview of the thought of the neoconservatives. See also the following: Nigel Ashford, "The Neo-Conservatives," *Government and Opposition* 16, no. 3 (1981): 353–69; Gillian Peele, *Revival and Reaction: The Right in Contemporary America* (Oxford: Clarendon Press, 1984), pp. 19–50; Louis Harap, "Right-Wing Intellectuals and Jews," *Jewish Currents* 34, no. 6 (June 1980): 4–9, 35–37; Kirkpatrick Sale, "Old Wine, New Bottles," *Mother Jones* 1, no. 4 (June 1976): 29–33, 50–55.

23. Walter Goodman, "Irving Kristol: Patron Saint of the New Right," *New York Times Magazine*, 6 December 1981, p. 90.

24. See the debate between Lionel Abel and Irving Kristol in *New Politics* 1, no. 2 (Winter 1962): 168–70.

25. Walter Goodman, "Irving Kristol," ibid., p. 202.

26. See the discussion, "Timerman and the Jews," in the *Nation* 223, no. 4 (8–15 August 1981): pp. 112–14.

27. Irving Kristol, *Reflections of a Neoconservative* (New York: Basic Books, 1983), p. xiii.

28. Ibid., p. 249.

29. Ibid., p. 260.

30. Ibid., p. 271.

31. The biographical information on Norman Podhoretz is from Podhoretz's *Making It* (New York: Random House, 1969).

32. This transit is well documented in Louis Harap, "Commentary Moves to the Right," *Jewish Currents* 25, no. 11 (December 1971): 4–9, 27–33, 35.

33. See Paul Johnson, "The Race for South Africa," *Commentary* 80, no. 3 (September 1985): 27–61, and Louis Wolf and Fred Clarkson, "Arnaud de Borchgrave Boards Moon's Ship," *Covert Action* 24 (Summer 1985): 34–35.

34. Norman Podhoretz, "The Culture of Appeasement," *Harper's* (October 1977). See "Podhoretz's *Kulturkampf*" in *Inquiry*, 21 November 1977, p. 4.

35. See Christopher Hitchens's analysis in "On 'Anti-Semitism,'" *Nation* 235, no. 11 (9 October 1982): 325–26.

36. See the critique by Theodore Draper, "The Revised Version," *New Republic* 186, no. 30 (10 March 1982): 30–34.

37. Podhoretz, *Making It*, p. 96.

38. Norman Podhoretz, *Breaking Ranks* (Harper and Row, 1979), pp. 296–301.

39. Ibid., p .363.

40. See Kathleen Teltsch, "400 Intellectuals Form 'Struggle for Freedom' Unit," *New York Times*, 19 February 1981, p. A19, and John S. Friedman, "Culture War II," *Nation* 232, no. 15 (18 April 1981): 452–53.

41. Norman Podhoretz, "New Sport: Ridiculing the Yuppies," *Los Angeles Times*, 11 July 1985, pt. 2, p. 5.

42. Midge Decter, "Liberalism and the Jews," *Commentary* 69, no. 1 (January 1980): 31.

43. Owen Harries, "A Primer for Polemicists," ibid. 78, no. 3 (September 1984): 57–60.

44. Gertrude Himmelfarb, "The University and Its Discontents," in *Our Country and Our Culture: A Conference of the Committee for the Free World*, pp. 46–52 (New York: Orwell Press, 1983).

45. See Nathan Glazer, *Affirmative Discrimination: Ethnic Inequality and Public Policy* (New York: Basic Books, 1973).

46. See Paul L. Montgomery, "Criticism of Israel among U.S. Jews Seems to Be Rising," *New York Times*, 15 July 1982, p. 10; advertisement, "A Call to Peace," ibid., 4 July 1982, p. E7; and Nathan Glazer and Seymour Martin Lipset, "Israel Isn't Threatened," *New York Times*, 30 June 1982, p. A23.

47. See Hilton Kramer, "The Blacklist and the Cold War," *New York Times*, 3 October 1976, sec. 2, pp. 1, 16, 24, and ibid., 17 October 1976, sec. 2, pp. 12, 28.

48. Hilton Kramer, "Professor Howe's Prescriptions," *New Criterion* 2, no. 8 (April 1984): 1–5. See the response by Robert Boyers, "The Neo-Con-

servatives and the Culture," *Salmagundi*, no. 66 (Winter–Spring 1985): 192–204. See also Pinsker, "Revisionism with Rancor," pp. 243–61.

49. The biographical information is based on the author's interview with Alfred Kazin, May 1981, New York City.

50. Alfred Kazin, "Saving My Soul at the Plaza," *New York Review of Books*, 31 March 1983, p. 40.

51. See the discussion of Lynn's article in Mark Shechner, "Rhapsody in Red, White and Blue," *Nation* 238, no. 24 (23 June 1984): 759–61.

52. The biographical information is drawn from the author's interview with Lionel Abel, May 1981, New York City. See also Lionel Abel, *The Intellectual Follies* (New York: Norton, 1984).

53. See n. 24.

54. Lionel Abel, "A Critic without a Country," *New Criterion* 3, no. 2 (October 1984): 82.

55. Geoffrey Sampson, "Censoring 20th Century Culture: The Case of Noam Chomsky," *New Criterion* 3, no. 2 (October 1984): 7–16.

56. Editorial, *New Republic*, 29 October 1984, p. 3.

57. See Alan Wald, "A Trans-Atlantic Smear Campaign against Chomsky," *Guardian*, 3 April 1985, p. 19; Noam Chomsky, "Chomsky's Defense," *New Republic* 191, no. 26 (24 December 1984): 2; Noam Chomsky, "Chomsky and 20th-Century Culture," *New Criterion* 4, no. 1 (January 1985): 81–84; Alexander Cockburn, "Disgusting Case," *Nation* 229, no. 21 (22 December 1984): 670–71; and Christopher Hitchens, "The Chorus and Cassandra," *Grand Street* 5, no. 1 (Autumn 1985): 106–31.

58. Committee for The Free World, "Report on Activities: The Committee for The Free World, September 1980–September 1981," p. 2.

59. Novak's background is atypical for the New York intellectuals, but he was a New Leftist in the 1960s and is a neoconservative today. See the two-part essay by Peter Steinfels, "Michael Novak & his ultrasuper democraticapitalism," *Commonweal* 110, no. 1 (14 January 1983): 11–16, and ibid. 110, no. 3 (11 February 1983): 79–85.

60. This publication has referred to feminists as "ugly," called liberal women faculty members "professorettes," published without authorization the membership of the Gay Student Alliance, and carried an article on affirmative action allegedly in "Black English" under the title, "Dis Show Ain't No Jive, Bro." See David Kupferschmid, "Alternative Papers Turn Conservative," *Los Angeles Times*, 27 December 1984, pp. 1, 18; Fran R. Schumer, "The New Right's Campus Press," *Nation* 234, no. 13 (3 April 1982): 395–401; Peter H. Stone, "The I.E.A.—Teaching the 'Right' Stuff," ibid. 233, no. 8 (19 September 1981): 231–34.

61. Jason Epstein, "The CIA and the Intellectuals," *New York Review of Books* 8, no. 7 (20 April 1967): 16.

62. Stone, "The I.E.A.—Teaching the 'Right' Stuff," pp. 231–35.

63. William Barrett, *The Truants* (New York: Doubleday, 1982), p. 237.

64. Ibid., p. 197.

65. Hilton Kramer, "Partisan Culture, Partisan Politics," *New York Times Book Review*, 7 February 1982, pp. 32–33.

EPILOGUE

1. Noam Chomsky, *American Power and the New Mandarins* (New York: Vintage, 1967), p. 325.

2. Hannah Arendt, unpublished lecture at the New School for Social Research, 1947 or 1948, Library of Congress, Washington, D.C.

3. Daniel Aaron, "Edmund Wilson's Political Decade," in *Literature at the Barricades*, ed. Ralph Bogardus and Fred Hobson, p. 186 (University: University of Alabama Press, 1982).

4. Raymond Williams, "Alignment and Commitment," *Marxism and Literature* (New York: Oxford, 1977), pp. 199–205.

5. Robert Tucker, ed., *The Marx-Engels Reader* (New York: Norton, 1978), p. 717.

6. Philip Rahv, *Essays on Literature and Politics*, ed. Arabel J. Porter and Andrew J. Dvosin (Boston: Houghton Mifflin, 1978), pp. 341–45.

7. Ibid., pp. 352–53.

8. Mark Krupnick, "He Never Learned to Swim," *New Review* (January 1976): 37.

9. Ibid., p. 39.

10. Rahv, *Essays on Literature and Politics*, pp. 335–40.

11. Ibid., p. xii.

12. Krupnick, "He Never Learned to Swim," p. 38; Noam Chomsky to AW, 2 April 1986.

13. For a more detailed analysis of the problems of socialist political commitment, see Alan Wald, "Marxism and Intellectuals: Towards a Critical Commitment," *Changes* 6, nos. 11–12 (November–December 1984): 14–21.

Index

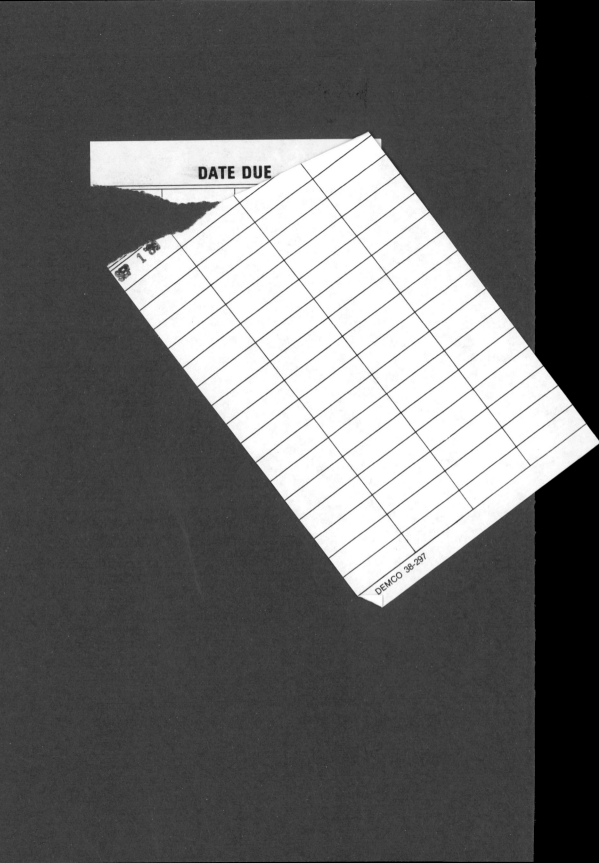

DATE DUE

DEMCO 38-297